On the ESSENCE of LEGAL CONSCIOUSNESS

Studies in Russian, East European, and Eurasian Law

William E. Butler (Series Editor)

1. Butler, W. E., *Russian Law and Legal Institutions*. 3d ed.; 2021. ISBN 978-1-61619-648-6

2. Il'in, I. A., *On the Essence of Legal Consciousness*, 2d revised ed., edited & transl. W. E. Butler, P. T. Grier and Paul Robinson. 2023. ISBN 978-1-61619-679-0

The Vinogradoff Institute • Penn State Dickinson Law

On the ESSENCE of LEGAL CONSCIOUSNESS

Ivan Aleksandrovich Il'in

(Доктор государственных наук)

Sometime Professor, Moscow Lomonosov State University

SECOND REVISED EDITION

Edited, Introduced, and **Translated** by

William E. Butler

John Edward Fowler Distinguished Professor of Law
Penn State Dickinson Law
Emeritus Professor of Comparative Law, University College London
Foreign Member, National Academy of Sciences of Ukraine and
National Academy of Legal Sciences of Ukraine

Philip T. Grier

Thomas Bowman Professor Emeritus of Philosophy and Religion
Dickinson College, Carlisle, Pennsylvania

Paul Robinson

Professor, University of Ottawa

TALBOT PUBLISHING

Clark, New Jersey

ISBN 978-1-61619-679-0

TALBOT PUBLISHING

AN IMPRINT OF
The Lawbook Exchange, Ltd.
33 Terminal Avenue
Clark, New Jersey 07066-1321

Please see our website for a selection of our other publications and fine facsimile reprints of classic works of legal history
www.lawbookexchange.com

Library of Congress Cataloging-in-Publication Data

Names: Il'in, I. A. (Ivan Aleksandrovich), 1883-1954, author. | Butler, William Elliott, 1939- editor, translat | Grier, Philip T., 1942- editor, translat | Robinson, Paul, 1966- editor, translat
Title: 0 On the essence of legal consciousness / Ivan Aleksandrovich Il'in, Доктор государственных наук, Sometime Professor, Moscow Lomonosov State
University ; edited, introduced, and translated by William E. Butler, John Edward Fowler Distinguished Professor of Law Dickinson Law, Pennsylvania State University Emeritus Professor of Comparative Law, University College London Foreign Member, National Academy of Sciences
of Ukraine and National Academy of Legal Sciences of Ukraine; Philip T. Grier, Thomas Bowman Professor Emeritus of Philosophy and Religion Dickinson College, Carlisle, Pennsylvania; Paul Robinson, Professor, University of Otta
Other titles: O suschnosti pravosoznananii͡a Engl
Description: Second revised editi | 1 Clark, New Jersey : Talbot Publishing, [20 | Series: Studies in Russian, East European, and Eurasian | Includes bibliographical references and ind
Identifiers: LCCN 2022054407 | ISBN 9781616196790 (hardcover)
Subjects:
Classification: LCC K230.I44 A3613 2023 | DDC 340/.1--dc23/eng/20230105
LC record available at https://lccn.loc.gov/2022054407

Printed in the United States of America on acid-free paper

Dedicated to Yury Trofimovich Lisitsa

We dedicate this second revised edition to Yury Trofimovich Lisitsa, the preeminent Il'in scholar. His extraordinary efforts over four decades and the assistance of his wife, Ol'ga Vladimirovna Lisitsa, and his son Andrei Lisitsa, have catalyzed the assembly, annotation, and publication of the collected works of I. A. Il'in in some thirty-seven volumes, thereby establishing a permanent foundation for Il'in Studies. Among his many services, he was instrumental in the return of the Il'in archive to its author's home institution, Moscow Lomonosov State University, where it is permanently housed and catalogued in the Department of Rare Books and Manuscripts of the Academic Library. Through assiduous investigations, Dr. Lisitsa has been able to gather and publish extensive materials relating to the family histories and biographies of Il'in and his wife, Natalia Nikolaevna Il'ina. We are indebted beyond measure to Dr. Lisitsa for setting, through the example of his own work, an exemplary high standard of research and writing on Il'in, notable for its seriousness and sophistication.

CONTENTS

Preface and Acknowledgments

This volume brings to an international readership a revised version what is perhaps the most impassioned and prescient work ever written by a Russian legal philosopher and jurist in support of the rule of law. Although Ivan Aleksandrovich Il'in is a remarkable figure for many reasons among twentieth-century Russian philosophers, theologians, historians, and jurists, perhaps his writings on legal consciousness are his most important and portentous for Russian society as a whole. If we are in an era of global development in which there is to be renewed emphasis upon the freedoms of the individual vis-à-vis the State, as many believe, what Il'in has to say on the subject will resonate strongly in this broader conversation.

Il'in arrives belatedly in the English language, Apart from four essays on music criticism published in 1955 (a field in which he was no less accomplished), Il'in has been accessible only to those who command Russian, German, or, exceptionally, French, and even then primarily in circles in which Russian émigré literature was disseminated. For entirely different reasons he has achieved a substantial readership in his native Russia only during the past three decades. The full measure of his prodigious intellectual legacy will not become accessible even there until the publication of his Collected Works is completed (37 volumes to date and continuing). The Grier translation from the Russian of Il'in's original two-volume commentary of the philosophy of Hegel has revealed a broader and different interpretation of Hegel than that contained in Il'in's own later, truncated German edition, which was previously used more or less exclusively by Western scholars. It is entirely appropriate in this volume to turn to Il'in's most original and influential contribution to the theory of law.

We are indebted to a number of individuals. Tatiana Poltoratskaia (1921-2016) generously gave permission and blessing to translate Il'in's treatise on the essence of legal consciousness and the predecessor essay devoted to concepts of law and power. The last and fragments of the first originally appeared in *The Journal of Comparative Law*, VII (2012), pp. 63-107. Comments on the manuscript by our spouses, Maryann Gashi-Butler and Ella Grier, were much appreciated, together with their encouragement to complete the work. Our collective debt to Yury T. Lisitsa, recorded in the Dedication, and Olga V. Lisitsa, is one owed by all "Il'inites" to that indefatigable family.

It would be remiss not to pay tribute to Clifford Haka and his colleagues, past and present, at the Michigan State University whose foresight enabled the Il'in Archive to be preserved and safeguarded for nearly three decades and eventually repatriated to Moscow Lomonosov

University.[1] We are obliged to the staff of the Moscow University Library for the opportunity to consult the galleys of Il'in's work, which offered considerable insight into the process of its intellectual journey.

Alexis Klimoff offered invaluable comments and details on the manuscript, and we benefited from the writings and reactions of Dr. Robert Williams on the occasion of an Il'in Conference in Spring 2013 at Moscow. Some of the introductory materials in this volume were originally aired at that Conference.

Il'in has received notice and some notoriety in western commentary on Russian affairs since the first edition of this translation appeared. Most of the commentary has ignored Il'in's contributions to legal theory, but rather concentrated on positioning Il'in among his political contemporaries in emigration or the use of his publications in Russian political circles during the past decade. To address these aspects of Il'in, we have invited Dr. Paul Robinson to join the collective authorship and added his essay to this second revised edition.

In addition to the Robinson Introduction, we have revised the introductory chapters to incorporate new information obtained in the decade or so since the appearance of the first edition and reordered the chapters. Minor infelicities have been rectified, together with the fruits of recent archival discoveries about the origins and completion of the original manuscript translated herein.

[1] The costs of transporting the Il'in archive from East Lansing to Moscow State University were paid by Viktor Vekselberg, the noted Russian magnate and philanthropist. See Marlene Laruelle and Margarita Karnysheva, *Memory Politics and the Russian Civil War: Reds Versus Whites* (2021), p. 96. The Archive amounted to 37 boxes weighing 486 kilos in aggregate transported by Aeroflot. See Olga V. Lisitsa, «К истории поступления архива И. А. Ильина в Научную библиотеку МГУ им. М. В. Ломоносова» [On the History of Receipt of the I. A. Il'in Archive in the Scientific Library of the Moscow Lomonosov State University], in Il'in, Собрание сочинений: О возрождении и обновлении России [Collection of Works: On the Rebirth and Renewal of Russia] (2021), [XXXIII](3), p. 519.

Introduction

On 28 September 1922, the steamship *Oberbürgermeister Haken* set sail from the port of Petrograd (St Petersburg), bound for Germany. On board were some 60 leading Russian intellectuals with family – scientists, economists, jurists, and philosophers – whom Russia's revolutionary Bolshevik government had decided to expel from the country. Among them was a Moscow law professor, the fiercely anti-Bolshevik Ivan Aleksandrovich Il'in. For a long time, Il'in's work attracted little attention in the West compared to that of some other passengers, such as philosopher Nikolai Berdiaev (1874-1948) and economist Boris Brutzkus (1874-1938). His works were accessible only to Russian speakers. However, in the past twelve years Il'in's works have finally begun to appear in English. The first was Il'in's doctoral thesis *The Philosophy of Hegel as a Doctrine of the Concreteness of God and Humanity*,[1] translated by Philip Grier and published in 2010. Since then, several English versions of Il'in's other books have appeared, namely: *The Singing Heart: A Book of Quiet Reflections*;[2] *Foundations of Christian Culture*;[3] and *On Resistance to Evil by Force*.[4] The re-publication in this volume of the Grier translation of *On the Essence of Legal Consciousness* marks a further step in making Il'in's work available to an English-speaking audience. It also provides students of law and politics with access to an original study of what remains an important issue: the spiritual foundations of a stable, law-based State.

Since the dissolution of the Soviet Union, Il'in has become the subject of considerable scholarly interest in Russia, with the publication of numerous books, articles, and dissertations devoted to him and his work. In the West, by contrast, he remained a relatively obscure figure until the President of the Russian Federation, Vladimir Putin, cited him five times in his speeches, thereby drawing scholars' attention to him.[5] In October 2021, Putin said "I read Il'in, I read him to this day. I have his book lying on my shelf, and I pick it up and read it from time to time".[6] Although Putin did not say which of Il'in's books he had in mind, a likely candidate is a collection of essays written for the White Russian military émigré organization ROVS, published under the title Наши задачи [Our Tasks].

1 I. A. Il'in, *The Philosophy of Hegel as a Doctrine of the Concreteness of God and Humanity*, transl. Philip T. Grier (2010). 2 vols.

2 Ivan Ilyin, *The Singing Heart: A Book of Quiet Reflections*, transl. Alexandra Weber (2016).

3 Ivan Ilyin, *Foundations of Christian Culture*, transl. Nicholas Kotar (2019).

4 Ivan Alexandrovich Ilyin, *On Resistance to Evil by Force*, transl. K. Benois (2018).

5 For a discussion of these, see Oksana Drozdova and Paul Robinson, "In Others' Words: Quotations and Recontextualization in Putin's Speeches", *Russian Politics*, II, no. 2 (2017), pp. 227-253.

6 Valdai Discussion Club Meeting, *Kremlin.ru*, 21 October 2021 (available online).

Following the lead of Timothy Snyder, a historian at Yale University, Western commentary has tended to focus exclusively on some statements that Il'in made in the 1920s and early 1930s that were supportive of certain aspects of fascism. From these Snyder and others have drawn the conclusion that Il'in was a fascist.[7] They have, however, failed to mention Il'in's many other statements and actions pointing in a quite different direction. In particular, they have failed to mention *On the Essence of Legal Consciousness* or even to give any indication that they have read it. This is a striking omission. For *On the Essence of Legal Consciousness* reveals an Il'in very different from the thinker depicted in current popular discourse.

On the Essence of Legal Consciousness is in many respects a "liberal" book, possibly the most liberal of all Il'in's major works. Il'in's most recent Russian biographer, Igor Evlampiev, called it "the main work of the entire school of Russian liberalism",[8] "a magnificent model of an original philosophical elaboration of the problems of law and the State on the basis of the principles of liberalism",[9] and "the culmination of the development of Russian liberalism in the nineteenth and early twentieth centuries".[10]

Evlampiev is not alone in characterizing Il'in as having been a liberal, or at least as having adhered throughout his life to certain core liberal principles. Il'in's one-time student and first biographer, Nikolai Petrovich Poltoratskii (1921-1989), described him as a "liberal conservative". So does contemporary Russia's most prominent Il'in scholar, Iurii Lisitsa (who has edited over forty volumes of the philosopher's work).[11] Others paint Il'in as a proponent of "moderate conservative liberalism",[12] or as "belonging to the school of classical liberalism".[13] Paul Valliere has commented that "to deny that liberal values occupied a central place in

[7] Timothy Snyder, "God is a Russian", *The New York Review of Books*, 5 April 2018, pp. 51-52 (available online); Timothy Snyder, *The Road to Unfreedom: Russia, Europe, America* (2018); Anton Barbashin and Hanna Thorburn, "Putin's Philosopher", *Foreign Affairs*, 20 September 2015 (available online).

[8] I. I. Evlampiev, *Ivan Il'in* (2016), pp. 14-15.

[9] Ibid, p. 32.

[10] Ibid, p. 180.

[11] N. P. Poltoratskii, Иван Александрович Ильин [Ivan Aleksandrovich Il'in] (1989), p. 153; Iurii Lisitsa, «Ильин искал сущность свободы как подобия божия в человеке: Интервью с Юрием Лисицей» [Il'in Searched for the Essence of Freedom as the Likeness of God in Man], Самопознание [Self-Knowledge], no. 2 (2015), p. 12.

[12] Egor Kholmogorov, «Правый гегелянец в окопах Сталинграда» [Right Hegelian in the Trenches of Stalingrad], Самопознание [Self-Knowledge], no. 2 (2015), p. 24.

[13] Liubov' Ulianova, «Скрытое славянофильство в творчестве Ильна» [Concealed Slavophilism in the Creative Work of Il'in], Самопознание [Self-Knowledge], no. 2 (2015), p. 38.

his [Il'in's] political thought is a mistake … For the same reason, it is a mistake to call Ilyin a 'fascist philosopher' … A rule-of-law state in Russia was always his goal".[14]

In reality, no modern political label suits Il'in well. Evlampiev noted that "Il'in's work is extraordinarily varied".[15] Given the manner in which he combined seemingly incompatible positions, words such as "contradictory" and "paradoxical" abound in scholarly analyses of Il'in's writing. Il'in managed to be simultaneously liberal and authoritarian, as well as a monarchist who spent his years in exile vehemently denouncing the Russian émigré monarchist movement. As Philip Grier has observed, Il'in "combined the most extreme Slavophilism in general with a strong commitment to the rule of law",[16] an almost unique combination (Slavophiles tended to prefer custom over law) but one which was typical of him. Selecting individual passages of Il'in's writings and portraying them as encapsulating the entirety of his worldview is profoundly mistaken.

Part of the problem is a natural tendency to try to fit people into neat categories. Yet the "isms" often used to describe political ideologies (liberalism, conservatism, fascism, and so on) are poorly defined and overlap considerably. Russian thinkers often fail to fit neatly within any existing category. In the aftermath of the Great Reforms of the mid-nineteenth century, for instance, many liberals, while wanting to expand civil liberties, viewed representative institutions with suspicion, seeing them as liable to be dominated by conservatives. They therefore preferred to support autocracy as a mechanism for reform. Many liberals also looked on the peasant commune – the bastion of rural conservatism – fairly positively, seeing it as a means of maintaining order in the countryside. By contrast, the so-called "aristocratic opposition", a supposedly reactionary force, supported the creation of an elected legislature (believing that they would dominate it) and argued in favor of abolishing the commune and reordering the rural economy along free market lines (believing that they would be the primary beneficiaries). The "reactionaries" were sometimes more "liberal" than liberals. Groups across the political spectrum espoused ideological combinations that do not fit easily with Western conceptions. Daniel Field noted that in the circumstances of mid-nineteenth century Russia,

> Doctrines naturally clustered together in Western Europe were in conflict in Russia … the espousal of constitutionalism or laissez-faire economics was regarded, often correctly, as an attempt to perpetuate the dependence of the peasantry and the dominance

[14] Paul Valliere, "Ivan Ilyin: Philosopher of Law, Force, and Faith", in Randall Poole and Paul Valliere, *Law and the Christian Tradition in Russian Thought* (2021), pp. 321, 325.

[15] Evlampiev, note 9 above, p. 8.

[16] Philip T. Grier, "The Complex Legacy of Ivan Il'in", in James P. Scanlan (ed.), *Russian Thought after Communism: The Recovery of a Philosophical Heritage* (1994), p. 167.

> of the nobility. … [A reformer] could not … embrace the whole bundle of liberal doctrines. Different men, grasping different parts of the bundle, naturally came into conflict.[17]

This phenomenon continued in later periods, with Russian thinkers bundling together ideas that in the West appeared to be mutually contradictory. Following the Russian revolution of 1917, many Russian philosophers who had previously held liberal democratic views shifted ground. They retained their belief in the paramount importance of the individual and individual freedom, but viewed liberalism and democracy with great scepticism, as being ill-fitted to protecting individual freedom and liable to collapse into communist or fascist totalitarianism. Il'in is a case in point. Although he perhaps took things to an extreme, he was not alone. He quarrelled with many of his émigré colleagues, most notably Berdiaev; they tended to share the same basic view that Russia's problems were spiritual in nature and thus the solutions needed to be spiritual too and were not to be found in the adoption of Western liberal democratic institutions.

Such views were the product of pre-revolutionary liberal idealism combined with historical circumstances. Prior to the 1917 revolutions, Russian liberal thought contained two main strands – positivism and idealism.[18] Positivists were the majority. They argued that the only valid knowledge is that which can be empirically verified. This led to the conclusion that religion or morality should not determine truth or what should be done, as they are not scientifically verifiable. Positivism also tended towards historical determinism and the view that human societies are subject to scientific laws according to which they all progress towards more rational forms of organization and eventually converge. Liberal positivists viewed the West as being the home of such rational forms of organization and therefore argued that Russia was destined in due course to become like the West.

Against this, a small group of idealist philosophers argued for the primacy of affairs of the spirit. In 1903 a group of such thinkers came together to produce a book entitled *Problems of Idealism*, edited by Pavel Novgorodtsev (1866-1924), a professor of law at Moscow University. In this they argued that the positivists were making the error of drawing an "ought" from an "is" – for instance, by concluding that because Western Europe "was" more advanced than Russia it represented something that Russia "ought" to be. In addition, Novgorodtsev denounced historical determinism for implying the "necessity for individual persons to bow down before this general course of history and recognize its inevitability

[17] Daniel Field, "Kavelin and Russian Liberalism", *Slavic Review*. XXXII (1973), p. 60.

[18] For a discussion of the differences between the two, see Vanessa Rampton, *Liberal Ideas in Tsarist Russia: From Catherine the Great to the Russian Revolution* (2020).

and beneficence".[19] Historical determinism, he said, implied that "the general course of events is everything and the individual is nothing".[20]

The idealists sought to ground liberalism in morality. This can be seen in their attitude towards law. Positivism views law as being law precisely because it has been deemed to be law by a recognized authority that has the power to enforce it. Legal rights are rights because the State has deemed them to be rights, not because they exist in some metaphysical sense. The idealists challenged this, arguing that law needs to be connected to morality, more specifically to natural law. Thus Petr Berngardovich Struve (1870-1944), one of the contributors to *Problems of Idealism*, wrote that natural law "lies at the heart of any true liberalism ... Natural law is not only the ideal but also the desirable law ... [I]t is absolute law, rooted in an ethical understanding of the concept of the person and its self-determination".[21] Meanwhile, Novgorodtsev wrote of a "crisis of legal consciousness" brought about by "decades of dominating legal positivism that had reduced [law] to positive law, that is, order of the State authority". This, said Novgorodtsev, had produced a "legal nihilism", in which people had no respect for the law because they regarded it as being entirely "the product of force".[22] The solution, claimed Novgorodtsev, was a "revival of natural law".

Struve and Novgorodtsev played an active role in the Liberation Movement that sought to pressure Tsar Nicholas II into granting a democratic constitution. They subsequently joined the liberal Constitutional Democratic (Kadet) party. Just as many other liberals, they then swung politically to the right following the 1917 revolutions. Within a few months of the Tsar's overthrow in March 1917, many Kadets were calling for a military dictatorship. At a meeting of the Kadet central committee in January 1918, Novgorodtsev asked fellow party members which they valued more: liberalism or democracy. If it was the former, they should abandon the latter and support a dictatorship, which could then enact their liberal program.[23] The party accepted his argument, and formally expressed its support for a military dictator. "If nothing is left of our democratism, then that is an excellent thing", Novgorodtsev remarked

19 P. I. Novgorodtsev, "Ethical Idealism in the Philosophy of Law (On the Question of the Revival of Natural Law)". In Randall Poole (ed.), *Problems of Idealism: Essays in Russian Social Philosophy* (2005), p. 275.

20 Ibid, p. 276.

21 Petr Struve, «В чем же истинный национализм?» [Wherein is True Nationalism?], in Petr Struve, На разные темы (1893-1901 гг.): Сборник статей [On Various Topics (1893-1901): Collection of Articles] (1902), p. 538.

22 Andrzej Walicki, *The Flow of Ideas: Russian Thought from the Enlightenment to the Religious-Philosophical Renaissance* (2015), p. 734.

23 William G. Rosenberg, "Russian Liberals and the Bolshevik Coup", *The Journal of Modern History*, XL, no. 3 (1968), p. 345.

in May 1919, adding that, "what is needed now is dictatorship, a force for creating authority".[24]

Struve, meanwhile, became foreign minister in the anti-Bolshevik White government of General Petr Nikolaevich Wrangel (1878-1928) in the Crimea in 1920. After Wrangel's defeat, Struve went into exile, where he established good relations with Il'in. He moved into the conservative camp, playing a leading role in organizing an émigré congress designed to endorse the leadership of Grand Duke Nikolai Nikolaevich (1856-1929). In 1933, welcoming Hitler's rise to power in Germany, he gave a speech arguing that liberty and democracy were not the same and that non-democratic regimes often proved better at defending liberty than democratic ones. Struve's biographer, Richard Pipes, noted that he "was prepared … to give Hitler the benefit of the doubt".[25] Only in 1938 did he change his mind and denounce the German dictator.

As this brief history demonstrates, Il'in's political development fitted a pattern. A student of Novgorodtsev's at Moscow University, he followed his teacher along the path from liberal democracy to dictatorship. At the same time, he preserved his belief in the central importance of individual freedom, as revealed by a number of essays that he wrote in Switzerland after taking up residence there in 1938 (for instance, his 1939 articles "Freedom"[26] and "The Free Person").[27] This raises the question of whether Il'in's beliefs changed dramatically over time, or whether the changes were largely superficial while his core values remained unaltered.

In this regard, it is worth comparing *On the Essence of Legal Consciousness*, the bulk of which was written in 1918, with *Our Tasks*, which was written between 1948 and 1954. The latter is undoubtedly more pronounced in its stress on Russia's unique character and more obviously hostile to the West. It tends to be more openly suspicious of Western-style democracy and more forthright in its demands for a dictatorship in post-communist Russia, at least for a transitional period. But there are similarities between the works, with some sections of *Our Tasks* being almost identical to passages in *On the Essence of Legal Consciousness*. For instance, in both books Il'in discusses the difference between a "corporation" (an arrangement in which people make decisions collectively) and an "institution" (an arrangement in which decisions are made for people by those in authority.) In *On the Essence of Legal Consciousness*, Il'in wrote:

[24] Rosenberg, *Liberals in the Russian Revolution: The Constitutional Democratic Party, 1917-1921* (1974), p. 416.

[25] Richard Pipes, *Struve: Liberal on the Right* (1980), p. 416.

[26] Il'in, «Свобода» [Freedom], in I. A. Il'in, Новая национальная Россия: Публицистика 1924-1952 гг. [New National Russia: Publicist Works 1924-1952] (2019), pp. 577-580.

[27] Il'in, «Свободный человек» [The Free Person], in Il'in, ibid., pp. 632-635.

> The State as it is historically realized combines within itself the features of a corporation with the features of an institution ... It is clear that the politician, organizing the State, must set out every time from a true estimation of the actual level of legal consciousness in a given country, determining in accordance with that level the vital combination of 'corporation' and 'institution' which will be best for the State in the given circumstances.

And in *Our Tasks*, he wrote:

> The State, in its healthy realization, combines within itself the features of a corporation with the features of an institution ... This means that the politician, organizing the State, should consider above all the level of legal consciousness present in a given country at a given time, determining in accordance with this the vital combination of institution and corporation which is best 'in the real conditions of life'.[28]

This points to considerable consistency in Il'in's views over time. Indeed, it is noteworthy that although Il'in spent some time amending *On the Essence of Legal Consciousness* in the last years of his life, the final version is not significantly different from the original. The book retains its relatively liberal character. Had Il'in truly turned his back on the core principles he held as a young man, he had ample opportunity to remove those principles from the later version of *On the Essence of Legal Consciousness*. Yet he did not. Because its content reflects both his earlier and later thinking, *On the Essence of Legal Consciousness* is thus an excellent tool for examining the continuities in Il'in's thinking.

Perhaps the most fundamental principle uniting all of Il'in's work is his belief in the primacy of spiritual over material concerns. As he wrote in *On the Essence of Legal Consciousness*, "However great the significance of the material factor in history ... the human spirit is never reduced, and never will be reduced, to a passive, non-acting medium subordinated to material influences ... It is impossible to organize the world of matter not having organized the world of the soul".[29] Likewise in *Our Tasks*, he wrote:

> The political and economic cause of this catastrophe [the revolution and its aftermath] are undeniable. But its essence is much deeper than politics and economics; it is spiritual. It is a crisis of Russian religiosity. A crisis of Russian legal consciousness. A crisis of Russian military loyalty and firmness. A crisis of Russian honor and conscience. A crisis of the Russian national character. A crisis of the Russian family. A great and deep crisis of all Russian culture.[30]

28 Il'in, Наши задачи [OurTasks] (1956), I, pp. 82-83.

29 Il'in, see below, pp. 115-116.

30 Il'in, note 29 above, II, p. 611.

It followed, Il'in concluded, that the main task was "to instill in the people a new Russian spiritual character".[31]

On the Essence of Legal Consciousness applies this thesis to the ideal of pre-revolutionary Russian liberal thinkers – a rule-of-law State. In line with the idealist, natural law tradition discussed above, Il'in viewed such a State as resting on the existence of the appropriate spirit in the people. A rule-of-law State, he argued, depends neither on the enforcement of law by force nor on the existence of this or that type of political institution, but rather on people recognizing the law as right and necessary and voluntarily subordinating themselves to it. It is the presence of this "legal consciousness" that makes a State strong and stable and liable to protect the natural rights of its citizens. The development of this legal consciousness will be difficult, however, if the State abuses its authority and if positive law strays too far from natural law, thereby discrediting positive law and encouraging disobedience.

The starting point of natural law, according to Il'in, is the fact that "every person is *distinctive and singular in his own way*".[32] Everyone lives in solitude, in that what exists inside their souls is inaccessible to others. Each person senses the world entirely independently. This meant, Il'in argued, that "*freedom of the will is essential* … The fundamental dignity of the human consists in living a spiritual life independently of any heterogeneous encroachment and pressure … *Free self-determination* in spirit is the deepest law of this life".[33] Natural law therefore gives everybody an "inalienable right" to spiritual freedom.

From this Il'in concluded that "Positive law by its very essence is an organized attempt to formulate natural law",[34] and that the purpose of the State is the realization of natural law, in other words, "guaranteeing *to the entire population and to each individual* their natural right to a distinctive self-determination in life, that is, the right to *life* and, moreover, to *a worthy* life, outwardly free and inwardly self-sufficient".[35]

This is a classically liberal position. However, Il'in then moved away from what nowadays would be considered liberalism in that he contended that the construction of such a State is difficult and that democracy is far from the optimal tool for the task. As he wrote, "the sole and objective *end* of the State is so elevated and requires from the citizenry such a *mature legal consciousness*, that historically speaking, nations turn

[31] Ibid, p. 613.

[32] Il'in, see below, p. 152.

[33] Ibid, p. 153.

[34] Ibid, p. 168.

[35] Ibid, p. 218.

out to be incapable of it".[36] Il'in argued that democracy may produce high quality government if the people have a sufficiently developed legal consciousness, but if they do not, the results may be catastrophic. This position reflected his own experiences living in Russia during the revolutions and in Germany in the 1920s and 1930s. He concluded that the form of the State must reflect the existing legal consciousness of the people. Where that consciousness is particularly distorted, some form of dictatorship may be necessary, albeit one that will seek to bring the State in line with natural law and develop the people's legal consciousness so that they will in due course be capable of self-government.

Unfortunately, Il'in did not provide a single, consistent definition of what he meant by legal consciousness. In *On the Essence of Legal Consciousness* he defined it as "a particular type of instinctive sense of right in which a person affirms his own spirituality and recognizes the spirituality of other people".[37] In a 1923 lecture entitled "The Problem of Contemporary Legal Consciousness," he described it as a conviction that there are limits to behavior, a understanding of what one can and cannot do, and of what one should and should not support.[38] Elsewhere, though, he wrote in terms suggesting a broader definition, including matters such as patriotism, honor, loyalty, religious faith, a sense of rank, and so on. This widens the meaning of legal consciousness far beyond law. Grier links Il'in's concept of legal consciousness to the work of Friedrich Carl von Savigny (1779-1861). Another point of reference is the Georg Wilhelm Friedrich Hegel (1770-1831) concept of *Geist*, usually translated into English as "spirit", a term which occurs regularly in *On the Essence of Legal Consciousness.* Anthony King described *Geist* in the following way:

> For Hegel ... *Geist* referred broadly to the consciousness of a people of itself and the world in which they lived. It referred to a people's self-understanding. It denoted the practices which a people regarded as appropriate, the kind of social intercourse in which that people engaged and, finally, the kind of world there was for that people. This consciousness was not just a system of logical categories; it was the living force of this people, sustaining them as a coherent social group, motivating every belief and action. Although a much looser translation, Geist might be better rendered as 'culture' in the anthropological sense. It refers to the distinctive lifestyles which various human groups have historically adopted, and to the shared understandings which underpin them.[39]

36 Ibid, p. 227.

37 Ibid, p. 185.

38 Il'in, Проблема современного правосознания [The Problem of Contemporary Legal Consciousness] (1923), pp. 9-10.

39 Anthony King, *The Structure of Social Theory* (2004), p. 104.

King's description of *Geist* fits well with what Il'in seems to mean by legal consciousness. In line with King's rendering of *Geist* as "culture", rather than "legal consciousness" a better translation of Il'in's term правосознание might be "legal and political culture". Il'in viewed every nation as having been imbued by God with its own particular *Geist*, producing a rich diversity of forms. "This is good. This is beautiful", he wrote: "The grasses and the flowers in the field are diverse. The trees and the clouds are diverse. God's garden is rich and beautiful; it has abundant forms, and glitters with colors and views".[40] Because forms of government should reflect the national legal consciousness, that is, the national culture, it followed, in Il'in's eyes, that they should be equally diverse. "It would be stupid to propose a monarchist or aristocratic order for Switzerland or the United States", he wrote.[41] But likewise, it was stupid to propose Swiss or American-style democracy for Russia.

There is a contradiction in Il'in's thinking here. On one hand, his answer to the question "what is best?" is that it depends on circumstances and that there is no solution which is best for everyone. On the other hand, it is obvious that he did have preferences. Although he admitted that liberal democracy suited the Swiss and Americans, there can be little doubt that it was not his preferred form of government, not just for Russia but as a general rule. Il'in complained that the liberal democratic legal consciousness divided nations up into competing interest groups rather than binding them together in pursuit of the common good. By contrast, what he termed a "monarchical" legal consciousness put the common good above individual interest and was associated with service, honor, rank, religious faith, and other concepts that Il'in held dear. In his short work "The Bases of the Struggle for National Russia", Il'in spoke of a "healthy legal consciousness", saying that Russia needed people who were Christian and honest, exhibiting self-control, discipline, and a sense of rank.[42] When Il'in wrote of the dictatorial State gradually developing the people's legal consciousness so that it became capable of self-government, it would appear that he did not envision self-government as being something akin to modern liberal democracy. Rather his preference was for a monarchical-democratic hybrid, founded on what nowadays would generally be considered quite conservative values. This would feature a strong monarchical executive, a weaker, elected, legislature, and guarantees of civil liberties.[43] One may doubt whether such a hybrid was practical.

[40] Il'in, note 29 above, I, p. 270.

[41] Ibid, p. 131.

[42] Il'in, Основы борьбы за национальную Россию [The Bases of the Struggle for National Russia] (1938), p. 44.

[43] Il'in laid out the design of such of a state in Il'in, Основы государственного устройства: Проект основного закона России [Foundations of State Structure: Draft Basic Law of Russia] (1996).

This is not the only weakness in his thesis. Il'in seemed to put great faith in the possibility of a benign dictator who could lead Russia away from communism and towards the kind of State that would embody the natural law. But he never explained how one could ensure that the dictator would act in this way. One suspects that the transitional dictatorship would in reality prove to be not so transitional. Instead of leading the people towards self-government, it would seek to keep itself in power, in the process acting in a way that undermined the development of a healthy legal consciousness.

Modern Western readers will for the most part probably reject Il'in's authoritarian tendencies as well as many of his more conservative values. Still, they may find much of use in his ideas concerning natural law and the purpose of the State. They may also find useful his idea that a rule-of-law State rests on more than formal institutions and requires an appropriate political and legal culture, specifically freely-given recognition of and obedience to the law. Contemporary Russia, for instance, has all the formal trappings of a liberal democracy but in practice is something different. Arguably, its institutions do not work in the manner foreseen by their creators due to the prevailing state of legal consciousness. In this regard, it is interesting that Il'in's critiques of Russian political and legal culture were remarkably similar to those of modern-day Russian liberals, many of whom regard their country's fundamental problem as being the illiberal culture of the Russian people. This is not just a Russian phenomenon. Efforts by Western States to promote democracy and liberal institutions abroad have often floundered when it has become apparent that the institutions in question do not fit local realities. The recent experience of some Western States has shown that institutions by themselves do not guarantee honest behavior by political leaders but are dependent upon obedience of unwritten rules and conventions. In other words, they depend on the existence of a certain legal consciousness. When leaders emerge who choose to ignore the rules, and when large numbers of people embrace that, the system comes under stress. In an era in which many commentators speak of a "crisis of liberalism", they might also be speaking of a crisis of legal consciousness. *On the Essence of Legal Consciousness* retains its relevance.

On the Essence of Legal Consciousness represents an attempt to fuse principles such as the rule of law and the absolute value of the person with the realities of the enormous political upheavals of Il'in's time. It represents an invaluable source for understanding the thought of Ivan Il'in and his contribution to political and legal philosophy.

Ivan A. Il'in: Russian Legal Philosopher

Ivan Aleksandrovich Il'in[1] was born at Moscow on 28 March (10 April) 1883. His parents descended from paternal and maternal members of the gentry, or nobility, Alexander Ivanovich Il'in. The stature of nobility was acquired by the Il'in family through I. A. Il'in's great-grandfather, Ivan Il'ich Il'in, who on 2 September 1793 was elevated to the rank of college counselor; on 25 April 1796 the dignity of nobility was conferred upon him.[2]

Ivan Il'ich Il'in left to his descendants a manuscript entitled "Catechism: To my son Ivan Ivanovich Il'in My Parental Blessing".

[1] The surname "Il'in" is transliterated variously in western sources: Il'in is the version followed here, using the Library of Congress transliteration system, but other versions include: Ilin (omitting the soft sign), Iljin, Ilyin, and so on.

[2] For background on Il'in, see: L. Chamberlain, *The Philosophy Steamer: Lenin and the Exile of the Intelligentsia* (2006); A. F. Kiselev, Иван Ильин и его поющее сердце [Ivan Il'in and His Singing Heart] (2006); O. A. Kudinov, Конституционные проекты Белого движения и конституционно-правовые теории российской белоэмиграции (1918-1940 гг.), или За что их расстреливали и депортировали (для тех, кто хочет понять смысл права) [Constitutional Projects of the White Movement and Constitutional-Legal Theories of the Russian White Emigration (1918-1940), or for What They were Shot and Deported (for Those Who Want to Understand the Meaning of Law)] (2006); V. I. Lafitskii, Богарне: судьбы и загадки истории [Beauharnais: Fates and Mysteries of History] (2d ed.; 2013); N. N. Leont'eva and N. T. Tarumova (comps.), «Поэзия Московского университета: от Ломоносова и до ...» ["Poetry of Moscow University: From Lomonosov up to ..."] (2011); Iu. T. Lisitsa, «Иван Александрович Ильин: Историко-биографический очерк» [Ivan Aleksandrovich Il'in: Historico-Biographical Survey], in Lisitsa (ed.), И. А. Ильин: Собрание сочинений [I. A. Il'in: Collection of Works] (1996-), pp. 5-35; Iu. T. Lisitsa (comp.), Иван Ильин и Россия: Неопубликованные фотографии и архивные материалы [Ivan Il'in and Russia: Unpublished Photographs and Archival Materials] (1999); Iu. T. Lisitsa and O. V. Lisitsa, Иван Ильин: провозвестник грядущей России [Ivan Il'in: Prophet of the Future Russia] (2005); Iu. V. Mukhachev (ed.), Российской научное зарубежье: Биобиблиографический справочник [Russian Scientific Abroad: Biobibliographical Manual] (2011); N. P. Poltoratskii, Иван Александрович Ильин: Жизнь, труды, мировоззрение [Ivan Aeksandrovich Il'in: Life, Works, World Outlook] (Tenafly, New Jersey, 1989); Iu. I. Sokhriakov, «Ильин Иван Александрович» [Il'in, Ivan Aleksandrovich], in A. N. Nikoliukin (ed.), Литературная энциклопедия русского зарубежья (1918-1940) [Literary Encyclopedia of the Russian Abroad (1918-1940)] (1997), I, pp. 197-201; A. Sharipov, Русские мыслитель.Иван Александрович Ильин. Творческая биография [Russian Thinker: Ivan Aleksandrovich Il'in, Intellectual Biography] (2008); I. Shevelenko, Материалы о русской эмиграции 1920-1930-х гг. в Собрании Баронессы М. Д. Врангель (Архив Гуверского Института в Стенфорде) [Materials on the Russian Emigration of the 1920-1930s in the Collection of Baroness M. D. Wrangel (Archive of the Hoover Institution in Stanford) (1995) (Stanford Slavic Studies, IX); V. A. Tomsinov, Мыслитель с поющим сердцем: Иван Александрович Ильин: русский идеолог эпохи революций [Thinker with a Singing Heart: Ivan Aleksandrovich Il'in: Russian Ideologue of the Era of Revolutions] (2012); T. N. Zhukovskaia (comp.), Евгения Герцык: лики и образы [Evgenia Gertsyk: Faces and Images] (2007); and the Il'in Archive and Library, Moscow State University; Archive of the Russian State Library.

Held by the Il'in family in a red leather folder, the document is dated 16 September 1814 and relates: "You know from what estate I came. You see what I have achieved, my teacher being fifty years of experience". It would follow from this observation that Ivan Il'ich Il'in was born in 1764.[3]

Ivan Ivanovich Il'in (1795/99-1865), I. A. Il'in's grandfather, served in the Russian artillery. In 1824, having achieved the rank of lieutenant, he transferred to civilian service and undertook special assignments for Governor-General A. D. Balashev (1770-1837). Then he served in a number of engineering posts in construction subdivisions; in 1841 he became a major in a construction detachment on the railway and then directed the construction of the Great Kremlin Palace, built between 1838 and 1849 and designed by a group of architects headed by Konstantin Andreevich Ton (1794-1881). When construction of the Great Kremlin Palace was completed, Emperor Nicholas I (1796-1855) appointed Ivan Ivanovich Il'in to the post of Commandant of this building with the official title "Major of the Gates of the Great Kremlin Palace". Documents list Ivan Ivanovich as a lieutenant-colonel in 1851 and colonel in 1855. This post of Commandant Ivan Ivanovich held throughout his lifetime (the post was extinguished upon his death), residing on the territory of the Kremlin with his wife, Liubov Petrovna Puzyreva (1811-1885), six sons, and three daughters. The fifth son, Aleksandr Ivanovich Il'in (1851-1921), was the father of Ivan Aleksandrovich Il'in.

Aleksandr Ivanovich Il'in, born 29 August 1851, was christened on 6 September; his godfather was the heir to the throne, Grand Prince Alexander Nikolaevich, who became Emperor Alexander II (1818-1881). Aleksandr Il'in graduated from the Tula Gymnasium in 1870 and enrolled at the Law Faculty of the Imperial Moscow University, graduating in 1874. Initially a candidate for a judicial appointment, in 1875 he moved on to the Department of Heralds as a provincial secretary and by 1883 had become a sworn attorney attached to the Moscow Judicial Chamber. In 1885 Aleksandr Il'in inherited land in Riazan Province from his mother and became and remained active until 1917 in various zemstvo affairs.

I. A. Il'in's mother, Karolina Louisa (Ekaterina Iul'evna) Schweikert (1858-1942), graduated from the Moscow Fourth Women's Gymnasium and in 1879 was authorized to act in the capacity of a "home teacher" with the right to teach those subjects which she had studied at the Gymnasium. Her father (and I. A. Il'in's grandfather) was Julius Schweikert von Stadion (1805-1876), who came from Wittenburg, in Saxony. He maintained the family tradition by studying medicine at Leipzig University and defended a dissertation there in 1831. A year later he removed to Russia and accepted the position of family doctor on the estate of Prince Aleksandr

[3] Pages from the "Armorial" which record the Arms of the Il'in Family relate that Ivan Il'ich took up State service in 1758; if accurate, this date would suggest that Ivan Il'ich was born not later than the early 1740s. Probably this was a copying error and should have read 1785. His son to whom the Catechism was addressed had reached age 19 in 1814.

Borisovich Kurakin (1752-1818). In 1842 he passed the medical examinations at Moscow University and in 1853 defended a doctoral dissertation on infantile pneumonia. He married Katarina Kuster (1824-1890); there were eight daughters of the marriage. The third of these, Karolina, married Aleksandr Il'in in 1880 and, upon converting from the Lutheran to the Russian Orthodox faith, came to be known as Catherine. She gave birth to five sons,[4] of which Ivan Aleksandrovich Il'in was the third.

Childhood and Student Years

When Ivan Aleksandrovich Il'in was about three or four years of age, his parents rented an apartment in a building owned by Count Sergei Dmitrievich Sheremetev (1844-1918) that overlooked the Kremlin. It was presumably a dilapidated structure, for it was replaced not long after the Il'in family moved on after six years to other quarters. Nonetheless, the location left an enduring impression on the young man – the chimes of the Kremlin bells, the majestic views of the Kremlin walls and towers, walks through the Aleksandrov Garden at the foot of the Kremlin ramparts and within the territory of the Kremlin itself. Small wonder that I. A. Il'in chose a view of the Kremlin walls for his bookplate design. As he later wrote of the view of the Kremlin from the fourth floor of the Sheremetev apartment: "Six years of patriotic feelings and admiration"[5] – and the home of his grandfather for several decades. Summers after 1890 he often spent at the Bykovo estate of his uncle, Nikolai Ivanovich Il'in (1837-19?) and was married in 1906 in the Bykovo church.[6]

After two years of being tutored at home, I. A. Il'in was enrolled in the third grade at the Moscow Fifth Gymnasium, well regarded at the time, and five and a half years later transferred to the Moscow First

[4] In addition to Ivan Aleksandrovich: Aleksei (1880-1913); Aleksandr (1882-after 1919); Iulii (1889-1901); Igor (1892-1937).

[5] Letter from I.A. Il'in to E. E. Klimov, Spring 1950, published in Собрание сочинений: Письма. Мемуары (1939-1954) [Collection of Works: Letters, Memoirs (1939-1954)], p. 50.

[6] The Il'in Bykovo estate was originally part of lands granted by Peter the Great to Illarion Vorontsov, father of Count Mikhail Illarionovich Vorontsov (1714-1767), and later belonged to Ivan Illarionovich Vorontsov-Dashkov (1790-1854). Master of Ceremonies attached to the Court of Emperor Nicholas I. Legend has it that Nikolai Ivanovich Il'in won the Bykovo estate at cards, but more likely purchased it in 1874 from the Vorontsov-Dashkov family. Nikolai Il'in was a member of the Board of the Moscow-Kazan Railway and is memorialized by the "Il'inskaia" railway stop just beyond Bykovo. His grandson, Mikhail Andreevich Il'in (1903-1981), was a noted art historian who wrote numerous works, including studies of church architecture in Bykovo, where nearby ecclesiastical edifices are attributed to the architects Vasilii Ivanovich Bazhenov (1737-1799) and Matvei Fedorovich Kazakov (1738-1812). See V. V. Gritskov (ed.), Быково [Bykovo] (Zhukovskii, 2005), pp. 57-58, 109-124. This work consists of excerpts from others devoted to Bykovo and includes two essays by M. A. Il'in. For two decades W. E. Butler owned a dacha situated on a land plot once part of the Il'in Bykovo estate.

Gymnasium, by consensus the finest in the city. He graduated in 1901 with marks of distinction in theology, Latin and Greek, mathematics, mathematical geography, physics, history, geography, French and German, and deportment, obtaining lower results in Church Slavonic and logic. The School awarded him the Gold Medal for his class, which translates as being ranked the best student.

Il'in applied for admission to the Law Faculty of the Imperial Moscow University in July 1901, but not without tribulations and controversy at home. He preferred the faculty of philology, despite a lower result in his studies of Church Slavonic; his father wished him to enroll in an engineering school and had arranged for extra tutoring in mathematics to this end. Ultimately, the law faculty was the compromise between father and son.[7] In this turbulent year for the Il'ins, I. A. Il'in's younger brother, Iulii, died from a blow to the head sustained during a fight at the Gymnasium.[8]

Approaching his legal studies reluctantly, I. A. Il'in's skepticism of legal education was initially reinforced by what he deemed to be "boring" courses on Russian legal history, "abstract" courses on political economy, the "dry" teaching of Roman law. Only Professor Pavel Ivanovich Novgorodtsev (1866-1924) intrigued him in his course on the "Encyclopedia of Law" and its introduction to the philosophy of idealism, little understood at the time. Unlike Professor Dmitrii Iakovlevich Samokvasov (1843-1911), who simply read aloud from the assigned readings and was quickly abandoned by his audience, Novgorodtsev was a gifted lecturer who introduced new materials supplementing the required texts.

I. A. Il'in gravitated towards the history of the philosophy of law gradually. In October 1902, under the guidance of Professor Sergei Nikolaevich Trubetskoi (1862-1905), the Student Society of Historical Philosophy held a solemn inaugural meeting at Moscow University. Il'in participated actively in the organization and within a short period the society had attracted a membership exceeding one thousand. The Society had its own library and reading room, met regularly to hear and discuss reports on the history of the philosophy of law, and contemplated the publication of its own journal. Il'in, however, was simultaneously drawn to another branch of law, fascinated by the lectures of Ivan Khristoforovich Ozerov (1869-1942), the Professor of Financial Law. He befriended Ozerov, sought him out for advice, borrowed books from his personal library on the history of the cooperative movement and on factory legislation in Russia, and thought seriously about writing a history of the Russian factory. A serious attack of bronchitis interrupted his studies

7 Ibid., p. 352.

8 See A. Sharipov, Русские мыслитель. Иван Александрович Ильин. Творческая биография [Russian Thinker: Ivan Aleksandrovich Il'in, Intellectual Biography] (2008), p. 16.

for three months, however, and Il'in was despatched to recuperate at the family country estate in Bolshie Poliany. He took with him a number of books on the history of philosophy: Wilhelm Windelband (1848-1915) on the history of ancient philosophy; Novgorodtsev on the history of the philosophy of law; and Plato's Dialogues. These books changed the course of his life and persuaded him to abandon any interest in financial law in favor of legal philosophy.

As it happened, Il'in's oral examination on the history of the philosophy of law in Spring 1903 was given by Novgorodtsev. The questions were concerned with Plato. Novgorodtsev listened to the replies with amazement and gave a 5+ (equivalent to a starred first in England, or an A+ in the United States). Sensing that his examiner was well-disposed towards him and aware that Novgorodtsev was a notoriously severe examiner, Il'in seized the moment to request, and obtained, permission to visit Novgorodtsev during office hours at home to discuss further studies of the history of the philosophy of law. On Sunday mornings, from 10:00 to 12:00, Novgorodtsev organized talks on philosophical topics and invited young lecturers, students, and magister candidates from the Law Faculty, together with young legal practitioners who continued after their student years to maintain an interest in matters of philosophy or acquaintances of Novgorodtsev who simply wanted to chat about interesting subjects.

On his first visit to Novgorodtsev, Il'in spoke of his plans for studying the history of the philosophy of law. "How much time would you wish to devote to my subject-matter?", asked Novgorodtsev. "My entire life", replied Il'in. "Very well, we for our part will do everything possible to assist you in your lessons and your situation", said Novgorodtsev, and promptly set his first assignment: to write a work about Plato. Il'in later recalled: "His seminars were crowded, lively, with impassioned meetings of Marxists, narodniks, idealists, and an atmosphere of common trust in the true, balanced, internally vibrant and outwardly restrained leader".[9]

Il'in's studies at Moscow University proceeded in turbulent times. From 1901 onwards the student body was absorbed by revolutionary sentiments, constantly holding gatherings, meetings, or demonstrations on virtually a daily basis and involving themselves increasingly in political campaigns. These were events that led Sir Paul Gavrilovich Vinogradov (1854-1925) in due course to emigrate and seek an academic position in England. On 5 December 1904 Il'in took part in a demonstration organized by the Moscow Student Executive Committee to protest the breaking up of a student demonstration in St. Petersburg. Il'in was among those arrested, interrogated, and released after nearly a month in custody along with the others detained at the time.[10]

9 Il'in, «Памяти П. И. Новгородцева» [In Memoriam P. I. Novgorodtsev], Русская мысль [Russian Thought], no. IX-XII (Prague, 1923/24), pp. 370-371.

10 Tomsinov, note 2 above, p. 14.

Diary entries suggest that Il'in was torn between an intense desire to pursue his studies and to be involved in the political events of the day. Some companions who recalled his activities of that time believed that he was a Bolshevik. On one occasion Il'in was reported to be seen storing a bomb in his apartment. He did attend and sometimes presided over political meetings at the University, but the balance of evidence and probabilities suggests that those who believed him to be a Bolshevik Party member confused him with his eldest brother Aleksei Il'in (1880-1913), also a jurist who was a member of the Russian Communist Party (Bolshevik). If Ivan Il'in was seen carrying and/or concealing a bomb,[11] it was undoubtedly to temporarily assist his brother, rather than to pursue his own ends. Aleksei was exiled to Siberia, returning in 1909, and died of typhus. In addition to being dedicated to the pursuit of learning, moreover, I. A. Il'in was during these times distracted from politics by another event in this life: he had fallen in love with Natalia Nikolaevna Vokach (1882-1962), the lady whom he married and whom at this time he courted single-mindedly.

Natalia Vokach-Il'ina was born into the nobility; her mother was a sister of the noted legal historian, Sergei Andreevich Muromtsev (1850-1910). Her father, Nikolai Antonovich Vokach (1855-1905) graduated from the Moscow University Law Faculty and served as a gunner in the I Grenadier Artillery Brigade. After being discharged into the reserve, he took a position with the Moscow Commercial Court and eventually became a sworn attorney in the Moscow Judicial Chamber. He was descended from emigrants from Serbia who during the reign of Ivan the Terrible (IV) had come to Russia as physicians. The rank of nobility for the Vokaches dated from the 1730-40s, when one of them took part in elevating Empress Elizabeth Petrovna (1709-1762) to the throne and then supporting her short-lived successor, Peter III (1728-1762). Empress Catherine II did not forgive or forget Vokach disloyalty to her. The Vokach family was forced to move to Prussia, where one of them eventually became a professor at Leipzig University. After the death of Catherine II in 1796, the son of the Leipzig professor returned to Russian service. Over marriages of several generations in the Vokach family, Natalia Vokach-Il'in acquired Dutch, Serbian, and German ancestry mixed in with Russian. Her interests were philosophy and aesthetics, and she studied art history.

At the end of May 1906, Il'in received a diploma with first class honors from the Moscow University, an academic achievement accompanied by an invitation to remain at the University to prepare for the professoriate at the Chair of Encyclopedia of Law and History of the Philosophy of Law. His petition to the Law Faculty for the requisite support required a recommendation signed by two professors. Novgorodtsev and Evgenii

[11] Rumors to this effect, however, persisted, even when Il'in was in emigration. Professor N. N. Alekseev is among those named as continuing to spread them. See Kiselev, note 2 above, p. 19.

Nikolaevich Trubetskoi (1863-1920) obliged as follows in a joint letter of support:

> I have been acquainted with Mr. Il'in since he passed into the second year and began under my direction to study philosophy in the classical works of ancient and modern times. His first work written on the topic of the political ideals of Plato showed at once that I have in this person a talented and thoughtful pupil attracted by the subject-matter of his lessons. From then and until the end of the course Mr. Il'in was among the most avid visitors and participants of my practical lessons and continued in addition his own studies of philosophy. These lessons were not interrupted when together with comrades and the entire University he lived through the alarming days of student disturbances. His last exceedingly well-substantiated and extensive work – "The Doctrine of Kant on the Thing-in-Itself in the Theory of Cognition" – was written in recent years when the general strike and impairment of academic life meant that many were unable to settle down and were deprived of the opportunity to engage in scholarship. Exceedingly lively and attractive, he is moreover distinguished by a rare diligence and great dedication to scholarship. The works written by Mr. Il'in show that he successfully combines a certain gift of generalization with the capacity for assiduous and careful analysis.[12]

Partly to cover his options if his academic studies did not proceed as planned, Il'in registered as an aide to the sworn attorney and privat-docent at the Moscow University Law Faculty, Igor Aleksandrovich Kistiakovskii (1868-1920), "without the intention to work in the Advokatura". On 27 August 1906 he married Natalia Vokach in the church at his uncle's estate in Bykovo.[13] In September 1906 the Council of Moscow University accepted Il'in's petition to remain at the University in order to prepare for the professoriate, which meant that he would commence studies for the magister examination in the history of the philosophy of law. His course of study was set out in a formal Instruction prepared by his supervisor, Novgorodtsev, as was the practice in those times, and formally approved by the Law Faculty. Il'in was directed to read some general surveys on the subject and the original works of certain of the greatest thinkers, together with a number of recent ones. Among the last were those devoted to positivist sociology, including Herbert Spencer (1820-1903) and Rudolf Stammler (1856-1938).[14] In his yearly progress report (1907), Il'in indicated that he had read several times more than the required minimum

[12] РГИА, fond 733, opis 153, delo 224, l. 254.

[13] Natalia Vokach's cousin, Evgenia Kazimirovna Gertsyk (1878-1944), reported on this marriage in her memoirs but seemingly confused Ivan Il'in with his brother and believed that Natalia had married a revolutionary member of the Social Democratic Party. Ivan Il'in throughout his lifetime did not join any political party. See Zhukovskaia, note 2 above, p. 240.

[14] РГИА, fond 733, opis 153, delo 224, l. 255.

during his first year of studies.[15] His studies of Plato were summarized by Il'in in an 84-page manuscript submission entitled "The Ideal State of Plato in Connection with His Philosophical Views".

Of the modern philosophers, Il'in devoted his principal attention to Immanuel Kant (1724-1804), Johann Fichte (1762-1814), and Friedrich Schelling (1775-1854). He summarized his readings in three written submissions, the first of which comprised 307 manuscript pages ("The Doctrine of Kant on the Thing-in-Itself in the Theory of Cognition"). The second was entitled "Doctrine of Fichte the Elder on Self-Consciousness. Prerequisites and Aspects for a Gnosiology of the First Period. Attempt at Differentiation", and comprised 324 pages. The third had not been completed by the end of the reporting year, but was well underway: "Schelling's Doctrine on the Absolute (Subject. Thing-in-Itself, Spirit. Organization. Being. History. State. God)".

In addition, together with his wife, Il'in had translated into the Russian language Rudolf Stammler (1856-1938), *Die Theorie des Anarchismus* (1894) and Paul Eltzbacher (1868-1928), *Der Anarchismus* (1900).[16] During 1908, Il'in completed his lengthy essay on Schelling and a number of other essays on individual philosophers ("The Idea of the Concrete in the Philosophy of Hegel"; "The Doctrine of Rousseau on a Common Will"; "The Doctrine of Aristotle on Slavery"; and "On the Methodology of the State Sciences").

In his capacity as supervisor, Novgorodtsev was required to assess the quality and progress of Il'in in his magister studies. In a positive evaluation dated 25 September 1908, Novgorodtsev recounted Il'in's diligence and mastery of the subject, while expressing concern that the self-imposed workload was so arduous that he feared for Il'in's health.[17] Il'in commenced the magister examinations on 20 February 1909 and upon their completion in May, was awarded an "extremely satisfactory". The time had come to petition the Faculty of Law to be sent abroad for the usual two-year "academic visit" in foreign universities to continue preparations for an academic appointment and to write his magister dissertation. Novgorodtsev wrote in his supporting letter: "I petition the Faculty of Law to render support in this respect to a young and very promising scholar".[18]

15 РГИА, fond 733, opis 154, delo 14, l. 128-139.

16 At the request of the publisher, Il'in, then 23 years of age, met with Leo Tolstoy (1828-1910), then 78 years of age, to ascertain whether Tolstoy might be willing to write a preface to Eltzbacher's book. The meeting occurred at Tolstoy's home in Yasnaia Polyana in 1906. Tolstoy did not agree to prepare a preface.

17 РГИА, fond 733, opis 154, delo 14, l. 127.

18 РГИА, fond 733, opis 154, delo 376, l. 12.

The original intention was that Il'in should travel abroad from 1 January 1910. For various reasons there were delays in formalizing his documents that led to his departure being deferred, according to some sources, for more than an entire year. Il'in took advantage of the delay to commence his teaching career. In spring 1909 he had been invited to deliver lectures at the Moscow Commercial Institute, of which Novgorodtsev had been the Director since 1906. From September 1909 Il'in also began to offer lectures and seminars on the history of the philosophy of law at the Moscow Higher Women's Legal Courses, a private institution founded by Varvara Aleksandrovna Poltoratskaia (1845-1923). These appointments enabled him to lecture and to earn a living, and if he and his wife were temporarily short of funds, they had established a line of credit with the private international lawyer, Mikhail Isaakovich Brun (1860-1916), "who was like a father" to them.[19]

Upon the recommendations of L. M. Lopatin, E. N. Trubetskoi, and Gustav Gustavovich Shpet (1879-1940), on 23 January 1910 Il'in was unanimously elected a full member of the Moscow Psychological Society (founded 1885), established to promote the development of psychology and related sciences (ethics, aesthetics, logic, philosophy of law, pedagogy, and others). Meetings were held at regular intervals to hear reports; from 1889 the Society published its official organ, Вопросы философии и психологии [Questions of Philosophy and Psychology], containing the minutes of meetings, texts of reports, and scholarly articles. Il'in's first substantial contribution to scholarship appeared in this journal – "The Concepts of Law and Power".[20]

In November 1909 Il'in delivered two "probationary", or "trial", lectures at Moscow University and in December 1909 was confirmed in the rank of privat-docent. During spring 1910 Il'in offered his first course at the University on the "General Methodology of Legal Sciences" at the Chair of Encyclopedia of Law and History of the Philosophy of Law.[21] He frequented the various literary and philosophical "circles" so fashionable in Russia at the time – evening or weekend meetings in private homes that assembled the most diverse participation – professors, journalists, artists, writers, musicians, and others absorbed by the lively issues of the day and the ultimate fate of Russia.

[19] Il'in, Собрание сочинений: Дневник. Письма. Документы (1903-1938) [Collection of Works: Diary, Letters, Documents (1903-1938)], p. 36.

[20] Il'in, «Понятия права и силы. Опыт методологического анализа» [The Concepts of Law and Power: An Essay in Methodological Analysis], Вопросы философии и психологии [Questions of Philosophy and Psychology], no. 21 (1910), pp. 1-38; transl. by P. T. Grier in I. A. Il'in, "The Concepts of Law and Power: An Essay in Methodological Analysis", *Journal of Comparative Law*, VII (2012), pp. 63-117.

[21] See Shevelenko, note 2 above, p. 98, reproducing an autobiographical sketch by Il'in dated 24 April 1932.

Towards the end of January 1911 Il'in departed[22] for Europe in the company of his wife, Natalia. The Instruction prepared by Novgorodtsev on behalf of Moscow University for the trip stipulated that Il'in was being sent abroad to prepare a dissertation on the subject "The Crisis of Rationalist Philosophy of Law in Germany in the Nineteenth Century" and to become familiar with the nature and methods of university instruction in the universities at Berlin, Heidelberg, Freiburg, Halle, Göttingen, Marburg, and Paris. A number of specific professors whose lectures Il'in was recommended to attend were named in the Instruction.[23] Correspondence preserved in the Il'in and other archives indicates that the couple visited Berlin, Munich, Dresden, Bamberg, Nuremberg, Bologna, Florence, Rome, Naples, Vienna, Göttingen, Paris, Brittany, and Cologne. By early May 1911 they had returned to Göttingen to commence the academic activities for which they had been sent abroad. In his later autobiography, Il'in said that he gave reports in the German language in Heidelberg, Freiburg, and Göttingen.[24]

In the meantime, while they were in western Europe matters at Moscow University were in turmoil. On 11 January 1911 the Council of Ministers of the Russian Empire had adopted a decree severely limiting the autonomy of the universities and prohibiting student meetings and assemblies on university premises. In the event of a violation, the police were authorized to take prompt and resolute measures to intervene on university premises. In protest against these measures the Rector and Pro-Rector of Moscow University offered to resign, and for this they were dismissed from their administrative and professorial positions. This prompted more than 21 professors and more than one hundred lecturers and privat-docents to resign, including Il'in and his supervisor, Novgorodtsev.

The Il'ins returned to Russia in May 1912, spending some months in the family country estate and then returning on 20 September 1912 to find accommodation – on this occasion an apartment in the outbuilding behind

22 There are conflicting dates of departure. Some sources say that the Il'ins left at the beginning of 1910. See Sharipov, note 2 above, p. 38. Others say their departure occurred at the end of 1910. See Iu. T. Lisitsa, «Иван Александрович Ильин» [Ivan Aleksandrovich Il'in], in Il'in, Собрание сочинений в 10 томах [Collection of Works in Ten Volumes] (1993), I, p. 11; A. F. Kiselev, Иван Ильин и его поющее сердце [Ivan Il'in and His Singing Heart] (2006), p. 23. However, a Letter from Il'in to L. Ia. Gurevich dated 25 January 1911 was apparently sent from Moscow and certainly not from abroad, given the content of the letter, whereas a letter sent to Gurevich on 2 February 1911 was sent from Berlin. See Il'in, note 5 above, pp. 39-44. In all it would appear that the Il'ins had at least sixteen months in Europe. Except, however, Il'in in his autobiography of 1932 wrote: "1910-1912 spent on an academic visit abroad: summer in Heidelberg (with Professor Windelband, Professor Jellinek, and Professor Lask); winter in Berlin (with Professor Zimmel); summer 1911 in Gõttingen (with Professor Husserl); and winter 1911-1912 in Paris and Berlin". See Shevelenko, note 2 above, p. 98.

23 РГИА, fond 733, opis 154, delo 376, l. 13-14. The discrepancy in dates is quite material: did the Il'ins spend sixteen or twenty-eight months in Europe.

24 Shevelenko, note 2 above, p. 99.

what is now the Institute of State and Law of the Russian Academy of Sciences. Il'in resumed his lecturing at Moscow University. He offered a course entitled "Introduction to the Philosophy of Law" and a seminar on the general methodology of the legal sciences. His courses on the same subject-matter continued at the Poltoratskii Higher Women's Legal Courses, and he offered tutorials on philosophy at the home of Professor G. N. Gabrichevskii. In all he was teaching for sixteen hours per week.

The Dean of the Moscow University Faculty of Law at this time was Pavel Vasilevich Gidulianov (1874-1937), professor of canon law and Director from 1911 of the Lazarev Institute of Oriental Languages. Il'in recalled how the Dean cornered him one day in the faculty common room and offered advice to the young privat-docent. Il'in should "simplify" his teaching, not complicating it with "unnecessary depth and detail". Students should be "allowed to pass" through the University without out making life difficult for them. Il'in was urged to accelerate his dissertation because a chair was vacant. Copy over your article on "Concepts of Law and Power", Gidulianov advised, and submit it for the magister degree. Il'in did not reply to the first advice, but as for the second, he said that he was preparing a large work on Hegel and did not intend to change his topic.[25]

Il'in's relations with Novgorodtsev deteriorated after his return from Europe as various colleagues tried to persuade Il'in to become involved in intrigues against Novgorodtsev. For a time Novgorodtsev, who was made aware of the intrigues, refused to support Il'in's reappointment as a lecturer at the Moscow Commercial Institute. Eventually, good relations were restored, and from 1 November 1913 Il'in was appointed an adjunct docent in the Chair of State Law at the Moscow Commercial Institute. He immediately became the most popular lecturer, attracting up to 1,200 students to his lectures, of whom 900 remained at the end of the semester.

The two years preceding the First World War were in many respects the happiest for Il'in. He was a popular lecturer in several institutions,[26] delivered reports in learned societies, studied in the libraries, wrote articles in books, attended the theatre and concerts, and visited intellectual evenings at the homes of sundry colleagues. His scholarly interests concentrated upon psychology and philosophy. In those years he was attracted by those philosophers who addressed various idealist systems and individualist conceptions. In 1911 he published an article on the idea

[25] Recounted in Il'in, Собрание сочинений: Письма. Мемуары [Collection of Works: Letters, Memoirs] (1999), p. 335.

[26] Looking back over the years 1912 to 1922, Il'in recalled that he had lectured at several institutions in addition to Moscow University, the Higher Women's Courses, and the Moscow Commercial Institute. He mentioned additionally the Shaniavskii People's University, the Cooperative Institute, the Higher Musical-Pedagogical Institute, and the Rhythmic Institute. See Shevelenko, note 2 above, p. 99.

of the individual in the teaching of Max Stirner (1806-1856).[27] This was followed in 1912 by an article on Fichte the Elder[28] and another on the concept of courtesy.[29]

Il'in's main preoccupation during this period, however, was his intended magister dissertation on Hegel. His interest in Hegel was piqued in 1908 when Il'in commenced readings on Hegel's "Phenomenology of Spirit". Looking back on this period, Il'in wrote in his introduction to the German-language Swiss edition of his dissertation: "I quickly sensed an enormous profound thought, honorable efforts in quests for truth and clarity, a wealth of views on the spiritual life and history of mankind".[30] Il'in completed his dissertation in 1916; it was published at Moscow two years later and used for his dissertation defense. He had devoted, he said, eight years of his life to fully comprehending the sources (twenty volumes, 8,000 pages of text) and scrupulously documenting his interpretation.[31] He had confined himself to original genuine texts written by Hegel in his own hand or dictated, verified, found to be mature, and handed over for printing. All of the texts required "… slow reading, a spiritual "loupe", concentrated meditation, and complete understanding".

Il'in undertook his studies of Hegel at a time when Hegelianism was enjoying a minor renaissance in Germany,[32] following a steady decline throughout the second half of the nineteenth century. In Hegelian philosophy Il'in saw the richest mine of major truths capable of illuminating the deepest secrets of the universe. Il'in saw his study of Hegel as an essential prerequisite for approaching Hegel's ideas on State and law: "The philosophy of Hegel is an integral metaphysical doctrine devoted to a single subject-matter and created by a single method. A study of his philosophy of law and State must commence with a mastery of this single and general metaphysical foundation".[33] The general value and purpose of his work he set out as follows:

27 Il'in, «Идея личности в учении Штирнера: Опыт по истории индивидуализма» [The Idea of the Individual in the Doctrine of Stirner: Essay on the History of Individualism], Вопросы философии и психологии [Questions of Philosophy and Psychology], no. 22 (1911), pp. 55-93.

28 Il'in, «Кризис субъекта в наукоучении Фихте Старшего: Опыт систематического анализа» [Crisis of the Subject in the Scientific Doctrine of Fichte the Elder], Вопросы философии и психологии [Questions of Philosophy and Psychology], no. 23 (1912), pp. 290-344.

29 Il'in, «О любезности: Социально-психологический опыт» [On Courtesy. Socio-Psychological Essay], Русская мысль [Russian Thought], no. 33 (1912), pp. 1-36.

30 I. A. Iljin, "Preface", in *Die Philosophie Hegels als Kontemplative Gotteslehre* (Bern, 1946).

31 Ibid.

32 On this phenomenon, see Il'in, «О возрождении гегельянства» [On the Renaissance of Hegelianism], Русская мысль [Russian Thought], no. 33 (1912), pp. 35-41.

33 The Theses to Il'in's dissertaton are set out in Il'in, Собрание сочинений: Философия

> On the threshold of new quests and achievements, in the struggle for spiritual purity, for authenticity of experience and objectivity of cognition, it is natural for philosophy to turn to its past in order to find inspiration, and a valedictory, in its greatest works. The genuinely great and significant always remains a hearth for spirit, capable of lighting new fires and giving a true sign of new, forthcoming triumphs. A work of genius functions like a door for anyone seeking access to the object itself, but one must know how not to screen oneself off from the object with this door, but rather to open it for oneself and for others; to open it in order to begin the struggle for independent and authentic experience and for true, objective knowledge. In this lies the supreme and fundamental task of the history of philosophy.[34]

He was severely critical of what had been written about Hegelian philosophy during the nineteenth and early twentieth centuries: "They speak and write about Hegel, but do not know precisely what he taught and what he wanted; the literature about him has an abundance of the most curious views and misunderstandings".[35] Subsequent writings were no improvement: "Marx, Engels, and so-called leftist Hegelians understood nothing from Hegel; they confused and distorted everything, such that they cannot be called Hegelians".[36]

In Spring 1914 Il'in's friend, Petr Bengardovich Struve (1870-1944), defended his magister dissertation in the field of economics: "Economy and Price: A Critical Study of the Theory and History of Economic Life". The official opponents were Professor Ordinarius Nikolai Alekseevich Kablukov (1849-1919), from the Chair of Political Economy and Statistics, and Professor Extraordinarius Andrei Kallinikovich Mitiukov (1871-after 1928), from the Chair of Roman Law. In complicity with Dean Gidulianov, they had decided to create difficulties for Struve by reason of his liberal views. Kabluklov spoke weakly and made no impression on the audience. Mitiukov accused Struve of plagiarizing from the Russian and Ukrainian philosopher Aleksandr Afanasevich Potebnia (1835-1891), but Struve easily refuted that accusation. Il'in had word of the impending scandal in advance and warned Struve what was afoot. During the defense and after the opponents had spoken, Il'in took the floor to say that although "I am not an economist and do not feel myself called upon to raise objections, I have attentively considered the methodological part of your work and consider it to be philologically brilliant and persuasive.

Гегеля как учение о конкретности Бога и человека [Collection of Works: The Philosophy of Hegel as a Doctrine of the Concreteness of God and Humanity] (2002), I, p. 397.

34 Il'in, *The Philosophy of Hegel as a Doctrine of the Concreteness of God and Humanity*, transl. P. T. Grier (2010), p. 5.

35 Note 3 above, I, p. 10.

36 Ibid., II, pp. 465-466.

When your work appears in foreign languages, we will be proud of you as we are now proud of you in Russia".[37]

On 8 May 1914 Il'in travelled in from the country estate to the Faculty of Laws to prepare for a visit abroad and to ascertain his teaching schedule for the forthcoming semester. He learned that his seminar on the general methodology of legal sciences had been cancelled and his lecture course on the introduction to the philosophy of law had been made an elective rather than, as before, compulsory. He perceived this as retaliation for his positive intervention in Struve's dissertation defense. The two remained close friends for the rest of their lives.

In spring 1914 Il'in delivered a report on Hegel to the Petersburg Philosophical Society.

First World War Years

When the First World War commenced, the Il'ins were in Vienna. Il'in either placed a trunk in storage or had a trunk sequestered by Austrian customs; the materials are ambiguous. Whatever the precise details, Il'in was unable or failed to take his dissertation research notes and manuscript with him. The Il'ins made their way home via Switzerland, Italy, Greece, Serbia, and Bulgaria, eventually arriving in Odessa. By 20 August 1914 Il'in was in the Crimea, depressed by the fact that the dissertation notes he had prepared from foreign sources available in Vienna but not in Russia were now beyond his reach and concerned about being called up for military service. In the end Il'in rewrote as best he could what remained in Austria, but he was unable to replicate in full all the sources consulted in Vienna, as he complained in his dissertation.[38]

Making a formal inquiry as to whether he would be called up, Il'in was advised that having the title of "magister" and a "permanent" lectureship at the university would exempt him from military service. The problem was that he was still not a magister and was not lecturing at the Moscow University. Having returned to Moscow on 10 September, Il'in learned that lecturing at the Moscow Commercial Institute would also exempt

[37] Il'in, note 5 above, p. 337. Dean Gidulianov officially informed Il'in that "The Faculty found your behavior inadmissible and decreed to announce to You a strict reprimand ... It was in vain to speak of the freedom of scientific views, the proper form of my address, and the merits of the classical work of P. B. Struve". Cited in Kiselev, note 2 above, p. 27. Il'in later listed himself as an "unofficial opponent" of the Struve dissertation. See Shevelenko, note 2 above, p. 99. In Spring 1914 Il'in also acted as an official opponent for the magister dissertation of A. A. Rozhdestvenskii on the "System of Subjective Public Rights".

[38] See Il'in's letter to his cousin, L. Ia. Gurevich, dated 19 February 1915. Il'in, note 5 above, p. 87; Grier, note 34 above, I, p. 271. Il'in described the materials in February 1915 as amounting to six or seven sheets or quires (it is unclear which, but probably quires) being replaced by him and a further six or seven to be written. In his dissertation, however, Il'in describes his notes as "detained by war" and irreplaceable in Russian sources. Il'in later in his autobiography said that part of his work on the philosophy of Hegel "perished in Austria", which "I wrote anew over two years". See Shevelenko, note 2 above, p. 99.

him from call-up, but Novgorodtsev refused to offer a position as there was no vacancy. Il'in then gathered his belongings and reported for duty at a military post. He was there informed that pursuant to a secret circular of the Ministry of War, all docents were exempted from military service. He was directed to return to his academic life.

In October 1914 Professor E. N. Trubetskoi organized a series of public lectures in Moscow on the "ideology of war". Il'in delivered one on the spiritual meaning of warfare.[39] The audience was small, and when Il'in was leaving after completing his lecture, a semi-drunk policeman approached him and said: "You know, professor, I wanted to interrupt and terminate your lecture when you touched upon the pogroms perpetrated by the mobilized reserves, but your eloquence won me over". Trubetskoi and Il'in left Moscow together for lectures in other Russian cities. In November 1914 Il'in delivered a lecture on the basic moral contradiction of war to the Moscow Psychological Society which later appeared in the Society journal.[40] Later he incorporated the piece in a larger work on the resisting of evil by force.[41]

The War did not interrupt the operation of institutions of higher education in Russia. Il'in continued to teach at the Law Faculty of Moscow University, Higher Women's Courses, and the Moscow Commercial Institute for 17 hours per week. Work on his dissertation continued. Indeed, Il'in published between 1914 and 1917 a number of journal articles based on his dissertation research. He was deflected from this in early 1915 when he agreed to write several sections on the general doctrine of law and State for the fourth edition of a basic introductory text intended for gymnasium students.[42] In this project he collaborated with Mikhail Nikolaevich Gernet (1874-1953), Ivan Borisovich Novitskii

[39] Later published as a pamphlet. See Il'in, Духовный смысл войны [Spiritual Meaning of Warfare] (1915).

[40] Il'in, «Основное нравственное противоречие войны» [Basic Moral Contradiction of War], Вопросы философии и психологии [Questions of Philosophy and Psychology], no. 25 (1914), pp. 797-826. The journal in which the article appeared was the subject of arrest by military authorities. Il'in appealed to the Procurator of the Moscow Judicial Chamber, and the arrest was removed. See Shevelenko, note 2 above, p. 99.

[41] Il'in, О противлении злу силой [On Counteracting Evil by Force] (Berlin, 1925).

[42] The first edition was published in 1907 under a different title. See V. M. Ustinov, M. N. Gernet, and I. B. Novitskii, Основные понятия русского государственного, гражданского и уголовного права: Общедоступные очерки [Basic Concepts of Russian State, Civil, and Criminal Law: Generally-Accessible Essays], preface by V. M. Khvostov (1907; 3d ed.; 1910). Gernet and Novitskii became well-known Soviet jurists. Vladimir Mikhailovich Ustinov successfully defended a dissertation for the degree of doctor of State sciences in 1907 and probably took the initiative to write the general introduction to Russian State, civil, and criminal law, adding Il'in as a co-author to the fourth and last edition. He was executive editor of the newspaper Утро России [Morning of Russia]. In 1919 he was sentenced to death in connection with the Tactical Center Case, replaced by deprivation of freedom for five years, but did not serve. He lectured in the Faculty of Social Sciences at Moscow University in 1921-1922.

(1880-1958), and Vladimir Mikhailovich Ustinov (1870-1941). The book appeared in that year, and the chapters written by Il'in have been published separately in his collected works.[43]

In 1916 Il'in was elected to the Board of the Society of Junior Lecturers of Moscow University, and in 1917, Chairman of the Society. As for the Hegel materials which remained in Austria, Il'in had no choice but to rewrite the relevant parts of the dissertation as best he could and accept the delayed completion.

Revolution and Civil War

In common with the great majority of the Russian intelligentsia, Il'in initially welcomed the February 1917 Revolution as an act of liberation by the Russian people that would save the Russian Empire from ruin. Russian unity was the key, he believed; caused by the War, this unity awakened an "ancient feeling of motherland" and introduced an awareness of unity between the State and the people. The will of the citizen ceased to concentrate upon special private interests of an individual class and was transformed into a general-political unity. The Russian people, he said, had completed the task initiated in 1905 and found their united will: to rescue the Motherland against attack and exercise a free authority of the people.[44]

For three months or so, Il'in took part in the events of the revolution, helping to organize various occasions and speaking out publicly. On 5 March 1917 Il'in addressed the Moscow Law Society on the subject: "The Struggle for Law Before the Court of Normal Legal Consciousness". By June 1917 he was exhausted. He wrote to his cousin, Liubov Iakovlevna Gurevich (1866-1940), on 5 June 1917 that: "I can do no more. And indeed the doctor has ordered this", as he decided to leave the field of revolutionary struggle and to write.[45] Retreating to the Il'in country estate at Vyropaevok, Il'in wrote a series of eight pamphlets under the general title of "Tasks of the Moment" that were published in late summer and autumn. These were not linked with any particular political party or movement, although they were remunerative.[46] Il'in called his missives

43 Il'in, «Общее учение о праве и государстве» [General Doctrine on Law and State], in Il'in, Собрание сочинений в десяти томах [Collection of Works in Ten Volumes] (1994), IV, pp. 47-147.

44 Il'in, «Партийная программа и максимализм» [Party Program and Maximalism], in Il'in, Собрание сочинений в десяти томах [Collection of Works in Ten Volumes] (), IX-X, p. 77.

45 Letter to L. Ia. Gurevich of 5 June 1917, reproduced in Il'in, Собрание сочинений: Дневник. Письма. Документы (1903-1938) [Collection of Works: Diary, Letters, Documents (1903-1938)], p. 92.

46 A pamphlet at the time published for general consumption in an edition of 100,000 or more copies in summer 1917 might engage a royalty in excess of 1,000 rubles per printed signature.

"squibs for the people". In a letter to Gurevich, Il'in described himself as follows: "Under the old regime I was a bourgeois radical and federalist-democrat (more or less) outside the parties. Now I am non-party … Especially now I am a patriot favoring a genuine aristocratic spirit".[47]

Il'in supported the February 1917 Revolution only because he saw good in it for Russia. He hoped and believed that Revolution would lay down the prerequisites for a renewal of Russian society. He supported the Provisional Government and favored the convening, at the end of the War, of a Constituent Assembly to establish a new State system. A man of intense emotions and passions, it is no surprise that by spring 1917 Il'in already was disappointed with the course of the Revolution. Looking back a decade later, in 1927, Il'in in some recollections penned at the time recalled a conversation in spring-summer 1917 with P. B. Struve. Il'in wanted to know whether Struve believed that the Investigative Commission formed by the Provisional Government into the affairs of the Russian Imperial family had found a basis for considering that the Tsar or Tsarina had committed treason. Hearing from Struve the reply: "No, nothing, absolutely nothing", Il'in inquired on what basis Miliukov on 1 November 1916 had delivered a speech in the State Duma on the subject of "Stupidity or Treason?" Struve's reply astonished Il'in. Miliukov, said Struve, also had no grounds for the accusation in the first place and raised the question because the Constitutional Democratic Party believed it was politically expedient at the time to raise insinuations against the royal family. Il'in promptly changed the subject.[48]

By October 1917, Il'in was thoroughly disillusioned with revolution. On 12 October 1917, in a public address to the II Moscow Meeting of Public Figures, Il'in said: "What remains of the revolution? The revolution has been transformed into the mercenary plundering of the State".[49] He lamented the anarchy and lack of respect for authority: "The fall of the old order created in revolutionary circles the assurance that anyone who wishes is empowered to rule in the person of the State. The power to rule and to command has come to be regarded as a masterless thing which may belong to each and all, to the first who grabs and seizes it … legal order is maintained only by inertia and an old reserve of fright".[50]

Once the Bolsheviks had come to power on 26 October 1917 (7 November 1917), Il'in looked back on the events from February to

[47] Note 45 above, p. 93.

[48] The occasion is recounted in Il'in, Собрание сочинений: Письма. Мемуары (1939-1954) [Collection of Works: Letters, Memoirs (1939-1954)], [XIV], p. 328.

[49] See Il'in, Собрание сочинений в десяти томах [Collection of Works in Ten Volumes] (1999), IX-X, p. 182.

[50] See his article five days before the Bolshevik Revolution: Il'in, «Чего ждать?» [What Are We Awaiting?], Утро России [Morning of Russia], 21 October 1917.

November 1917 as nothing other than a terrible nightmare.[51] He witnessed the actual battles in the streets of Moscow during the Bolshevik seizure of power. Recalling in 1930 the combat at the end of October 1917, he mentioned the skirmishes in the streets, the armistice, the surrender and handing over of weapons, the anatomy theater in the University filled with corpses gathered from the streets, faces of the wounded filled with incomprehension. The Bolshevik coup Il'in perceived as a turning point in the fate of Russia and in his own life. Paradoxically, the coup was a catastrophe for his country but a new life for him. Just as most other Russians, Il'in believed the Bolsheviks would remain in power but for a short time. But by December 1917 Il'in's attitude towards the incipient Constituent Assembly had changed diametrically from cautiously positive to implacably negative. His colleagues Fedor Fedorovich Kokoshkin (1871-1918) and Professor Novgorodtsev had been elected deputies to the Constituent Assembly. Encountering them on the street, Il'in implored them not to attend the Assembly and "… participate in that abominable and disgraceful institution".[52] Already, Il'in apprehended that the struggle against Bolshevism would be a lengthy one and a positive result not achieved through institutions and organizations.

The ultimate causes of the "Russian catastrophe" Il'in addressed in a speech to a public meeting in February 1918 at the Society of Young Lecturers of Moscow University. His subject was "patriotism". Russia had fallen, he said, not by reason of economic or technical backwardness. The Russian shortcomings were not material, but spiritual. He identified four major ailments sustained by the Russian soul in all strata of the population, in every Russian person. The future of Russia, he said, depended upon overcoming these "ailments".

The first was the "lack of a strong and mature legal consciousness". The Russian people, said Il'in, "do not know law [jus]; they do not understand that is has objective content; they do not see its objective significance; they do not acknowledge it, do not respect it, they do not impute to themselves the duty of voluntary compliance with it; they do not motivate their behavior by law; they observe it only because of fear or mercenary motives; they do not know how to live with it; they do not create it nor struggle for it".[53] The second ailment followed from the first and became evident during the revolutionary events of 1917: the failure of the Russian people to comprehend the essence of the State and a lack of knowledge and skill of how to build one. Russians, Il'in said, did not know how to distinguish the State from State power, and power from the

51 Il'in, «Кошмар» [Nightmare], Утро России [Morning of Russia], 10 November 1917.

52 Il'in, «Встречи и беседы» [Meetings and Conversations], in Il'in, Собрание сочинений: Письма. Мемуары (1939-1954) [Collection of Works: Letters, Memoirs (1939-1954)], [XIV], pp. 328-329.

53 Il'in, «О патриотизме» [On Patriotism], in Il'in, Собрание сочинений: Справедливость или равенство? [Collection of Works: Justness or Equality?] (2006), [XXVII], p. 354.

person who governed it. They failed to understand that the Russian State is they themselves, that the State exists in them, through them, and in the form of them. They did not feel themselves to be included in their own State; they had no consciousness of State unity, no will to support the State, no ability to preserve it. They did know how to fear State power when the State was strong; they knew how to criticize it, suspect it, but not trust it; they knew how, when necessary, to bribe it.

The third ailment, said Il'in, was a failure to understand the essence of democracy coupled with a distorted attitude towards the people. Democracy in Russia had been transformed into a system of bribery. The major ailment, however, in Il'in's eyes was a lack of true patriotism. A love for one's fatherland, he believed, must underlie legal consciousness, the health of statehood, and a normal democracy.[54] Bolshevism (and Il'in was far from alone among the Russian intelligentsia in coming to this perception) as a phenomenon had its roots in the world outlook and psychology of Russian society and therefore could not disappear without leaving some trace. Some Russians believed the proper course of action was to emigrate or to engage actively in armed combat against Bolshevism. Il'in recommended the last course and later said that had he not been exiled from Russia, he would have been in active struggle to eliminate Bolshevism in his homeland.

Igor Aleksandrovich Il'in (1892-1937), a sworn advokat before the 1917 revolutions, remained in Soviet Russia and found a place under the new system. He was arrested in 1937, accused of engaging in anti-Soviet propaganda, and shot. His relatives were told that Igor had perished in 1943 on the front. He was rehabilitated in the 1950s. Another brother, Aleksandr Aleksandrovich, left Russia for the United States before, during, or shortly after the 1917 revolutions and apparently remained there. Under the Russian Provisional Government from February to October 1917 and initially under the Bolsheviks the universities and other educational institutions continued to operate more or less normally and cautiously. It was less a coup and more like a change of cabinet, said one observer.

While readying his dissertation for publication and defense, Il'in devoted much of his time to the subject first mentioned in his address on patriotism: legal consciousness. He lectured on the subject extensively during 1916 and 1917 in a number of Moscow educational institutions and public occasions.[55] By the end of 1917, within days after the October Revolution, the text of his book may have been more or less completed in

[54] Ibid., pp. 356-357.

[55] It has been aptly observed that the lectures and efforts of Il'in and others were the non-Bolshevik answer to agitprop. The intelligentsia "went to the people" out of a "... love of culture and social and political idealism. Their aim was to teach and encourage an appreciation of Russian culture and help spread its benefits to the long deprived and illiterate masses". See L. Chamberlain, *The Philosophy Steamer: Lenin and the Exile of the Intelligentsia* (2006), p. 43.

galley proofs; the tides of fate were such, however, that the book appeared only posthumously in 1956 in a Russian language text and appears in the present volume for the first time in English.

"Legal consciousness" was understood by Il'in in a much broader sense and context than modern Russian legal doctrine does. Given its scope and range, Il'in's work on legal consciousness might well have been entitled: on the essence of law and State. Modern Russian legal doctrine shares a narrower understanding of legal consciousness: the aggregate of knowledge, ideas, views, notions, feelings, and moods relating to law.[56] Soviet approaches to legal consciousness strongly reinforced this approach.[57] For Il'in, though, legal consciousness was linked not only with law, but with society as a whole, with the entire life of society.

By spring 1918 Il'in's monumental magister dissertation on Hegel was in print just in time for his dissertation defense. Earlier efforts to complete the printing had apparently for various reasons not come to fruition. Il'in finally turned to Georgii Adolfovich Leman-Abrikosov (1887-1968), who agreed to assist. In his unpublished manuscript memoirs held by the Russian State Library, Leman-Abrikosov wrote as follows on this affair:

> I cannot recall where and how we became acquainted. But somehow he came to me as a publisher – later he called me his "editor" – with a request to publish his work on Hegel. At the time his work had been completed and some Jew known to him gave him money to print it. However, for some reason this printing did not transpire, and his request was to continue this unrealized printing and bring it to completion. I with delight assumed this task and indeed brought it to successful completion. Success, in particular, consisted of his having within a short time to defend his work as a magister dissertation, and he implored me to have the second volume printed before the day of defense. This I succeeded in doing".[58]

Il'in's defense of his dissertation is legendary in its own right. The defense was scheduled for 19 May 1918 at the Law Faculty of Moscow University at 14:00 hours. A month or so before the scheduled defense an event occurred which nearly frustrated the entire occasion. On 15

[56] See, for example, M. N. Marchenko, Теория государства и права [Theory of State and Law] (2009), p. 798.

[57] See Iu. K. Pogrebnaia, Кризис современного российского правосознания [Crisis of Contemporary Russian Legal Consciousness] (2013).

[58] ОР РГБ, fond 218, K. 1272. Item 5, list 2. Although not published until 2010, the memoirs of Leman-Abrikosov are believed to have been written no earlier than 1957. The "Jew" referred to was Vladimir Bary, whose grandfather, Veniamin Matveevich Bary, graduated from a Talmudic School in Königsberg. He intended to be come a Rabbi, but converted to Lutheranism. See Il'in, Собрание сочинений: О возрождении и обновлении России [Collection of Works: On the Rebirth and Renewal of Russia] (2021), [XXXIII] (3), p. 582. An excerpt from the Leman-Abrikosov memoir is published in Ibid., pp. 322-331.

April 1918 Il'in was arrested pursuant to an Order issued by the All-Russian Extraordinary Commission and held in custody. The arrest was occasioned by testimony from a Lieutenant Dmitrii Antonovich Gromov, who had been detained in connection with a case concerning a counter-revolutionary organization that was allegedly forming a "Voluntary Army". This organization had been established at the end of 1917 by a group of persons led by Countess Aleksandrovna Nikolaevna Lanskaia and had divisions in a number of large Russian cities, including Moscow and Petrograd. By spring 1918 the organization had supplied regiments headed by Ataman Aleksei Maksimovich Kaledin (1861-1918) and General Lavr Georgievich Kornilov (1870-1918) with more than 2,000 volunteers, uniforms, and supplies.

On the eve of Il'in's arrest in Moscow, a leading American engineer, Woldemar (Vladimir) Aleksandrovich Bary (1887-1979),[59] was arrested as a leader of the "Voluntary Army" organization. At an interrogation on 14 April 1918, according to some sources conducted by Feliks Dzerzhinskii (1877-1926) himself, Bary said with respect to Il'in: "Privat-docent Il'in I know personally, but I have no knowledge of what relations he has with the organization of Countess Lanskaia. I know only that Il'in is at the head of those who wished to continue the war with Germany, that is, belonged to an organization of Allies".[60] Nothing was said about Il'in belonging to a counter-revolutionary organization, nor indeed of the others arrested in the case: V. V. Krivoshein and K. M. Khalafov. Among Bary's papers and accounts, though, was an entry dated 30 November 1917 in Il'in's own hand: "8000 – Iv. A. I. 30 November".[61] This entry led the investigators to believe that Il'in had received money from Bary to be transferred to the officers being sent to the Don military theater. Thus commenced Case No. 93 against Il'in, Bary, Krivoshein, and Khalafov.

[59] Russian language materials refer to Bary as "Vladimir"; his United States passport and census documents refer to him as Woldemar; stockholder records of the Sikorsky Aviation Corporation mention him as "Vladimir"; and reports of Vice Consul John Lehrs to his superiors in the Department of State refer to him as "Woldemar". However, McFadden refers him unaccountably as "John Bary", although the sources McFadden used do not use this name. McFadden also misidentifies the repository of the Francis Papers, which are at the Missouri Historical Society (St. Louis), and not the Missouri State Historical Society (Columbia). See David W. McFadden, *Alternative Paths: Soviets and Americans, 1917-1920* (1993), pp. 133-134.

[60] Cited in Il'in, Собрание сочинений: Дневник. Письма. Документы (1903-1938) [Collection of Works: Diary, Letters, Documents (1903-1938)], [XIV], p. 583.

[61] The sum of "8000" is designated, but not the currency. The Russian investigators and later researchers seem to have assumed that the figure referred to Russian currency, and not to United States dollars. If a "subsidy" to White forces was truly involved, one would perhaps expect a hard currency transaction. On the other hand, if the transaction were not in rubles, one would expect the currency to be designated. In a separate case during an interrogation of 5 November 1918 Ill'in acknowledged that he received the 8,000 rubles to pay for printing his dissertation but in late January 1918 he repaid Bary because he found a publisher, Georgii Adolf' Leman, who was prepared to publish the book and pay a royalty. Nikolai Petrovich Tarasov (1897-1982), Il'in said, was a witness to the repayment.

At his interrogation by the All-Russian Extraordinary Commission on 21 April 1918, Il'in denied any knowledge of Gromov, but admitted that he was acquainted with Bary and Countess Lanskaia. He also firmly rejected any suggestion of an affiliation with a counter-revolutionary organization. He swore to the investigator that he had never belonged to any political party and never worked for any political organization. Quite apart, he said, from a general inclination not to engage in political organizations, his health and lecture commitments (twenty hours per week) precluded any such activities. He intended, he added, to publish three books in the imminent future.[62]

On the following day, 16 April 1918, the Board of the Society of Young Lecturers of Moscow University petitioned the All-Russian Extraordinary Commission for Il'in's immediate release on the grounds of ill health and teaching commitments at the University and elsewhere in Moscow. The Board in its petition acknowledged its readiness to act as surety for Il'in. On 18 and 19 April additional petitions were received from Higher Women's Legal and Historical-Philological Courses and other Moscow institutions. These petitions produced results. On 24 April 1918 Il'in was released into the custody of the Board of the Society of Young Lecturers on condition of agreeing to return to the investigator at his first request.

On 27 April 1918 the Il'in case was transferred to the Revolutionary Tribunal. The conclusion to indict charged that Il'in, together with Vladimir Aleksandrovich Bary, Vasilii Vasilevich Krivoshein, and Konstantin Moiseevich Khalafov, were involved in the activities of a counter-revolutionary organization and therefore were guilty of a "plot against the Russian Soviet Republic". At a session of the Investigative Committee attached to the Moscow Revolutionary Tribunal held on the same day a decision was adopted to satisfy the petition of the defenders of Krivoshein and Konstantin Moiseevich Khalafov to be released from custody. The United States Vice Consul, John A. Lehrs (1888-1961), was present at this session and requested that V. A. Bary be released under surety to him and granted "… those rights which have been provided by the Dekret of the Revolutionary Tribunal with respect to all citizens of the Russian Republic".[63] The Russian defenders and the Vice Consul

62 His dissertation on Hegel was divided into three parts, but ultimately was published in two volumes.

63 Documents of the VChK, GPU, NKVD, published in Il'in, Собрание сочинений: Дневник, Письма, Документы (1903-1938) [Collection of Works: Diary, Letters, Documents (1903-1938)] (1999), [XIII], p. 384. These are reproduced again in greater number and together with the documents relating to the others accused. See Il'in, Собрание сочинений: О возрождении и обновлении России [Collection of Works: On the Rebirth and Renewal of Russia] (2021), [XXXIII] (3), pp. 7-231. The Department of State of the United States took exceptional measures between November 1917 and September 1918 to understand what was happening in Russia and substantially increased their staffing, especially in the provinces, for this purpose. For details, see D. A. Langbart, "'Spare No Expense': The Department of State and the Search for Information About Bolshevik Russia, November 1917-September 1918", *Intelligence and National Security*, IV (1989), pp. 316-334. Vice Consul Lehrs was part of that undertaking. In June 1918 Lehrs requested

simultaneously petitioned to have the matter now treated as an inquiry, and not a preliminary investigation. The Investigative Commission decreed to transfer the case for further investigation to the Political Section of the Investigative Commission attached to the Moscow Revolutionary Tribunal.

Thus ended Il'in's second arrest in Soviet Russia. He was now able to defend his dissertation. The printer delivered several copies of volume two of the dissertation on the morning of 19 May 1918, the very day of the defense, to the Faculty of Law at Moscow University. The legend, however, continues. One of the two official opponents for the magister dissertation was Il'in's supervisor, Pavel I. Novgorodtsev. Il'in learned on 18 May 1918 that Novgorodtsev was likely to be arrested. He warned Novgorodtsev about this and strongly urged him not to spend the night at home, when the arrest was likely to occur. On the morning of 19 May it became clear that Il'in's apprehensions were well-founded. The police had raided Novgorodtsev's apartment at night, conducted a search, and left officers to await Novgorodtsev's return. At 14:00 hours all assembled at Moscow University for the dissertation defense, but Novgorodtsev had not arrived. Under the regulations, a defense could not occur if only one opponent was present, in this case Professor E. N. Trubetskoi. When Novgorodtsev arrived half an hour late, the defense commenced. It lasted for four hours. In an exceptionally rare outcome, Il'in was awarded the degree of magister for volume one of his work on Hegel, and the doctor of State sciences for volume two.[64]

the Council of People's Commissars to issue licenses for United States consular officials to carry firearms. When no reply was received to this request, on 27 June 1918 Lehrs went directly to the Russian Foreign Minister, Georgii Vasilevich Chicherin (1872-1936), and Karl Radek (1885-1939) to demand the weapons authorizations. Radek answered that Feliks Dzerzhinskii and the Cheka refused to issue them, regarding the American consular personnel as counter-revolutionaries. The annoyed Lehrs replied that he would arm the consular personnel without the required licenses. Radek replied that if this were done, the American consular officials would be shot on sight. Lehrs replied that anyone seeking to remove weapons from the consular personnel would themselves be shot and then walked out of the conversation. Lehrs was then "reassigned" away from Moscow to Ambassador David R. Francis in Vologda. Lehrs prepared a "Memorandum" on the incident with Radek dated 29 June 1918, and Radek prepared his own account of what transpired, duly forwarded to DeWitt Poole on 28 June. Poole reassigned Lehrs to Vologda "... for his personal safety". See the Lehrs Memorandum and accompanying Soviet materials in the David R. Francis Papers, microfilm edition, Reel 10. Also see McFadden, note 58 above, p. 134. Ambassador Francis used Lehrs frequently in his communications with Chicherin and the eventual move of the United States Legation to Archangelsk. See D. R. Francis, *Russia from the American Embassy 1916-1918* (1921; reprint ed., 1970), p. 259. Lehrs served from 1921 to 1923 with the American Relief Administration in Russia and at various times as Vice Consul in Switzerland and Spain. On the ARA, see American Relief Administration, Russian Operations Records, Box 52, Folder 2, Hoover Institution Archives.

64 The dissertation defense was reported in glowing terms by V. M. Ustinov, «Диспут И. А. Ильина» [Dispute of I. A. Il'in], Заря России [Dawn of Russia], no. 34 (5 June (23 May) 1918), p. 1; republished in Il'in, Собрание сочинений: О возрождении и обновлении России [Collection of Works: On the Rebirth and Renewal of Russia] (2021), [XXXIII] (3), pp. 77-78.

The investigation of Il'in for counter-revolutionary activity arising out of his April arrest continued throughout the summer. On 23 July 1918 Il'in was summoned by the Investigative Commission attached to the Moscow Revolutionary Tribunal to appear for interrogation as an accused in the case. Il'in at the time was not in Moscow. He and his wife were visiting the country estate of a friend. Accordingly, Il'in did not appear when summoned. A second summons was despatched to him on 30 July, and he again failed to appear. The Investigative Committee then issued an order for Il'in's arrest on 10 August, which was executed on the following day. It appears that he was held in custody for more than two months, although correspondence from Il'in suggests that within this period Il'in may have been at liberty for three days. He was ultimately released on 17 October 1918 and three days later was lecturing again in Moscow educational institutions.

On 3 November 1918 Il'in was arrested once more with regard to the same case. The investigator in the case stated in his conclusion to indict dated 28 November 1918 that in view of the circumstances Il'in "... should be confined in a concentration camp".[65] Not long before his pending trial, Il'in was released probably because the institutions at which Il'in was lecturing petitioned for him to be allowed to resume his duties. On 19 December 1918 Il'in was summoned to a session of the Moscow Revolutionary Tribunal, which designated 26 December as the trial date but then postponed the proceeding to 28 December. The Tribunal completely exonerated Il'in, decreeing to "deem the participation of Citizen Il'in in a counter-revolutionary organization to be unproven, his explanations concerning his relations with Bary and Lanskaia to deserve trust, and that he himself is not dangerous to the revolution. The case concerning Il'in is terminated forever pursuant to the Decree of the VI Congress of Soviets on Amnesty".[66]

As for Bary and the other co-defendants, they had fled Moscow and their cases were considered *in absentia*. Bary was declared to be an enemy of the entire working people of mankind and if extradited to Russia or apprehended, to be shot upon the establishment of his identity. The two Russian co-defendants were sentenced to a similar fate. In the sanguinary spirit of the Russian Revolution, Bary's sentence was embellished with the following instruction: "any citizen to whom the liberation of mankind is dear and who encounters him on the planet should shoot Bary".[67]

How did Il'in escape execution by a Revolutionary Tribunal when others on a daily basis suffered this fate? The confluence of a number

65 The original text of the investigator's opinion is reproduced in Iu. T. Lisitsa (comp.), Иван Ильин и Россия: Неопубликованные фотографии и архивные материалы [Ivan Il'in and Russia: Unpublished Photographs and Archival Materials] (1999), p. 72.

66 The document is reproduced in facsimile in ibid., p. 73. Note that the outcome, formally speaking, was not acquittal, but that Il'in was "amnestied".

67 Note 45 above, p. 423.

of circumstances may explain the favorable outcome for Il'in. The accusation against Il'in was tenuous at best. Even the investigator did not recommend execution; he suggested confinement in a concentration camp. Such camps had been established by the Bolsheviks for persons suspected of counter-revolutionary views. The tenor of the proceeding suggests that the Tribunal wished to hear Il'in's explanations. The chairman of the Tribunal, A. M. Diakonov, said:

> As the comrade assessors are aware, the sole grounds for accusing I. A. Il'in is the testimony of witness Gromov, who has now recanted his testimony, saying that he does not remember. The comrade assessors shall hear the explanations of Il'in and decide whether to believe his words or not".[68]

Moreover, Il'in had retained the services of a skilled and experienced defender, Mikhail Iur'evich Goldman (1882-1938). The defense did not confine itself merely to showing that Il'in's involvement in a counter-revolutionary organization had not been proven. An affirmative position was launched to establish that Il'in represented no danger to the Revolution. Goldman told the Tribunal:

> During 1918, I. A. Il'in performed his lecturing activities to the greatest degree ... He delivered courses of lectures on philosophy, logic, history of political doctrines, and all those who truly wanted to know how and what Il'in thinks had the broadest opportunity to be persuaded of this. I am convinced that among his numerous audience there were communists and persons who support Soviet power not from fear, but from conscience. If any anti-Soviet elements had been truly noted in his activities, all those present would have had sufficient material for this.[69]

Perhaps, however, the principal factor influencing the favorable outcome was a letter written by the historian, Aleksei Ivanovich Iakovlev (1878-1951), on 24 August 1918 to Vladimir Il'ich Lenin, the Chairman of the Council of People's Commissars. Iakovlev's father, Ivan Iakovlevich Iakovlev (1848-1930), a Chuvash educator, had at one time cared for Lenin's brother, Alexander, and was close to the Ul'ianov family. In his letter A. I. Iakovlev informed Lenin about the so-called "Bary & Co." case before the Moscow Revolutionary Tribunal and that his colleague, I. A. Il'in, was among the defendants. This, Iakovlev said, was most certainly a misunderstanding very unpleasant for Il'in. Iakovlev then explained that among the arguments incriminating Il'in was the 8,000 rubles given him by Bary, which was indeed intended to help Il'in pay for the printing of his dissertation brilliantly defended in the past May. In addition, Iakovlev noted, Il'in was one of the most valuable lecturers in his School and was not in the best of health. Iakovlev assured Lenin that Il'in was not involved

[68] Ibid., p. 418.

[69] Ibid., p. 419.

in politics in any way and had no intention of becoming involved. Lenin was asked to terminate the proceedings in the case and to invite Iakovlev to chat about some interesting issues of current historical developments. Lenin did invite Iakovlev in for a meeting, and as a result a copy of Iakovlev's letter was passed by the Administrative Office of the Council of People's Commissars to the Moscow Revolutionary Tribunal to be "attached to the file of the case concerning Bary & Co.". It is probable that the Moscow Revolutionary Tribunal was influenced when deciding the Bary case with respect to Il'in by the presence of Lenin's letter in the file. Iakovlev undoubtedly also was aware that Lenin was interested in and attracted by Hegelian philosophy; it was no coincidence that Iakovlev mentioned Il'in's work on Hegel twice in his letter.[70]

A parallel proceeding (Case No. 1315) seems to have been instituted in November 1918 with respect to Il'in. On 3 November Il'in's apartment was searched, documents seized, and Il'in arrested. Il'in was interrogated on 5 November 1918, where he explained that he had received 8,000 rubles from Vladimir Bary and repaid that sum in late January 1918. The conclusion of the investigator, Vozdvizhenskii, was that the entire transaction was highly suspicious. He claimed that the sum was received by Il'in on "30 September 1917" and that the publishing contract was entered into on "28 September '18", by which time Bary had absconded. Moreover, said the investigator, Il'in signaled acceptance of the amount with his initials, not his full name. If the money was intended for legal purposes, concluded the investigator, there was no reason to conceal the transaction. Il'in knew Countess Lanskaia, acquired food products from her at reduced prices, and knew she was supplying the Cossacks. He recommended that Il'in should be confined "in a concentration camp". Il'in's exoneration by Extraordinary Investigative Commission for the Struggle Against Counter-Revolution on 28 December 1918 brought an end to this proceeding as well.[71]

On 29 August 1919 Il'in's arrest was again ordered (Case No. 113568) and his apartment searched. On this occasion it was apparently intended to implicate Il'in in the well-publicized case against an anti-Bolshevik underground organization, the "National Center", in which several leaders of the Kadet Party were involved. Il'in was not a member of that

[70] While the Bolsheviks were releasing Il'in, there is a certain irony in the fact that during the winter of 1918 Il'in was approached by a former justice of the peace, N. V. Iakushkin, who served as a volunteer during the War in a bacteriological laboratory. Iakushkin said that friends of his had at their disposal some containers of Asiatic cholera bacteria that might be used against the Bolsheviks. Iakushkin asked Il'in's advice. Il'in replied that the Bolsheviks "could and should be overcome only by spiritual, religious, and State, but not the mass dying of the people from epidemics". He gave analogous advice to White officers who sought Il'in's views on the use of poisonous gas against the Bolsheviks. See Kiselev, note 2 above, pp. 64-65.

[71] The documents concerning this affair were discovered by Iurii T. Lisitsa in the archive of the Federal Security Service and are reproduced in Il'in, Собрание сочинений: О возрождении и обновлении России [Collection of Works: On the Rebirth and Renewal of Russia] (2021), [XXXIII](3), pp. 232-246.

Party at any time. Il'in was tipped off and managed to be elsewhere when the authorities arrived.[72] According to some sources, Il'in was involved in supporting the cavalry raids of General Konstantin Konstantinovich Mamontov (1869-1920) by helping to cut telegraph lines.

Il'in's work on Hegel saved him from execution again in 1920. On 24 February 1920 Il'in was arrested in the case of the so-called "Tactical Center", a political association created to coordinate the activities of anti-Bolshevist organizations in the city of Moscow (Case No. 803). Two days later, after a brief interrogation, Il'in was unexpectedly released. Lenin had once more intervened. The evidence comes from several diverse sources. The head of the Administrative Office of the Council of People's Commissars, Vladimir Dmitrievich Bonch-Bruevich (1873-1955), related that shortly after Il'in had been arrested his office received a declaration that Il'in was ill and could not undergo prison confinement. Attached to the declaration was the two-volume set of Il'in's work on Hegel. Bonch-Bruevich immediately reported the matter to Lenin, providing him with the declaration, the books, and various materials assembled. Lenin "… devoted serious attention to this case, personally rang Comrade Dzerzhinskii, learned what the case was about, and took all measures to facilitate the lot and then to release this scholar-prisoner of the revolution. The books, which had not previously fallen into his hands before, he carefully studied with pencil in hand". Then Lenin said to Bonch-Bruevich, although Il'in's views are "not ours", his books "all the same are good".[73]

Another source, Karl Radek (1893-1938), said that when he visited Lenin, the last told him that Il'in had been arrested. Lenin immediately called the Cheka and said to Agranov, who was leading the investigation: "You once more have arrested Professor Il'in? This is a public scandal! Interrogate him at once, release him, and leave him in quiet!" Having been told this about himself, Il'in asked in wonderment: "What am I to him?" They replied that Lenin had read his book about Hegel and had a high opinion of the book. Il'in related in his own memoirs that "tame" communists had told him that he had a good notation at the

[72] The documents appear in Il'in, Собрание сочинений: О возрождении и обновлении России [Collection of Works: On the Rebirth and Renewal of Russia] (2021), [XXXIII] (3), pp. 247-251.

[73] Огонек [Small Light], no. 3 (20 January 1929), p. 2. One wonders whether Lenin knew, or recalled, that his own work on materialism and empirocriticism, published under the pseudonym "Vl. Il'in", had been savagely reviewed by I. A. Il'in in Русские ведомости [Russian Gazette], no. 222 (1909). According to other sources, the copy of Il'in's book on Hegel and other materials were delivered by Nikolai Petrovich Tarasov (1897-1982): "After the arrest of Il'in, N. P. wrote an application, took two volumes of the book on Hegel, and went to Lenin. Passed all this to the secretary. They replied that Il'in would be freed. A memo of Lenin to Dzerzhinskii exists: 'Il'in, although not ours, but talented, release him'". Cited in Iu. T. Lisitsa, «Иван Александрович Ильин: Историко-биографический очерк» [Ivan Aleksandrovich Il'in: Historico-Biographical Survey], in Lisitsa (ed.), И. А. Ильин: Собрание сочинений [I. A. Il'in: Collection of Works] (1993-), I, p. 27.

GPU: he was considered to be an Hegelian. Il'in replied that this was a misunderstanding. He was never an Hegelian and Karl Marx had nothing in common with Hegel. He was told to keep quiet and not object. Being a Hegelian was his protection. While living abroad in emigration, Il'in later learned that Lenin said to his protégés: "Write about Marx as Il'in wrote about Hegel! Why do you not write thus? Because you cannot!"

These anecdotes are confirmed by two unrelated considerations. First, there are materials in the Central Archive of the Federal Security Service of the Russian Federation, where "Talon No. 356" directed the head of the indoor prison to immediately release Il'in from custody. The document was issued on the basis of an order from Agranov dated 26 February 1920. During his interrogation on the occasion of this arrest, Il'in was asked about his political sympathies. His reply: "I will be sympathetic to any State authority which nurtures a normal legal consciousness in the people".[74] Second, Lenin's personal library contains a copy of Il'in's dissertation; it is a reasonable speculation that this is the copy of the book that came to Lenin as described above and that Lenin read, underscored, and annotated it.[75]

Il'in was elected to the Moscow (later All-Russian) Union of Writers.[76] In autumn 1921 all lecturers in the field of philosophy who were not members of the Communist Party were dismissed from the faculties of social sciences (which the universities had been renamed in 1919) and transferred to an Institute of Philosophy attached to the university. Il'in was among those affected. The academic year 1921-1922 was his last in Russia: he offered two seminars: one on the philosophy of Hegel and the other on the method of philosophy. By early 1921 the defeat of the White Guard in the Russian Civil War left Il'in without any hopes that Russia would be rescued from Bolshevism. Il'in's father died in November 1921.

[74] Note 45 above, p. 427. In his interrogation at the time, Il'in said that he had given a report on the "Religious Foundations of Legal Consciousness in which I had tried to ascertain the religious (not confessional) nature of normal legal consciousness leading a person along an extra-Party and above-class path towards nurturing in oneself feelings of own dignity, inner self-discipline, mutual respect, and trust. I guide myself in so doing by convictions of non-Party ideology, not anticipating anything good from the civil war, class embitterness, or policy of coercion and revenge". Il'in, Собрание сочинений: О возрождении и обновлении России [Collection of Works: On the Rebirth and Renewal of Russia] (2021), [XXXIII](3), pp. 256-257. When enumerating the reasons for deporting Il'in, the List of candidates indicated that "In the Spring of this year he visited illegal meetings in the apartment of Professor Avinov, were he delivered abstracts and reports of a counter-revolutionary character". Ibid., p. 272.

[75] See item No. 1074, Библиотека В. И. Ленина в Кремле: Каталог [Library of V. I. Lenin in the Kremlin: Catalog] (1961), p. 159. As the catalog demonstrates, Lenin marked and annotated his books and placed ownership inscriptions and stamps on them. The anecdotes are consistent with Lenin's routine reading practices.

[76] «Ильин Иван Александрович» [Il'in Ivan Aleksandrovich], in Iu. V. Mukhachev (ed.), Российской научное зарубежье: Биобиблиографический справочник [Russian Scientific Abroad: Biobibliographical Manual] (2011), p. 306.

In addition to his lectures and seminars, Il'in delivered in the early 1920s a series of lectures on the philosophy of religion at the Psychological Society, of which he had become the chairman in 1920, succeeding Lev Mikhailovich Lopatin (1855-1920). On the fortieth day after mourning his father, he delivered a lecture on the "Religious Meaning of Sincerity". His mother was in the audience. The lecture later became chapter 19 of his treatise on the axioms of religious experience.

Il'in was elected to the Board of the Moscow Law Society in 1921. The Society had done little since 1917 and was considered to be dormant. After a five-year interval, the Society began to meet in spring 1922. Il'in delivered a lecture on the "Basic Tasks of Jurisprudence in Russia".[77] Legal science, he said, must be built not simply as a science about "law", but a science concerning "law in a normal legal consciousness". Jurisprudence should be placed on the firm ground of genuine legal experience.

Banishment from Russia

On 4 September 1922 Il'in was again arrested. The order had been issued more than two weeks previously, on 16 August, as part of a general round-up of Russian intellectuals. But Il'in was not to be found at his Moscow home; he spent the summer of 1922 at the family country estate or the estate of Mikhail Vasilevich Nesterov (1862-1942), the artist who painted the remarkable portrait of Il'in. It took some time for the police to locate him.

This arrest was unlike the others. Modern scholars see the episode as an

> … attempt of the authorities to establish strict ideological control, having removed from the country the intellectual elite – those people who might think freely, autonomously analyze the situation and express their ideas, and also often criticize the existing regime. They did not want to "stick to" their convictions or change them, they thought, wrote, and spoke as their conscience dictated, remaining free under conditions of a strengthening non-freedom. By an independent word they attempt to persuade of their rightness, however this turned out for them personally.[78]

In spring 1922 the Bolsheviks had begun to prepare an extensive offensive to banish abroad those members of the Russian intelligentsia who

[77] The text was published as Il'in, «Основные задачи правоведения в России» [Basic Tasks of Jurisprudence in Russia], Русская мысль [Russian Thought], no. VIII-XII (Prague, 1922), pp. 162-188, edited by P. B. Struve.

[78] M. E. Glavatskii, «Философский пароход»: год 1922-й: Историографические этюды [The "Philosophy Steamer": The Year 1922: Historiographical Studies] (Ekaterinburg, 2002), pp. 24-25.

were considered to be potential opponents of the Bolshevik policies.[79] The III session of the All-Russian Central Executive Committee, held from 12 to 26 May 1922, confirmed the 1922 Criminal Code of the RSFSR. That Code included among the punishments that might be assigned: "expulsion from the limits of the RSFSR for a term or in perpetuity". Among the crimes that might be punished by expulsion was "propaganda and agitation in the direction of assistance to the international bourgeoisie". The criminal offense of the "arbitrary return" to the RSFSR after such expulsion was the death penalty.

Il'in's name figured on the list of candidates drawn up for exile, falling into the category of "active anti-Soviet intelligentsia" in Moscow who were "subject to exile abroad or to determined points in the RSFSR". With respect to Il'in personally, it was noted: "Definitely anti-Soviet". The List of "active anti-Soviet intelligentsia" was confirmed on 10 August 1922 by the Politburo of the Central Committee of the Russian Communist Party.

Upon being arrested on 4 September 1922 (Case No. 15778), Il'in was immediately interrogated by an officer from the IV Section of the Secret Division of the State Political Administration (GPU). Il'in's replies during the interrogation, which survive in the Central Archive of the Federal Security Service, suggest Il'in was rather candid: Q: "Tell us, Mr. Il'in, your views on the structure of Soviet power and the system of the proletarian State?" A: "I believe Soviet power to be an historically inevitable formalization of a great socio-spiritual ailment which has matured in Russia over several centuries". Q: "Your views on the tasks of the intelligentsia and so-called public?" A: "The task of the intelligentsia is to nurture a new world outlook and legal consciousness and to teach it to others; the task of the old Russian public is to understand its unfoundedness and to begin to exist anew". Q: "Your views of political parties in general and on the Russian Communist Party, in particular?" A: A political party builds a State only when and only insofar as it sincerely serves above-class solidarity; I am deeply convinced that the Russian Communist Party, in neglecting this principle, is harming itself, its cause, its power, and Russia".[80] Upon completion of the interrogation, Il'in signed the usual undertaking not to leave Moscow without the authorization of the GPU

[79] Some believe the initiative has origins dating back to 1919. For a succinct summary of the origin and sequence of events based on security service archives, see V. S. Khristoforov, «Высылка ученых и деятелей культуры из России в 1922 г. в документах ГПУ» [Exile of Scholars and Cultural Figures from Russia in 1922 in the Documents of the GPU], in L.S. Fleishman (ed.), Русский Берлин: 1920-1945 [Russian Berlin: 1920-1945] (2006), pp. 39-65. With respect to Il'in, see the documents published in Il'in, Собрание сочинений: О возрождении и обновлении России [Collection of Works: On the Rebirth and Renewal of Russia] (2021), [XXXIII](3), pp. 258-293.

[80] For the documents, see V. G. Makarov and V. S. Khristoforov (comps.), Высылка вместо расстрела: Депортация интеллигенции в документах ВЧК—ГПУ 1921-1923 [Banishment Instead of Shooting: Deportation of the Intelligentsia in Documents of the VChK—GPU 1921-1923] (2005), pp. 239-240.

and to return to that institution on 5 September no later than 12:00 hours. He was then allowed to return home.

When Il'in returned to the GPU on the following day, he was handed the text of a Decree that indicated he would be accused as follows: "he from the moment of the October coup and to the present time not only had not reconciled himself with the Workers-Peasants' power existing in Russia, but had not for a single moment ceased his anti-Soviet activity, and had intensified his counter-revolutionary activity at a moment of external difficulties for the RSFSR".[81] He was taken into custody and required to sign a document under which he agreed: "1. To go abroad at his own expense according to the Collegium of the GPU; 2. Within seven days after release to wind up all his personal and official affairs and obtain the documents necessary to travel abroad". Upon the expiry of the seven-day period, Il'in was to appear again at the GPU. The document ended with the caution: "I have been told that the failure to appear within the said period will be regarded as flight from custody with all the consequences arising therefrom …". Il'in further acknowledged by his signature that he agrees "not to return to the territory of the RSFSR without the authorization of agencies of Soviet power" and that Article 71 of the 1922 RSFSR Criminal Code engaging capital punishment for a violation had been drawn to his attention.

On 11 September Il'in was released to arrange his personal and official affairs within seven days, to appear at the GPU upon the lapse of that seven-day period, and to depart abroad.

Together with his wife, Natalia, and what luggage he could manage, on 26 September 1922 Il'in boarded the steamer *Oberbürgermeister Hacken* en route for Stettin, Germany.[82] The previous day he had bid farewell to his mother, Ekaterina Iul'evna Il'ina (1858-1942) at the railway station in Moscow. He was never to see her again, being left to communicate by infrequent letters, unsigned, delivered surreptitiously by hand through friends and acquaintances.[83]

In August 1923 word was received that the Presidium of the All-Russian Central Executive Committee had decreed to deprive Il'in of Russian citizenship and to confiscate all his personal property.[84]

[81] Note 45 above, p. 435.

[82] On the expulsion of the Russian intelligentsia generally see Chamberlain, note 55 above.

[83] She lived with her son Igor. The fact that her son Aleksei had helped conceal a well-known Bolshevik from the Russian authorities in 1905/06 enabled her to save her husband from execution by the Bolsheviks and later to receive a State pension.

[84] Руль [Helm], no. 815 (5 August 1923).

Exile in Berlin

Upon docking in Stettin, the Il'ins moved on to Berlin – the European center of Russian emigration during the 1920s. A paradoxical location for the Russian émigré community in the view of many, for Germany had been the principal adversary of Russia during the First World War, just ended, and partly, if not primarily, responsible for the downfall of the Russian Empire. The Il'ins found accommodation in the western Charlottenburg district, where perhaps some two-thirds of the 300,000 Russians in Berlin, a substantial number of whom were Jewish, lived at the time. Russian restaurants opened in abundance, three vodka manufacturers, literally dozens of Russian bookshops and publishing houses,[85] and six banks. Recalling his times there, the Russian/American novelist Vladimir Nabokov (1899-1977) wrote: "for fifteen years of life in Germany I did not become closely acquainted with a single German, did not read a single German newspaper or book, and never felt the slightest inconvenience from not knowing the German language".[86]

On the very day that the Il'ins arrived in Berlin, the "Second Congress of Russian Jurists" commenced its deliberations. This Congress was formed to establish a dimension of continuity between the prerevolutionary Russian legal community and those jurists who had emigrated.[87] One of the burning issues of the day, destined to endure for decades, was the legal status of Russian emigrants, who had become in many instances stateless persons. To the extent they continued to be governed by or have legal capacity under the law of their former State, the question was: which law? Imperial Russian law (which continued to be in force in the Baltic countries and eastern Poland, for example), or Soviet law? The Congress was resolute in deciding that Russian law in force up to 25 October 1917 should apply to those Russians in emigration. The extent to which emigration meant a "parting" with Russia was addressed by Il'in in a lecture to Russian professorial deportees on 14 November 1922. In the spirit of his earlier views on legal consciousness and patriotism, Il'in stressed that there is a parting only with the geographical and ethnological substratum, but not with the Fatherland. With his customary elegance, he

[85] Russian publishers in Berlin were constantly opening, merging, closing. During the early 1920s, their numbers ranged from 30 to 87. See A. V. Startsev, «Русский Берлин» в 1921-1923 гг.» ["Russian Berlin" in 1921-1923], in Культурная миссия российского зарубежья: История и современность [Cultural Mission of the Russian Abroad: History and Modern Times] (1999), p. 79.

[86] V. V. Nabokov, Собрание сочинений в четырех томах [Collection of Works in Four Volumes] (1990), IV, p. 284.

[87] The First Congress of Russian Jurists was held at Moscow in May 1875. See Сборник статей: Первый съезд русских юристов в Москве в 1875 году [Collected Articles: First Congress of Russian Jurists in Moscow in 1875] (1882). On Russian participation in international congresses, see A. V. Vinogradov (ed.), Россия на международных форумах и конгрессах XVII – начала XX века [Russia at International Forums and Congresses XVII-Early XX Century] (2021).

affirmed: "Wherever I am and whatever I do, my Fatherland is always in me as the spiritual essence of my soul, of me myself".[88]

Shortly after arriving in Berlin, Il'in was invited to remove to Prague and join the Russian Juridical Institute, then under the directorship of his former supervisor, Professor Novgorodtsev. The position offered an income and stability that undoubtedly was attractive, but Il'in preferred war-torn Germany. He joined instead the newly-formed Russian Scientific Institute in Berlin, which functioned until 1937.

The official opening of the Russian Scientific Institute took place on 17 February 1923. The Institute combined three faculties: law, commercial, and historical-philological. The first Director was Professor Vsevolod Ivanovich Iasinskii (1884-1933). Il'in served on the organizational committee, together with Iulii Isaevich Aikhenvald (1872-1928), Nikolai Aleksandrovich Berdyaev (1874-1948), Sergei Konstantinovich Gogel (1860-1933), Georgii Dmitrievich Gurvich (1894-1965), Avgust Isaakovich Kaminka (1865-1941), Lev Platonovich Karsavin (1882-1952), Aleksandr Aleksandrovich Kizevetter (1866-1933), Nikolai Onufrievich Losskii (1870-1965), Mikhail Aleksandrovich Taube (1869-1961), Semen Liudvigovich Frank (1877-1950), and others. Il'in anticipated that the majority of students would be pupils from Russian Junker schools created by the Chief Command of the Russian Army, which had retreated from the Crimea to a camp in the Balkans. The intention was to offer instruction in law and other disciplines more or less according to the syllabi of Russian prerevolutionary universities. Il'in agreed to lecture in the courses on encyclopedia of law, history of the philosophy of law, and the history of ethical doctrines, all in the Russian and German languages. He held the post of Dean of the Law Faculty for the academic year 1923-24. His activities annoyed the Soviet Government sufficiently so that in late July or early August 1923 the Presidium of the All-Russian Central Executive Committee decreed to deprive Il'in of his rights of citizens and confiscate all of his personal property.[89] In 1924 Il'in was elected an associate of the School of Slavonic and Eastern European Studies of the University of London, then part of King's College London.[90]

The formal opening of the Russian Scientific Institute featured a public lecture by Il'in on the "Problem of Contemporary Legal Consciousness". The substance comprised the first chapter of his contemplated book on the subject.[91] He told the students that the "historical epoch being experienced

[88] For Il'in's address at a celebratory evening of the German Red Cross and Society for the Study of Eastern Europe, see Il'in, note 79 above, pp. 233-234.

[89] Reported in Руль [Rudder], no. 815 (5 August 1923); reproduced in Iu. T. Lisitsa and O. V. Lisitsa, Иван Ильин: провозвестник грядущей России [Ivan Il'in: Prophet of the Future Russia] (2005), p. 15.

[90] Ibid., pp. 20-21. Also see Il'in's autobiography, in Shevelenko, note 2 above, p. 101.

[91] The lecture was published as a separate booklet. See Il'in, Проблема современного правосознания [Problem of Contemporary Legal Consciousness] (Berlin, 1923). 32 p.

by peoples should be thought of as an era of spiritual unmasking and review". Russian jurists, he said, should commence a spiritual review so as to be able to live by law and move towards a State which is comprehended by modern mankind. This meant that contemporary legal consciousness should be the focus of scholarly attention, analysis, and diagnosis. Always and for all times, he counseled, legal consciousness is the real and sacred foundation of society and the State. The modern legal crisis is historically linked with the process of secularization of the entire spiritual culture, with the process of the dying out of the religious spirit therein.[92] Some of these ideas were explored in a cycle of lectures delivered during the winter and spring of 1928.[93] He continued to refine them in connection with an intended, but uncompleted, substantial work on the correlation between legal consciousness in a republic and in a monarchy.[94]

Although Il'in is traditionally labeled a conservative and a monarchist, and not without reason, Il'in was attracted by and inclined towards a monarchical form of government because in his eyes the head of State in a monarchy is an individual not bound by any class or political groupings. A monarchy is not an end in itself, but desirable because the monarch is a tsar who is above parties, classes, and estates. During the 1929/30 academic year at the Russian Scientific Institute, Il'in offered a lecture course entitled "Concepts of Monarchy and Republic". He took the position in that course that a tsar exists for the country and for the nation, and not the country for the tsar.

On 4 October 1924 Il'in wrote to the former Commander-in-Chief of the Armed Forces of the South of Russia, Lt. General Baron Petr Nikolaevich Wrangel (1878-1928) to say that he was completing a new and short book on resisting evil. This was not a political pamphlet, but a philosophical work which nonetheless would be readable and accessible to all. Il'in wished to dedicate the book to the Russian White Army and its leaders and sought Wrangel's consent to do so. Wrangel replied on 12

92 The principal ideas expressed in his lecture Il'in published as "Der Bolschewismum und die Krise des modernen Rechtsbewuβtseins", *Archiv für Rechts- und Wirtschaftsphilosophie*, XIX (1926/26), pp. 26-44; reprinted in *Archiv für Rechts- und Sozialphilosophie*, LXXXVII (2001), pp. 61-71. A Russian-language translation appeared in Il'in, «Большевизм и кризис современного правосознания» [Bolshevism and the Crisis of Contemporary Legal Consciousness], in Il'in, Собрание соыинений в десяти томах [Collection of Works in Ten Volumes] (1998), VII, pp. 7-26.

93 See Il'in, «Мировые причины русской революции» [World Causes of the Russian Revolution], in Il'in, Собрание сочинений: Кто мы? О революции. О религиозном кризисе наших дней [Collection of Works: Who Are We? On Revolution. On the Religious Crisis of Our Days] (2001), pp. 190-216.

94 Il'in wrote the introduction and first seven chapters, of an intended twelve. These were published posthumously by N. P. Poltoratskii, initially as an article and then as a separate book, in the United States. See Il'in, «О монархии» [On Monarchy], Русское Возрождение [Russian Renaissance], no. 1-4 (New York, 1978); Il'in, О монархии и республике [On Monarchy and a Republic] (New York, 1979).

October that he saw no reasons to object and would be, on the contrary, delighted if Il'in chose to do so.

The book was published in June 1925 at Berlin with a print run of 2,000 copies. Baron Boris Gustavovich von Köppen financed the volume. The book addressed two interconnected issues: "May a person aspiring to moral perfection resist evil by force and sword? May a person believing in God and accepting His universe and his place in the world not resist evil by sword and force? The book was partly aimed against Tolstoyan doctrines of non-resistance and pacifism. Il'in distinguished between personal evil and public or social evil. Christian teachings, he said, that counseled one to love thine enemy and forgive insult had in view the personal enemies of an individual, but not the enemies of God, of everything Divine. The book generated sharp polemics and divisions in Russian émigré circles which festered for years.[95]

In early May 1925 Petr Bengardovich Struve, Il'in's former classmate at University, invited Il'in to come to Paris to celebrate the opening of a new émigré newspaper, Возрождение [Renaissance] and to deliver a lecture on the occasion. Il'in at the time had just returned from Prague, where he had lectured.[96] His health was not the best, he replied to Struve, but he would come with Natalia to be treated by Dr. Manukhin. The newspaper published its very first issue on 3 June 1925. Struve, in his capacity as editor, invited Il'in to become a regular contributor, an invitation warmly accepted. The newspaper sent Il'in to Italy in September and October 1925 to gather materials on that country and report on the new leader, Benito Mussolini (1883-1945) and Italian fascism. Returning to Berlin on 9 November, Il'in began to publish articles in the newspaper from December. Seven were devoted to Italian developments under the general title "Letters on Fascism". Nine articles in seven months addressed the essence of fascism, the domestic and foreign policies of fascist authorities, the struggle of Italian fascists with the masons, a biography of Mussolini, the Tyrol problem, and others.

Struve did not accept all of Il'in's submissions. His article criticizing the group around Grand Prince Kirill Vladimirovich (1876-1938),

[95] Among the reviewers in the Russian émigré press were N. A. Berdyaev (1874-1948), P. Struve (1870-1944), V. V. Zenkovskii (1881-1962), F. A. Stepun (1884-1965), Iu. Aikhenwald (1872-1928), Boris Suvorin, and Z. N. Gippius (1869-1945). For references, see Iu. I. Sokhriakov, «Ильин Иван Александрович» [Il'in, Ivan Aleksandrovich], in A. N. Nikoliukin (ed.), Литературная энциклопедия русского зарубежья (1918-1940) [Literary Encyclopedia of the Russian Abroad (1918-1940)] (1997), I, p. 199. Also see N. P. Poltoratskii, И. А. Ильин и полемика вокруг его идей о сопротивлении злу силой [I. A. Il'in and the Polemic Around His Idea on Resisting Evil by Force] (London, 1979).

[96] The precise legal status of the Il'ins seems to have been that of a stateless person, in the case of Ivan Il'in, because his citizenship was withdrawn in 1923. His wife did not suffer a similar sanction. Most likely the Il'ins traveled on provisional passports issued by the Organization for the Defense of Russian Refugees in Germany. In 1924 the Il'ins had a joint passport issued by this organization valid for a six month period. Reproduced in Lisitsa, note 2 above (1999), p. 20.

putative heir to the Russian throne, was rejected. Il'in reacted badly. He implored Struve for a "guarantee" that his submissions would be accepted; otherwise, he would cease to contribute. Struve was able to placate Il'in, and their collaboration continued so long as Struve remained the editor, until 18 August 1927. On that day he resigned, citing disagreement with the owner and patron, the oil magnate Abram Osipovich Gukasov (1872-1969). Some 23 collaborators followed Struve, including Il'in.

Struve's departure as editor of Возрождение [Renaissance] enabled Il'in to turn to a project long dear to his heart. A patron had appeared, recently departed from the Soviet Union but with financial resources reasonably intact, who admired what Il'in wrote and was prepared to back a monthly ideological journal. Il'in accepted the offer to become the editor-in-chief personally. The identity of the patron is obscure, but believed to be N. Gromov.[97] In a letter to his friend in Prague, Nadezhda Nikolaevna Krámáře, Il'in said that the journal should be for the "Russian patriot irrespective of his past and his location".[98] On 23 June 1927 Il'in reported to Struve that the money for the journal had been received and the name chosen: Русский колокол: Журнал волевой идеи [Russian Bell: A Journal of Resolute Ideas].

Il'in adhered to these basic notions in the lead editorial of his first issue. The journal was conceived, he said, as an "ideological-philosophical and political-publicist" journal. Simple and readable, the journal would establish the purpose of the entire imminent struggle for Russia for decades to come. It should inspire all sound elements of Russia, abroad and within the country. It should be a State and national journal, but one encompassing all aspects of spiritual culture. A future Russia should not be a restored facsimile of prerevolutionary Russia; it must have regard to the historical changes in the appearance of Russian material.

The first issue appeared at Berlin on 22 September 1927 and the second on 28 November 1927. By May 1930, nine issues had appeared in all with a print run of no less than 1,000 copies – thereby exceeding the circulation of all Russian émigré publications to that date. Il'in himself wrote forty of the articles. The journal was distributed throughout the world, from Kharbin in Manchuria to San Francisco, from Calcutta and Teheran to Athens and Paris. At its peak the journal had 120 persons around the world working to circulate the publication on a voluntary and unpaid basis. Il'in likewise worked without remuneration, devoting his time, energies, creative resources, personal life and leisure to the project. Within a year, however, his patron was fed up with émigré intrigues and rivalries and withdrew his support from the various warring émigré groups. From summer 1928 Il'in was obliged to seek support from other Russian emigres. Among those to whom he appealed was his friend, the composer, Sergei Vasil'evich Rachmaninoff (1873-1943). Rachmaninoff obliged

97 This is the informed speculation of Iu. T. Lisitsa, See note 46 above, p. 559.

98 Ibid., p. 263.

with a one-off donation of 800 marks but was unable to offer permanent subsidies.[99] Igor Ivan Sikorsky (1889-1972), the aviation pioneer, and his wife Elizaveta wrote in 1930 with a commitment to support the journal with a US$25 monthly contribution. The last, ninth, issue appeared in April 1930. Il'in planned the tenth and eleventh numbers, to be composed of his own articles, but these issues never appeared. Russian emigration, Il'in wrote to Rachmaninoff on 2 December 1928, was poor; it did not purchase enough issues and delayed paying for them.[100] The worldwide depression put an end to any possibility of continuing the journal. The journal was revived in 2012, with continuous numeration (issues no. (1)10, (2)11, (3)12 ...).

The first decade of Il'in's sojourn in emigration was, perhaps, the most intensive in his lifetime. In addition to lecturing at the Russian Scientific Institute, he routinely traveled to lecture throughout Europe – Austria, Belgium, France, Switzerland, Czechoslovakia, Latvia, and various cities in Germany. Between autumn 1922 and the end of 1932, according to a list that he compiled, he delivered no less than 105 lectures in the German language on the topics of Russian culture, Bolshevism, Soviet domestic policies, and Soviet-German relations.[101] The list did not include his numerous lectures in the French language, and those in Russian delivered in various Russian émigré organizations. The winter of 1929 was especially arduous. The fatigue was genuine, but so too was the satisfaction. The depression had its expected pernicious effects, however. Russian émigré organizations which had supported needy Russians folded for lack of funds; Russian educational institutions in Europe were under threat for the same reason.

[99] Nikolai Medtner (1880-1951), Rachmaninoff, and Il'in form an interesting triangle. Il'in and Medtner corresponded voluminously about music (three to four volumes of the correspondence are to be published in 2022/23 as part of the Il'in Collected Works), and Rachmaninoff made crucial financial contributions to Il'in's publishing activity, as he did with other members of the White emigration. Il'in and Medtner will not have failed to comment on Rachmaninoff's music. Medtner "is regarded as closest to Rachmaninoff in musical style", and the two "genuinely admired each other's music". In exile, "they developed a friendship", but notwithstanding Rachmaninoff's tireless efforts to further Medtner's career", their disparities in fame and income "sometimes cast a cloud over their relationship". They "pictured themselves as comrades in arms", persevering in the face of critics who dismissed each new work as old-fashioned and dedicated respectively the Rachmaninoff fourth concerto and the Medtner second concerto to one another. See Marina Frolova-Walker, in *Rachmaninoff and His World* (2022), p. 35 (Bard Music Festival Program). Also see Simon Morrison, in Philip Ross Bullock (ed.), *Rachmaninoff and His World* (2022), p. 173; Rebecca Mitchell, *Sergei Rachmaninoff* (2022) (Critical Lives), pp. 145-168.

[100] Lisitsa, note 46 above, p. 332.

[101] He mentions his arduous lecturing activities in his autobiography. Indicating that he lectured in the Russian language at Prague, Paris, Brussels, and Riga; in the French language at Brussels and Leger, and in the German language at Bern, Basel, Zurich, Aarau, and Innsbruck in addition to lectures in Germany. On one occasion in 1928, he had an audience of 14,000 in Berlin. Many lectures were held in Catholic and Protestant churches. See Shevelenko, note 2 above, p. 101.

The Russian Scientific Institute had paid its lecturers regularly through 1932. Il'in received about half of his annual income from the Institute; the other half was covered by royalties for publications and lecture fees. The living conditions of the Il'ins in Berlin were tolerable. In the summers they traveled throughout Europe. Il'in even had enough to help defray personally the costs of *The Russian Bell.* Circumstances changed from 1932. The Russian Scientific Institute was unable to pay lecturers. Illness forced Il'in to cease public lectures. The financial position of the Il'ins deteriorated considerably.

The accession of the Nazis to power in Germany led to Il'in and other Russian emigres of his orientation beginning to experience persecution. By spring 1933 the Gestapo sought to identify Il'in as a "Francophile". The Gestapo suggested that Il'in should become an informer and report regularly on the Russian community in Berlin. Il'in rejected the suggestion. In August 1933 his premises were searched by the Gestapo, he was detained for some period, and cautioned against participating in any political activity under threat of confinement in a concentration camp. In April 1934 the Gestapo suggested that Il'in engage in anti-semitic propaganda within the émigré community; again a refusal. In reprisal, his lecturing at the Russian Scientific Institute was suspended, and in August 1934 he was dismissed from the Institute.

Notwithstanding this turn of events, Il'in remained in Germany. The sole organization within which he might continue to propagate his views and earn a living was the church. Until February 1938, Il'in regularly spoke in evangelical churches and cathedrals on the roots of the modern crisis in religion and the martyrdom of the Russian Orthodox Church. The Gestapo renewed its efforts against Il'in in August 1937, not least because of dozens, if not hundreds, of denunciations of Il'in by members of the so-called Russian National-Socialist Movement. Il'in was twice summoned in October 1937 by the Gestapo for interrogation. He was asked: Did he not serve the Bolsheviks in Moscow? Il'in replied, no. Why then, the question followed, was Il'in not shot at once and banished only after five years? Il'in replied: God did not allow this. The Gestapo changed tack and accused Il'in of being a "secret mason"; Il'in denied any involvement in matters masonic.

Il'in was summoned again by the Gestapo in February 1938. On this occasion he was taken by car to the Gestapo premises by Marina Aleksandrovna Deriugina (1916-2003), the sister of Aleksei Aleksandrovich Kvartirov (1911-1980), a pupil of Il'in in Berlin. Deriugina waited for Il'in outside in her car; had Il'in been arrested, she would have followed instructions given to her in that event. Again rejecting Gestapo suggestions that he collaborate with them, he was formally prohibited from making any public speeches in the German and Russian languages under threat of confinement in a concentration camp. Informing Rachmaninoff about what had transpired, Il'in said that he had learned from a reliable source that the Gestapo wished to force Il'in to accept German doctrines on racism and to use his name and his efforts in a future conquest of Ukraine. By May 1938 Il'in realized that he had no future in Germany and began preparations to depart. He vacated his apartment, placed their belongings in temporary storage, obtained an entry visa for Switzerland without difficulty, obtained from the German authorities a Ruckreissichtvermerk until 1 December, and arranged for his literary royalties to be transferred to the account of the Akademisch-Philosophischer Verlag at the Schweizerische Bankgesellschaft in Zurich. On 9 July 1938 he and Natalia left for Switzerland with assistance from Kvartirov and Deriugina. His departure was unobstructed. He was able to gather his things, furniture, paintings, library, and, most important, his manuscripts, which alone filled several suitcases. Il'in was not expelled from Germany; his passport contained a notation that would have allowed him to return. This technical legal possibility Il'in knew to be dangerous, if not chimerical.

Wartime Years in Switzerland

From July to November 1938 the Il'ins lived at Locarno Monti in a villa belonging to Mrs. Schmidt-Varenna. Il'in submitted a request to the Swiss cantonal authorities to reside permanently in that country. On 8 August 1938 Il'in received a request from the Swiss immigration authorities to indicate on what basis he had received a visa from the Swiss Embassy in Berlin, where he wished to reside (in Zurich proper or in the Zurich Canton), his income and financial status, and whether he had a bank account. If permission to reside were granted, Il'in was advised that he would be required to post a minimum bond of 4,000 Swiss francs in a Zurich bank. The Il'ins did not have that sum of money, but it was made available by Rachmaninoff. As matters were pending, the Il'ins sought an extension of their visa from 1 October to 1 December 1938, which was granted. As their place of permanent residence, the Il'ins chose the municipality of Zollikon and removed there on 31 October. The Zollikon municipality gave Il'in authorization to live there for a year on 23 November, but the cantonal police five days later annulled this authorization and suggested that Il'in return to Germany. Il'in appealed this annulment and on 1 December received final authorization to remain in and take up residence (but not settle) in Switzerland. On 7 December his furniture and books were released and the following day they moved to their rented apartment. By 10 December 1928 they were in their new home. Thus commenced the final period in Il'in's life.

The Swiss were cautious about their new Russian guest, which made life for the Il'ins initially no less difficult than it had been in Germany. Il'in was allowed to engage only in scholarly activity and undertake research. He was prohibited from collaborating with a Swiss periodical publication or from engaging in any other activity – change of profession, use of his profession for a different purpose, undertaking household work where women's labor was not used, or any other office in the city. He found the restrictions onerous and discriminatory. Poor health complicated his situation. In the end, Il'in's talents as a writer and lecturer proved to be his salvation. Having a fluent command of the German language, Il'in began to lecture to German-speaking Swiss in people's universities and at learned societies or cultural organizations, and once more in churches. After the Second World War commenced, there was among the Swiss a renewed interest in Russian history and culture; and the Russian émigré community in Switzerland was pleased to have an eminent Russian professor in their midst. Each occasion, of course, required clearance from the Swiss *Fremdenpolizei* and any discussion of political matters was off limits. Just as generations of Russians before him, including Lenin, Il'in was able to take advantage of the Rubakin Library and borrowed books from it by post.[102]

The restrictions on publishing in Switzerland under his own name Il'in evaded by adopting pseudonyms, as he had previously done in Russia and Germany: Peter Just, R. K. [Russisch Korrespondent?], K. P., S. L., Julius Hefer, Iulii Schweikert, Alfred Normann, Old Politician, or simply anonymously. Among the Russian-language journals open to him was Новый путь [The New Way], published by the Russian Labor Christian Movement, together with a supplement Голос русской молодежи [Voice of Russian Youth]. As for the War itself, Il'in rejoiced in victories of the Russian Armed Forces, which he saw as triumphs of the Russian people and not of the Soviet State or Communist Party. As the War drew to a close in 1944-45, he resisted any notion of "Russian" designs on western Europe by "Moscow"; any such designs, which he doubted, would be "Soviet" designs engendered by the Bolsheviks.

Under his own name, however, Il'in was permitted to publish in Switzerland a series of essays on the essence and distinctiveness of Russian culture, having wanted for years to do so under the inspiration of Ivan Sergeevich Shmelev (1873-1950).[103]

From 1945 he became ill more frequently, finding succor in his writings, in the flames of creativity, which distracted him from bodily pain and distress. He wrote book after book, some of which he published. While still in Berlin, in 1938 he had succeeded in publishing a German-language work on his philosophy of life.[104] A second volume followed in 1943 (Bern)[105] and a third in 1945 (Zurich).[106] Among the works completed

102 Nikolai Aleksandrovich Rubakin (1862-1946) formed a remarkable personal library of more than 200,000 volumes in Switzerland which he made available to the public. Upon his death, it was purchased by the Soviet Government and repatriated to the Soviet Union. See A. E. Senn, *Nicholas Rubakin: A Life for Books* (1977).

103 Il'in, *Wessen und Eigenart der russischen Kultur* (Zurich, 1942).

104 A second edition of this appeared at Berlin in 1939. A Russian translation appeared in his Collected Works.

105 The Russian version which Il'in prepared was published posthumously by his widow in 1958 and again in his Collected Works.

106 The Russian text was not published at the time. A translation appears in the Collected Works (1998), VIII, pp. 341-564.

was an abridged German-language edition of his 1918 edition on Hegel. Although widely described in the literature as a "German translation", for Il'in the German language was as native as his Russian. He did not "translate" his work into German, he wrote it in German, drawing, of course, on his original version. Of immense financial and moral support to him in this endeavor, and to the Il'ins generally throughout their residence in Switzerland, was Charlotte Bareiss. The precise amount and duration of financial assistance is unknown, but the fact itself is beyond dispute.

Final Years in Switzerland

Il'in devoted much time and effort in the postwar period to the future of Russia. He never doubted that sooner or later the Soviet system would crumble. For Il'in, the question was what sort of State and government should post-Soviet Russia have. As best he could, he followed the course of Soviet affairs and events attentively. His thoughts on the future Russia he set out in a lengthy series of articles in the weekly newspaper of the émigré organization, "Russian All-Military Union" under the general rubric of «Наши задачи» [Our Tasks]. He sent the text of the articles to Aleksei Aleksandrovich von Lampe (1885-1967) in Paris; if necessary, a discussion followed by correspondence. The final versions were then sent to Brussels for approval by General Aleksei Petrovich Arkhangelskii (1872-1959), who was the head of the Russian All-Military Union, whereupon they were published without any indication of authorship.[107] Il'in's authorship was disclosed after his death. The articles were collected in a two-volume edition published at Paris in 1956.[108]

Collectively, the articles addressed what Il'in saw as the most significant, fateful events of Russian history, the most controversial issues of Russian social life, the distinctive elements of the Russian national character, the catastrophe of the Russian revolutions, the paths for a Russian renaissance, the threats Russia was likely to encounter in the future, the organization of a post-communist Russian State, and issues of federation, democracy, elections, totalitarianism, fascism, and others.

Il'in's other great work of the postwar era was devoted to axioms of religious experience. He first thought of producing a work on the history and philosophy of religion back in 1919-20 when he had prepared lectures for his course "Introduction to the History of Religions" at Moscow University. He worked on the project intermittently over the years, but set about producing a final product in 1946. In 1951 he offered the completed manuscript to the YMCA Press in Paris. The YMCA Press declined to publish, saying that their publication program was full for

[107] Il'in later explained that he had published these articles anonymously from April 1948 in the name of the Board of the Organization. The articles, he said, needed to speak for themselves without any indication of authorship. When the necessity arises, he said, "... I will replace the anonymity with my full signature". Il'in, note 35 above, p. 176.

[108] They have since been published at Moscow in the Collected Works of Il'in.

the forthcoming year; Il'in suspected the conspiratorial hand of Masonic influences in their decision and the unpopularity of his ideas in Masonic circles.

Il'in turned for assistance to Vladimir Petrovich Riabushinskii (1873-1955), who agreed to help and quite literally became blind as a consequence of working with the manuscript. The book appeared at Paris in 1953, printed in the old Russian orthography.[109] This was Il'in's last great work of scholarship. He lived to see the publication, but in completing it, he seems to have understood that the end of his days was approaching.

Epilogue

By 1950 Il'in's friends in emigration were beginning to pass away. Shmelev died on 24 June, having for more than a quarter century shared with Il'in joys and sorrows, thoughts about Russia past and Russian culture, through correspondence and occasional holidays together. On an exceedingly hot day in late July 1952, Il'in strolled out to post a letter. The ensuing heart attack required three months of treatment in hospital. Upon returning home, he could no longer work at his previous pace nor easily move about. He hurried to complete those books he had written, especially his treatise on the monarchy, and continued to produce articles for the Russian All-Military Union bulletin. Among the works placed in final form was his long-awaited book on legal consciousness. An application for a Rockefeller grant to support publication was not successful.

In November 1954 he was hospitalized with another heart attack. The doctors were not unduly concerned, but Il'in had a premonition of impending death and made his peace with the world. He died on 21 December 1954. He was buried in the Zollikon Cemetery, joined by his wife Natalia in 1963.

On 3 October 2005 the Il'ins were reinterred (together with General Anton Denikin (1872-1947) and his spouse), at the Cemetery of the Don Monastery in Moscow,[110] the same cemetery where his devoted friend, I. S. Shmelev, was reinterred. A plaque in his honour was unveiled on 9 April 2008 in central Moscow on the original building of the Law Faculty at Moscow University. The Il'in library and personal archive were returned

109 Il'in, Аксиомы религиозного опыта: Исследование [Axioms of Religious Experience: A Study] (Paris, 1953). 2 vols. The book has recently been republished in Moscow in the modern script. Il'in doubtless would have objected. He wrote on another occasion: "To print my work in the new orthography would be murderous to the meaning because a whole series of religious texts and philosophical theses would be distorted by mixing words and concepts ... ". Il'in, note 22 above, p. 124. For a western study of Il'in's religious thought, see Wolfgang Offermans, *Mensch, werde wesentlich! Das Lebenswerk des russischen religiösen Denkers Ivan Iljin für die Erneurung der geistigen Grundlagen der Menschheit* (Erlangen, 1979). x, 305 p.

110 S. L. Myers, "For a New Russia, New Relics", *New York Times*, 9 October 2005.

from exile at Michigan State University in East Lansing, Michigan,[111] and solemnly accepted on 22 May 2006 by the Cultural Fund in Moscow and on 20 November 2006 at Moscow University – pursuant to his wishes. The Il'ins were repatriated at last to their beloved homeland.

[111] See *MSU News Bulletin*, no. 18 (1 June 2006), pp. 1, 4; reproduced in [C. H. Haka], *The Ivan Aleksandrovich Il'in Papers and the Michigan State University Libraries* (East Lansing, Michigan: Michigan State University, [2013]), pp. 40-41.

The Origins of Il'in's Treatise on the Essence of Legal Consciousness

The intellectual legacy of Ivan Aleksandrovich Il'in had, until 2010, been available only in the Russian, German, and French languages, all of which were effectively native tongues for the author. The Grier translation of Il'in's monumental dissertation on Hegel was the first appearance of Il'in in English.[1] The present chapter addresses his second appearance in the English language and the first in his capacity as a legal scholar rather than a philosopher[2] and adds new data based on archival sources previously unavailable to our understanding of Il'in and his writings.

On the Origins of Il'in's Monograph on Legal Consciousness

From 1916 onwards Il'in's principal scholarly preoccupation in Russia was with the first "disease" of the Russian people identified in his celebrated public lecture on patriotism in February 1918: the lack among the Russian people of a mature legal consciousness. His magister dissertation was essentially completed. On 5 June 1917 he wrote to his cousin, L. Ia. Gurevich: "I am finishing my book "On the Essence of Legal Consciousness" (it will appear in the autumn)".[3] By then, however, whatever many have been the position in manuscript, the book was only partly in galley proof and remained so until February 1919. Although some sources have suggested that a printed book existed by 1918, a careful examination of what evidence survives would suggest that these survivals are various forms of galley proofs.

The basis for suggesting that the book as such existed in 1918 appears to be an item catalogued as item 110 in the Il'in Library.[4] The catalog entry reads: О сущности правосознания. – [M.]: [1916-1918]. – 110 c. The annotation to the catalog entry records the dimensions of the volume: 14,5 x 21,8. The "binding" is wrappers from the proofs themselves held together by a barbarous piece of black tape or leather scrap. An inscription

1 This observation disregards a posthumous publication of three essays by Il'in included in R. Holt (ed.), *Nicolas Medtner: A Memorial Volume* (London, [1955]).

2 Extracts from the present work appeared in the *Journal of Comparative Law*, VII (2012), pp. 63-107.

3 Il'in, Собрание сочинений: Дневник. Письма. Документы (1903-1938) [Collection of Works: Diary, Letters, Documents (1903-1938)], p. 92.

4 See I. L. Velikodnaia (ed.), Каталог библиотеки Ивана Александровича Ильина [Catalogue of the Library of Ivan Aleksandrovich Il'in], I. V. Ovchinkina, comp. (2011), pp. 58-59.

(probably of R. M. Siehle) in black ball-point pen reads in Russian: "I. A. Il'in. On the Essence of Legal Consciousness – Moscow. 1916-1918". A further inscription in Russian says: "In this Moscow edition 10 chapters of the same work published fully in 1956". At the end of each of the ten chapters a date is indicated in pencil (Il'in?), as follows:

"p. 13: November 1916; addition: 165;
p. 22: November 1916;
p. 33: November 1916;
p. 41: November 1916;
p. 53: November-December 1916;
p. 63: December 1916;
p. 75: January-February 1917;
p. 83: February 1917;
p. 92: end October 1917 (during uprising of Bolsheviks in Moscow);
p. 110: February-July 1918.
Traces of reading: pencil and black ink marks".

The rationale for treating this item as a book would appear to have been: the item was included as part of the Il'in library and not the archive; the item was, after a fashion, bound, however primitively; the item was paginated consecutively; Siehle, probably when inventorying the item for shipment to Michigan State University, treated the item as a book and reinforced this impression with his annotations on the item itself.

The rationale for reconsidering this attribution would be as follows: the paper on which the item is printed and the type setting are identical to other galley proofs of this item in the Il'in archive; the item was bound up for working purposes, probably as the most complete, if not the last, set of proofs to come from the printing house; the item contains no evidence of having been part of a print run of the final book; the item contains no publication data that would routinely be included in a published book; no record exists anywhere of a copy of this title being published; nothing in the Il'in archives or library otherwise indicates that the book on legal consciousness was published in this text, format, or form. Although a comprehensive comparison has not been undertaken, the so-called "reading marks" appear to be more in the nature of proof corrections than emendations placed by a reader.

Why Il'in never published his completed manuscript in Soviet Russia can only be the subject of conjecture. Many reasons are possible, including financial, difficulties in finding a printing house, and the political climate of the day. More puzzling is the fact that he did not publish the volume in exile. Certainly, he thought about and planned a version devoted to this subject-matter. He wrote to General P. N. Wrangel on 5 April 1923: "In the coming months I will print my books written and forged in a Satanic smelter, – on the essence of legal consciousness and on the monarchy".[5] The reference, however, is probably not to the book on legal consciousness written from 1916-19, but to the volume that treats aspects of legal consciousness and appeared at Berlin in 1924.

Il'in's close friend, Roman Martynovich Siehle (sometimes Zile), who knew Il'in from 1928 until his death in 1954 and was in constant correspondence with him, said in a memorial address delivered in 1955:

> In 1919 Il'in completes his study on the essence of legal consciousness;[6] these were delivered in the form of a course of lectures at Moscow higher educational institutions and discussed more than once in sessions of the Moscow Law Society and in private meetings of the Muscovite docents and professoriate. But this book, entitled "Doctrine on Legal Consciousness", has still not appeared. However, this is not merely an invaluable contribution to legal doctrine, but a genuinely new, living word about that spiritual atmosphere which law and State require in order to flourish.[7]

All the evidence suggests that Il'in had continued to prepare the publication of his work on legal consciousness up to his death in 1954. The book was not something that he had laid aside and forgotten. His widow, Natalia, guided the Russian-language version of the work through press at Munich in 1956.[8] A comparison of the galley proofs dating from 1919/1922 and the text published in 1956 indicates that the texts are substantially identical, subject to certain later changes made by Il'in over the next three decades or so.

But that observation relates to the first ten chapters; there are 22 chapters, including the Conclusions, in the 1956 version. The question remains as to whether Il'in had completed ten or twenty-one or even twenty-two chapters by late 1919 or whether he wrote chapters eleven onwards after 1919 either within or outside Russia. Further examination

5 Letter of I. A. Il'in to P. N. Wrangel, 5 April 1923, cited in V. G. Bortnevskii, Избранные труды [Selected Works] (Leningrad, 1999), p. 134.

6 Siehle was aware of galley proofs dated February 1919 and emendations thereon, although the essence of the work seems to have been completed by spring 1918.

7 The text of the Siehle address to the Russian All-Military Union on 1 May 1955, held in Casablanca, is published in Il'in, Собрание сочинений в десяти томах [Collection of Works in Ten Volumes] (1993), II(2), p. 416. The full text is published from archival sources in Il'in, Собрание сочинений: О возрождении и обновлении России [Collection of Works: On the Rebirth and Renewal of Russia] (2021), [XXXIII] (3); see especially pp. 371-373. Siehle's observation is not consistent with what he later indicated on the bound proofs of this book reposing in the Il'in private library, which would suggest that Siehle's notes on the bound proofs were made not in 1955, but ca. 1966 when the materials were being inventoried and packed for shipment to the United States.

8 Il'in, О сущности правосознания [On the Essence of Legal Consciousness] (Munich, Tipo. I. Pochaevskii in Munich, 1956. 223 p. See note 4 above, item 111. This volume was republished in full in Il'in, Собрание сочинений в десяти томах [Complete Collection of Works in Ten Volumes] (1994), IV, pp. 149-414.

in 2022 of the Il'in archives in Moscow by Andrei and Iurii Lisitsa have identified Chapters 21 and 22, duly typeset, and titled respectively "Legal Consciousness and Religosity" and "Conclusion". Il'in, we know, lectured on religosity in 1922 at the home of Professor Avinov, and this was duly noted when the Cheka cited reasons to expel Il'in from Russia later that year. This would seem to be confirmation that Il'in had completed the entire work before he emigrated abroad and that the work had been set in galley proofs. In his correspondence over the years with Nikolai Medtner, Il'in mentioned working on his book devoted to legal consciousness, but presumably this meant that he was polishing the text rather than originating *de novo*. When Il'in applied for a Rockefeller Foundation grant in 1952, a more or less complete copy of the book in galley and manuscript form was cobbled together for the purposes of the unsuccessful application.[9] Ultimate publication was achieved in 1956 unless and until an earlier date can be demonstrated.

The Role of Woldemar A. Bary

On or about 30 November 1917, Woldemar (Vladimir) Aleksandrovich Bary (30 September 1887-23 December 1979) transferred to I. A. Il'in the sum of "8,000".[10] This entry in the Bary accounts served as the grounds for suspecting that Il'in (and Bary) were involved in a plot against the Soviet Government and the Bolsheviks and that these funds were intended to be passed on by Il'in to someone in support of White armies in southern Russia. Il'in's explanation was simple: the monies were a gift from Bary to help him publish his book. Which book(s)?

At the time of the gift, Il'in was working on two major projects: the first was his dissertation on Hegel, intended to be printed in three volumes but later combined into two; the second was his work on legal consciousness. By late November 1917 both works were known to be in galley proofs. Il'in customarily did not confine himself to making technical corrections on his galleys; he would polish the prose and insert sundry refinements of the text at this stage. He did, in fact, engage in a measure of rewriting. The funds from Bary, in other words, could have been intended to help defray printing costs of one or the other, or both, books.

How Bary and Il'in came to be acquainted is not disclosed by the available materials. They were not far apart in age (about a four-year age difference) and of the same generation. The Bary firm was, it would

9 We are indebted to Iurii Lisitsa for details of his latest discovery, communicated by several e-mails to Butler, Grier, and Robinson between 3 August and 17 September 2022 (on file with the authors).

10 The entry in the accounts does not specify the currency. Russian sources have treated the sum as being in rubles. Exchange rates at the time, judging from United States Embassy correspondence, fluctuated from ten to twelve rubles per dollar. If the sum was in rubles, Il'in was given roughly between US$650 to $800, which would be more or less consistent with what seemed to be the cost of printing his dissertation. If the sum were in dollars, it would have been extravagantly in excess of printing expenses.

seem, successful and profitable in its various engineering activities, well regarded for the innovation and quality of its boilers and other products, and known throughout the Russian Empire.[11] Whatever the precise details, Bary was actively supporting the White Guards and not well disposed to the Bolsheviks. He may have been willing to lend material support to the White movement; his firm was ultimately nationalized by the Soviet authorities in 1918 and 1919.

Il'in is known to have experienced difficulties with printers during 1917. Whether these were financial issues or others is not a matter of record. Nor is it clear how advanced the composition of the Hegel volumes was between 30 November 1917 and the ultimate delivery of the books for the Il'in dissertation defense on 19 May 1918 – a period of five and a half months with Christmas and Easter holidays in between and the disruptions of the incipient civil war and armed conflict. Even under normal circumstances the setting, proofing, and printing of the two large Hegel volumes and the setting and proofing of the essays on legal consciousness, whether at the same printing house (which seems unlikely) or not, was an heroic achievement. Unless the 8,000 "rubles" was flagrantly extravagant in comparison with its alleged purpose (which seems not to have attracted the attention of the Moscow Revolutionary Tribunal or the investigator as being the case), Bary is owed a considerable debt by intellectual and legal history for his role in helping two important contributions to ultimately appear.

The Bary (sometimes: Bari) family originated in France and removed to Lithuania and then Russia proper. Woldemar A. Bary was the grandson of Veniamin Matveevich Bary, who originally intended to become a rabbi, and the son of Aleksandr Veniaminovich Bary (1847-1913), a citizen of the United States and Russian entrepreneur-engineer. Born in St. Petersburg, according to family legend A. V. Bary was the godson of Alexander Humboldt (1769-1859). A. V. Bary personally knew and corresponded with Karl Marx (1818-1883), As a result, he attracted the attention of the III Section of the Imperial Russian Police. He emigrated from Russia to Switzerland in 1862, where he graduated from the Zurich Polytechnic, and then went sometime between 1865 and 1870 to Detroit and Philadelphia in the United States, where he founded an engineering firm. In 1875/76 he won a competition to design pavilions for the World Exhibition in Philadelphia commemorating the centennial of United States independence. Bary befriended the Russian delegation to the Exhibition, especially Vladimir Grigorievich Shukhov (1853-1939), and in 1877 was elected a corresponding member of the Pedagogical Council of the Imperial Technical School in St. Petersburg. In that same year

11 On the Bary family, see A. B. Efimov, G. B. Efimov, and M. V. Efimova, «Иван Александрович Ильин и семья А. В. Бари, встречи в начале XX века» [Ivan Aleksandrovich Il'in and the Family of A. V. Bary, Encounters in the Early XX Century], published in Il'in, Собрание сочинений: О возрождении и обновлении России [Collection of Works: On the Rebirth and Renewal of Russia] (2021), [XXXIII] (3), pp. 496-508, for some details.

the Bary and his wife, Zinaida, of German extraction but with roots and relations in Russia, returned to St. Petersburg. Bary co-founded "Bary, Sytenko & Co." to build equipment for the oil industry. Several years later he established a firm called the "Technical Office of Engineer A. V. Bary". The firms flourished. A. V. Bary's widow, Zinaida (15 February1854-18 February 1940), inherited the business in 1913. When the firm was nationalized by the Russian authorities in 1918-19, it was Zinaida's property that was taken.[12] The settlement ultimately reached with respect to the nationalization of the Bary property resulted in tax litigation in the courts of the United States.[13]

Woldemar Bary was one of nine children. He was directing the Bary interests in 1918 on behalf of his mother. He was taken into custody by officers of the All-Russian Extraordinary Commission against Counter-Revolution, Sabotage, and Speculation on Sunday, 14 April 1918. The United States Vice Consul, John A. Lehrs, was summoned by telephone during the search of the Bary home and appeared while the search was underway. Lehrs lodged a formal protest that the search was being performed without the United States Consulate General having been notified. According to Lehrs, the search produced "... a great amount of correspondence ... most of which was returned later in the day; ... four revolvers and ... two swords, one of them a present to Countess Lanskaya from the Cossacks, having an inscription to that effect engraved upon it".[14] Lehrs repaired at once to the office of the Extraordinary Committee, where he was received by Feliks Dzerzhinskii. Lehrs demanded to see the charges against Woldemar Bary. This request was declined until instructions were received from the Council of People's Commissars. Later that same day Lehrs met at 17:00 hours with the People's Commissar for Foreign Affairs, Grigorii Chicherin, to lodge a verbal protest "... against the house of an American citizen being searched without the knowledge of the Consulate General", to request a meeting with Woldemar Bary, and to be apprised of the charges. The Vice Consul was notified by telephone that evening of the charges, confirmed by letter the following day: "supplying officers with money for the purpose of joining the counter-revolutionary troops of Kaledin and Korniloff in the

[12] Zinaida Bary was a United States citizen by virtue of her husband, A. V. Bary's, naturalization. She entered the United States on 16 October 1925 via Rotterdam and two years later executed a one-page will bequeathing all her property, wherever situate, to her son, Woldemar A. Bary. She died in New York County; her will was not offered for probate until June 1958; Letters Testamentary were granted to Woldemar Bary on 8 May 1959.

[13] See Estate of Bary v. Commissioner, 24 T.C.M. 1790 (1965); affirmed: 368 F.2d 844 (1966).

[14] J. Lehrs, "Memorandum re Woldemar Bary's Case", David R. Francis Papers, microfilm edition, Reel 9. The Memorandum was composed on 17 April 1918 and sent on to Ambassador in Petrograd on 19 April 1918.

Don district ... storing of fire-arms without license ... [and] purchase and storage of false documents".[15]

The following day Lehrs met with Woldemar's brother, Victor, and his sister, Catherine Bary (d. 1978), who was engaged to marry Vasilii Vasilevich Krivoshein, charged in the case together with Woldemar Bary and Ivan A. Il'in. Victor Bary knew that Woldemar was in communication with officers and "helped them out with money", had "suspicions that these officers were connected with some counter-revolutionary movement", and therefore had objected strongly "... to those officers calling on his brother at their office". Victor believed that Woldemar in giving money to officers had "... acted merely out of charity". As for the revolvers, Victor Bary said that these had been "... purchased and borrowed from friends for the purpose of self-defense, which was of vital necessity in connection with the attempt the anarchists made on Victor Bary some time ago". Victor knew nothing of the false documents, but Lehrs believed these documents had been explained to him by Woldemar in an earlier conversation. Woldemar had said that "... he would procure for himself a false document which would enable him to leave Russia at the last moment as a Russian citizen".

At this point, the matter took a sudden and unexpected turn. Catherine Bary succeeded in arranging a meeting with her brother Woldemar when the Vice Consul was unable to do so. She used the good offices of the investigator in the case, Moisei Solomonovich Vengerov, who seemed to want to ingratiate himself with Woldemar and Catherine. On 16 April Victor Bary informed Vice Consul Lehrs that a confidential offer had been received: Woldemar Bary would be released if Victor Bary paid 150,000 rubles (the exchange rate about this time was twelve rubles to the United States dollar). Victor Bary reported the offer to his lawyer and to the Vice Consul.

In the meantime, Vice Consul Lehrs pressed Chicherin to arrange a meeting with Woldemar Bary. At 21;00 hours Lehrs received a telephone call at home from Woldemar Bary to say that Investigator Vengerov would grant a meeting at once. They had forty-five minutes together. Lehrs was shown Bary's dossier in which he observed papers and notes in Bary's handwriting purporting to account for money being spent for dispatching officers and members of a strike force to the south. Woldemar Bary's explanation was that the money was contributed during the early days of October 1917 when the strike force members were not considered to be counter-revolutionary. The investigator said that had the United States Consulate not intervened, it would have been easy to destroy the evidence; however, the Consulate having protested the search and arrest, the Extraordinary Committee was keen to prove that there were grounds for the measures taken against Woldemar Bary. The investigator promised not to refer to this compromising evidence and to regard the Vice Consul's interview with Woldemar Bary as unofficial. He further suggested that

[15] Ibid.

the Vice Consul make an application to Leon Trotsky and request that Woldemar Bary be released on surety to the Consulate General.

Vengerov then left Bary and the Vice Consul together alone: "Mr. Bary told me that his case was very serious and that he implored the Consulate and the Embassy to take immediate measures to release him".[16]

Lehrs did not trust Vengerov and was "… inclined to think that he is dishonest". On 17 April Lehrs was informed through official channels that he might see Woldemar Bary at 12:00 hours on 18 April. Lehrs replied that Catherine Bary already had a meeting with her brother, but did not disclose his own meeting with Woldemar. In the meantime, Consul Maddin Summers on 16 April 1918 had informed the Secretary of State of the United States, Robert Lansing (1864-1928), through the United States Consul at Vladivostok, about the arrest of Woldemar Bary by cablegram and sought instructions: "Have demanded Bary be allowed counsel and that member consular staff be present trial … Shall I inform Government of serious displeasure United States Government if American citizen convicted and punished by Revolutionary Tribunal. Similar cases are likely to arise in the near future".

The United States Consul General in Moscow, DeWitt Clinton Poole, approached a Russian sworn Attorney, Aleksandr Semenovich Tager (1888-1939), to act as defense counsel in the forthcoming proceedings.[17] Lehrs did indeed attend the public session of the Investigative Commission attached to the Moscow Revolutionary Tribunal on 30 April 1918, where Tager acted on behalf of Bary and Nikolai Konstantinovich Murav'ev (1870-1936) represented Il'in. Illness prevented Il'in from attending, who submitted a medical certificate to this effect. Murav'ev sought to separate the accusation against Il'in from those accusations against the other three defendants. The Tribunal denied this petition.

Tager then petitioned the Investigative Committee attached to the Revolutionary Tribunal to consider the proceedings to be an inquiry and to launch a fully-fledged preliminary investigation, releasing the defendants in the meantime while the preliminary investigation proceeded. Vice Consul Lehrs supported this petition. The Investigative

16 Ibid. The Moscow press was conversant with what was happening with Bary and Il'in and reported in some detail on the substance of the charges. See Свободная Россия [Free Russia], no. 16 (17 April 1918), p. 3; no. 17 (18 April 1918), p. 4, reproduced in И. А. Ильин: Собрание сочинений. Дневник. Письма. Документы (1903-1938) [I. A. Il'in: Collection of Works. Diary. Letters, Documents (1903-1938)] (1999), pp. 586-587.

17 Tager, a graduate of the Moscow University Law Faculty, became a sworn advokat who took part in several political trials between 1912 and 1917. From February 1917 he served as a jurisconsult of the Extraordinary Investigative Commission of the Provisional Government and was a member of the Commission of the Provisional Government on law reform of the court and advokatura. Following the October 1917 Revolution, he served as defense counsel in the Moscow Revolutionary Tribunal and in 1933 published a volume on the Beilis Trial. On 15 April 1939 he was executed for counter-revolutionary activity and rehabilitated on 4 April 1956 by Ruling of the Military Division of the USSR Supreme Court.

Committee decreed to satisfy the petition and to refer the case for further investigation to the Political Section of the Investigative Committee. Bary was released on surety to Vice Consul Lehrs. In his three-page letter to Ambassador Francis on 30 April 1918, then in Vologda, reporting the latest news, Maddin Summers added a postscript in hand: "Bary was released today on bail".[18]

Lehrs believed that the charges against Woldemar Bary were part of an extortion scheme with respect to the Bary family. He lodged complaints to this effect and apparently succeeded in having two officials of the Extraordinary Commission arrested. This led to an interesting issue of international law which Dewitt Poole (1885-1952) raised with the Consular Corps in Moscow. The Revolutionary Tribunal requested that Lehrs appear "in the case of attempted extortion growing out of the Bary case". In Poole's view, international law was "perfectly clear" that a consular officer cannot refuse his evidence in a criminal case provided the official business of his office is not discussed. Poole sought instructions from Washington on the matter, but in the meantime the Revolutionary Tribunal was advised that Lehrs would be permitted to give his testimony to a commissioner sent to the Consulate General of the United States for that purpose. It was, Poole said, "highly desirable that Lehrs should give his testimony which will be very damaging to those who originally instigated the charges against Bary ...".[19]

When Lehrs was reassigned to Vologda later in June 1918 as a result of a contretemps with Karl Radek (1885-1939), the United States Consul in Moscow, DeWitt Poole linked the Bary Case with his concerns about the personal safety of Lehrs. Poole reminded Ambassador David Rowland Francis (1850-1927) that "... Lehrs was instrumental in connection with the Bary case. As one of these was a special investigator of the Extraordinary Commission against Counter Revolution, which is an instrument of pure terror, I have been fearful for some time that Lehrs might become the victim of some act of revenge".[20]

The subsequent movements of those released on surety are obscure. By 15 June 1918 Poole referred in a letter to Ambassador Francis to the "... military side of the Krivoshein group" and that "negotiations between that group and the German representatives here have taken on a much more definite character within the past few days". The Krivoshein Group had apparently been addressed by a German colonel in uniform who promised troops "... to support a coup d'etat against the Bolsheviks".[21]

[18] Letter Summers to Francis, 30 April 1918. David R. Francis Papers, microfilm edition, Reel 9.

[19] Letter of Poole to Francis, 7 June 1918. Ibid.

[20] Letter of Poole to Francis, 1 July 1918. David R. Francis Papers, microfilm edition, Reel 10.

[21] Letter of Poole to Francis, 15 June 1918. Ibid.

Bary did not remain in Russia to tempt the fates of the Revolutionary Tribunal. He reportedly escaped from Moscow disguised as a woman[22] and made his way back to the United States, via Vladivostok, for on 5 March 1919 he married Natalia ("Nina") Mikhailovna Anikin at the United States Consulate in the City of Vladivostok. He did not appear for his trial in December 1918, nor did his co-defendants, except for Il'in.[23]

After returning to the United States, Bary made the acquaintance in the early 1920s of the Ukrainian aircraft designer and inventor, Igor Sikorsky (1889-1972), who later founded Sikorsky Aviation Corporation. The Sikorsky helicopters became and remain world renowned.

Bary joined Sikorsky[24] and became initially the Treasurer and later Vice President of Sikorsky Aviation, helping to facilitate the company's relocation from New York[25] to Pennsylvania. Upon retirement, Bary lived in Bushkill, Pennsylvania, for the remainder of his life. Bary acquired a number of United States patents, including for an apparatus for electrolytic protection of vessels against corrosion (No. 2,193,667: 12 March 1940); an inflatable dome structure (No. 2,837,101: 3 June 1958);[26] and a closed track airport (No. 3,173,634: 16 March 1965). After Nina Bary's death, Woldemar Bary remarried in 1973 Valentina Bary (24 September 1904-29 October 2002).[27]

22 A. Palomino, "From Russia With Love: An Immigrant's Story", *The Joint Archives Quarterly*, XXIII, no. 1 (Spring 2013), p. 1. The Bary Family Archives are held at the Joint Archives of Holland, Michigan. The Certificate of Marriage between Woldemar Bary and Natalia Anikin was issued by the American Consular Service in Vladivostok; the marriage ceremony was performed by the Rev. John F. Smith, of the YMCA, who was authorized by the laws of the State of Ohio to perform such a ceremony.

23 Bary published "The Engineering Industry in the U.S.S.R.", *Nature*, CXLVIII, no. 3749 (6 September 1941), p. 283; *Engineering*, 15 August 1941.

24 According to Bary's obituary, he "founded the Sikorsky Aircraft Corporation of Stanford, Conn., in 1921, sold it to Pratt & Whitney and became vice president of the Sikorsky Division. He built the first amphibious aircraft and was a pioneer in amphibious aircraft transport. In later years he was a consultant for major airlines. He was a member of the Greek Orthodox Church of Delaware Water Gap". See *The Pocono Record*, 24 December 1979, p. 14, col. 1. A biography of Sikorsky indicates that Sikorsky Aero Engineering Corporation was formed on 5 March 1923 with temporary offices at 114 East 25th Street, New York City, and Woldemar Bary acting as Treasurer. Very possibly Bary, Sikorsky, and others operated as an unincorporated entity or within another corporate personality prior to 1923. Sikorsky arrived in the United States on 30 March 1919. See F. J. Delear, *Igor Sikorsky: His Three Careers in Aviation* ([1969]), pp. 89-98.

25 The United States Census for 1940 (reported 19 April 1940) records Bary and his wife resident in New York City and Bary earning a salary of US$1,300 per year. Bary lived in Bushkill, Pennsylvania, for nineteen years prior to his death, which would place his arrival there about 1960.

26 See L. Wiegler, "Tearing into the Metrodome: Are Other Air-Pressurized Stadiums Unsafe and Outmoded?", *Scientific American*, 20 January 2011.

27 *The Holland Sentinel* [Holland, Michigan], 30 October 2002. Valentina Bary was born in Dubno, Russia, and emigrated from Czechoslovakia to the United States in 1968.

Riabushinskii

In Il'in studies the name of Vladimir Pavlovich Riabushinskii (1873-1955) is deservedly celebrated for his role in arranging the publication in Paris of Il'in's treatise on the axioms of religious experience. Both Riabushinskii and Il'in had collaborated with P. B. Struve in publishing the Paris daily newspaper Возрождение [Renaissance] and co-signed Struve's letter of resignation dated 17 August 1927.[28] He also was a frequent contributor to Il'in's Русский колокол [The Russian Bell].[29]

The Riabushinskii family, however, was previously associated with Il'in in their capacity as printers. The surviving proofs of Il'in's work on legal consciousness bear the stamp of «Товарищество типографии Рябушинских» [Partnership of Riabushinskii Printing House].[30]

The Il'in Personal Archive

It is well established that Il'in hoped and expected that his personal archive and library would one day return to the University from which he graduated and by which he was employed. That this actually happened was the outcome of a carefully conceived and executed program by Il'in himself, his wife, Natalia, and his friends who survived him. Having been taught a severe personal lesson by having his Hegel dissertation manuscript, notes, and materials confiscated in Austria at the outbreak of the First World War, which then had to be rewritten or reconstructed, all the evidence suggests that Il'in took care to retain and preserve his papers and his books for posterity. This was consistent with his general view set out in an article entitled "A Matter of Keeping":[31] "Our archives and museums should never be transferred in ownership to foreign powers. We ask them to help us to keep them. We request acknowledgement, respect, and hospitality, but not seizure. That collected should have one purpose – return to Russia, unified and liberated".

When Il'in died on 21 December 1954, all author's rights and rights of inheritance passed to his widow, Natalia Nikolaevna Il'ina. She was not abandoned and forgotten in widowhood, as all too often can happen. Il'in's pupils and friends of the family gathered in support. On the second

28 The letter is reproduced in full in A. V. Lomonosov, «Возрождение» [Renaissance], in A. N. Nikoliukin (ed.), Литературная энциклопедия Русского зарубежья. 1918-1940. Периодика и литературные центры [Literary Encyclopedia of the Russian Abroad. 1918-1940. Periodicals and Literary Centers] (2000), II, p. 67.

29 See V. V. Sapov, «Русский колокол» [The Russian Bell], in ibid., p. 397.

30 The stamp appears on p. 49 (dated 16 November 1917) and p. 65 (dated 21 February 1918) of a set of galley proofs amateurishly bound together, probably by Il'in himself, for working purposes.

31 See Il'in, «Дело хранения» [A Matter of Keeping], in Il'in, Собрание сочинений в десяти томах [Collection of Works in Ten Volumes] (1999), IX-X, p. 412.

anniversary of his death these individuals created an informal association known as the "Ivan Aleksandrovich Il'in Society".[32] A constitutive document was drawn up which set out their purposes and aims: to render all and every assistance to the cause of keeping and preserving, publishing and republishing, and disseminating the works of Professor I. A. Il'in, as well as to promote the extensive dissemination of his ideological legacy".

The founders, in addition to Natalia Il'ina, included Elena Fedorovna von Baumgarten (1891-after 1970), who then lived in Zurich; Roman Martynovich Siehle (1900-1971), who lived in Germany; Aleksei Aleksandrovich Kvartirov (1911-1989), who resided in Geneva and then relocated to the United States; and Konstantin Evgen'evich Klimov (1896-1974), who lived in Canada.

Baumgarten was a medical doctor and director of a clinic in Zurich where Il'in was treated and eventually died. By 1956 she was a pensioner.

Siehle was a pupil who had been a follower of Il'in since 1928 in Berlin. He intended to write a book about Il'in (and may have preserved papers for that purpose) and served as the permanent secretary of the Society.

Kvartirov had been a pupil of Il'in in Berlin. Together with his sister, Marina, they helped the Il'ins successfully depart Germany for Switzerland in 1938. Both Marina and her husband, Mikhail Georgievich Deriugin (1914-1982), a clergyman in the Russian Orthodox Church Abroad, were members of the Society.

Konstantin Klimov was a noted musician, professor of music at Laval University in Quebec, and brother of the artist and art historian, Evgenii Evgen'evich Klimov (1901-1990). The Il'ins had helped the Klimov family, who had emigrated from Russia in 1921, during their relocation after the Second World War to Germany and Canada.

The initial Society members drafted an Appeal to Russian émigrés to help preserve the Il'in legacy. Specific projects were mentioned, including the need to publish manuscripts unpublished, to reissue works long out of print or destroyed, to assemble his various articles and reissue them in collected form, and in general to prepare and publish a complete collected works of Il'in. The Society was exceedingly cautious and careful in selecting individuals who might wish to be associated with them. Ultimately the following became members: A. D. Bilimovich (United States); Professor V. S. Il'in (cousin of Ivan Aleksandrovich, Venezuela);

[32] See on this episode Olga V. Lisitsa, «Миссия содружества имени Профессора Ивана Александровича Ильина» [Mission of the Professor Ivan Aleksandrovich Il'in Commonwealth], in S. V. Kornilov (ed.), Идейное наследие И. А. Ильина и современность: Сборник научных трудов [Ideological Legacy of I. A. Il'in and Modern Times: Collection of Scholarly Works] (2008), pp. 29-40. The term "society" is a loose translation here of what would be more literally and properly conveyed as "commonwealth". The organizers, it would seem, deliberately chose a vague term that would enable them to pursue a common aim without being required to register an organization under Swiss law, with all the costs, technicalities, risks, and formalities such a body would entail.

Professor Alfred A. Swan (Swarthmore and Haverford colleges, United States); Professor P. D. Il'inskii (United States); Archpriest Mitrofan Znosko-Borovskii (Morocco); E. E. Klimov (Canada); G. A. Alekseev (United States); G. V. Ofrosimov (Switzerland); F. A. von Shultess (Switzerland); Archpriest Sergii Shchukin (United States, Canada); G. V. Mesniaev (United States); I. N. Gorianov (Germany); A. I. Buld (United States); M. A. and M. G. Deriugina (Austria); R. M. Trakhtenberg (Switzerland); A. A. Tenson (Germany); A. N. Tsurikov (Germany); and V. A. Boss (Switzerland).

A number of measures were taken simultaneously. Some of Il'in's books and manuscripts began to be published, including the work on legal consciousness. It was decided to microfilm part of the collection. Nine microfilms were made, containing about 10,000 pages with additional notes; in all, about one-seventh of the archive. Four copies were made of the microfilms. Where should the microfilms be stored? This was all being undertaken during the Cold War when there existed literally a nuclear balance of terror. The Society members feared the consequences of a nuclear conflict. It was decided to disperse the microfilms around the world. One would remain in Switzerland with Natalia Nikolaevna Il'ina, and another in New York with Kvartirov. But New York began to be viewed as unsafe – a likely target in the event of a nuclear conflict. It was decided that a "backwoods" site would be appropriate in the United States: East Lansing, Michigan, was the choice.

In 1961 Natalia's health began to deteriorate rapidly. She needed constant supervision and care. The Il'in apartment was vacated; all the Il'in belongings, including the library, archive, and everything else, were packed in boxes and stored in the Baumgarten clinic in Zurich; Natalia herself was placed in a home, where she passed away in 1963. The Commonwealth then began to seek a permanent site for the archive and library. A number of possibilities were considered and rejected (Columbia University in New York was rejected by Natalia because she was not impressed by the curator of the archive; the Russian Museum in San Francisco was in a wooden building, which was not deemed sufficiently safe; the Hoover Institution at Stanford University was prepared to accept the archive provided that after 30 years title to the materials would pass to the Institution, which was absolutely contrary to Il'in's wishes). Zurich itself was a possibility, but there was no appropriate building.

In late 1963 or early 1964 a new plan emerged. K. E. Klimov suggested that Aleksei,[33] the son of E. E. Klimov, also a member of the Commonwealth, who was completing his studies of Russian language

[33] Aleksei, or Alexis, Klimoff (b. 1939) is Professor Emeritus of Russian Studies at Vassar College (1971-2012) and sometime Professor of Russian in the summers at Middlebury College (1981-1997) in Vermont. He received his B.A. and M.A. at Michigan State University and Ph.D. at Yale University. He is the editor of *One Day in the Life of Ivan Denisovich: A Critical Companion* (1997); co-author of *The Soul and Barbed Wire: An Introduction to Solzhenitsyn* (2006) (with Edward E. Ericson); among others.

and literature at Michigan State University under the direction of Professor Poltoratskii, be considered a possible guardian together with his professor. Inquiries were made of Poltoratskii. He was amenable. The University would be asked to cover the costs of transporting the Archive from Europe to the United States. In October 1965 Poltoratskii traveled to Zurich to meet with the Swiss members of the Society. The meeting went well, Poltoratskii was invited to join the Society, and Poltoratskii's negotiations with the Director of the Michigan State Library, Richard Chapin, proceeded smoothly and successfully. Poltoratskii reported the conditions would be as follows:

> [1]. The Archive would not be sold to nor bestowed upon Michigan State University, but would be provided to the University for temporary use;
>
> [2]. After the liquidation of the Communist regime in Russia, the Archive should be transferred to Moscow University;
>
> [3]. Il'in's books should insofar as possible be kept together and not distributed throughout the collection;
>
> [4]. A small portion of Il'in's correspondence should remain under seal and be used only upon the expiration of a designated period of time;
>
> [5]. The materials of the Archive should be kept in conditions normal for such materials;
>
> [6]. Poltoratskii would be assigned to watch over the keeping and use of the materials;
>
> [7]. The Michigan State Library would pay the expenses for transporting the Archive and Library to East Lansing from Zurich.

Of these conditions, only the second caused some discussion. What might the "liquidation of the Communist regime in Russia" mean exactly? The phrase was ambiguous and might give rise to difficulties in the future. It was decided that the "fall of communism" should be understood to mean the absence of a one-party dictatorship pursuing such goals as world revolution, or the establishment of Communism, Socialism, or Anarchism all over the world; the permanent establishment of a national Russian governmental system; clear guarantees that national political opinion, scholarly research and teaching, and religious and church activities, were to enjoy complete freedom.[34]

On behalf of the Society, Elena Fedorovna Baumgarten took over the discussions with Michigan State. She was now in advanced years and wished nothing more than to bring the matter to a conclusion.

[34] This was the formulation set out in the Letter from E. de Baumgarten to the Director of Libraries, Michigan State University, Richard E. Chapin, dated 7 May 1965. Reproduced in [C. H. Haka], *The Ivan Aleksandrovich Il'in Papers and the Michigan State University Libraries*. East Lansing, Michigan: Michigan State University, [2013], p. 10.

Michigan State accepted the conditions laid down by the Society. Roman Siehle agreed to pack the Archive and books for carriage. An inventory was prepared to ensure that nothing was lost. The shipment arrived in East Lansing in 1966. For three years it was kept under seal until the construction of the new library premises was completed. In 1969 the materials were transferred to the Department of Rare Books and Manuscripts in the Library.

Professor Poltoratskii in the meantime had accepted an invitation to join the University of Pittsburgh.[35] He nonetheless complied with his obligations to watch over the Archive, undertook his own research in the materials, and published a number of works on Il'in, including a biography. In 1990 Poltoratskii traveled to Leningrad to deliver lectures on Il'in. These were received with great acclaim, but he fell ill there and passed away in his Leningrad hotel.

The perestroika processes underway in Russia brought Il'in and his works for the first time to the attention of the Russian general public. The ultimate intention of the Society began to be realized: the publication of the Complete Collected Works of Il'in. This became possible because Aleksei Klimov, the student of Poltoratskii and now Professor of Russian Literature at Vassar College near New York, undertook the immense task of making a full inventory and photocopies of the entire Il'in Archive. These were carried over in batches to Iurii and Olga Lisitsa and served as the basis for publishing the Complete Collected Works of Il'in, of which going on thirty-seven volumes have appeared to date.

The individual now acting for the Society was Tamara Mikhailovna Poltoratskaia (1921-2016). She agreed to the reinterment of the remains of Ivan and Natalia Il'in in the cemetery of the Don Monastery in 2005. It was natural that the Archive, comprising some 70,000 pages of material, should follow. The materials were received for processing in Russia on 27 May 2006 and were transferred on 20 November 2006 to the custody of the Department of Rare Books and Manuscripts of the Moscow University. The books (630 titles) came in two lots, in 2006 and in 2008. The mission of the Society, solemnly undertaken in 1956, was successfully completed to the credit of all concerned a half century later.

35 Professor Nikolai Petrovich Poltoratskii was born at Istanbul, Turkey, brought up in Bulgaria, graduated from the Sofia Russian Gymnasium, and attended various universities in Bulgaria, West Germany, and France, specializing in philosophy, Russian studies, and history. He arrived in the United States in 1955, specialized in Soviet studies, headed the Russian program at Michigan State University for nine years and more than twenty years at the University of Pittsburgh. See Haka, ibid., p. 8. His scholarly publications included a biography of Il'in published in the Russian language at Tenafly, New Jersey, in 1989.

The Il'in Private Library

The Il'in family were book people who esteemed books to study, acquire, and treasure. We know little of the Il'in personal library in Moscow prior to their departure nor the extent to which they carried books into exile as part of their luggage. Il'in's own property was confiscated in 1923 by Decree of the Soviet Government; what property precisely fell victim to the decree and whether books were part of that property is not a matter of record. Evidently there were personal "confiscations" of professorial libraries. The story is told by Il'in of an incident in the Institute of Philosophy arising out of the Bolshevik practice of seizing professorial libraries and distributing the books among their members. One Bogolepov, a pupil of Ozerov, had seized the latter's library; Riazanov-Goldendakh had taken the library of S. N. Bulgakov; someone else had taken Novgorodtsev's books.[36] Russian scholars were generous in lending books to one another; the seizures made it difficult to say with accuracy from whose personal library a particular title had originated.

Before departing abroad in 1922, Il'in had given to the Library of Moscow University fifteen books and offprints, six autographed. Additional Il'in materials had been acquired incidentally with the personal archives of Sof'ia Nikolaevna Shil' (1863-1928) and Aleksandr Sergeevich Akhmanov (1893-1957), a former student of Il'in. These have been added to or linked with the Il'in Archive and Library and are recorded in the Catalog of the Il'in Library. What the Il'in Library might have become had the Il'ins either remained in Russia or had possessed the financial resources to acquire books on a substantial basis can only be imagined. Il'in did succeed in removing all of his books from Germany to Switzerland, and presumably the Library remained intact while in the United States.

The affection and emotional attachment of Il'in for his library is evident in two respects: special bindings and his exlibris. His Hegel dissertation is present in the Library in a fine leather binding, probably Russo/German, without a binder's label but plainly superior work. A number of volumes, bound at Zollikon, Switzerland, bear a binder's ticket or mark. The exlibris designed by Klimov (see below) for the Il'ins together is pasted in to about two-thirds of the volumes and was doubtless printed cliché in Switzerland. The idea of having an exlibris may have originated with the designer; the fact that the Il'ins greatly loved and admired the exlibris is demonstrated by the simple fact that they used the bookplate extensively in their library – a library that they intended one day should return to Russia.

[36] See A. M. Sharipov, Русский мыслитель: Иван Александрович Ильин. Творческая биография [Russian Thinker: Ivan Aleksandrovich Il'in. Intellectual Biography] (2008), p. 89.

Ovchinkina gave a rough classification of the books in the Il'in library as follows: (1) belles-lettres, principally Russian and Russian-émigré titles: 76 authors, 266 titles; (2) history, principally Russian, including in foreign languages: 69 authors, 110 titles; (3) art: 34 authors, 72 titles; (4) religion and theology: 16 authors, 19 titles; (5) philosophy: 10 authors, 14 titles.[37] The number of titles on philosophy and law is striking for being so few.

As a reader, Il'in took full advantage of his books. He made marginal notations frequently in pencil or in pen. Among those often appearing in Russian were: "Russia", "people", "triviality", "nonsense".[38] Natalia Il'ina was more reserved in her observations, usually confining them to two horizontal marks in the margin or, rarely, a notation; these occurred principally in books on history or in those devoted to the poetry of Pushkin, Lermontov, or Zhukovskii. For those interested in reading patterns, the Il'in collection promises rich insights.

The Il'in library and the predominance of belles-lettres and Russian history within it provide occasion to consider their friends and acquaintances, many of whom presented books to the Il'ins. Among their dearest friends was the writer Ivan Sergeevich Shmelev (1873-1950). They did not know one another in Russia; they met in Berlin and maintained a lively correspondence. Shmelev routinely sent warmly inscribed books to the Il'ins. Among composers and musicians the Il'ins were close to the Medtners from their days in Moscow. Il'in had defended the works of Emilii Karlovich Medtner (1872-1936)[39] vigorously against critical attacks launched in the press by Andrei Belyi (1880-1934; pseudonym of Boris Nikolaevich Bugaev) in 1917 and actively promoted Nikolai Medtner's music. It was entirely appropriate that the jubilee volume published to honor Nikolai Medtner (1879-1951) should reproduce three of Il'in's critical appreciations.[40] They corresponded frequently from 1915 until Medtner's death. The Il'in copy of Medtner's book is extensively annotated.[41]

The Klimov family became close to the Il'ins through the Medtners. Il'in accepted and used the exlibris designed by E. E. Klimov, assisted

37 I. V. Ovchinkina, in note 5 above, p. 12.

38 Ibid., p. 13.

39 M. Ljunggren, *The Russian Mephisto: Study of the Life and Work of Emilii Medtner* (Stockholm, 1994). Emilii was a Russian publisher and influential member of the Russian symbolist movement.

40 The three essays by Il'in were: "A Study of Medtner"; "Medtner's Fairy Tales"; and "Sonata Form in Medtner", published respectively in R. Holt (ed.), *Nicolas Medtner (1879-1951): A Tribute to His Art and Personality* (London, [1955]), pp. 163-188.

41 See N. K. Medtner, Муза и мода (Защита основ музыкального искусства) [The Muse and Fashion (Defense of the Foundations of the Art of Music)] (Paris, 1935). Item 183 in Ovchinkina, note 4 above, pp. 87-88.

the Klimov family materially after the Second World War, endeavored to arrange exhibitions of Klimov's paintings in Switzerland, and sought to develop patronage for his works. When the Il'ins traveled on holiday, especially during the interwar period, they arranged to spend time with these individuals.

Others with whom Il'in corresponded and accepted as friends included: the actor and director, Konstantin Sergeevich Stanislavskii (1863-1938); the painter Mikhail Vasilevich Nesterov (1862-1942), who had produced a remarkable image of Il'in; the composer Sergei Vasil'evich Rachmaninoff (1873-1943); Baron Petr Nikolaevich Wrangel (1878-1928); Aleksei Aleksandrovich von Lampe (1885-1967); and Boris Aleksandrovich Nikolskii (1885-1962).

Although on several occasions Il'in vigorously denied being a poet, he wrote verse frequently from his student years at Moscow University on in to later life. A number of his verses have been considered to be worthy of publication.[42]

On the Il'in Bookplate

The initials "E.K." (the same in Russian and English) conceal the identity of a bookplate designer unknown to Western bookplate literature yet appear on the bookplate design belonging to Ivan and Natalia Il'in.

The initials stand for Evgenii Evgen'evich Klimov, known in Canada and the United States as Eugene Klimoff (he preferred the soft "ff" in the English spelling of his surname, as have so many Russian émigrés, to the Library of Congress transliteration "v" – technically more correct). Klimov was born on 8 May 1901 in the City of Mitau, then part of the Baltic segment of the Russian Empire. His father was a lawyer. Upon completing his secondary education at Novocherkassk in 1918, he enrolled at the Don Polytechnic but was forced by the Russian Civil War to interrupt his studies. He enlisted in the Russian Navy, serving at Novorossiisk and Sevastopol, and by some miracle escaped the mass repressions experienced by the White Russian forces after the fall of the Crimean Peninsula. In 1921 he was permitted as a native of the Baltic region to return to Riga, Latvia, where he was accepted for further studies by the Latvian Academy of Arts. Upon graduating in 1929, he worked as a teacher of art and art history at the Lomonosov Lycée, a Russian-language institution, in Riga. He offered instruction in drawing and art history.

He traveled frequently during this Latvian period, including abroad, completing his own graphics and paintings and visiting art museums. He studied techniques of icon painting under the direction of a master who

[42] V. I. Lafitsky, Богарне: судьбы и загадки истории [Beauharnais: Fates and Mysteries of History] (2d ed.; 2013), pp. 124-126; N. N. Leont'eva and N. T. Tarumova (comps.), «Поэзия Московского университета: от Ломоносова и до ...» ["Poetry of Moscow University: From Lomonosov up to ..."] (2011), pp. 290-292.

worked in the Old Believer tradition, Pimen Sofronov (1898-1973), and took part in a group project to decorate a church with frescos. Exhibitions, museum work, and study groups were part of the cultural milieu for the Russian community of Latvia, and he took an active role in these.

In 1944 he was invited to the Kondakov Institute in Prague, a center for icon restoration, and in 1945, three months after the Soviet Army occupied Czechoslovakia, fled with his family to the American occupation zone of Germany. There in a Bavarian village he spent four years. He resettled in Canada in 1949, choosing by reason of his command of the French language to base himself in Quebec. He resumed his teaching career in art history, private art lessons, Russian language instruction, public lectures, and frequent appearances in the Russian émigré press. During the 1960-70s he visited Europe often, and the Holy Land in 1964. An automobile accident took his life on 29 December 1990 in his ninetieth year.[43]

So far as the record discloses, the bookplate for the Il'ins is the only one known to have been designed by "E.K.".[44] Eugene Klimoff first met Ivan Aleksandrovich Il'in in 1931, when Il'in visited Riga to deliver some public lectures. Although Il'in returned several times more for this purpose, friendship with the Klimoff family (as opposed to being acquaintances) developed from 1935, when Il'in spent much of the summer at a large dacha in rural Latvia that the Klimoffs had rented. Surviving correspondence suggests that the Il'in bookplate was not commissioned from the artist, but rather was a gift, perhaps an expression of gratitude for assistance extended by the Il'ins to the Klimoffs when they were refugees after the Second World War in Germany. Il'in sent food parcels from Switzerland together with touching letters of support and encouragement during those difficult times.

In a letter dated 13 January 1949[45] Il'in promised to send E.K. a picture of the Kremlin palace. This would suggest the scheme of designing a bookplate was underway. On 17 August 1949 Il'in commented on a draft design rather severely. By the time of the third letter the Klimoffs were in Canada. Il'in gave a detailed critique in early Spring 1950 on a further version which implied that the final design had not been agreed. Perhaps the final version was done in late spring of 1950. A letter of April 1950 from Il'in requests quite a different bookplate design (an eagle on a cliff), but there is no indication that E.K. ever attempted a design along these lines.

[43] Biographical data is drawn from A. Klimoff, *Eugene Klimoff. Selected Works* (Riga, 2006) and correspondence with Alexis Klimoff, who was kind enough to share recollections of his father with me.

[44] Alexis Klimoff has a dim and perhaps unreliable recollection that his father may have undertaken a woodcut or wood engraved bookplate in the late 1940s or early 1950s, but no copy, if it was ever made, is known to have survived.

[45] Iu. T. Lisitsa (ed.), И. А. Ильин. Собрание сочинений. Письма. Мемуары. 1939-1954 [I. A. Il'in. Collected Works. Letters. Memoirs. 1939-1954] (1999), [XIV], p. 34.

A variant of the bookplate also is illustrated here. Correspondence in the archive suggests there may have been another, probably without the name of Il'in's wife. Natalia Nikolaevna Il'ina was a noted historian in her own right. Her work criticizing theories of the Scandinavian origins of the Russians appeared at Paris in 1955 and was reissued in Russia in 2010.[46]

The bookplate has only recently become known to Russian bookplate collectors.[47] A copy has been presented by Alexis Klimoff to the Special Collections Division of the Moscow University Library and is found in 461 books in the Il'in private library. The dimensions of the bookplate are 7.5 x 9.2 cm. (P1).[48]

46 N. N. Il'ina, Изгнание норманнов: очередная задача русской исторической науки [Banishment of the Norsemen: Routine Task of Russian Historical Science (Paris); reprinted in V. V. Fomin (ed.), Изгнание норманнов из русской истории [Banishment of the Norsemen from Russian History] (2010), pp. 19-136: "The Norman theory does not give a satisfactory explanation of those events which disturbed our country in the ninth century and were noted in the early news of the Russian chronicle". Ibid., p. 120.

47 The first illustration was as the cover design for two previously unpublished works by Il'in on State structure and constitution for a post-Soviet Russia. See I. A. Il'in, Основы государственного устройства. Проект Основтного Закона России [Fundamental Principles of State Structure. Draft Basic Law of Russia], ed. Iu. T. Lisitsa (1996). The bookplate appears in color in a collection of unpublished photographs and archival materials edited by Lisitsa, Иван Ильин и Россия [Ivan Il'in and Russia] (1999), p. 160, together with family photographs of the Klimoffs and two pencil sketches by E. K. of Il'in. Il'in bookplates are illustrated in Ovchinkina, note 4 above, p. 7. Also see W. E. Butler, "The Il'in Bookplate by E. E. Klimoff", *The Bookplate Journal*, X, no. 1 (N.S., 2012), pp. 34-37.

48 Each entry in the Catalog of the Il'in Library indicates the presence of any bookplates, labels, or other evidence of provenance, whether of the Il'ins or anyone else. Many are illustrated. Among them is an inscribed copy of a book in French by P. P. Vinogradoff, who held the Chair in comparative law at Oxford University. See note 5 above.

I. A. Il'in and the Rule of Law

The main text translated herein constitutes perhaps the most impassioned defense of the rule of law ever penned by a Russian legal theorist.[1] More specifically, it contains an outline of all the essential elements required for a well-ordered State such that the rule of law could in practice be realized, the rule of law itself being the chief defining characteristic of the well-ordered State.[2] These ideal elements are specified by Il'in as comprising the legal consciousness of the general population, the legal consciousness of the ruling authorities, the legal consciousness of jurists, and the necessary conception of the State as an ideal to be shared by them all. The work contains detailed examinations of the inevitable damage to the political and legal order caused by corruption or lack of development in any one of these individual elements. Each is examined separately as a potential source of "disease" for the entire political order.

The author of the text, Ivan Aleksandrovich Il'in (1883-1954), received his formal higher education in the Faculty of Law of Moscow University (Diploma 1906; Magister exam 1909; Magister and Doctorate, 1918), began lecturing there as a *privat docent* from 1910, and as a professor from 1918. In 1920 he was elected head of the Moscow Psychological Society (the main philosophical association in Russia). However in autumn 1922 he was exiled by the Bolsheviks, under threat of execution, along with more than sixty other prominent intellectuals considered irreconcilable to Soviet power, on the now infamous "philosopher's ship".[3] He and his wife spent the remainder of their lives in exile in Germany and Switzerland.

The portrayal of the well-ordered State and legal system advanced here by Il'in here was in the main not derived from contemporary experience. It was constructed, rather, on the basis of general reflections on political history, on legal theory, and on philosophy, including that of ancient Greece. On the other hand, the various diseased states of populations and political orders, leading in some instances to their complete collapse,

[1] For a fuller appreciation of why such a strong commitment to the ideal of the rule of law should be an exception rather than the rule in the history of Russian legal thought, see Andrzej Walicki's classic account, *Legal Philosophies of Russian Liberalism* (1987), esp. chapter 1 on the sources of Russian legal nihilism.

[2] Along the way Il'in deals with many traditional issues treated in the philosophy of law: the concept of law, natural law and positive law, the critique of legal positivism, the validity of legal norms, the criteria for genuine authority of the law, conscientious objection and civil disobedience, criminal guilt and responsibility, punishment, the necessity of loyalty to the State ("patriotism"—on condition that the State be genuinely committed to realizing the rule of law), and the practical problems of cultivating respect for the law as well as the rule of law in actual human communities.

[3] There were actually two such ships, the *Oberbürgermeister Haken* and the *Preussen*, on which many of the anti-Bolshevik intellectual elite were exiled in autumn 1922, all under threat of execution, accompanied by numerous family members.

were generally taken from contemporary experience. Il'in was an astute observer of the various political disasters of European history in the twentieth century. He experienced more than his share of them personally.

He first lived through the declining years of an enfeebled Tsarist autocracy, experiencing the revolution of 1905, the February revolution of 1917, and finally, the Bolshevik revolution of October 1917 – followed by four years of exceptionally bloody military conflict, followed by the consolidation of power by a fanatical Bolshevik dictatorship. Expelled from Soviet Russia, he landed in Weimar Germany and lived through the spectacular economic collapse of that society. During the first year of Mussolini's full-blown version of Fascism (1925), Il'in was sent by Petr Berngardovoich Struve (1870-1944), the Editor of the émigré journal Возрождение [Rebirth] to observe this new form of politics in person for two months (September and October), gather materials, and articulate his impressions in a series of essays for Struve's journal. From 1933 to 1938 he lived through the emergence of the Nazi regime in Germany. He had survived multiple life-threatening encounters with the Bolshevik Cheka (soon renamed the GPU) in the cellars of the Lubianka and other prisons, and now was subjected to repeated interrogations by the Nazi Gestapo, which threatened to send him to a concentration camp. The political and legal deformities of twentieth century European history were well known to him. He was finally able to witness the events of the Second World War and its aftermath from the relative security of Switzerland (1938-1954), where for the first time in his life, at age fifty-five, he encountered a functioning democratic political system.

By the time Il'in began to write this work in 1916, the Russian Empire was well on its way to disintegration as a consequence, *inter alia*, of its disastrous involvement in the First World War. That process was completed by the abdication of Emperor Nicholas II and the two successive revolutions of 1917. Il'in regarded the second of these, the October Revolution, as the culmination of an utter catastrophe for Russia. The "State" erected by the Bolsheviks, and subsequently Stalin, was radically defective according to Il'in's conception. He never ceased predicting its inevitable collapse for reasons specified in this text.

Just as the major ancient Greek philosophers, Il'in was convinced that a well-ordered State could be constructed only on the basis of the well-ordered souls of its individual members. The focus on "legal consciousness" was, among others, a device for specifying the nature of the well-ordered soul as well as the nature of the well-ordered State. By formulating his argument in terms of "legal consciousness" Il'in was joining in a discussion that had been pursued on the continent of Europe since the early 1840s. That concept (*Rechtsbewußtsein*) figured prominently in the writings of Friedrich Carl von Savigny (1779-1861) that gave rise to the Historical School of nineteenth-century German jurisprudence. Before the nineteenth century was out, that School had contributed to the shaping of legal thought throughout the European continent, including the legal thought of Russia.[4]

In Savigny's conception, directly influenced by Johann Gottlieb Herder's (1744-1803) doctrine of the "*Volksgeist*," each distinct culture of Europe was defined by a "common consciousness of the people" unique to it. That consciousness was expressed first by the language intrinsic to it, by its folk tales and verbal arts, as well as its phonetics, lexicon and grammar. It was this conception that lay behind the countless investigations of local dialects, folk tales, and forms of village life for which the nineteenth century was famed. Savigny also argued that the "common consciousness" of a culture was equally manifest in its sense of justice and its expectations concerning the normal incidents of its law, properly administered. He held that the only valid source of law in a given culture was this "legal consciousness" of its inhabitants, originally expressed primarily in symbolic acts at public ceremonies whereby rights were created or extinguished, punishments administered, and so forth. This represented the "*youthful*" phase in the development of a particular legal culture, an expression of the legal sense "natural" to it.

However, such a primitive legal culture would be defective in its language and the logical exactitude by which it was expressed. A mature legal system must have developed into the *learned* phase, wherein highly trained specialists (and legislators attentive to them) formulate the legal instincts of the population in terms of formalized codes. This constitutes in effect a second species of "legal consciousness" that is highly refined by comparison with the "legal consciousness" of the population at large. The scholars' formulation of the legal system as a whole in the form of a code or codes constitutes *Recht*, the genuine and ultimate form of that people's law. However, a "learned" system of law which had lost touch with the original "natural" or "common" legal consciousness of the population could never be counted as valid. This was in effect an elaborate argument on Savigny's part to the effect that no single "universal" code of law such as the Roman could be considered valid for any non-Roman population, and thus no codification of German law based primarily upon the Roman system could be considered valid for Germany (this was among the major practical issues agitating German legal thinkers during the first half of the nineteenth century).

Thus, there are tacitly two somewhat distinct forms of legal consciousness in Savigny's theory: that of the general population and that of the legal scholars. Closer inspection reveals a third quasi-distinct form of legal consciousness in his theory: that of the ordinary rulers/legislators. This is so because the members of this group are unlikely to be identical with the set of sophisticated legal scholars. The legal consciousness of the emperors, senators, and legislators entrusted with the task of *enacting* (as

4 For recent accounts of Savigny's career see Benjamin Lahusen, *Alles Recht geht vom Volksgeist aus* (2012) and Joachim Rückert, *Friedrich Carl von Savigny: Leben und Wirken (1779-1861)* (2014).

Gesezten—rules of positive law) and enforcing the law is not identical with that of the scholar-jurists whose articulation of the *Recht* is presumed to be the ultimate embodiment of the system. The lawmakers and enforcers may be acting on behalf of particular interests, out of transient concerns, or from simple ignorance; as a result, the *Gesetzen* may become "a baleful corruption of the *Recht*".[5] Thus Savigny's theory originally points toward three distinguishable aspects of legal consciousness, or perhaps even three distinct forms thereof.

By the end of the nineteenth century, these three aspects or forms of legal consciousness had figured in countless discussions of legal theory, and they were still present and recognizably distinct as separate themes in German and other jurisprudential literature as late as the eve of the First World War and beyond. This may be taken as a mark of the continuing influence of the Historical School many decades after its founding.

To these three well-established notions of legal consciousness Il'in added a fourth: "political legal consciousness," which amounted to a reflection on the ideal form of the State as a political association (as well as the various deformities to which it is liable in practice). This notion was adopted from an influential work of his professor and mentor, Pavel Ivanovich Novgorodtsev (1866-1924), *The Crisis of Contemporary Legal Consciousness*, published a few years earlier.[6] Through an examination of these four forms or aspects of legal consciousness Il'in was able to articulate a relatively complete theory of the State and law as ideals, the thoughts, attitudes and motivations required of the various participants in such a well-ordered political and legal association, as well as of the many deformities to which each was liable in practice. He characterizes these various deformities as "diseases" capable of bringing about the destruction of the State.

Indeed, Il'in's detailed account of the fundamental causes leading to the deformation or destruction of States in recent European history (see especially chapters fourteen through twenty) was arguably unprecedented at the time in the depth and precision of its moral and psychological

[5] F. C. von Savigny, *Vom Beruf unserer Zeit für Gesetzgebung und Rechtswissenschaft* (1814; 2d ed., 1828; 3d ed., 1840). The second edition was translated by Abraham Hayward as *The Vocation of our Age for Legislation and Jurisprudence* (1831; reprint ed.: New York, 1975). See p. 32.

Although Savigny was an opponent of what he understood by the natural law tradition, his own theory offers some support for a diminished analogue of that doctrine by introducing a distinction between the *Recht* and *Gesetzen* and suggesting that the former serves as the objective standard for the validity of the latter. Il'in, on the other hand, explicitly reintroduced a doctrine of natural law as a central feature of his theory.

[6] P. N. Novgorodtsev, *Кризис современного правосознания* [Crisis of Contemporary Legal Consciousness] (1909; reprinted by the Institute of State and Law, Russian Academy of Sciences, under the editorship of Academician V. N. Kudriavtsev in 1996). This was Volume 2 of an intended 3-volume work under the collective title *An Introduction to the Philosophy of Law*. Volume 3, *On the Social Ideal*, appeared in 1917, but volume 1 was never published as such.

insights. Without specifically naming the nineteenth century Tsarist Russian State, he supplies a remarkably subtle and penetrating account of the decades-long, gradual weakening of political bonds within it, to such an extent that the will to preserve it, on the part of much of the population, had ultimately evaporated. His account invokes moral, spiritual, and political failings on the part of the citizenry as well as the ruling authorities, where the failures on one side led to corresponding reactions by the other in an accelerating downward spiral of reciprocal action and reaction, culminating in the death of the State and mutual calamity. He provides a similar analysis of the deformities of totalitarian politics in the twentieth century which is applicable to the Nazi "State" no less than to the Stalinist version of statehood. The grounds of his certainty that no such State could endure in the long run are convincingly articulated.

Il'in began his work with the observation that behind the cataclysm of world war and its consequential upheavals was to be found "*a disordered and embittered human soul*"[7] and that recovery from these disasters depended ultimately upon a re-ordering of the human soul. Such a re-ordering he believed to be possible only on the basis of a life lived "*from a single objective center, moved by an authentic love of Divinity as the supreme good*". For the individual soul to achieve such a life was for it to enter into the life of "spirit". Hence one of the central preoccupations of the text: what it means for a (potentially disordered and embittered) individual soul to achieve the life of spirit. Indeed, the mature, developed form of legal consciousness is but a consequence of the achievement of spirit—i.e., of a plurality of individual souls that have grown together into a single common spirit, or in Hegel's famous phrase: "An 'I' that is a 'We', and a 'We' that is an 'I'".[8]

As Il'in makes clear in the penultimate chapter, the Divinity he has in mind is that of a generally Christian worldview, but apparently not so narrowly sectarian as to be restricted merely to Russian Orthodoxy, or even Orthodoxy in general. However, there is no reference to either of the other major monotheisms in this context. At another level however, the concept of "spirit" seems to acquire a dimension of universality, as Il'in bases his "grounding" of natural law on a *universal and inalienable natural right* of every individual to a freely and self-sufficiently created life of spirit [одухотворенной жизни].[9] Presumably such a natural right would be entirely non-sectarian.

It is evident that the inspiration for much of Il'in's talk of "spirit" and "Divinity" is as much Hegelian as Biblical. The Divinity that Il'in has in mind serves principally as the standard of the good, the true, and the beautiful in the proper ordering of human conduct. There are numerous

[7] I. A. Il'in, *On the Essence of Legal Consciousness*, p. 129 below.

[8] G. W. F. Hegel, *The Phenomenology of Spirit*, transl. A. V. Miller (1977), p. 110.

[9] See the concluding pages of chapter five.

invocations of Hegel's conception of spirit scattered throughout the text in the form of direct or oblique references to his short-hand definition of spirit as the "I" that is a "We", and a "We" that is an "I". This is entirely appropriate because Il'in's conception of the basis for the rule of law as a consequence of the maturation of legal consciousness all around presupposes a more detailed account of what it is for a plurality of individual selves ("souls") to grow into a common, shared spiritual unity, a *community* in a strong sense of the word.[10] And Hegel's philosophy offers what is probably the most thoroughly developed account of "spirit" in this sense to be found in the literature of modern philosophy. Moreover, that Il'in appreciated this point is left in little doubt by his two-volume 1918 commentary on the philosophy of Hegel.[11] Nevertheless, for whatever reason, in this text Il'in did not expressly name Hegel as the source of this conception of spirit.

It must be acknowledged, however, that there is a conspicuous impediment in the text to the straightforward assertion that Il'in was fundamentally appropriating an Hegelian account of the formation of spirit. In Chapter Five Il'in commits himself to a fundamentally Cartesian *cum* Leibnizian account of the nature of the individual self and bases his justification of natural law doctrine on this account. Since the justification ("grounding") of natural law doctrine was one of the central aims of his treatise, this essentially dualistic Cartesian account of the nature of the individual self cannot be regarded as a dispensable element in his theory. But neither can it be reconciled with an Hegelian account of the formation of spirit. For Hegel, the individual self is *already spirit*—i.e., *finite, subjective* spirit, but spirit nevertheless. It is comprehensible that subjective spirit should develop to the point of participating in objective spirit, and ultimately in absolute spirit. But for Hegel the being of such a finite individual spirit is ultimately *derivative* from infinite being (the doctrine of the "ideality of the finite"); finite being cannot be conceived as entirely distinct from infinite being. Il'in, on the other hand, treats the being of each finite individual self as *complete* and *distinct*. That introduces an apparent contradiction within his account which cannot obviously be overcome. On this particular question Descartes and Hegel cannot be reconciled. At first glance (and second) there is no way of overcoming this *aporia* in the text.[12]

[10] For an enlightening discussion of this aspect of Hegel's thought, see Robert R. Williams, *Tragedy, Recognition and the Death of God: Studies in Hegel and Nietzsche* (2012), esp. Part I.

[11] For example, see I. A. Il'in, *The Philosophy of Hegel as a Doctrine of the Concreteness of God and Humanity*, Volume Two, *The Doctrine of Humanity*, transl. Philip T. Grier (2011), pp. 115ff. and 228ff.

[12] Why Il'in himself might not have perceived this as a contradiction can perhaps be explained by his questionable interpretation of Hegel's philosophy as aspiring to be a monistic system, but actually failing to avoid dualism. For a discussion see Philip T. Grier, "Ivan A. Ilyin: Russia's 'Non-Hegelian' Hegelian", in Marina F. Bykova, et al. (eds.), *The Palgrave Handbook of Russian Thought* (2021), pp. 317-327; and esp. Giacomo Rinaldi,

It is worth reflecting on the audience Il'in would have had in mind, especially during his later years. By then the majority of the émigré Russian intellectuals of his generation would have been deceased, or past the point of active participation in the political affairs of the emigration. Any hope of influencing developments inside Russia had long since vanished anyway. Access to his works was strictly forbidden inside the Soviet Union. He was certainly capable of producing the work in German, but did not. So for whom was he struggling to complete this project, despite very frail health, at the end of his life? The most accurate answer that can be given, one that is only marginally speculative, is this: he was writing for the citizenry of a future post-communist Russian nation in the immediate aftermath of the collapse of the Soviet regime. It must not be forgotten that Il'in was unwavering in his conviction that the Soviet "State" was so radically defective that it was bound to collapse eventually from its own internal defects and failures. Il'in's hope was that at such an historical juncture his future Russian countrymen would take up the enormous challenge of constructing a viable State aimed at realizing the rule of law.[13] Such an endeavor would have little hope of success in the absence of clear and adequate conceptions of the State and of the rule of law as ideals to guide the process of construction. Il'in believed that he could supply both, via his discussion of all the necessary facets of "sound legal consciousness" in a form intrinsically adapted to Russian culture. That in all likelihood was the ultimate purpose of the book.

Il'in on "The Concepts of Law and Power"

In this essay from 1910,[14] his first significant publication (also translated herein in the Appendix) in a major professional journal, Il'in wrestled with the challenging question of whether a pure concept of law could be disentangled from the various manifestations of law as an actuality in the world, each one of which appeared necessarily to involve some admixture of law with power. He approached the problem as one of *appropriate methodology*, taking note of the fact that the field

"Neo-Kantianism versus Hegelianism: Ivan Aleksandrovich Il'in's Interpretation and Critique of Hegel's Philosophy", *Jahrbuch für Hegelforschung*, XXI (2020), pp. 11-100.

[13] It should not be forgotten that during his years of residence in Switzerland Il'in had been engaged in writing and circulating among the Russian emigration a total of 215 short individual essays (eventually gathered together and published in two volumes after his death entitled *Our Tasks*) each addressing some aspect of the situation Russia would find itself in upon the collapse of the communist regime, and attempting to supply guidance as to what would have to be done in order to reconstruct a reformed Russian state, society and church. These were necessarily addressed to his future countrymen.

[14] Translated in the Appendix to this volume as I. A. Il'in, "The Concepts of Law and Power: An Essay in Methodological Analysis". The original appeared as "Понятия права и силы: опыт методологического анализа," in *Вопросы философии и психологии*, XXI (1910), book 1, pp. 1-38. It was subsequently revised and published in German as "Die Begriffe von Recht und Macht: Versuch einer methodologischen Analyse", in *Archiv für systematische Philosophie* [Berlin]. Sonderabdruck, Band 18 (1912), pp. 63-88, 125-44.

of legal studies had in his day expanded to embrace two non-traditional methodologies: sociology and psychology. Sociology of law had been gradually taking shape as a distinct approach to the study of law in the final decades of the nineteenth century, with Russian legal theorists numbered among its pioneers. Similarly, beginning in the late 1890s the Polish-Russian legal theorist, Lev, or Leon, Petrazhitskii (1867-1931), had been developing a sophisticated theory of law as a phenomenon of individual psychology. These newly-emerging approaches were taking their places alongside the established methods of the *historical* study of the law and the *political-teleological* approach to it. Il'in further differentiated the *philosophical* investigation of law from *legal dogmatics*.

Il'in thus distinguished several separate methodologies for the study of law. He was interested in the question of which of these pairs of methodologies were, at least in part, mutually compatible, and which might be wholly incompatible. Further, he wished to know whether the concepts of law and power could be kept distinct within any of these methodologies. Hovering over this entire series of questions was his fundamental concern: whether there was any available methodology capable of elucidating law in its pure form, with no admixture of power. To any such (possible) methodology he applied the label "*juridical*". The fundamental aim of the essay can thus be reformulated as finding an answer to the question: is there a distinctively *juridical* methodology for the investigation of law in its pure state, and if so, what would be the nature of that methodology?

He first developed an answer to his own question concerning whether law as an actual phenomenon in the world could ever be found pure of any admixture with power. On the basis of an apparently sound set of arguments, he concluded that in principle this must be impossible. Therefore, if a *juridical* investigation of law is to prove possible, i.e., a pure theory of law, it will necessarily have to operate at some level of abstraction from empirical phenomena as such. On the other hand, he simultaneously concluded that the phenomena of law-as-power can (and must) be examined on the real plane by the various familiar methods of investigation. He also insisted that it is vain to expect that any single definition of law ("methodological monism") will prove satisfactory across all these various forms of inquiry, and instead cited a list of prominent German and Russian legal theorists, all of whom recognized the inevitability of some sort of "methodological pluralism" in this matter.[15]

Turning to the fundamental question of whether a *juridical* theory of law is possible, he began with the basic observation that "*law is a norm* or *an aggregate of norms*". By a "norm" he meant "*a judgment establishing a certain order as obligatory*", whereas by an "order" he

[15] See p. 349 footnote 4 (he enumerates P. Laband, G. Jellinek, E. Lask, and M. Weber among the German legal theorists, and P. Novgorodtsev, A. Alekseev, Th. Kistiakovskii, and G. Shershenevich among the Russian).

meant "a certain standing relation among elements of a multiplicity". If such a standing relation among elements of a multiplicity is judged to be *valuable* independently of whether it is currently actual or not, then we can say that such an order is *obligatory*.[16] Thus a law is both a norm and a judgment, that is, "*a judgment ... which establishes a certain order ... as obligatory*".[17]

The most striking feature of Il'in's analysis of law as a norm and a judgment is his conclusion that both forms of investigation, the normative and the logical, "may be completely abstracted from any temporality or actuality whatever, that is, move in an order alien to being and reality".[18] This is so because a norm can be analyzed in a purely formal relation, according merely to the *content* of the prescription, independently of whether it is effective or not, or whether it has been applied. This is so because the *norm itself* is to be distinguished from *the consciousness of a norm*. Thus one may inquire into the content of the norm simply as a *conceivable content*, without respect to whether it is being thought by any particular person, that is, in abstraction from any temporal or causal dimension.

Similarly, the *logical make-up* of a judgment, and the judgment's *being thought by someone*, are quite distinct matters. The investigation of the former can be carried out in complete abstraction from the temporal conditions of the latter. Thus, the *normative* examination of the law can be carried out in complete separation from its political, sociological, historical, or psychological examination; and the *logical* examination of the law can be carried out independently of a psychological one.[19] Hence the *juridical* investigation of the law is carried out in complete abstraction from everything real, from any "ontology" as such.[20] In this methodological order one can ascribe to the law neither being nor non-being, for the predicate "real" is dead for this order.[21]

It is obvious that to carry out such a "juridical" investigation of the law presupposes a subtle and complex approach to the problem. First, one must grasp the *untheorized* legal norm in the temporal circumstances of its historical occurrence as law-and-power. Then one must theorize the abstracted norm (that is, abstracted from issues of power, temporality, actuality) merely as a conceivable content, in order to carry out a *juridical* investigation of it as a pure norm, and then *reintegrate* that theorized content with a political, sociological, historical or other conception of the

16 See the beginning of Chapter Three, pp. 354-356.

17 See p. 357 below.

18 See p. 358 below.

19 See p. 359 below.

20 See p. 360 below.

21 Ibid.

norm, in order to see the phenomenon whole. Il'in defended the necessity of this rather subtle and complex intellectual exercise on the grounds that *only* on the basis of such a "juridical" investigation of a norm can one properly identify the subject matter appropriate to a sociological, psychological, political, or historical investigation of the law.[22]

This very first published essay by Il'in attracted the attention of a leading legal and social theorist, the Ukrainian Bogdan Aleksandrovich Kistiakovskii (1863-1920), who discussed Il'in's essay at length in a major work on *The Social Sciences and Law*.[23] Kistiakovskii devoted several pages to a summary and critique. He declared it to be an important essay on the pure logical analysis of law and compared it with Hans Kelsen's work *Hauptprobleme der Staatsrechtslehre* published the following year (1911), which was also an attempt to work out a pure theory of public law from a strictly "normative-logical" standpoint. Kistiakovskii eventually declared Il'in's work to be fundamentally flawed. It might be possible to defend Il'in's essay against some of Kistiakovskii's critique if one instead were to read Il'in's essay against the background of Edmund Husserl's *Logical Investigations*, as an early attempt at a phenomenological analysis of law.[24] To pursue this point here, however, would take us too far afield.

In any event, Il'in made no pretense of having developed a complete theory of law. He explicitly declared that his essay was merely aimed at establishing an essential methodological *preliminary* to such a theory. As such, it still offers interesting material for reflection.

Il'in on Natural Law

For Il'in, the rule of law as an ideal was inseparable from a modernized doctrine of natural law. His defense of the rule of law rested on his conviction that the justification of law could never be grounded entirely in the mere happenstance of some existing body of positive law, a product of the contingencies of history. Rather, law could be grounded only in an objective idea of the essence of law as an ordering of relations among individual human beings required by the unconditional right of each individual to the free, self-directed pursuit of a spiritually worthy

[22] See pp. 360-364 below.

[23] B. A. Kistiakovskii, *Социальные науки и право: очерки по методологии социальных наук и общей теории права* [The Social Sciences and Law: Essays on the Methodology of the Social Sciences and the General Theory of Law] (1916), pp. 301-317. This was a 700-page collection of many of his previously-published journal articles, his *magnum opus*. See Walicki, note 1 above, Ch. VI, esp. pp. 342-348, and Susan Heuman, *Kistiakovsky: The Struggle for National and Constitutional Rights in the Last Years of Tsarism* (1998).

[24] This is quite plausible in that Russian interest in Husserlian phenomenology emerged in the early years of the twentieth century, earlier than in any other country outside of Germany. Volume One of Husserl's *Logical Investigations* was published in Russian translation in 1909. However, Il'in was easily capable of pursuing Husserl's thought in German, and evidently did so in conjunction with his graduate studies in the years 1906-1909. At some point he made extensive notes on volume two.

life, that is, a life aimed at the knowledge of truth, the creation of beauty, the flourishing of genuine goodness, and the achievement of an objective religious faith ("To ground law means to demonstrate that it is in practical terms necessary on the path of a human being to the realization of the supreme good. This means to demonstrate that the fundamental laws of being of the human spirit are such, and that the essence of the supreme good is such, that law as an objectively obligatory rule of external conduct is the necessary form of their coming together").[25]

Sound legal consciousness involves the exercise of this basic right on one's own behalf and the simultaneous recognition of a duty to respect the identical basic right of every other human being. Consequently, an objective order of legal relations guaranteeing the exercise of this right to every individual is intrinsically obligatory. That, roughly, is what Il'in means by "natural law". That such an ordering of legal relations could be conceived to be *objective* follows from Il'in's *juridical* investigation of law in the essay on "The Concepts of Law and Power".

According to the juridical point of view, a legal norm is simply an *objectively conceivable content*, and the judgment contained therein can be grasped from a logical point of view merely as the connection between two concepts (a subject and a predicate in the simplest case).[26] Neither the norm nor the judgment is thought in connection with historical circumstances or even in terms of a particular psychological instantiation. The content of natural law, Il'in supposes, could thus be articulated as a system of norms, grasped objectively from the purely juridical point of view, entailing the equal basic right of every individual to the pursuit of a spiritually worthy life. Il'in clearly presupposes, without discussing the presupposition, that such a system as a whole is objectively possible and that it would spell out the universal requirements of natural justice. Such a system of natural justice would be intrinsically obligatory for rational beings and thus authoritative for all. The authority of any body of positive law would ultimately rest upon the plausibility of its claim to be genuinely aimed at articulating the requirements of natural law, whatever the current deficiencies of that particular system of positive law might be.

Il'in's work *On the Essence of Legal Consciousness* was originally conceived as part of a now little-remembered movement aimed at the revival of natural law beginning in the 1890s, primarily in Germany and Russia. The two figures usually credited with initiating this movement are Rudolf Stammler (1856-1938) ("natural law with a changing content") and Leon Petrazhitskii ("the rebirth of natural law"). The former was German; the latter was born in Poland, educated in Kiev and Germany, and was living and working in Germany at the time he originally conceived his contribution to this movement. Stammler's attempted revival of a modernized natural law doctrine was strictly and explicitly neo-Kantian,

25 Chapter Five, first paragraph.

26 Il'in was thinking specifically in terms of Aristotelian logic.

whereas Petrazhitskii attempted to launch what he conceived as an analogue of natural law doctrine in the form of a new "science of legal policy", that is, a largely empirical investigation of what law "ought" to be at various stages of social development in order to realize certain ideal values.[27] By 1897 Petrazhitskii had moved to St. Petersburg and begun teaching in the Law Faculty of St. Petersburg University, soon to become a major influence on Russian jurisprudence and a prominent member of the Russian Liberal movement. He was widely acknowledged as the leader of the "St. Petersburg school of jurisprudence".

The leader of the "Moscow school of jurisprudence" was Pavel Novgorodtsev. He and his colleague, Evgenii Trubetskoi (1863-1920), were professors in the Faculty of Law of Moscow University. Both were teachers and mentors of Il'in, as well as prominent activists in the Liberal movement. Novgorodtsev, seconded by Trubetskoi, was well known for his advocacy of a revived doctrine of natural law.[28] As opposed to Petrazhitskii's positivism, Novgorodtsev argued that the foundation of natural law had to be located in some trans-empirical, trans-historical source: Kant's supreme principle of pure practical reason. Although Novgorodtsev never attempted to work out the details of a revised doctrine of natural law himself, he tirelessly advocated this conception as the only appropriate, objective foundation for such a doctrine.

Il'in's treatment of natural law thus followed the general spirit, if not the Kantian letter, of Novgorodtsev's view. In Chapter Five of *On the Essence of Legal Consciousness*, Il'in did attempt to sketch rather briefly what a "new" doctrine of natural law might look like, but the sketch is too cursory to be treated as a distinctive theory of natural law in its own right; there are only hints of what a fully developed theory might have contained. Nevertheless, Il'in unambiguously lent his support to the broader trend of advocacy of natural law for which the Moscow school of jurisprudence was particularly known in the first two decades of the twentieth century. This intriguing development in Russian legal thought was soon cut off by the ideological controls imposed by the Bolsheviks in the aftermath of the civil war, and thereafter could be pursued only by a few solitary spirits such as Il'in in emigration. The further career of the revived idea of natural law on German soil during the twentieth century is a complex and interesting story with several chapters, which cannot be pursued here.

However, the reader of these texts by Il'in should understand that his defense of a revised doctrine of natural law was by no means the quixotic preference of an isolated thinker simply nostalgic for a "lost" intellectual tradition, but a tendency of legal thought well supported by major

[27] As Walicki, note 1 above, reports (p. 307), as early as 1902 V. M. Hessen [Gessen] had published a wide-ranging summary of the effort in Germany and Russia to revive the natural law tradition in some revised form. See V. M. Gessen, *Возрождение естественного права* [The Revival of Natural Law] (1902).

[28] On this point see Walicki, note 1 above, pp. 299-311.

developments in the contemporary jurisprudence of Germany and Russia. There were prominent legal theorists in both countries who rejected the claim that an adequate account of the authority of law could be supplied on the basis of any merely positivist conception.[29] These theorists all supposed that the ultimate authority of law could be grounded only in some trans-empirical principle of reason such as Kant's categorical imperative, or some universal ideal (for example, of justice, or of love).

Many of these theorists were confronting a deeper underlying issue: the relation between the rational and the historical in the theory of law. That problem had been placed on the agenda early in the nineteenth century by the competing perspectives of two professorial colleagues at the University of Berlin: Savigny and Hegel. Savigny had stated the case for the primacy of the historical in his *Vom Beruf unserer Zeit für Gesetzgebung und Rechtswissenschaft* (1814).[30] In 1820 Hegel undertook a fundamental critique of Savigny's historicism in his *Elements of the Philosophy of Right*,[31] arguing that the Historical School failed to grasp the role of the genuinely rational in the law. Indeed, Hegel's account of the relation of the rational and the historical amounted in effect to the very sort of "modernized" doctrine of natural law for which many later theorists claimed to be searching at the turn of the century.[32] Notwithstanding his extensive use of the concept of "legal consciousness," Il'in's explicit embrace of a revised version of natural law was thus a deliberate step away from Savigny's Historical School in the direction indicated by Hegel (although Il'in seems to have been no less influenced by his neo-Kantian mentor, Novgorodtsev).

In the two texts translated herein Il'in has advanced some interesting proposals for distinctive approaches to some of these perennial issues in the philosophy of law. Admittedly, most of Il'in's proposals would require further development before being entered into the lists of contemporary debate in the philosophy of law, but some are arguably worthy of such further development. Even if one were to conclude that he has not

29 There is still much to be said on behalf of this view, notwithstanding the current dominance of legal positivism in English-language literature.

30 See note 6 above, English translation by Hayward. To be sure, von Savigny had acknowledged the necessity for the subsequent systematization, i.e., the further development, *post factum*, of each distinctive body of law that had emerged historically. That process involved the introduction of a kind of (bounded) rationality in each system of law.

31 G. W. F. Hegel, *Elements of the Philosophy of Right*, transl. H. B. Nisbet, ed. Allen W. Wood (1991). See esp. §§3, 4, and 211.

32 However, Hegel's solution of this problem was effectively unavailable for discussion at this point, given the widespread neglect (ignorance) of Hegel's thought toward the end of the century, especially in Germany. This was ensured by the dominance of neo-Kantianism, an intellectual movement premised on the "necessity" of going "back to Kant" (i.e., skipping over the thought of his German Idealist successors). Consequently, the philosophy of law, especially in the English-speaking world, has yet to engage the debate between von Savigny and Hegel in a serious way, even two centuries later.

supplied an enduring solution to any of the fundamental problems in the philosophy of law, his discussion of these issues remains valuable if only as a reintroduction to an era in the history of legal thought that was particularly rich in the variety of viewpoints it offered on perennial issues of fundamental significance in the philosophy of law.[33]

[33] A particularly well-informed overview of the state of legal philosophy in Europe on the eve of the First World War can be found in Morris R. Cohen's essay "On Continental Legal Philosophy: Philosophical-Legal Literature in French, German and Italian: 1912-1914", in Cohen, *Law and the Social Order: Essays in Legal Philosophy* (1933), pp. 286-318.

The Concept of Legal Consciousness: Origin and Transformations

The concept of legal consciousness[1] has a lengthy and complex history in theories associated with the civil law systems of a number of European countries over the nineteenth and twentieth centuries. It originally stemmed from the German historical school of jurisprudence in the first half of the nineteenth century, specifically from their claim that the ultimate source of any people's law (*Recht*) was its distinctive *Volksgeist,* its common consciousness. Each such distinctive cultural nation was said to possess its own distinctive legal consciousness (*Rechtsbewußtsein*). Stemming from its German origins, the concept of legal consciousness was widely adopted over much of the European continent, ultimately morphing into several closely related variant concepts. On the other hand, the concept was largely absent, or barely acknowledged, in the legal theories of the (primarily anglophone) common law systems of the world during the same time frame.

Yet if one pauses to consider in the abstract the variety of issues which might motivate the use of that concept, it would appear that no theory of law could be considered complete without some explicit treatment of the phenomena of legal consciousness. At its most basic level, "legal consciousness" might be simply a formulation of the commonsense idea that a person's or a people's actual awareness of law must play a significant role in the operation of any functioning legal system: how could any legal system be imagined to function *if its supposed subjects were unaware of its existence*? At some fundamental level there could be no such thing as a legal system without the presence of *some form* of "legal consciousness" on the part of those subject to it.

Further reflection leads to the realization that "legal consciousness" would necessarily prove to be a multi-layered, many-faceted phenomenon, susceptible of many different emphases. To what *extent* would the

1 "Legal consciousness" is not an adequate translation of the term, but unfortunately will have to serve for present purposes. The problem is that the other languages of interest here (Russian, German, French, Italian, Latin) all possess the *paired* terms *право, закон; Recht, Gesetz; droit, loi; diritto, legge; ius, lex*, which English lacks. The first member of each pair carries some suggestion of a connection between "law" and "the right" ("justice"), or the law as an ideal, or the law as an integral whole, whereas the second member refers more simply to law as written, or the rules being enforced. The terms being investigated – правосознание, *Rechtsbewußtsein,* and so on – all employ the *first* term of the pair, not the second. To explore the implications of this much-belabored terminological distinction would require more space than can be devoted to the problem here. However, the usual assumption that the absence of the paired terms in English makes no fundamental difference to our understanding of the nature of law is not clearly supported by the respective histories of legal theory within the civil and the common law traditions.

population have to have an *accurate* understanding of the nature of the prevailing legal system in order to be said to have a "legal consciousness" adequate for that system? Could the "actual legal system" be anything fundamentally other than what prevailing "legal consciousness" took it to be? Would popular legal consciousness necessarily have to match up to just those elements of law actually recorded in normative legal acts and enforced by officialdom?

Might legal consciousness be shaped in part by an *ideal* of what law *ought to be*, or would it be restricted merely to the operative "positive" law in a given system? Would a fully developed legal consciousness include a *justification of the authority* of the existing legal system? Would such a justification have to be restricted to the actual foundational documents, or historically given premises, of that particular legal system, or might it include elements which transcend these (for example, something like natural law)? Would it be expected to contain an adequate answer to the question: "why ought I obey the law?"

A further, critical dimension of the problem is revealed if we ask: "how is legal consciousness *acquired*"? What is the process of formation (*socialization?*) through which a legal consciousness is shaped? (when does it succeed? when does it fail?). How many factors might there be in such a social process? How could they be identified? And are we talking about the consciousness of an *individual*, of a *group*, or of an entire *society*? If we plan on comparing the legal consciousnesses of different groups or cultures, *along how many dimensions might they differ*? If societies can be distinguished by their characteristic modes of legal consciousness, can such differing modes of legal consciousness explain fundamentally divergent forms of social order?

Seen from this perspective, some conception of the role played by legal consciousness must be a necessary element in a complete account of the efficacy of any functioning system of law. It is also unsurprising that at times the theme of legal consciousness has been connected with doctrines of *natural law* (although there need be no necessary connection with such doctrines). Thus, legal consciousness, properly understood, turns out to be an important nexus for the examination of any system of law, and a necessary element in multiple approaches to the study of law, notwithstanding the general neglect of the concept in anglophone legal theory.[2]

The concept of legal consciousness (*Rechtsbewußtsein* in German) was a familiar theme in legal theory on the continent for at least eight

[2] A recent examination of relations among several of these approaches to the study of law was carried out in W. E. Butler and P. T. Grier, "Legal Consciousness: Some Comparative Legal Aspects", *The Journal of Comparative Law*, VII (2012), pp. 40-62. Some parts of that study have been used here in revised form. For example, we would no longer defend the suggestion made there that the dominant influence of the historical school may have stemmed primarily from the 1840s. On this point we are entirely persuaded by the work of Mathias Reimann.

decades in the nineteenth and early twentieth centuries. As an explicit preoccupation of legal theory it appears to have emerged in German jurisprudence about 1840, near the apogee of the influence of Savigny's historical school, and was soon reflected in the legal thought of a number of other European countries influenced by the emerging German model of *Rechtswissenschaft*. Since the conclusion of the First World War, explicit treatment of the theme on the continent has gradually attenuated. However, this appears to be more a phenomenon of scholarly forgetting or systematic neglect, owing to a shift of attention to other theoretical issues and perspectives, rather than to any definitive rejection of the concept as intrinsically flawed or irrelevant to legal theory. Indeed, it is difficult to see what could constitute grounds for a fundamental rejection of "legal consciousness" as a necessary feature of anything constituting a functioning legal system. Quite apart from the ever-present issue of which school(s) of jurisprudence are dominant among the university faculties of law and their graduates at any particular point in time, historians of law in Germany have displayed a continuing and lively interest in the historical school throughout the twentieth century, and there is evidence of a recent up-tick of interest in some of the doctrines of the historical school among German scholars.[3]

Legal Consciousness (Rechtsbewußtsein) in the German Historical School

It appears that the systematic employment of the term *Rechtsbewußtsein* in German legal discourse, and the ultimate source of all subsequent discussions of "legal consciousness" throughout Europe in the nineteenth and twentieth centuries, can be traced to the influence of Friedrich Carl von Savigny (1779-1861) and his "historical school" of jurisprudence. That tradition could be said to date from 1814, when Savigny published *Vom Beruf unserer Zeit für Gesetzgebung und Rechtswissenschaft* [On the Vocation of our Age for Legislation and Jurisprudence].[4] In

[3] See, for example, the several works by Joachim Rückert on this topic, including his *Friedrich Carl von Savigny: Leben und Wirken (1779-1861)* (2014). See also Benjamin Lahusen, *Alles Recht geht vom Volksgeist aus* (2013), including the biblography there of works on Savigny and the historical school.

[4] F. C. Savigny, *Vom Beruf unserer Zeit für Gesetzgebung und Rechtswissenschaft* (1814). There were two more editions in Savigny's lifetime: 1828 and 1840. The English translation by Abraham Hayward (1831) was of the second (1828) German edition.

Mathias Reimann has pointed out that four main texts were actually involved in the development and presentation of von Savigny's conception of legal science: 1. (1802-1803): *Juristische Methodenlehre*, ed. G. Wesenberg (1951); 2. (1814): *Vom Beruf unserer Zeit für Gesetzgebung und Rechtswissenschaft* (already cited); 3. (1815): the introductory essay in the journal von Savigny co-founded with Karl Friedrich Eichhorn, "*Über den Zweck dieser Zeitschrift*", *Zeitschrift für geschichtliche Rechtswissenschaft,* I, p. 4; 4. (1840): *System des heutigen römischen Rechts*, vol. 1. See Mathias Reimann, "Nineteenth Century German Legal Science," *Boston College Law Review*, XXXI (1990), p. 837, n. 61. See also Reimann, *Historische Schule und Common Law: Die deutsche Rechtswissenschaft des 19. Jahrhunderts im amerikanischen Rechtsdenken* (1993).

that work Savigny laid out the fundamental program for what was to become the "historical school". Given that this text went through three editions between 1814 and 1840, it is reasonable to assume that this is the single most important source of the historical school's influence. However, Savigny restated his conception of the method appropriate to jurisprudence (*Rechtswissenschaft*) in volume one of his influential *System des heutigen Römischen Rechts* (1840-1849). There is reason to believe that this publication later in his career was responsible for the still greater influence of his school. Moreover, there is some evidence that, contrary to a widely shared impression, especially among English-speaking legal theorists, the influence of the historical school actually persisted, if somewhat attenuated, at least through the end of the First World War and to some extent beyond. The influence of that school at its height extended throughout much of Europe, given that nineteenth century German legal science was widely regarded as the most advanced on the continent, and served as the model, or indeed the matrix, for legal thought in a number of other countries.[5]

His *System des heutigen Römischen Rechts*[6] was generally regarded as the masterwork of von Savigny's long career. Various earlier works by von Savigny had received significant accolades, beginning in 1803 with his study of the Roman law of possession, which was said to have revolutionized the study of Roman law in general. In addition to the 1814 work *Vom Beruf unserer Zeit für Gesetzgebung und Rechtswissenschaft*, his five-volume *Geschichte des römischen Rechts im Mittelalter*[7] (1815-1831) further distinguished him as the leading Roman law scholar of his time. However, the appearance of the eight-volume *System des heutigen römischen Rechts* represented the full maturation of his systematic jurisprudence, addressing a wide range of issues in contemporary legal scholarship. Despite the fact that various legal thinkers toward the end of

[5] Reimann's study, "Nineteenth Century German Legal Science," cited above, is an admirably thorough and comprehensive study of the development and influence of nineteenth century German *Rechtswissenschaft*, which, he argues, must be understood as essentially identical to the original program of von Savigny's historical school. This *Rechtswissenschaft* remained the object of widespread attention by legal scholars throughout Europe in the nineteenth and early twentieth centuries (Il'in's work, translated herein, is yet another reflection of this phenomenon, one of the later ones). By the turn of the century, German *Rechtswissenschaft* was being discussed by leading American legal theorists operating in the very different common law tradition. However, Reimann argues, for various reasons these American commentators seem never to have fully grasped the nature of the development. Their characterizations of "legal science" in Germany were generally wide of the mark. In what follows we rely upon Reimann's work at a number of points.

[6] Friedrich Carl von Savigny, *System des heutigen Römischen Rechts* (1840-1849). 8 vols. (A ninth volume contained indexes to the first eight volumes). Available in English translation as *The System of the Modern Roman Law*, transl. William Holloway (1867). (Both are available in full text online).

[7] F. C. von Savigny, *The History of the Roman Law During the Middle Ages*, transl. E. Cathcart (1829; reprinted 1979). Apparently only volume one has been translated into English.

the nineteenth century attempted to move away from some fundamental premises of that framework, it may be argued that the cataclysm of the First World War was necessary to clear the intellectual and moral space within which a fundamentally different framework for thinking about law could take over.

That von Savigny's use of the term *Rechtsbewußtsein* was the main occasion of its inception into German legal discourse (and indeed the German language) is attested by an entry in the *Deutsches Wörterbuch* (1854-) of the Brothers Jacob and Wilhelm Grimm, which was ultimately destined to become the master historical dictionary for the German language. That original edition of the dictionary contained a short entry for *Rechtsbewustsein* [sic]: "n. *bewustsein* [sic] *in bezug auf sittliches oder gesetzliches recht*" ["Consciousness in reference to ethical or statutory law"] followed by an example taken from volume one (1840) of von Savigny's *System des heutigen Römischen Rechts*, p. 32: "*das rechtsbewusztsein* [sic], *welches jedem aus seinen früheren verhältnissen inwohnt*".[8]

This particular dictionary entry, attributing the inception of the term *Rechtsbewußtsein* to the first volume of von Savigny's *System des heutigen römischen Rechts*, carries with it exceptional authority, given that both brothers Grimm studied law under von Savigny himself as students at the University of Marburg in the first decade of the nineteenth century and remained close to him for the rest of their lives. In 1840 Savigny appealed to Frederick Wilhelm IV (1795-1861) to secure appointments for both brothers at the University of Berlin, enabling them to rejoin him (and where they all remained until the ends of their lives, which were separated by only a few years).

Further confirmation of this account of the inception of the term *Rechtsbewußtsein* can be found through the statistical frequency diagrams available at the Google N-gram facility online, if one assumes that the inception and increasing frequency of usage of the term *Rechtsbewußtsein* in the German language are associated with the still-expanding influence of the historical school, as we believe to be the case.[9] The frequency curve for the term *Rechtsbewußtsein* drawn for published German literature between 1800 and 2000 through the Google facility shows an

[8] "[T]he consciousness of law dwelling in each one from their previous circumstances". A second example was taken from p. 415 of that same volume.

[9] The N-gram facility is available at http://books.google.com/ngrams. It produces more or less instantaneous frequency curves for occurrences of terms or phrases in works digitized by Google in the given language (to obtain an accurate graph in this case one must combine the graphs for the two alternate spellings of *Rechtsbewusstsein* and *Rechtsbewußtsein*, in order to allow for a reform of German orthography. A few additional occurrences are picked up by adding the third much less common variant spelling *Rechtsbewustsein*—the original spelling in the *Deutsches Wörterbuch*). There is no way to ascertain what fraction of all the published materials in a given language has been digitized by Google, but evidently the fractions are quite large. The frequency statistics given for each year are relative to the total number of words published in that year, so that the statistics across years are comparable.

abrupt inception of the term about 1840, a rapid increase in usage during the 1850s, with a continuing series of peaks extending to a few years after 1900, a slightly declining rate of usage in the decade prior to the outbreak of the First World War, followed by a single dramatic spike in the year 1919 (coincident with the debate over the Weimar Constitution?), followed by a gradually lessening of overall relative frequency of usage continuing to the present (with no frequency peaks after 1920 quite equaling those between 1840 and 1920).

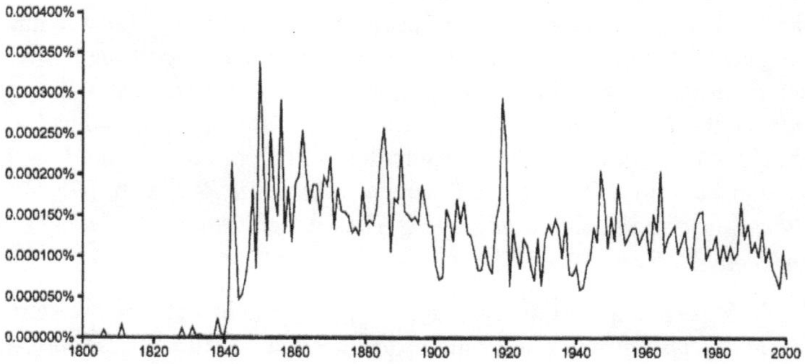

Law as a Cultural Phenomenon

The association of the term *Rechtsbewußtsein* with Savigny's historical school of jurisprudence is readily understandable. Savigny was strongly influenced by Herder's notion of a *Volksgeist*, the "spirit of a people." Each distinct culture of Europe was said to be characterized by a "common consciousness" unique to it, differentiating it from all the others. Such a common consciousness is expressed initially through the emergence of a distinctive language (grammar, lexicon, phonetic system, and so forth) which is the common property of all who share that same consciousness. Savigny argued that the legal sense of a people is analogous to its language, in that each cultural group gives rise to a distinctive conception of law intrinsic to its specific identity, its common consciousness,[10] and that the resulting legal consciousness (*Rechtsbewußtsein*) of each individual is shaped by this common consciousness.[11]

Savigny thus insisted that law is a *cultural* phenomenon, meaning that genuine law can be found only as existing in the actual practice of an individual society, having from the earliest history of that society

[10] "[T]he common consciousness of the people is the peculiar seat of law". See Savigny, note 4 above, Hayward translation, p. 19.

[11] "Rather is it the spirit of a people, living and working in common in all the individuals, which gives birth to positive law, which therefore is to the consciousness of each individual not accidentally but necessarily one and the same." Savigny, note 6 above, Holloway translation, p. 12.

"already obtained a fixed character, peculiar to [its] people like their language, manners and constitution".[12] Indeed, he insists that law, language, manners, and constitution "have no separate existence" but are "inseparably united in nature".[13] "That which binds them into one whole is the common conviction of the people, the kindred consciousness of an inward necessity, excluding all notion of an accidental and arbitrary origin".[14] Law is thus intrinsically connected with the "being and character of the people", and as an expression of the life of that people it constitutes an *organic whole* whose the inner coherence requires examination as a *system.*

The Developmental Stages of the Law and the Role of Legal Scholarship

From the beginning Savigny recognized that his theory of the origin of law in cultural consciousness could not alone account for the mature form of a modern legal system. "Young nations, it is true, have the clearest perception of their law, but their codes are defective in language and logical skill,"[15] he acknowledged. In its development, each distinct system of law exhibits two successive phases, the first of which he termed "*natural* law" (in a sense different from the usual meaning), and the second, *learned* law.[16] In the first phase, most pronounced in the "youth" of the nation, law is a lively expression of the "common consciousness of the people";[17] its symbolic acts whereby rights were created or extinguished were the chief manifestation of the existence of law, and their solemnity and weight were palpably felt by the population.[18] In the second, *learned* phase, the law acquires a more refined and systematic *verbal* formulation. The transition from the first to the second phase in the development of law involves the gradual transition from symbolic enactments to verbal formulations, and a transition from the common consciousness of the people to a distinct branch of knowledge in the hands of learned jurists. Though a mature, living legal system would never entirely lose its connection with the

12 Savigny, note 4 above, Hayward translation, p. 24.

13 Ibid.

14 Ibid.

15 Savigny, note 4 above, Hayward translation, p. 42. More specifically, he held that it was in the "youth" of such nations that the spirit of the law was likely to be manifest in its full individuality: "In the history of all considerable nations we find a transition from circumscribed, but fresh and vigorous individuality, to undefined universality. The law undergoes the same, and in it, likewise, the consciousness of nationality may, in the end, be lost." Ibid., pp. 135-136.

16 Ibid., p. 29.

17 Ibid., p. 28.

18 Ibid., p. 26.

common consciousness, it would assume an increasingly technical form the coherence of which could only be articulated by these same learned jurists whose role in the maintenance and development of the law is indispensable. The common consciousness of the people (the "natural" phase) is the original and, in some sense, ultimate seat of law; however, the learned phase comes to be seen in a different sense as the primary seat of law once the system is fully developed and mature. Savigny believed that the essence of a mature, living system of law (that is, *Recht*) could only be found articulated in the writings of the best professional scholar-jurists operating within that same tradition.

This conception of the development and maturation of law, within the civil law tradition, emphasizes the dominant role of legal scholars, as opposed to legislators or sitting judges, in the codification of specific bodies of law in collections which are relatively complete, coherent, and clear. From the jurisconsults of ancient Rome, to the commission appointed by the Emperor Justinian to produce the *Corpus Juris Civilis*, to the Glossators and Commentators of the medieval Roman law tradition, to the authors of Frederick the Great's *Landrecht of 1794,* to the scholars who dominated the proceedings of Napoleonic codification commissions culminating in the *Civil Code of 1804*, to the German professors of law who shaped the proceedings of the commission charged with writing the *Bürgerlicher Gesetzbuch* of 1896, the civil law tradition has been formed through a series of systematic compilations of bodies of law assembled by scholarly legal experts who were themselves neither legislators nor sitting judges, but whose formulations of the law have been accepted as authoritative.[19] To be sure, in the modern period these codifications have required formal enactment by sovereign national legislatures in order to come into force; however, modifications introduced at the stage of legislation have tended to be marginal at most. The *system* of the law expressed as a complete, coherent, and clear code, or set of codes, i.e., *Recht*, has traditionally been the work of professional scholars, and not legislators or judges. As John Henry Merryman (1920-2015) observed: "The civil law is a law of the professors".[20]

Despite Savigny's insistence that the system of Roman law could never be substituted for the common legal consciousness intrinsic to the Germanic people, his account of the *development* of law appears to be inspired by the ancient Roman example. It was the scholar-jurists serving on the Emperor Justinian's commission who were responsible for articulating Roman law in the systematic form, the *Corpus Iuris Civilis*, in which it was handed down to posterity.[21] It was these scholar-jurists

[19] In von Savigny's view, Germany in the early nineteenth century lacked such a group of appropriately learned and culturally-informed legal scholars rooted in *German* (as opposed to Roman) legal consciousness, and for that reason as of 1814 he strongly opposed any immediate attempt to codify German law.

[20] John Henry Merryman, *The Civil Law Tradition* (2d ed.; 1985), p. 56.

[21] Moreover, in the Emperor Justinian's edict, all previously-accepted legal principles

who, on the basis of an intimate knowledge of the history of their own legal tradition, i.e., a deep immersion in its fundamental *Rechtsbewußtsein*, were able to articulate its principles as a coherent totality, identifying its "leading axioms" and outlining the appropriate treatment of particular cases from such "axioms".

Such a fundamental *Rechtsbewußtsein* took the form of a holistic "living intuition of the institutions of the law in their organic connection, so that whenever the necessity arises for the rule to be conceived in its logical form, this must be first formed by a scientific procedure from that total intuition".[22] For the legal scholar to produce a "rational" explanation and justification of a particular positive rule of law, it must be derived from a general principle shown to be inherent in and necessary for the coherence of that specific "total intuition" of the institutions of law definitive of a specific people (to attempt to justify a positive rule of law merely on the basis of some abstract, universal principle of reason, or merely upon the basis of an alien, allegedly "common", body of law such as the Roman, would amount to jurisprudential malpractice in his view).[23]

From this picture of the development of ancient Roman law Savigny developed a distinctive view of the essence of law as *Recht* (право), as opposed to *Gesetz* (закон). In his view the essence of a mature and living system of law (*Recht*) could be found only in the writings of the best jurists operating within the tradition in question. Its interpretation and development could only be fully entrusted to their hands. They alone could be trusted to have grasped the fundamental, organically-interconnected principles of that distinctive legal tradition originally contained in the "common consciousness of the people", to have articulated these principles as a mutually consistent whole, and to have shown how they are to be applied to specific cases. The learned jurists thus form a kind of priesthood (not Savigny's term) through which alone *Recht* can be articulated with confidence. Neither emperors, senates, nor legislatures can be ultimately trusted with this task, as their enactments (*Gesetzen*),

not endorsed in the *Corpus Juris Civilis* were nullified. The new codification was to be regarded henceforth as the one universal and permanent statement of valid fundamental law for all the peoples of the Roman Empire. In furtherance of this aim, all further learned commentary on the law beyond that provided in the *Corpus Juris Civilis* itself was forbidden. See Merryman, note 20 above, p. 7. Napoleon similarly hoped to forestall any further commentary on the Napoleonic Code. Ibid., p. 59.

22 Savigny, note 6 above, transl. Holloway, p. 13.

23 To be sure, Savigny argued that *certain parts* of Roman law had, centuries earlier, become absorbed in German *Rechtsbewußtsein*; thus those parts were no longer "alien". However, in assessing the relevance of Roman law for the healthy development of contemporary German legal consciousness, it was first necessary to separate the "still living parts of that Roman element" from "the part of it which is in fact dead, and, merely through our misunderstanding, still drags on a perturbing show of life". Savigny, note 6 above, transl. Holloway, "Preface", p. v.

being random products of particular interests, transient concerns, and/or ignorance may "become a baleful corruption of the law" (*Recht*).[24]

From Savigny's perspective, there appears to be an historically "best moment" in the life of a society for the codification of its *Recht*. For example, he believed that Roman law had reached its peak of organic development in the so-called "classical" period of the early third century A.D., in the work of the jurists Aemilius Papinian (142-212), Gnaeus Domitius Annius Ulpian (c. 170-223 or 228), and Julius Paulus (2-3 centuries). By the time of the compilation of Justinian's *Corpus Iuris Civilis* three centuries later, there was already a sense of a living tradition about to be lost and in danger of being corrupted.[25] Conversely, he believed that in early nineteenth century Germany, there had not yet emerged a sufficiently strong tradition of legal scholarship embodying a specifically German *Rechtsbewußtsein* to undergird the process of codification.

Forms of Legal Consciousness

It is important to recognize that, according to Savigny, what the Roman scholar-jurists articulated as the system of Roman law constituted *Recht*, and not merely *Gesetzen*. The latter took the form initially of edicts by the magistrates, more particularly by the praetors, though principles applied consistently by successive praetors might eventually be woven into official scholarly summaries of the law and thus become elements of the *Recht*. But in referring, for example, to the *Corpus Iuris Civilis* as an articulation of the *Recht* by the scholar-jurists of the Roman or Byzantine empire, as the "learned" phase in the development of Roman law, Savigny was invoking a conception of "legal consciousness" quite distinct from that of the "youthful" or "natural" phase of legal consciousness. Thus, there appear to be two incipient versions of *Rechtsbewußtsein* in Savigny's theory.

[24] Savigny, note 4 above, transl. Hayward, p. 32. It was a fundamental thesis of Savigny's tract that Germany at the time (1814) had not developed the requisite *Rechtswissenschaft* for legal scholars to be in position to guide legislatures adequately in the process of codification (i.e., the articulation of *Recht* and its transformation into *Gesetz*). And to attempt the codification of law in this condition was likely to bring about far more harm than good. One could argue, however, that over the course of the nineteenth century, German jurisprudence developed the major elements of just such expertise, and that by the time the codification of the German civil law was undertaken, in a newly unified nation, in the last quarter of the nineteenth century, German *Rechtswissenschaft* was indeed adequate to the task. The career of a figure such as Bernhard Windscheid (1817-1892) is testimony to such an account: he was widely viewed as one of the greatest of the Pandectists. Guided by the Roman Pandects, and inspired by the achievements of German *Begriffsjurisprudenz*, he systematized private law to a remarkable degree. He then sat on the preliminary commission for the design of the *Bürgerliches Gesetzbuch*, the original form of which was said to reflect to a great extent the structure of Windscheid's textbook.

[25] Ibid., chapter IV, "Roman Law".

As we read further, it transpires that there are implicitly *three* forms of *Rechtsbewußtsein* to be found, because the *Rechtsbewußtsein* of the emperors, senators, and legislators entrusted with the task of *enacting* (as *Gesetzen*) and enforcing the law is not identical with that of the scholar-jurists whose comprehension of the *Recht* is the ultimate embodiment of the system. As already noted, the lawmakers and enforcers may be acting on behalf of particular interests, out of transient concerns, or simple ignorance. Thus, the *Gesetzen* may become "a baleful corruption of the *Recht*".[26] Consequently, the *Rechtsbewußtsein* of the rulers-legislators may be distinctly inferior to that of the scholar-jurists, and both these forms of *Rechtsbewußtsein* are in some sense distinct from that of the general population.

In most of the subsequent legal literature across the continent influenced by the historical school, one finds a continuing echo of each of these three forms of legal consciousness. For example, these three forms of *Rechtsbewußtsein* reappear in Puchta as the ultimate sources of three different kinds of law: customary law (*Volksrecht*) emanating directly from the people, statutory law (*Gesetzesrecht*) produced by the legislators, and the law of the jurists (*Juristenrecht*) formulated by legal science.[27] On the eve of the First World War, we continue to find analogues of these three types of legal consciousness (and sources of law) in the works of Eugen Ehrlich and Ivan Il'in.[28]

History and System in Savigny's Legal Thought

Savigny's insistence on the organic wholeness of the society and its way of life, as encapsulated in its law, leads to a further fundamental characteristic of the historical school which is little noticed in English-language legal literature: that any such body of law must be presumed to possess a distinctive internal *coherence* and *systematicity* simply from the fact that it represents the settled way of life of a specific, persisting, organically whole human community.

In Savigny's case it was ancient Roman society that provided the model of a complete, functioning legal system expressive of an established way of life. His own exhaustively detailed studies of Roman law set the pattern for much of nineteenth century German jurisprudence.[29]

26 Savigny, note 4 above, transl. Hayward, p. 32.

27 Reimann, note 4 above, p. 860. He refers to Puchta, *Das Gewohnheitsrecht* (1828-1837). 2 vols. No page citation.

28 See below.

29 Savigny held that the "strict historical method of jurisprudence" did not "consist, as some recent opponents have strangely maintained, in an exclusive admiration of the Roman law; nor in desiring the unqualified preservation of any one established system, to which, indeed, it is directly opposed, as has been shown by the above judgment on the Austrian code. On the contrary, its object is to trace every established system to its root,

Because the Roman law actually in use emerged from, evolved with, and successfully supported the life of ancient Roman society as a whole, it could be presumed to constitute a coherent, organically complete system appropriate for that way of life.

One implication that might be drawn from the foregoing analysis is that the standard practice of referring to Savigny's school simply as "historical" is substantially misleading. It would be more accurate to refer to this as the "historico-systematic" school of jurisprudence. As Savigny remarks, "a two-fold spirit is indispensable to the jurist; the historical, to seize with readiness the peculiarities of every age and every form of law; and the systematic, to view every notion and every rule in lively connection and cooperation with the whole, that is, in the only true and natural relation".[30] If anything, he considered the task of a *systematic* examination of law to be even more exacting than the *historical*:

> In every triangle, namely, there are certain data, from the relations of which all the rest are necessarily deducible: thus, given two sides and the included angle, the whole triangle is given. In like manner, every part of our law has points by which the rest may be given: these may be termed the leading axioms. To distinguish these, and deduce from them the internal connection, and the precise degree of affinity which subsist between all juridical notions and rules, is amongst the most difficult of the problems of jurisprudence.[31]

The fact that Savigny's theory contained *both* these elements—the cultural/historical *and* the systematic, *Geschichte und System*—constituted the defining feature of the new *Rechtswissenschaft* emerging in early nineteenth century Germany. Indeed, according to Reimann, it was Savigny's successful merging of these two elements into a coherent, if complex, conception of method for legal scholarship that constituted the emergence of German *Rechtswissenschaft* in a fully mature form.[32] Savigny thus "became the true founder of modern German *Rechtswissenschaft*".[33] That widely-admired, much-studied model of jurisprudence was inseparable from the original program of Savigny's historical school.

As Reimann noted, Savigny's grand methodological synthesis harbored a number of inherent tensions – between the organic and the

and thus discover an organic principle, whereby that which still has life, may be separated from that which is lifeless and only belongs to history". Savigny, note 4 above, p. 137.

30 Ibid., pp. 64-65.

31 Ibid., pp. 38-39.

32 Reimann, note 4 above, p. 840 and *passim*.

33 Ibid., p. 852.

systematic, the historical and the logical, the real and the ideal,[34] but each of them was arguably kept within bounds by the sophisticated and balanced treatment of each within Savigny's original grand vision.

However, by approximately mid-nineteenth century that grand synthetic vision had begun to give way to a certain division and specialization of labor. By that point a rough consensus of opinion had developed among many scholars to the effect that the specialized investigations into the history of Roman and Germanic law called for by Savigny's conception of jurisprudence had basically been accomplished.[35] Some scholars concluded that this left them free to concentrate more on developing the systematic side of Savigny's project, leading to the form of jurisprudential practice that came to be called "*Begriffsjurisprudenz*" or "conceptual jurisprudence".[36] Georg Friedrich Puchta (1798-1846) and Rudolf von Jhering (1818-1892) (in the first phase of his career) were leading practitioners of this conceptual jurisprudence. Another group of scholars, of which Karl Adolf von Vangerow (1808-1870) and Bernhard Windscheid (1817-1892) were leading exemplars, undertook the development of an elaborate modern system of private law modeled on the Roman Pandects. Inspired by the conceptual jurisprudence developed by Puchta and Jhering, Windscheid and others produced an admirably complete and internally coherent system of modern private law, which incidentally provided the basis for much of the great German Civil Code (BGB) of 1900.[37]

Another branch of legal scholarship that emerged from the aforementioned division of labor were the "Romanists" and the "Germanists," two groups of legal historians who took up the detailed study of original legal texts from each of these two traditions, in the process setting standards of professionalism in writing on legal history that became widely emulated models outside of Germany as well as within. These Romanists and Germanists were less concerned with the immediate implications of their work for contemporary legal theory and practice, but interested in the pursuit of legal history for its own sake. In these respects they too were merely pursuing a limited dimension of Savigny's original synthesis.

Nevertheless, as Reimann repeatedly emphasized, the nineteenth century German practitioners of all of these approaches—conceptual jurisprudence, the Pandectists, Roman and German legal history—were aware that their research projects had evolved from von Savigny's original

34 Ibid., p. 894.

35 Ibid., pp. 862, 864.

36 Ibid., p. 859.

37 Ibid., pp. 866-867.

grand synthesis and therefore in some sense still constituted extensions of that project.[38] As Reimann observed:

> Nineteenth century German legal science followed Savigny in all essential regards. It looked only to positive law. It was interested mainly in its organic essence and considered only carefully selected data. And finally, it was determined to find and to develop the logical structure in law. This made "*Rechtswissenschaft*" a peculiar mixture of positivism, idealism, and formalism.[39]

Moreover, it will be argued below that the commonly encountered reports of the "death" of the historical school sometime in mid-nineteenth century Germany are in some respects significantly exaggerated. Reimann argued persuasively that most German legal theorists in the latter part of the nineteenth century were still conscious of Savigny's original program as the ultimate source of their projects; there is also good evidence that important legal writers as late as the eve of World War I were still aware of the parameters of Savigny's program in its original form, and in developing their own views continued to take account of it. Two examples of such authors – Eugen Ehrlich and Ivan Il'in – will be discussed below.

The Obscurity of Rechtswissenschaft in American Gaze

The widespread supposition that the impulse of the historical school was exhausted by the mid-nineteenth century has led to some significant misunderstandings of the nature of nineteenth century German *Rechtswissenschaft*, especially on the opposite side of the Atlantic. In the late nineteenth and early twentieth centuries, various American legal scholars were attempting to sort out recent developments in German legal thought. Among the salient developments encountered was the so-called "*Begriffsjurisprudenz*". For the most part failing to grasp that this project was conceived by its practitioners as an extension of the "systemic" dimension of Savigny's original project (on the supposition that the "historical" dimension had largely been accomplished by that point), some American commentators attempted to make sense of *Begriffsjurisprudenz* as a free-standing exercise of legal thought on its own. Struck by the pronounced emphases on the elucidation of fundamental concepts and general principles, and the attempt to place subordinate concepts and principles in proper relation to the more fundamental and general ones, and the presentation of the whole as a complete *system* of law, American observers tended to conclude that the entire project was an exercise in deductive logic, akin to philosophically-based, deductive theories of natural law. A common translation of "*Begriffsjurisprudenz*" was

[38] Ibid., pp. 874-875. According to Reimann, "All major versions of jurisprudence after Savigny and until Jhering were variations on these basic themes" [of history and system] (p. 875). Mathias is presumably referring here to the second stage of Jhering's career, when he turned to a purposive "interest"-based theory of law late in the nineteenth century.

[39] Ibid., p. 889.

"mechanical jurisprudence", as in Roscoe Pound's famous 1908 essay by that name.[40]

In that article Pound attempted to characterize the main developments of recent German legal theory, taking note of its claim to constitute a "science".[41] The "scientific" jurisprudence that Pound wished to criticize was one which took science to be "a rigid scheme of deductions from *a priori* conceptions".[42] Pound believed that such a conception of science, involving "the method of deduction from predetermined conceptions" was dominant in German jurisprudence until the last quarter of the nineteenth century in "both the historical school of jurists and the philosophical school".[43] The difference between these two schools, according to Pound,

> lay in the manner in which they arrived at their fundamental conceptions. The former derived them from the history of juristic speculation and the historical development of the Roman sources. The latter, through metaphysical inquiries, arrived at certain propositions as to human nature, and deduced a system from them. This was the philosophical theory behind the eighteenth-century movement for codification.[44]

The philosophical theory that lay behind the eighteenth-century movement for codification, and which resulted in the Prussian Civil Code, was the elaborate natural law system of Christian von Wolff (1679-1754) (published in 8 volumes). Pound appears to have believed that some such approach was still being pursued by some in Germany as late as the third quarter of the nineteenth century. He thus appears not to grasp that it was precisely the collapse of the method of natural law theory at the end of the *eighteenth* century which led to the development of Savigny's historical school, and that it was in multiple respects founded upon a rejection of natural law theory.[45]

Precisely what Pound understood of the differences between "the historical school", "the philosophical school", and *Begriffsjurisprudenz*, or relations among them, cannot be clearly discerned. In any event, all supposedly involved rigid deductive systems of one sort or another, and accordingly deserved to be dismissed as "mechanical jurisprudence". He argued that any such conception of science was by now (1908) outdated and should be replaced by a pragmatic, sociological approach

40 Roscoe Pound, *Columbia Law Review*, VIII (1908), p. 605.

41 Pound, "Mechanical Jurisprudence", quoted from George C. Christie and Patrick H. Martin (eds.), *Jurisprudence: Texts and Readings on the Philosophy of Law* (1973), pp. 828-832.

42 Ibid., p. 830.

43 Ibid., p. 831.

44 Ibid., p. 832.

45 Reimann, note 4 above, pp. 842-846.

to jurisprudence as well as to judicial decision-making. All this tends to suggest that Pound never had a clear grasp of the nature of the historical school or of its central role in the development of nineteenth century German jurisprudence. That, in turn, would imply that the true significance of German *Rechtswissenschaft* escaped him, and therefore that many of the subtleties and complexities, as well as much of the sophistication, of nineteenth century German *Rechtswissenschaft*, were not well comprehended in early twentieth century American legal scholarship. Clarifying this entire episode appears to have been one of the primary motivations behind the work of Mathias Reimann cited here.

Evaluating a Legal System: the Historically Real and the Ideal

Since Savigny rejected both the classic positivist account of law as the command of the sovereign, and traditional natural law doctrine (mainly in the form represented by Wolff's formulation of it), the question of how to understand Savigny's theory in relation to each of these traditions bears further investigation.

Despite Savigny's explicit rejection of the positivists' command theory of the law, later scholars nevertheless came to view the historical school as an essentially positivist theory in a different sense. It was the first branch of Savigny's two-fold conception of method which could later be construed as a kind of "positivism": namely, that the law in question was to be discovered entirely through painstaking *historical* investigation of cultural phenomena (and not to be "adduced" philosophically from allegedly universal principles). One might further conclude from this that the element of the "ideal" had consequently been eliminated from Savigny's conception of law. However, neither conclusions could be unambiguously sustained. First, such a "positivist" reading of Savigny's theory could have arisen only if the importance of the historical dimension was inflated to such a degree as to obscure the systematic dimension of the method. Keeping both dimensions in proper perspective, one can see an appropriate rejoinder to such "positivistic" readings: a certain element of the "ideal"—though an ideal supposedly peculiar to each culturally distinct people and its way of life – was always preserved through the notions of *organic wholeness* and *system*, that is, through the second dimension of Savigny's conception of method.[46]

One can argue that achieving a reasonably complete and accurate description of a legal system as reflecting the way of life of an (historically) existing society as an organic whole should obviate the need for any independent evaluative judgments on the part of the investigator as to "good" or "bad" elements of that system. Any mutually contradictory or genuinely dysfunctional elements arising in such a legal system would presumably be noticed eventually by its practitioners/subjects, and

[46] Reimann is particularly clear on this aspect of the problem. See Reimann, note 4 above, pp. 886-891.

steps to resolve or eliminate them should be apparent in the historical record. Thus, an exhaustive historical *description* of that system as an organically-functioning whole, i.e., as a *system* of law, should ultimately provide adequate guidance on any legitimate topic of jurisprudential theory, without the need to introduce any extraneous or independent scholarly judgments as to what was "good" or "bad", "just" or "unjust", in the functioning of such a system.[47]

Because such a body of law emanates from the consciousness of the people whose law it is, this must in some sense be thought of as "chosen" by that people and hence to reflect their collective judgment about what is "good" in the way of social order for them. To this extent, such a body of law (their *Recht*, but not necessarily every element of their *Gesetzen*) could be presumed to incorporate an "ideal" form of their way of life. In this way one could suppose that the tendency of the historical school was to locate the ideal as by definition embedded in the organic way of life reflected in the society's distinctive *Recht*.

Although Savigny was firmly opposed to traditional "natural law" conceptions deriving the law from timeless and universal philosophical principles, in practice Savigny's theory could be seen as lending aid and comfort to a renewal of a natural law doctrine in one crucial respect: his insistence that the (positive) *Gesetzen* are likely to constitute "a baleful corruption" of the *Recht* suggests the idea of a higher, objective standard by which existing statutes can and should be assessed. In Savigny's conception, *Recht* could not claim universal validity, being an historical expression of the culture of a particular people, but it might achieve a kind of objectivity where its scientific (*rechtswissenschaftliches*) articulation as a system constitutes a true and accurate reflection of the original legal culture. In that case it would rightly serve as a standard by which the adequacy of individual positive laws (*Gesetzen*) could be measured within that same culture. And given this theoretical background, plus the centrality of *Roman* law for so much of the history of European legal practice after the eleventh century, it might seem only a short step to the (technically unjustified) assumption that the concepts and institutions of Roman law possessed a kind of "universal" significance after all. But this last conclusion is the one that Savigny most strenuously resisted, for it directly contradicted his central thesis concerning the essential distinctiveness of the *Rechtsbewußtsein* of each cultural grouping. The most compelling conclusion might be that Savigny's theory cannot be accurately described either as a "positivist" or as a "natural law" theory in any of the standard meanings of those terms, but seems to exhibit a certain shadow of each, depending upon whether we focus upon the "historical" or upon the "systematic" dimension of his method.

In one of his most telling conclusions, Reimann remarks that

[47] See ibid., pp. 879-880 and 890-891.

> At the core of Savigny's historical theory of law lay the conviction that the principles were all internally consistent because they were all part of the same organic whole of one true law for the entire (cultural) nation. This was because the legal principles reflected basic patterns of the common legal consciousness [that is, *Rechtsbewußtsein* – PTG]. The scientific jurists had only translated and condensed them into the logical form.[48]

The possibility of developing a coherent summary of *Recht* as a *codified system* of law (as opposed to a mere listing of *Gesetzen*) thus rests on the prior possibility of describing the society whose law it is as a coherent (organically) organized whole. Only if the forms of life adopted in the society as a whole manifest some shared comprehension of what is required, forbidden, or permitted would there appear to be the possibility of formulating such a codified system. But that was what *Rechtsbewußtsein* represented for Savigny.

The Subsequent Fate of the Historical School

Given Savigny's exceptionally able representation and defense of his point of view, the program of the historical school set the dominant agenda for German jurisprudence for much of the nineteenth century and beyond. There is evidence that its spell was not completely broken until after the end of the First World War, when new constitutions were being drafted for Germany and Austria under radically altered political circumstances, amid new intellectual cross-currents generated by such diverse legal theorists as Hans Kelsen (1881-1973) and Carl Schmitt (1888-1985).[49]

[48] Ibid., p. 886.

[49] Hans Kelsen taught public law and legal philosophy at the University of Vienna beginning in 1911, becoming a full professor in 1919. In that same year the Austrian Chancellor, Karl Renner (1870-1950), asked Kelsen to produce several drafts of a possible new Austrian constitution, one of which was adopted and remains the basis of the Austrian legal system to the present. Kelsen's most influential works were *Hautprobleme der staatsrechtslehre entwickelt aus der lehre vom rechtssatze* (1911); *Allgemeine staatslehre* (1925); and *Reine Rechtslehre* (1934). In the second and third of these works Kelsen developed a systematic positivist account of the nature of a legal system, which remains to this day one of the most influential formulations of legal positivism.

Carl Schmitt is primarily remembered as a prominent legal and political theorist of the German Nazi regime. Not always appreciated, however, is the fact that the main outlines of his legal and political theory were well developed long before the Nazis came to power. In a series of works published before 1924, Schmitt had developed a powerful indictment of parliamentary democracy as an inevitable fraud, had argued vehemently that all written law was fundamentally and necessarily indeterminate (thus rendering the liberal ideal of the rule of law incoherent), and (by 1927) had claimed that political order could only be based upon the arbitrary *decision* of a leader who would define the nation's *enemies*, and formulate national policy accordingly. Schmitt's main works include *Gesetz und Urteil* (1912); *Der Wert des Staates, und die Bedeutung des Einzelnen* (1914); *Politische Theologie* (1922); and *Die geistesgeschichtliche Lage des heutigen Parlamentismus* (1923). Debates between adherents of Kelsen's positivist, but fundamentally liberal, conception of the law and State, and Schmitt's radically anti-liberal conception of law and State were a prominent fixture of German intellectual life from the late 1920s through the 1930s; at the time, Kelsen's

Nevertheless, it seems clear that the dominance of Savigny's historical school began to be challenged in certain respects around the middle of the nineteenth century. Precisely when and why (and to what extent) that dominance began to diminish raises complicated issues. Because it is known that other, competing, schools began to emerge by the mid-nineteenth century, or at any rate before the last quarter of that century (e.g., *Begriffsjurisprudenz*, Jhering's theory of law as the expression of a social interest, various versions of legal positivism, the sociology of law, and others), one is sometimes left with the impression that these alternative doctrines began rapidly displacing the historical school and that long before the end of the nineteenth century it had been more or less completely replaced by some combination of these successor schools. Indeed, Reimann speaks of "the demise of von Savigny's original program around the middle of the century" and the "waning influence of von Savigny's original conception of the historical school" when *Begriffsjurisprudenz* emerged in the middle decades of the century.[50] But at the same time, he points out that all major versions of jurisprudence after Savigny and until Jhering, that is, Jhering's second, sociological phase focused on law as the expression of a social interest, were variations on Savigny's basic themes.[51]

Thus, the question of the "after-life" of the historical school is considerably more complicated that most short accounts of the matter would seem to imply. Even the emergence of clearly competing points of view, such as Jhering's social-interest theory of the law, did not necessarily put an abrupt end to the influence of the historical school. The arrival of a new theory of law on the scene, incompatible in major respects with a previously dominant theory, does not in itself guarantee that the influence of the previous theory has been abruptly erased. The new theory may simply push the older theory partially or temporarily into the background, where it remains available for consideration, albeit discussed less frequently than before. Something like this may have befallen the historical school in the latter part of the nineteenth century. Indeed, the "after-life" of the historical school may have extended until about 1920.

That Savigny's theory was still influential as late as the eve of the First World War can be seen in a series of German publications dating from the years 1912 to 1914, actively debating the contemporary relevance of the historical school. Savigny's conception was energetically attacked in 1912 by Hermann Kantorowicz (1877-1940) in the essay "*Was ist uns Savigny?*" [What is Savigny for Us?].[52] That publication brought forth

position came to be regarded as a suspect, minority view (although in the larger sweep of time the fates of the two positions have been reversed).

50 Reimann, note 4 above, pp. 880, 864.

51 Ibid., p. 875.

52 Hermann Kantorowicz, "*Was ist uns Savigny?*", in *Recht und Wirtschaft* (1912) (also

a vigorous defense of the historical school in 1914 from Alfred Manigk (1873-1942), *Savigny und der Modernismus im Recht* [Savigny and Modernism in Law].[53] Eugen Ehrlich's work *Grundlegung der Soziologie des Rechts* (1913) (to be discussed below) showed a strong continuing influence of some of Savigny's fundamental ideas. We are suggesting that Il'in's work on legal consciousness, commencing in 1916, should be viewed as further evidence of the continuing influence of Savigny's approach to legal theory in this period.

By the eve of the First World War, we were long past the point when it seemed plausible to characterize the underlying unity of *Rechtsbewußtsein* in terms of an organic cultural *Volksgeist* such as posited by Savigny. However, developments in this time frame suggest that some analogue of Savigny's *Rechtsbewußtsein* remained a possibility in the eyes of some contemporary legal theorists. At a minimum any such proposed analogue had to satisfy two conditions: to identify some underlying unity expressed in the forms of life constitutive of the society or societies in question, and this underlying unity also had to be manifested as a dimension of the collective consciousness of society if it were to form the basis for an alternative doctrine of *Rechtsbewußtsein.*

Early in the twentieth century the Austrian legal theorist Eugen Ehrlich supposed that such an underlying unity could be identified in terms of the market economic institutions increasingly coming to dominate much of western European life. Ehrlich is regarded as one of the founding fathers of the sociology of law; however, he was still recognizably working within the framework of a modified version of historical school jurisprudence as late as 1913. One of his modifications of Savigny's theory consisted in down-grading the significance of the *Rechtsbewußtsein* of the legal scholars and of officialdom, tending to merge them into a single category, and restoring the *Rechtsbewußtsein* of the general population as the continuing, primary source of law. The other modification involved replacing the cultural *Volksgeist* by the shared experience of operating the economic institutions of a contemporary market economy.

The *Rechtsbewußtsein* of the general population was conceived as the product of their immediate involvement in the formal as well as the informal operations of the myriad economic institutions making up a complex modern society at the turn of the century. Presumably, the underlying dynamics of market economies were increasingly forcing themselves into the consciousnesses of European citizenry and governing their activities. Conceiving of *Rechtsbewußtsein* in these terms carried

separately published in 1912. 45 p.) Eugen Ehrlich's work *Grundlegung der Soziologie des Rechts* (1914) showed a strong continuing influence of some of Savigny's fundamental ideas.

[53] Alfred Manigk, *Savigny und der Modernismus im Recht* (1914). See Morris R. Cohen, "On Continental Legal Philosophy: Philosophical-Legal Literature in French, German and Italian: 1912-1914", in Cohen, *Law and the Social Order: Essays in Legal Philosophy* (1933), pp. 286-318.

the significant implication that it was no longer restricted to separate and distinct cultural nations, as in Savigny's original conception, but could be conceived as a common consciousness extending over numerous societies, so long as all of them were operating at approximately similar levels of economic development. Ehrlich's conception of a popular *Rechtsbewußtsein* could thus potentially embrace much of the western European world as he knew it.

In similar fashion, beginning in 1916, Ivan Il'in focused upon *Rechtsbewußtsein* (правосознание) as the central theme in his account of the nature of law, exploring the same three forms or aspects that have been hallmarks of the doctrine since its inception in the writings of Savigny. However, like Ehrlich, Il'in no longer regarded the assumption of the essential distinctiveness of each cultural entity as a wholly defining feature of the theory. Instead he treated the objective content of *Recht* (право) as intrinsically universal, grounded in the objective requirements of "spirit" which are likewise universal, even if manifested somewhat distinctively in each of the national cultures. Thus Il'in supposed that the underlying unity reflected in *Rechtsbewußtsein* could be conceived in terms of some universal dynamic of the human spirit in which all humans participate at some level of consciousness.

In this way these early twentieth-century echoes of Savigny's theory dispensed with his assumption of the distinctiveness of each linguistically separate nation's legal culture, often regarded as the most conspicuous hallmark of the historical school, and yet continued to reflect other characteristic, recognizable themes of that school.

Il'in's Conception of the Landscape of Legal Theory at the End of the First World War

Taking into account all the various developments in recent and contemporary jurisprudence of which Il'in seemed to be aware, it is possible to assemble a list of major influences upon his thinking as of the period from 1916 to 1918, when he set about writing an early version of *On the Essence of Legal Consciousness*.

First, it is evident that the general framework of his thinking still reflected the influence of Savigny's Historico-Systematic school, now largely shorn of the once-definitive assumption that each distinct cultural nation possessed its own distinctive conception of law, replaced by a more universalist conception of legal institutions. Nevertheless, the framework of Savigny's three distinguishable forms of legal consciousness remained fundamental to his thinking.

It is also clear that Il'in was influenced by the contemporary effort to restore a version of natural law doctrine. This was characteristic of the "Moscow" school of jurisprudence headed by his mentor Novgorodtsev at Moscow University, but not confined to Russian legal thinkers alone at the time.

Il'in's first important published essay in jurisprudence, "The Concepts of Law and Power," (published as an appendix in this volume) demonstrates how Il'in assessed the state of jurisprudential theory as of 1912. There he showed a clear awareness of several distinctive approaches to the study of law, some sharing over-lapping concepts, and other approaches so different from one another that a question fundamental for one approach could not even be meaningfully formulated in another. In that essay he distinguished *psychological* approaches from *sociological* ones, and *historical* approaches from *political*. He specifically rejected the idea that any single approach could be treated as fundamental, dispensing with the suggestion that a "methodological monism" was possible in the law; methodological "pluralism" was inevitable. No single approach could claim to be exclusively correct; only all of them together might lay claim to presenting an exhaustive comprehension of law.

Both the psychological and the sociological approaches were characterized in some detail in the essay, suggesting that Il'in viewed them as particularly important contemporary conceptions of the law, which was, of course, an accurate reflection of recent developments in legal theory. Below there follows a summarized contemporary version of sociological jurisprudence in the work of Eugen Erlich, and a version of psychological jurisprudence in the work of L. I. Petrazhitskii, both contemporaries of Il'in, to illustrate these new developments. Each found a distinctive application for the term "legal consciousness", thus contributing to the continuing development of that concept.

Eugen Ehrlich: An Early Sociological Theory of Law

In the early twentieth century the legal theorist Eugen Ehrlich (1862-1922), author of *Grundlegung der Sociologie des Rechts* (1913)[54] and generally regarded as among the most important founders of the new *sociological* approach to law, was agitated by a version of the same problem formulated by Savigny in 1814: what is the fundamental source of law? Just as Savigny, he too distinguished the legal consciousness of the general population from the formalized codes of statutory law and the rulings of the professional jurists. Unlike Savigny, however, Ehrlich was inclined to merge the second and third forms of *Rechtsbewußtsein* (that is, that of the scholar-jurists, on one hand, and the official legislators and executors of the law, on the other) into a single "professional" *Rechtsbewußtsein* which Ehrlich condemned as inevitably destined to be fragmentary, overly-abstract, and in certain respects misleading – concerned merely with written formulations of law – in contrast with the true substance of the "living law" to be found only in the informal understandings of the general population whose members actually operated the countless smaller associations that collectively made up the (fundamentally economic) fabric of society as a whole. Moreover, the

[54] Ehrlich, *Fundamental Principles of the Sociology of Law*, transl. Walter L. Moll (1936; reprinted 1962).

commonality of economic institutions across multiple societies at similar levels of development made plausible a greater commonality of legal forms across cultural borders. Nevertheless, Ehrlich still supposed that the *Rechtsbewußtsein* of the society at large was the ultimate source of law. Thus, despite Ehrlich's fundamental disagreement with some specific tenets of Savigny's historical school, he is recognizably operating within the general framework set by the historical school and takes the centrality of *Rechtsbewußtsein* as a given.

Born in Czernowitz, on the eastern border of the Austro-Hungarian empire, he received his legal education at Vienna, where he taught and practiced for some years before returning (1897) as Professor of Roman Law to the university at Czernowitz. He remained there until World War I, when he moved to Switzerland to escape successive military invasions of his home province. In contrast to either Durkheim or Weber, Ehrlich succeeded in laying out his sociology of law in a relatively accessible and complete form in a single clearly-written monograph.[55]

Ehrlich came to the conclusion that the real institutional basis of any actual legal system, what he termed the "living law", could not be identified with codes and statutes, courts, or even the legal functions of the State, but was found only in local custom and the accepted "juristic" practices of the countless smaller associations and groups making up the real life of society. He distinguished three different types of norms operative in essentially all legal systems: (1) the abstract "legal propositions" (*Rechtssätze*) found in formal codes and statutes, which were primarily the concern of courts and were known to the general population, if at all, only in a vague and superficial manner; (2) "decision rules" (*Entscheidungsnormen*) addressed to judges and jurisconsults, governing procedures for the formal resolution of conflicts among individuals and groups in society; and (3) by far the most extensive and substantive category, "social law" (*gesellschaftliches Recht*), the originally non-formalized but vital, functioning, inner principles for the ordering of human associations, beginning with the most primitive familial, clan or tribal associations up through those countless associations making up the most complex of contemporary societies.[56] "The inner order of the associations of human beings is not only the original, but also, down to the present time, the basic form of law".[57] By contrast, "legal propositions" or "legal norms" are a later, derivative, and in many ways subsidiary phenomenon. "The legal proposition not only comes into being at a much later time, but is largely derived from the inner order of the associations. In order to

[55] There is evidence of a revived interest in Ehrlich's sociology of law among English-speaking authors. See M. Hertogh (ed.), *Living Law: Reconsidering Eugen Ehrlich* (2009); Roger Cotterrell, *The Sociology of Law: An Introduction* (2d ed.; 1992). See also Manfred Rehbinder, *Die Begrundung der Rechtssoziologie durch Eugen Ehrlich* (2d. ed.; 1986). A concise critique can be found in Georges Gurvitch, *Sociology of Law* (1947), pp. 116-122.

[56] Gurvitch, note 55 above, pp. 117-119.

[57] Ehrlich, note 54 above, p. 37.

explain the beginnings, the development, and the nature of law, one must first of all inquire into the order of the associations. All attempts that have been made until now to comprehend the nature of law have failed because the investigation was not based on the order of the associations but on the legal propositions".[58] Ehrlich viewed all previously established, formal jurisprudence or *Rechtswissenschaft* as, at most, a partial and ultimately failed attempt to grasp the reality of law as a whole, mainly because its declared subject matter, *legal propositions* (i.e., codes and statutes), was at best only a small fragment of that whole, and not the real substance of the living law.

Attempting to summarize his entire doctrine in a single quotable sentence, Ehrlich stated: "At the present as well as at any other time, the center of gravity of legal development lies not in legislation, nor in juristic science, nor in judicial decision, but in society itself".[59] Ehrlich's notion of "living law" would obviously be more closely connected to what others have called "legal consciousness", because the "living law" refers especially to the informal understandings, expectations, and requirements involved in the internal ordering of the countless associations making up the bulk of society. Ehrlich further noted a significant connection between what he called the "living law" and the basic content of natural law, which he regarded as largely a summary of prevailing social relations and institutions[60] (although he did not focus upon the term "legal consciousness" as a technical term in this work, he did employ it in a sense clearly related to the meaning it had acquired in the context of Savigny's historical school).

L. I. Petrazhitskii: The Origin of Law in the Human Psyche

In the early twentieth century, a number of Russian legal theorists actively participated in discussions of legal consciousness (*Rechtsbewußtsein*, правосознание). Il'in's contribution to this theme, and its connection with Savigny's historical school, have been outlined above. There was a second, more unusual, strand of reflection on legal consciousness which stemmed from the work of Lev Iosifovich Petrazhitskii (1867-1931), the influential Polish-Russian legal theorist who taught in the Faculty of Law at the University of St. Petersburg from 1897 to 1917.[61]

[58] Ehrlich, note 54 above, pp. 37-38.

[59] Ehrlich, note 54 above, "Foreword", p. xv.

[60] "The attempt of the law of nature school to do this manifestly amounted to a finding of norms, i.e., juristic science. It is true, it was a juristic science which was based, in the main, on the living law, and whose relation to the existing law was one of comparative freedom, but, by no means, of absolute independence; for it presupposed the existing social and economic order which, for the most part, has arisen and taken shape under the influence of the existing law". Ehrlich, note 54 above, p. 419.

[61] A full chapter on Petrazhitskii can be found in A. Walicki, *Legal Philosophies of*

Just as many legal theorists, he was determined to identify the fundamental form, the ultimate *reality*, to which all further phenomena in the life of the law could be traced. He concluded that, rather than "a command backed by force", "statutory law", "the common consciousness of the people", "a codification by experts,", or any other commonly held conception, the ultimate reality of law was to be identified (and explicated) wholly in terms of the psychic states of individuals.

Petrazhitskii was a sophisticated theorist, determined to set the study of law upon a fully scientific foundation. His general philosophical orientation was toward positivism (though he was a firm critic of legal positivism), with a distinct inclination toward psychologism. He believed that legal theory would be unable to make progress until a "clear and precise definition of the concept of law"[62] had been attained, and he believed that he had solved that problem in the form of a purely *psychological* theory of the nature of law. To carry out this entire project successfully, he found it necessary to revise existing empirical theories of human emotion and motivation, which he found inadequate for his own theoretical purposes. In order to make the methodological foundations of his own project clear, he supplied an elaborate account of the principles of concept formation in empirical science, and set these in the context of his own account of the general logic of empirical inquiry. All of this theoretical apparatus was then turned to the problem of elucidating the ultimate source of law.

He argued that in reality all the material necessary for a completely successful solution of the problem was at hand, and it required no reference to anything of a "transcendent" nature. According to Petrazhitskii,

> The fundamental, fully reliable material directly given to us for the cognition of the essence of law is our internal psychic acts.
>
> The point is that law (no one denies this) is a phenomenon not of the external, material world, as, for example, a stone, a tree, but a phenomenon of the spiritual world, a psychic phenomenon, a phenomenon of our soul; therefore we can directly acquaint ourselves with its nature only ... within our soul, i.e. by means of the observation, comparison, and analysis of our own psychic states and movements.[63]

Drawing out some of the more striking implications of his account, Petrazhitskii emphasized:

> That the account established above of the concept of a norm of law, of a legal relation and its elements, does not in general

Russian Liberalism (1987), Chapter IV.

62 Л. И. Петражицкий: Теорая и политика права: Избранные труды [L. I. Petrazhitskii, Theory and Policy of Law: Selected Works], ed. E. V. Timoshina (2010), p. 250.

63 Ibid., p. 251.

> necessarily presuppose the existence of an organized social union, for example, a state, the recognition of norms or legal relations on the part of people around us, the existence of courts, the legislator, or similar phenomena, ideas of which are usually connected with the concept of law, particularly in the mind of jurists.[64]

On the contrary, he claimed, it is necessary to recognize as the fundamental manifestation of law the mere consciousness of an obligation or of a claim "which exists only in the soul of a single person and does not encounter recognition or agreement on the part of social authority, a court or in general of anyone else whomever, except one who experiences these psychic states".[65]

For example, an Earthling visiting Mars, whose knife was taken and not returned by some Martian, might be convinced of a duty on the part of the Martian to return the knife, even if such a duty was no part of the Martian's consciousness, and was not recognized by any third person on Mars. The Earthling's conviction of the existence of a legal duty on the part of the Martian would nevertheless be "fully appropriate" on Petrazhitskii's conception of law.[66] Similarly, if a superstitious person or lunatic were to conclude a contract with the devil, selling his soul, even though the devil does not exist in reality, there would be an operative norm of law prescribing the fulfillment of the contract, a legal relation, rights and duties, objects of rights and duties, two subjects, and so on.[67] In short, "Law is a psychic phenomenon, and its elements are elements of a psychic act, and not any sort of objects existing outside of the psyche".[68]

Throughout most of the nineteenth century *Rechtsbewußtsein* referred to some form of *collective* consciousness. The *Volksgeist* was treated as fundamental, and the individual manifestations of it as derivative.[69] Petrazhitskii reversed this relation, treating the phenomena of the individual psyche as fundamental and the collective manifestations of such phenomena in society as derivative in his account of the ultimate source of law.

Having located the ultimate source of law among the phenomena of individual psychology, Petrazhitskii then turned to a more sociological perspective, advocating the creation of a new science of "legal policy"

[64] Ibid., p. 259.

[65] Ibid.

[66] Ibid.

[67] Ibid., p. 260.

[68] Ibid.

[69] Remembering Savigny's declaration, for instance: "Rather is it the spirit of a people, living and working in common in all the individuals, which gives birth to positive law, which therefore is to the consciousness of each individual not accidentally but necessarily one and the same". Savigny, note 6 above, transl. William Holloway, p. 12.

which would investigate the most appropriate directions for the planned development of the law. This science of legal policy (a science of what the law ought to be in the future) would require, first, a systematic study of the psychological impact of law on the motivation and conduct of the individual, expanding into an investigation of the psychological laws of character formation under the influence of various legal orders.[70]

The development of this science would then provide a basis for legislators in the future to tailor their formulations of law to the existing stages of social development of a given population in such a way as to promote the continued development of legal consciousness in an appropriate direction. The goal of that development would be the gradual elimination of the necessity for the legal regulation of human conduct, culminating in the "attainment of a completely social character, the complete domination of active love in humanity".[71] This stated goal of universal active love is of course not established by means of scientific investigation but is "axiomatic."

In a later work Petrazhitskii described this proposed science of legal policy as equivalent to the restoration of the neglected study of "natural (rational, ideal, philosophical) law" which used to fulfill that "important and high mission which a future science of legal policy must serve", and which existing "practical-dogmatic jurisprudence" dedicated to the "interpretation and systematic reworking of existing positive law for the requirements of practice" is incapable of providing.[72]

Legislators and expert scholars in the future, armed with Petrazhitskii's new empirical science of individual psychology, would be able to elucidate the stages of development of legal consciousness (правосознание) and identify the appropriate policies at each stage necessary to encourage the realization of the ultimate level of правосознание, in which the need for external legal regulation of human conduct would have been transcended by a universal ethic of love.

70 Hugh W. Babb, *Boston University Law Review*, XVII (1937), p. 815. The whole of Babb's article is devoted to an examination of Petrazhitskii's proposed science of legal policy. It is based on «Введение в науку политики права» [Introduction to the Science of Legal Policy], which he published in Kiev: Киевские университетские известия [Kiev University News], no. 8 (1896), pp. 1-99; no. 10, pp. 99-169; (1897), no. 9, pp. 169-250. This was a translation by Petrazhitskii of the Preface to his *Fruchtverteilung beim Wechsel des Nutzungsberichtigten* and parts of the Appendix to *Die Lehre vom Einkommen*, previously published in Germany. Babb's article was also based on К вопросу о социальном идеале и возрождении естественного права [On the Question of the Social Ideal and the Renaissance of Natural Law] (1913), and on a manuscript entitled "The Policy of Law," originally written in Polish about 1925, subsequently translated into Russian and then English (bibliographic data not given). The first two works have recently been reprinted in note 62 above.

71 Babb, note 70 above, p. 813.

72 Petrazhitskii, Введение в изучение права и нравственности: основы эмоциональной психологиии [Introduction to the Study of Law and Morality: Fundamental Principles of Emotional Psychology] (3d ed.; 1908); reprinted in note 62 above, p. 380.

*Legal Consciousness (*Правосознание*) in the Bolshevik Revolution*

Shortly after the successful seizure of power by the Bolsheviks on 26 October 1917 (old style) at St. Petersburg in Russia an issue of legal consciousness arose: should the positive Imperial Russian law be retained in force, at least in part, or should there be a complete break with the old legal order by repealing Imperial Russian legislation and supplanting it with something else. Anecdotal evidence indicates that Lenin, himself a law graduate, was hesitant about so drastic a measure as complete abrogation. Consulting his People's Commissar of Justice, whose deputy was Mikhail Andreevich Reisner (1868-1928), a protégé of Leon Petrazhitskii (Petrazycki) and devotee of the latter's theory of intuitive law,[73] Lenin was persuaded to support a version of Dekret No. 1, "On the Court", terminating the operation of laws of the Russian Empire contrary to the ideas and principles of the Revolution and to substitute in their place a "revolutionary legal consciousness".[74] The anecdote was related as follows:

> "After the Bolshevik Revolution, Reisner ... was appointed Vice-Commissar of Justice. In this capacity, as reported by Timasheff, he used Petrazycki's theory of intuitive law 'to persuade his superior, the Commissar of Justice, that it was possible to abrogate uno actu the legislation of the Tsarist regime and of the Provisional Government, since a substitute already existed in the form of

[73] Reisner had reinterpreted Petrazhitskii's theory of intuitive (as he called it) law from a Marxist perspective long before the 1917 Russian Revolutions. See M. A. Reisner, Теория Петражицкого: Марксизм и социальная идеология [Theory of Petrazhitskii: Marxism and Social Ideology] (1908); transl. by H. W. Babb in J. N. Hazard (intro.), *Soviet Legal Philosophy* (1951). Both at the time in 1917 and subsequently some Russian and Ukrainian jurists have preferred to use the term "intuitive", rather than "psychological", to describe Petrazhitskii's theory. For them, "intuitive" seems to mean "spontaneous", that is, the spontaneous and instinctive reactions of the proletariat to the course of events. This would, in our view, be a seriously misleading perception of Petrazhitskii's theory, which postulated, first and foremost, the constant and persistent re-shaping of legal consciousness along directions discovered through his new concept of "legal policy", culminating in a society which no longer required law and legal institutions. Law would be replaced by love.

Reisner's work on Petrazhitskii in 1908 was evidence of Reisner being a "Bogdanovist", that is, a follower of A. A. Bogdanov (real name: Malinovskii) (1873-1928), as was Lunacharskii. On "Bogdanovism", see S. V. Utechin, *Russian Political Thought: A Concise History* (1964), pp. 208-213.

[74] The relevant passage in the Dekret on the Court of 22 November (5 December) 1917 provided: "5) Local courts shall decide cases in the name of the Russian Republic and shall be guided in their decisions and judgments by laws of the overthrown governments only insofar as such have not been repealed by the Revolution and are not contrary to a revolutionary conscience and revolutionary legal consciousness". See Декреты советской власти [Dekrets of Soviet Power] (1957-), I, p. 125. The Dekret was signed by V. I. Lenin (1870-1924) and by Commissars: Aleksandr Grigor'evich Shlikhter (1868-1940), Aleksandr Gavrilovich Shliapnikov (1885-1937), Iosif V. Stalin (1879-1953), Nikolai Pavlovich Avilov (N. Glebov) (1887-1937), and Petr Ivanovich Stuchka (1865-1932).

the intuitive law of the working class. Reisner's advice was embodied in the decree On Courts (7 December, 1917), according to which the new courts had to render decisions on the basis of the enactments of the 'Workers' and Peasants' Government' and of the revolutionary consciousness of the judges which was supposed to coincide with the ideas on justice held by working men. Since, at that time, the enactments of the new government were scarce and unsystematic, the other source, revolutionary consciousness had to prevail".[75]

Lest this be considered a unique and isolated event in Russian experience, it should be observed that a similar issue arose when the Soviet Union was dissolved in December 1991. The transition inaugurated by Mikhail Sergeevich Gorbachev (1931-2022) during the mid-1980s towards a "socialist market economy", the term "socialist" later being dropped, has required an adjustment of legal consciousness on the part of the Russian population towards the introduction of legal values associated with a rule-of-law State, democracy, and a market economy that differed fundamentally from those previously propagated. Legal consciousness has accordingly been used actively in two senses within the Russian context: one to characterize those legal values and concepts of law and justice deeply embedded in the national character and culture of a people; the other to characterize the antithesis – an infinitely supple and flexible loyalty and dedication to Communist Party policies and actions, whatever they may have been, as they emanated over time.

Petrazhitskii was in a position uncommon for a legal theorist. Unsympathetic to those who had seized power, convinced that these events boded a terrible catastrophe for Russia, deeply attached emotionally to his Slavonic Russian and Polish roots, he departed Petrograd for Warsaw in early 1917, leaving behind the precious manuscripts of his work in progress. His psychological theory of law, however, was about to be "hijacked" by those in power and to be deployed in perverted forms for nearly three-quarters of a century in support of a movement that he despised. In short, some of his ideas concerning the nature of law were about to be implemented, in part by some of his students and followers.

The Bolshevik response to their dilemma of what to do with the "old" legal system and its enactments was not prescribed by the prerevolutionary writings of Marx, Engels, and Lenin, who had devoted most of their

75 Walicki, note 61 above, pp. 287-288. Reisner deflected criticism of Lunacharskii and Stuchka for drawing upon Petrazhitskii's theory of intuitive law: "The guilt attributed to Luncharskii I must to an important degree take upon myself inasmuch as I was the person whose lot it was, in conversation with him, (a) to attest the necessity of organizing revolutionary justice (which Lunacharskii put forward), and (b) to point out the fact that ... revolutionary law is already existent and in being, notwithstanding the absence as yet of any legislation confirming it ... this was the intuitive law of our revolutionary masses ... which ... as the class law of the insurgents ... comprises completely the entirely of the appropriate legal consciousness ... Everyone knows that the turn of the revolutionary masses to intuitive law vindicated itself magnificently". Hazard, note 73 above, pp. 86-87.

attention to diagnosing the ills of a capitalist society and little to what administrative and legal structure should follow if Revolution proved to be successful. The initial reaction set out in the Dekret on the Court was twofold: to create a proletarian law and court that would administer the commands of a proletarian State and to form within the workers' State a "revolutionary", or a "socialist", or a "communist" legal consciousness that would create, inculcate, and nurture a new legal consciousness consistent with Party policies and values. The new legal consciousness was expected to inform the interpretation and application of the new proletarian law and any survivals of the past not deemed antithetical to the Revolution.

This was a transition that required explanation and justification to the public at large. Some imagined an immediate transition to a classless society in which the State and law would be superfluous; others expected a gradual adaptation of pre-existing rules and institutions. Lunacharskii was among those who seized the baton of explanation. A society, said Lunacharskii, is not a unified whole. A society is composed of classes with antagonistic interests and with diverse mentalities and legal consciousnesses.[76] Ruling classes create courts and laws in their own interests, punish those who encroach upon their privileges, and persuade the people to accept this state of affairs by infusing into their consciousness a belief that their legal order is a manifestation of "justice". So long as the proletariat remains a victim of the law made by its masters, the proletariat is deprived of the opportunity to formulate its own legal consciousness; it cannot create its own ideal of court and legal code in a vacuum.

The revolutionary class, said Lunacharskii, bring a new legal consciousness and a new concept of good and evil. The revolution is a fact of juxtaposing a new law to the old one. The creation of a new civil and criminal law, a new State structure, new agencies of power, including courts, formulates and materializes the new revolutionary legal consciousness. The Revolution was an opportunity for a new legal consciousness to be translated into reality, a new customary law to be created, deducing this from the "sources of the same spiritual movement that led the proletariat to the victorious revolution". In support of these views, Lunacharskii invited "our enemies" to read a few paragraphs from the writings of the theorists whom they recognize as "authorities in the field". These paragraphs, he said, sound "as though they were written yesterday, as though they were written specifically in defense of the type of courts that we are forced by the existing circumstances to create". Among those quoted was "Professor Petrazhitskii, in whom official Russian science takes pride as one of the greatest authorities in Europe"

[76] Vyshinskii later emphasized the class nature of legal consciousness: "... the 'legal consciousness' on which the bourgeois judiciary is based is nothing but a *bourgeois* consciousness". See A. Ia. Vyshinskii, «Еще раз о социалистическом правосознании» [Once Again on Socialist Legal Consciousness], Рабочий суд [Worker Court], no. 5-6 (1925), pp. 196-200; translated in M. Jaworskyj, *Soviet Political Thought: An Anthology* (1967), p. 200.

and who described vividly the relationships between the "positive" written law and the "intuitive law" of the new social forces:

> The simultaneous existence and functioning of the positive (written) law with the intuitive law (with the ideal of the new classes) is possibly only if there is a general agreement between them; if the discord reaches a certain degree, then the disintegration of the positive law becomes inescapable; in a case of opposition, the disintegration is brought about through a social revolution.[77]

The Revolution postulated by Petrazhitskii occurred, said Lunacharskii, on 25 October 1917, and he quoted Petrazhitskii again to describe the consequences of such a revolution: "it reaches a fanatical hatred of the existing order with its laws, and ultimately it arouses an explosion – the Revolution". Petrazhitskii, said Lunacharskii, was not alarmed by such manifestations of the new, popular, and revolutionary legal consciousness. These would include, according to Petrazhitskii:

> However repulsive the guillotines of the Revolution and the destruction of the cultural centers are, they are an inescapable result of the insulted popular sense, a spontaneous vengeance for the suppression of rights, i.e., people's inner legal consciousness.

For Lunacharskii, Petrazhitskii was a prophet. The conclusion, he said, is obvious: the people engender a new intuitive law which calls for the destruction of all organs of the old law that are perceived by them as complete injustices. This intuitive law, reflecting the class interests of the proletariat and newly emerging social structures, can be distinctly formulated only in the process of direct, revolutionary legal creativity.[78]

A proper study of legal consciousness in the Soviet context remains to be undertaken.[79] The early approach of the Bolsheviks to legal consciousness apparently continued to attract criticism. One of the signatories of the Dekret on the Court felt the need to explain the reliance

77 Lunacharskii cited L. Petrazhitskii, Теория права и государства в связи с теорией нравственности [Theory of Law and State in Connection with the Theory of Morality] (Petersburg, 1909). One presumes he was likewise under the influence of Reisner, who had emphasized what he considered to be materialistic aspects of Petrazhitskii's thought in his 1908 work. See Reisner, note 9 above. This was certainly Reisner's view; Reisner claimed in 1925 that "with the citation of certain scientific materials" – probably his 1908 work – he had managed to convince Lunacharskii that "… the revolutionary government had to rely on the legal consciousness of the revolutionary masses and how Lunacharsky in turn had succeeded in gaining the support of Lenin for this view". See Walicki, note 61 above, p. 288, citing Hazard, note 73 above, and both relying upon Reisner, Право, наше право, чужое право, общее право [Law, Our Law, Foreign Law, Common Law] (1925).

78 Lunacharskii's views are summarized from his article «Революция и суд» [Revolution and the Court], Правда [Truth], no. 193 (1 December 1917), translated in Jaworskyj, note 76 above, pp. 52-56.

79 The wealth of material to be explored is addressed in Iu. K. Pogrebnaia, Кризис современного российского правосознания [The Crisis of Modern Russian Legal Consciousness] (2013).

on revolutionary legal consciousness: the Dekret "... was an answer to the attempt to retain old laws that, although burned, were still living in people's minds. On the other hand, this was an answer to our right-wing Marxists, who reproached us for having anarchistic tendencies, namely for our rejection of the laws of earlier governments".[80]

By the mid-1920s, Stuchka observed:

> Perhaps there is not a single word from the dictionary of law which has been so widely disseminated after the October Revolution as the word "legal consciousness". We encountered revolutionary, socialist, even communist legal consciousness at every step, but it cannot be said that all or even the majority of comrades understood it.[81]

Whatever role the concept of revolutionary legal consciousness continued to serve throughout the 1920s and early 1930s, in the popular mind the concept had become a means for rationalizing any behavior of the authorities, lawless or lawful, for anything done could be said to be justified as consonant with the requirements of revolutionary legality. Following the adoption of the 1936 USSR Constitution, insofar as the concept was discussed a new appellation was applied: socialist legal consciousness. Although a comprehensive account of the history of legal consciousness in the Soviet period remains to be done, all preliminary indications are that the concept receded into the background and atrophied from the mid-1930s to the late 1950s.

From the mid-1950s onward legal consciousness experienced a revival in émigré and Soviet legal doctrine apparently for entirely independent reasons. Il'in's widow and friends succeeded in bringing his long-awaited work on the subject to publication in the Russian language at Munich in 1956, but any impact of the work was confined to the aging Russian émigré community. There is no evidence to date that the work was disseminated in the former Soviet Union, even in samizdat form; in published form, of course, Il'in's book was completely unsatisfactory for ideological reasons; any discussion of it would have been unacceptable, not to say dangerous. Nonetheless, by the late 1950s the Soviet Communist Party

[80] P. I. Stuchka, «Пролетарское право» [Proletarian Law], in Октябрьский переворот и диктатура пролетариата [The October Upheaval and the Dictatorship of the Proletariat] (Moscow, 1919), pp. 24-28; translated in Jaworskyj, note 76 above, p. 74. Stuchka later added: "The aggregate of our decrees has never embraced, and does not now embrace, the entire of sphere of legal relations; that is why we introduced the idea of a revolutionary legal consciousness". Stuchka, «Марксистское понимание права» [Marxist Understanding of Law], Коммунистическая революция [Communist Revolution], no. 13-14 (November 1922); translated in Jaworskyj, note 76 above, p. 92. Stuchka was soon criticized for introducing "revolutionary legal consciousness" into a single concept of legal theory, for revolutionary legal consciousness was an "anti-Marxist vagueness". See I. Podvolotskii, Марксистская теория права [Marxist Theory of Law], intro. N. A. Bukharin (1923), pp. 163-187; translated in Jaworskyj, note 76 above, p. 106.

[81] P. I. Stuchka, «Правосознание» [Legal Consciousness], in Энциклопедия государства и права [Encyclopedia of State and Law] (1925-26), III, p. 446.

leadership had decided that the USSR had entered the phase of societal development known as the "building of a communist society" in which law and State would, as Karl Marx had predicted, commence the process of "withering" or "dying" away.

This process of "dying away" would be accelerated by the transfer of classical State functions to non-State bodies: the principal examples were the transfer of some law enforcement functions to people's guards[82] and comrades' courts.[83] This might have been an opportunity for the Party to encourage an investigation of societal factors that would promote cohesion and an awareness of law and legal values among a population that was supposedly to witness the beginning of the dismantling of the State. The concept of legal consciousness, one might suppose, could have been marshalled for this purpose. The campaign to build a communist society in the Soviet Union by 1980 disappeared with the removal of Nikita Sergeevich Khrushchev in October 1964 and with that event also the potential deployment of legal consciousness in the service of the construction of communism. "Soviet Man", it would transpire, as a jurisprudential and psychological construction, stood mostly apart from the conversation about legal consciousness.

Nonetheless, Russian and Ukrainian legal scholars returned to the subject of legal consciousness in its own right, quite independently of the writings of Petrazhitskii and Il'in, in the late 1950s[84] and again in the post-Soviet period. These days legal consciousness is viewed as a "category of jurisprudence that is inextricably linked with law and an element in the mechanism of legal regulation".[85] It is widely regarded as an indispensable component of legal culture and a special form of a larger social consciousness.[86] Modern Russian and Ukrainian jurists are

[82] On 2 April 2014 the Russian Federation adopted the Federal Law on the Participation of Citizens in the Protection of Public Order. This Federal Law institutionalized the formation of people's guard units, which had continued to operate in post-Soviet Russia without new legislation. The Law is translated in W. E. Butler, *Russia & The Republics: Legal Materials* (2006-).

[83] See W. E. Butler, "Comradely Justice in Eastern Europe", *Current Legal Problems*, XXV (1972), pp. 200-218.

[84] Among the studies of this era were: I. E. Farber, Правосознание как форма общественного сознания [Legal Consciousness as a Form of Social Consciousness] (1963); G. S. Ostroumov, Правовое осознание действительности [Legal Consciousness of Reality] (1968); E. I. Lukasheva, Социалистическое правовое сознание и законность [Socialist Legal Consciousness and Legality] (1973); V. A. Sapun, Социалистическое правосознание и реализация советского права [Socialist Legal Consciousness and the Realization of Soviet Law] (1984); N. A. Bura, Функции общественного правосознания [The Functions of Social Legal Consciousness] (Kyiv, 1986); N. Ia. Sokolov, Профессиональное сознание юристов [Professional Consciousness of Jurists] (1988); among others.

[85] O. F. Skakun, in V. Ia. Tatsiy (ed.), *The Legal System of Ukraine: Past, Present, and Future*, transl.W. E. Butler (2013), I, p. 638.

[86] A recent definition suggested that legal consciousness is a specific normative form of

inclined to distinguished between a "professional legal consciousness" of lawyers, judges, and other legal professionals and a "regional legal consciousness" of the population in given geographical areas.

Although the works of Il'in are now accessible to this conversation, for the most part the dialogue concentrates upon the cognitive dimension of the human intellect with respect to mastering a knowledge of law – a special form of social consciousness called "legal consciousness": "... a relatively autonomous and most rationalized component of the legal system of society accumulating all preceding socio-legal experience while preserving a certain degree of adjustment and reproducing this in legal practice, science,and education".[87] The conclusions of Il'in are seen to have been the following:

(1) the reflex of legal consciousness is a specific form of social consciousness that incorporates the legal knowledge of people, their thought, feelings, and emotions, and determines their attitude towards surrounding legal phenomena;

(2) legal consciousness in and of itself is generated by objective conditions of human life and at all stages of historical development is the product of a reflection of their social being;

(3) reflexive legal consciousness is the major regulator of human behavior in society, which suggests that any study of individuals, social groups, or society as a whole necessarily engages an encounter with the phenomena of legal awareness or consciousness of various kinds of social relations, suchc as power and subordination, poverty and wealth, and others;

(4) legal consciousness imparts to human activity in the legal domain a purposeful character that enables human behavior to be shaped and directed towards achieving results set out by society or a specific individual.[88]

social consciousness that reflects and influences legal reality and forms certain notions and judgments about municipal and international legal phenomena on the basis of legal traditions and social experience in the system of ideas, views, doctrines, including a mentally aware and unaware attitude towards them, the legal behavior of subjects of law, the activity of law enforcement and other agencies reinforced by feelings, emotions, motives, aims, and will as a process sof self-reglation of a behavioral act achieving a socially significant purpose with respect to the operation of law. See F. Sh. Iambushev, Правовое сознание в механизме правового регулирования общественных отношений [Legal Consciousness in the Mechanism of Legal Regulation of Social Relations] (2003), p. 60; cited in Skakun, note 85 above, p. 638.

87 Pogrebnaia, note 79 above, pp. 6-7.

88 See L. V. Grineva, «К вопросу о рефлексии правосознания в формировании правового государства» [On the Question of the Reflex of Legal Consciousness in Forming a Rule-of-Law State], История государства и права [History of State and Law], no. 5 (2011), p. 2. Also see P. P. Marchenia, «Общественное правосознание в отечественной истории» [Social Legal Consciousness in Fatherland History], Вестник Московского университета МВД России [Herals of Moscow University of the Ministry

The decision of the early Soviet leadership to bring "legal consciousness" into play in order to redress the sins of the prerevolutionary legal order has meant that the dialogue concerning the content and meaning of legal consciousness has in the twentieth century been principally a domestic Russian dialogue carried on in a literature unexplored, from this vantage point, by foreign legal scholarship and, indeed, unknown to western legal scholarship. For the most part, the discussion of legal consciousness in post-Soviet doctrine is reminiscent of an episode in "authoritarian" and "post-authoritarian positivism".

Given the current preoccupations of western comparative legal scholarship with "legal culture", it is remarkable that considerations of "legal consciousness" have remained largely outside that dialogue. Some are inclined to dismiss the entire discussion as essentially "Marxist" in origin and character, ignoring the roots of the concept in nineteenth and early twentieth century legal philosophy. Although there is some awareness of "consciousness" in comparative legal analysis,[89] the term "legal consciousness" is rarely encountered and explored even less. Consider, for example, the proposition that Western and East Asian cultures differ in individualism and collectivism – such differences expressed, *inter alia*, in respective legal systems, rules, and institutions, that such differences may be partly indebted to culture-gene coevolution,[90] and that the modern legal history of right-bank and left-bank Ukraine is typically characterized as evidence of divergent emphasis given to individualism and collectivism.[91]

In light of this long and variegated history of the concept of legal consciousness, we must be wary of attempts by any one field of inquiry to arrogate for itself an exclusive claim to the investigation of the subject. Although in contemporary English-language scholarship, the term would appear to be the more or less exclusive property of empirical legal

of Internal Affairs of Russia], no. 1 (2006), p. 158; D. Chuikov, «Понятие правосознания» [Concept of Legal Consciousness], История государства и права [History of State and Law], no. 21 (2007), p. 39.

[89] See H. Patrick Glenn, *Legal Traditions of the World* (2d ed.; 2004), pp. 55n., 150.

[90] See J. Y. Chiao, K. D. Blizinsky, V. A. Mathur, and B. K. Cheon, "Culture-Gene Coevolution of Empathy and Altruism", in B. Oakley, A. Knafo, G. Madhavan, and D. S. Wilson (eds.), *Pathological Altruism* (2012), pp. 291-299.

[91] See, for example, the dichotomy suggested in Ukraine in the domain of civil law as between East and West. The East is said to be characterized by the "absolute primacy of collective, community, State interests over the individual, a despotic type of power, an egalitarian and regulated social ethic, a significant statization of economic life and low development of private ownership, and the ethical-normative and socio-legislative function of religion", whereas the West of Ukraine is characterized by a "powerful institution of ownership playing a decisive role in economic life, socio-political pluralism, separation of powers, self-government, and secular nature of power, competitive and personalist social ethic, religion as absolute values directed towards comprehending the "Absolute". See E. O. Kharitonov, in Правовая система Украины: история, состояние, и перспективы [Legal System of Ukraine: History, Present, and Future] (Kharkov, 2011), III, p. 83.

sociology, it is clear that there are normative dimensions of the concept that can be properly treated only within a more traditional jurisprudence, and others that would appear to be the proper concern of philosophy of law. At the same time it has to be seen as a crucial dimension of the study of legal cultures, and hence equally crucial for the comparative study of legal systems.[92] Properly understood, legal consciousness must be seen to inhabit a critical territory necessarily contiguous with several fields of inquiry at once, and to be an essential component in the complete description of any functioning legal system. It is possible that the neglect of this concept in so much contemporary legal scholarship can be traced to a widespread lack of clarity about its provenance, and an equally widespread uncertainty about who "owns" it.

[92] Most modern western treatments of comparative law and legal theory have little to say, if anything, about legal consciousness. No mention is made as such in M. Adams and J. Bomhoff (eds.), *Practice and Theory in Comparative Law* (2012); M. Bussani and Ugo Mattei (eds.), *The Cambridge Companion to Comparative Law* (2012); W. L. Twining, *General Jurisprudence: Understanding Law from a Global Perspective* (2009). On occasion the term is used to mean "legal awareness" in substance rather than "legal consciousness", a fine distinction that can sometimes be pushed too far. See, for example, the subsection entitled "The Legal Consciousness of Merchant Capital", in J. Adelman, *Republic of Capital: Buenos Aires and the Legal Transformation of the Atlantic World* (1999), pp. 227-235.

A Note on the Translation

As suggested above in the essay on "The Concept of Legal Consciousness," Il'in's text *On the Essence of Legal Consciousness* cannot be intelligently read without consistently maintaining the distinction between *право* and *закон* (analogous to the distinction in German between *Recht* and *Gesetz*). Because English does not possess these paired terms designating two different conceptions of law, translators often adopt the policy of simply translating them both as "law". One could at least mount an argument that this policy does no particular harm in the context of the common-law tradition of legal theory. However, in the context of the civil law tradition, where the distinction is permanently and deeply rooted, any such argument falls at the first hurdle. And because the present text is firmly fixed in the civil law tradition, some device must be adopted to maintain the distinction throughout. Given that Il'in uses the term "право" [*pravo*] more frequently than 'закон' [*zakon*], the former has been translated simply as "law". To signal the fact that Il'in has used the term "закон" it is always translated by using a subscript "z" following the term "law" (i.e., law_z).

It is useful to note that Il'in uses the term "закон" in two different contexts. The first, and by far the most common, is in referring to statutory law, which he usually describes as the "positive" law, as contrasted with "natural" law. However, the term "закон" arises in the context of references to "the $laws_z$ of nature" or even, occasionally, "the $laws_z$ of spirit". "Law_z" in this sense refers to observed regularities in phenomena which are conditioned (in some sense) by contingent circumstances. Il'in is entirely consistent in restricting the use of "закон" to these two contexts throughout.

A second challenge to the translator arises in the case of another pair of terms which Russian and other languages possess, but which, again, English lacks. Russian possesses *two* terms, both of which are usually translated into English simply as "object", without distinction: "предмет" [*predmet*] and "объект" [*ob'jekt*]. These are more or less exactly parallel to the pair of German terms "*Gegenstand*" and "*Objekt*". For some subject matter this practice of ignoring the distinction arguably does little harm. However, in certain philosophical contexts the two terms reflect an important, systematic difference between two conceptions of objectivity, and to ignore the terminological distinction is to fail to grasp a significant aspect of the philosophical argument.

In this text it is clear that Il'in is generally using the term "объект" (and the corresponding adverbial and adjectival forms "объективно" and "объективный") in discussing things the *value* or *being* of which is *unconditioned*, that is, not relative to or dependent upon some other thing or condition. Thus, what has "objective being" in this sense depends upon nothing else for its being; and what has "objective value" in this sense has value *in itself*, or *intrinsic* value, independent of a relation to anything other than itself. Such being or value transcends the realm of ordinary, contingent existence.

On the other hand, what is "objective" in the other sense [предметный] pertains to things or states the existence of which belongs to the realm of the contingently existing. For example, knowledge of the laws of nature could be described as "objective" [предметное] if it accurately reflects the regularities of contingent events in nature. However, both the objects of nature and the state of my understanding of them have *conditions* (of different types), in the absence of which neither could be what it is, or be explained. In such contexts Il'in almost invariably uses forms of "предмет" and not "объект".

Some device must be adopted to preserve this distinction if all of the obviously intended philosophical implications of Il'in's discussion are to be kept in view for the anglophone reader. The least obtrusive such device seems to be to introduce the systematic (mis)spelling "objekt" (along with the alternative forms "objektive" and "objektively") whenever "объект" (or one of its forms) occurs in the text. Thus "предмет" and its various forms will be translated with the standard spelling of "object" ("objective", "objectively"), whereas "объект" and its forms will always be (mis)spelled with a "k".

There are a few instances where it is not entirely clear that Il'in has consistently maintained the distinction between two types of objectivity just drawn. However, in the overwhelming majority of cases the distinction does appear to be consistently maintained, and thus to ignore it would be a defect in the translation.

For a more extensive discussion of some of the intricacies of translating Il'in's philosophical texts, the reader may refer to the "Notes on the Translation" (pp. lxii-lxviii) in volume one of my translation of Il'in's *The Philosophy of Hegel as a Doctrine of the Concreteness of God and Humanity* (see the Bibliography below).

A final stylistic note concerning the text of the translation: there are two sets of footnotes, those belonging to Il'in and those supplied by the translator/editor. Il'in's footnotes are relatively few in number and are signaled by asterisks in the text. My own footnotes are numbered and intermixed with Il'in's. For ease in distinguishing the two at a glance, Il'in's footnotes are printed in a bold font, whereas mine are printed in a normal font.

I. A. IL'IN

ON THE ESSENCE OF LEGAL CONSCIOUSNESS

(1919 &) 1956

Chapter One
The Problem

The historical epoch now being experienced by the nations must be comprehended as an epoch of great *spiritual unmasking and revision.*

The calamity of world wars and revolutions,[1] which has overtaken the world and shaken the entire life of nations to its very root, is in essence a natural phenomenon, and therefore it can have only natural causes and grounds. But everywhere nature flares up, where it, once ignited, seizes possession of people's affairs and fates, everywhere that people find themselves helpless before its blind and shattering upsurge, there is everywhere hidden the imperfection, or immaturity, or degeneracy, of the *spiritual culture* of humanity: for the business of this culture consists precisely in subordinating every element of nature whatever to *its* law, *to its* development and to its *end.*[2] A natural calamity always reveals the *defeat*, the limitation and the failure of spirit, for the creative transformation of nature remains its highest task. And however great this calamity, and however vast and overwhelming the sufferings caused by it, the human spirit must *accept* its failure and in the very acuteness of its suffering discern a call to rebirth and regeneration. But that means comprehending the disaster befalling us as a great *spiritual unmasking*.

The nature that by now has involved humanity in the immeasurable misfortune of great wars and upheavals is the nature of *a disordered and embittered human soul.*

However great the significance of the material factor in history,[3] with whatever power the needs of the body rivet to themselves the interest and attention of the human soul,[4] the human spirit is never reduced, and never will be reduced, to a passive, non-acting medium subordinated to material influences and the demands of the body. Moreover, a blind, unconscious obedience to these influences and demands diminishes spirit's dignity, for its dignity consists in being *a creative cause*, *creating* its life in accordance with higher ends, and not in being a passive medium

[1] This chapter was originally written in 1916, in the midst of the First World War. As of 1953, now in the aftermath of the Second World War, when the manuscript was finally completed (chapters 11 through 22), Il'in obviously saw no need to modify the description of the depths of global disorder he had penned almost four decades earlier.

[2] In some respects Il'in seems to be presupposing a generally Hegelian perspective in this work, if only in outline. This theme of spirit emerging from nature, transcending it, and subordinating nature (especially *human* nature) to itself is consonant with the general outlines of Hegel's philosophical system. However, in the main, the argument that Il'in constructs here is distinctively his own.

[3] Presumably a reference to the central thesis of Marxist "historical materialism".

[4] Evidently a reference to Plato's *Phaedo* at 83d.

of natural processes in matter. Every influence entering into the human soul ceases to be a dead weight of causality and becomes a living inducement, attraction, reason, subject to spiritual transformation and rational guidance. To the very essence of the human spirit belongs this gift: to apprehend, interpret, transform and direct anew every influence intruding from without. And to the extent that the human spirit does not possess this gift in sufficient measure, to that extent natural elements of the world oppress it and fracture its life; to that extent its *immaturity* is unmasked and revealed, to that extent new *tasks* and the possibility of new *achievements* open up before it.

But in order to take possession of this gift and use it in all its world-transforming power, the human spirit must take possession of *its own nature*: the nature of the irrational and semi-rational soul. It is impossible to organize the world of matter not having organized the world of the soul, for the soul is the essential creative instrument for organizing the world. A soul submissive to chaos is powerless to bring about a cosmos in the external world: for a cosmos is created in accordance with higher *ends*, while a psychic chaos rushes about, confused, among a multiplicity of trivial, contradictory "ends," obedient to blind instinct. The unsettled soul retains a real potentiality for spirit: it perceives and refracts, but does not transform and direct anew the influences intruding from without. Its "ends" remain passive marks of causal pressures, and their confusion is always fraught with new calamities. Internally unsettled in its tasks, strivings, and abilities, the human soul vainly seeks salvation in mastery over the external world: in technically conquering matter, it creates for itself only a new helplessness; in overcoming external nature, it prepares an insurrection of internal chaos; its successes forge the mould for a new, unexpected defeat.

Presently, before our eyes, the modern world repeats the path of ancient suffering; the new experience leads to old conclusions. These conclusions once again teach that self-knowledge and the self-transformation of the human spirit must lie at the basis of all life, so that life should not fall victim to chaos and degradation; they teach that the inner disintegration of the human soul renders social order impossible and that disintegration of social organization leads the life of a people to ignominy and despair.[5] And still more, these conclusions teach that the formal orderedness of the individual soul and of the social economy doesn't make the life of a human being secure from substantive degeneration and criminal ways. Through all the sufferings of the world the ancient truth arises and flares up, and summons people to a new understanding, recognition and realization: *the life of a human being is justified only when his soul lives from a single, objective center, moved by an authentic love of Divinity as the supreme good.* This love and the will born of it lies at the base of the entire developing spiritual life of a human being, and outside of it the soul wanders, becomes blind, and stumbles. *Outside of it* knowledge becomes

[5] These are familiar Platonic themes, drawn in particular from the *Republic*.

a parody of knowledge, art degenerates into an empty and banal form, religion is converted into a dishonest self-intoxication, virtue is replaced by hypocrisy, law and the State become instruments of evil. Outside of it a human being cannot find a single suitable *end in life* that would convert all of his "activities" and "business" into a single *affair of Spirit* and would assure the human spirit of its victory. Only a vital and authentic craving for Perfection ensures this victory, for it is itself the source of the greatest *power*, invincible by any "circumstances" whatever, and introducing order into the inner and the outer world. This is explained by the very nature of spirit: it is that *creative power of the soul that seeks authentic knowledge, virtue and beauty, and intuiting the Divinity as the real focal point of any perfection whatever, cognizes the world in order to realize His law in it as its own.* But the soul, ever preserving within itself the potentiality for spirit, can convert this possibility into actuality only when within the soul there flares up, as a holistic and joyous fire, a love for the Divine and a craving *to become Spirit*, to find a path to it, and to reveal it to others.

History shows that it is not easy for a human being to find this path, that it is difficult to follow it, and easy to lose it. The chaos of trivial desires and petty ends imperceptibly disperses the powers of the soul, and human passions extinguish its fire. The soul loses its access to spiritual contents and therefore cannot maintain the form of spirit: for it can be in the shape of spirit only when it lives authentically by means of spirit's real contents. Having lost the shape of spirit, it becomes a victim of its own chaos and gets carried away by its spinning to collapse and calamities. And then its task is to perceive in these very calamities and sufferings its own falling away from God, to hear His call, to recognize His voice, and subject its own false path to unmasking and reexamination.

At present philosophy has the great and responsible task of initiating this reconsideration and unmasking. Such a staggering spiritual failure of humanity as a stream of unheard of wars and unprecedented revolutions witnesses with unquestionable power and clarity to the fact that *all* aspects of spiritual existence lived and developed along false paths, that *all of them* are in a state of deep and severe crisis. Humanity lost its way in its spiritual life, and chaos overtook it with unheard-of calamity. This witnesses to the fact that *the very mode of spiritual life was false*, that it must be reexamined to the roots, and renewed and regenerated from the roots up.

And if the task of organizing a peaceful and just community of people on earth is a task for law and legal consciousness, then the contemporary crisis lays bare above all *the profound disease of contemporary legal consciousness.*

In the souls of people there are always such aspects that can for a long time not attract sufficient attention to themselves, dwelling in obscurity from generation to generation, only partly recognized. This occurs not only because these aspects possess in their very essence an instinctive character and are, as it were, crowded out from the field of consciousness;

and not only because they are in themselves spiritually insignificant or secondary in practical terms and, as it were, get lost among other equally inessential nuances of life—but also because the cultivation of them requires a particular effort of will and attention, while their spiritual significance, in terms of their basic nature, stands opposed to the self-interestedness and myopia of everyday consciousness.

One can always find quite a few people prepared to be sincerely surprised at the fact that in them dwells a certain worldview, that they possess their own particular *aesthetic* taste, that they stand in a certain constant relation to the voice of *conscience*, that they possess a *legal consciousness* characteristic for their souls. And meanwhile each person, independently of his age, education, intellect and talent, lives by these aspects or functions of the soul, even when he himself has no suspicion of it. In such case his judgments and actions are formed directly under the guidance of instinctive attractions and impulses and express the structure of his psyche, his personal character, his individual level of life, despite the fact that he perhaps knows nothing of this and does not even suppose that people inevitably have a worldview and a legal consciousness, that they inevitably live according to an aesthetic taste and a conscience. A limited, narrow, obtuse worldview remains a view of the world; undeveloped, perverted, bad taste makes an aesthetic choice in its own way; a suppressed, deadened conscience, not listened to, still struggles and calls from within, and a deformed, unfree, weak legal consciousness directs people's acts and creates their relations throughout life.

It is impossible for a human being not to possess legal consciousness; everyone who realizes that there are other people in the world besides himself possesses it. A human being possesses legal consciousness independently of whether he knows it or does not know it, values this asset or looks upon it with disdain. The entire life of a human being and his entire fate are formed with the participation of legal consciousness and under its guidance; moreover, to live means for a human being to live by means of legal consciousness, within its function and within its terms: for it always remains one of the great and necessary forms of human life. It also lives in the soul even when positive law is as yet lacking, when there is as yet neither "law$_z$" nor "custom", when no "authority" whatever has yet spoken of "rightful," correct behavior. A naive, half-conscious, immediate conviction that not all the external acts of people are equally admissible and "correct," that there are completely intolerable actions and there are "just" outcomes and decisions—this conviction, as yet unaware of the distinction between "law" and "morality", lies at the basis of any "law$_z$" and "custom" and genetically precedes any law-creating activity. And even in those cases when the content of custom and law$_z$ is defined by the self-interest of the powerful, when law is "unjust" or "bad" law—at its basis lies nevertheless an immediate conviction of the necessity and possibility of distinguishing "correct" and "admissible" from "incorrect" and "inadmissible" behavior and of regulating people's lives on the basis of this generally-obligatory criterion.

In this is revealed the distinctive tragi-comedy of living under law: deformed, perverted legal consciousness remains legal consciousness, but it perverts its content; it addresses the *idea* of law, but takes from this idea only a *schema*, uses it in its own way, abuses it and fills it with unworthy, perverted content; there arises *unjust law* [*неправое право*][6] which however is called "law" and is presented as law, compromising the very *idea* of law in people's minds and undermining faith in it.

This tragicomedy is characteristic not only of law-creating activity; it is the tragicomedy of the entire spiritual life of humanity. Every person possesses within his exclusive individual inner experience the sole medium connecting him with the heights of spirit—with the true, the good, the beautiful, with revelation and the law—and the sole source for cognizing them and for judgements concerning them; each one knows concerning these objects only that which he has independently and authentically experienced and creatively verified.* And so people continually forget about these fundamental conditions of spiritual activity: they do not seek authenticity in experience and objectivity in research, but base themselves on personal inclinations and satisfy themselves with subjective opinions. And as a result of this there arises an unworthy and comical spectacle: people make judgments concerning what is most important and supreme, not knowing what they judge; each one makes claims, and encroaches, having no basis for it; supra-personal self-manifesting truth [сверхличная очевидность][7] is replaced by personal certainty; there arises an endless multiplicity of disagreements, the mind wanders, vacillates, and arrives at a fruitless "subjectivism" and a groundless "relativism". Belief in the possibility of genuine knowledge, in the unity of the good, in the objektive value of beauty, in the possibility of genuine revelation, in just and spiritually true law, is lost, and with it inevitably the will to discover the true path to the cognition and realization of these supreme contents withers. Personal interest remains the sole guide, and life imperceptibly degenerates.

This objektivity of the content of the object as it relates to law can be described such that in the external relations of person to person there is a certain *unitary and objektive rightness* [правота] which it is possible to cognize only through *inner experience*, through an *authentic, objective examination and disclosing of natural law*. The experience of natural law is inherent in every person, but for the majority it remains a vague, uncertain and unrecognized "feeling of right", as it were an "instinct for the right" or in the best case an "intuition of right". To become aware of the content of this natural law and to disclose it means to initiate a mature *natural legal consciousness*, to make it an object of *will* and justified

6 Alternatively, "unrightful law".

*** Comp. my work *The Axioms of Religious Experience*, chapters 1-3. See also the three speeches "The Religious Meaning of Philosophy".**

7 Очевидность (roughly speaking, "self-evidence") was a technical term for Il'in, used fairly frequently, and is probably best translated as "self-manifesting truth."

emotion, i.e., to convert this unitary and objektive rightness into a needed and desired end in life—it means to develop and realize in oneself a natural legal consciousness.

In particular, a *natural legal consciousness* as the object of knowledge of the "most" "genuine" unitary *law* itself must lie at the basis of *any* judgment of "law" and of any legal or judicial [правового и судебнаго] decision, and for that reason it must also lie at the basis of those "laws$_z$" which are established in various communities and States by authorized representatives under the name of "positive law". The more developed, mature, and profound the natural legal consciousness, the more perfect will be in such a case both "positive law" and the external life of the people guided by it; and conversely: vagueness, inconsistency, lack of objectivity and weakness of natural legal consciousness will create "non-objective," i.e., senseless, false, unjust "positive law" not corresponding to its prototype. Then the "law," unitary and true according to its idea, bifurcates and enters into a peculiar internal contradiction with itself: natural legal consciousness does not affirm what a knowledge of positive law speaks of, and as a result the soul acquires *two* different legal consciousnesses, for side by side with natural legal consciousness there arises a *positive legal consciousness*, not corresponding with it in terms of content. Such a bifurcation of the law, such a contradiction of legal consciousnesses, witnesses, of course, to a spiritual failure befalling a human being: he doesn't succeed—owing to lack of will or insufficient ability—in becoming aware of the content of natural law and placing it in the unshakable foundation of any judgement concerning "positive" law; but since the ability always depends upon the heart which loves, and upon the will which forges and cultivates the ability, then all that great spiritual failure in the matter of law-creating activity rests upon the universal, historically stable *hardening of hearts and lack of will to just law* [*правому праву*].[8]

[8] This formula, "*правое право*" ("just law" or "rightful law") – at first glance a somewhat odd formulation, involving the adjectival form and the noun form of the very same word – should remind us of a possibly influential precedent in the German language: the notion of *richtige Recht* developed by Rudolf Stammler in his widely read work *Die Lehre vom den richtigen Rechte* (1902); translated as Stammler, *The Theory of Justice* (1925). "*Richtig*" would be "right, correct or just"; thus the formula "*richtige Recht*" could be translated as "just law" or "right law". The primary meaning of the German term *Recht* itself is "right," but it has the further meanings of "law" or "justice", so the English translation of Stammler's title as "The Theory of Justice" is supportable. These linguistic features point to a close linguistic connection in both German and Russian among the notions of "justice", "rightness", and "law" in the sense of *право* or *Recht* (but not of *закон* or *Gesetz*). Linguistically as well as conceptually there would appear to be little to choose between translating the Russian phrase *правое право* as "just law" or as "right law", Such phrases came easily to Il'in, as he was developing a version of natural law theory.

Stammler (1856-1938) was Professor of Law at Halle from 1885 to 1916. He developed a distinction between the *concept* of law, which he described as essentially formal, and the *ideal* of law which was justice. He conceived the task of legal theory as a search for a theoretically valid ideal of justice with which law ought to conform and was consequently regarded as attempting to revive a version of natural law doctrine. However, he insisted that this ideal content of law was not fixed but variable, depending

From this it is already clear that normal legal consciousness leads not to a bifurcated, but to a unitary and holistic life, and if that consciousness sees before it an historically given bifurcation of law, then it wholly devotes itself to the struggle for a unitary, just law [*правое право*] and for the restoration of its own inner, objective spiritual unity. At the same time, it, as a spiritually true and *holistic relation of the soul to the Law*, is not reduced to "consciousness" and "cognition", but lives always in the form of a will to perfection, justice [справедливость] and right [право], awakened by the heart and conscience. Normal legal consciousness *knows* its object; it is a knowing will to the law, *recognizing* it in its objektive significance and obligatoriness, and recognizing it because the will recognizes its *end*. Therefore, normal legal consciousness is above all a will to law as an end, and for that reason also a will to the law; and from this the necessity arises for it to *know* the law and the necessity to realize it in life, i.e., *to struggle for the law*. Only in this holistic form does legal consciousness appear as *normal legal consciousness* and become a noble and inexorable power, nourishing itself from the life of spirit, and in turn determining and cultivating spirit's life on earth.

Normal legal consciousness can be depicted as a particular mode of life by which the soul lives, *objectively and truly* experiencing the law in its fundamental idea and in its singular modifications (institutions). This order of psychic life is of course something ideal, though not in the sense that this "ideal" would be unrealizable. On the contrary, this mode of life is already given *in embryo* to each person, and depends upon each of us to become aware of, develop and establish this embryo in ourselves. And in this self-training the closest dependence is discovered between the "awareness" and the vital "strengthening": the investigation of normal legal consciousness succeeds only in the presence of a creative will to the law as an end, but precisely an objective cognition of this end strengthens the vital will to it.

The scholar putting before himself this task enters inevitably into a struggle with a whole multiplicity of prejudices: a *relativist viewpoint on the law* will be perhaps the most persistent of them.

Seemingly, the very conditions for the creation and realization of the law favor this prejudice. Within the law, apparently, everything is relative. Human consciousness gets accustomed surprisingly easily

upon the differing histories and cultures of specific nations. Reduced to a slogan, this became "natural law with a changing content", a doctrine well known to most European legal theorists in the early twentieth century. Il'in's conception of a body of "natural law" lying at the foundations of positive law, which in the ideal case would mainly reflect and articulate that natural law, seems in some ways strongly reminiscent of Stammler's theory (it is known that Il'in was familiar with some of Stammler's work: *Wirtschaft und Recht* was assigned to him as required reading in the Faculty of Law, and he also reported that he had translated Stammler's brochure on *Die Theorie des Anarchismus* into Russian. See V. A. Tomsinov, *Мыслитель с поющиь сердцем* [The Thinker with a Singing Heart] (2012), pp. 23-25. Given that *Die Lehre vom den richtigen Rechte* was Stammler's most widely-discussed work, and lay squarely at the center of Il'in's field of interest, it is reasonable to assume that he was familiar with it.

and firmly to the idea that the law is "conditioned" by time and place, interest and power, persistent will and blind chance. What is "now" and "here" the law may "tomorrow" and "here", or "now" and "there", not be law; what is forbidden today may be permitted tomorrow and perhaps imposed as obligatory a month from now; organized interest becomes a power and pronounces as "just" what tomorrow will be overthrown as an "accidental" confluence of circumstances. Within the archives are preserved piles of "outmoded norms" and entire codes, and a resourceful mind, serving a momentary interest, is able to interpret and adapt "prevailing" law however one wishes. The content of the law is always sufficiently "indefinite" and "conditional", and its meaning is always "provisional" and "relative".

Contemporary legal consciousness grows and lives in this conviction; it is deeply penetrated by relativism and doesn't know about itself that it can and must be other. The conviction that law is something "relative"—both in terms of its content and its obligatoriness—arises imperceptibly, unconsciously, and for that reason is rooted in souls particularly strongly and deeply: this conviction converges with selfish and myopic interest, is nourished by it, and in its turn, serves such interest. There arises a vitally important vicious circle: darkness begets evil, and evil supports the darkness. "Educated" and uneducated circles of people identically decline to believe in the objektive value of law and do not respect its prescriptions; they see in it either an unpleasant constraint, or in the best case, a convenient means for defense and attack. Legal consciousness is reduced to a stock of unreasoned bits of information from the sphere of positive law and to the ability to "make use" of them; but behind this "knowledge" and "use" it conceals in itself the most profound failures and defects, inward degeneracy and spiritual impotence.

A blind, self-interested, unprincipled, and impotent legal consciousness directs the life of humanity. And thus these diseases of legal consciousness unleashed the natural element of the soul and prepared its spiritual failure.

The life of spirit requires indeed a profound re-examination and renewal.

Chapter Two
Knowledge of the Law

Normal legal consciousness is by no means reducible to *a true knowledge of positive law*. In general it is not reducible to "knowledge" alone, but includes within itself all the fundamental functions of psychic life: above all will, and moreover, in particular, *the spiritually cultivated will*; and then also feeling and imagination and all the civilized and order-producing functions of the human soul. It also cannot be reduced to the experience of "positive law" alone, but always approaches it with a certain higher, objective criterion; finally, it is not a passive state but vitally active and creative. For that reason mere knowledge of positive law, a true comprehension of it, does not guarantee the presence of normal legal consciousness.

And all the same this knowledge is essential. A people not knowing the "laws$_z$"[1] of its country leads an existence outside of law, or is satisfied with self-made and unstable rudiments of law. People who do not know their duties are also not in a position to observe them, do not know their limits and are helpless against extortion by a "warlord", a usurer or a robber; people not knowing the bounds of their authority transgress them arbitrarily, or yield in cowardly fashion to power; people not knowing their prohibitions easily forget any restraint and discipline or turn out to be doomed to legal irresponsibility. Ignorance of positive law leads inevitably to the arbitrariness of the powerful and the intimidation of the weak. What is more, they render impossible a life within law and according to law. People remain in the condition of animals or of things reached by no voice appealing to what is "permitted", what is "required", and what is "prohibited", even though it is forbidden to them "to speak of ignorance of the law$_z$"; and not being responsible, they cannot even lay claim to an irresponsibility degrading to humanity.

It is necessary and fitting for a people to know the laws$_z$ of their country; such knowledge enters into the make-up of life under law.[2] Law speaks in the language of consciousness and addresses consciously aware beings; it asserts and negates, it formulates and requires—in order that people *should know* what is asserted and what rejected, and *become aware* of the formulated requirements. And one to whom it "permits", "prescribes", and "forbids" is a *subject* of legal powers, obligations and prohibitions, i.e., a *subject of law*. The very *essence*, the very *nature of law,* consists in being created by consciously aware beings and *for* consciously aware beings, *by thinking subjects* and *for thinking subjects*.

[1] The subscript 'z' signals that the Russian term translated was a form of *zakon* (equivalent to the German *Gesetz*); the term "law" or "legal" without the subscript translates the Russian *pravo* (*Recht*).

[2] The Russian phrase is правовой жизнь, more literally "a legal life."

For this reason that form of life in which knowledge of their law is not accessible to a people is absurd and dangerous: when, for example, among a people there are illiterate individuals, or when the law is inscribed in a foreign tongue, or when the text of the laws$_z$ remains inaccessible for a people,* or when the meaning of the law is expressed in a manner too complicated, intricate and incomprehensible. Then in the best case there arises between the people and the law a hierarchy of greedy intermediaries levying a special tribute for "finding" the law and servicing popular ignorance to their own profit; it is advantageous to them to render clear matters obscure, rather than to clarify what is obscure, to rescue a "hopeless" case and introduce falsehood into the court; and in their "experienced" hands the interpretation of the law$_z$ is soon converted into professional misinterpretation. Thus, the population's legal consciousness degenerates, owing to the impossibility of absorbing the law directly into consciousness. It is inadmissible for a human being not to be a subject of the law, for the very essence of law consists in its addressing every responsible human being, if only with prohibitions and prescriptions. And accordingly, it is impossible that a subject of law should be an inanimate thing, an insect or an animal, for law presupposes the capacity for knowledge, understanding, and a corresponding self-control.

However the knowledge of positive law as such only stands on the height when it is *objective*. This means that in addressing the law one must approach it seeing in it *an objektively given content, possessing its finished and definite meaning*; this meaning, previously thought out by someone (the legislator?) and vested with words and phrases must now be *precisely elucidated and understood without distortion*. For one who wishes to really know the positive law, it is necessary to understand that it is above all *given* to him in a ready, completed, established form, as a particular *object* with specific characteristics and properties. This *object*, just as any *object*, demands that perception, attention and thought be adapted to it and have learned to see and understand it. This study, just as any movement toward the *truth,* requires that same conscientious and unbiased "theoretical" approach that characterizes science and is cultivated in scientific instruction.

This does not mean, however, that this approach is characteristic just of the scientist and only of the scientist. No, on one hand it is possible for there to be learned jurists who do not elevate themselves to the theoretical study of law; they are interested in it only in the measure and from the viewpoint of its practical application, and casual "requirements of life" dominate their scientific activity. In their classrooms they educate trainees who are able but lacking in scientific principles, and such educators, often unaware of it themselves, retard the growth of true legal consciousness in the country. On the other hand, a conscientious and unbiased approach

*** Hegel gives the example of the tyrant Dionysius who hung the text of the laws$_z$ so high that no one could read it. Hegel, *Grundlinien der Philosophie des Rechts* (1833), p. 278.**

to the explication of the "precise meaning of the law$_z$" is accessible not only to the "learned" jurist, but also to a simple human being; a lack of general or legal education may hinder him in the *realization* of this precise explication, the absence of ability and practice may hamper him, but an awareness of the importance and necessity of such an unbiased interest in the content of the law, of such a "disinterested" understanding, of such a careful explication, may characterize him in the highest degree.

There is always present in developed legal consciousness an unshakable certainty that *the right and the law$_z$ possess their own definite content* and that each of us attending to the law and encountering its binding decrees, has above all the task of elucidating and understanding without distortion this *objektive content of the law*. And in this certainty people are not mistaken. It is characteristic of the law in its mature and developed form to possess the appearance of norms, that is, *of a thesis expressed in words and establishing a certain order* of external conduct as having juridical significance (for example, of permissions, orders or prohibitions).* A norm of the law appears to the human mind not simply in the form of a coherent grammatical sentence; behind its words is always hidden a definite content from which it is evident that it is a rule of conduct and not the description of *a singular fact* and not a formula *of positive law$_z$*, which speaks of that order which is being realized in actuality. That content is expressed in a legal norm as considered and determined by thought, such that behind each word of the grammatical sentence is hidden a logical *concept with its particular content*. A legal norm by its very essence combines two more or less complex concepts: *prescribed, permitted or forbidden conduct* and the concept of *the human subject* whose form of activity is regulated by this. From this stems the necessity of *an objective logical and normative* examination of the law.

An objective reading and study of legal norms begins with the recognition that every norm as *a logical thesis* and *a rule of conduct* possesses its own objektive content, adjusted to a precise and appropriate understanding.

As a *thesis* connecting two *concepts*, a legal norm stands in the order of meanings subordinate to the law$_z$ of identity and the law$_z$ of contradiction, and subject therefore to formal-logical examination.** It

* **I attempted to develop and justify this viewpoint in detail in the essay "The Concepts of Law and Power," in *Problems of Philosophy and Psychology*, 1910, number 1. This essay was published also in the form of a separate brochure.** [A translation of this essay can be found in the "Appendix" to this volume].

** **By "meaning" I understand here not "metaphysical essence", and not "absolute value", and not "creative end", but the purely "logical", identical, abstract (from the mode and the act of thought), non-spatial and non-temporal, non-sensory, non-figurative content, insofar as "the objective" and "the ideal" are specifically grasped by an act of pure thinking. A complete explication of its nature requires of course an independent investigation. Unfortunately this term is abused in the philosophical literature, particularly by intellects unaccustomed to differentiated thinking and striving to construct a "system" on the basis of a single term with vague content.**

is necessary to disclose *each* concept hidden behind the verbal text of the norm in a clear and distinct enumeration of the specific and generic characteristics. Here nothing "goes without saying": it is essential to put into question the accuracy of every characteristic in each concept and to impartially *verify the logical content understood in it.*[*] This task is logical-anatomical; the commentator studies and discloses one and the same unknown meaning of a legal norm objektively hidden behind the words "having significance" (or "having had significance" in the past); he exposes theoretically the meaning content of positive law, not pursuing in this any practical end. And the more faithful he remains to this theoretical task, the more exhaustive, consistent and unbiased his analysis, the higher and more refined will be the level of *knowledge of the law*, and correspondingly, of *law-creation,* and of *legal consciousness* in the country. Exploring all the twists and turns of the laws$_z$, determining the variability of the terminology (one concept having two names), uncovering the instability of thought (one name concealing behind itself two different meanings), discovering the presence of concepts with indeterminate content, logically empty and superfluous terms, erecting a classification of juridical concepts and laying bare the limits of meaning of the legal code—he may be positive that his work is essential in the matter of the perfecting of the law and the catharsis of legal consciousness: it creates the scientific basis for the practical interpretation and application of the law, it uncovers logical defects in the formulas of positive law, it facilitates rooting out self-serving misinterpretation, it exposes defects in legal thinking in the country, it elevates the technique of law-creation.

[*] Here arises a complicated problem: from where does one take the material for these logical definitions? After all, positive law often employs juridical terms, not defining them, as though their meaning "goes without saying" and would be known to everyone. Highly advanced scientific theory and legal consciousness make superfluous any excessive burdening of norms with logical definitions: the legislator (but not the scientific commentator) can consider that many terms are already established in science and assimilated by popular legal consciousness in their settled and definite meanings. And all the same it should be recognized that the more complete is the law in the formal sense, the more it is thought out and the more explicit definitions there are contained in its norms, for in scientific theory there always remains something disputed, and in legal consciousness there are things unsettled and subject to the influence of private interest. This does not mean that the law must exhaustively stipulate and pedantically regulate all the singular details of life; no, there will always be much left to the discretion of the legal consciousness of the person applying the norms of law. However, what is *stated* and established in a norm must be disclosed and fixed in it unambiguously.

No matter how broadly a commentator utilizes the comparative study of the norms of that same codex, explanatory documents of the legislator, incontrovertible for the given scientific theory, and all means leading to an understanding of the *objective meaning* of a law$_z$, he will always have in remainder a certain aggregate of indefinable terms, and his task is to plainly distinguish the *precise meaning of the law$_z$* obtained by him from an *interpretation* personally suggested by him. All the power of logical commentating must be directed so as to *have in view*, to understand and set apart the meaning given in the law$_z$ from any addition whatever, no matter from what noble considerations it sprang.

Quite deliberately people began to express legal rules of conduct in the form of *logical theses* and record them. It is not only that "*verba volant, scripta manent*" (spoken words vanish, what is written remains). Living together, people turn to the creation of thought-out legal theses and formulae precisely in order to *preserve*, repeat and disseminate widely a once-discovered "correct" resolution of an argument or a conflict, and to *consolidate* the "correct" mode of conduct found: "let it be *just the same* in all identical cases". But it is precisely *thought* that possesses the particular capability of capturing, securing and preserving its contents, bringing them to maximal clarity and definiteness, and imparting to them inner logical consistency: for it makes of them *meanings* and subsumes them under the laws$_z$ of *identity and contradiction.* Only owing to this can law be successfully solving such tasks as: the preservation and accumulation, clarification and simplification of the rules structuring life; the disciplining of instinctive impulses and arbitrary encroachments through the power of rational *identity*; the gradual schooling of people to *self-limitation* and the gradual enlargement of a *dispute-free* sphere of human relations; and finally, the just "*equalization*" of that which is identical in the lives of people. Law takes the form of objektive meaning in order to introduce into social life the principle of a *rational, peaceful and just order*. And anyone who in the capacity of a consistent subjectivist, who does not perceive in law an obligatory meaning, and reduces everything to more or less unstable subjective "conceptions" and "interpretations", negates this mission of law and contributes to its failure.

To this logical investigation of law is closely adjoined the objective investigation of a norm as a *rule of conduct*. It is clear that one can comprehend a rule only after its logical meaning is disclosed, and frequently the juridical research institute merges the two investigations into one.

Each legal norm is established by *authorized* subjects, and moreover in an *established*, previously planned procedure outside of which it cannot acquire its significance.[*] [3] To investigate a rule of conduct means above all to find an objective, exhaustive answer to these two formal questions: by whom and by which procedure (whether appropriate) it was established. An objektive and convincing resolution of these questions is extraordinarily important for legal consciousness: there may be norms encroaching on the *status of, and the value of, meaningful*, binding "operative" norms, without *any basis whatever*. Not every "dictate of external authority" is capable of giving birth to a legal norm; arbitrary dictates and orders exceeding the competence of the one giving the orders, or simply based on a relation of brute force (e.g., the anti-legal orders of a conqueror in occupied territory) are possible. And indeed a developed

[*] **This is related also to norms of "customary law", arising when a law-applying agency formulates, recognizes as binding, and applies a simple custom as a legal relation.**

[3] The Russian term is *значение* which would normally be translated as "significance". However, in this context it is unmistakably close in meaning to "validity," a point which should be continually borne in mind.

legal consciousness is always able to grasp where law begins and ends and where arbitrariness arises; and, having resolved that question, it is always able to draw appropriate practical conclusions: where it is appropriate to acknowledge and submit, and where it is appropriate to oppose arbitrariness and brute force with all the might of the true believer and up to the heroism of a principled rebelliousness. And history shows that such a legal consciousness managed time and again to have its own way and to defeat enemies by the power of spiritual rightness. Thus does knowledge of the right enter organically into the very essence of a life lived under law.

To investigate a legal norm as a rule of conduct means, furthermore, to establish its *content* exhaustively. The content of each such norm conceals in itself two criteria for the examination of human life: the *first* criterion establishes precisely which actions and statuses of people possess legal significance, i.e., are subject to legal qualification or legal scrutiny and can be "lawful" or "unlawful" (as distinct from juridically "indifferent" or "irrelevant"); the *second* criterion establishes precisely what constitutes the legal significance of these actions or statuses. This legal significance can be reduced to the fact that for certain subjects there are established certain powers, obligations, and prohibitions indicated in the content of the norm. Thus each norm indicates *precisely which actions and statuses of people* establish *which particular* powers, obligations and prohibitions *for precisely which* subjects. This determines the content and the compass of a rule of conduct: certain precisely defined conduct is permitted, required, or forbidden to precisely designated people in precisely defined circumstances. Such a rule is frequently accompanied by a sanction, i.e. an indication of those mandatory expected consequences which must befall a violator of the norm. To investigate a rule of conduct means to find an objectively exhaustive answer to these four questions (or, correspondingly, twelve questions):[4] what, to whom, under which circumstances, and with what sanction it is required, forbidden, or permitted.

Such a thorough analysis obviously requires a research institute, systematic thinking, and methodological work. A true knowledge and understanding of positive law is in the highest degree an arduous and responsible matter, as is all movement toward the truth. The responsibility of the learned jurist requires particular attention, because in the midst of its objektive and unbiased work there often bursts in the clamorous voice of the everyday struggle for existence; and the covert whisper of personal, group or class interest may weave itself in. Motives extraneous to the matter at hand often endeavor to entice the jurist-theoretician onto a path of obsequious accommodation: the growth of legal consciousness compels the powerful and the domineering to seek a legal basis for their power and rule, even where admittedly there can be established no more

[4] The twelve questions would be: *What* is being required, forbidden or permitted?; *To whom* is it being required, forbidden or permitted?; *Under which circumstances* is it being required, forbidden or permitted?; and *With what sanction* is it being required, forbidden or permitted?

than the *outward appearance* of the law. As a counterweight to this, the jurist-theoretician is obliged to remember that the business of scholarship being performed by him must be carried out objectively: he does not concoct, make up, or specially "prep" his results, producing "strains in the law_z". He uncovers the meaning, significance, and content of the positive law objektively, exposing it in all its virtues and deficiencies. He uncovers not only aspects of it already existing in practice, but also those which up to now have remained hidden from sight, concealing within themselves the possibility of new conflicts, perplexities, misinterpretations, and mischief. He does not wait on practical occasions, although he is able to make use of them scientifically; the objektive content of the law is given to him as an object even when a code has not yet been put into effect. People who do not believe in the autonomy and power of pure theoretical knowledge, in its spiritual value and practical importance, can of course disregard such an analysis of the law, considering it a manifestation of lifeless scholasticism. But woe to the person—both physician and patient—studying anatomy only to the extent of the "casual", that is, incidental, demands of life ...

Popular legal consciousness can stand on the heights only when juridical science also stands there. Where jurisprudence is non-objective and biased or, still worse, ignorant and corrupt, there the very core of legal thought degenerates, and respect for the law is soon lost. The theoretician then approximates to the type of the old scrivener,[5] and owing to his "scientific" pettifoggery, legal consciousness soon fades away. In judgments concerning the law an instability and a malignant vagueness set in; everything in the intellect fragments and vacillates; and it is difficult to expect anything from the "earth", when its salt is losing its potency.

A lively contact between juridical science and the consciousness of the masses is the second condition for the development of legal consciousness. The content of positive law must be not only "accessible" to the populace such that each one in every case *could* without difficulty determine his legal powers, obligations and prohibitions; it must be *actually introduced* into the consciousness of the populace in all its determinateness and unambiguous clarity. Legal consciousness consists above all in a person knowing of the "existence" of positive law and of his being "bound" by it; and, further, knowing that the meaning of this law is one and determinate, unalterable by personal arbitrariness or casual interest, and that its content is "such and so". It is essential that everyone actually know according to the law what he "may do", "must do", and "cannot do", so that he, as it were, should perceive with his own eyes the boundaries of his legal "status" with confidence, that they can be altered *in accordance with law, but not contrary to law, and not through evasion of it.*

[5] The Russian term is *подьячий*: also a clerk, notary, or petty government official (especially in old, Muscovite Russia).

It is also clear what a great significance the popular teaching of law and the cultivation of legal consciousness in the schools has for the life of the nation.[6] Generally accessible textbooks of law are indispensable; the teaching of jurisprudence in high schools is indispensable; a required course in legal consciousness taught in institutions of higher education for students of all faculties is indispensable. The presence of a cadre of travelling lecturers and consultants paid by the city or the district councils and free to the populace (similarly to doctors, veterinarians, and agronomists) would have great significance. It is essential to do everything to *bring the law nearer to the populace*, in order to strengthen mass consciousness of law, so that the populace should understand, know and value its laws$_z$, so that it should voluntarily observe its obligations and prohibitions and fairly make use of its legal powers. Law must become a factor in life, a standard of real conduct, a power of the national soul.

And indeed if it be agreed to name the objektive content of positive law its meaning, and the subjectively assimilated content of it its concept, then it would be possible to say: positive legal consciousness consists above all in human beings experiencing a *concept* of positive law *adequate* to its *meaning*. However, legal consciousness would by no means be exhausted by this.

[6] By this time Il'in had made a personal contribution in this cause. One of Il'in's earliest scholarly efforts was a textbook on law for high school students: *Общее учение о праве и государстве: Основы Законоведения* (General Doctrine on Law and the State: Fundamental Principless of Jurisprudence] (1915). 106 p. (Il'in's part only).

Chapter Three
The Significance of Positive Legal Consciousness

The second basis for legal consciousness consists in the fact that positive law is experienced as having *objektive significance*. It has a unified and definite content, characterized by a particular form of "significance" in the life and affairs of a given community of people. This can be provisionally expressed as follows: positive law takes upon itself the responsible task of indicating to people the "*objektively best*" mode of external conduct and "binding" them by means of this indication. How is this to be understood?

A person for the first time encountering the legal regulation of life finds out that among his possible and actual actions and statuses not all of them have legal "significance": that there are those which are in one way or another referred to in law—"stipulated"[1] activities and statuses; and those of which "nothing is said"; and that to the stipulated activities and statuses are ascribed some sort of particular quality, such that certain characteristics, changes, consequences, and so forth are associated with them. And the first thing that strikes his consciousness is that all these characteristics, consequences, conclusions, and so forth *maintain their significance* even in the event that he does not wish to acknowledge them, even if he should act as though he knew nothing of them, or as though they "did not exist at all". It turns out that their "significance" does not require his consciousness, consent, or acknowledgement.

Even before he himself envisaged his future activities and thought about his behavior and statuses, they were in large part stipulated, described, and sorted out in a general way by other people, independently of whether this corresponded to his personal interests, desires, and intentions or not; and at the same time it was established that some of his activities, behavior, and statuses are "important" and are to be taken into account, whereas others are indifferent; and that among the number of stipulated ones, some deeds are "prohibited" for him, such that although he is able to carry them out, he dare not; others are "imposed upon him as a duty", such that, although he could fail to perform them, he *must* carry them out; and a third are "left to his discretion"; however, with the proviso that if he carries them out, he will then not be "permitted" to "take them back" or "annul" them under any circumstances by his own desire alone. He sees that his life is woven into some sort of a net such that in practice he does not have to take it into account, but that it does not become torn because of that, and does not disappear. And, moreover, this net by no means possesses a material character: one can never see it, touch it, or destroy it by physical means. One can find out about it only from written

[1] *Предусмотренные*; stipulated or provided for in advance, anticipated, foreseen, specified or defined in advance.

rules, but in these rules nothing is said about him personally, nor about anyone else in personal terms. "People in general" are spoken of, and "behavior in general" or "actions in general", and from this it "follows" that he too is entangled in an invisible net of some sort of "significances" and "duties". And without difficulty he convinces himself that indeed one can frequently ignore these "duties": do what is prohibited, evade duties, exceed what is permitted. Often "nothing is even due" for this (*lex imperfecta*); occasionally something unpleasant is "due", but one manages to evade it.

The legal net, like every net, has empty spaces; it does not fetter a person by the hands and feet. Law not only does not stipulate *all* activities and statuses of people, but does not even attempt to do that; and concerning what is stipulated, it cannot operate like the laws$_z$ of nature. Law cannot make what is "prohibited" not doable, what is "obligatory" inescapable, "what is permitted" accessible; it prohibits, requires, permits; finally, it threatens with unpleasant consequences and carries them out where it is able; but it is powerless to put a person in that position of *inescapable necessity* in which he would dwell as a natural phenomenon: as a living part of the world a person can only live *by* the laws$_z$ of nature, combining them to his benefit or to his detriment; he is powerless to violate them, but as a *subject of law* he can interweave legal deeds with illegal ones, *lawful with unlawful, violating* law, violating its rules and even slipping through the empty spaces of the legal "net" (for example, the life of a band of robbers).

But then in what does the "significance of law" consist? Should not we really call law$_z$ only what is *inviolable*, only what is unshakably fixed like a fate, leading the compliant and forcibly dragging along the obstinate? What sort of "significance" can be ascribed to law if it is in its very essence violable, if there is the possibility of transgressing and evading it, if it does not put a person in an inescapable position, but merely threatens with unpleasantnesses, which it often does not manage to impose? What do all these "characteristics" and "qualifications" mean, all these "mays", "musts", and "must nots", if it is possible to evade and laugh at them? In what consists the *power* of this *law$_z$*, if in the order of external, material-corporeal existence it so often winds up powerless?

For an individual with an undeveloped legal consciousness all these doubts are sufficient to relegate the significance of law to the sphere of illusions, delusions, fantasies or, in the currently fashionable word, to the sphere of "phantasm".[2] Law *does not possess* objektive significance,[3] as it also does not possess an objektive, meaningful content; however, *it seems to people* that both the one and the other are in it, and, yielding to this

[2] Il'in's reference to the "currently fashionable" term "phantasm" would almost certainly have been widely perceived at the time as pointing to Petrazhitskii, who introduced the term as a prominent part of his technical vocabulary.

[3] In the remainder of this paragraph Il'in is outlining a view that he himself regards as false.

illusion, they *imagine* that they are dealing with something objektively significant and with objective standing. Meanwhile, they need only to examine closely their personal "experience" to be convinced of their mistake: everything is exhausted by their *subjective experiences*, their emotions and the work of imagination, creating various "phantasms".*

Law as something objektive only "seems" such to people; it is like a phantom or an apparition: one need only collect one's spirit, examine it closely—and it turns out to be a play of affects and fantasies; it is like a "double," perturbing a frightened imagination; and perhaps for one not able to unmask this "double" and overcome it with the power of one's own will and thought, it is appropriate to undergo a cure ... by means of an *objective self-blinding, and a relativist naiveté*.

Any legal consciousness whatsoever comes to an end precisely here, for *to become aware of law* is not the same as to possess a tangle of subjective emotions, devoted to a reaction to supposed "commands" and "authorizations". The entire problem *of law* begins only where it is admitted *that not everything which appears lawful is in fact lawful*, only where to subjective opinion concerning law and the infringement of law is opposed the *objektively subsisting, objectively determinate, self-significant* law. [We can speak of legal consciousness in the objective sense][4] only where *disagreement concerning law* is possible, that is, where controversy concerning the legal truth, based upon one and the same meaning of the statements [is possible]—therefore [it is possible] only where the *object itself* exists, and the object has an objektive *meaning* given to adequate understanding. But meaning is grasped not by affect, and not by emotions, and not by the imagination, but by *thought*. And law is not experienced in the form of random and, in terms of content, unfounded "normatively attributive" stimuli and impulses,[5] but

4 The words inserted in brackets here are interpolations by the present translator for the sake of greater clarity.

5 "Normatively attributive stimuli and impulses" are technical terms in Petrazhitskii's theory of law. Normative or imperative impulses would lie behind a feeling of *moral duty* (where the beneficiary of one's possible action has no corresponding *right* or *enforceable claim* on one's benevolence); imperative-*attributive* impulses would underlie convictions of *legal duty* (where one's *duty* toward another is accompanied by a corresponding *right attributed* to the other, where the other is viewed as having an *enforceable claim* for the

*** This view, betraying the profound sickness of Russian legal consciousnesS, was put forward and developed by Prof. L. I. Petrazhitskii. The imperishable contribution of his works was a brilliant and precise descriptive analysis of legal experience; however, this analysis is by no means exhaustive, and remains silent about what is most important: the experience of the *objektive elements of law*. The author consistently defends *relativism* in the understanding of *law* and realizes a *personal subjectivism* in the understanding of experience; as a consequence of this, legal consciousness is converted in his analysis into an *emotional imagining of law*; meaning and value as self-sufficient objects are not examined at all, and defects of *personal* legal and philosophical experience acquire a principled-theoretical interpretation. All this forces one to recognize that a *scientific overcoming of his theory is essential for the true and creative development of Russian legal consciousness.***

is *objectively* perceived and *soundly tested* by the will as an objektively significant institution. Outside of this there is not and cannot be any "legal consciousness"; there will be only non-objective and unfounded judgements of *supposed* law and vague phantasms on themes more or less *similar* to law.

In order to possess a mature legal consciousness, it is essential to undergo in the soul a particular experience which can be indicated as follows: it is above all *an immediate, authentic and distinct experience of something intangible as having objektive significance.** Such an experience, verified and refined by the method of intuition, inevitably gives rise to a *conviction* of the actual presence of an *object* with an objektive significance, and the attempt to grasp this object by thought inevitably forces one to recognize in it its own proper objektive meaning, self-identical and immanent within it, given to appropriate understanding. Such is the schematic path to the assimilation of the essence of positive *legal consciousness as such.***

Thus the development of legal consciousness requires above all work on the broadening and refining *of one's inner spiritual experience*. In this regard a life under law underlies the general and fundamental law of spiritual development and is, like religion, philosophy, science, art, and moral creativity, a variety of the one vital-spiritual activity. But if that is so, then not just any human being, standing on any level of mental and spiritual development, is competent to judge of the concepts and essence of law, and his "objections" against the objektive significance of law will not have any force and persuasiveness, if at the basis lies a boundedness or shakiness of *his personal spiritual experience*. The majority of disputes between relativists and philosophers are based precisely on the fact that the former do not cultivate in their inner experience the objektively subsisting and significant elements, and for that reason do not "see" them, and deny their presence, often not even understanding what, strictly speaking, is at issue.

performance of the duty). Moral duties are "unilateral" whereas legal duties are "bilateral"; to be convinced that one is bound by a *legal* duty (as distinct from a moral duty) is to simultaneously *attribute* a corresponding *right* to another.

*** Such an experience can and must be acquired not only in and for legal consciousness, but also in other spheres having to do with objektively significant objects. Such is, above all, religion; further: theory of knowledge, investigating the nature of truth and cognitive self-evidence, ethics, investigating the nature of good and conscience, and aesthetics, investigating the nature of beauty and artistic taste. The soul possessing such philosophical culture has a ready basis for mature legal consciousness, and in this is discovered, by the way, the significance of philosophical culture in the matter of the development and growth of true legal consciousness.**

**** "Positive legal consciousness", that is, the objective experience of positive law, is distinguished both here and in what follows from natural legal consciousness, however not because these two consciousnesses are opposed and incompatible; on the contrary: natural legal consciousness, as is revealed below, constitutes the deepest ground of positive legal consciousness.**

The development of legal consciousness requires that *each one of us discover the objektive significance of law with the force of self-manifesting truth.* It consists in that qualifications, delimitations and decisions, once having obtained the fully-weighted nature of *law* and its "virtue," *preserve this significance of legal correctness, accuracy and obligatoriness regardless of accidental ignorance, disagreement, or even systematic insubordination from the side of one or another subject of law.*

If, *for example, there are in a country uneducated people knowing nothing* of the existence of *law* in general and not knowing that each of them possesses their own legal "status", that is, possesses a determinate sphere of *legal* powers, duties, and prohibitions, each of them nevertheless retains this sphere with all its consequences. It might happen that *everyone forgets* about some *legal* norm—citizens who must observe it, and the agencies of the State that must apply it—but it as before remains at all times a rule of conduct, retains its meaning and its content; and when they remember it, they will be convinced that the forgetting did not extinguish its objektive significance. But if *ignorance* does not extinguish the law, then disagreement is powerless to suppress or alter it. Any person, restricted by law in his selfish interest, is inclined to grumbling, protest, and disagreement; however, the very essence of law consists in the fact that the bribe-taker, thief, usurer, lawless ruler, and counterfeiter cannot by their "disagreement" alone extinguish the law and render their conduct lawful. The criminal law upholds all of its prohibitions, regardless of the abundance of unapprehended thieves and highly-placed bribe-takers; constitutional law is not distorted and does not "vanish" because there are ministers inclined to violate it; international law retains all of its significance regardless of the fact that it is all too often circumvented in times of peace and not observed in war.

This objektive significance[6] of law is clearly expressed in the fact that the moment of its "establishment" and the moment of its "cancellation" must receive and do receive a strict formal determination. From the normative point of view, law possesses not an "historical genesis" and not a "psychological origin"; it has a *foundation*, determining its significance: it is a certain set of events (for example, the initiation, discussion, approval, promulgation of a law_z, or, the signing and distribution of an instruction, or, the recognition, formulation and application of a custom),

[6] By this point in the text it becomes increasingly clear that Il'in's notion of the "significance" of a norm has a very close connection with the contemporary conception of the "validity" of a norm, the establishment and removal of which are specific, datable events.

***Law as an aggregate of norms is generally not subject to temporal change and development. When one speaks of the development of law, by this should be understood: 1) either the development of legal consciousness and changes in the understanding of legal norms (a real process taking place in time), 2) or the cancellation of an old legal norm and the establishment of a new one replacing it (an ideal-valuational fact, conditioned by temporal events). I attempted to raise this problem in the essay "The Concepts of Right and Power".**

the actual realization of which serves as the *foundation* or *condition* for a rule becoming a "significant" norm of law.* Norms of law "flare up" and "go out" in connection with moments of time, that is, in determining relations with strictly defined temporal events; however, both their "flaring-up" and their "extinguishing" possess not a subjective-psychic nature, but an objektive-evaluative one: thus a judge, mistakenly applying a norm that has been repealed, *believes* that he is applying *law, but in actual fact* he is not applying it, but erroneously committing a nonsensical act; people not knowing of the introduction of freedom of assembly and fearing to attend a meeting, see a prohibition where in *actual fact* there is a legal power, and so on.

It is essential for each individual to verify, and once and for all to confirm in personal authentic experience, with all possible immediacy and clarity, this irreducibility of law to personal *psychic* states,[7] this independence of its significance from irrelevant "ignorances" and "disagreements" and from relevant "violations". One must *make certain* of this on the basis of one's own proper "powers", "duties", and "prohibitions"; one must ascertain that, in rejecting the objektive meaning and objective knowledge of law, a person deprives himself of that basis on which *alone a life under law is possible*: he then no longer has any reason, nor any theoretical or life-derived ground to *argue* about law and *lawlessness*, to be indignant about *arbitrariness*, to appeal to the *court, to insist* on his rights of political freedom, to repudiate by right his *supposed* duty, *to protest* against the violation of his *property* rights, and so forth. For where is the *criterion* for my legal rights, if the content of a legal norm is deprived of any objektive, *self-identical meaning*? And in what consists the significance of *my* right, if the significance of right *in general is* a product of subjective fantasy? A consistent "subjectivism" must have excluded itself from a life under law or hypocritically appealed to objektively significant law, chuckling at the credulity of its audience.

It is clear that he will not succeed in excluding himself from a life under law, for even the most consistent and formal renunciation of his legal powers would not free him from legal *duties and prohibitions*, and as a consequence the deplorable mixture of hypocrisy and naiveté determines his fate to the end.

Law and legal consciousness begin and end where begins and ends the question: "*and what in fact* possesses *legal significance and in what does it consist*?" The judge, the official, the lawyer, and the citizen—if they do not pose that question and do not reach an objective resolution of it – *are not living by law and are not creating law*, and their legal consciousness stands at the lowest level.[8] They are satisfied with surrogates of law, and

[7] Here too Il'in is emphasizing his opposition to Petrazhitskii's characterization of law in terms of individual psychic states.

[8] In contemporary terms, Il'in is stating that absent an agreement on the formal conditions of validity for a legal norm, the participants are not sharing in a fully developed, mature legal system.

falsify it. One who avails himself of the incompetence of the judge, the venality of the official, the "flexibility" of the lawyer or the illiteracy of the neighbor in order to realize his unlawful interest, giving out what is not law for *law*, thinks and acts like a sophist of the lowest order, supposing that "truth is what I am able to convince others of". He works at the degeneration and degradation of the common life.

Quite a bit of time was needed for people to arrive at a mature verification and conviction that these "formulae" and "theses" conceal behind themselves rules or norms with *objektive significance*. The objektivity of this significance consists in that it is truly *inviolable and immutable,* from the very establishing of the norm to its revocation. It is possible not to observe that conduct which the norm requires, and it is possible to violate its prescriptions; a person can slip out of legal bonds and ties, and even "laugh at" them. But the significance of a norm as a "binding", "operative", *significant* law, its *legal significance*, remains essentially inviolate and immutable. One who pays income tax, having cheated the treasury in his declaration, is still *obligated de jure* just as before to pay more than he paid; the deserter is still *subject to military duty* just as before; the criminal in hiding is still *subject to judgment* and perhaps punishment, just as before. Law is violable in the sense that persons to whom it is addressed retain the capacity for self-sufficient direction of their own conduct, and for that reason can fail to perceive in its requirements a reason for a corresponding decision. People may fail to follow the voice of the law, openly transgressing its requirements or hiding from them in a cowardly manner. There is no *inescapability* in practice here: a legal regime is not a convict prison, and a life under law is not a mechanical system. Both the one and the other would be beneath the dignity of humanity and its rational spirit. But, at the same time, the significance of law is such that it actually places a human being before a certain "*normative-evaluative*" inescapability: he is in fact presented with the possibility of insubordination, but there are no *means* for him to alter or extinguish the *anti-legal* nature of his action. A violation of law remains a violation of law even in the case that *no one knows* about it, and even when the one committing it remains in ignorance (for example, an accidental killing on a hunt, taken by everyone to be suicide), and this can be changed neither by "the time limitation on prosecution" (not to mention the "time limitation on punishment"), which establishes the concept of the "statute of limitations for a *crime*), nor amnesty, which creates not the fiction of "the non-criminality of the act committed", but the fiction that "no *criminal act* was committed".

People with a developed and refined legal consciousness not infrequently experience the *anti-legality* of an action as a particular stain, really inhering in it; for them this is not only "the result of an ideal evaluation from the viewpoint of a legal norm": such conduct is actually experienced by them as an *objektively* "dark" matter, and they remain firmly convinced that one cannot rid oneself of this anti-legality by any means, not even by a justificatory verdict of a jury in court: no matter by whom a crime was committed (by the accused or by another hiding in obscurity), whether the criminal should be punished or not—all the same it remains an *objektively anti-legal* action.

In a consciousness having consistently thought through this objektivity of a significant law, there can arise a credible image according to which upon every stipulated human action or status there rests a certain "tonguelet of flame" expressing its legal significance by its color: a blue flamelet expresses the legality of the action or status, red—its anti-legal character.[9] If one may be permitted this image, then a life under law will appear in the form of a multiplicity of blue and red flames, flickering, changing their color, going out and flaring up anew. These flames burn with a blue color regardless of whether people see them or not, and if they do see them, regardless of whether they accurately distinguish their coloring or, like color-blind people, do not gain an understanding of the objektive nature of their colors. It is clear that establishing a new norm does not immediately extinguish the previous flames and does not change their nature, because *the law*$_z$ *is not retroactive*. It is also clear that the application of a law consists not in a law-applying subject igniting and extinguishing flames at his discretion, and furthermore arbitrarily choosing which specific flame to ignite—blue or red; no, his task consists in examining objectively and accurately whether a flame already burns above a given status and activity, and if one burns, which one in particular. His determination may be objektively true or objectively false, for, for example, the blue flame of an innocent man condemned remains blue to the end, notwithstanding that everyone accepts that it is red and the condemned will spend the rest of his life in prison. And if this image were

9 This somewhat startling passage is presumably inspired, at least in part, by Petrazhitskii's doctrine of "emotional *projection*". Petrazhitskii attempted to develop a complete account of all the essential phenomena of law at the level of *individual psychology*. As this account was intended to be a *causal*, empirically scientific, one, he framed it in terms of *impulsions* ("appulsive" and "repulsive" emotions), also referred to as "motor irritants" or stimuli "provoking" (causing) certain specific experiences and (under some circumstances) actions of the individual subject. According to Petrazhitskii, "Legal and moral experiences, and corresponding moral and legal appulsive and repulsive emotions, have such common properties as to justify the formation of a higher class of emotions embracing both legal and moral impulses—*emotions of duty, of obligation: ethical emotions*".

"Motor provocations, aroused in us by different objects (by perceptions or ideas of them) or experienced with reference to them, communicate to corresponding perceptions or ideas special hues, a special tinge, so that the very objects appear to us in a corresponding particular shape, as if they objectively possessed the special underlying qualities. This phenomenon (which has place also in cases and provinces of emotional life) we call *emotional or impulsive projection* or *phantasy*". Leon Petrazhitskii, *Theory of Law and State in Connection with Morality*, (1907, 1908), pp. 33-37, 38, 39; quoted from a translation by Hugh W. Babb in his article "Petrazhitskii: Science of Legal Policy and Theory of Law", *Boston University Law Review*, XVII (1937), p. 793; XVIII (1938), p. 538. Thus, the idea of a certain action as a moral or legal *duty* in some way *binding* me to performance might present itself to me subjectively as an image tinged with a specific hue, signaling the appulsive or repulsive emotion aroused by that idea, independently of whether I am objectively bound by such a duty. Il'in evidently wishes to add the claim that there are such things as the unchanging *objective* hues of the action in question, reflecting the objective status of the action as something required or prohibited, "regardless of whether people see them or not". Il'in was everywhere concerned to "correct" what he saw as the "subjectivist" or "relativist" implications of Petrazhitskii's psychological account of law.

to find access for itself to the soul of the individual and were accepted by the soul, then it would not be able to believe that the truth in the matter of law is "the result of a legal pleading".

This objektive significance of law must not be confused in general with its *power* or effectiveness in life. The significance of law correctly established and not repealed, consists not in people knowing it, understanding it, and deriving from this knowledge motives for corresponding conduct, but in the fact that it preserves in itself a certain *correct standard* and a certain correct rule of conduct, which retains its correctness even when people do not know and do not want to know it. If legal consciousness stands on the lowest level, then the *practical "effect"* of law suffers greatly from that, but the *significance* of it as a standard and a rule is not thereby diminished.

In exactly the same way, if the greater part of a legal code consists of laws, lacking "sanctions," or if the legal order established in the norms is actually not "put into practice", or the regime supporting the realization of law disposes of a weak or inactive apparatus of "coercion", the *objektive significance* of law by no means disappears and is not diminished. *Law* can retain its obligatory, "binding" *significance* and nevertheless not fulfill its *purpose*; such will be the case if between a significant law and legal consciousness there arises discord and alienation. Law then appears powerless in life and fails to achieve its end: consciousness of it either *still* does not influence, or *no longer* influences people's conduct, and its requirements remain appeals in a void.

All this can be expressed as follows: *law is in need of legal consciousness in order to remain a creative, vital force, and legal consciousness is in need of law in order to acquire an objective basis and objektive truth.*

Law only realizes its purpose when legal consciousness takes cognizance of it, fills itself with its content, and permits new knowledge to influence the life of the soul, determine its decisions and guide the person's conduct. Then *law* becomes *a force in the inner* life of a human being, and through it also in his *external* life.

However for that it is necessary that law in its objektive meaning content and in its objektive significance should not only be *grasped in thought and verified in experience, but also acknowledged by the person's will.*

Chapter Four
Recognition of Law

The spiritual purpose of law is *to live in people's souls*, "imbuing" their experiences with its content, and in that manner forming in their consciousness inner *impulses* acting on their life and on their external form of activity. The task of law is *to create motives* for *better behavior in the soul of a human being.*

For the resolution of this spiritual task it is by no means indifferent what these new motives are, what their nature is, and of what quality they are. Admittedly, in jurisprudence there is a view that *motives of behavior* are important in the moral sphere and not important for living under law: all that law requires is an external legal [легальный] form of activity, from whatever impulses it springs; for "law" the disposition of a human being is indifferent, if only he observes the limits of his legal "status". But if one takes this formal and nearsighted view and consistently puts it into practice, then a profound degeneration of law and legal consciousness inevitably arises. The motives for legal behavior can be indifferent only for that sort of consciousness that pulls law away from its fundamental *highest end* and limits its essence to the superficial appearance of a "good" order. Separated from its ultimate task and *from the root of true legal consciousness*, law of course turns into an unprincipled, self-sufficing means; it then limits its spiritual purpose, turning away from the problem of *the content and quality* of life under law, and deteriorating into an empty formal appearance; it is sufficient for it if people obey it out of laziness, observe it out of self-interest, do not break it out of fear; it is sufficient for it if "judging by appearances" everything is "satisfactory", even though behind that appearance is concealed a profound inner degeneration, and behind that satisfactoriness there are approaching disasters and collapses. That view mistakenly takes the *formal indication of a violation of law*, and the limit beyond which criminal prosecution is admissible, for the very *essence of law*; it constitutes a hidden example of "negative definition".

In contrast to this it is essential to recognize that law can realize its spiritual purpose *only when legal consciousness stands on the height*, and its height is measured not only by the knowledge of law, but also by the *recognition* of it, and, moreover, recognition not "from fear", but "from conscience", and not by blind habit, but from sighted, rational *conviction.* Only *a free recognition of law* is not degrading for a human being; only it can fittingly carry out the task of law-creation; only it will find for itself a true ground in the human spirit; only it will be able to reach the final end: the perfection of positive law.

The *recognition* of positive law consists in a human being, having perceived its *objektive content and* its *objektive significance as the self-manifesting truth, voluntarily imposing as a duty upon himself* the observation of its rules, and *cultivating* in that direction not only his own conscious decisions, but also his own immediate, instinctive desires and impulses. In this way he accomplishes a distinctive *spiritual assumption* of positive law, and this assumption requires a particular maturity of mind and will, a particular equilibrium of soul, because it must be accomplished with a *distinct consciousness of the ever-possible profound imperfections of positive law*: this assumption must be sighted, free from idealization and therefore without fail a creative, *transformative* assumption; but just for that reason it requires great steadfastness, self-control and resolute discipline.

The recognition of positive law is hindered by the circumstance that people do not perceive its spiritual *value* and vital *necessity*.

If we leave on one side people who are mentally lazy and indifferent, who generally perceive nothing and do not trouble themselves with "perspectives", then those who *deny law* make up two large groups: some do not recognize law *only in part*, from naive self-interested motives; others deny law *on principle*, by a conscious or instinctive idealism, avoiding "compromises" in life.

The *first* variety of people make up the great majority. Strictly speaking, such a person does not deny law, but recognizes it only *one-sidedly*, only to the extent that it corresponds to *his* interest. Thus, he insists on his powers, but at the same time is always ready to exaggerate them by misinterpretation; he does not like to clarify his duties and is always ready to slip out of performing them; and if fear does not force him to keep within the boundaries of what is prohibited, then carelessness or self-interest will easily turn him into a violator of law or even a criminal. Such a person firmly knows that *others* are "obligated" to him and *what they* do not "dare to do", but he is constantly ready to forget that he is "obligated" to others, and what *he* "does not dare to do". In defending his own interest, he becomes indignant and protests, appeals to "principles", to "law" and "justice", and quickly turns into a predator the moment the law is not managing to shield someone else's interest, or into a liar the moment it succeeds in doing that. Insisting that "this is mine", he is always ready to add, of someone's else's belongings, "and that is also mine." Law is "sacred" for him only so long as the law is going *his* way; in other words, it is for him not "sacred" at all. The entire question of "law" is for him a question of how to arrange for himself a more advantageous and provident "state of affairs" in life, whereas the principle of reciprocity (mutualism) says nothing to his myopic soul: he is incapable of understanding that *his* empowerments live and are nourished by *others'* obligations only thanks to the fact that *others'* empowerments live and are nourished by *his* obligations; he does not understand that the legal order is as it were a net of subjective legal cells, everywhere adjoining and supporting one another, that each cell is whole and living *only so long as* the neighboring cells are whole and living, that the maintenance of the common and single legal order is *a single common concern* and that this concern requires above all that no one trample on the limits of his own legal status. The wise saying that "the freedom of each ends at the limits of the other's freedom" means nothing to this person.[1]

Such an attitude toward law represents one of those diseases of legal consciousness from which only the rare individual is fully free. One need only ask oneself, who among us does not experience a certain negative, unpleasant affect before the thought of "my duty", "my obligation" (provided that duty does not conceal behind itself an "advantageous" empowerment)? And can one guarantee that this negative affect has no influence *whatever*, even unnoticed and unconscious, on the choice of a line of conduct? Of course, the degree of this influence depends on the level of legal consciousness and determination of will; however the disease may also be concealed in nuances.

And thus among those who deny law disinterestedly and on principle, it is appropriate above all to pay attention to those who do not recognize law from a naive or myopic self-interest. To observe their form of activity, to understand its essence and the universal instinctive inclination toward it, is to become convinced that the historical growth of positive legal consciousness is one of the most effective and powerful means of struggling against it—it means to learn a sobering lesson and an instructive argument directed against a supra-legal "idealism". No matter how bitter and harsh this sounds, law and a legal order are essential as a kind of "muzzle" for the self-interested evil will and for the predatory instinct. And everyone must detect this self-interested instinct in himself and say of himself: "yes, for me too positive law is necessary". For the social *animal* a conception of the strict limit of what is permissible and impermissible is essential, in order not to fall into a *struggle of everyone with everyone*, and that idea is as old and inescapable as the world.

The contemporary view of law, asserting this necessity and defending positive law, falls, however, into a profound mistake, reducing all legal consciousness to a *settled habit of taking account of the orders of the external plenipotentiary authority* and obeying them.[2] This view is mistaken because obedience to an external authority as a motive determining the activity of a person is not commensurate with his spiritual dignity, and, moreover, in *all* spheres of spiritual life: in knowledge and in morality, in art, in religion and in law. The most fundamental and profound essence of what humanity always fought for in the name of *freedom* consists in the possibility of *autonomous and voluntary self-determination* in spiritual life. The loss of this inner ease and voluntariness inevitably leads to a distortion of spiritual life, and if a person experiences law only as a *manifestation of someone else's will*, striving to bind and

[1] Il'in here adopts a standard conception of freedom familiar from seventeenth and eighteenth century political and legal theory, ignoring alternative doctrines of freedom that emerged, e.g., from nineteenth century German Idealist philosophy. However, this more usual and older conception of freedom is well accommodated to the form of relations among solitary psyches that he sketches as the human condition in the following chapter.

[2] "The contemporary view of law" referred to here is evidently legal positivism.

limit him, then he loses his spiritual *freedom*; and together with it also genuine *self-respect.*

Indeed, legal consciousness, experiencing law as alien, as a pressure coming from without, as compulsion, and perhaps even as coercion, as a kind of perpetual shackle imposed by a powerful hand on personal life, remains *unfree and oppressed by its own unfreedom.* Of course, the authoritative pressure of law can lead to self-interested desire being precluded from realization; impending unpleasantnesses and threats frighten it away, so that gradually it becomes constrained and suppressed. As a result, the naive, self-interested trampling under of law is gradually reduced to a minimum and cedes its place to a peculiar "acknowledgement"[3] of it and a forced observance; but this unfree, anxious, wary and half-intelligent "acknowledgement"[4] will be far from a genuine, free, and spiritually-thought-through *recognition* of law. The disease of naive self-interest cedes its place to the disease of a tested, experienced, and suppressed self-interest, and nothing more. Legal consciousness, having grown only to an *external legality*, remains an immature legal consciousness.[5]

Indeed, long and continuous training, proceeding from generation to generation, can habituate the soul to a conscious observance of legal$_z$ forms and legal$_z$ limits in deeds. Obvious or covert theft will become the exception, and the blossom of a fruit tree, growing beside a main road, will peacefully turn into a mature fruit that touches the passer-by; arrogation of the law to oneself [самоуправство] disappears, deliberate violation of rights will be a rarity; the citizenry will consult weekly, concerning everything, with a personal contract lawyer,[6] and gradually, with particular satisfaction at the legality of their conduct, litigate against one another in an intelligent, fair, and just court; the epoch of petty bribes and large-scale theft will be forgotten, and people will cease to see any special daring in unpunished violation of law; finally, duty, private and public, will become an habitual form of life ... And behind all this, externally sparkling legal order may be concealed *the legal consciousness of a resentful slave.*

Self-interested desire does not disappear and is not extirpated because it encounters external prohibitions, threats, opposition or even punishment. True, it learns "not to dare" and conceals itself from the superficial glance, but precisely for that reason it accumulates gradually,

[3] Instead of the usual *признание* ("recognition"), Il'in here employs the unusual alternate form *признавание* (here translated as "acknowledgement").

[4] *Признавание.*

[5] In this and the following paragraphs Il'in is spelling out his critique of the consequences for legal consciousness of the doctrines of legal positivism that he considered dominant at the time.

[6] *годовым адвокатом*: a lawyer hired by contract for a period of one year.

persisting unsatisfied, not overcome—beaten but not persuaded—and concentrates in the soul, tincturing the whole of life in traces of restrained, hidden *bitterness*. It assumes and observes a legal$_z$ form in relations, but is silently oppressed by it, experiencing it as a shackling chain. Keeping quiet, self-interested desire as before continues to look for persons or situations unprotected or insufficiently protected by law and fills in these gaps with activity which, although it does not diverge from the "operative" law$_z$, entirely contradicts *the spirit and aim of law*; the predatory and power-seeking soul as before seeks for itself a helot and finds it in the person of the unorganized proletarian, the colonial of a different nationality or the defenseless foreigner. Such a legal consciousness continually *engages in hatred* and awaits only for the external legal authority to remove from him, even for a time, the restraining prohibitions, and the call to war, for example, signifies for him that in the person of "enemies" there is a group of absolutely legally disqualified people for whom "the law$_z$ is not written": in relation to them everything is permitted and every kind of violence is considered allowable by law. Thus, the well-trained slave, schooled at home to elementary honesty, does not consider it shameful to steal from a neighbor, and, becoming like him, contemporary legal consciousness willingly divides people into "ours" and "others", punching deep holes in the "just" interpretation and "equal" application of law.

Such a legal consciousness was *obliged* to take account of law and *submitted*, but *did not accord recognition* to that to which it submitted. It experienced the legal reaction as an opposition, as an active rebuff, threatening resistance to the end, that is, as a *force*; and it recognized the *force* of law, but not its *worth*. It learned that one must *know* the law, and perhaps even that it has *objektive significance*, but it did not learn a *sighted, rational conviction of the spiritual value of law*. It did not turn into *a will to law, grounded in a will to its end*. Moreover: it concealed in itself a *will to lawlessness* and a certainty that *everything is permitted to might*. It taught itself to profess hypocritically that *might is there where law is*, and retained an unshakable certainty that *law is there where might is*. Could it have been otherwise, when it submitted to law only because it sensed *the might of its organized pressure*? Such a legal consciousness, strictly speaking, is entirely alien to the *idea of law*, although perhaps it experiences the *concept* of law adequately to its *meaning*: the selfish instinct of the human created *its own might* so long as it did not experience the opposition of an *alien* organized *might*; it yielded to it and learned that *this might is law* and that one must submit to it, and in the soul of a contemporary civilized human being, having submitted to external authority, there remained the half-conscious conviction that *law is nothing other than organized might*. Can one be surprised that, for example, contemporary German science is permeated by this view no less than the legal consciousness of the submissive philistine?[7]

[7] Il'in is presumably expressing his contempt for the legal positivism which was generally thought to be the dominant view of law among German theorists at this time.

But the legal consciousness of the slave is characterized precisely by the fact that he *submits, without recognizing and without respecting*. The power binding him is an external power, proceeding from another, alien to him; it requires from him obedience and not recognition, subordination and not respect. Is not it all the same which motives force the slave to work with the exertion of all his strength? And if the motives do not matter, why not crack the whip over his head? Aristotle said that it is characteristic for the slave to understand others' thoughts, but not to have his own, for the slave receives directions from others concerning what he is to do and how he is to behave. He submits while gnashing his teeth, yielding to violence, and not to reasoning. He does not yet know of his inalienable spiritual right *to recognize and not recognize* another's dictate: fear and habit lead him in a yoke, and perhaps a consciousness that his *submissiveness is degrading both for him and for his master* glimmers only dimly in his soul. Such a consciousness is the *beginning* of legal consciousness.

The immediate task of contemporary legal consciousness is to free itself from these traits characterizing the soul of a slave. And, above all, it is essential to understand that this liberation cannot come from anywhere outside: the slave, having become a freedman, carries into freedom the entire mode of his previous life and fills the free form with the desires, rights and deeds fitting for a slave. No kind of legal and political reform can *by itself* remake the psyche of a human being habituated to passively submitting while gnashing his teeth and not knowing that genuine self-governance grows only from the depth of a *free will which respects itself*. The motives according to which a human being observes the law are not only not indifferent, but include within themselves the very *root of legal consciousness*, and if these motives are such as to trample and abase the freedom of spirit and deprive a person of *respect for himself*, then legal consciousness turns out to be decomposing at its own root. Blind obedience to command from fear and self-interest puts a human on the level of an animal, incapable of law and devoid of legal consciousness.

It befits a human being to choose one of two paths: either to *reject* law on principle: exclude oneself from a life under law and oppose to the predator and the aggressor the idea of a *lawless existence*; or *to recognize law on principle* and derive from this recognition the logical conclusions.

However, in order for such recognition to take place, an objective and convincing spiritual basis must be present.

Chapter Five
The Grounding of Natural Law

In order that a human consciousness should be able to recognize law and carry out the spiritual acceptance of it, law must be *grounded.* To ground law means to demonstrate that it is *in practical terms necessary on the path of a human being to the realization of the supreme good.* This means to demonstrate that the *fundamental laws of being of the human spirit* are such, and that the essence of the *supreme good* is such, that law as an objektively obligatory rule of external conduct is the *necessary form of their coming together*. In other words, law is necessary because without it a person's spirit will be deprived of the possibility of realizing the supreme good in his own life. And if law cannot be accorded recognition until it has been grounded to a sufficient degree, then the identification of it as *a necessary form of spiritual being* must make *creatively accepting it*[1] obligatory.

From the very beginning it may seem that such a grounding of law is impossible. Anyone who is acquainted with the content of positive law and with the methods of its realization has probably more than once experienced a profound disillusionment, has been filled with a feeling of protest and indignation. One can even assume with confidence that the principled denial of law and the State are fostered by this indignation. One who has lived under the burden of a totalitarian regime and terror;[2] who has thought over the essence of material inequality and understood the regular connection between the sizes of the harvests in a country and the quantity of crimes against property; who is acquainted with the essence of the previous Russian suit for divorce; who has been in a convict prison and has heard the rattling of chains on human beings; who knows what corporal punishment is, and has had contact with a person condemned to capital punishment; who saw all that and understood that it is *also* carried out *in accordance with law*—such an individual possesses sufficient psychic motives to no longer trust in a single formulation of the problem of the spiritual justification of law. The profound defects and vices of positive law—as in the very order of its establishment, so also in

[1] Or: *creatively taking it up*. It is clear from the context that Il'in has in mind not a passive but an *active* acceptance of law, a *taking up* of law as a project willed by an autonomous rational being committed to the development of his or her own spiritual life.

[2] "totalitarian regime and terror" are an addition to the 1956 edition. In the 1919 edition the phrase was "a despotic regime". Il'in had personal experience of both: he was arrested by the Cheka/GPU six times between 1918 and 1922, being held for various periods of time in the cellar of the Lubianka, before being forcibly exiled to Germany by the Bolshevik regime in September 1922, under threat of execution. Then, after the Nazis came to power in Germany, Il'in was regularly subjected to interrogation by the Gestapo (between 1934 and 1938) and threatened with arrest and transport to a concentration camp, before finally escaping to Switzerland in 1938.

its content and application—always form the greatest obstacle on the path to spiritually accepting it.

This obstacle would, of course, be insuperable and ineliminable if positive law *in its very essence* were connected with *senseless content and an inadmissible form of establishment*, or if the very essence of law consisted in some people imposing their will on others, still more by means of "compulsion" and "coercion". But such an understanding would be false: it would confuse the historically given content of law with certain imperfect although widespread means of establishing it, with the fundamental nature of law itself. And in the meantime history shows that law can have a content which is more unsatisfactory and less unsatisfactory, less free and just and more free and just; moreover, it can acquire a content fully corresponding to the dignity of the human spirit (for example, all norms and statutes guaranteeing "personal inviolability" and freedom of spiritual life). Further, the history of law witnesses to the fact that the forms of its statutes change, and change moreover in the direction of extending the self-activity of peoples, the self-determination of groups and the self-government of individuals. Finally, it is natural that to the degree that, as the element of externally-authoritative command in law yields its place to the element of *self-obligation* in the widest sense of that word, to that degree the recognition of law increases and legal consciousness grows stronger, while the threat of disagreeable consequences loses its realistic character and gradually ceases to be a factor of life.

It is essential to draw a strict demarcation between *the fundamental essence of law* and its historical realizations. The fundamental essence of law is expressed in terms of *an objektively significant rule of external social conduct.* An historical realization of this possibility can be distinctive; it can pour a different content into this rule; it can put forward various means for the establishment of law; it can make the establisher of law one, a few, many or all; it can appeal to various motives of psychic life.

Thus, law in its very essence has *objektive significance*; it is established and extinguished not by means of "individual caprice", but by means of "constitutional authority". However, by this it is not yet said that at the foundation of this significance may lie *only* the will of *other* people. On the contrary, only the personal acceptance and recognition of law imparts to life under law its true dignity and completeness. Of course, it also happens that positive law is established by the discretion and decision of a few plenipotentiaries, who turn out to be "other" in relation to the rest; but if the rest participate in life under law only through a *consciousness* of norms and *obedience* to them, but not through *recognition* of them, then in their souls a repressed, disfigured legal consciousness takes shape, and law itself, while not losing its objektive significance, loses its spiritual truth and, perhaps, even its spiritual worth. It is fitting for a human being to *recognize* a rule to which he submits, and only such a *conscious recognition* can secure for law a living observance. Political philosophy long ago perceived this and more than once addressed the idea of a "social contract", trying to construct a foundation of law on this either historical or systematic "presumption". But this problem is not solved in this way: law must be *recognized by each in a conscious spiritual decision*, and not in an unconscious, taciturn passivity; on one's own, and not in the person of one's legendary ancestors.

Further, law by its very essence regulates the external conduct of people, creating particular *motives* in their souls: it always addresses a comprehending and willing consciousness as a *guide* for the external actions of a human being. However, by this is not yet said at all that law always and inevitably appeals to the motives of fear, calculation, profit, ambition, and so forth in the souls of people, and that its sanctions consist in threats and compulsion. By now there are quite a few norms in positive law lacking such a sanction, and one can say with certainty that a positive legal order deriving its vital force *only from a sanction*, is striding rapidly to its own degeneration. Fear diminishes a human being, and once aroused, fear easily turns into a resentful impudence; compulsion nurtures in souls a faith in coercion and a hope in force; personal selfishness and class interest by no means always coincide with law, and ambition is a motive created as it were precisely to transgress law and trample it under. It is worthy for a human being to *respect* that rule to which he submits, and to submit to it precisely *out of respect*. Moral philosophy already long ago recognized this in its sphere, and time and again turned to the idea of "*autonomy of the will*" as the sole basis of moral conduct. But the idea of autonomy does not at all have a specifically moral character; it is deeper than the sphere of ethics, for it lies at the foundation of *all* life of the human spirit.

All this can be expressed thus: the *historical existence of law* does not in itself exhaust *all possible forms* of it, does not determine its *normal structure* and does not establish in itself its worthy, *ideal* aspect. Similar to the way in which, on all other paths of a *creating and perfecting* human being, the concept of the object is defined not only through the description of *already realized* things and conditions but also through the study of *the ideal* as the guiding end and *of the possible* (that is, of the realizable), so it is also with law. The philosophy of law, formulating the essence of law and achieving its grounding, has in view not only the *concept* of law fixed in the content of historically realized norms, but also the *idea* of law, given in the *experience of a systematically purified legal consciousness, the objectively-intuited supreme end of law and spirit*. The essence of law is not exhausted by the content of positive law; law is created by an end-proposing humanity, and he who strives to cognize this fundamental *nature of law*, must intuit not only the "stages" badly assembled in the past, but also the supreme *end* of the entire ascent. In grounding law, philosophy must set out from *normal legal consciousness*, that is, from that sort of *objective experience* that is wider and deeper than a simple knowledge of positive law. This objective experience must have in view *the fundamental function* of any law as such and show that this function is essential in the life of the human spirit. To ground law does not mean to justify everything historically realized, but to show that law in its *generic essence* and in its *positive form* deserves spiritual recognition and acceptance on the part of *every human being.*

What is the basis for this acceptance?

To humanity, living on the Earth, there is inherent a *mode* of existence such that it makes *law a necessary form of its being.* This mode of existence is determined by a particular correlation of *multiplicity and unity, identity, difference, and commonality.*

Specifically, humanity lives on the Earth in such a way that one human being always remains a *psycho-physical other-being* to another, and all people together constitute *a multiplicity of identically solitary but distinctive spiritually-creative monads, connected by a common basis of existence.*[3] Such a structure of being, given from nature, makes *spiritual life* possible only on the condition that humanity is able to organize its *external life* on the ground of *objektively significant rules, which maintain a free and just order in the existence of this multiplicity.*

Indeed, humanity constitutes a multiplicity of spiritual centers, each of which conceals itself in mysterious fashion in a single thing, central for it and serving it specifically, called *its body*. Each spiritual center, needing its own body in order to live at all and manifest itself, experiencing the body's needs as *its own*, and therefore devoting the greater or lesser part of its energy to their satisfaction, turns out at the same time to be *isolated* from other spiritual centers precisely by this – *for it* – central thing. Each soul experiences with the force of *immediacy* and exceptional authenticity only *its own states* and instinctively concentrates its attention, affect, and doings on them; concerning other centers, and events within them, each gets to know them only mediately, through bodily perception of states expressed bodily as well; all this, pertaining to others, is experienced as alien, incomparably less trustworthy and authentic. Not only psychically but also physically, each remains to every other an *other-being*: the immediate process of life, its beginning and end, psychic and bodily states, abilities and actions, in a word, the entire fate of each one, is separate and particular; each of the "indivisible" spiritual beings is *individual and a distinct existence*, here repetition is impossible, for every moment of life is irretrievable, unrepeatable, and already experienced by each in his own way. For that reason every person is *distinctive and singular in his own way*, regardless of the abundance of separate, abstractly taken, similar traits. And despite the constant everyday conscious and unconscious

[3] Il'in here invokes the Leibnizian concept of the "windowless monad" which is able to have awareness of the structure of the world around it only indirectly through the coordination of its internal perceptions with those constituting the structure of every other entity/event in the world. However, the monad can be directly aware only of its own internal perceptions.

intercourse, each human being makes his way and realizes his fate in profound and inevitable solitude.[4]

This *solitude*, identically present in each and all, is expressed *psychically* in the fact that the individual life of the soul proceeds in an enclosed isolation and inaccessibility for another's soul, in a distinctive "darkness" for the other. No one experiences "my" states as "his own", immediately accessible to him – no one besides me myself; no one can "admit" anyone else into his own soul; no one may have "common" experiences with anyone else, but only "similar" ones; no one may perform volitional or mental exertions for another or "loan" to the other his experience and his disposition. Each knows of the other's soul only to the extent that it "presents itself" or "expresses itself" in the other's body.

Further, this *solitude* is expressed *spiritually* in the fact that the supreme good can be realized by humanity *only in the form of a multiplicity of parallel, solitary, ascending processes*. This realization of the supreme good—the cognition of *truth*, the creation of *beautiful images*, the flowering of genuine *goodness*, the achievement of objective *religious faith* and, finally, the holistic *spiritualization* of soul and body—requires above all a self-sufficient, authentic, and objectively-adequate *experience* of that which proceeds toward realization. Here a mature, personally experienced, and systematically purified inner and outer-inner experience is essential, which can be endured and forged *by each independently*. No one can take away from another's soul the burden it independently bears, the burden of solitary seeking and creativity. *Self-activity in seeking and self-sufficiency in discovery* is the fundamental law of spiritual life: from this self-sufficiency begins *scientific knowledge*, placing the individual soul face to face with the object itself. With it begins authentic *religious faith*, eliminating intermediaries between the individual soul and the Divinity. With it begins *ethical* practice, taking upon oneself the decision, the responsibility and the guilt; in a word, *the whole of spiritual life* and personal maturity are determined by the moment when a person places his individual—experiencing and creating—psychic center in immediate

[4] Il'in's emphasis here upon the solitude of individual human existence apparently reflects a theme of philosophical conversation at the time between himself and his wife, Nataliia Nikolaevna Il'ina (*née* Vokach). She was an historian and philosopher in her own right, and wrote a 158-page manuscript in 1916 entitled «Одиночество и общение [Solitude and Communion] It has been published as an appendix in a supplementary volume of the Собрание сочинений [Collected Works] of Il'in, ed. Yu. T. Lisitsa, pp. 587-665. That volume is entitled Философия как духовное делание [Philosophy as a Spiritual Doing] (2013). Although unnumbered, that volume is in fact the 29th in the series, and is so-described in the editor's introduction.

The date of composition of this essay by Nataliia Nikolaevna coincides precisely with the beginning of Il'in's work on the first ten chapters of *The Essence of Legal Consciousness*. See also the essay by Yu. T. Lisitsa, «Радости общения», «Одиночество и общения», «Бытие как общение» у И. А. Ильина, Н. Н. Ильиной и Митр. Иоанна Зизиуласа [The Joys of Communion, Solitude and Communion, Being as Communion by I. A. Il'in, N. N. Il'ina, John Zizioulas) in Исследования в русской философии и культуре [Investigations in Russian Philosophy and Culture], ed. S. B. Kornilov (2010), pp. 52-53.

relation to the world and life. *A freedom to seek and to find* is essential for spiritual life, as air is for the body. In accordance with this law, spiritual life only possesses its authentic significance and its own true value when its driving motives are nourished by its own personal-individual inclinations and interests, such that the pressure of another's will, even if noble and righteous, does not have a decisive significance in that creativity. Here *freedom of the will* is essential—not in the sense of indeterminism, but in the sense of the absence of external, alien commands and prohibitions. It is freedom to voluntarily and self-sufficiently discover and recognize the true in truth, to see the beautiful in beauty, to make certain of and to convince oneself of the objektive characteristics of the good, to come to believe in received revelation. The fundamental dignity of the human consists in living a spiritual life *independently* of any heterogeneous encroachment and pressure, and at the same time *in an objectively creative manner*. *Free self-determination* in spirit is the deepest law of this life and at the same time the sole path to the authentic realization of the supreme good; in it lies the highest meaning of all reformations, of any liberation and emancipation, of any individualism and political self-governance.

In this way the one process of the spiritual life of humanity internally falls apart into a multiplicity of isolated, self-sufficient and distinctive processes, each with an individual character. All of these solitary individual processes stand in a co-existence and a more or less incomplete *interaction*. This means that they, *identically* solitary and *identically* conditioned by connection with an individual body, with the material environment and with each other, have a *common basis of existence*. This basis is *common* for them in the precise and strict meaning of the word: each person has the grounds to say of *the space* in which its body lives and moves, of *the air* which he breathes, of *the sun* which warms him, of *material things* which are needed by him for various bodily and psychic requirements—"this is necessary for my being" and, further, "*this is mine and for me*"; and all together – recognizing this straight away, and simultaneously of everything together—point *truly* to the *common basis* of existence and state an indefinite, unlimited *claim* on this basis. And thus this single external-material basis of existence, common to all, leads inevitably to *an encounter among a multitude of claims*.

Driven by the primordial instinct of individual and family self-preservation, each singular soul appears in the form of an *aggressive will*, turns toward the common basis of existence and draws around himself circles of his own unrestrained self-assertion. This self-assertion constitutes not only a psycho-physical but also a *spiritual* necessity. In order to exist *with dignity*, that is, *to live with growing spirit*, it is essential above all to exist: in order to exist, for each singular individual it is necessary to *function self-sufficiently* in the external world, *to create* what is needed and *protect* what has been created. The circles drawn by each one around himself, will sooner or later, but inevitably, come into contact and collide; a conflict of claims inevitably gives rise to the question of the *justice* of the claims, and the arbitrary establishment of one's own boundaries comes to an end: the question of the *rightful* claim is already the question of *law*, now resolved in a mature way by recognition of the determinate *legal status of each subject.*[5]

In this way the presence of a *common* basis and environment for a multiplicity of *separately* existing *subjects* leads to the creation of law. And if the complete isolation of people in these surroundings (similar to Leibniz' "windowless" monads) would have made law unnecessary, *the impossibility of communicating* through these surroundings, to understand one another and agree with one another, would have made law impossible. Such communication of people with one another, given the collision of their arbitrary claims can of course end up in the form of physical violence, deterrence, deception and extended struggle. However, all these outcomes, degrading for the human spirit, do not eliminate the question of law, but give it a distorted and deformed resolution. To live in the certainty that "those who are right are always powerful and cunning", does not mean to reject "rightness" in general, but it means to decide the question of right on a *sham* foundation. For at the foundation of any judgment of what is "right", at the foundation of any norm, and consequently at the foundation of any *legal norm*, of any empowerment or duty, necessarily lies a certain openly or secretly recognized value: "what ought to be" is always "what ought to be" precisely because its content exactly reproduces the form and content of the value. Thus what ought to be in ethics is determined by the form and content of the good itself; what ought to be in aesthetics—by the form and content of beauty; what ought to be in knowledge—by the form and content of truth, and so forth. However, this value frequently yields its place to deliberate or semi-deliberate surrogates: for example, to personal or class interest, to popular prejudice or biased doctrine. Then the question of "what is right" receives a more or less false resolution, and "what ought to be" acquires a more or less false grounding: *badly grounded rules of conduct* are formed. Thus, in positive law there are quite a few such norms, which have more or less false, at times savage, and at times degrading foundations or, if you will, *sham values*. The scientific disclosure and reconsideration of them could at times give stunning results. Nevertheless, positive law *can* and must receive, and receive little by little, a content corresponding to that value which makes it essential. The guarantee of this is that it has a particular, internal connection with natural law.

[5] Il'in's treatment of this problem has a precedent in volume one of Savigny's *System of the Modern Roman Law*, transl. Holloway. There Savigny argued that "Man stands in the midst of the outer world, and the most important element to him in this surrounding of his is the contact with those who are like him, by their nature and destination. If now in such contact free natures are to subsist beside one another mutually assisting, not hindering themselves, this is possible only through the recognition of an invisible boundary within which the existence and activity of each individual gains a secure, free space. The rule by which those boundaries and that free space are determined, is the law" (§52; p. 331, original German edition). However, this conception of a necessary sphere of protected free action for each individual is common to numerous early modern political and legal theorists, and Il'in does not indicate any particular source for his view.

The value lying at the foundation of natural law is the *worthy, internally-self-sufficient and externally free* life *of the entire multiplicity of individual spirits* composing humanity. Such a life is possible only in the form of the *peaceful and organized equilibrium* of the subjective centers making claims: an equilibrium identically guaranteeing to each the possibility of a spiritually worthy life and therefore disturbing that equilibrium only on the side of *justice*.

The singular human being is the sole possibility of an inspirited life; to lead such a life, creating it self-sufficiently and freely, is the *basic and unconditional right of each*. It can be called a *natural* right, because it expresses the essential *nature* of the spiritual life of the human: it can be called an *eternal* right because it maintains its significance for all times and peoples; it can be called an *inalienable* right because any derogation or trampling of it distorts spiritual life and destroys the dignity of the human.

This natural, subjective right belongs *to each* human being, however small, ill or bad he may be. The mystery of solitary being is inviolable, and no penetrating diagnosis whatever is able to substantiate the qualification of a human being as having lost his natural right. Accordingly, humanity appears in the form of a multiplicity of subjective *centers of natural right*, where each encloses within itself or envelops a natural-right- capable center of spiritual life. The peripheral contiguity and correlativity of these centers turns them into a distinctive system of natural-right delimitation and natural-right meanings. All of humanity participates in this system, independently of space and of State affiliation: in it there is neither Hellene nor Jew, nor are there those without right or those excluded. It is deeper than any positive right and all positive-right divisions and demarcations. It is a system of spiritual-natural correlations: of universally-human spiritual *brotherhood* and of natural *equality*.

The recognition of such a natural right for every human being as a possible center of the distinctive and autonomous life of spirit affirms, actually, the principle of legal *duty* and legal *equality* in the life of people. People *are not equal* to one another in body or in soul; neither are they equal in terms of the content of their spiritual life, regardless of the fact that they are turned toward the very same objective centers of spirit before the face of which they live, even when they turn away from them and forget about them; but each is equal to every other in terms of his own right to a dignified life. The circle of free self-assertion, defining the natural-law status of each, stretches no farther than to the limit of the neighboring centers, similar to it in terms of spiritual significance and compass. And any deviation from this *equilibrating* justice in the *distributive* direction must have an objektive foundation in the properties of individual spirit and an objective limit in the spiritual autonomy of the person.

The right to lead a spiritually-dignified life is not reducible to not having deliberate obstacles to existence or "having the possibility of endeavoring not to perish". To lead a spiritually-dignified life means to have not only "one's daily bread", but also that *leisure* which Aristotle required for a person "free from nature". In precisely the same way the self-sufficiency of spirit presupposes a *right to education* and the development of the soul and to the *self-governing* of a human being as a free subject of right. A consistent, analytical disclosure of ideas of *a living spiritual being, of spiritual freedom, of spiritual self-activity, of spiritual dignity and equality* can establish an entire system of natural, subjective rights and duties, forming together what it is appropriate to call *natural law*, the common normative formulation of which permits one to speak of natural law and in an objektive sense. This single natural law in itself turns out, of course, not to be adapted in itself to different conditions of place, time, to particular conditions of life, and so forth, but fully yielding to such adaptation; it constitutes the natural and spiritually true foundation for any draft law. In this sense it can, if you will, be characterized as "formal", that is, as comparatively more general than any positive law. But if one adheres to the strict juridical usage of words and understands by the content of *objektive law* the empowerments, duties and prohibitions established by it; and by the content of *subjective law*, the permitted and prohibited deeds, then true natural law turns out not to be "formal" but *substantive*.

To recognize that the spiritual life of humanity is possible only given the assertion of this natural right means to recognize such a right both for oneself (but not only for oneself), and for all others (but not only for others). This means, further, to recognize both for oneself and for others a *duty*, correlatively corresponding to that right, for in truth every right-capable [правовая] cell is nourished in its powers by the duties of others, and conversely; and each of them is whole and alive only so long as its neighbors are whole and alive. This means, finally, to recognize the *objektive significance* behind those rules, formulated by thought, in which are articulated and established the legal [правовые] boundaries of personal status. In accordance with this, the objektive significance of natural law obtains two roots: the *value-objective*—through its connection with the life of spirit, and the *subjective-living*—through its connection with a personal, self-obligating recognition.

The recognition of natural law, founded on a sighted and rational conviction of its spiritual necessity, is the condition under which the personal spirit of a human being, in obeying it, remained *free*. The freedom of spirit is not disrupted because a person independently perceived and recognized the rational groundedness of the rule: on the contrary, his self-determination receives from this its own true, objective content. The rule's being recognized does not absorb or abolish its *objektive significance*: it is preserved, and consists in the fact that the recognition of it gives objektive rightfulness to the one who recognized it, and non-recognition remains powerless to change anything in its objektive content and significance. Happy is he who perceived and recognized it: the honor fell to his lot to impart life and power to authentic spiritual value, and at the same time affirm in this his own autonomous self-determination. And conversely, painful and sorrowful is the state of one who has to encounter this value in a socially-heteronomous manner and submit to it, not obeying voluntarily, pursuing false goals. For the fate of natural law is to await from people for a long time and in vain an independent and voluntary recognition, and to perennially receive the form of positive law so as to be fitting for souls in a socially-heteronomous condition. Natural law can be perceived and recognized by each one in his own, solitary, objectively-spiritual experience; but in the majority of cases people do not get that far, and then they are faced with encountering natural-legal requirements in that form which is imparted to them by positive law —formulating them, truncating and even distorting their essence—referring to the external authority of plenipotentiary individuals, and, perhaps, even threatening with unpleasant consequences.

Heteronomous establishment, approximateness of content, and the possibility of threatening sanctions: these distinguish positive law from natural law and require for the former a particular grounding.

Chapter Six
The Grounding of Positive Law

Law in its original, "natural" sense is nothing other than a *necessary form of the spiritual being of a human.* It indicates that order of equal, *free self-sufficiency of each* in which alone spiritual life is possible on earth. From this it follows that law in this sense could be extinguished or become unnecessary only if the basic mode of human existence were to change, that is, if humanity ceased to be *a multiplicity of self-sufficient subjects*, united *by a shared basis of external life.*[1]

The matter stands otherwise with positive law. *Its* necessity is based on a certain immature state of human souls, which can change over the course of time. However until it changes, positive law will exist as *an expedient form for the maintenance of natural law.*

This necessity arises as a result, first, of the inalienability and indiminishability of natural law, and second, from the absence in people of the ability to regulate their external life by means of autonomous self-obligation.

Natural law as a necessary form of spiritual being is the most precious possession of humanity. Outside of this form there is no path either to wisdom, to virtue, to Divinity, or to the ultimate and highest satisfactions of spirit. Every diminution of natural law degrades human worth; each violation of it is spiritually contrary to nature. Therefore it is essential to guard and to uphold it against those who violate it and don't recognize it; it is essential to protect it, affirming it through *collective, organized recognition, proclamation and realization.* This collective establishing of natural law as universally obligatory imparts to it, however, the character of a *heteronomous rule*, in particular for all those who do not recognize it and do not take it into consideration. They encounter an organized *external authority* prescribing, permitting and forbidding various external actions, and accompanying their decrees with threatening sanctions, that is, *with an indication of the possibility of forcible opposition to the violator.* From long and bitter experience people have become convinced that a purely autonomous self-obligation grows in souls with extraordinary slowness, extending over many generations, that it is characteristic of humans to recognize *their own empowerments*, exaggerating their limits

[1] Il'in here implicitly distances himself from Petrazhitskii's view that law as such was destined to disappear as a means of social regulation in the highest stage of development of human social conscience, to be replaced by universal mutual love. Il'in is prepared to concede that *positive* law in the sense of a form of external coercion imposed upon the individual to regulate behavior might eventually prove superfluous, but even in a world where every individual freely exercised appropriate self-governance, the positive law would remain, if only as an objective reflection of the requirements of natural law. In the interim it remains a necessary form of tutelage heteronomously imposed upon the naive egocentrism of uncultivated souls.

and not realizing their spiritual essence; but not particularly characteristic to recognize at the same time their *duties*, and the empowerments *of others*, that this recognition of others' rights is forged within souls only as a result of prolonged frictions, as a result of that life and death struggle for "mutual recognition" of which Hegel once spoke with such perspicuous wisdom.[2] This bitter experience teaches that a human being is in need of a fencing in of his spiritual center *by rules of external behavior, upheld by a social, externally authoritative order.*

Humanity exists in the form of a multiplicity of psychic-spiritual centers, in need of external security and inviolability for the sake of a free self-determination proceeding from within, and at the same time standing within a particular order of coexisting claims; in this form humanity began its life without any awareness of the laws of its being, and without the presence of the spiritual skill of mutual recognition. The life of the singular soul in the majority of cases is determined even up to now by a naive egocentric inclination in which a human being in the best case experiences the limits constraining him of another's status as an onerous inconvenience. And meanwhile it is impossible to "set aside" the realization of natural law and the vocation of a human being for spiritual life, until such time as people have learned not to reciprocally trample on its limits._

And thus the fundamental task of positive law consists in *accepting within oneself the content of natural* law, unfolding it in the form of *a series of rules of external conduct*, fitted to the conditions of a given life and to the needs of a given time, imparting to these rules *a semantic form and verbal consolidation* and, further, *penetrating into the consciousness and the will of people* as *authoritative binding commands*. In this way the ideas of *the obligatory and the prohibited* must be inculcated in the naive egocentric soul; and if morality and religion attempt to achieve a self-sufficient and active awakening of the soul from the depth, and meet with assistance from the side of science and art in this, positive law takes upon itself the elementary and comparatively crude task of *habituating human beings from without to an initial, external, regulated self-limitation.* For that it turns to the idea of a socially-organized, plenipotentiary *external authority*, subordinated to rules. It is essential that people, *in the beginning at least*, become accustomed to acknowledging this external authority and its legal commands. It is essential that the predator and the aggressor encounter from without an organized and imposing opposition based on the idea of *rightness and legal power*. A conscious, principled instruction that "this is inadmissible," and "this is obligatory" made by one person to another with a sense of rightness and spiritual worth and supported

2 A reference to Hegel's famous discussion of the "dialectic" of Lordship and Bondage (also referred to as the "Master/Slave dialectic") in Part A of the section on "Self-Consciousness" in *The Phenomenology of Spirit*. The fundamental significance of Hegel's doctrine of mutual recognition has been recognized only comparatively recently in English-language Hegel commentary: see Robert R. Williams, *Recognition: Fichte and Hegel on the Other* (1992), and Williams, *Hegel's Ethics of Recognition* (1997).

by the organized decision "not to permit" and "to insist," is in truth one of the most powerful means of social training. The presence of such an *external reaction* to external conduct and *the necessity to take account of the organized directives of others* constitute the basic scheme of positive law. To one who does not feel the summons of spirit and the force of good in self-sufficient internal experience, and who himself is unable to locate the natural-law limits for his own claims, has to find out about these limits by way of a socially heteronomous demarcation of limits.

This does not signify, however, that the heteronomous character of positive law excludes autonomous self-obligation. On the contrary, positive law possesses the more spiritual truth the more fully it is adapted to the fundamental laws$_z$ of spiritual life, and above all to the law$_z$ of its *self-lawfulness*.[3] *To ground* positive law means to demonstrate its applicability for a spirit living self-lawfully; *to organize* positive law means to find and create for it the form of creative self-lawfulness; *to overcome* positive law means to imbue it with a normal legal consciousness living self-lawfully, and by that means to make it superfluous.

Thus positive law is acceptable for a self-lawfully living spirit because it, according to its own fundamental and guiding idea, its own *end*, serves the self-lawfully living spirit. Positive law as a norm is established by living spiritual beings for the protection and strengthening of the self-activity of living spiritual beings. Precisely for this reason at the basis of any positive law lies the recognition of the human being as a *subject* possessing the capacity for law and the capacity for action, that is, a recognized sphere of juridically significant self-sufficient volition. Outside the recognition of a human being as a subject there is not and cannot be law. Of course, people by no means understood straight away that a human being cannot fail to be a subject of law. Thus the conception of the Roman jurist attempted to equate *unfree and dependent subjects of law* to animals and tolerated the idea that "a slave is a thing", and, not noticing the objective mistake and contradiction, this conception asserted on behalf of slaves a certain, though scant, circle of legal powers, ever enlarging it over the course of time.[*] If positive law regulates the method of establishing and of abolishing slavery, if it asserts on behalf of the slave-owner a legal power, then it is compelled to recognize tacitly

[3] *Самозаконность* (self-lawfulness), that is, obeying a law one prescribes to oneself, hence a synonym of *autonomy* (auto-nomos). The term might be translated more explicitly as "self-lawgiving"; however, Il'in quite frequently uses the term in adverbial constructions, and "self-lawgivingly" (!) would be too clumsy in English. On the other hand, "self-lawfully" works reasonably well. Il'in used this term *самозаконность* (and the adverbial form *самозаконно*) quite frequently in his commentary on Hegel, a portion of which he also translated into German himself. In German he uses both *Eigengesetzlichkeit* and *Autonomie* more or less interchangeably to translate *самозаконность*. The term "autonomy" also figures prominently in this chapter.

[*] **On the contradiction between the *theory* of law and *positive law* in Rome, I. A. Pokrovskii supplies detailed information in his work *История Римского права* [*History of Roman Law*]. (1913), pp. 174, 285-298.**

on behalf of the slave a correlative legal obligation, and if it recognizes that a slave can stand in *cognatio servilis*, that he can buy, give, possess *obligatio naturalis*, and even "his own slaves" (*servi vicarii*), then it thereby recognizes correlative obligations and empowerments on the part of *other* subjects of law, both of the free and also of slaves.

Positive law is developed under conditions such that its content is subjected to the influence of self-interested will, ignorance, false theory and lack of ability.[4] And nevertheless, however great and even monstrous the deviations and distortions introduced into its content by these factors, by its very nature it *preserves within itself a fundamental core of natural law*, for the service of which it is called into life. Positive law cannot fail to express the nature of that spiritual sphere that creates it; it can *attempt* to ignore its constitutive laws$_z$ and will inevitably fall into contradiction, for spiritual life is such that it inevitably sooner or later blazes up with the fire of its nature, tears away the shrouds distorting it, and cancels the contradictions oppressing it. Thus it is impossible for positive law to categorize a living, conscious subject as a thing: the objektive law$_z$ of spiritual life lying in the foundation of any positive law and guiding its development is stronger than any interest and any theory.

Positive law is acceptable for an autonomous will because by its very essence it *remains always a "modification" of natural law*. And even when this system of positive law is senseless and distorted, when it forgets its generic essence and tramples on it, a nucleus of natural law continues to lie at its basis. The old doctrine that "law serves freedom" should be accepted not only in a normative sense, that is, that it *ought to* serve freedom, but also in the sense of inductive generalization: positive law in actuality always demarcates the spheres of free volition, striving to secure and reconcile them in a certain balanced order. A rational and good will has the task of detecting this nucleus of natural freedom in it, purifying it of false admixtures, developing and strengthening it. In exactly the same way the assertion that "law serves equality", is by no means merely a publicistic slogan: positive law, regardless of what personal, estate and class privileges it grants, always and inevitably realizes the function of equalization. This is expressed not only in the leveling character of "general" rules, which require that identical things be categorized identically, but also in that all personal legal states (statuses) mutually condition and "nourish" each other: all of them are identically correlated one with the other (correlativity), mutually require one another and support each other (mutuality). A rational and good will has the task of detecting this nucleus of natural equality in positive law, purifying it of unjust violations and creating a spiritually grounded order of just equality. Finally, the modern catchphrase "law is founded

4 It is not inappropriate to compare Il'in's account of the relation of the imperfect "positive" law (*закон*) to the requirements of "natural" law (*право*) which it ought to express, to von Savigny's account of the relation of *Gesetz* to *Recht*. *Recht* serves as the standard to which the *Gesetzen* should conform, but the latter may in fact amount to "a baleful corruption of the *Recht*".

on self-governance" is by no means merely a postulate. Positive law according to its very essence addresses the rational will of a human being as a *self-governing center*; the fundamental objective of law is that every individual should govern his external conduct in accordance with the requirements and prescriptions of law. And in the final analysis nothing can replace this spiritual self-governance, proceeding from an individual center of life. Positive law arises *as a consequence of* a deficiency of this self-governance in people's souls; it is created *in order* to cultivate, to assist, to consolidate this self-governance; and thus a rational and good will must understand and undertake this task of positive law and help it manage the task.

That is why to place positive law on the height and organize its realization means to create for it *the form of self-lawfulness*. Positive law fulfills its purpose when *the simple awareness* of its rules forms in the human soul the *motive* for obeying it, that is, when the individual spirit accepts it on the basis of *self-obligation*. The capacity of the individual will to govern the life of a person can be inculcated and developed only where it is regularly exercised and systematically carried out. Suppressed by external authority, oppressed by threats and fear, accustomed to expect orders and permissions in all things, the will becomes accustomed "not to dare" and lives passively; the center guiding its life shifts from within to somewhere outside of it, it loses the ability to have "its own motives" and "its own decisions" and its legal consciousness loses its creative connection with law.

Normal legal consciousness consists in a person *governing* his own conduct *himself, but in accordance with positive law*. That is why legal consciousness can stand on the height only where law organizes life as *a school of self-governance*. The principle of self-governance is *the sole* principle: the creative maturity of the individual and the creative maturity of a nation—both in internal matters and in external politics—are identically determined by the capacity for self-governance. Where the solitary self-activity of the will is *not* developed, there social self-governance drags out a pitiful existence. And conversely, social self-governance can inculcate genuine legal consciousness in the soul of a person. The autonomy of the individual will and political autonomy are mutually connected. A nation leading an ignorant and unsober life is incapable of organized self-governance. But precisely there where a chasm lies between those ruling and those being ruled, national legal consciousness will inevitably be dragging out a pitiful existence. Legal consciousness matures and grows only when this opposition does not exist; only where political organization begins with the empowered citizen, where governance of the nation is at the same time the self-governance of the nation, where the one being governed knows and feels himself to be self-governing, such that obedience to positive law leaves him free. The problem of positive law can be solved only in such a way that organized external (social) self-governance habituates the person to organized internal (individual) self-governance; the self-activity of the human completes this task in terms of morality and spiritual culture.

It is clear that only to *autonomous legal consciousness* can it be given to freely accept positive law. Rules of conduct issuing from external authority will always be necessary, but especially until such time as a rational and good will understands the *necessity* for them, becomes reconciled to them for the nucleus of natural rightness hidden within them, and *takes* upon himself – as his cross and his fate – the task of their *creative transformation*. Positive law must itself adequately and without distortion uncover and realize through itself the laws of spiritual being, following them not only in organizing the method of establishing law, but also in the content of its rules, and being situated in a creative correspondence with morality, as the social-practical basis of the life of autonomous spirit. In this light the growth of legal consciousness turns out to be in the closest connection with the transformation of positive law. It is absurd and impossible to cultivate autonomous legal consciousness while settling on unfree, unequal, unjust, and fully heteronomous law; for a voluntary and creative recognition of positive law is accomplished the more easily the more freedom, justice and autonomy there is in its norms. The perfecting of law is itself already a powerful factor in the development of legal consciousness. And thus, foreseeing the prospect of this development one can say that positive law will become less and less needed to the degree that it itself approaches the spirit and meaning of *natural law*, while legal consciousness will grow, becoming deeper and stronger.

It is clear that the overcoming of positive law does not coincide either with its anti-lawful violation or with its lawful cancellation, or with the principled negation of it. It is a complex process of *the growing of the soul into law* or *of the assimilation of law by consciousness and will*. Consciousness here precedes will and uncovers the spiritual-natural roots of positive law; by this it gives to the will the basis for *accepting* positive law and opens up to the will *the goal and path* for overcoming it. It turns out that heteronomous regulation is admissible only for the sake of the protection of the autonomy of spirit and for the sake of the training of the individual soul to true self-governance in external conduct; that at the basis of positive legal consciousness must lie *natural legal consciousness*. Consciousness discovers that for the will there are two possible paths. First, the mature systematic path which consists in the will autonomously accepting natural law as the highest spiritual value and subsequently turning to the recognition and creative transformation of positive law; on this path legal consciousness grows in the soul from its deep and natural roots. Second, the ordinary empirically-accidental path which consists in the will encountering positive law on the basis of heteronomy and not perceiving in it anything other than externally-authoritative prescription. Here again there are two outcomes: the will can recognize positive law in its objective significance or can fail to recognize it. And depending on for which motives the will recognizes or rejects it, the legal consciousness of a person will take a more or less immature or diseased form. For all outcomes of the second path the overcoming of positive law remains an unresolvable problem.

In order to overcome positive law, legal consciousness must not only recognize its objective significance, but *perceive and accept its true basis*. It must understand that the root of this significance lies not in "power", and not in "class interest", and not in an "emotional phantasm",[5] and not in "the will of other people", and not in "impersonal social authority", and not in "the will of the State", but in *the objektive worth of natural law*. Positive law has objektive signficance because in its depth is hidden the *spiritual rightfulness and natural law* of the human being; its significance is founded on its worth, and its worth is determined by the worth of natural law. Mature legal consciousness constantly experiences in positive law the presence of something not *relative*[6] in its significance and is at times at a loss to point out what precisely evokes this feeling in it: for "the will of other people", even if "fully empowered" "by third parties", by itself alone cannot impart to its commands this *unconditional significance*. Objectively investigating and verifying its experience, legal consciousness assures itself that the hidden inner worth really does not abandon law, even if it is false or unjust in its content.[7]

This worth is by no means a product of the imagination or, more precisely: what presents itself to the imagination, and thought and feeling, is here something actually *objektively* subsisting. Positive law, even when false, that is, having distorted the prototype hidden within it, is experienced by legal consciousness as an *imperfect manifestation or immature formula of natural law*, as the creation of a humanity vaguely and helplessly searching for unconditional spiritual rightfulness [правота]. Perhaps it happened that people failed to find this rightfulness and in their searching lost their way: continued to talk about it, but already wanted something else; or perhaps they wanted it but searched for it where it does not dwell. And, as a result, there arose a false formula, an imperfect rule, an unjust decision of a disagreement over claims. This manifestation may be false, this formula may be false; but if natural law is to be found and formulated in perfection and truth, then it will be and must be found *precisely through the creative acceptance and transformation of an imperfect formula*, and through the purification of it, achieved through hard life experience, helping to obtain the true path. The new formula will take that same place which is now occupied by the unsuccessful formula; it will take over the significance of the latter, which must be preserved without derogation and without wobbling; it will say something different, and say it in a different way, but will speak of the same thing: of freedom of the person, of justice in the enforcement of law, of the self-governance of the human spirit. A

5 An apparent reference to Petrazhitskii's theory of law.

6 That is, something having ***absolute*** (unconditional) significance, and not something the significance of which is relative to some further value or condition.

7 Il'in further clarifies his objections to any version of legal positivism here. He insists, by implication, that the ultimate motive for obeying the law cannot be found in any merely formal or institutional-historical circumstances, but only in terms of the ***objective content*** implicit in the positive law.

developed and mature legal consciousness sees in positive law the primal glimmer, as it were, of natural law and therefore prizes it: such a legal consciousness does not "defend" positive law against reform, rather the reverse; but it *obeys* it pending repeal.

To this motive for the recognition of an incompletely expressed minimum of natural law, affirmed in the shape of positive law, there is joined another motive, based on a sense of justice. If positive law, incorrectly formulating *others'* obligations, *correctly* expresses "my" legal empowerment, then "I" accept it: for if "I" were not to accept it and not to protect "myself" with it, then "my" spiritual personality, most certainly, would long ago have faded out of earthly life. Besides, "I" already availed myself of the security guaranteed by it long before "I" had time to understand its necessity for "my" existence. But if "I" agree to assert "my own" legal *empowerment* on the basis of imperfect legal norms, then "I" thereby *already enter* into the net of political and social legal *mutuality*, and in turn must accept the reverse side of this imperfect order of law.

The imperfection of positive law is the *common* scourge of people, associations, States, and all of humanity; and one who accepts it up to the extent of his own interest, uses, observes and perhaps defends it to that extent, and then knows how to evade and escape it the moment another's rightful interest lays upon him an uncomfortable duty or a constraining obligation, according to the principle of mutuality—that one exercises the greatest hypocrisy. In this lies the deep meaning of that tacit consent which Rousseau pointed out.

Normal legal consciousness, accepting positive law as a phenomenon and a promise of natural justice, always finds within itself the power [силу] to recognize a lawful finding and verdict, when it is spiritually false and unjust *in relation to the one recognizing it*: precisely to the extent that "my" interest is derogated or trampled on by the law, "I" can freely recognize and accept this injury, if only this recognition is not a renunciation of "my" spiritual worth. Such an upholding of positive law is an act of struggle for *the triumph of natural law.* That is why the figure of Socrates, accepting the unjust verdict of the Athenian court and calmly drinking the poison in the name of a celebration of unjust law, remains forever the most profound summons to the overcoming of a positive legal order for the sake of the natural one.

Normal legal consciousness is a creative will to the goal of law.

Chapter Seven
The Struggle for Law

Normal legal consciousness is a *volitional* state of the soul, active and creative; it seeks in life a free, true and just [справедливого] law[1] and compels the human to struggle for its discovery and realization.

In this struggle "effective" positive law is accepted as the latest stage achieved by law-creating humanity in the matter of the maintenance and formulation of natural law. Consciousness perceives not only the *objektive* meaning of positive law, but also *the objektive idea of natural law* and places before itself the task of bringing this "meaning" into correspondence with the "idea".[2] This means that normal legal consciousness, commencing the struggle for law, must realize *three* self-sufficient acts of cognition: first, to establish the objective *meaning* of positive law; second, to formulate in explicit form the objektive *idea* of natural law; third, to detect the hidden, but *incomplete* presence of the *idea* in the meaning, and find such a formula for meaning as would reproduce the essence of the idea precisely and without distortion. As a result of this, the law-creating soul forms within itself two concepts of law: the concept of positive law, corresponding to its meaning, and the concept of natural law, true to its idea. Behind these two subjectively experienced concepts are hidden, objectively speaking, *two* objektively significant legal values apparently dwelling in mutual divergence or even opposition. To a superficial glance there is revealed an "unavoidable" dualism of "positive" and "natural" law, such that a conscientious but not thoughtful person might perceive here a hopeless situation for legal consciousness. However, a third act of law-creative cognition cancels this "hopeless dualism" and indicates a way out and a direction for the entire struggle: natural law lies in a concealed fashion at the base of positive law, present in it first as a certain "minimum of rightness" [правоты]; second, in the shape of its own fundamental categories; and third, in the form of an immanent but incompletely resolved task. The unity of positive and natural law *is already given*, although in embryo, and *yet to be given* in its holistic and realized form.

And thus to the extent it is "yet to be given" for realization, legal consciousness actually has before it a certain duality, though not a hopeless one. To the extent that positive law in its prescriptions and formulas diverges from the requirements of natural law, to that extent are revealed

[1] The Russian phrase here (in the 1956 edition) is "*оно ищет в жизни свободнаго, вернаго и справедливаго права*," changed from the original version (in the 1919 edition) of "*оно вызывает к жизни настойчивую и непобедимую волю к свободному и правовому праву*": i.e., "it summons to life a persistent, invincible will to free and rightful law".

[2] This distinction between the "meaning" of positive law and the "idea" of natural law appears to invoke something like Hegel's notion of an idea as rationally structuring the actual (i.e., not a mere mental *representation* of something actual).

two "proper" orders of law, in appearance identically claiming objektive obligatoriness and objektive significance. Expressing this conflict in the image of "quiet[3] flamelets", one can say that legal consciousness sees in many states, deeds and relations of people *two* different flames, one of which, small, expresses a positive-legal qualification, and the other one, large, expresses a "natural-legal" qualification; such that the small blue flamelet, indicating the "positive" rightfulness of the act, may burn alongside the large red flame signifying the "natural" wrongfulness of that same action, and conversely. The obligation of the "jurist" may turn out to be in essential contradiction with the obligation of the human being living according to "natural" legal consciousness, and this may give rise to a split within a conscientious soul. It is characteristic of normal legal consciousness always to scrutinize the color of *both flames* with objective attention and that makes it particularly vulnerable to such conflicts. It is clear that the pretensions to co-existence of the two flames must come to an end in an objectively-grounded and principled resolution of their dispute.

The conflict between natural and positive law must be resolved in favor of the *former*, and, moreover, because the objektive significance of positive law is determined at its root by the spiritual worth of natural law, that is, first, by the real and substantive presence in it of spiritual-natural rightness; second, by the formal possibility, and its vital objective, of being a true and exact formula of natural law. Positive law by its very essence is *an organized attempt to formulate natural law*; the spiritually vital importance of this matter, an awareness of its seriousness, and the certainty that such a formula is unitary, constitute that *spiritual* foundation which impels people to concentrate on the strictly formal regulation of the very order within which law is created. It is clear that positive law in all cases of divergence turns out to be a *surrogate* of natural law, and if this divergence sharpens to the point of *conflict*, then positive law may appear to consciousness in the role of "false" law, pseudo-law, or an "impostor". When such a conflict is discovered, there ensues a period of *temptation* for legal consciousness: the concept of law bifurcates; positive law begins to lose its aura of rightness, and if the idea of objektively significant natural law does not live in minds with sufficient distinctness and force, then the "principled" dethronement *of any and all law* turns out to be at the doorstep. Law begins to be depicted as a "simple manifestation" of power, force and violence, as an instrument serving the organized dominance of the propertied class; it is gradually discredited in logical, but unseeing critical analysis, and an unseeing skepticism leads to its categorical rejection. There begins a more or less profound *crisis of legal consciousness*, which *may* lead to the degeneration of life under law, but

3 "*почиющих*". This somewhat overworked image of "flamelets" is continued from Chapter Three (see footnote 9 there), and was apparently inspired by a passage in Petrazhitskii. Here large red or blue flames attached to actions from a natural-law perspective are contrasted with small red or blue "flamelets" attached to actions from a positive-law perspective.

must lead to a deeper grounding and understanding of law and to the birth of a *new* legal consciousness.*

The conflict between natural and positive law is resolved in the vital *struggle for law*: in the creation of law. This struggle, depending on its immediate and paramount task, can have two forms: it can be a struggle for "law in the objektive sense" (that is, for the renewal of legal norms) and a struggle for "law in the subjective sense" (that is, for the maintenance and realization of just empowerments, duties and prohibitions). It is clear that these two tasks not only do not exclude one another, but the one mutually presupposes and grounds the other.

The usual, healthy path of struggle for new, better *objektive law* (that is, for "new laws$_z$") is the path of *law-making*: false, unjust, obsolete laws$_z$ and institutions are abolished and instead of them, by means of the peaceful, organized realization of those external deeds by which are conditioned the "initiation" of new norms, *a new, better law* is established. Normal legal consciousness considers this mode of struggle for objektive law the best because its simple realization in itself strengthens and inculcates in people's souls a *will for* and *confidence in law*: the circumstance that life under law *itself* opens up a path to the perfecting of law, that *obedience to positive law* itself can advance positive law toward "natural" correctness and, by the same means, toward its overcoming—this circumstance in itself summons, as it were, toward its recognition. The significance of positive law is inviolable; but all norms entering into its make-up, according to their general, fundamental essence, are subject to abolition and replacement by new ones. Law possesses the capacity to renew itself on its own inner paths, and so long as this capacity is preserved, legal consciousness faces the prospect of peaceful and organic development.

Accepting the path of such a renewal of law, normal legal consciousness begins always with a conscientious attempt to uncover and formulate that *natural law* which must lie at the foundation of new norms. Such an attempt is necessary precisely because every positive norm, as already demonstrated above, takes upon itself the responsible task of indicating to people the *best* conduct, obligatory for them. This idea of "best" by no means coincides with the concepts of the most "convenient", "advantageous", "useful", and so forth: what to various people are "useful", "advantageous", and "convenient" are different, whereas the legal idea of the "best" has a single, objective content. This "best in law" can be at variance with all present "traditions", "creeds", "prejudices", not excluding also "social opinion". The scholar-jurist and in particular the philosopher of law must uncover this idea scientifically and make its content a common possession. People creating and formulating new

* **P. I. Novgorodtsev provides a formulation and illumination of the problem of the crisis of contemporary *political* legal consciousness in his work *Кризис современнаго правосознания* [Crisis of Contemporary Legal Consciousness] (1909), especially pp. 1, 5, 13, 15, 16, 392, 393.**

legal norms must cultivate in themselves a particular "act"[4] of legal consciousness, or, conditionally speaking, *of legal conscience*, verifying or even for the first time formulating this idea and forcing the inclusion of it in the foundation of new norms as a true and objectively grounded value. A true legislator is *an artist of natural rightness*, its seeker and servant. For him the "best" is always what is best *in actual fact and in itself*: for he is guided by *a good will*.

However, it may turn out that the healthy and normal path to the renewal of the laws and the State order is inaccessible for the one who began the struggle for law. The social group ruling a given State may not consider reform useful, just or necessary, whereas the State structure may not possess sufficient "flexibility" to provide for a renewal of the laws under any circumstances. Then the normal path turns out to be closed and the struggle for "objektive law" enters upon a new path.

It turns out that the norms of positive law acquired the anti-natural character of being *unrepealable* or *unchangeable*, while the "incorrectness" characteristic of their content becomes the scourge of life. The consciousness of a human being sees that it is enslaved by an imperfect and perhaps even degrading life and that the conflict between positive and natural law does not submit to resolution: law [право] cannot be developed further *in accordance with right* [по праву], while a matured legal consciousness cannot return to its previous state. And thus arises the necessity to find another method of *law-creation*; and there remains the path of an *immediate realization of new subjective rights.*

This path consists in the *subject, directed by his own legal consciousness to the goal of law, asserting for himself other empowerments, obligations and prohibitions* than those which belong to him at the given moment on the basis of the norms of *effective positive law*. Further, recognizing these empowerments, obligations, and prohibitions as his own, he sets about the *immediate realization* of them. Legal consciousness forges for the subject a new status, belonging to a new, officially not yet established legal order, and sets itself the task of living according to this

[4] Il'in's conception of philosophical method, developed at some length elsewhere, centers upon his Husserl-inspired conception of a "philosophical act" which involves an *intuitive seeing* with the mind's eye of an object of thought which is subsequently described and analyzed in its pure givenness, with no admixture of the philosopher's own theories, assumptions, or biases concerning the supposed nature of the object, and without reference to the philosopher's *consciousness* as the medium of that experience. An "act of legal consciousness" would be a specific instance of the more general category of "philosophical acts" which consist of three stages: 1. the philosopher invokes in herself the real experience of the object that she wishes to investigate, 2. enters into the content of the object being studied, engaging in a systematic intuitive inspection of it in its givenness, 3. undertakes an analytical description and rational-logical explication of the experienced and inspected content. In an "act of legal consciousness" the object of the (inner) experience would presumably be the idea of some particular feature of natural law in its objective givenness. For a fuller discussion of Il'in's conception of philosophical method, see the "Translator's Introduction" to I. A. Il'in, *The Philosophy of Hegel as a Doctrine of the Concreteness of God and Humanity*, Trans. and Ed. Philip T. Grier, Volume One: *The Doctrine of God* (2010), pp, *xxxi-xxxviii*.

new status.[5] It anticipates the new, more just legal order, as it were, and hastens its inception, hurrying to meet it. The natural-law law$_z$[6] of universal correlativity, and the mutuality of legal spheres[7] forces him also to recognize new empowerments, obligations and prohibitions *for other* subjects and in this way to make all the consistent deductions. Legal consciousness finds a heroic way out of the developed conflict, recognizing every subject as a member of *two* different legal orders *at once*: one, repudiated in terms of content, but not abolished, and retaining a "positive" significance, and another recognized in terms of content, but not yet established, not affirmed, and perhaps even not yet formulated—however, true, just, better, and therefore often having the *worth* of natural law.

Conflict and duality, ineliminable through the creation of new legal norms, are accepted and creatively overcome by consciousness; the open encounter between positive and natural law, leading always to the subordination of the former to the latter, becomes organized in the process of *implementation in life*; this is done so that the external encounter should bring in its train their *inner* encounter—in the souls of those blind and deaf to natural rightness [правоте]—and, as a result of this the establishment of new law. On this path natural law is realized *as though it already were* positive law; in practice it is implanted in life so as to become a real mode of life and conduct. Natural legal consciousness asserts itself as a living *power* in the certainty that it is a rightful power [правая сила] and that victory over the stagnating and weakening unrightful law [неправым правом] is at hand for the power of this rightfulness [прваоты].

This path of struggle for law is occasionally perceived and depicted as a path of *the violation of law* or as a path of *violent* overthrow of an old legal order. However, such a viewpoint is in essence superficial and false: first, the element of "violation of law" and the element of "*violence*" may be *completely absent* in such a mode of struggle; second, the present violation of law may be a violation not of "law in general", but only of *positive* law, and moreover, in the name of natural law; that is, it may possess the character of an act not of destroying the legal order, similar to all punishable violations of law, but creating and perfecting a life under law and according to law.

Thus, first, a voluntary change of personal status is accepted in principle by positive law itself, insofar as it is recognized that a human being has not

[5] Il'in supplies some concrete examples of such conduct just below.

[6] The "law" (закон) of universal correlativity and mutuality pertaining to the legal sphere is a feature not of the positive-law order, but of the required structuring of relations among spiritual centers which gives rise to the content of natural law.

[7] This is a reference to the doctrine of the inevitably separate "centers" or "spheres" of individual existence articulated in Chapter Five, their potential for mutual infringement upon one another, and the necessity for an order of law which guarantees to each what is essential to their individual being.

only a "legal capacity", but also a "dispositive legal capacity", and among law-forming facts is included *the expression of will*. By means of formal expressions of one's own will each person with dispositive legal capacity can ensure that he will have *more or less* those or other empowerments and obligations, whereas positive law remains unviolated (*secundum legem*). No one can prevent people from making use of this possibility in order to bring their positive-legal status closer to the natural-legal one. Moreover, this possibility always remains within their disposition, that is, even when the normal path to legislation is open and accessible. There is no necessity whatever to passively wait until the law$_z$ or administrative disposition has placed upon me a just [справедливую] obligation, or cancelled my unjust empowerment, especially if I myself feel and am conscious of what is just and what is not. In the majority of legal relations one can find a way out that at once or gradually extinguishes my unnatural empowerments and introduces my natural obligations.

Every person, if he is guided by natural legal consciousness, will seek and find the possibility of bringing his positive-law status closer to the natural. He may *immediately cease to practice* his "non-natural" empowerment and then extinguish it by *a renunciation*; thus in its time natural legal consciousness impelled some landowners to "set free" their peasants and compelled L. N. Tolstoi to refuse the author's copyright to his works. He can, further, *transfer his empowerments to others* in the measure to which he feels these empowerments to be unjust; such is the inner meaning of many "donations" to good causes, of the Christian "distribution of property to the poor" and L. N. Tolstoi's posthumous distribution of the land at Yasnaia Poliana. Further, each one can, following natural legal consciousness, *take upon himself* the fulfillment of *another's obligations*, pay a tax for a poor person, substitute for a sick companion at work or, as was accepted formerly, "go as a recruit"[8] in place of a brother with a large family. Legal consciousness can impel each one to voluntarily place upon himself property obligations, augment others' empowerments at the expense of his own obligations, allow his own unjust rights to expire through limitation of action, volunteer for war, take upon himself this or that responsible service to the nation, etc. Normal legal consciousness, which in general impels one not to avoid assuming and performing *public empowerments and obligations*, but, on the contrary, to seek them and take care of them, gradually teaches a person to experience public *empowerments* as the *obligations* of a citizen, and public *obligations* as inalienable *empowerments*. The natural-law solidarity of people illuminates anew the positive status of the person and renews his understanding from the depth: participation in legislation, administration and the court turn out to be *natural obligations* of the adult citizen, whereas personal and property responsibility is understood as a

8 That is, to the army. In Imperial Russia there was a system of mandatory annual quotas for military recruits imposed upon each district, village, etc. The term of conscription was normally 25 years.

precious *natural empowerment*: to uphold the life of his union through personal work and participation.

Each of us, in reexamining and revising our own positive-law "status" under the guidance of natural legal consciousness, will see that all such "renunciations", "alienations", and "self-obligations" are not, from one's own point of view, "supra-obligatory charity", leniency, or sacrifice, but a simple observance of natural rights [прав] and obligations and thereby a struggle for the realization of a natural legal order. What one does is suggested to him by an immediate feeling of law and a vivid consciousness of his own natural-law obligation. It is normal *legal consciousness* itself that impels him from good will to reexamine and purify his positive-law status and in this way step forward in life as a *volunteer for natural rightness* [правоты].

Entering upon this path, each of us is easily convinced that natural legal consciousness is called upon to guide not only the creation of *norms* of positive law, but also life in everyday *legal relations*, that the struggle with unrightful law [неправым правом] must *always* be led not only from the top, from the "general," through the norm, but also from below, from the "singular," through subjective law. Natural law not only "constructs" a political program for the more or less distant future, but also points to a line for *immediate* personal conduct; its realization is possible and obligatory *right now*, side by side with the positive legal order, *through* it where that is possible, and *in spite of* it—as a matter of morality, mores, custom—where it is impossible. Natural law is not a "distant" or even more, an "infinite" ideal;[9] no: for each of us it stands at the threshold of personal life as a near and immediate possibility, and it depends *upon us* to realize it at each step, not postponing this creative task with splendid hypocritical speech.

In this way it is possible that the element of "a violation of law" will be entirely absent in this law-creation: then this path leads *to a loyal* struggle for *natural law in the subjective sense*.

But further, second, history shows that in the life of a nation there occur confluences of circumstances under which the quickest and most direct path leading to the renewal of the legal order is a path *taking the deeds of a person outside the limits of positive law*.[10] In this case law-creation forsakes the way of strict loyalty and seeks other measures.

[9] Il'in appears to invoke here a critical echo of Kant's doctrine of duty as a perpetual "ought-to-be" not ultimately fulfillable, and rejects it in favor of a conception of duty somewhat closer to Hegel's. Hegel argued that the actual fulfillment of a Kantian duty would undermine the moral world view itself (*Phenomenology of Spirit*, p. 368 in the Miller translation (1977).] Il'in was familiar with the Kantian doctrine as well as Hegel's critique of it.

[10] At this point Il'in begins to develop a multi-faceted doctrine of civil disobedience aimed at the realization of natural law, or at a closer approximation of positive law to it.

These measures may possess a two-fold character in view of the fact that "beyond the limits" of positive law lie, on one hand, deeds "not stipulated" in its norms, and on the other hand, deeds directly forbidden.

In this case so-called "customary-law" creativity points to a precious way out for all of life under law, and not only in the "private" but also in the public sphere. The history of the English constitution witnesses to what an enormous life-transforming significance that path can have. The creation of juridical custom is a *lawful* means of the gradual *introduction into the limits* of positive law of those elements of life which lie *beyond its limits*, but which legal consciousness is in need of. The steady implementation of the *nonlegal* as the *legal* is accompanied by the understanding that "to act this way" is *necessary and correct*; it is truly one of the classic paths leading to the victory of natural law over positive. Actions and *states* not stipulated in advance gradually work their way into the legal order, become "stipulated" and "significant", and the previous order yields its place to a better one. With this outcome one is able to stave off the conflict between natural legal consciousness and positive law: a creative will finds the means for avoiding a rupture between them and does not see itself compelled to turn to *law-violation in the name of law*.

It is clear that a sharp-eyed anticipation from within the old order can quickly place normal legal consciousness before a dilemma: either repudiate one's creative task, or enter on the path of *direct violation* of individual norms of positive law. If normal legal consciousness under the pressure of this despair choses the second path, then it surrounds its decision by a whole series of conditions, remembering that in the name of which it struggles, and remaining true to itself. Neither this goal nor this obedience converts the violation of law committed into a lawful deed, but makes the one who commits it innocent by right, and the deed itself, a *non-punishable* violation of law.

In accordance with what was established above, the decision to permit a direct violation of positive law is accepted by normal legal consciousness only in the extreme case: for a deliberate violation of law contradicts the fundamental essence of legal consciousness, that is, the will to law. This decision is accepted, consequently, as though *contrary to will*; in any case, as a result of an inner struggle. The inner struggle arises as a consequence of the fact that the will to law breaks up into two opposing inclinations: on one side, the will to the end of law summons to rightful law [правому праву] and to the creative renewal of the legal order; on the other side, that same *will to the end of law* summons to the realization of the *inviolability of positive law*. Normal legal consciousness firmly knows that *respect for positive law* is the precious result of a long and painful process, and that to shake that respect means to destroy the abode of natural law already present and necessary in the future; it cannot strive for the destruction of law and, if one tolerates a *violation* of it, it is precisely in order to uphold it and not *permit its destruction.*

Therefore, legal consciousness, deciding to enter upon this path, preserves fidelity to itself only in the case that it observes the following conditions:[11]

first, if all other means of struggle for the renewal of false law have already been tried, exhausted and have not led to the necessary result. Legal consciousness can permit the violation of positive law only in an *extreme case* and, in particular, only after the struggling subject has transformed its personal positive status into a natural one;

second, if this decision is taken *not* out of purely personal or self-interested motives, but out of a *will to the common good*; legal consciousness sees in the creation and maintenance of a legal order a matter of great—*spiritual and common*—necessity, and not of individual profit, and therefore permits *personal* motives here only in the measure of their coincidence with the single, common spiritual interest;

third, if this decision flows from normal legal consciousness, that is, *from a will to the goal of law*. This violation of law loses its ordinary law-destroying character; it flows not from a will to lawlessness and not from an insufficient will to legal order, but from a deep and holistic will to law; it is directed *not against* law and legal order, but strives to create a positive law closer to the natural. It *does not* destroy the existing *legal structure*, precisely to the extent that it is a legal structure, and not a disorder distorting the nature of law; moreover it supports the present legal order as such, trying to correct those traits of it which threaten an actual, and furthermore general, collapse;

fourth, if this line of conduct violates only *certain enactments* of positive law, but does not strive to destroy it as a whole or install in its place a primitive absence of regulation in life. Legal consciousness protects positive law even when it decides to violate it in the name of natural rightness, and, not only to uphold the entire remaining system of effective law, but, perhaps, even to observe it at this time with particular zeal: as a skillful and experienced surgeon does not injure the tissue of a living body more than is necessary, and at the same time is concerned for the careful nourishment of the entire organism as a whole;

fifth, if this deed violates only those positive norms which *support the impossibility of abolishing or changing unrightful law*: such as precisely those norms of public (and only public) law which formulate and protect a political regime hindering the natural growth and purification of law. Then this line of conduct is understood not as a struggle with positive law, but as *a struggle with the impossibility of abolishing or changing its unrightful norms* [неправых норм], which then leads to the abolition of them in a *new* constitutional order;

[11] Il'in here sets forth six conditions all of which must be satisfied if an act of civil disobedience is to be justified. Where all six conditions are in fact satisfied, one can even speak of a "natural right" of disobedience of law.

sixth, finally, if this deed violates only unrightful norms of positive law, *but does not violate the natural rights of human beings: legal consciousness can tolerate the violation* of unrightful law to the extent of its wrongfulness and for the sake of reforming it, for it knows that what is violated is, in its unrightful manner, slow to disappear before the face of natural rightness; but it cannot tolerate *the violation of natural rightness* for the sake of its establishment and realization, for a means which destroys its end is a false and unrightful means: creating it tramples on the very essence of its end and carries guilt.

Such are the conditions under which the violation of a positive-legal norm doesn't contradict legal consciousness and which gives to a human being the natural right [естественное право] of disobedience of law.

And nevertheless such disobedience represents a violation of law which is subject to legal judgement and may be taken for crime.

Chapter Eight
Legal Consciousness and Criminal Guilt

A solution of the problem of criminal guilt and punishment is possible only on the basis of a holistic and mature doctrine of legal consciousness. The guilt or innocence of a person established by a criminal court is determined by nothing other than the *state of his legal consciousness*, that is, the relation of the will guiding him to the end[1] of law, and therefore also to law. Accordingly, the offender will be guilty in case he violated a norm of positive law due to *insufficient will to the end of law, and to law* as a necessary means, and will be innocent in case a true *order of law was his aim* and *his motive*. To recognize and consistently realize such an understanding of criminal guilt means to solve one of the great immediate tasks of criminal science and practice.

Formally speaking, the violation of a positive norm, by whatever motives it took place, is a violation of law, for it exceeds empowerments and does not observe obligations having *de jure* significance; if it thereby breaks prohibitions established in the norms of positive law on pain of punishment for guilt, the one committing it is subject to criminal responsibility, trial and judgement. However, a criminal court truly understanding its task and objectively investigating the deed of the accused, will not be in a position to find in it an element of legal guilt, to condemn the offender, and to impose punishment on him, if his deed resulted *from a good will, striving toward the end of law and toward law.*

According to such an understanding, uncovering the basic nature of the jury, and together with it also the essence of *any* criminal court, not all criminal violations of the law takes place in a guilty manner. According to the general rule, the accused *may be* found guilty only for a deed forbidden on pain of punishment, but that does not mean that he *must be* found guilty for *any* such deed: it is possible for there to be a violation of a *law*$_z$ in which the person committing it *is free from guilt*, but not because he was "not responsible" (that is, incapable of rational determination of the will), but on other grounds. The right is granted to the jury to decide the question of the presence of these grounds "solely" by "inner conviction", which is formed as a result of a "comprehensive evaluation of *all subjective conditions of guilt*".*

[1] The Russian term here is цель, which may be translated as "aim", "goal", "end", or "purpose". In this chapter it will be translated both as "end" and as "aim", depending on the context. This is in order to maintain (insofar as possible) a distinction between the *end* of the institution of the law as a whole, which Il'in will eventually connect with the idea of an end-in-itself or an intrinsic good, and will also come close to connecting with Aristotle's notion of an activity which contains its end within itself. On the other hand, when the context is that of the personal *aims and motives* of an individual actor, or even the *aim* of a particular law, "aim" or "aims" will be the preferred translation.

*** Compare: *Устав Уголовнаго Судопроизводства* [Rules of Criminal Procedure] (in prerevolutionary Russia), compiled by Shramchenko and Shirkovyi (6th ed., 1913), p. 804, addendum 1.2.3, pp. 809 and 810.**

These subjective conditions of guilt are always individual and distinctive, not only for each criminal, but also for each single crime. They possess not an outward corporal-physical character, *but an inner, psychic-spiritual nature*: thus, the jurors, having recognized that an outwardly law-violating deed is present and that it was indeed committed by the accused, may subsequently establish his innocence. The guilt of a person is determined by the inner state of his soul and spirit, and not by an outward deed, the factual presence and criminal stipulation[2] of which provides only a basis for the beginning of a preliminary investigation. The psychic-spiritual state of the accused is examined by the court from the standpoint of *consciousness and will*: he must be convicted if his deed resulted from "full awareness" and a "criminal will". However, that "awareness" which must be present for an accusation is not at all exhausted either by a knowledge of the illegality$_z$ of the given action, or by a distinct awareness of his deed, or by a full foresight of its consequence: there may be present not only the "intent", but deep and comprehensive premeditation concerning the action—and this need not hinder the jury from bringing a verdict of not guilty, given the presence of *certain subjective conditions*. In precisely the same way, that "criminality" of will which must be present for an accusation is not at all determined either by a causal connection between lively desire and the vital consequence of the action, or by a natural weakness of will of the accused, or by a decision or an intention to commit the prohibited action: a "transgressing" will is thereby still not at all a "*criminal* will" and the jurors can bring a not guilty verdict for a premeditating violator of a prohibition, but, of course, given the presence of *certain subjective conditions*.

These subjective conditions, exculpating the accused *despite everything else*, are concealed within *his legal consciousness* and are determined by those *motives and aims* which brought to life the forbidden action. This means that the verdict of the jurors depends not on whether the accused knew that he was violating a norm of positive law, and whether he wanted to violate it, but on *precisely what pushed him into this, and what aim he pursued*. Resolving the question of guilt, the court must examine and establish: *what were the aims and motives possessing the soul of the accused during the action, and in what relations these aims and motives stand* to the aims and motives of *normal legal consciousness*. Here again it is found that motives and aims enter into the very essence of both *obedient* and *transgressing* legal consciousness; they determine the culpability of a person. Normal legal consciousness possesses *its own* aims and lives according to *its own* motives; in what do these aims consist, and what sort of motives these are, the law$_z$ does not say, and legal theory to this day has not explained. The law$_z$ leaves it to the "*conscience*" of the jurymen* to know of this, and manifests in this way a great trust in the human spirit. In order to be worthy of this trust, the jurors, just as

[2] Предусмотренность. This term was introduced in Chapter Three (See footnote 1).

* **See ibid., p. 804, addenda 2[1] and 4[2].**

the legislator, must accomplish in themselves an act of *legal conscience*, objectively witnessing *by which objektively-best contents a normal legal consciousness lives*. They must, as it were, "sense" to the extent of their power the fundamental *idea of law* and its end and, to do that, internally invoke a *good will* as the natural basis of legal consciousness. A sensitive and conscientious person, performing as a juryman, carries out a profound inner work: for a person has one conscience, and its testimony on law (in the capacity of "legal conscience") inevitably sets in motion its ultimate ethical depth; precisely this work and only this work can make of a judge[3] in a criminal case *an artist of natural rightness*.

And thus, the judgement of a person's guilt or innocence is a result of a (vague or distinct, imaginative or objective) comparison: of motives and aims actually presented with the motives and aims of normal legal consciousness; and if one conditionally equates the presented content of the aim with the content of the volitional motive (the latter is always more complicated, unconscious, non-rational), then it will be possible to say: *criminal guilt is determined by a discrepancy between the subjective will giving rise to the violation of law, and the sole objektive end of any law, while the degree of guilt is determined by the degree and the conscious awareness of this discrepancy in the given action of the accused.* A person is guilty in the case that his will, having brought about the violation of law, tramples on *the end of law.* Consciousness of this lives not only in every objective judgement of a jury, but also in the hearts of simple people: they know that people, carried away by passions, *often* trample on the end of law, but at the same time not infrequently avoid criminal violation of the law. They know that *those guilty by law and before the law* are far more numerous than those who are actually tried, and that on the other hand, there are quite a few persons tried, and perhaps even convicted, who have committed an "innocent" violation of law. That is why the folk wisdom advises "not to refuse to have anything to do with prison" and calls those who have been convicted "unfortunates".

But if that one is guilty whose transgressing will trampled on the end of law, then this can also be expressed as follows: the guilty will tramples on *the essence of law*, because what constitutes the *essential nature of law* is determined precisely by its *end.* This essence of law, as already demonstrated, lies at the foundation of *positive law* and is concealed within its depth; therefore, the question of guilt can be formulated as whether the accused, in violating a positive-law prohibition, strove to violate and trample on what constitutes the *essence of law* hidden in it, that is, the natural-law basis of the positive norm. He will be recognized as guilty if his will was drawn toward that.

All of this can be expressed by saying that the spiritual *wrongfulness* [противоправность] of the deed, constituting the guilt, does not coincide with its formal *unlawfulness*, [неправомерность] supposing only

[3] By the term "judge" Il'in may still be referring to the juror exercising judgement as to guilt or innocence.

the beginning of a criminal reaction: the will, *having transgressed* the prohibition and having committed the illegal action, may be recognized as *not criminal*, that is, *not wrongful*, and consequently, as a *non-guilty will*. On the contrary, guilt consists always in the *wrongfulness of the direction of will*, that is, in the more or less conscious and audacious placing of his own private aim *above* the end of law, in the trampling of the latter for the sake of realizing the former. In other words: the accused is guilty in case he violated a norm of positive law for the sake of his own private aim, which is incompatible with the free, just and peaceful life of a community of people. That one is guilty who violates positive law, proceeding from an aim which is *wrongful in the highest sense*; and *the degree* of his guilt depends upon what form that wrongfulness took in his soul: did it reveal a level of direction of will *usual* for an accused (the legal consciousness of an "habitual" criminal), or was that direction of will an *exceptional* deviation, and moreover *repeated* (the legal consciousness of a "recidivist"), or *accidental* (the legal consciousness of an "accidental" violator), and further, did this wrongful direction of will have at the moment of the crime the character of an *intention repudiating* the end of law (an absence of legal will) or it was just carelessness that neglected the end of law (a defect of legal will); and finally, to what extent this wrongfulness took shape "consciously", that is, to what extent this consciousness was involved and absorbed in serving the wrongful will (gradations of defects in knowledge and awareness of higher and lower wrongfulness). All these varieties of *guilty legal consciousness must, of course, find a classification for themselves.*

In this way the term "guilt" qualifies a *state of the criminal will at the moment of committing the prohibited deed.* From this it is already clear that the question of *punishment* must be separable in court from the question of guilt and examined independently: for punishment is imposed on the person not at the moment of committing the crime, but after a certain interval of time, in the course of which the state of the transgressing will may have changed radically. A person transgressing a prohibition due to defect or absence of legal will or consciousness could experience through his own deed or when brought to justice a certain renewing and regenerating upheaval of soul cultivating in him a healthy and steadfast legal consciousness. In committing the crime, he was guilty and at that time, perhaps, was in need of an organized influence on his legal consciousness; and perhaps, had the forms of mutual social training been more completely developed, and brought about an organized reaction to bad actions in the form of "criminal morality" and "mores", then his legal consciousness would not have led him to the dock at all. However, at the moment of the judgment he, perhaps, may already have no need at all for outside influence on his legal consciousness or, if it is needed, then in the mildest and most solicitous form.

Criminal punishment has and only can have one sole purpose: *the compulsory training of legal consciousness*. To sentence a person to punishment means to recognize that his legal consciousness is *in the given moment* in such a state that it is necessary for him that his consciousness be subject to obligatory, publicly organized cultivation and strengthening; this means to recognize that he cannot be left, without further measures, to the usual normal life characteristic of a person as a *self-governing* spiritual center; it means to recognize that during the period between the crime and the judgement he was not able independently to cognize the *wrongfulness* of his transgressing will and overcome its power by way of self-training. But in order to recognize this, the present state of his legal consciousness must be subjected to a particular independent examination, either in court or in a particular collegium competent in the examination of legal consciousness and in the means of its active cultivation. "Punishment" is proper for one who cannot, is unable or unwilling, to conquer a wrongful will in himself; but this means that punishment is already not "punishment", but a socio-pedagogical measure and that the character of this measure must be strictly individualized in its application.[4]

Given such an understanding of criminal guilt, it turns out that not only is an "innocent" violation of a prohibition possible, but also *a "guilty" transgression which is not subject to punishment*. The question of "guilt" and the question of "punishment" are posed and resolved separately, but in strict sequence, so that the recognition of guilt does not yet decide the question of the punishability of the guilt, while a sentence of punishment is possible only after the examination of the *present* legal consciousness. At the same time, "punishment" loses its opprobrious character and is not measured out by a formal scale; its immediate aim remains the *correction of legal consciousness*, and on the basis of this rejects all measures of retribution[5] not strengthening but undermining legal consciousness, or still more, ending his life (capital punishment). The contemporary criminal process turns out to be deeply unsatisfactory, and even the jury is receiving a substantial rearrangement: its basic idea—"an intuitive judgement, according to the conscience of a free collegial legal consciousness, of the direction of will of the accused"—is revealed in all its significance and depth and is receiving a deliberate differentiated realization; moreover, the task of a criminal court is established as one and universal for all of its forms: on the basis of an external act violating a positive-law prohibition, to investigate and examine the *legal consciousness* of the violator, establishing the *wrongfulness* of his will at the time of the deed (guilt) and the time of the judgement (punishability). It is clear that given this resolution of the problem, the institution of a "conditional sentence", the doctrine "of the dangerous state" of the criminal and the intensified reform of the penitentiary system receive their true basis and full recognition. The jurymen will understand *what* they are requested to do, and will not be compelled to ascertain the *absence of guilt* where it *was* obvious, but

[4] Il'in here declines to follow Hegel's account of the nature of punishment, and adopts what amounts to a utilitarian doctrine instead.

[5] If any further clarification were needed, Il'in's rejection here of "all measures of retribution not strengthening but slackening legal consciousness" appears to distance himself from Hegel's doctrine of punishment, which is frequently labelled a "retributivist" view (though of course not in the primitive sense of "an eye for an eye").

has now been spiritually overcome by the accused. The criminal court can set out from the certainty that "law" is *not* the same as "a given positive law", and that legal consciousness is not a blind will toward submission to historically given positive norms, toward obedience to unjust law no matter what and under any circumstances whatever. Only a recognizing, sighted and creative obedience to law is capable of maintaining its content and the very life of spirit at the peak.

It is natural that a criminal court, correctly understanding its task and objectively investigating the deed of a person as a holistic manifestation of his legal consciousness, will not recognize the accused to be either guilty or deserving of "punishment" if it is convinced that *the violation of the prohibition sprang from a will toward law and its end.* Not encountering hindrances in the erroneous organization of the process, in false theories and extraneous tendencies, the sharp-sighted eye of justice will inevitably see and openly recognize *behind the apparent disobedience of law the sincere and convinced service to Law.* It will establish here the absence of any *infringement* of the essence of the legal order and verify only the presence of a more or less successful *creative legal seeking.* There cannot be criminal guilt in a deed not violating natural rightness and summoned to life by an authentic will toward the end of law and toward the perfection of positive norms. The complete absence of flexibility in the constitution, the use of other paths, the presence of a will to a *general* and principled recognition of positive law complete those conditions in which legal consciousness did "*transgress*", but remained *free from criminal guilt*: in the struggle with the impossibility of repealing unjust law, with the inflexibility of a constitution, legal consciousness does not abandon the public-legal path, but carries out a forced transition from the legislated order to another, representing a complex combination of the ordinary legal order, of immediate anticipatory application of *legis ferendae*,[6] and of an initial, instituting proclamation.

In this way, in the struggle for natural law and for a worthy life, legal consciousness does not see itself as having abandoned the path of Law even when it decides to violate this or that positive prohibition. It recognizes that in violating "the law" it realizes the Law, and that to convict and to sentence the bearer of this legal consciousness is possible only for, or in consequence of, an erroneous organization of the criminal court, or in the form of an extra-legal reprisal [внеправовая расправа]. If "punishment" is a measure of compulsory training and the strengthening of a sick or weak legal consciousness, then here it turns out to be unnecessary: legal consciousness which is able for the sake of Law and law [Права и права] to take upon itself according to Law the burden of a violation of law and preserve its innocence of criminality, is in need not of correction, but of objective study and imitation. And is it not natural that one studying this outcome is reminded of the figure of Socrates, proposing a just

[6] future law.

punishment for himself before the Athenian jury sentencing him —in the form of the table of honor in the Prytaneum?

Chapter Nine
The Basis of Sound Legal Consciousness[1]

From everything I have said up to now, it must already be clear that there is such a thing as sound legal consciousness. It is something broader and deeper than "consciousness" as such. In legal consciousness not only "knowledge" and "thought" participate, but also imagination, will, and feeling, and the entire human soul. It is insufficient to correctly know one's empowerments, obligations, and prohibitions; there are people who know them perfectly well and constantly abuse this knowledge in order to exceed their empowerments, minimize their obligations, and remove prohibitions from themselves. It is necessary not only to know all this, but also *to recognize* them by way of *self-imputation*; and having recognized them, to possess sufficient strength of will *to observe what is recognized.* One must turn to one's own *instinct* and *habituate* it to "obedience to law$_z$" or "fidelity", and this proves possible only for one in whom a *spirituality of instinct* dwells, sufficiently strong and definite to master the *spiritual meaning of law*, its end and its function.

It is vain to think that *spirit and instinct* might be inimical to one another: that they might be incompatible and set in an eternal struggle.[2] That does not correspond to the actuality. Of course, there are people who, living almost without spirit, are indifferent to the spiritual principle and spiritual contents; they live by spiritually-indifferent instinct, which guides all their activity. But in them as well spirit may suddenly flare up in the depth of instinct and lead them to what is unusual for them: a manifestation of conscience, of prayer, of an artistically true choice, of a sense of law or justice, of charity, of generosity, or of love. And the task of genuine cultivation consists precisely in awakening the spiritual principle in human instinct from childhood; moreover, not in the sense of a habit imposed through discipline, but in the sense of a *free joy and a free preference*.

Somewhere in the depth of the unconscious lives the sacred capacity of a person to distinguish *the better* from *the worse*, to prefer the better, to rejoice in it, to desire it and love it. From this begins the spirituality of a human being; in this consists the life of spirit. At the same time,

[1] The title of this chapter in the 1919 edition was simply: "The Basis of Normal Legal Consciousness". In the 1956 edition Il'in appears to have recognized that he was dealing with an additional aspect of legal consciousness, beyond what he had described previously as "normal", and he distinguished this additional aspect here by the phrase "*sound* (*здоровое*) legal consciousness". Consequently, he had to rewrite the introductory paragraphs of the chapter.

[2] Il'in is evidently rejecting here the Kantian conception of a necessary incompatibility of reason and inclination. He is able to do this so straightforwardly one presumes because his discussion is also informed by a very detailed knowledge of Hegel and Hegel's thorough-going rejection of this aspect of the Kantian standpoint.

speaking of "the better", one must intend not the subjectively-pleasant or convenient, but *the objektively more perfect* in the artistic, ethical, social or religious sense. To humanity is given from God and from nature a certain *instinctive sensorium*[3] *for the objektively better*; to bring up the child means to awaken and to strengthen this instinctive sensorium in the child for the whole of life. In art this is called artistic feeling or "taste"; in ethics, conscience, or a feeling of justice, or else an organic goodness of soul; in science, a sense of truth or sometimes the self-manifesting truth; in religion, a thirst for Perfection, prayer, or sometimes an intuition of God; in social life this is expressed in a sound and strong legal consciousness.

For that reason it would be possible to describe legal consciousness as a natural sense for law [права] and right [правоты] or as a particular spiritual attunement of instinct in relation to oneself and to other people. Legal consciousness is a particular type of *instinctive sense of right* in which a person affirms his own spirituality and recognizes the spirituality of other people; hence the basic *axioms of legal consciousness*: a sense of one's own spiritual worth, the capacity for self-obligation and self-governance, and the mutual respect and trust of people in one another.[4] These axioms teach a person independence, freedom, compatibility, mutuality, and solidarity. And above all, and most of all: *a spiritual will.*

It would be possible to say that legal consciousness is an instinctive will to spirit, to justice, and to every kind of good. But precisely for that reason, its living root must be sought in religious feeling and in conscience. One can, of course, imagine legal consciousness outside of religion and outside of conscience, but this would be something somewhat similar to will deprived of heaven and earth; it would be a disciplining of inclinations, but not a creative principle of life, nor one of high quality; a callous form deprived of the gift of love and the gift of intuition.

Law in its fundamental essence is a form of spiritual life on earth necessary for a human being; or otherwise: a necessary form of the "encounter" between the supreme good and the human soul. Law [право] is above all the right [право] of a human being to be an independent spirit, the right to being and the right to freedom, the right of self-sufficiently turning to God, to seek, to find, to profess and to realize the perfection seen and preferred. In a word: law is an attribute of spirit, its mode of life, its necessary manifestation. And legal consciousness is a will to true law and to the one, supreme *end of law* as such.

This connection between *law and spirit* is so genuine and essential that without a recognition of it—clear and mature, or immature, only a presentiment of it—a life of *normal legal consciousness* is impossible. Only *the spiritual life of humanity* is in need of *natural and substantively-*

3 Чувствилище.

4 These three "axioms of legal consciousness" will prove to be fundamental features of Il'in's theory of law and the State. Two full chapters will be devoted to the elaboration of each of them below (Chapters 15-20).

perfected law; only the soul, possessing the organ for (conscious or unconscious) spiritual life, is capable of normal legal consciousness. The *human-animal* can get along entirely without law; he will bring about a triumph of naive force. For humanity as the *creator of an economy* it is impossible to live outside of law, but at the same time it is possible to limit oneself to merely a superficial appearance of the right [правоты], to merely a *sketch* of law, cultivating and applying bad and unjust "positive" norms. Only to humanity as a *creator of spiritual life* is normal legal consciousness accessible; only to humanity is it given to seek and find *rightful law* [правое право],[5] for only to humanity is the *end* of law and its living source opened.

To solve the problem of legal consciousness means to establish and formulate that unconditional foundation which makes its being necessary, its inner structure normal, its content spiritually true and worthy, and its power vitally creative and invincible. This foundation must be not an abstract principle, suitable for a philosophical construction but powerless in the actual life of humanity; it should be sought among the vital inclinations and motives fundamental to every human being, expressing at the same time *the spiritual essence of the human* as such. Only a *motive flowing from the very nature of the human as a spiritual being*, and constituting that nature, could be such a foundation. It is clear that this motive as a manifestation of the fundamental and universal living will of the human could not be filled with just any sort of transitory, or accidental, or purely subjective content, but must be chained to a substantial, permanent content which is accessible to everyone. Such a universal inclination in life is given to every living human being in the form of *the will to spirit and to spirituality*.

No matter how dark and meagre the life of the soul, no matter how base and crippled its usual contents, it always possesses states in which its *will to spirit* is revealed, even when it does not think of this, is not aware of it, and pehaps does not even know in general that spiritual life is possible. These states reveal the attraction of soul now to *the form of spirit*, now to its *content*.

Every human being as such has an intrinsic attraction toward a vital *self-sufficiency and self-activity*, toward an autonomous self-determination; the significance and maturity of the individual soul are determined above all by the depth and compass of this autonomy. This self-lawfulness[6] in its simplest form extends only to the everyday

[5] Alternatively, "just law".

[6] Самозаконность: following a law prescribed by the self for the self; thus also, *autonomy* (see also Chapter Six above, footnote 3). This passage reflects a more Hegelian conception of freedom than a Kantian one. Both view freedom as autonomy. However, Kant sees autonomy in conduct governed not by natural inclination but by the moral law alone (the law of pure practical reason) which I prescribe to myself. From the Kantian standpoint autonomy lies exclusively on the one side of the dualism of reason and nature. For Hegel one is free only if one is self-determining, that is, not dependent on anything

functions of the human: the physiological, the economic, and the routine psychic sides of life, and to that extent, not finding for itself a worthy content, self-lawfulness often finds expression in purely subjective manifestations: in fancy, caprice, arbitrariness, obstinacy, self-will, and a fetish for originality.[7] These inferior manifestations of distinct being, in themselves still not spiritual, reveal, however, *the formal potential for spirit*: the search for an autonomous life is already an attraction to spirit, for self-lawfulness is precisely *its* constitutive form. But this search is not more than a "potential", because true achievement and satisfaction is possible only on unconditional objective contents; the inferior contents leave the soul always impoverished, precisely because they easily carry it away to *empty form*, that is, to an independence without content, on the path of exorbitant love of power, criminal ambition, and unrestrained cupidity.

In just the same way there is present in every person an attraction to finding a certain content in life *indisputable in terms of its value*, and clinging to it through their *faith* and their *love*; the significance and maturity of the individual soul is determined by the objektive worth of this content and the intensity of personal attachment to it. This content is usually chosen by people from the sphere of everyday existence, from the physiological, economic, and the psychic-domestic aspects of life, and to the extent that people bring about a substantive degeneration of spirit, faith becomes a non-objective superstition, joy in life is connected with the ephemeral and banal, the power of love remains an instinctive attraction, grows into an abnormal passion or degenerates into an aimless melancholy. The spiritual content is replaced by a more or less worthless and pitiful surrogate, while the soul gives birth to a sterile boredom (*taedium vitae*) or drags itself out in the hollows of animal passion. And nevertheless this need for a "principal," beloved, unconditional life-value reveals in humans a *substantial potential for spirit*: the search for this potential is already an attraction toward spirit, for unconditional value is an objektive property of *spirit's* content and objects. But such an attraction is no more than a "potential": only an *autonomous and objective* search can provide a support in life which is unconditional in

other than oneself. However, what turns out to be finally other than myself is subject to substantial adjustment over the course of individual and historical experience. What initially presents itself as wholly other to me (whether psychological experience, natural conditions, economic processes, political and legal institutions, Divinity, etc.) may prove in the long run to be structured in accordance with the very same conceptual categories which I recognize as constitutive of my own being, and thus not wholly other after all. Thus the boundary between self and other is not fixed, but is "negotiable" through individual learning and historical experience. Il'in also adopts Hegel's conclusion that genuine autonomy ("spirituality") is achieved only when the content of my thinking objectively reflects what is ultimately real, that is, the true infinite, God, or absolute spirit. At the culmination of this process the self would find itself "at home" in what initially presented itself as other, and hence autonomous (free) in that it is determined by nothing which is ultimately other than itself.

[7] Оригинальничание.

terms of value and power, a creative act, and not a passive clinging, an objectively-true choice, and not an accidental determination of the soul by a pleasant content. The absence of such a search always returns the soul to the slavery of inferior contents and therefore makes it *a victim of self-delusion*, allowing one to take the trivial for the great and the insignificant for absolute value.

However in all these manifestations of spiritual distortion and degeneration of content the wise and sharp-sighted eye will be able to recognize the original and primordial *attraction to spirit*, to its *self-lawful* mode of life and to its *absolutely valuable* objective contents. This attraction in all its evident vagueness and unconsciousness is the lowest and most elementary stage of the *will to spirit*. The wise mentor must find this obscure will in each soul in order to transform it into a higher state, into a definite and conscious, life-determining and mighty will to spirit, that is, to *a free and active life dedicated to objective knowledge and the self-active realization of higher, unconditional values.* Each human being does not merely "possess a soul", but is himself *an individual spirit*, that is, a self-active center of a possible and already present spiritual life (although in the rudimentary forms of "the self-manifesting truth", "conscience", "taste", "profession of faith", and "legal consciousness"). To be a human being means to be an individual spirit and consciously or unconsciously to *want* to be one. But to want to be an individual spirit means to be in need of *natural*, and then also of *positive law*, and this means to possess—consciously or unconsciously—*a will to law and to its end.*

The will to spirit, that is, the will to autonomous life, dedicated to the absolutely valuable, is precisely that motive which lies at the basis of *normal* legal consciousness and which *must* lie at the basis of *any* legal consciousness as such. It is that universal motive which is already immanent in every person and which in its true development and deepening inevitably forges in the soul the *will to the end of law*.

Thus the will to spirit, single and whole in its essence, leads to law and to its end in all three possible forms of what attracts it: *objective, individual, and social.*

The *objective* attraction of will to Spirit requires that in the life of a person in general be realized true knowledge, genuine goodness and objektive beauty as the law$_{z}$ and presence of the Divinity. But this realization, as already shown above, is possible only in the form of a multiplicity of identically solitary and distinct individual processes, flowing, according to their external existence, into a single, common environment and requiring for that reason *legal delimitation*, that is, law. The will to Spirit is a will to its necessary conditions; such conditions are: the mutual belonging of individual spirits within natural law, and the organization of their external co-existence within positive law. Spirit is the end of law, whereas law is its necessary means; not any law whatever, but only spiritually-true, free and just law. Thus does normal legal consciousness arise.

The *individual* attraction of will to spirit, requiring that "my personal life" apprehend an absolutely valuable content and realize in it the form of autonomy, leads to that very result. In order for me to lead a spiritual life, it is necessary, first, that the center of my spiritual willing be protected from forcible encroachments from without; second, that I have time for and access to the spiritual environment already created and realized. *Legal guarantees of personhood and the legal organization of a worthy life* are essential "to me" as a creature moved by the will to spirit. Right law [*Правое право*] also remains an essential means when the end is the being of *individual spirit*. And the path to normal legal consciousness is opened up anew.

Finally, the *social* attraction of will to spirit requires that others, and moreover *all* others, forge for themselves autonomous self-determination in absolutely valuable contents. This spiritual flourishing of others and everyone is for "me" not only a *subordinate end*, essential for "my" spiritual growth, enrichment and protection, but also a *self-sufficient* end which "I" acknowledge both in a purely spiritual, and in a purely ethical way.The objective will to Spirit is deeper and broader than the will to its individual realization and flourishing "in me". One who really loves Spirit as a self-sufficient object naturally and imperceptibly lives through love for the entire throng of actual and possible individual spirits, and this love of his obtains the entire depth of ethical and religious justification. It is clear that such a seeking of spirit *in all and for all* forces the will to concentrate with particular force on the creation of *a common and just legal order*. The spiritual union of people, revealing through itself the spiritual unity of humanity, is one of the most substantive bases of normal legal consciousness; it discloses with self-manifesting truth the *spiritual* nature of law and society, and lays bare in the depth of legal consciousness its ethical root.

Thus only *a will to spiritual life as the supreme good* can be the true basis of normal legal consciousness.

Normal legal consciousness approaches law not from the viewpoint of private,[8] purely personal interests, but setting out above all from its fundamental, sole and universal *end*. Law as a totality of objektively significant rules of external social conduct is created by people for the sake of this single and universal end, which consists in *the protection and organization of the spiritual life of humanity on earth*. The necessity of law is its necessity for the life of spirit; the content of law is determined by the fundamental laws of spiritual life; the creative life of law is its life in the human spirit and for the sake of the human spirit. For that reason any law whatever must be recognized as the more perfect the more fully and precisely it expresses these laws$_z$, the more successfully it organizes the peaceful and just equilibrium of subjective spheres making claims, and the more quickly and painlessly it inculcates autonomous legal consciousness in souls.

[8] *Частных*. This could also mean "particular".

Normal legal consciousness accepts law, cultivates and perfects it, moved by a will to its supreme *end*, that is, *to spiritual life and its organization*. It perceives in this life, dedicated to the free, objective acquisition and realization of the highest, unconditional values, *the supreme good*, and in accordance with that extends its volitional affirmation to everything that necessarily leads to its correct realization. *Normal legal consciousness is the will to law, proceeding from the will to spirit.*

This will should be understood not as a "decision" of only one consciously-rational part of the soul, but as a holistic striving, involving also the non-rational, inmost recesses of the soul and deriving precisely from them its life force. Such a state of holistic, harmonious, and rationally-justified desire, directed to the supreme and universal good, is in itself one of the highest achievements of the ethical life of humanity. And this means that normal legal consciousness can be developed and strengthened in the soul only in connection with its common moral and ethical cultivation.[9] This cultivation must fasten the vague and elementary "spiritual will" to the instinctive root of life and show it the objective path to an unconditional content worthy of it. It must introduce legal consciousness into the life of the *ethically good soul*.

Legal consciousness can be examined separately from morality and ethical life as a sphere situated alongside the entire sphere of ethics.[10] Then it will be discovered that legal consciousness and ethical consciousness are particular manifestations and aspects of the spiritual life of humanity, similarly determined by the mode of being, the tasks and the limits of the human spirit.[11] However, such an isolated examination,

[9] The distinction here is between моральный (moral) and нравственный (ethical). This distinction tracks Hegel's contrast between "morality" (Kantian moral philosophy) which he systematically criticized as an abstract and formal conception of moral life—though a necessary stage in the progress toward an adequate form of ethical life--and "ethical life" itself or *Sittlichkeit*, which was his own account of the rational forms of the family, civil society and the political state. Il'in almost always uses the term "нравственный" rather than "моральный", as though preferring Hegel's account to Kant's, although he does not explicitly discuss the problem in this text.

[10] Not "нравственность" but "этика" here. This is the first occurrence of the latter term, and Il'in seems to intend it as a way of referring simultaneously to both morality and ethical life.

[11] Il'in may be tacitly referring to Petrazhitskii's psychological theory of a special category of "bilateral passive-active experiences" which he termed "emotions" or "impulsions", among which he numbered "ethical" experiences, which he further sub-divided into "moral" and "legal" experiences. The former were experiences exhibiting "imperative" norms, and the latter, "imperative-attributive" norms. Having distinguised the special sub-category of motivational experiences characteristic of law, Petrazhitskii seemed to imply that the study of law could proceed mainly via the more exacting and detailed study of just these psychic experiences. See Hugh W. Babb, "Petrazhitskii: Theory of Law", *Boston University Law Review*, XVIII (1938), pp. 529-547. Il'in, while willing to grant that there could be "methodological" reasons for investigating these separately up to a point, insists here that the study of law as a whole required comprehending it in its relations to the ethical as well.

permissible for methodological considerations, in no way leaves out of sight the circumstance that in the real life of spirit these aspects stand in necessary and fruitful interaction, and that the resolution of spiritual tasks is possible only given a holistic and harmonious mode of life.

On one side, the very *will to spirit* in its true significance takes shape as the mature result of personal and social ethical culture. Thus it arises only as a result of a reconciliation of the rationally-conscious power of the soul with the unconscious inclinations of instinct, and moreover not only in terms of their disciplining, but in terms of their *substantive regeneration and spiritualization*; will remains always a variety of the one and universal principle of *love* in its purest and most noble—Christian—form; it requires unceasing self-restraint and a distinctive, refined selflessness; finally, it blossoms freely and bears fruit only where there is present a high social level, creating an ethical atmosphere of objective service.

On the other side, spiritual life in itself is always an instrument for moral training of the soul and a source of its ethical power. Objective service to unconditional values keeps the soul in a sort of purgatory, teaching it self-knowledge and self-possession, forging in it the capacity for self-restraint and training it for the *selfless joy of objective perfection.* At the same time, this service imparts to the soul that power and that authority which is given only as a result of an actual objective possession, and that confident serenity which is produced only by the merging of one's own fate with the fate of the authentically real supreme good.

Finally, the ethically mature will brings with itself and to spiritual service and legal consciousness a great gift: the art of the objective investigation of "conscience," on which *any* objective cognition in general can train and orient itself. In particular, a developed and deepened ethical will can sometimes by itself absorb and replace by its own motives the will to law: thus, for example, the recognition of others' rights to freedom and to a worthy life can flow not only from a consciousness of the essence of spiritual life and the universal mutual connection of subjective spheres, but also from the deepest source: a spiritual love toward every manifestation of living spirit.

Thus in the holistic life of the soul *the will to the good* nourishes from itself and serves *the will to spirit*; and conversely. This cannot be otherwise because the good in itself is included in the make-up of spiritual objects and its life in the soul is already the real life of spirit.

And both these wills, each separately and jointly, generate and cultivate *a will to just law*. But in the order of *grounding*, the will to spirit, as the more general and constitutive state, has superiority and determining significance. The will to the good in the final analysis tends toward replacing "law" with itself and making it unnecessary. On the contrary, the will to spirit *affirms law* and legal consciousness in its own essence.[12]

[12] Il'in appears to be implicitly criticizing Petrazhitskii's conception of the ultimate fate

Legal consciousness, grasping its own spiritual root, finds its substantial basis and the source of its content. It accomplishes as it were an act of self-cognition and once and for all ceases to see in law an enemy lying in wait and a tyrant. It knows henceforth to what it submits, and recognizes its objective significance; it submits to that which it recognizes as necessary and which it respects, in which it places spiritual value. A person living by such a legal consciousness, possesses in it an organ of law which can resolve the apparently most hopeless problems of life under law. Thus, precisely legal consciousness, intuiting the *end* of law and realizing in itself an act of legal conscience, is capable of that individualizing discretion in the application of law which must be based on an authentic and objective legal intuition and not allow the *summum jus* to be turned into the *summa injuria*. Just such a legal consciousness is able to find the correct way out of the necessity to obey an unjust law [неправому праву] and the impossibility of transforming its injustice [неправоту] in a lawful way. It is capable of resolving the problem of legal guilt and pointing out to positive law its ideal.

Such legal consciousness, proceeding from a will to spirit and nourished by a will to the good, begins inevitably to restructure the social life of people on principles of *spiritual self-governance, a sense of one's own dignity, respect, trust and justice*.

True patriotism and a feeling for the idea of the state[13] will be its mature fruit.[14]

of law here. According to the latter, law only exists because of a lack of cultivation of the human psyche, which is ultimately destined to be raised to a completely social state in which human conduct will be completely dominated by an active love. At this point law will have made itself superfluous and have been abolished. See Hugh W. Babb, "Petrazhitskii: Science of Legal Policy and Theory of Law", *Boston University Law Review*, XVII (1937), pp. 809-810. Il'in's "will to the good", left to itself, would apparently tend in a similar direction. However, he insists that the "will to spirit" is "the more general and constitutive state" and "has superiority and determining significance". And the "will to spirit *affirms law* and legal consciousness in its own essence". As the will to spirit is fundamental for the grounding of law, and law is explicitly involved in its essence, it would appear that law is destined to be a permanent feature of the human situation according to Il'in.

13 Государственность.

14 It is interesting to note that in the printed galleys of this text (the first ten chapters) found in Il'in's personal library, immediately following the final sentence of this chapter, Il'in penciled in the following note: "End of October, 1917 (during the Bolshevik insurrection in Moscow)".

Chapter Ten
On Patriotism

The will to spirit, that is, the desire to lead a spiritual life for oneself and to secure it for others, is *the unconditional and universal* basis of legal consciousness.[1]

It is *unconditional*, first, because it is directed to a supreme and self-sufficient value which serves nothing higher, but itself constitutes the ultimate end of human life. For a human being it is worth living in the world only in order to be spirit and to serve the Divine Spirit; outside of this his life is pointless and degrading. But then the will, directed at this object, which is unconditional in its significance, is lacking neither in justification nor in grounding: it is *fully* right and *objektively* right and is in this sense unconditional.

It is unconditional, second, because it is intrinsic to every person, independently of conditions of place, time or nationality. There is no person who would have been deprived of it, for it constitutes the very essence of "the human". A human-like creature, entirely free of it, might be subsumed under the concept of the human only from a zoological point of view.

Further, the will to spirit is *universal*, first, in terms of the make-up of those subjects for whom it is *intrinsic* and whose legal consciousness it in one way or another motivates. It lives in *all* people, now concentrating on an empty form of spirit, now becoming exhausted from its unformulated content, manifesting itself in endless variety and differing value. The bellicosity, the tatooing, the totemism of a savage witness in their own way to its immaturity, just as its maturity is revealed in any just law, in a painting by Leonardo da Vinci, or in the philosophical doctrine of Hegel.

It is universal, second, in terms of the make-up of those subjects which it *recognizes*, including them in the sphere of legal association and union. The will to spirit is a will to all of its individual hearths, those already extinguished and those not yet ignited, actual and possible.[2] It leads the

[1] This chapter, on the theme of patriotism, was presumably written in approximately the same time frame (February 1918) within which Il'in delivered a major address "On Patriotism" at a public meeting (in the great physics auditorium) of the Society of Young Lecturers of Moscow University (we know that the preceding chapter was written during October 1917, and the first ten chapters were all in galleys by some point in 1919). The 1918 public address is published in *И. А. Ильин: Собрание сочинений* [I. A. Il'in: Collected Works], ed. Yu. T. Lisitsa, in the unnumbered supplementary volume entitled *Справедливость или равенство?* [Justice or Equality?] (2006), pp. 353-374. The contents of this chapter and of the address of 1918 are not identical, but there is a significant overlap of themes and conclusions, as one would expect. However, the passionate eloquence of the spoken address, delivered a few months after the definitive collapse of the Russian State in the disorder of October 1917 is remarkable.

[2] Il'in here (and at various places below) makes extended use of the image of the central (sacred) hearth in the ancient Greek Prytaneum. The fire, which was perpetually kept burning there, tended by the king and his household, symbolized the living unity of the polis. Upon the founding of a new colony, the fire in its central hearth was kindled from the

soul out beyond the conditional boundaries of any historically composed social group and forces a person to really experience and become aware of a *universal human* inter-connection possessing a *natural-law* character.

The will to spirit has significance "for all," but not in the sense that all people in fact know of it and consciously live by it, but in the sense that all people *ought* to live by it and *are able* to devote themselves to it as supreme. Its rightness [правота] and significance do not depend on subjective recognition or non-recognition; it is *subjective* in terms of its source and manifestation, but *objektive* in terms of value and object. And precisely the unconditionality of its significance raises it to that sphere in which are revealed the horizons of the universal compass common to all humanity.

Moved by the objective will to Spirit, a human is, imperceptibly for himself, drawn into the natural-law order of *universal human* brotherhood. Each one of the entire throng of individual spirits is perceived by him as a living abode of Spirit, as a self-sufficient and distinct hearth of spiritual life. Connected with each one of those spiritual hearths by threads of natural-law and positive-law co-belonging, he recognizes this legal connection, respects and supports it as an essential condition of his own and others' spiritual lives. In this way the basis of normal legal consciousness makes a person a member of the *single world-wide legal community*, a "citizen of the universe".

It would appear that for such a legal consciousness the division of people into particular legal, territorial, national, and State communities would have no significance. Any such union of people rests upon a division of the world-wide legal community such that the single and unconditional *natural* legal order is divided into a multiplicity of particular and conditional *positive* legal orders and correspondingly, of States. But spiritual brotherhood and natural-law connectedness do not die out and cannot die out even though humanity over all the centuries of its existence has not been able to organize a stable world-wide union on the basis of *positive international law*.

If someone were to express this by saying that "a citizen of the universe" cannot be a *patriot* and that rejecting the native land for "internationalism" is the last word of normal legal consciousness, such a conclusion would be completely false.[3]

fire in the Prytaneum of the original polis. Analogously, the fire in each individual hearth within the polis could be viewed as an extension of the central sacred fire, which is what Il'in seems to have in mind here.

[3] If, as was apparently the case, Il'in finished composing the previous chapter just as the Bolsheviks staged their insurrection in the name of the coming international proletarian revolution, we may assume that Il'in was writing this chapter on patriotism in the immediate aftermath of that insurrection, or at some point in early 1918. According to its adherents, the Bolshevik "revolution" would have been an important step toward relegating the ideology of nineteenth-century nationalism and national chauvinism, which had culminated in the catastrophe of the First World War, along with nation-States themselves, to the rubbish

In actuality, the problem of patriotism must be posed and resolved in terms of normal legal consciousness. To possess a native land means to possess a particular, self-sufficient, natural-law union, not coinciding with the world-wide, universal human community, and to grant it preference in the matter of love and service. This union rests upon a certain preferential spiritual homogeneity and closeness of people, while the spiritual homogeneity creates that preferential--living and effective--patriotic union, which always possesses a natural-law character, and usually issues in a positive-law organization. The patriotic union of people possesses at its root a spiritual character, taking shape and flowing into the forms of law and the State.

One can say that true patriotism is born from that same source as normal legal consciousness: from *the spiritual nature of humanity* and from *the will to spirit.* The love of a patriot is dedicated to that same object that law serves: spiritual life, its organization and flourishing. But, nourishing the spiritual will from the depth by the power of passionate feeling, patriotism at the same time focuses it on a separate, particular object and manifestly limits the compass of its immediate activity; and thus this *patriotic limitation of the will to spirit* must be comprehended and justified in its essence. Patriotism must be grounded as a *necessary and true manifestation of the will to spirit.*

For the resolution of this problem it is not sufficient to establish its empirical necessity and its acceptability for positive legal consciousness; neither the one nor the other yet uncovers the most fundamental and deep root of love for the fatherland.

The empirical conditions of human life make *necessary* the division of the world-wide community into particular territorial, national and State communities. The spatially scattered nature of humanity on the face of the earth and the economic necessity of settled labor and settled life are the main basis for this division: humankind inevitably lives in the form of a multiplicity of spatially-differentiated "provinces". The sole external basis of existence common to all humanity (above all, space and land) not only unites people, but also disjoins them; knitted together by blood and ancestral ties, groups of people are imperceptibly drawn into local, limited tasks and gradually work out a local, limited mode of demarcation and an ordering of individual claims and spheres. Climate and race naturally reinforce this spatial differentiation and integration of humanity; the economic division of labor and the exchange of goods trains the will

heap of history. From Il'in's perspective, the simultaneous crises of Russia's devastating defeats on the battlefield, the collapse of the Russian State, and the apparent triumph of the Bolsheviks, with their ideology of proletarian internationalism, would all have conspired to make the question of the meaning of true patriotism a burning one. In order to oppose these forces, as Il'in was determined to do, it would have been essential to re-think the meaning of patriotism in a way that could be defended in the face of all these contemporary developments, raising it to the status of a permanent and universal human value, which is precisely what this chapter attempts to do, in the process also linking it indissolubly to the concept of genuine legal consciousness.

to unity and organization; the similarity of interests, way of life, and customs completes this knitting together, and the joint organization of defense forges a common authority and discipline.[4] Thus are formed an entire series of independent legal centers, State communities, and positive legal orders. An instinct for self-preservation, the brevity of individual life, the limitation of individual receptivity, forces a human being with all the content of his life to cling wholly to a single definite social group, to seek support and mutual help *precisely* from it and *only* from it, to the detriment of and in opposition to the universally-human unity. *Need and fear* summon to life the first glimmers of "patriotism," but the empirical inevitability of such a "love for the fatherland" still says nothing of its spiritual essence or of its philosophical grounding.

Positive legal consciousness can impart to such a patriotism a certain spiritual sanction. A heteronomous legal order, uniting one single territorial, national or economic community, solves within its own boundaries and in its own way the spiritual task of *natural law*: it educates a person to the idea of an objektively-significant order, founded upon compatibility and reciprocity, and leading to freedom and justice. Unity, built upon need and fear, receives in this an elementarily-spiritual and moral illumination. A person having grown up in a certain legal order, is conscious of himself as wholly *obligated* to the legal consciousness of his fellow-citizens and the legal culture of their fatherland: the native land acquires for him the significance of a positive-law establishment, already having provided for his existence and now protecting his spiritual life. Thanks to this, the affiliation with a certain political union begins to define itself not only by need and fear, but by a feeling of *duty, honor, and gratitude*. The life interest of the "patriot" acquires moral meaning, and an attraction to the native land: a natural-law basis. True, a political union, educating its citizens, reduces the natural-law reciprocity, limiting it to the compass of a single community. However, legal unity *within* the State by no means excludes legal association stretching *beyond* its limits: political patriotism establishes the *paramountcy* of legal culture, but by no means its *exclusivity*. Citizens of other communities and States remain in principle subjects having legal capacity, and a world-wide union of nations on the basis of international law is recognized as the next task for humanity: this union takes shape slowly over a long period, ascending from the small to the large, from the periphery to the center, from a *multiplicity* of positive-law orders to a *single* positive-law order.

However, all these considerations still do not uncover the most fundamental and deep root of patriotic love abrogating the world-wide

4 This could be read as a one-sentence summary of Hegel's doctrine of civil society and the political State in his *Elements of the Philosophy of Right*. Il'in may well have felt a particular affinity for Hegel's treatment of the topic of patriotism as an essential element of the rational idea of the ethical State. For Il'in's own more detailed summary of those aspects of Hegel's thought, see his *The Philosophy of Hegel as a Doctrine of the Concreteness of God and Humanity*, Volume Two: *The Doctrine of Humanity*, transl. and ed. Philip T. Grier (2011), Chapters 18-20, especially pp. 143-155.

natural brotherhood, due to feeling, and will, and action. Love for the native land must be comprehended as a *creative act of spiritual self-determination*, for only in this form does it achieve true height and maturity, imparting the ultimate sanction to "need" and "duty" and "honor" and "gratitude".

In order to love one's own fatherland, it is essential to *discover it and really experience* that it is actually "my fatherland". Evidently this experience is gained by the majority of people without seeking, as a result of a habit arising naturally and imperceptibly from the conditions of life around them. But precisely owing to this, the *spiritual* essence of patriotism remains very often subconscious. Love for the native land lives in souls in the form of a non-rational, objectively indeterminate inclination which either completely dies down and loses its force given the absence of "appropriate stimulation", or blazes up with a blind and anti-rational passion which does not remember the spiritual relationship, wandering about in the darkness, muffling both the summons of good will and the voice of legal consciousness. This blind passion shares the fate of all passions the clarification and purification of which a person doesn't work at: it imperceptibly degenerates and diminishes the person.

It degenerates either into an empty form of belligerent chauvinism and stupid national self-importance, or into a blind partiality to empirical trivialities, or into a hypocritical enthusiasm, concealing a personal or class greed. A person harboring in himself such a patriotism does not know either *what* he loves or *why* he loves it. He follows not spiritual-political motives, but a herd-political instinct; and the life of his feeling vacillates, as in a genuine animal, between sterile apathy and rapacious outbursts.[5]

A person can spend his entire life within the boundaries of his State and not acquire his own native land, so that his soul will be to the end patriotically empty and dead; and this failure or incapacity will lead him to a distinctive spiritual orphanhood, to a creative groundlessness and sterility. For the acquisition of a native land is an *act of spiritual self-determination*, indicating to a person his own creative ground, and conditioning therefore the spiritual fruitfulness of his life. Such a person will never love his native land, because he never acquired it.

But it might be that a person, not having acquired his own native land, lives his entire life mistakenly considering himself a patriot: then the object of his love will be *not* the fatherland, but something else, taken by him for the fatherland. Such a surrogate can be any of the usual contents and conditions of life, to the extent that it is taken separately, in isolation from its spiritual meaning and significance. Not one of them, taken by itself, constitutes a "native land": not the spatial nearness of people living

[5] Il'in's conception of genuine patriotism sets forth such strict conditions for its manifestation that one assumes only a relatively small spiritual elite could possibly qualify as genuine patriots. What passes for "patriotism" among the majority is condemned by Il'in in quite striking terms here.

side by side, nor the blood relation of descent, nor national or racial affiliation, nor the customary way of life, nor economic unity, nor nature, nor the commonality of positive law and the State. The presence of each of these conditions still does not indicate to the person his spiritual native land, and conversely: patriotism can be formed in the absence of any of these contents. A long life in a foreign land does not make it a native land, regardless of the habituation to a way of life and a nature and to a stable legal community; the tie of blood and nation doesn't resolve the question of a native land for people of mixed origins; membership in a State can be involuntary and produce in the soul a steadfast "anti-patriotic" tension. This means that a *native land* is not defined by and not exhausted by these contents: it is *larger and deeper* than each of them separately and all of them together. That is why the figure of the protestant Roger Williams, who broke away from everything that is normally considered a fatherland, and created for himself a new, genuine native land, will remain forever a living summons to a deepened understanding of patriotism.

If these empirical bonds by themselves do not exhaust the essence of a native land, they nevertheless can all *acquire* that spiritual significance which makes them a worthy object of patriotic love. Then they become a true external sign of *the spiritual bond* uniting people, and through it they acquire a sacred meaning and arouse in souls a patriotic cult. For true patriotism it is not adherence to the external conditions and forms of life that is characteristic, but a *love of spirit* hidden in them and manifesting itself through them. What is important is not "external", but "internal", not the superficial appearance, but the innermost essence. What is important is *precisely what* is loved in the beloved and *for what* it is loved. And thus the true patriot will be one who acquires for his feeling an object *actually worthy of a self-sacrificing love and service.*

One can say that the true patriot loves his fatherland not with the usual blind partiality, motivated purely subjectively and attaching to its object a supposed value; but with a spiritual, sighted love proceeding from the recognition of an actual, not a supposed, *objektive worth* present in the beloved object. To love the native land means to love something that in actual fact objektively merits love, such that the one loving it is *right* [прав] in his feeling, and in serving it, is *right* [прав] in his service. Moreover, the object referred to as the native land is so objektively and unconditionally excellent in itself, that the soul, having found it, having acquired *its native land, cannot fail to love it.*

A person cannot fail to love his own fatherland; if he does not love it, then this means that he did not find it and does not possess it. For the native land is found precisely by the *will to spirit,* while spirit is the self-sufficient and supreme excellence. One may not see it and not know it, *but having seen and known it, it is impossible not to fall in love with it.* The native land is acquired precisely by a living and immediate spiritual *experience*; a person deprived of it will also be deprived of patriotism. The soul, futile in the search for truth, lifeless in the creation of the good, powerless in the intuition of beauty, religiously empty and politically indifferent, has no spiritual *experience*, and everything that is spirit, and everything that is from spirit, remains always for the soul an empty word, an objectless sound. Such a soul will not find a native land, but in the best case will be satisfied through life with a surrogate of it, and its patriotism will remain a subjective passion. To possess a native land means precisely to possess it *through love*. But not through that love which knows of the worthlessness of its object and therefore, not believing in its own rightness or in itself, is ashamed of itself, and of it; and suddenly exhausts itself under the pressure of a new passion. Patriotism is intrinsic to that soul which *through living experience felt the objektive and unconditional worth of its object*. Such a soul objectively knows that its beloved is the most excellent thing in the world, living in people and creating through people. The fire of this feeling is ignited in the soul from a single, simple, but authentic contact with the spiritual object. To find the native land means really to experience this contact and carry away in the soul the burning fire of this feeling. It means to undergo a kind of spiritual conversion: to discover in the object an unconditional value, actually and objektively intrinsic to it, and to cling to it with will and feeling; to discover in oneself a genuine craving for this highest thing and the capability for selflessly celebrating its perfection, to love it and serve it. This means, finally, to unite *one's own life with its life and one's own fate with its fate*.

That is why at the basis of patriotism lies an *act of spiritual self-determination*. A person generally defines his life by *what he considers his most beloved object*. Then a new State takes hold of him, in which his life is filled with beloved contents, clinging to him and to their source. In view of this, a true love always gives the capacity for self-sacrifice, for it forces the loving person to love his object *more than himself*. And thus if a person acquires an object for such a love, actually worthy of this love in terms of its objektive value, and if this object is *the spiritual life and spiritual property of his nation*, then he becomes *a true patriot*. He carries out an act of spiritual self-determination by which he, *in a holistic and creative state of the soul, identifies his fate with the spiritual fate of his nation*.

That to which my love for the fatherland is directed is the *spiritual life of my nation*, its creative formations and its necessary conditions (material, cultural and political). Not simply the nation as such, but the nation leading a spiritual life, and not simply the life of the nation as such, but a genuinely spiritual and spiritually elevated life, and not simply all the conditions of life—land, and climate, and economy, and organization, and government, and laws,—but all that as given for spirit and created by spirit and for the sake of spirit. Spiritual life is that *for which and for the sake of which* one can and must love one's nation, fight for it, and perish for it. Through spiritual life everything acquires its true significance and authentic value. In it is the essence of the native land, that essence which is worth loving more than oneself, through which it is worth living precisely because it is worth dying for. In actuality it is worth merging one's life and one's fate with it, because it possesses objektive value *before the face of God*. The spiritual life of my nation and its creations are important, necessary and precious *in themselves*, and for that reason also *universal*: not only for me but *also* for me, and for my nation, but not only for my nation; always also for everyone, for all people who are living or someday will live.

Uniting one's own fate with the fate of one's nation—in its achievements and in its degradation, in danger and in well-being—the true patriot identifies himself not with the multitude of empirical individuals; he doesn't merge with the life of the ignorant masses, taking them for *the nation*, and does not sacrifice himself to the mercenary interests of the poor or the rich mob; he by no means bows before the "multitude" as before something superior and more powerful, supposedly gifted with a wise and infallible will.[6] No, he merges *his spirit with the spirit of his nation*, and empirical individuality naturally and imperceptibly follows from that identification. Similar to the way in which the body of a person is alive only so long as it is ensouled, so the soul of the genuine patriot can live only so long as it is *creatively inspired* in unity with the spirit of its nation. For between him and his nation there is established not only a spiritual union, but there is revealed a direct *unity in spirit*. And this unity he conveys by the word "we".[7]

Such an identification cannot be created artificially, arbitrarily or deliberately. It can be formed only *involuntarily*; it arises *by itself, naturally, as though blossoming in the soul*. But this apparently irrational blossoming has its profound and rational laws$_{z}$.

Above all, it must be experienced by each person *independently and in his own way*. No one can point out to another person his nation—not the educator, not the friend, not social opinion, not the political authority. Patriotism is a spiritual state, and therefore it can arise only independently as something *autonomous*—in personal, but authentic and objective spiritual experience. Any injunction coming from without can only hinder this experience or lead it to an ill-fated simulacrum. It is impossible to love by compulsion or by another's orders; love can arise only "by itself", in *an easy and natural objective joy, conquering and touching the soul.* This objective joy either spreads over the person—and then he becomes a *living organ of the beloved object* and is not burdened by this, but rather celebrates his happiness; or it passes his soul by—and then nothing can help him.

At the base of such a fusion lies forever a certain *uniformity in the ways and means of spiritual life*. The patriotic unification of people rests upon a certain *co-belonging* of them, as necessary, natural and sacred,

6 This would appear to be Il'in's judgment on the spiritual worth of the Russian Populists' idolization of the *Narod* (the People), the Marxists' idolization of the Proletariat, and so on.

7 This remark may be an echo of Hegel's famous characterization of *Geist* (spirit) in the *Phenomenology of Spirit* as "The 'I' that is a 'we', and the 'we' that is an 'I'." See Hegel, *Phenomenology of Spirit*, transl. A. V. Miller (1977), p. 110.

just as the spiritual object and spiritual way of life is necessary, natural and sacred to the person. The burden of empirical existence is overcome only through creation, that is, the making of new objective values through suffering and labor; only the impulse to spirit, only the realization of spiritual states, liberates a person; personal fear and personal loss are outweighed only by that love and that rejoicing which are devoted to an imperishable, divine content. And thus in this spiritual creativity, each nation possesses its own substantive characteristics. These very nodes of empirically-given character—conditioned by race, nationality and language, climate and nature, social structure and upbringing—are disentangled and unbraided in a distinct way in each nation, and it converts these threads into a spiritual fabric in a distinct way. In the struggle of the soul with its limitation and with its adversity, with its passions and with its impossibilities, each individual composes for himself *a particular spiritual path*. But this path of suffering spirituality unites the individual soul through identity and proximity with other souls *of a single national womb*. The threads of *spiritual likeness* bind people more deeply, and for that reason also more strongly, than any other threads. The very mode of personal inspiration, the very rhythm of spiritual life in its intuition and action, the very degree of craving and satisfaction, the very upsurge of despair and glorification—all fasten together the souls of one nation through likeness and proximity. And this likeness leads to people being bound together by a deep, mutual attraction, forcing them to value their life together, to establish it, and to perfect its organization. An identity of spiritual life leads imperceptibly to an intensive *intercourse and interaction*, and this in its turn gives birth to new creative efforts, and new achievements, and a *new likening*. Spiritual likeness gives birth to spiritual unity, and conversely. And the whole of this process of spiritual "symbiosis" rests on the *commonality of the spiritual object*. There is no deeper union than in the identical intuition of the one God, but precisely such a union of people lies at the base of true patriotism.

Each spiritual act possesses its own particular structure, being composed in its distinct way from thoughts, feelings, will, imagination and sensation. It is clear that to each spiritual act there is opened in a distinct way a single and objektive object, both in the cognition of the truth, and in the creation of beauty, and in the realization of the good, and in political unity. And thus every nation nurtures and realizes *spiritual acts of a particular, national structure* and for that reason creates an entire spiritual culture in its own way: it investigates scientifically and philosophizes in its own way, sees beauty and cultivates aesthetic taste in its own way, yearns and prays in its own way, loves and dies, creates virtue and realizes the lowland of vice in its own way. And every achievement of it—personal and material, in thought and in feeling—becomes a new link forging its unity and its unanimity. Every spiritual achievement of a nation is a single *hearth*, common to all, from which multiplies, without diminishing, the fire of spiritual combustion; such that the entire system of national spiritual culture appears in the form of a multiplicity of common, kindled fires, by which each can and must ignite the fire of his own *personal spirit.*[8] And this flame, leaping over to new hearths, preserves its primordial homogeneity—in rhythm, in power, in coloration, and in the entire character of combustion. Nations take shape in distinctive spiritual unities, and as a result of this, the spatial, racial and any other empirical bond acquires its own true and profound significance—an objective-spiritual co-belonging.

That is why the national genius and his creativity frequently turn out to be predominantly an object of patriotic love. The life of national spirit, forming the very essence of the native land, finds for itself in the creative genius a concentrated and mature expression.[9] He speaks *on behalf of* himself, but not only *for* himself, but for the whole of his nation; and that of which he speaks is an object common for all, but unclear to the majority; and *what* he says about it is the true word, revealing both the nature of the object and the essence of the national spirit; and *the way* in which he speaks of it releases the constraint and languor of the national spirit, for his word is carried along by the authentic rhythm of national life. The genius lifts the burden of his own nation, the burden of its misfortune, of its searching, of its life, all of its *onus essendi*;[10] and having lifted it, he triumphs in such a way that his victory becomes—on the paths of immediate or mediated intercourse—the source of a victory for everyone connected with him by a national-spiritual likeness. To him is given that power for which whole generations yearned, and for the sake of which they suffered in the past; and from this power will come forth spiritual help for whole generations in the future. The creative achievement of the genius indicates the path for all those leading a semi-creative life, freeing them through perception, artistic identification and imitation. That is why the genius forever remains for his nation a living source of spiritual liberation, joy and love. He is that hearth on which, having broken through, the flame of national spirit blazed up; that leader, who opens for the nation access to God, a Prometheus, making a present of heavenly fire, an Atlas, carrying on his shoulders the spiritual heaven of his nation. His act is an act of *national self-determination in spirit*, and descendents gather around his creativity as to a single and common altar of national liturgy.

The genius places his nation before the face of God and articulates for it and on its behalf the symbol of its objective faith, its objective intuition, knowledge and volition. He reveals and affirms by this the national spiritual unity, that great spiritual "we" which constitutes the very essence of the native land. Genius is that creative center which creates for the nation the spiritual objectivity of its being: it justifies the life of its nation

[8] See footnote 2 above, in this chapter.

[9] Though no specific "genius" is named, one assumes that Il'in may have had in mind such creative geniuses as Pushkin in the case of Russia, Goethe in the case of Germany, Shakespeare in the case of England, Cervantes in the case of Spain, and so forth.

[10] *Onus essendi*: the burden of existence.

before the face of God and in this way becomes the *true founder of the native land.*

One who speaks of the native land means—consciously or unconsciously—the *spiritual unity of his nation.* He means something that remains present and objektive, despite the death of individual subjects and the change of generations. The native land is something *unitary for the many*; each of us can say of it: "this is *my* native land", and will be correct, and everyone can say at once concerning it: "this is my native land, this is our native land", and they will also be correct.[11] The native land is an object uniting in itself *all* of its sons, such that each soul is united with it by a thread of living connection, and this connection is preserved even when the soul for some reason does not cultivate it, disdains it, or distorts it. It is not within the power of a human being to cease being a force, capable of and summoned to spiritual life; it is not within the power of a human being to break away from that spiritual environment which nurtured him, to extinguish his national-spiritual cast of mind and make himself *objektively* deprived of spirit and native land. But in order to find his native land and blend with it by feeling, and will, and life, it is necessary above all to *live by spirit* and cultivate it in oneself, and further, it is necessary to realize objective self-cognition or at least acquire an objective self-feeling *for oneself and one's nation in spirit.* It is necessary to truly sense one's spiritual life and the spiritual life of one's nation and really assert oneself in the powers and means of the latter. This means to recognize that the objectivity and distinctiveness of my personal spirit is connected *by likeness, intercourse, and commonality* with the spiritual culture of my nation such that *its* creators and *its* creation are *my* achievements. My path to spirit is the path of my native land; its ascent to God is my ascent. For I am identical with it and inseparable from it in turning to the Divinity. In this lies the religious root of patriotism.

Such a merging of the patriot with his native land leads to a splendid and fruitful identification of their spiritual energies. In this identification the spiritual life of the nation is strengthened by all the personal powers of the patriot, and the patriot obtains an inexhaustible source of creative energy in the nation-wide spiritual ascent; and this mutual nourishing, returning the powers ten-fold, gives a person an unshakeable *faith in his native land.* In merging my life with the life of my native land, I experience the spirit of my nation as an unconditional *good* and an unconditional *power*; and at the same time *I* identify myself with this *living power of the good.* I sense that I am borne by it, that I am powerful through *its* power, that I am right through *its* rightness, that I am victorious through *its* victories. I sense and know that *I* become a living vessel or, according to Hegel, a living organ of my fatherland in its ascent to spirit and to God. And on this path *love for the native land* is united with *faith* in it, so that the true patriot cannot doubt the approaching flourishing which awaits his native

[11] Again, the echo of Hegel's "'I' that is a 'we', and a 'we' that is an 'I'" seems unmistakable.

land in the future. Whatever happens with his nation, he knows through faith and vision, living experience, and the victories of the past, that his nation will not be abandoned by God, that the days of humiliation are temporary, whereas spiritual achievements are eternal, that the weighty hammer of history will certainly forge from his fatherland a mighty and victorious sword of Damascene steel. It is impossible to love the native land and not believe in it, for the native land is a living spiritual power, in which it is impossible not to believe. But only he can believe in it who lives *through it, together with it, and for the sake of it*, who joined with it the sources of his own creative will and spiritual well-being.

It is clear that in such a merging and identification that psychological atomism within which life on earth is available to a human is imperceptibly overcome.* This overcoming consists, however, not in atomism disappearing and the human being ceasing to be an enclosed psychic monad. No, the mode of empirical being is preserved, but along with it arises a powerful, creative unity of people in *a common and jointly created* object: in *national spiritual culture*.[12] All the spiritual property of our native land is one for all of us and common to all of us: both the creators of spirit, and the creations, and all the essential conditions and forms of spiritual creativity, in science, and in art, and in ethical life, and in religion, and in law, and in the State. Each of us lives through them, independently of whether he is aware of this or not, and whether he believes that the center of his life lies in these contents or not. In the spiritual culture of our native land we are all *one*; in it is objectified the best that is in each of us; through its creations is the individual spirit of each of us populated and enriched and creatively aroused; it causes the *psychic solitude* of people to fade to the background, and yields primacy to spiritual unification and unity.

Such is the essence of the native land. And given such an understanding of it, it is discovered with one's own eyes that a person deprived of it will actually be doomed to a distinctive spiritual orphanhood and *homelessness*, that the acquisition of it is truly an act of spiritual self-determination, that to possess a native land is happiness, and to lose one's connection with it is a great sorrow, that to love the native land and feel a yearning for it is not shameful, and that, on the contrary, a person naturally takes pride in his fatherland.

And precisely for this reason patriotism is fully acceptable for religion and in no way contradicts world-wide brotherhood.

A true patriot loves *the spirit* of his nation, and takes pride in it, and sees in it the source of greatness and glory precisely because it is *Spirit*,

[12] Il'in's attempt to depict the process of forming an *actual* "We" of spirit here from a multitude of separate, isolated "monads" raises the problem alluded to in my introductory essay on "Il'in and the Rule of Law".

* **See Chapter Five.**

that is, that it is excellent with the highest excellence, radiating *to all* peoples and nations and deserving from their side *the same love and pride*. Each true spiritual achievement – in knowledge or in virtue, in religion, in beauty, or in law—is a *universal human* achievement which can and must unite in itself the views, the feelings, the thoughts, and the heart of *all* people, independently of epoch, nation or citizenship. A true spiritual achievement transcends the empirical sub-divisions of people, and for that reason leads people themselves beyond these boundaries. It witnesses to a certain highest and deepest affinity of them, to a certain authentic unity of the human race which abides, despite all sub-divisions, borders and wars. It witnesses to the fact that patriotism itself flourishes in the deep womb of universal human spirituality, and that there is a summit from which opens up a universal human brotherhood, a brotherhood of *all* people before the face of God.

To love the native land means to love its *spirit* and through it all the rest, not merely "the soul of the nation", that is, its national character, but precisely the *spirituality* of its *national character and the national character of its spirit.*[13] One who has no idea what spirit is, and does not know how to love it, also does not have patriotism, but rather only an instinct for group and national self-preservation. But one who knows how to love spirit knows its supra-national, universally-human essence; therefore he *is not able to hate and despise other nations*, for he sees their spiritual power and their spiritual accomplishments. He loves in them the *spirituality* of their national character, even though the national character of their spirit may be foreign to him. And this love for a foreign spirit and its achievements in no way hinders him in loving his own native land.

And thus only that one is able to love his native land who is unable to hate and despise other nations, for only he knows what spirit is, and without that it is impossible to love one's own fatherland truly. The true patriot loves in his own nation that which all other people *ought* to love—and *will* love when they learn of it—but for the same reason he also loves in other nations that which constitutes the true source of *their* greatness and glory. The true patriot not only is not blind to the spiritual achievements of other nations, but he strives to comprehend and assimilate them, to introduce them into the spiritual creativity of his own native land, in order to enrich its life, to intensify its path, and to heal the possible incompleteness of its achievements.

That is why love for *one's own* fatherland does not dissolve and does not disappear in this supra-national rejoicing in every—also foreign—spiritual achievement. This openness of the individual soul to *all* achievements is a direct path to true patriotism: only that one knows how to love his own native land who has at least once felt that the universe could

[13] This contrast between *national* soul and *national* spirit parallels the distinction between *individual* soul and *individual* spirit: *soul* would necessarily characterize only the individual (nation or person), that is, each soul is distinct from every other; whereas *spirit* would be shared in common by many individuals (nations or persons).

actually be the fatherland of the sage.[14] And conversely, only that one can unhypocritically speak of "the brotherhood of nations" who has been able to find *his own* native land, assimilate its spirit, and merge his fate with it. It is clear that in his own native land the true patriot loves not only the spirituality of its national character, but also *the national character of its spirit*, experiencing this general character of his nation as *his own*, and himself and his own creativity as rising to supra-national achievements precisely on the distinctively-national paths of his nation.[15] The patriot feels that the life of his individual spirit is at once dissolved in the spiritual life of his nation, as it were, and at the same time gathered from it and concentrated into living individual unity; he cultivates this distinctive and marvelous unity and treasures in this way the spiritual "we", participation in which can only introduce his individual achievements into the tissue of universally-human spiritual life. Patriotism is the rightful [правая] and true love of the individual "I" for that national "we" which elevates it to the great universal human "we"; this is the real spiritual unification of the individual and the nation in the great womb of the universally-human.[16]

This unification of a human being with his nation takes shape always in the form of a *legal relation,* and usually takes the shape of a *political union*. And when this political unity of people is created by *normal legal consciousness*, set in motion by love and will to spirit, then patriotism imparts to the soul the whole power necessary for the heroic defense of one's native land, and yet at the same time, does not permit it to lapse into the savage, aggressive greediness of the international bandit.

Thus for normal legal consciousness the *entire* human race enters into the legal order, into this living net of subjective legal cells; and love for one's fatherland does not lead to a negation of the natural right [права] to existence and to spiritual growth of other nations. The right of others does not end for him where the interest of "my" nation begins, and the right of "my" nation does not stretch to the boundaries of its "power", but only to the limits of its *spiritual necessity*. Each nation has the inalienable natural right to lead a *nationally-autonomous* life, for autonomy constitutes the very essence of spirit, and every nation in the struggle for its national autonomy is right before the face of God. Only the struggle for a spiritually distinct being can ground the necessity for war, but even when that necessity is proved, war is experienced by normal legal consciousness

14 This appears to be an oblique reference to the Cynic and Stoic idea of a "cosmopolis", a universal "city" transcending all particular historical cities. It was said to be the true polis in which all genuine philosophers, that is, all of the wise, held citizenship, and hence became *cosmopolitans*.

15 This appears to be a version of the commonplace observation that the greatest writers and poets, those achieving universal significance in their art, paradoxically embody the essence of their national culture to the highest degree: for example, Shakespeare, Goethe, Pushkin, Cervantes, to mention only the most standard examples. The same point could be made with reference to certain composers, painters, sculptors, and others.

16 This appears to echo Hegel's characterization of *Geist* (spirit) in the *Phenomenology of Spirit* as "The 'I' that is a 'we', and the 'we' that is an 'I'." See footnotes 7 and 11 above.

as genuine fratricide. Love for *spirit* spurs a person to defend *his* life, its dignity and its necessary conditions, and love for the spirit *of one's own nation* is capable of moving him to taking on himself the heavy guilt of fratricide, repugnant in essence and in terms of conscience and normal legal consciousness.* But then the opponent is not left without rights even in the very battle; and the warrior, guided by normal legal consciousness, acquires in combat the appearance of a knight.

Only an immature or diseased legal consciousness could cultivate patriotism as a blind, extra-ethical frenzy, forgetting that an extra-ethical ecstasy is needed only in order to loosen the bonds of an animal self-interest degrading to a human being, and blindness is needed only in order not to see this personal degradation. The clash of nations is in fact not simply a clash of mutually exclusive self-interested encroachments, as both the "sober" man in the street and "wise" politicians often think; it is in its essence a clash of *natural rights*, requiring their own recognition and normative regulation. And since a *natural right* always remains *a rightful* [правым] *claim of spirit to a worthy life*, then a resolution of this clash by means of force is spiritually contrary to nature, for spirit relies not upon the "power" of things, or circumstances, or weapons, but *on its worth* and *the rightfulness of its claim*. And war serves to disabuse people, blinded to the point of rage, of belief in the possibility of resolving a dispute over spiritual claims by means of brute force.

The clash of rights [прав] is *a dispute over the right*, [праве] and a dispute over the right *can* be resolved only by way of legal organization and *must* be resolved on the basis of natural law. Therefore the struggle for international law must be carried out precisely not by arms, but by way of international organization, and the spiritual purpose of war is precisely to convince people of the worth and the necessity of this path. That is why patriotism, nurtured by spirit and closely linked with normal legal consciousness, cannot perceive in war a true means of struggling for right. To love one's native land does not mean to consider it the sole focal point of spirit; for one who asserts that does not know what spirit is, and does not know how to love even the spirit of his own nation. There is no individual and no nation that could be the sole focal point of spirit, for spirit lives in all people and in all nations. Not to see this means to be spiritually blind, and for that reason to be deprived both of patriotism and of legal consciousness. This path of spiritual blindness is in truth an "extra-ethical" path, alien to genuine love for the native land, for true patriotism is love which is not blind, but sighted, and its soaring on high is not alien to the good and justice, but is itself one of the highest ethical achievements.

*** See my essay "Основное нравственное противоречие войны" [The Fundamental Ethical Contradiction of the War], *Вопросы философии и психологии* [Problems of Philosophy and Psychology], no. 5 (1915).**

Chapter Eleven
On Political Legal Consciousness

The mutual spiritual belonging of peoples, tribes, and nations naturally leads them to the organization of life on the bases of a common law, a common ruling authority[1] and a common territory. *The homogeneity of spiritual life, the compatibility of spiritual creativity, and the commonality of spiritual culture* comprise the deepest, the authentic, basis of all political union. Precisely this bond—the most subtle and at times least conscious and perceptible—creates the most powerful, most indissoluble, unconditional and sacred unification of people into legal and political[2] alliances. The State is defined by the fact that it is the *positive-legal form of the native land*, and the native land is its *creative, spiritual content*. From this follows the essence of the State, its mode of being, its grounding, its end, its means, and its normal structure.

From time immemorial people have lived in political alliances, and the dimensions of political experience accumulated by them are enormous. All of history is a series of great objective lessons suffered by humanity in the matter of social construction; and it would seem that these lessons

[1] The term translated here as "ruling authority" is власть. It would be equally well translated as "ruling power", especially since the root meaning of власть is simply "power". However, the same Russian term can also carry the meaning of "authority". This opens the door to a troublesome ambiguity, as the question of the *legitimacy* of the rule in question can be formulated precisely as the choice between describing it as mere "*power*" or as "*authority*". A ruling *power* may compel outward conformity to its orders through nothing more than naked coercion; such a rule would not have *authority*, however *effective* it turned out to be. On the other hand, a ruling *authority* would secure conformity to its orders, for example, through the willing consent of the governed. To be sure, "legitimacy" is an ambiguously used term in English: some authors use it merely to mean *the effective exercise of systemic power*. A "legitimate" ruler is one able to maintain effective conformity of the behavior of the population to its orders. But that merely papers over the fundamentally important question of the *motive* for conformity to the orders of the ruler(s): *coercion* (that is, a universal fear of the punitive consequences of disobedience), or *willing consent* (based upon a conviction that the system operated by the rulers is generally in the common interest and therefore has a claim upon the allegiance of its subjects). Because in this and several of the following chapters, Il'in will be discussing this very topic of the two different motivational grounds for obedience to rulers, it follows that he will sometimes be discussing a ruling *power* and at other times a ruling *authority*. Presumably, Russian readers of the term власть simply cope with the inherent ambiguity of that term; the English translation, on the other hand, will alternate between "ruling power" and "ruling authority", wherever the context makes it clear that one or the other meaning is most appropriate.

[2] The term translated here as "political" (and also in the title of the chapter) is *государственный*, the adjectival form of the term for "State" (*государство*). A more literal rendering of this phrase would be "legal and State alliances [or unions]". However, at various points in the text, it seems clear that Il'in is using the adjectival form of "State" more or less interchangeably with "political" (*политический*). Noting this, plus the fact that the nominative and the adjectival forms of "State" do not differ in English, tending to produce confusion in some contexts, it has seemed preferable to use "political" at times for the adjectival form.

would have taught people both an abstract understanding of systems of State, and a practical ability to create and maintain political alliances. Nevertheless, to this day, the learned political theorist struggles to specify those categories on which his subject matter stands, and the practicing politician to this day repeats old mistakes and not seldom steers his ship with an uncertain and inexperienced hand.

These mistakes are explained not only by accidental oversights or personal incapacities, but by common and fundamental *defects of political legal consciousness.*

People have still not assimilated the fundamental axiom of all politics, according to which law and the State are created *for the inner world* and realized through none other than *legal consciousness.* Both in theory and in life a *formal* understanding of the State still rules, distorting its nature and destroying in souls all the fundamental principles of citizenship. In accordance with this understanding people construct political life as if it were reduced to certain mechanically-realized *outward deeds* torn away from the inner world and from the spiritual roots of humanity. The presence or absence of these outward deeds must in their view be guaranteed by any means whatever, and at any price: through violence or fear, self-interest or punishment; and everything supposedly reduces to this: if only people obey, if only they pay taxes, if only they do not commit crimes and do not incite disorder, nothing else matters. The State is understood as a structure of *outward* life, and not *inner.* In this way it cuts itself off from legal consciousness and, feeding on superficial layers or evil powers of the soul, is distorted in its content and fragmented in its foundations. It is led away from the authentic element of national life, is concentrated in the volitions and actions of a narrow circle of rulers, and is transformed for the rest of the citizenry into an unintelligible system of deadening constraint alien to them. Membership in the State begins to be experienced as a hated shackling chain, and the rulers seem to them permanent prison-guards.

If law is powerless and meaningless outside of legal consciousness, then the State is *degrading, ephemeral, and dead* outside of a *political form of thought.* For in actual fact not only its roots, but also its everyday life possesses an inner, psychic-spiritual nature. It is absurd and pernicious to think that a human can live by outward deeds separated from inner conditions; or that the State can exist in a dignified fashion, mechanically registering its "subjects", establishing for them obligations and duties and not transforming them into *citizens*, participating by *consciousness, will, feeling and action* in the creation of a unified, rationally-organized life. The State is not an external thing among things; and its being is not of a material-corporeal character, even though its natural and economic "substrate" is material, and its personal make-up has a bodily existence. The State is something *of the spirit* and something *for the soul.* It is *the spiritual unity of people*, for at its basis lies *a spiritual bond*, destined *to live in souls and create within them motives for the right external behavior.*

In the awareness of this lies the primary foundation of any system of statehood and politics; in the realization of this lies the primary condition for its true flourishing. The political form of thought is a variety of *legal consciousness*; in this everything fundamental is already said.

The political form of thought does not reduce to a knowledge that "there exists a State in the world" to which "I belong". But it begins from just that.

Every human being pretending to intellectual and spiritual maturity must take account of whether he is a member of some State, and of which one, precisely? And to what does that obligate him and empower him? And what does it mean in general "to be a member of a State"? Outside of that the political distinction of a citizen from a savage, and even from an animal, may remain elusive. In general, a human being who *does not know* of his membership in a State, or does not know precisely to which State he belongs, dwells in a state of primitive naivete and political incompetence. In his soul the seed of the State has not yet germinated. The savage, deprived like a child of political self-consciousness, may actually not know of the very fact of his citizenship; but precisely because of that he *in no way leads a political life*, and is not even capable of it. It is senseless to expect from him a political volition or act, when he is spiritually so feeble as to be incapable either of political loyalty or political treachery. Strictly speaking, such people do not enter into the State, but are only *numbered among* its members; they are in fact those "citizens *in spe*"[3] who remain, perhaps for life, in a half-slave, half-subject condition, politically distinguished from animals only by this "possible future".

Obviously a political union having in its make-up a large quantity of such half-savages leads a sham existence: the rulers "enumerate" the subjects, issue commands and exact demands from them as if they were capable of politically intelligent acts. And meanwhile, the political feeble-mindedness (*imbecillitas*) of a primitive soul makes it a senseless tool for another's will: this tool can "break" at the critical moment or cross over suddenly to other hands, serving other ends, and then it will destroy the State's business. A person harboring in himself a political feeble-mindedness, ignorant of his citizenship or not understanding its nature, only seems to be a rational being; and any political organization counting on his reason and on his will, is doomed to a sad end.

However, that is not all: it is necessary to *acknowledge* one's membership in a definite State, that is, accept it *through will and feeling*, treasure it and cultivate it. Political membership must be *consciously accepted* by each separate citizen and *recognized* by him in an *unfettered, free decision*; and this decision must lead each to a spiritual act of *voluntary self-obligation*, or, what is the same thing, to an act of spiritual

3 "citizens *in spe*": Citizens *in hope*, i.e., future possible citizens.

imputation to oneself of public-law powers, obligations, and prohibitions. Outside of this, disintegration inevitably awaits the State.

It is necessary to keep in mind that political membership is defined, generally speaking, not by a free and one-sided decision of the citizens, but by heteronomous[4] legal rules, imposing their determination on a person *prior* to his decision and *without* his consent. Even before my birth it was juridically established that the being presently born in my person would belong to such and such a political union; so that later my "ignorance" would be powerless to change anything in that, while my unilateral "refusal" would always be insufficient to extinguish my citizenship. Membership in a State possesses an objektive significance and does not depend on the will of the individual person. But precisely in this is revealed a danger characteristic of any law: *the spiritual purpose of citizenship* and its *vital effectiveness* are in need of precisely what its formal meaning does not require—a living, substantive, willed acceptance, filling and realization. Citizenship not accorded recognition by the person creates a tragic illusion: a dead or ephemeral political union. To the objektive meaning is counterposed a psychic emptiness or a spiritual lie and a sham; and this inevitably destroys any meaning of citizenship and any life of the State.

One cannot be a member of a political union *despite* one's own feeling and desire; that means to convert one's own life into a system of manifest and concealed semi-betrayal, destroying from within that same union which a citizen ought to be creating and maintaining. A State possessing such members in its make-up commits the greatest mistake in preserving for them the title of citizen; it deceives itself and prepares its own disintegration.

However, it is equally absurd to be a member of a political union *contrary to* one's own feelings and desires; that means to turn oneself into a dead, fixed thing, mechanically carrying out certain outward motions according to an alien will and an alien decision. A State prepared to be reconciled with such a condition of the citizen distorts the very essence of *political union*, for political union is created precisely through the *will*, nourished by *feeling* and led by *consciousness*.

The political form of thought, politically tempered feelings, the political direction of the will—all these together form the necessary and real basis of a living State; or rather, *the authentic tissue of its life*. It is like the air that it must breathe, and without which it suffocates and perishes. Where this does not exist at all, there is no State, but merely the empty appearance; and the first serious difficulty will not be long in revealing

4 Kant in his ethical theory distinguished between *autonomy* and *heteronomy* of the will. An *autonomous* will prescribes the law to itself; a *heteronomous* will is determined by a factor found outside of itself. Thus, a "heteronomous legal rule" would be one which originates not in the subject's own will but in some other source (this of course leaves open the possibility that the subject may subsequently judge the content of the rule to be something which he ought to impose upon himself).

it. A person creates the State precisely through *consciousness, feeling and will*; not "simply" by means of outward acts, but by means of those *motives* which stimulate him to act in this way and not otherwise; not only from legal norms or the power of coercion, but through the lasting, solid and substantively-true *exertion of soul and spirit.*

In order for the State to exist in the form of an "external" social organization, it must live in the *souls* of people, occupying their *attention*, attracting their *interest*, continuously forcing their *thought* to work, their *will* to exert itself, their *feeling* to blaze up. A nation for which political life is without feeling, without will, without thought, is politically dead and sterile; its political organization "has validity"[5] and "exists *de jure*", but does not have *spiritual existence*. Such a nation, strictly speaking, does not lead a political life at all; for political life is a variety of *creative spiritual work*. One can say that the State as an object created by human beings corresponds to its purpose and worth only if it is created by an *appropriate organ*, and moreover, an organ standing at the proper height. A vicious will, maimed or impotent feeling, a feeble or ignorant consciousness are not in *a condition to build political life*. For a State is an organized unity of *spiritually-solidary* people, *comprehending in thought* their spiritual solidarity, *accepting it with patriotic love and supporting it with a selfless will.*

Such is the true position of things: outside of *thought*, political legal consciousness is vague and objectless, while the State is formless and immature: outside of *feeling*, political legal consciousness is superficial and powerless, while the State is unstable and subject to atomization; outside of *will*, political legal consciousness is passive and inert, while the State is doomed to a loose and extensive vegetative existence. A nation which is so uncultivated in rationality as to understand neither its own unity nor the nature of political union; so indifferent or dead to feeling as not love its own native land, its political form and independence; so timid or weak of spirit as not to possess a will to spiritual-political sovereignty—such a nation *does not have a State*: it is politically amorphous and its political existence is a tragi-comic illusion.

But in order for human thought, feeling and will to be creatively brought back to living creatively through the political bond, a *spiritual acceptance* of the State must be brought about. Each human being, dwelling in a state of naive self-seeking, must accept the State, at first on the basis of *egoistic self-interest*, and then from *objective-spiritual interest*.

Above all, he must assure himself through independent and authentic, always hard and tormenting experience that he is personally interested in the existence and maintenance of the State. He must come to know and

[5] The Russian phrase is *имеет значение*, that is, has "significance". However, as pointed out in a previous chapter, Il'in's use of legal "significance" is very close to the contemporary notion of legal "validity". In this particular context, "significance" would obscure the obviously intended meaning.

be convinced that he himself is urgently in need of political union; that his own fundamental and daily needs lead him to recognition of the State; moreover, his private egoistic interest is by itself already within certain limits nothing other than the interest of the State *itself* and of the *entire* State as a whole; that, finally, his very life is impossible outside of or apart from a political organization.

In this initial, self-interested acceptance of the State, humanity slowly and gradually—enduring over the centuries the experience of feudalism, civil war and class struggle—learns *a public-law and patriotic lack of selfishness*. It learns that life possesses not only the dimension of personal self-interest, but also the dimension of *spiritual worth*, dispensing supreme judgment over all "interests"; it learns that the State is something not only "useful", but *spiritually righteous and spiritually necessary*; that it is impossible to be a human being, that is, an individual spirit in the full and true meaning of this word, and not participate with one's personal powers in the life and activity of a politically organized union. And, having simply become convinced of this, a human being obtains a sufficient, and at the same time compelling, basis *to recognize* the State and *voluntarily* accept its laws as a matter of self-imposition and obedience.

The State is necessary and acceptable because positive law is necessary and acceptable:* the immature state of human souls afflicted by naively-vicious egoistic inclinations and incapable of motivating their outward behavior through an independent recognition of natural rightness—makes the State a necessary and expedient means for the maintenance of *natural law* through its declaration and imputation of *positive law*. The inalienability and indiminishability of natural rights, from one side, and the extremely limited ability of people for autonomous self-obligation from the other, lead to the organization of such unions, which must establish and defend the order of natural law by means of heteronomous legal rules, and maintain their observance by the power of external, universally-recognized ruling authority. The unified ruling power of the union, fully empowered by law and itself subject to law, acquires an obligation: to formulate natural law in the form of objektively-significant,[6] universally-obligatory rules of outward conduct (i.e., in the form of positive law), in order that these rules should penetrate into the consciousness and will of people and engender in them motives to proper conduct.

In accordance with its fundamental idea the State is *a union of spiritually-mutual belonging of people, tribes and nations, united for the sake of the heteronomous realization of natural law*. This means that the State possesses a *single, objective, and higher end*, and that only a free, willing acceptance of this end makes a human being truly a citizen.

[6] That is, objectively *valid*.

* **See Chapter Six.**

Thus the State in actual fact possesses such a single higher end, which it *must* serve and which it in fact—with more or less success—*does serve*. To the unsophisticated, superficial eye it may of course seem that people in their *political* activity pursue a multitude of different ends; such that not only for each separate individual is there his own particular "political" end, but that one and the same individual can *arbitrarily* change his "political" ends, giving himself to them by turns, and selecting them one after the other. And each of these subjective and relative ends, regardless of their *content* and their *worth*, will possess a political character thanks merely to the fact that someone will wish to realize it through the *means of State power*. Given such an understanding, what is crucial is not the question of *what* this or that individual wants, but the question of *in what way* he intends to achieve it. Any end, the most absurd, self-interested and anti-political [противогосударственная][7] end will turn out to be a "political" [политическою] end, while activity leading to its realization turns out to be political [государственною] activity. *A formal understanding of statehood* and politics, satisfying itself with the empty signs of an "organized power" and "general rules", breaking away from the natural-law basis of any State and sticking to its positive-law form, becomes reconciled with *any* interest, sanctifies *any* desire, permits *any* encroachment – thus degrading both the nature of its own object and the very life of humanity.[8] Political formalism implants in the souls and in the activities of people the most unprincipled *political relativism*; and, as a result of this, entire generations of people grow up in the certainty that "in politics everything is permitted" and that by means of the authority of State power "everything" can be "concealed". And humanity, from time

[7] Reading "*противогосударственная*" for "*пртивогосударственная*."

[8] Il'in is here explaining a central doctrine in his theory of the State: the distinction between a genuine State (ruling authority) and a merely formal approximation of it (ruling power). The genuine State is a political union of people sharing a common spiritual culture the end of which is the realization of natural law through a system of positive law. Such a State possesses genuine authority. A merely formal conception of the State, on the other hand, is satisfied by the presence merely of organized power and general rules (that is, positive law) where these have no intrinsic connection to natural law—thus, merely a "*ruling power*" (it is useful to compare Il'in's doctrine with Passerin d'Entrèves' distinction between the State conceived as a system of *authority*, and the State conceived as a system of *power* in his classic work *The Notion of the State: an Introduction to Political Theory*). Il'in seems to imply that a State as a ruling authority could be considered to possess *legitimacy* so long as it genuinely pursued the true end of any political union, that is, the realization of natural law, regardless of whether this was properly appreciated by its citizenry. Thus, if the legal consciousness of the citizenry were less than fully developed, it might fail to grasp the legitimacy of the State, even as the rulers were rightly carrying out their obligation to raise the level of legal consciousness in the citizenry. In such a situation the rule of an elite, itself possessing a fully developed legal consciousness, might be legitimate, that is, possess *authority* and not mere *power*, even in the absence of an appropriate recognition on the part of the citizenry—*so long as the ruling authority remains committed to the end of realizing natural law*. The commitment to the intrinsically political end of the realization of natural law is thus the ultimate distinguishing mark of the genuine State, the State as ruling authority, and not merely ruling power.

to time reaping the fruits of this degradation, continues blindly to hold on to such an anti-natural tradition and absurd practice.

In contrast to this, normal legal consciousness, already since the time of Plato and Aristotle, asserted and will assert the *unity and objektivity* of the political end.[9] The term "political" points not only to the *path* of the organized exercise of power, but above all to a certain *higher value*, served by the State. So that from all the ends with which people ascend to power, only those ends will be *political* which correspond to this highest value. An "interest" which is "political" from the formal point of view, may be *in actual fact anti-political*; and activity which is "political activity" by its outward appearance, may *in actual fact* be completely *antagonistic to the State*. Politics is by no means an empty form of the "organized exercise of power"; no, it possesses a particular *content* constituting it. The State is not at all a social mechanism, indifferent to what it creates; no, it possesses its own particular *substantive-determinate* task. If the State does not realize it, or realizes something quite other, then it not only ceases to be a State "in idea," but in actual practice falls apart and perishes. The State possesses its own objektive nature, which is determined by its objektive end and which cannot be destroyed or flouted with impunity. Those who do not understand this are incapable of political activity; those who fail to follow this prepare a tragic end for themselves and their State. The State conceals within itself a certain fate immanent to it, and this fate brings woe and requital, both to the politically-unwise ruler and to the politically-blind nation.

[9] Il'in appears to be identifying his conception of natural law as the ultimate political end with Plato's Form of the Good as the ultimate object of knowledge of the Philosopher King.

Chapter Twelve
The Essence of the State

The objektive nature of the State is determined by its highest end, its sole and unchangeable mission. This mission consists in the *protection and organization of the spiritual life of the people belonging to a given political union.* The protection of spirit consists in guaranteeing to *the entire population and to each individual* their natural right to a distinctive self-determination in life, that is, the right *to life* and, moreover, to *a worthy* life, outwardly free and inwardly self-sufficient. The organization of such a life together, and, moreover, on the bases of *law and authority*, constitutes the sole political end that the State serves. Only a true understanding of this *end* opens access to an understanding of *the means and the structure* of a political union.

The fundamental nature of this end, that is, precisely what makes it *political*, consists in its *unity and commonality for all citizens.*

The protection of the individual, as a creative center of spiritual life, is something in which everyone obviously has an interest, if seemingly only *for oneself and about oneself*; inasmuch as it becomes clear that every individual has an *egocentric* attraction to freedom, that every individual seeks to ensure *for himself his own* natural rights. This means that many people have *similar* or even *identical* ends, not coinciding, however, in the single unified and common end. There are as many ends as there are people; since each is for himself. In the determination of *his own* interest each may "agree" with another; but these interests *do not flow together* into a unified and common one. In other words, here is similarity, and, possibly, even agreement; but there is no *solidarity*, for *identical* interests are not united into a *common* one. And meanwhile *political* activity is nothing other than *solidary activity in the name of a common end.* The absence of it destroys the political union and converts the people into a multitude of disconnected *atoms*. Then an egocentric attraction leads to egoistic activity; a similarity of interests gives rise only to a *parallelism and competition*; and, in the end, spiritual atomism and self-seeking remain the final word of this anti-political disorder.

The essence of the State consists in the fact *that all its citizens* have, despite many different opposing or identical interests and ends, *a single, unified end and one common interest.* Of that end, each one *can* say "that is my end", and will be correct; but each *must* add: "not *only* mine". And everyone can say at once: "this is *our common* end"; and, having said that, everyone will be correct. But this also means that this end is *common.* The multitude of bodily and psychically separate people desire *one and the same thing*, such that it will either be had *at once by all*, or *no one* will have it. Each one desires equally by himself and in his own way; "interest" as a personal experience remains distinctive and plural. But the object of the desire is *the same for all* and can be created only in an organized, *joint* and *not* solitary work. The commonality of the end creates a commonality of ways and means; and the basis of political activity is given.

This solidarization of interests arises in such a way that each member of the union comes to understand the unrealizability of *his* end without the realization of the identical ends of *others*, and moreover, of *all* others. An individual spiritual center, needing a definite and secure sphere of free volition, becomes convinced that his powers are supported and nourished exclusively through the obligations and prohibitions of others, and that at the same time they are limited everywhere by others' powers. All subjective legal "statuses" are, as it were, mutually contiguous everywhere, forming a living system of mutual support and limitation. Each cell is whole only so long as the neighboring ones are whole; and since all the cells are connected through each other with all the rest, a violation of one of them violates thereby all the others, or, in any event, places all the others under threat.* Precisely this correlative (connected) and mutual (reciprocal) coexistence of all subjective-legal cells persuades people that the very *form of legal connections* is not only *identical* for all but is something *common to all*. Thus to create a demarcation and protection for each *pair* of subjects means to establish a *limit common* to both; moreover, this means to establish a *deciding organ common* for both, that is, a legal authority creating and applying the law; and finally, a *rule common* for both, that is, a legal norm or a code of norms. In other words, to organize a legal order means to create a single common union (the political "we"), with a single common legal power ("our" government), and a single common system of law ("our" laws). The *organizing* task of the State consists precisely in this, and *everyone* is *identically* interested in the realization of it. Each person is identically interested in the common concern; or, what is the same thing: *all are solidary*. On this solidarity – precisely on it and on nothing else — the State is founded; *political activity* consists in the discovery of such solidarity and service to it.

It is clear that this solidarity on the question of the legal *form* of life receives its sanctification from the depth of spiritual content – nationally unified and patriotically common. The State is a variety of organized living-together; and at the basis of any shared life of people, if it is not degrading for them and not ephemeral, lies a *spiritual homogeneity* and a commonality of *spiritual culture*. That is why at the basis of any powerful and spiritually-productive political union lies a spiritual solidarity of the sons of the common native land. Love for the fatherland is a love for that same *national spirit*, the joint and combined life which the State organizes and protects. The *feeling* of the patriot is devoted to that same thing that is served by the *thought and will* of the statesman. The politician standing on the heights manages that concern in which *his entire nation finds its solidarity*; and if he manages it with the fire of his own soul, then he is a patriot. The patriot actively working to organize the spiritual life of his nation, managing the social form of its flourishing, is because of that

* **See Chapters Three and Four.**

a statesman, a national-political builder, and leader. Politics outside of patriotism is objectless, absurd and ruinous; patriotism outside of the State is impracticable, impotent, and formless. Thus: *the State is the positive-law form of the native land; while the fatherland forms the true content of politics.*

Precisely the struggle for the *spiritual culture* of the nation is what imparts to the State the highest and the ultimate justification before the face of Divinity; none other than the *spiritual* content of patriotism imparts to the State its natural rightness, *contrasting* it to universal brotherhood and, at the same time, *reconciling* the state with that brotherhood.* In the struggle for their spiritual culture the citizens of the State are at once sons of their native land and champions of the universal concern; they are in essence citizens of the *national city of God*, and, at the same time, creators of world culture, recognizing the universal concern as their own. The State, as *an instrument of spiritual life*, not only does not contradict the universal unity, but directly *creates* it; for any unification of people is holy and secure only to the degree that it possesses a spiritual nature – but precisely for that reason it does not split people up into irreconcilable groups, but connects them in a higher unity. Creating and organizing the life of the *national spirit*, each State is an organ of *universal spiritual life* common to the entire world.[1] And obviously, to the extent that the state distorts its nature and organizes not a life of national spirit, but national greed and aggression, to that extent it becomes an instrument of disintegration, calamities, wars and universal degeneration.

Thus, *spiritual solidarity* is the authentic and real basis of the State. Precisely on this basis the State must be understood and realized, as a living system of *brotherhood*, not only not contradicting Christianity, but corresponding to the spirit of the gospel doctrine.[2]

[1] This claim might at first glance appear to be a puzzling one; but its meaning becomes clear when we set it within the framework of Hegel's holistic logic of the concrete universal, the particular and the individual. A particular State organized in terms of the political unity of its members committed to the realization of spirit as its ultimate end, would be a moment of, or a manifestation of, universal spirit itself. The universal (spirit) would exist only in the form of the various particulars reflecting it, but the shape of each particular (moment) of the whole would be determined by the self-particularizing universal itself. So each particular realization of a genuine state would be a further *concretion* (individualization) of the universal itself; but a particular State which *failed* to reflect, or distorted, the conceptual structure of the universal would constitute a *degradation* of that universal. That Il'in should be thinking here in terms of the structure of Hegel's speculative concept should not be surprising, given that he spent the previous eight years writing a major two-volume commentary on Hegel' system, focusing particularly upon the *Logic*.

[2] This tight connection Il'in draws between the genuine State and the Christian community of faith ("the national city of God") is mainly *asserted*, rather than explained and defended, in this chapter (but see Chapter Twenty-One). It is clear that Il'in dismisses out of hand the possibility of any purely secular account of the ultimate end of the State, and sees the realization, the protection, of "spirit" as its ultimate end, because that is equivalent to

* **See Chapter Ten.**

To lead a political life, or what is the same thing, to be a genuine citizen, means *to experience a living, indissoluble identity between the interest of the State and one's own proper interest; and through this, to recognize as one's own proper interest every spiritually-true interest of each of one's fellow citizens.* The fundamental content of political life reduces to this.

In fact, the first thing that makes a person a citizen is *acceptance of the State's end.* To accept the State's end means to experience it as *one's own*; it means not only to "reconcile" oneself with it or "consent" to it, but to recognize it as one's own end, and to no longer counterpose it to one's own interests. This is possible only on the condition that the personal interest of a person draws him to the same thing to which the concern of the State leads. And for that it is necessary either that the State lower itself to the content of personal, private self-interest, which would mean for the State degradation and destruction, or that the individual elevate himself to the content of genuine State interest. This means that the citizen must be a patriot, seeking for the spiritual culture of his nation to flourish: then the fundamental end of his life in itself coincides with the sole and the objektive end of the State, and as a result, a living, indissoluble *identity of interests* is easily and naturally established.

the realization of a natural law order in his view. "Spirit" functions at three levels in this account: as the state of the individual soul which has risen to the objective truth of being, as the community of faith mutually shared by the citizenry, and as the Divine itself present in the world through the community of faith. Although Il'in nowhere acknowledges this explicitly, it is evident that this particular doctrine of "spirit," including the doctrine of the three levels of subjective (individual), objective and absolute spirit, echoes Hegel's political philosophy to a striking extent.

Hegel likewise dismissed the possibility of a purely secular justification of the State as tending to atheism, but also ruled out theocracy as incompatible with the realization of that individual freedom which is the ultimate justification of the modern State. As Peter Hodgson observed, summarizing Hegel, "Whereas religion is the *knowledge* of the highest truth, the truth that humans are free before God, the State is the *actualization* of freedom in the world. There can be only *one* concept of freedom that manifests itself in both religion and the State. Thus, religion is a foundation of the State, and the State is a telos of religion". See Peter C. Hodgson, *Hegel and Christian Theology* (2005), p. 196.

Hegel acknowledged that in the early history of the Christian church there was a tendency to turn its back upon the world, giving all to the poor, but that attitude could not be reconciled with the mission of the church to remain a presence in the world. In order to secure that presence, it was necessary (again quoting Hodgson) to deal with concerns "about family, property, laws, governance, etc. The church is not directly responsible for these matters, its principal domain being that of the salvation of souls. What is needed, however, is that "out of the womb of the church there be formed a free life, a civil and political life, stemming from eternal principles, a rational, worldly kingdom in accord with the idea of freedom and the absolute character of rights". Thus, the church does have an essential role to play in the formation of the body politic: it is the provider of ideals, goals, frames of reference; and the relation of the community of faith to the world is, as we shall see, an abiding concern of Hegel's". Hodgson, ibid., p.186. Hegel's discussion of these last points can be found in his *Lectures on the Philosophy of Religion*, ed. Peter C. Hodgson, transl. R. F. Brown, P. C. Hodgson, and J. M. Stewart with the assistance of H. S. Harris, (1984-1987), III, pp. 151-152. Il'in's various cryptic remarks on this subject in this chapter (and elsewhere in the text), including the closing remark concerning "Caesar and God," all appear to be consonant with a generally Hegelian posture on this problem of the relation of religion and State.

If the individual conceives himself above all as *spirit*, the concern of Spirit becomes for him the first and fundamental concern. And it is not a purely personal, and not a private, concern, but, in its essence it is identical for all and common to all, and, according to its social form of realization, a matter of politics and the State. To find in oneself a *spiritual interest* means to find in oneself a universally human and patriotic root, and a political direction of will. This means to confirm the basis of one's personality in that depth in which "*my* concern" merges inseparably with the concern of "my State", and the interest of "*my State*" is revealed as a universally human interest.

However, this acceptance of the State interest is carried out by no means merely as a matter of *self-sacrifice*, but also as a matter of *self-affirmation*: for the State, protecting and creating national spiritual culture *accepts, protects and nourishes the spiritual interest of each of its members*. Created for the sake of natural law, the State affirms the natural legal power *of each citizen*, protecting it as a distinctive, creative center of spiritual life and facilitating it in its autonomous self-determination. This means that each citizen finds in the State's end the entire fullness of his own spiritual interest recognized, observed and affirmed in such a way that his patriotic "self-sacrifice" is at the very same time an act of "self-affirmation": for his personal spiritual interest is not only not excluded from the universal-political one, but enters into it in its entirety, forms its very tissue. The spiritual rightness of any personal interest makes it an interest of the State itself; and so it stands even in the case that a historical State power for some reason does not recognize this, or turns out not to be in a condition to organize the satisfaction of every such interest. The interest of the State is composed of *all the spiritually-right* [духовно-правых] *interests of all the citizens*, and moreover, through this inclusion by the State, every spiritually-right personal interest turns out to be both *held in common and political*. Thus, everything necessary to the citizen for creative work and a dignified existence enters into the interest of the State itself, filling in the content of its sole end and its practical tasks. *The spiritual life of the nation is the spiritual life of all of its citizens*; and by this is determined the direction and the compass of political activity.

Given precisely this understanding, *the State* inevitably becomes the *instrument of brotherhood and solidarity*. Accepting the interest of the State as one's own, each individual actually assimilates *all* the ends and *all* the tasks of the State; here there are no limitations or reservations: the citizen as a true patriot does not divorce himself from his political union, *its* tasks from *his own* tasks, *its* fate from *his own* fate. But precisely through this he accepts and assimilates *every spiritually-right interest of each of his fellow citizens*; and, having accepted this, he experiences and regards this as his own proper interest, personal and urgent. A "private interest", if it is spiritually right, is already not merely an "interest", but *a natural right*, and not merely a "private interest", but a common and political one; and this means that there is no citizen in the State who would have a basis for relating to it with political indifference or passivity.

The interest of the State consists in maintaining and realizing all *the natural rights* of all its citizens; and for that reason involving the individual will in "politics" means involving it in the struggle for the natural right of each and every one. Therefore, the ascent of personal, private will to the political end is by the same token its *expansion in terms of compass and content*; and is at the same time its *liberation* from any purely individual, group or class self-interest—a liberation and a *purification*. For the political does not admit any purely individual, group, or class interest whatever, but either rejects it entirely or recognizes it as a true and just natural right and in so doing converts it into a common and political interest.

A truly political understanding rejects all private encroachment, all private desire, all class interests. For if a class interest has behind it a spiritual foundation, then it is *no longer* simply a "class" interest, but a common and political one; and then to insist upon its "class" character makes no sense: it would mean, already possessing the whole, to strive for its part; or from two universally-assertive judgments to derive a particular-assertive conclusion.[3] If a class interest *does not* have behind it a spiritual foundation and *does not* conceal behind itself a natural right, then no efforts whatever—not "organization", not "propaganda", not "agitation", neither lies, nor terror, nor insurrection, nor civil war, nor class dictatorship—can convert it into a common political or State interest; it remains a *private desire and an unjustified encroachment*, whereas a political party trying to vindicate it by all means will prepare a true destruction—of itself, of its class and its State, remaining "political" only in name.[4] For in practice it is *possible* to make of any State organization an instrument of any class interest whatsoever; but this means to slacken or even extinguish the will to political unification *in all the remaining classes* and by the same means to tear the living State to pieces. Fortunately such a form of activity harbors within itself its own impending doom: the objektive necessity of the State will not permit such activity to the point of its complete destruction, and the tactics of the encroaching class inevitably provoke in the nation a deepening and a purification of political legal consciousness, and together with that also a strengthening of the State system being trampled upon.

One can say that the State in general is constructed *not according to the principle of self-interest, but according to the principle of rightness; and not by the principle of conflict, but by the principle of solidarity.*

[3] That is, to violate that rule of Aristotelian syllogistic logic which states that no valid standard-form categorical syllogism with a particular conclusion can have two universal premises. To violate this rule is sometimes referred to as the "existential fallacy". The rules for Aristotelian syllogism would have been familiar to any philosophy student in the beginning of the twentieth century.

[4] Il'in obviously has in mind the history of the Bolshevik party, the Soviet "State system", and a Soviet Marxist theory of the State. This passage lends considerable insight into why Il'in remained certain right up to his death in 1954 that the Soviet State would eventually disintegrate from its own internal defects.

So that every time the principle of self-interested conflict is put forward onto the first plane of politics, or triumphs over the principles of right and solidarity, the destructive element becomes dominant and the State enters upon the path of destruction. The essence of the political lies not in the fact that citizens *fight* with one another, but in the fact that they *work together*; the State is a variety not of war and discord, but of unity and creative working together; and its formula is not "a compromise of self-interested encroachments", but a "coincidence of rightful and solidary directions of the will". According to its most fundamental essence, the State strives not to organize the collision of private or class interests and not to simply reconcile them, but *to exclude them*; and the everyday solidity of the State is determined precisely by that sphere of interests and political acts at the limits of which the struggle of classes dies down or does not arise at all (for example, a defensive war).

It is natural that, given an appropriate understanding of the State system and politics, the self-interested struggle among the citizenry or classes has no soil at all in which to arise. If every citizen considers his own and others' interests by the standard of their rightfulness, then he has no basis either to insist on his own unrightful interest, or to reject another's rightful claim. On the contrary, he is ready to accept every other rightful interest and abides in the certainty that his own rightful claims will be recognized by all other citizens. Just such an interrelation of citizens, composing the fundamental nature of *political union*, transforms the State into a living system of *brotherhood* and reconciles it with Christ's teaching on love.

One might have thought that the thousand-year practice of State systems would have sufficiently clearly shown the incompatibility of it with the spirit of Christ's teaching. At least, all the theories which reduce the State to an organization of violence, to "the sword" and fear, or convert the teaching of Christ into an ascetic morality, into "non-resistance" and sentimental sanctimoniousness, insist on that.[5] Letting slip from view, on one hand, the *spiritual* purpose and *ideal* essence of the State; on the other, the task of *creative transformation of life* placed upon the followers of Christ, these theories see an opposition where there is none. Of course, the historical experience of humanity has measured the entire great divergence between the empty, and for that reason distorted, form of the State system, and the empty, perverted form of the gospel doctrine; however this divergence, this opposition between the principle of "violence" and the principle of "ascetic humility" in no way resolves the fundamental problem. *Normal legal consciousness* not only does not exclude love for those near to one, but seeks and finds ways for the systematic organization of its social realization; for to accept every rightful interest of the other as one's own means precisely to relate to those near to one as to oneself. Political activity correctly understood not only does not exclude service to God, but, on the contrary, is in itself a worthy deference to Him "in spirit and in truth". The teaching of Christ

5 Tolstoy's moral and political theories are presumably the target of these remarks.

never summoned to a renunciation of the feeling of *one's own spiritual worth*; but precisely this rightful feeling lies at the basis of the human struggle for its natural right.* And conversely, normal legal consciousness not only does not encourage self-interestedness, as the motive power of human deeds, but assumes in humanity precisely that capacity to place God's concern highest of all, which Christ spoke of as the basis of all life.

In vain do the anarchists and other partisans of a supra-political "idealism" consider their criticism irrefutable and final: they repudiate only *an empty form* of the State which *should be rejected, even if one is not an anarchist*; but they lose sight of *the true content* of political activity, and therefore criticize what they do not understand themselves. A convinced anarchist is always a victim of his own political naivete: he judges the law and the State as though he understands, not only not understanding the subject, but also not even suspecting his lack of understanding; for understanding is given here only as a result of *an objective intuition of the end of the State and the essence of political union.* It is precisely naiveté that permits him to believe that, with the "abolition" of the State, *natural legal consciousness will suddenly mature* in the souls of people and will begin to determine their behavior by itself; for that reason positive law is not necessary; that life can be organized even completely outside of law; or, that law can be established without a generally recognized State power; that State power does not require the sanction of an organized compulsion, and so on. All this reveals that the anarchists are possessed by *a defective legal consciousness* and that their propaganda remains an extolling and a popularization of their own spiritual delusions.**

A correct understanding of political legal consciousness is not only not hostile to an ethically good will, but accepts its end and serves its objectives.*** Political life rests upon a *brotherly disposition* of the soul, and if this disposition disappears, then political life also degenerates. Law in practice serves not only "freedom",**** but also the "brotherhood" which was so ceremoniously, and at the same time so impotently, proclaimed by the first French revolution. But "brotherhood" is that mode of relation of human being to human being the deepest interpretation of which was given by Christ. For that reason the true politician possesses all the grounds to recognize himself—in terms of end and spirit—as Christian: for in normal legal consciousness "Caesar" and "God" form a living unity.

*** See Chapter Fifteen.**
**** See Chapter Four.**
***** See Chapter Nine.**
****** See Chapter Six.**

Chapter Thirteen
The Form of the State

The State, according to its *fundamental idea*, is a spiritual union of people having mature legal consciousness and authoritatively securing natural law in a brotherly, solidary collaboration.

Such is the *idea* of the State. But, historically speaking, it only very slowly acquires these conceptually true characteristics and often brings about, while preserving its name, a whole series of profound deviations. The correction of these deficiencies and distortions is possible only with the growth, purification, and deepening of *legal consciousness*, such that if the history of the State reveals progress in the sense of a growth of the *idea of the State*, then this progress must be understood as a *psychic-spiritual development of humanity*. The political structure and legal consciousness form an indissoluble unity, to such an extent that not a single reform is possible until a certain improvement in legal consciousness has reached maturity; and any reform not in proportion to the state of popular legal consciousness may turn out to be absurd and ruinous for the State. The sole true path to any reform is *the gradual cultivation of legal consciousness.*

Precisely in this way and only in this way is resolved the fundamental contradiction between *the idea* of the State and its historical *realization.* For, on one hand, the State lives through *the legal consciousness* of the nation; whereas the essential characteristic of legal consciousness is *the capacity for self-governance*; *from this, in theory, the State reduces to the self-governance of the nation.* However, on the other hand, the sole and the objektive *end* of the State is so elevated and requires from the citzenry such a *mature legal consciousness*, that historically speaking, nations turn out to be *incapable* of self-governance, of the realization of that end. And thus is revealed a great discrepancy between the ideal form of the State and its historical manifestation. Political philosophy must uncover the roots of this discrepancy; the ruling authority must find a path to heal it.

The problem reduces to the fact that in idea the State is a corporation, but in actuality it is *an institution.* The problem is resolved through combining the institution with the corporation, while maintaining the *aristocratic* nature of the State, however.

One needs to recognize the fact that history imparted to the State a particular positive-law form which does not fit among the usual categories of jurisprudence. It is indisputable that the State is something capable of completely independent *legal acts* (for example: a declaration of war, the conclusion of a treaty, the promulgation of a law, a confiscation); for that reason it must be recognized not as an object of law and not as a legal relation, but as a *legal subject* (a person). That is, of course, not a "natural person" (a spiritual individual, an individual legal subject), but a "juridical subject" (a socially-organized legal subject). However, this exhausts everything that the usual juridical categories can definitely express concerning the State.

Contemporary legal science knows two forms of juridical persons: "corporations" and "institutions". But the historical form of the State, strictly speaking, cannot be related to either of these groups.

The distinguishing feature of a corporation lies in the fact that its structure ascends from an *identical* interest to a *common* one based on the principle of *solidarity*; from many identically interested subjects, identically goal-setting and legally empowered – a *single subject* is formed, with a single common interest, a common goal, a common "substrate", with a single status as a legal subject, and a single system of action.[1] The interest and the authority, the interest and the goal-setting, the goal-setting and the acting, are inseparable from each other in the very essence of the corporation, and remain fused even when the corporation, from practical considerations, sets up within its own boundaries a whole series of subordinate institutions acting on behalf of its person. Within this corporate unity the interested parties establish by themselves their common goal, carry full authority themselves, and realize that goal in which they are interested through plenipotentiary activity.

On the contrary, the very essence of an *institution* consists in the fact that the interest and the legal authority, the interest and the goal-setting, the goal-setting and the actions are separated (or may be separated in pairs) from each other and are distributed among various subjects: the interested

[1] This term, *цель*, will generally be translated as "end" here, especially when Il'in uses it in such expressions as "the end of the State". His understanding of such an end seemingly approaches (without quite clearly reaching) Aristotle's distinction between two types of activites: those which contain their ends within themselves (such that, in effect, the activity becomes its own end, or an end in itself) *versus* activities the ends of which lie beyond the activities themselves. See *Nicomachean Ethics* 1094a. Perhaps the ultimate example of the former in Aristotle would be that complex of activities involved in the flourishing of the polis itself. This complex of activities contains its end within itself; thus in effect making that pattern of activities which constitutes the successful functioning (the flourishing) of the polis self-justifying. Examples of the second type of activity would be boat-building, house-building, etc. – or in the most general case, the transfer of wealth from others' pockets into one's own by whatever means – where the "external" goal of the activity (the boat, the house, the acquisition of wealth) alone confers value upon the activity. When Il'in talks about the "end of the State" in the ideal case, his description approximates Aristotle's first type of activity.

Where he speaks about the "goals" of *a corporation* (one corporation among many, or a "private-law corporation") or of *an institution*, the term he uses is still "*цель*", but the context would seem to justify the alternative translation of "goal", because these would generally involve objectives distinguishable from, lying beyond, the *activities* of the private corporation or of the institution themselves. It is when he assimilates the idea of the State to a *unique* corporation (a "public-law corporation") that he comes closer to Aristotle's first type of activity. It is instructive to consider the similarities and differences between Il'in's account of "private-law corporations" and "public-law corporations", on one hand, and Michael Oakshott's distinction between "enterprise association" and "civil association" in *On Human Conduct*, on the other (Oakshott is one of the few contemporary political theorists who fully appreciated the significance of Aristotle's distinction between activities which contain their end in themselves, and activities the end of which lies beyond the activity itself).

one does not formulate his own goal, but others formulate the goal for him, externally to him; neither does he possess the authority to act on behalf of this goal; the subject setting the goal may himself be completely uninterested in its realization and not have the authority to act to achieve it; whereas the one empowered to act may be completely extraneous to the institutional goal-setting and to an everyday interest in the given goal.[2] Precisely in consequence of this an institution is constituted *not* by the principle of the *solidarity of those with an interest*, but by the principle of *trusteeship* over them; unity does not include multiplicity within itself but counterposes itself to it; the identical does not ascend to the common; consciousness, recognition, legal empowerment of will and the action of those interested do *not* compose a legal being and a legal act of the institution, but remain indifferent and may be absent.*

One can understand the State *according to its fundamental* essence as a corporation, and not as an institution. Then its life will be realized precisely in the ascent from an identical interest to a common one according to the principle of solidarity; the citizens of it are bound by a common end (the spiritual flourishing of the native land and its organization on the bases of law), a common substrate (a territory and all the rest of "nature") and a common organization (a single union, a single State authority, a single system of legal norms, a single legal order). Then this bond must live in their consciousness, be maintained by their recognition, nourished by the authority of their will and realized through their action. The State, in theory, dwells not *above* the citizenry, but lives *within them.* It is created not only *for them* (that is, in their interest), but *by them and through them* (it is irrelevant for now by whom, how, and to what extent). They themselves accept that end which expresses their common spiritual interest and themselves experience that interest in the name of which they enter into a political union. The State exists *in the person of the citizenry*; such that all the citizens, as an organized political unity, *compose the State itself.* Citizens are not reckoned within it according to the principle of trusteeship; they do not stand opposed to it, but are included within it, summoned as participants and creators of the common end.

According to this view, the State is a corporation. However, it is not a private-law corporation, but a public-law one; and here begins a whole series of complications. Among the fundamental powers of the State is included the power to *authoritatively* direct the life of the political union: to authoritatively and definitively establish the legal norms and compulsorily apply them to relations among the citizenry. It is characteristic of the State to act in terms of positive law, that is, in a system of the organized exercise of power. It is fully empowered not

[2] A set of circumstances which might arise within any hierarchically-ordered corporate bureaucracy, for example.

* **Compare the position of patients in a clinic; lunatics in an asylum; the poor in an almshouse; the stipendiary confronted by the stipend; the subjects of an authoritarian State.**

to ask, but to require; it is *obligated* not to try to persuade those who disagree, but to authoritatively prescribe and forbid, keeping in view the possibility, the obligatoriness and the inevitability of compulsion. And in relation to this power, creating objectively-significant law, the citizens have the obligation of subordination and obedience; such that, formally speaking, their agreement or disagreement is irrelevant — both as to the significance of the norm, and to the significance of any personal legal status.

This public-law character of the State is expressed in the fact that it creates within its boundaries an entire series of institutions, fully authorized with power, and functioning formally *by the principle of trusteeship*. Obviously this imparts to the political union the character of authoritarianism and heteronomy, and likens the State not to a corporation, but to *an institution*. And in actual fact, historically, any State lives and functions as an institution.

A corporate structure requires from the citizenry above all a mature legal consciousness; for without it the common interest will remain unrecognized, the principle of solidarity will fall away, the interest and the goal-setting will drift apart, and as a result the State will either cease to exist or will turn into an institution. And indeed the State *always* had and always will have in its make-up citizens with immature legal consciousness; for even given a perfect structure there will be in it children and minors composing approximately half of the population, and perhaps also the psychically infirm. And since for them a proper political goal-setting will be out of reach, then the State will forever retain in relation to them (that is, for somewhat more than half of the citizenry) the character of an *institution*. History further joins to them *all* the citizens with immature legal consciousness, incapable in practice of participating in the life and activity of a public-law corporation. They are incapable of becoming aware of their own interest as political, and in consequence of this their consciousness, recognition, will, and action *cannot* create a legal being and a legal act of political union; the State remains for them an institution: that is, it continues to work *for* them, but creates its life *not through their volition*.

All this means that the State as it is historically realized combines within itself the features of a corporation with the features of an institution. Its structure will be the more perfect the higher and stronger is the level of legal consciousness in the country, and, correspondingly, the stronger will be the predominance of *the corporate spirit* above the spirit of a trustee-type institution. It is clear that the politician, organizing the State, must set out every time from a true estimation of the actual level of legal consciousness in a given country, determining in accordance with that level the vital combination of "corporation" and "institution" which will be the best for the State in the given circumstances (given the present territory, density of population, the make-up of political and economic tasks, the given level of legal consciousness in the country, and so on).

To find that historically best combination of "solidary self-governance and ruling trusteeship" means to correctly solve the problem of the organization of State *power*.

The nature of State *power* is determined by that *end* for the sake of which it is created; and this end is the end of *the State itself.* This means that political power serves the *native land*, that is, the flourishing of national spirit: in this service it acquires, formulates, protects, and secures *natural law*, imparting to it the form of a *positive law order*.

From this it is already clear that political rule places on a human being the greatest *responsibility*: the ruler, by his very vocation is a *legislator of natural rightness* [правоты]; therefore he must be capable of *objective comprehension* of Spirit and Law, or what is the same thing, he must possess a developed and deepened *legal consciousness.* The legislator, the organizer, the judge only stand at the peak of their vocation when they are guided by a will to the end of law, and therefore to *the law*; when they regard any positive law as a manifestation of natural rightness and themselves step forth in life as its students and creators.* This is precisely what Plato had in mind when he spoke of the "rule of philosophers" and of "the philosophizing of the rulers".

The one ruling must have a true understanding of the supreme end of the State and its means. His legal consciousness must have its root in *good will and patriotism*. He must firmly believe in the nobility of the State and in the vital spiritual necessity of political unity. He must combine in himself a refined *vision of law* with an unwavering will to its *authoritative realization*; a deepened *feeling of responsibility* with a capacity for imperative decision. The one ruling cannot be *without a will to rule*; but this will must not be an objectless love of power, but a living *inspiration from the idea of the State*. The ruler at his best sees in his public authority not a greedy, licentious advantage, but *an obligation and a responsible burden*. He does not halt before the burden of a vitally necessary compromise, but does not "contrive" justifications for it in the name of conscience, and does not distort the ethical nature of the State by the false doctrine that "a good end justifies any means". In a word, the one ruling must make of his will a living *instrument of the idea of the State*, or, what is the same thing, his soul must be *objectively possessed by the end of the State*. And any defect in his legal consciousness is fraught with heavy consequences for the entire political union. The one wielding authority, whoever he may be—legislator, ruler or judge—devoid of a sense of the State or of patriotism, possessed by an evil will, self-interest or class interest, without feeling for the law, not believing in the purpose and power of the State, and not recognizing his responsibilities, lacking in will, or cowardly, will always be a true disaster for his union: for his actions will undermine what is most important in political life: belief in the law and the will to the unity of the State.

* **See Chapters Seven, Eight and Nine.**

All this can be expressed in saying that in any State, and given any structure, *power must belong to the best people.*[3] In terms of its end and according to its essence the State is *aristocratic*; that is an unshakable axiom since the times of Confucius, Heraclitus, and Aristotle. A State which placed in power the worst people, or still more, one elevating social riff-raff to the top, experiences a fatal disease; the State "expelling" or executing its best people is in need of "a revolution" (Heraclitus); a State not able to select its best citizens is doomed to prostration and degeneracy. And given all that, the criterion by which the best citizens are identified is *not* conditional, *not* relative *and* not debatable: it is *the capacity for disinterested service to spirit and the capacity for the social organization of brotherhood;* the first is an ethical qualification, the second is a political qualification of an aristocracy. Political "*nobility*" is by no means the same as the "ancientness of the family", "nobility", or even more, "wealth"; it is a nobility of *will and of legal consciousness*. And all the "aristocracies" which have come about in history, but not satisfying this criterion, were a government of "the best" in name only.

Further, the very end of the State shows that power in fact *cannot and must not be realized by the entire nation conjointly* or *to an identical extent.*

In actual fact, the existence of a political organization is not in itself either a self-sufficient or a higher end of human life. The State is necessary in order that the protection of natural rights [прав] should give to human beings the possibility not only and not simply "to live", but to lead a life worthy of the human spirit. For that reason political activity cannot and must not devour the nation's energy more than is necessary; for in the final analysis the statesman remains not so much the immediate creator of spirit, as a servant of the nation and of its spiritual leaders. The nation establishes or accepts authority in order to live and create, but not conversely. Precisely for this reason the process of forming an authority is always a process of *social differentiation*, that is, the designation of a few persons authorized to realize the end of the State imperatively. To that is joined the *technical* impossibility of creating a ruling authority from a great mass of people: the ruling authority is above all a living, acting *unity*, requiring a single *direction of will* and, accordingly, the agreement of individual wills in the matter of common tasks and common means. This single direction of will is developed with all the more

[3] However anti-modern and unrealizable such an axiom of political life may appear, there is no room for doubt that Il'in was permanently wedded to this "aristocratic" conception of political rule. But it should be noted that Il'in by no means had in mind any actual hereditary aristocracy. Such aristocracies were very likely to place incompetents in power. By "aristocracy" he meant literally the "best people", people of the highest spiritual qualities; by what mechanism they were to be selected and placed in power is nowhere discussed in detail by Il'in to our knowledge. It is clear, however, that he was at least as much alarmed by the prospect of the "rabble" or the "mob" in power as Plato or Aristotle were by the *demos*. None of them ever endorsed the idea of a "pure" democracy. However, Il'in does actively consider mechanisms whereby immature political actors could be brought to a state of maturity.

difficulty the larger the number of people participating in it with their opinions, and the more the principle of *subordination* is crowded out by the beginning of *collusion*. Political history knows examples of how entire institutions, parties, and even regimes perished from inactivity and sterility because in the process of organization they violated the law of *economy of forces*. Finally, by no means every citizen possesses those qualities which are essential for power—a developed legal consciousness, a true understanding of the end of the state, incorruptible will, a scientific understanding of socio-economic processes, civic courage and a gift for organization. The capacity for power is an extremely high qualification of the individual soul, and given the contemporary historical level of humanity, people standing on such a level turn out to be exceedingly few.

All this can be expressed in this way: ruling in the person of the State always was and always will be connected with definite *spiritual "qualifications"*.* To reject this is possible only through misunderstanding, or as a consequence of complete incompetence in matters of State. Moreover, it is appropriate to put the question directly whether anyone rejects this political axiom in general. For so far as is known, no one ever put forward such an absurd assertion as that any citizen, as such, is capable of exercising the authority of public law, or what is the same thing, might possess the capability for public-law . On the contrary, all political writers and all political parties always recognized that among the citizens there are people, spiritually immature and spiritually bankrupt, whom it would be absurd and ruinous to entrust with State functions; and to find differences of opinion on this question would obviously be quite impossible.

In fact, to leave the exercise of the authority of public law to minors or psychically ill people would be so absurd and ruinous for the political union that no one would insist on it. Citizens who have not yet acquired a "mature and sound understanding", who have already lost it or never possessed it (fools) are naturally kept away from matters requiring such understanding. And such a removal rests, obviously, on the acknowledgement of political authority through a deed requiring a *spiritual qualification*. Disagreement begins only with the question of *the extent* of this qualification and of *the means* of determining it.

It would be useless to think that just any human being having achieved the age of twenty and not having obviously lost his mind, would be capable of constructing political authority. That would mean to place politics lower than any elementary trade or craft, requiring besides age and the absence of insanity, also the presence of an appropriate apparatus, the physical skill and at least a dim awareness of the end. And thus political activity, no less than any trade or craft, requires in addition to age and "not being insane", the presence of the appropriate *spiritual apparatus*, an awareness of the political end, and at least minimal

*** Not to be confused with social estate, property, professional, or religious qualifications.**

intellectual skill. It would be absurd to construct a political authority not being in possession of *political legal consciousness*; deplorable results will always be guaranteed: this will be either an anti-political authority, or a State powerlessness, or even—still worse—an anti-political State powerlessness. The first will take the form of a personal despotism or a class dictatorship; the second will create a regime of faintheartedness, concessions, excessive tolerance, and correspondingly, a regime of State atomization, that is, a misappropriation of power, a disintegration of the nation and the territory; the third will produce the worst structure—mob rule: the dominance of the inferior, led by demogogues. Political history knows all of these paths and possibilities; and in realizing them, gave and gives proof that *public legal capacity* is measured entirely by *political legal consciousness*.

Therefore, it is essential to recognize that historical States, *slowly and gradually* admitting the popular masses to public activity, are guided by a true instinct for self-preservation. A political union not observing this gradualness, risks its existence; it places its fate in the hands of political infants or political imbeciles, and its days are numbered. In this safe gradualness there is nothing politically reprehensible; on the contrary, there is profound sense and political wisdom in it. On the other hand, the behavior of ruling groups and classes is ruinous and criminal if they use the incompetence of people in order to replace state interest with class interest, and keep the population's legal consciousness at a low level. In this way they prepare calamity not only for themselves but for the entire State: they compromise the very idea of political unity, connecting it in the popular conception with the idea of class self-interest; they cultivate in the population a blind mistrust in *any* authority, deaf rage and dark avarice; they cultivate that Caliban, that rabble, which will one day, having lost its fear, try to abolish culture and the State, and *openly* replace political authority with self-interested arbitrary rule. Such behavior by ruling groups and classes witnesses to the fact that their own legal consciousness is far from corresponding to the necessary level; that *formal* legal guarantees against them are needed, for the best *substantive* guarantee--nobility of legal consciousness—is absent. And difficult indeed is the position of such a State, in which the ruling groups are incapable of ruling in an order of true political trusteeship, whereas the broad masses are incompetent either to assume power from them or to bring about *formal* legal guarantees. Such a State cannot be constructed according to the institutional model, but is not in condition to turn to the corporate structure either; and only social work on the development of legal consciousness can save it from a slow disintegration.

The danger of such an abuse of power witnesses of course not to the "non-necessity" of spiritual qualifications, but, on the contrary, to the unconditional necessity of them. The fundamental objective of the State structure consists in ensuring selection for rule of *the best* citizens; and one can say that the political maturity of the broad masses is defined precisely by their capacity for such a selection. State power must always and unconditionally possess an *aristocratic* character; it is the first, fundamental requirement, preceding all others. And the transition from a regime of political *trusteeship* to a regime of political *self-governance* makes sense only to the extent that it does not violate this fundamental condition.

Historically the State can be described as follows: in terms of *form* it is a public *institution*, slowly approaching toward a *corporation*; according to *spirit* it is a self-governing *corporation*, slowly drawing into itself wider circles and the popular masses. Political wisdom consists in maintaining the regime of trusteeship only to the extent of actual necessity, while at the same time working energetically on overcoming the political incompetence of the masses; or, otherwise, to cultivate in the masses the spirit of corporate self-governance and to reinforce this spirit through an appropriate political form. The objective of political trusteeship consists not in maintaining its wards in a state of spiritual immaturity, in a state of gullibility; but in the cultivation of the ward, imparting to him the capacity for self-restraint and self-discipline, the capacity for self-guardianship. For the State is strong and worthy not when the rulers drag the population toward a legal order against their wills, binding the people to a patriotic solidarity by means of fear and executions; but when the spirit of political patriotism and free political will live in the people themselves.

Accordingly, one of the fundamental tasks of ruling authority is the political cultivation of the people. This means that the broad masses must be drawn into political life *before* their competence in public affairs is formally affirmed; or, what is the same thing, only that individual can enter into the exercise of public *authorities* who has grasped and mastered his public *obligations and prohibitions*; for self-rule and self-organization presuppose great discipline in the masses, that is, an unwavering fidelity to obligations and prohibitions. In other words one can say that the broad masses of the population must be drawn into political life initially through legal consciousness, and only later through the political act. For a political act not growing out of a sound legal consciousness is ruinous and senseless; whereas a sound legal consciousness not finding expression in any sort of definite and formalized political act is by no means senseless and not ruinous—on the contrary, it remains a precious capability, the possibility for future achievements.

It can be acknowledged, of course, that a person who is not permitted at all to stand on his feet and walk will not learn to walk. However, a child who is placed on his feet by his tutor too soon, and urged to walk when he is not yet strong enough, will grow up with mutilated, crooked legs. This means that it is essential for the population to practice social self-governance; however, not in that sphere in which the will *definitively* constructs political life along fundamental life-determining lines. It is important for the population to become schooled in the construction and maintenance of social organizations; but it is absurd, harmful, and ruinous when that school of social self-governance, accustoming people to the alphabet of coordination and subordination, shifts into the sphere of fateful decisions and State policy. Politics tolerates neither childishness, nor games, nor dilettantism, nor maniacal experimentation. And what is appropriate in the sphere of private sociality—sports and clubs, philanthropy and cooperation—has no place in questions of national leadership and defense.

All this taken together gives us the possibility of illuminating the question of political form and the question of democracy.

Given careful treatment, this question falls into two distinct questions: the question of the *empirically most expedient* form and the question of the most *perfect* form.

There is not, and cannot be, a single political form most expedient for all times and for all nations. It is time to put an end to this dream-like and groundless prejudice. For political form is determined by the entire ensemble of spiritual and material facts for each separate nation, and above all, the level of legal consciousness present in it. For each given nation in each given epoch the most expedient one is that political form which best takes into account the maturity and firmness of political will present in it, and matches it with that combination of the corporate and the trusteeship principles which leads to and builds national life. And, moreover, that form must lead the nation toward the sole and objektive end of the State, and guarantee the aristocratic nature of rule. It is clear that here there cannot be a single solution; besides, it is possible that the most expedient form may turn out to be, *rebus sic stantibus*,[4] the least spiritually perfect form: thus, the rabble, as such, require despotic domination, and in the absence of monarchical presuppositions in a country, the State may turn out to be doomed to a form of tyranny.

The matter stands otherwise with the question of *the most perfect* political form.

Here one can definitely establish that the most perfect is that political form which corresponds to the fundamental and unchanging axioms of legal consciousness and appeals in the souls of the citizens to those axiomatic bases of civil life. Of such axioms one can point to three: 1) a feeling of one's own spiritual worth and its manifestations: self-respect, the principle of honor and of the spiritual dimension of life. 2) the capacity for resolute self-governance, and its manifestations: fidelity to principle, conviction, self-activity, discipline and duty. 3) mutual trust and respect—citizen to citizen, citizen to authority, and authority to citizen. And thus the most perfect is that political form which corresponds to these axiomatic fundamentals, appeals precisely to them and brings them into action, as a politically effective motive.

One could say that the most perfect is that political form which assimilates in itself the spirit of Christianity and absorbs the rhythm of political unity—with the principles of love, respect and trust, the principles of spiritual self-affirmation, self-sacrifice in earthly life, and

[4] "So long as things remain the same".

heroism. With such an approach the question of democracy will also be correctly illuminated.

Democracy is a *political structure* in which *power is organized by the principle of corporate self-governance.*[5] Everything essential follows from this.

A democratic structure is a mode of political organization. Consequently, as is also every other structure, it is valuable and admissible only to the degree that it does not contradict the end of the State. "The State" is a generic concept; "a democratic State" is a specific one. The species, having lost the marks of the genus, is nonsense; a State striving to be a democracy at the cost of its political being is an absurd and doomed phenomenon. In other words: if the intrusion of the broad masses into politics is ruining the State, then the State either perishes or finds within itself the power to halt this intrusion and put an end to it. Democracy as an anti-State principle possesses neither meaning nor justification; it is *mob rule*, i.e., the rule of the rabble, and by that its fate is already pre-determined.

This means that democracy is valuable and admissible only insofar as it brings about an *aristocratic* realization of the political end, that is, serves the *common* concern of *authority, law and spirit*. Democracy is neither a higher end nor a self-sufficient end; it is only a *mode* of selecting the few, *the best*, for power; and moreover *one* of the modes. As a mode of the *aristocratizing* of power, it is subject to a decisive evaluation; in this lies its test and from this proceeds its verdict. And if this verdict is negative, then the State either turns to other modes or perishes.

A democratic structure, by itself, is only a form: and therefore its value depends upon what content is injected into that form.

The so-called "people's will" possesses value only to the extent that it is *true to the political content*; outside of that it turns out to be only *a foolish craving of the crowd*; and the quality of this foolish craving does not become higher because many or even the majority are infatuated with it. Not every "need of the people" is sacred, because it happens that both the individual and the many have needs not deserving satisfaction. And thus politically competent people must be able not only to *recognize* their needs, but also to understand the nature of such needs, their *worth*, and then make a *selection* among them. And those needs which are spiritually true, must be comprehended as *common and solidary* and subsequently introduced into the framework of *public legal consciousness*, so that their *aristocratic realization* could be organized. Only in this significance is "the people's will" something *precious*, for the people cease to be a dark mass, a crowd, or the mechanical sum of classes and professions: it becomes a politically organized, spiritual unity, it steps forth as a single national spirit, truly and autonomously realizing its destiny.

[5] That is, a public-law, and not a private-law, corporation. See the distinction above in this Chapter.

In this way is resolved the question of the "form" of the State. It must be determined in the interaction of two fundamentals: the single, objektive political *end* and the *level of legal consciousness* present in the country. It must always ensure the aristocratic nature of authority and at the same time conform to the dimensions of self-governance of the people with the maturity and firmness of its political will. There is not and cannot be a single political form "best" for all times and peoples: it is time to extinguish this dream-like and groundless prejudice; it is time for political leaders and parties to join in wisdom, combining the spiritual authority of "the one" with the vision of "the many and the different ...". There is no single, best form: but there are fundamental, imperishable axioms of ruling authority and axioms of legal consciousness, on the observance of which must rest any legal organization. These axioms are determined entirely by the nature of the human spirit and law.[6]

[6] One should note that Il'in is enumerating *two* sets of "axioms": *axioms of legal consciousness*, of which there are three, all of which were enumerated above in this chapter; and *axioms of ruling authority*, of which there are six, all of which are enumerated in the following chapter. The three axioms of legal consciousness will be further examined in three separate pairs of chapters (fifteen through twenty) below.

Chapter Fourteen
The Axioms of Ruling Authority

The historical experience of humanity shows that the authority of positive law and of the rulers creating it rests not only on a social contract, not only on the plenary authority of the legislator, not only on the imposing effect of orders and threats—but above all, and most profoundly of all, on *the spiritual rightness* [правоте], or what is the same thing, on *the substantive truth* of the commands and norms issued.[1] Precisely this spiritual truth of the created law is always the best guarantee that the authority of the law and of the rulers will actually be acknowledged in the legal consciousness of the people and that their political strength will be joined with productiveness in life. Spiritual rightness in itself possesses in general a certain secret force which impresses even those who strongly oppose it, even when it seemingly remains a voice crying in the wilderness. This influence of rightness is explained by the fact that it possesses not only *spiritual value, but also a vital truth*; and in particular the study of natural law resolves not only the theoretical problem but also the urgent problem of human organization. A spiritually true law is true not only "in theory"; no, it truly resolves the *practical* tasks of sociality; it establishes that basis of life in relation to which the burning political questions and complications are only secondary modifications or particular cases. The true discovery of this personal and social *spiritual form* constitutes the deepest, and an unconditional, need of humanity. It is vain to think that any sort of ordinary political task can be truly solved outside of the affirmation of this spiritually-true form of life: outside of it any "solution" will be illusory—either a conditional postponement or a source of new calamities. Salvation lies in one thing: *the form of spirit must establish the act of legal consciousness, the content of the law and the structure of political power*. Legal and political life must be true to their own deep, ultimate roots; and these roots possess a spiritual nature.

This can be expressed as follows: it is necessary for people in their life together to abide by certain *elementary but sacred bases of law and the State*. Outside of this, not a single political organization will create anything other than destruction and suffering. These bases can be formulated as a series of *axioms*, and this series, descending from the surface to the depths, can be divided into two groups: one contains the *axioms of ruling authority*, and the other the *axioms of legal consciousness*.

Political rule consists in the socially-concentrated and juridically-organized *influence of the will* of some of the best, legally-empowered people on the will of others, the subordinated ones; moreover, those

[1] Commands and norms are not typically regarded in contemporary philosophy as possessing the property of truth or falsity; however, one can simply re-interpret Il'in's remark as referring to the "substantive truth" of the spiritual presuppositions invoked to justify commands and norms.

subordinated are bound not only by the *rightness and force [силою] of the ruling authorities*, but also by *their own legal consciousness*; this influence must serve the triumph of natural law, that is, its discovery and realization, as a single, common order of life.

This means that ruling authority, according to its specific essence, is *force*,[2] and moreover *force of will*, while according to its generic distinction it is *legal* force.

A ruling authority is above all *force*. This is expressed in the fact that it is the capacity to have an impact, and to influence. A ruling authority without force is a logically meaningless phrase, and in relation to the State a ruinous spectre, a phantom or a simulacrum; such a ruling authority is needed by no one, for it is deprived of genuine, vital reality; it is dangerous and fatal, because it leads the entire political union to destruction. In order for the State *to exist and to act* it must have this *authentic energy*, *concentrated and organized* into a living unity. The essence *of life* consists in action, and moreover in *purposeful action*; the capacity for such action is *a living force*. Therefore, to say "a forceful ruling authority" [сильная власть] is the just the same as to say "an authentic, living authority" or "a ruling authority corresponding to its nature and its purpose". A State with weak force is not capable of life. The weakening and enfeeblement of the State is its death.[3] For that reason, everything that constitutes the force of the ruling authority—*authority, unity, rightness of the end, the organization and the assiduity of the apparatus of coercion*—all that forms the very basis of the existence of the State.

In distinction from any physical force, State power is the force of *will*. This means that the mode of its action is by its very nature *internal*, *psychic*, and moreover *spiritual*. Physical force, that is, the capacity for the material-corporeal influence of one human being on another, is essential for State authority, but it by no means constitutes the fundamental mode of action intrinsic to the State. Moreover, the more perfected the State structure the less it turns to physical force; and precisely that structure

[2] The term translated here as "ruling authority" is власть, the more basic meaning of which is "power," hence also "ruling power" In relation to the context of political rule, власть may be properly translated either as "authority" or as "power." S.ince Il'in seems to be discussing both concepts at various times, it is necessary to alternate between them in the translation, depending on the immediate context. A further complication arises in the remainder of this clause when he asserts that "ruling authority, according to its specific essence, is *force*". The latter term is сила, which may mean "power" or "force". For the most part сила will be translated as "force" rather than "power", so as to preserve a distinction between the two Russian terms. However, there are a few instances where it seems advisable to translate сила by "power" because Il'in occasionally seemed to treat them simply as synonyms. These instances will be indicated with footnotes or by the inclusion of the Russian term in brackets in the text.

[3] It is perhaps worth remarking that Il'in had lived through the steady weakening of the tsarist autocracy from the Russo-Japanese war of 1904-1905, the revolution of 1905 (during his undergraduate years), the catastrophic defeats of Russian armies during the First World War, and the February and October revolutions of 1917. He had ample opportunity to observe and reflect upon the process of the weakening of the Russian State.

which is drawn toward the exclusive dominance of physical force undermines itself and prepares itself for destruction. The "sword" does not at all express the essence of State authority; it is only the most extreme and unhealthy of its means; it constitutes its *final* word and *the weakest of its supports*. There are situations and periods when a ruling authority without a sword is a useless and disastrous one; but these periods are exceptional and abnormal. Normally the force of the ruling authority lies not in the sword, but in the *authoritative influence of its willed imperative*.

The ruling authority is *the force* [сила] *of will*.[4] This force is measured not only by the *intensity and activity* of inward volitional exertion realized by the ruler, but also by the *authoritative inexorability of* its *external manifestation*. For that reason a person with an indecisive, vacillating, divided will, amenable to non-objective influences, soft and yielding, is incapable of ruling. The purpose of rule is to create in the souls of people a mood of certainty, decisiveness, impulsivity [импульсивность], and diligence. The one ruling must not only desire and decide, but systematically lead others to a concordant desiring and deciding. To rule means to somehow impose one's own will on the will of others; however, in such a way that this imposition is *voluntarily accepted* by those who submit. Ruling is a subtle, aesthetically compounded process of the interaction of a stronger will with a weaker will. This process creates an invisible and imponderable atmosphere of gravitation of the periphery to the center, of many uncoordinated wills into a single, organized leading will. The creation of such an atmosphere is a matter of particular art, requiring not only *intensity of will* but also a psychic-spiritual sagacity, a genuine perception of the *subconscious* life of others and an ability to *cultivate* it. The ruler must make of his will, first, a *force* [сила] *fixated objectively on the end of the State*, and second, *an actual and unified volitional focus on national life*. The life of the State consists in such *agreement of wills* (coordination) which, while remaining essentially a *voluntary coordination*, takes the form of a voluntary *subordination* (submission). Thus, the task of the ruler consists in training the will *by way of subordination* to *autonomous concord* and to satiate with the spirit of this voluntary coordination the subordinating form of the state idea.* Such is the volitional task of the ruling authority; and only on this basis can the State be transformed into an actual and non-degrading unity of wills.[5]

4 Власть есть *сила воли*. Alternatively: "The ruling authority is the power of will," or, still less happily: "The ruling power is the power of will".

5 Il'in's remarks on the psychology of ruling in this paragraph may also be tacitly revealing of his own sense of himself as a potential leader. The noted Russian philosopher and historian of philosophy, V. V. Zen'kovskii, provided the following impression of his first meeting with Il'in in the early 1920's in Berlin: "I saw I. A. Il'in at a congress of the Movement in Germany and must say that I. A. Il'in produced an extremely powerful impression on me. Outwardly he was extremely handsome, tall, broad-shouldered. With

* **See Chapters Four, Seventeen and Eighteen.**

To this is joined the *legal* character of State authority. It emphasizes that the *will of the State*, as a variety of human will, is not objectless and not unbound, but *objectively bound to ethical contents*. By this is determined the *spiritual* and not simply the social-psychological being of the State. The will of the people, separated out in the process of social differentiation and politically organized, preserves its *spiritual nature, its objektive end*, its *principles* and its *standard*. The State authority adheres to its own true spiritual nature only if it remains true to its end, to its ways and means; it acquires its sacred significance only from this ultimate spiritual, ethical and religious depth.

In these founding considerations are contained, essentially speaking, all the *axioms of ruling authority*. Taken together, they affirm that the fundamental nature of law and the State cannot be reconciled with just any ascent to power [власти]; that there are paths to power to enter upon which means to destroy both the ruling authority and the State. The struggle for State authority must under all conditions preserve its *political nature*; in the opposite case the path will ruin the achievement itself and the means will destroy its own end. The political possesses its own essential paths and forms, and people have never succeeded in violating and trampling on them with impunity.

The *first* axiom of ruling authority says that State authority cannot belong to anyone without *plenary legal authority*.

That is apparent from the fact that the legislator of natural right [правоты] must possess a particular objective and spiritual *competence*: only a spiritually-sighted human being possesses *the basis and the right* [право] to take upon himself the authoritative governance of social

a striking gaze, he somehow immediately riveted one to himself. But most remarkable in him was his eloquence, full of power and fire. He was a "flaming" orator; he spoke passionately at all times, and having captured the attention of the auditors, did not release them from himself for a moment. In the voice, in the intonations one felt a great power, but above all—*a capacity to subordinate one to himself*. This was a born leader, demanding unconditional subordination to himself; one could say submissiveness. Someone called him "a virtuoso of eloquence". But the point was not the eloquence of Il'in alone; his principal power lay in *the commanding tone*, and, moreover, in this command one always felt a certain *moral violence* over the thought and conscience of the auditors. Il'in did not try to convince, but "magically" subordinated the youth to himself; he wanted not a free joining with him, but an unconditional acceptance of his thought, his plans. Someone told me that for Il'in there were in the Russian emigration only three persons whose authoritativeness he recognized and understood: P. I. Novgorodtsev (his teacher), P. V. Struve, and A. V. Kartashov; all the rest he simply "did not recognize"; they were for him simply an empty spot.

"In Il'in there dwelled a fighter; he absolutely had to denounce someone, to slash, to flog, to break. But youth, in which at times there is encountered a sharp need to find a leader for themselves, if they were attracted by Il'in, then strongly; he was able to inspire them.

"As a thinker he was exceptional, but his faith in Orthodoxy (even in his final book *The Axioms of Religious Experience*) was forced, not from the heart, not from the whole spirit, but from the head". Translated from *Записки Русской академической группы в США* [Transactions of the Association of Russian-American Scholars in the USA], XXVII, pp. 25-26 (New York: Association of Russian-American Scholars in USA, 1967-1995).

life. In terms of political expediency this is required by a principle of *organization* which rests on a division of functions, on their distribution, on social consent and recognition. Moreover, legal consciousness requires that the ruling authority [власть] itself be perceived not as a force [сила] giving rise to law, but as a *plenary authority possessing vital influence* (force) [силы] only *in the measure of its rightness*. Law [право] is born not of force [сила], but exclusively of right [права], and in the final analysis, always from natural right. This means that brute force [сила], seizing power [власть], will be creating positive law only to the extent to which the *legal* consciousness of people *consents* (under the pressure of whatever considerations) to recognize its *plenipotentiary* force [силой].

Ruling power, completely deprived of *legal sanction*, is a juridically indifferent phenomenon: it does not possess a legal dimension. It must receive a legal sanction *both* from constitutional law *and* from the recognition of legal consciousness.

Ruling power, deprived of the sanction of law$_z$, arises in catastrophic events of disorganization or revolution; and then its task and its salvation lie in relying on the sanction of *legal consciousness* (its own and the people's) which is alone competent to create a *new* constitutional form and in this way to fill in the missing formal sanction. If it does not succeed in that and a new form is not created, then an inevitable destruction flowing from non-recognition of the ruling power and a deepening of the disorganization carries along with it both the defective ruling power and the State itself.

A ruling power deprived of recognition and respect is revealed in such situations as when an historically formed regime has exhausted and outlived itself, such that the legal consciousness of the ruling circles has fallen behind the growth of people's needs and the legal consciousness of society. The task and the salvation of such a ruling power consists in relying on the existing formal sanction of the law to renew its political direction of will and in that way to earn the sanction of legal consciousness. If it does not succeed in this, and the legal consciousness of the people does not accept it, then revolution will overtake it with all the dangers of the first outcome.

It is clear that a ruling power legally empowered *neither* by constitutional form *nor* by an accepting legal consciousness can only simulate the creating of law$_z$, government, and the court, for it remains a pretending and encroaching power; and even natural law incidentally proclaimed and asserted by it, remains either an abstract formula, or an imposed and dead convention of life. Obviously this first axiom of ruling authority, requiring legal empowerment, is supported by the vital mechanism of the State itself.

The *second* axiom of ruling authority asserts that the State authority, within the boundaries of each political union, must be *one*.

This is apparent from the fact that natural law expresses the essential form of spirit itself and that, therefore, it is itself *one*, as Spirit is one and His rightness [правота] is *one*. In terms of political expediency this requires the principle of State *unity*, binding the multitude of people precisely through their relation to the common and *sole source* of positive law.

One must understand the *unity* of State authority, of course, not in the sense of the unity of an "agency" or the undividedness of functions and competencies, but in the sense of the *unity of an organized direction of the will*, expressing itself in the unity of law attained and realized. Within the boundaries of a single union at one and the same moment, one and the same thing cannot be "law" and "not-law". Positive law by its very meaning is definitive, unambiguous, and unitary; its unity is a manifestation of natural rightness [правота] present in it and sanctifying it. And State authority, possessing the high purpose of formulating natural rightness [правота] in the form of positive norms, acquires from this the significance of *the sole and unique* competent source of the law; such that only a fully-empowered *association* with this authority could impart to an individual or an agency the competence to establish law.

Legal consciousness by its very essence cannot recognize as "legal" two mutually exclusive norms or commands. And, in just the same way, it cannot recognize two mutually exclusive ruling authorities, or two authorities in opposition to one another, as being equally "the State". In every political union the State authority, despite all of its branchings, is by its very essence *unitary*; the presence of *two* State authorities witnesses to the presence of *two* political unions. It may happen that these two "States" are only just now arising, or are dying out, or are fragments of a disintegrated political union; but if two newly-arisen ruling authorities do not merge into a single one, then sooner or later they will enter into a struggle for the members and the territory of a juridical person, and war between them becomes inevitable. For that reason a State within which *two* ruling authorities have arisen, faces a civil war and internal destruction; and it falls to legal consciousness to note the flouting of one of the axioms of ruling authority and to make a choice.[6]

The *third* axiom of ruling authority asserts that the authority of the State must always be exercised by *the best* people, satisfying ethical and political qualifications.[*]

This is defined by the magnitude, complexity and responsibility of the task the resolution of which presupposes that such a person be an artist of natural rightness. In terms of political expediency, this is required by the principle of the *authority* of the ruling power and the principle of the voluntary *recognition* of it on the part of the legal consciousness of those subordinated to it. Ruling power deprived of authority is worse than

6 There were instances of such temporary dual authority in Il'in's personal experience in both the 1905 and the 1917 revolutions.

* **See Chapter Thirteen.**

manifest powerlessness [безвластие]; a people rejecting the rule of the best on principle or not knowing how to organize and maintain it, are a *rabble*; and *demagogues* are its fitting leaders.

People become a *rabble* when they take charge of the affairs of State moved not by political legal consciousness but by private self-interest; but precisely for that reason they do not seek the best people and do not wish to convey power to them. *Anyone* can belong to a rabble: the rich and the poor, the ignorant and the "intelligentsia". A rabble is distinguished by *self-interested will and a crippled legal consciousness*, and in a revolutionary epoch, moreover, by making *political demands*. State power is for it only a convenient means for obtaining personal or class goals. The distinction between the public-law sphere and the private-law one, the priority of the public good over the private, the sacredness of public obligation—all that is beyond the rabble; precisely for that reason down through the centuries they take and give bribes, selling out and embezzling State business; they avoid onerous obligations by all means; they remain indifferent in times of social distress, and in troubled times revolt and pillage, easily changing leaders and flags. The rabble understands neither the purpose of the State nor its ways and means; it does not know the common interest and feels no solidarity; precisely for that reason it is incapable of organizing and maintaining discipline and is easily scattered at the first energetic opposition by State-organized forces. It is completely deprived of awareness of State unity and a will to political unification; and that is why, left to itself, it quickly falls apart into hostile camps and gangs and commences an unending civil war. Law is for it a question of power, cunning, and luck; and that is why, seeing power on its side, it displays insolence and quickly becomes impudent, while when losing, trembles and grovels. The rabble hates State power when that power is not in its hands; and, hating, submits out of fear; and submitting, expects and requires from it crumbs. But having set up its *own* ruling power, it does not know how to give it either respect, or trust, or support; it begins to be suspicious of it, becomes permeated by hatred for it, and in this way renders feeble and ruins its own anti-political handiwork.[7] And if it succeeds all the same in creating a certain likeness of a "regime", then this "regime" brings about under the aspect of "democracy" the triumph of greed over the common good, equality over spirit, lies over evidence, and violence over the law; this "regime" rests on flattery and graft, and realizes power for *demagogues*.

In the ranks of self-interested and ambitious people striving for power, heedless of everything, the *demagogue* occupies the lowest place: for he chooses the path which is most ruinous for the legal consciousness of the people. He addresses the rabble, seeks success from them, and receives power from their hands. In order to secure this "investiture", he uses all paths, not hesitating even to take those which destroy the State itself;

[7] "Anti-political" presumably because Il'in was thinking of a rabble setting up its own center of power in opposition to an existing State authority.

he appeals to the blind, anti-political self-interest so easily absorbing the ignorant soul and, igniting it to a state of passion, speaks to it the words of *flattery and bribery*. He addresses the *worst* there is in the human being and *places* this worst *at the basis of politics and ruling power*; he lowers affairs of State to the level of the rabble and its understanding, and builds his success on that. For that reason he is the worst enemy of the legal consciousness of the people and of the idea of the State.

The demagogue dims the consciousness of the mass, tossing to it anti-State "ideas" in the form of prepared popular slogans tempting to it; he corrupts its feeling, feeding it passions of hatred and greed; he perverts its will, directing it to anti-political and vicious aims. The demagogue creates a system for the gratification of the ignorant mass; he mobilizes the rabble where it already exists, and creates one where there was none. And in this gratification he naturally extols the rabble, depicting it as "the sovereign people", and praises its low craving and deeds, depicting its supposed loftiness and valor. In this way he cultivates *political venality* in souls: he convinces the rabble that political power is its commodity, which it can sell advantageously; and then it sets the price of this commodity in the form of "political" promises and bribes. The demagogue seeks to *buy* political power, as though that power actually belonged to the ignorant mob. And suborning it with anti-political, unrealizable and absurd bribes, he brings about the worst, because the most refined and depraved, form of political corruption; and at the same time he carries out a political fraud, for the absurd promise is certainly hopeless, while the realization of the anti-political bribe, if it were undertaken, would destroy both the corrupting demagogue and the already half-ruined political union. And thus, piling fraud upon bribery, the demagogues carry out an auction of state power.

Thus the violation of the third axiom of ruling authority gradually creates a regime of political depravity and perverts the aristocratic nature of the idea of the State at its very root.

The *fourth* axiom of ruling authority asserts that a political program can include only such measures as pursue the *common interest.*

This is apparent from the fact that State authority has the mission of affirming natural law, and natural law coincides precisely with the common spiritual interest of the nation and the citizen.* By way of political expediency this is determined by the fact that only service to the common interest transforms State power into an actual, authoritative center of political unity.

One can express this axiom thus: that the program of the ruling authority must be acceptable to *a mature political legal consciousness*; not simply for a "legal consciousness present in the people", but for its spiritually-true objective depth. To place oneself face to face with that

*** See Chapters Five and Twelve.**

depth of legal consciousness and with the common political interest constitutes the fundamental task of any honest political party.

A party is not a gang, not a band, not a clique, and not a coterie precisely to the extent that it strives to establish *political authority*, and not simply to seize power in the State. But a will to *political authority* is thereby a will to the political *end*, which includes within itself no private interest whatsoever as such, either of a person or of a class. For that reason a political party cannot be class-based *in terms of its program*: it must without fail represent *all classes* and hence be *above classes*.[8] For State authority is something *unitary* for all and *common* to all; and for that reason the program projecting its desired and future line of conduct can contain references only to *common* interests. A party *lacking* a *political* program, supporting a single class interest, is an anti-political party; it is incapable of functioning politically; if it seizes power it will conduct an absurd and ruinous policy and destroy the State sooner than the power of things will force it to hurriedly think up *political* additions to its anti-political program.

A mature legal consciousness is the sole power which can guarantee the *political nature* [*государственность*] of party programs. Given the presence of such a legal consciousness, one party can be distinguished from another not according to *whose* interest each of them defends, for all of them will defend one and the same interest: the interest of the State—but by the way in which *it understands* that sole and common interest. Then the struggle among the parties is no longer a competition of class claims, but an *argument over political understandings*. Then all parties want one and the same thing: the political good, that is, the good of all citizens, all classes, which is above classes; all parties carry *a single direction of will*; all parties *strive* above all to distinguish the political interest from private and class interest; and all of them recognize the impermissibility of constructing a program according to the principle of self-interest.

As a consequence of this, a party may and must be its own sort of *political purgatory*: it purges the will of its members from anti-political self-interest, tearing their near-sighted gaze away from immediate egoistic tasks and forcing them to search out the spiritual tasks of the nation and State: it will teach them *to conquer* personal and class greed *on the very threshold* of the political act: by this means it will train their souls for *the political direction of the will* and prepare the triumph of political *reason* over anti-political *passion*. The first task of the political party consists in growing in its members a true public legal consciousness and uniting them in a *political* like-mindedness. This will introduce into political life a necessary *spiritual hygiene*, for it frees it from foolish and blind passions. Not blinded by these passions, the party ceases to see an enemy in the other party, but finds in it a *collaborator* in political *understanding and construction*. The very distinction of programs ceases to be a scandal:

[8] Obviously Il'in would deny that any Marxist "party", not to mention the Bolsheviks, could qualify as a genuine political party.

for all programs are freighted with an identical direction of will to a single end. A mutual recognition of parties and classes is accomplished not by way of mutual pressure, threats, or violence, but by way of mutual political justification or acceptance. Politics loses the character of a *latent civil war* and achieves its true height.

Then the unity of the political end does not arise *as a result* of a struggle for power—as a "compromise" or a "resultant force"—but matures *on the threshold* of this struggle. The struggle for power already presupposes a unity in the direction of will in the citizenry and in the party. Only on this condition would the political struggle not divide the people, but unite them around a single source of law common to all and identically revered: a ruling state authority. The quarrel of different understandings, given the presence of common ends, ensures both the dignity of the subject and a creative collaboration of those with different opinions. And politics becomes now not a clamorous bazaar, but a search for responsibility and a school of natural right [правоты].

However, a normal ascent to power presupposes not only a *political* program, but its realizability. For that reason the *fifth* axiom of ruling authority asserts that a program of ruling authority may contain only *realizable* measures and reforms.

That is apparent from the fact that the mission of political authority must be vital and effective; its vocation is not to dream of a perfect structure, but to introduce into the lives of the people the maximum possible natural-law form. In terms of political expediency this is determined by the fact that chimerical and utopian plans not only undermine among the people trust in ruling authority, faith in political organization in general, and the will to political construction, but simply demoralize and ruin the State.

Whatever the ultimate causes of the unrealizability of a reform—whether natural causes, technical, or economic—in the eyes of a statesman they acquire a *political* character; because for him what is "possible" is only what can be realized *under the given level of legal consciousness of the people* by means of *an imperative legal organization*. This means that at any given historical moment, he can realize only a certain part of what, generally speaking, is necessary for the common good; and only this part can he include in the "agenda for the day". Violation of this axiom gives rise to the diseased phenomenon of "political maximalism" and leads the State to destruction.

Precisely the principle of "realizability" forces the party to have *two* programs: "maximal" and "minimal"; the first indicates that "ideal" in the name of which the second is required to be realized, while the second establishes the reforms realizable *rebus sic stantibus*,[9] that is, given present historical conditions. For that reason, the "maximum program", strictly speaking, is *not* a program; it describes a certain ideal end, which *cannot now be realized*; it enumerates those measures and reforms which

9 So long as things remain the same.

it will be possible to put into practice only when the minimum program and the structure indicated in it have been realized, and when, given this new structure, a *new legal consciousness* has been formed. The parties supporting such a division of programs are correct.

In social and political development there is a necessary sequence which can never be disregarded with impunity; and if parties begin to disregard it, then they set out on a path of ill-fated stupidities and destroy the State. A party erasing the distinction between a distant end, unrealizable given the present position of things, and the sequentially next necessary reform, is *politically incapable of functioning*. For, by including the maximal points in the agenda for the day, it deliberately gives to the voters *unfulfillable* promises and summons them to an admittedly *hopeless* struggle; it prompts people to "demand" what not only no one can "give", but the one "demanding" could not himself "take", or perform, or realize, even if everyone agreed not to interfere with him; the party prompts people to believe in the possibility of what *is impossible in actual fact*—through deception or self-deception; igniting passions, it arouses in souls an unquenchable claim, and sets up the one who believed for a heavy disappointment. Arguing for the possibility of the impossible, the maximalist begins, on one hand, to diminish, distort and pervert the distant *ideal end*; on the other hand, to distort and pervert the *surrounding actuality*, now keeping silent about adverse phenomena, now thinking up non-existent ones, and so on. In this way he enters on the path of unconscious or conscious political lies, and in doing so undermines the unity of the State, for he violates the essential trust of people in one another, both of the party in the leaders, and of the party to other parties, and, primarily, of the unorganized mass of the people to the parties and to the whole of politics in general. *An indifference to politics and a decline in legal consciousness* are the mature fruit of this tactic.

In actual fact, moving along this path, the maximalists infect others with this disease from which they suffer themselves: a distinctive illness of political perspective, a *foolish farsightedness*; it forces them to see the faraway as the nearby, and what is nearby they do not see at all. They always deal with an *imagined* reality, depicting it in such a way as to agree with their desires. Thanks to this, their judgement of events, ends, and means acquires the character of a continuous deviation from the truth and from expediency. They begin to *hallucinate* in politics and serve chimeras. They are guided by blind faith in the omnipotence of the "revolutionary act", in the creative power of destruction.[10] This faith draws them into a blind struggle for an unrealizable goal, while the blind struggle forces them to convulsively snatch at *all* means and not stop at any measures whatsoever. And the tragedy of this convulsive casting about from means to means, and this unscrupulousness about measures,

[10] Presumably a tacit reference to Bakunin's famous claim that, "The passion for destruction is a creative passion, too" (the concluding sentence of "The Reaction in Germany" [1842]).

lies in the fact that in the face of an unrealizable goal, all means, even the most unprincipled and foolish, are equally impotent.

Meanwhile, turning to any and all means, the struggle loses both an organized form and a political character. Sticking to unrealizable goals, the tactics of the maximalists turn away from the path of *public law* which ascends through the cultivation of legal consciousness and through a planned organization of the people, to a fully legally empowered ruling in the name of the State. It is clear that this path does not promise and cannot promise the realization of the maximal requirements; and the maximalists abandon it. They seek not law and not public empowerment, but actual possession, and they turn to the violation of *public and private* law—*through usurpation.* A political movement is transformed into a competition of powerful and skillful lawbreakers with one another, into a kind of triumph of "the law of the fist", into a *civil war*: people are seeking an improvement of life via theft, arson, massacres, armed attacks, reciprocal assassinations, and class terror. Blindness gives strength to helplessness and hatred, while hatred and greed do not permit one to come to one's senses and see things clearly. And only weariness and a general derangement of life can halt this process of blind self-extermination, while political destruction and the calamities connected with it remain for a long time a sad monument to the fact that the axiomatic basis of political authority was destroyed.

Finally, the *sixth* axiom of ruling authority asserts that State authority is *bound in principle by distributive justice*, but that it has *the right and the duty* to depart from it when, and only when, the maintenance of *the national-spiritual and political existence of the people* requires it.

That is apparent from the fact that the national spiritual culture is that common, fundamental principle of life apart from which individual spirit could not exist; the interest of that culture includes within itself any individual interest whatever, in the same way that the interest of an organism includes within itself and subordinates to itself the separate interests of all of its members. In terms of political expediency this is determined by the fact that the State, as a whole, has certain autonomous tasks the resolution of which sometimes turns out to be possible only under the condition of a rejection of a just consideration and protection of all the interests of all the groups and classes; *a proper and timely carrying out of justice might under certain conditions destroy the national and political existence of the people.*

The establishment of justice in the social life of people is undoubtedly one of the fundamental tasks of State authority: it flows from the very nature of law and the State. However, the real conditions of political existence may happen to be such that placing this task *higher* than all the others can bring the State to ruin and destruction. This means that within the complement of spiritually-true and just reforms there may turn out to be some which must be recognized as *politically unrealizable*. The State authority is not omnipotent: it is fettered by political unrealizability and is forced to conform to it. What is politically unrealizable is above all everything that *destroys the State itself*—in its organization, or in its personnel, or in its necessary "substrate"; and further, everything that *exceeds the existing powers [силы] of the legal consciousness of its people* and of their level of organization. The ruling authority must not and cannot carry out a reform destroying the very existence of the State or trampling on the life and autonomy of the national spirit. Maintenance of the State as the autonomous form of national spirit, as the dwelling and as the protective enclosure of national spiritual culture, constitutes that facet which is inviolable for State authority and before which anything must yield, even the most just and spiritually-true interest of the citizenry.

This becomes particularly obvious if, for example, one interprets social justice in the sense of "a formal equality of every citizen in every respect". The establishment of such a (leveling) "justice" would turn out to be ruinous for the State, and for that reason it must be recognized to be politically unrealizable. The life of a politically-organized people is a profoundly differentiated process, *resting on* distinctions in capabilities, occupations, and ways of life, and in turn *creating* these distinctions. A formal leveling can only destroy this living and concordant unity of differentially-acting forces. The State, as a *spiritual* union, is interested not in eliminating spiritual distinctions among people, but in securing for these distinctions a free, creative outcome, fullness of being and reconciliation in life. Given this task, a formal leveling will always be spiritually unnatural; the aristocratic essence of the State excludes it in the sense of political acceptability.

However in actual fact, social justice is not at all reducible to a formal leveling of the citizenry. It consists in an *impartial, objective consideration, recognition and protection of each individual spiritual subject in all his essential attributes and well-founded claims*. This means that the essence of it lies not in a blindness to human differences, but in the *recognition* of them and in *the accommodation to them*. Social justice does not at all "equalize" people, that is, does not "assert" their "sameness", which in reality does not exist, and does not "make" them identical, which is in actual fact impossible. It requires, first, identically objective impartiality in the examination of human similarities and differences; second, the stable content of those measures and standards by which this examination is conducted; third, a real correspondence between the given distinctions and the legal and life consequences connected with them. It is clear that justice in such a "distributive" sense requires *legal inequality*, and creates it, connecting, for example, public capability (voting, service) with certain spiritual qualifications, or introducing a progressive income tax.

And thus, speaking in terms of principle, *ruling authority is bound by distributive justice*, and a self-interested trampling on it will never go unpunished. A regime upholding unjust privileges without sufficient grounds is an anti-political regime: it compromises the dignity of State authority and undermines the will to political unity. Such a regime cannot be strong, because it cultivates those centrifugal forces which sooner or later will destroy it, and raises the question of the very existence of the State. And then, either the political union will perish or its supra-class nature will be re-established. This can be expressed as follows: that any retreat of the ruling authority from justice, any failure to satisfy a spiritually-true interest of a citizen must be explicitly justified by an objective showing of the *political unrealizability of the opposite course*: a just interest can be and must be left unsatisfied, either "pared down" or "deferred", if its satisfaction threatens the very existence of the State or will inflict harm on national-spiritual development. One must never introduce in the name of justice such a political order as would ruin the State itself or destroy and extinguish the spiritual life of the people: for justice serves spirit, and not spirit, justice. It is absurd to bring about a political "inner contradiction", knowing in advance that it will be doomed in life: it is not worth struggling for a just life in such a way as to destroy both justice and life. Equalization of property, particularly in the conditions of capitalist production, and given a low level of legal consciousness, can serve as an example of such political unrealizability.

Such are the fundamental axioms of ruling authority. And one can say with certainty that the future fate of the idea of the State is connected with their assimilation and realization.

Chapter Fifteen
The First Axiom of Legal Consciousness

All axioms of ruling authority can be essentially reduced to the fact that in the final analysis politics as a living activity always serves *spirit*, asserting "right law" [правое право][1] and creating a political union for the sake of it. *A worthy and creative life of the human spirit* remains the highest *end* of politics, while positive law and the organization of the State remain the *means*. Politics stands on the peak only when it remains true to its supreme end.[*] This means not only that it must serve the protection and organization of the spiritual life of the people, but that this *service* itself must be accomplished on paths *worthy* of spirit and *observing its laws*$_z$. It is absurd to resort to means which destroys the end; it is senseless to protect the life of spirit, while trampling on its essence and extinguishing its fire.[2] A politics which is destroying spiritual life or at least not facilitating its cultivation and blossoming, is a profound contradiction in life: it not only departs from its end, but *cuts off the source of its own life* and in this way commits itself to degeneration and death. For politics in its true significance is brought about by the best, most substantive, and deepest powers of the soul, that is, *by spirit*, and serves that very same thing that brings it about. And for that reason it must not trample on but observe the laws$_z$ of spirit.

The spiritual is that state of the soul which is the perception, experience, and realization of supreme, objective value.[**] Such a state, transforming the soul into a living organ of Divine life, reveals to a person his purpose and at the same time points him toward a fitting and necessary *form of existence* for him. A person's claim on these forms of life spiritually necessary for him is a well-grounded, true *legal claim*, or, what is the same thing, it has *natural law* behind it. From this it is clear that spiritual life is not conceivable outside of *righl law* [правого права] and that the experience of natural law, as of objektive value, is in itself a *spiritual state*. This connection between *spirit* and *law* can be expressed as follows: *the essential forms of spirit* constitute the *bases of legal consciousness*. And one who objectively experiences law will discover that at its basis always lies a living and rightful *claim of the human being to spirituality*, or, what is the same thing, a claim to a certain *spiritually-necessary form of life*. But if the necessary and true forms of spirit constitute the bases of legal consciousness, that is, its necessary

[1] Alternatively, "just law".

[2] Evidently another reference to the sacred central fire in the Prytaneum of an ancient Greek polis, a symbol of the unity of the polis, as the fire in every individual hearth was supposedly ignited from the one sacred fire. See Chapter Ten, endnote a.

[*] **See Chapters Ten, Eleven and Twelve.**
[**] **See Chapters Five, Six and Nine.**

motives and *modes of life*, then theoretical expression ascribes to it the form of an *axiom*.

The axioms of legal consciousness are its fundamental *truths*, to which correspond in life the fundamental *modes of being, motivation and action*. Wherever there is legal consciousness, these modes of life are present; and the more mature the legal consciousness, the more these modes of life turn out to be conscious, stable, and, as motives, stronger and purer. The more spiritual is the person, the truer is he to the laws$_z$ of his spirit; such that these universal laws$_z$ or modes of life are simultaneously *constitutive forms* of human spirit, and in their pure and holistic aspect, its *norms*. A person lives by these laws$_z$ even when spirituality flares up in him incidentally, weakly or unconsciously; then he realizes them in a distorted way, fragmentarily, obscurely and helplessly. But in a *spiritualized soul* these modes of life and activity are transformed into the principal and the sole ones; and then they form a habitual and stable level of the person—his atmosphere, his character, sometimes imperceptible both to himself and to others. The laws$_z$ of spirit form then something like an artistic form of the soul, inseparable from all its contents; this form is invisibly present in each movement of feeling, in each decision of the will, in each manifestation and action of the person; the soul as it were blossoms and flourishes according to the laws$_z$ of spirit, for they have become the soul's own laws$_z$. The norms become, as it were, real modes of life and legal consciousness achieves its complete maturity.

Such axioms of legal consciousness are: the law$_z$ of *spiritual worth*,[3] the law$_z$ of *autonomy* and the law$_z$ of *mutual recognition*.

The form of human life is defined basically by the fact that a human being is not simply a living creature, and not only a creature endowed with psychic capacities, but a *spiritual* creature. True, at the lowest level the spiritual nature of the human being remains in a potential state, and has the aspect of an awakening capacity, or a developing, but not yet objectively formed, inclination. However, in such a form as well, the human soul remains a living *spiritual creature*, that is, not only the capacity for objectively-valuable contents, but also a power possessing the mode of life essential for these contents. A human being, even the most primitive, conceals within himself *a will to spirit, the form of spirit, and the capacity for spirit*.* And precisely in this way is affirmed the first

[3] The Russian term is *достоинство*, which may be translated as "worth", "merit", or "dignity" in this context. Any of these three alternatives could be made to serve, but "worth" and "dignity" seem the best choices. There is little to choose between them. At times one of them seems to fit the context best; at others, the other. Rather than alternate between them though, we have chosen to translate *достоинство* inflexibly as "worth". "Worth" seems marginally the better choice, not so much in this chapter as in certain later ones.

* **See Chapter Nine.**

and the deepest basis of his being and his activity—a *spiritual worth* intrinsic to him and a live feeling of it within himself.

The feeling of one's own worth is the essential and authentic manifestation of spiritual life; it is a sign of that *spiritual self-assertion* without which neither the struggle for law nor political self-governance, nor national independence is thinkable. A citizen deprived of this feeling is politically incapable of functioning; a people not moved by it is doomed to terrible historical humiliation.

The sense of one's own worth is generated in a person's soul as the result of an authentic, although elementary and formal *spiritual experience*. Such an experience assures the person that he is actually *capable* of the realization or perception of something unconditionally *valuable*; that it is given to him to experience a real encounter with a vital task and in this encounter to accept and support the burden of labor and responsibility. Even if in the least degree, even if obscurely and unconsciously, even if in the life of elementary instinct—a human being must feel himself a bearer of a certain "mission", with honor coming from the task predestined for him; standing face to face with a certain danger, or with an alien power, or even with a difficult routine task, he must connect his *personal self-respect* to *overcoming* it, and emerge from this situation as a victor. In the face of the counteracting or encroaching powers of other-being, a person must accomplish the exertion of his best and fundamental powers and *stand one's ground in the struggle*. And then the feeling of his own worth is affirmed in him. It is clear that this feeling acquires a *spiritual* character and a *spiritual* significance precisely when the person has a live feeling that he stands before the *highest* values and the ultimate mysteries of life, that is, before the face of God; and this feeling arises when the mission itself and the overcoming itself actually possess the dimension of *absolute value*. In order to feel and to affirm *one's own spiritual worth* it is necessary in fact to make certain of one's capacity for the perception and realization of *the objektive, highest* value. This means that a person must experience *a real encounter with the divine contents*, to experience and recognize their *affinity with one's own personal nature*, and to affirm *them in* oneself and *oneself through them*. Thus, a religious person gains his spiritual worth in that *humility* with which he accepts the will of God as his own, and through which is revealed to him his authentic *unity* with God, his highest, absolute significance; thus, the ethical worth of a person is affirmed precisely in the fact that he vitally unites "himself" with "his" conscience and in *service* to the good finds his actual, *personal calling*; thus the spiritual worth of the scholar and of the artist is determined precisely by the fact that they merge their personal interest with the concern of supra-personal, self-manifesting truth,[4] and voluntarily devote themselves to the objective service of truth or beauty. Only personal

4 The Russian phrase is *сверхличной очевидность. Очевидность* (loosely speaking, "self-evidence") was used by Il'in as a technical term, the more precise meaning of which is probably best expressed as "the self-manifesting truth".

experience, spiritual both by form and by content, gives rise in a person to *a sense of spiritual worth*: the soul must feel that it actually stood and stands before the face of God; that it found in itself a good will toward the divine contents, for it saw and fell in love with them; that it affirmed this will in itself, and through it, affirmed its spiritual worth.

A christian accomplishes this discovery and affirmation every time that he reads the Lord's Prayer, dwelling in it with heart and will: "Our Father" ..., for in this prayer he exalts himself to God, in order to confess before His face His spiritual Fatherhood, and his own sonship in relation to Him. Through this he accomplishes the affirmation of his spiritual worth.

The soul must know of itself that this highest task and highest responsibility did not overwhelm it, but strengthened its powers and shaped its life: such that it can, even having suffered a collapse, once again find its affinity with the divine contents and once again affirm them in itself and itself through them. *The self-affirmation of the soul in the absolutely-precious* [ценном] *object* always was and always will be the sole source of the feeling of one's own spiritual worth.

Of course this *spiritual self-assertion* can be experienced not in distinct thought but in obscure affective form. Further, it is experienced by each one individually, and for that reason differently; each one realizes it in his own way. Thus, it may come about in early childhood or at a mature age; it may develop quickly and easily, or as the result of a long and tormenting process of the spirit struggling with the foolish inclinations of the soul; a person may almost not succeed, or not succeed at all, or it may be accomplished in deep old age. But it is unconditionally necessary for a worthy life, both for personal and for social life.

Spiritual self-affirmation consists in a person finding the correct resolution of the conflict between *spiritual vocation and the instinct of self-preservation*. The first awakening of spirit in a person disrupts in him the naive, zoological wholeness of the soul and convinces him that the instinct of self-preservation, with its immediate preference for self and near-sighted self-interest always threatens to captivate the soul in a state which is degrading to its spiritual worth. A human being stands higher than an animal to the extent that spirit stands higher than the instinct for self-preservation. For that reason a worthy life of a human being requires that spirit accomplish a certain disengagement from naive and self-interested instinct, counterpose himself to it and keep it in check. That does not mean, however, that such a victory may or must lead to an enfeeblement of the conquered instinct. No; *a worthy* life remains above all *a life*; and a person can maintain and defend his life only by following his instinct for self-preservation. From this stems the necessity not only to master one's instinct and subordinate it to spirit, but also to *vindicate* it before the face of spirit, to sanctify it and release it within the necessary bounds. Instinctive self-interest in a person should not be subjected to extermination and not to "abolition", but to spiritual comprehension and justification, or, what is the same thing, to recognition and reconciliation, and inspired employment. But in order for that to take place, it is necessary for a person to apprehend *his own self as a certain value* which is worth defending in the struggle for existence: a person must carry out a *spiritual self-affirmation* and through it justify the instinctive self-centering of his soul. And thus do matters stand not only in personal life, but also in national life: there is no *life* for a person on earth in the absence of an instinct for personal and national self-preservation; but there is also no worthy life for him on earth in the absence of spiritual *restraint of*, and at the same time *justification of*, this instinct. And this justification is given only through the assertion of *one's own spiritual worth.*

Spiritual worth, its true perception and affirmation, is the deepest root of mature character and sound legal consciousness. For law, according to its deepest essence, is a necessary *attribute of spirit*: *its* claim, *its* sphere of freedom, *its* empowerment, *its* limit, *its* rule, *its* free obedience. And the value of law, its significance, its binding competence, is determined in the final analysis precisely by the value of the spiritual *contents* and spiritual *states*. Law is either an everyday convention, created by force and easily getting along with hypocrisy and simulation; or it is something authentically valuable, irrevocable and sacred, and then at its basis must lie, and actually lies, something *objektively sacred*, a certain unconditional and highest value. And thus, a true experience of law is an experience of it as an attribute of this highest, sacred value. A true understanding of law is an understanding of its spiritual nature and its spiritual purpose; such an understanding is characteristic only for one who *himself lives* by this purpose and who has become aware of and affirmed *in himself* this spiritual nature. Indeed, law is inconceivable and impossible apart from the legal *subject*, that is, without that being *for whom* it exists, *to whom* it belongs, and *through* which it exists. But this being, creating law as something which is *his own and for himself*, must be *in need* of law, must guard within himself its *standard* and *criterion*, must experience it as his own *necessary attribute*. It must itself be *worthy* of law and at the same time it must create such a law as would correspond to its own proper worth. But this worth of law and its subject is the worth of *spirit*: *its* content, *its* mode of life, *its* states.

That is why a sound legal consciousness rests entirely upon the sense of one's own spiritual worth. Only a subject knowing, or at least feeling, its own spiritual worth can respect the law and, at the same time, create such law as would not be degrading for a human being, would not distort the mode of his life, would not cater to his vicious and ruinous inclinations. Law and the State create the form of life; and in order to choose a *worthy* form, it is necessary for *the subject himself* to be *a living hearth of spiritual worth.*[5]

[5] Il'in here, as before, makes use of the image of the fire in each individual hearth in the polis being ignited from the sacred central fire kept burning in the Prytaneum. (See Chapter Ten, footnote 2.)

One can say: for a human being as a subject of law and a creator of law, it is necessary *to respect oneself.*

To respect oneself means to recognize one's own worth; and moreover, precisely one's *spiritual* worth; and in recognizing it, to prize it, take pride in it and preserve it in life and in deeds. For this it is essential to experience oneself as a *force for the good*: precisely as a *force* capable of affirming and creating, of struggling and overcoming; precisely as a force for the *good* capable of distinguishing good from evil, choosing and determining itself to the good. A subject of law possesses a basis to respect himelf because he is a *spiritual subject*, that is, a living focal point of *the will to spirit and to the good*, or, what is the same thing, a *force for the good*; this living spiritual force is in need of law and creates law, as its essential living form and that is why this form must protect the worth of its creator and express his natural respect for himself. And just as the worth of individual spirit depends precisely on *that by which* he lives (the supreme value) and *how* he lives (the order of autonomy), so also his respect for himself must be *socially self-sufficing*, determined entirely by his *personal objective experience*. *At the basis of normal legal*$_{p}$ *consciousness lies an objectively grounded* but *socially self-sufficient respect of the subject for himself as a spiritually beneficent force*. A person honoring in himself the spiritual principle [начало], will recognize it and value it regardless of how others regard it; and another's lack of respect or even scorn will not shake either his real spiritual worth or the corresponding feeling of respect for himself.

The sense of one's own spiritual worth and, flowing from it, one's own respect for oneself is necessary both for the individual *citizen, and for the nation* as a whole, and for the *State authority and the army*; it is necessary in private, and in political, and in international life.

This feeling, dwelling in the soul of the citizen, is the deepest and truest guarantee that his behavior will be in the highest meaning of the word objective, that is, it will correspond to the *end* and to the *prescriptions* of law. A consciousness of the fact that "I am spirit", and the presence of a will to spirit, compels a person to *value* the law, as the necessary form of spiritual life, to prize it and observe its prescriptions. Moreover: *the feeling of one's own spiritual worth, in itself, already conceals within itself a living will to the end of law*, that is, to the protection and flourishing of spiritual life. To be spirit and to treasure one's spirituality means to be in need of law, to recognize it and to possess the strongest and purest *motive* prompting one to loyal conduct. Spirit is the *end* of law; and law is the *form* of spirit and its *means*. Precisely for that reason the feeling of one's own spiritual worth creates in the soul the most powerful stimulus to law and a legal order.

Objective legal conduct will be that which corresponds to the objektive *end* of law, and therefore to its prescriptions. And thus a human being is in continuous need of a living motive and a strong stimulus which would compel him to observe objective conduct, that is, not to deviate from the end of law. This motive must be so mature and strong that it could endure any temptation arising out of foolish, self-interested, and anti-social inclinations. In order not to surrender to these inclinations, their ingratiating summons and sly whispering, a person must master the *spiritual dimension* of life and activity, which would give to him the possibility of distinguishing the higher from the lower, the worthy from the unworthy, the unconditional from the conditional, the significant and sacred from the vulgar, the spiritually-necessary and right [правое] from the personally-important, the "needed" from the "useful". He must further truly become aware of the *end* of law, which consists in the protection and organization of life, a life dedicated to the highest, the worthy, the unconditional, and the significant.* He must recognize the rightness [правоту] of this end and its advantage over other possible ends; and in turn, there must be formed in his soul a vivid *scale of the ends of life*, as more valuable and less valuable; moreover, such that law as an end, *unconditional and universal* for all people, and as also desired *by him personally*, would receive preference over any *conditional and purely personal* end. And if in the soul such a scale of *ends* takes shape according to their *value* and a corresponding scale of *desires* according to their *strength*, then the person will acquire a stable stimulus toward undeviatingly lawful conduct.

This signifies that objective conduct in law rests entirely upon the *spiritual self-awareness* of a person and on his *feeling of his own spiritual worth.* Precisely on this basis and only on it can be formed that civic character which will always be a true creator and builder of social and political life. Only a spiritually mature person can be a true citizen and patriot;** for only he lives by that for which it is worth dying; only he has something which is actually worth loving more than oneself; only he possesses a sufficient ground and motivation to defend the spiritual culture of his country voluntarily and with all his powers. The soul of a citizen must be sufficiently *strong in love* for spirit and *firm of will* to pick up and carry the burden of political responsibility; for that soul there must also be an impartial direction of the will and true convictions, and a vital fearlessness. But such an adamantine political character is possible only on a certain *unconditional basis*, on the basis of an unshakable spiritual self-awareness and worth. Such a basis the vast majority of people can find *only in religion*, which opens access to spirit even for the most elementary soul. That is why a living religion always was the most powerful and true source of a worthy legal consciousness; and the history of humanity more than once showed how a people, having forgotten God, destroyed their State.

A citizen in possession of mature spiritual self-awareness comprehends and illuminates all the elements of his legal status as a subject

* **See Chapter Five.**
** **See Chapter Ten.**

[субъективно-правового статуса]: all of his legal empowerments, obligations, and prohibitions.[*]

Thus, he feels himself *worthy* of all his *legal empowerments* and perceives these empowerments as means essential to him for the assertion of his spiritual personality. He pours into them the energy of his will and creates from them the living form for his own spiritual being. Property empowerments arouse in him not greed, not an inclination to ascetic renunciation, but a feeling of personal and social responsibility and a will to their lawful use. Political empowerments, leading him into the living system of political rule, are perceived by him as his sacred *obligations*:[**] obligations to further by word, by voting, and where necessary by compulsion, the autonomous, supra-class and aristocratic organization of one's State.

He accepts, further, the entire burden of his legal *obligations*, voluntarily imputing to himself the duty of performing them. The feeling of one's own worth arouses in him a consciousness of his own responsibility, while the mutuality of obligations and legal powers, the mutual bond of legal cells[***] and the solidarity of all in relation to the sole and common legal order[****] arouses in his soul a steadfast will and a keen readiness for the observance of one's obligations. He pours into his legal$_p$ obligations the energy of his will and nourishes others' legal empowerments through them, not from fear but from conscience, maintaining through them the personal legal form of other spiritual beings. His property obligations arouse in him not malice, not a desire for evil to befall others, not an inclination to litigiousness, distorted interpretations or bribery, but a feeling of legal incontestability, indisputability, respect and responsibility. Political obligations, introducing him to a living system of political subordination, are perceived by him as his integral *legal empowerments*:[*****] empowerments to assist through property, deeds and life the spiritual organization and flourishing of his native land. Thus, tax obligations are for him a precious *right* to support his native land through contributions to its treasury within his means; military obligation is conceived by him as an honorable *right* to defend the spiritual culture of his nation with weapon in hand, and so on. A citizen steps forward as a volunteer for the State "military draft": patriotism is a living creative power, and desertion by and large turns out to be excluded.

Finally, *being prohibited* does not oppress the soul filled with a feeling of its own worth. Such a soul either observes its prohibitions easily and naturally, perceiving behind them the objektive and indisputable end of law and not *stooping to crime*. Or the soul, having exhausted all loyal

[*] **See Chapter Seven.**
[**] **See Chapter Seven.**
[***] **See Chapters Four, Five and Six.**
[****] **See Chapters Nine and Twelve.**
[*****] **See Chapter Seven.**

paths leading to the renewal of law, resolves on a political violation of law in the name of the idea of law and its end; but such a violation of law not only does not degrade, but affirms and deepens its spiritual worth.

Precisely respect for one's self as spirit lies at the foundation of the vitally important struggle for subjective right [право]. The feeling of one's own worth establishes in this struggle, as it were, two facets: first, the facet from which begins the impossibility of *waiving* one's rights—such are all rights of personal freedom; and second, the facet from which begins the impossibility of *insisting* on one's own rights—such are all "non-natural," unjust [несправедливые] legal empowerments, degrading for others, and for that reason degrading also for the one legally empowered.[*] There are rights which it is impossible to renounce, while preserving respect for one's own spirit; but there are rights which it is impossible *not* to renounce from a sense of one's own worth. And the best people time and again witnessed to the truth of this—both in word, and deed, and death.

The feeling of one's own spiritual worth excludes in general all crooked paths of life. Thus, above all, it cannot be reconciled with a *lie*, witnessing to an insufficient respect for oneself, to insufficient courage or trust. Whether a person says not what he is thinking; or does something other than what he says; or does not do what he says, undermining the value and force of his pronouncement; or, finally, remains silent, dissembling—the sense of one's own worth turns out invariably to be protesting; for a person is an organic unity of spirit, soul and body and the renunciation of this unity diminishes the worth of spirit. Respect for oneself cannot abide either flattery, degrading to both the flatterer and the flattered; nor bribery, perverting the motive of conduct and corrupting the very basis of legal consciousness; nor violence, negating the idea of law, as the idea of spiritual autonomy; nor unprincipled life *compromises*, bordering on betrayal. Concluding a vital, or in particular, a political, compromise is in general a special art requiring genuine *respect for oneself* and a true *allegiance to the object*. Precisely these two conditions establish the limit of admissibility of a compromise: never consent to a means which excludes one's end or demeans its worth; never make a concession in the sphere of ideas, ideals, or convictions; never measure one's concession by the standard of interest, even if grounded, even if common.[6] Precisely the sense of one's own spiritual worth is that living force which does not permit political consent to be converted into an unprincipled deal of mercenary personal interests. The business of spirit is not the business of commerce, and politics is precisely the business of spirit; the idea of the State is a *beneficent force of history*, possessing its own immanent laws[z], and for that reason it threatens all those trading in politics with unmasking and "ruin".

[5] It seems fair to note that Il'in himself was viewed by some of his contemporaries as singularly unwilling to compromise on what he viewed as points of principle.

[*] **See Chapter Seven.**

The feeling of one's own spiritual worth, necessary for the individual citizen, determines through itself the spiritual level of *the nation as a whole*. The spiritual culture of each nation in its own development and in its content, depends on whether the trait of *respect for oneself* is characteristic of it or not characteristic. National spiritual culture can grow, deepen itself, and grow strong on worthy, objective contents, only given the condition that *respect for oneself* is the property not only of selected individuals, immediately creating that culture, but also of the broad mass of the people. For without respect for oneself, there cannot be faith in one's powers [силы]: and without faith in one's powers there cannot be a genuinely spiritually-creative flight and blossoming. In this connection it is natural for a person to respect in himself not only his own personal spiritual power, but also its *national character*.* It is necessary for him to respect *in himself* the spiritual power of his own *nation* and to respect his *nation*, as a great energy of spirit nourishing his *personal* powers. Respect for the national "we" is the basis of true respect for the personal "I."[7]

National self-respect is inculcated in the nation slowly and over a long period. Initially it penetrates the souls of a few; it begins as it were from the atom; and only over the expanse of whole generations can it be strengthened and formed into that "atmosphere" of spiritual being from which each new individual obtains his upbringing, support and sanction. In order to create this "atmosphere"—this spiritual solidarity, this objective life, permeated by mutual confidence—each nation must suffer through a great test of individual and collective *self affirmation* and absorb this experience. It is necessary for the nation as a living unity to succeed in this *self affirmation of spirit*: so that its culture should accumulate an entire pantheon of spiritual *achievements and victories*—personal and objectivized, as in religion and virtue, so also in art, and in political construction, so also in war for the native land. Precisely in the creation of this spiritual "pantheon" a nation affirms and forms its native land, creating it in spiritual exertions, ascents and sufferings, acquiring it through victories and love.** A nation lacking its spiritual "pantheon" has not yet accomplished national self affirmation: it has not yet justified itself before the face of God; it has not yet proved to itself its own right to self respect; and in consequence of this its feeling of its own spiritual worth remains in an immature, weak, problematic state: it can easily vacillate in the hour of trial and carry the nation into ill-fated collapses.

Still more essential, still more deeply necessary is the feeling of one's own worth for any *State authority*. In the very idea of the "State" and in the very idea of "ruling authority" is placed the principle of spiritual

[7] This is yet another echo of Hegel's definition of spirit: "The 'I' that is a 'We', and the 'We' that is an 'I'." See Chapter Ten, endnote f.

* **See Chapter Ten.**
** **See Chapter Ten.**

worth: for the worth of the State is determined by its end, whereas the worth of ruling authority is established by its being recognized and its social rank. State authority is precisely a *force* [сила] *for the good** and a *spiritual force*; but precisely for that reason its vitally important success is determined by its *spiritual rightness* [правоту] *and its nobility*.[8] To recognize in itself this spiritual rightness and this nobility, means in general *to assert one's power* [власть]; for State power this means to accomplish one's spiritual *self-assertion*. This self-assertion of State power does not coincide with the spiritual self-assertion of its individual representatives: for individuals replace one another and exit to the grave, whereas State power maintains its unity and continuity. For that reason its self-assertion must take the form of a mature and solid *tradition*, rooted in the legal consciousnesses of the *majority* of individuals; this traditional volitional and emotional self-regard must enter into the soul and infect each one who joins in public legal empowerment or carries out public activity. State power stands on the peak only where contact with it arouses respect for oneself even in one for whom in ordinary life it is not characteristic to respect oneself to a sufficient degree. It is not possible to rule without respecting in oneself *the sovereign* and his *dignity*. The very essence of State power consists in a distinctive spiritual impressiveness, without which there remains only naked physical power, terror and mutual humiliation. That is why *respect for oneself* enters into the very essence of State power: it must know and profess before everyone—in word and deed—its highest vocation, its rightness and the nobility of its direction of will. It must preserve its spiritual worth, as a national-political treasure, as the root of political legal consciousness and the political being of its nation.

It is clear that also the army, as the concentrated embodiment of the power of the State, must place the feeling of its own worth at the very basis of its life.[9] The army, as an element of the being of the State, is an organized multitude of people, systematically *training themselves for victory, and for the sake of it—to death and to killing in the name of the political end*. Precisely in this way is determined its worth and its tragic nature. Each member of the army, each soldier, regardless of his high or

[8] Beginning with this sentence it becomes necessary temporarily to translate власть as "State power" rather than "State authority", despite the fact that Il'in is clearly describing a State in possession of genuine and deserved authority, because the remainder of the paragraph plays upon the notions of "force" [сила] and "power" [власть] as *attributes* of (authoritative) *State power*.

[9] It is enlightening to set Il'in's remarks on the army in the context supplied by Paul F. Robinson, *The White Russian Army in Exile, 1920-1941* (2002), esp. Chapter 11. During the 1920s and early 1930s in Germany, Il'in came to be known as the "theorist of the White Idea," writing extensively on the political, legal, and military situation of the remnants of the defeated White army situated in Europe. His views were particularly appreciated by General Wrangel', who had commanded a significant portion of those forces during the Russian Civil War.

* **See Chapter Fourteen.**

low rank, must carry in his soul an *understanding* of the political end and a volitional and emotional *acceptance* of it. An army can exist only in that degree to which a politically-patriotic legal consciousness inspires it. Such a legal consciousness remains always a *will to the political end*; and this will also produces a preparedness for State *service*. For that reason service in the army must be permeated with a living *inspiration by the idea of the State*. The soldier is a citizen who has taken upon himself the concentrated *burden* of the citizen's calling and being: for he is the living fulfillment of the force [силы] of the State, a living instrument of State *will*, *an organ* connecting his concern with the question of personal *life and death*. But *a living* instrument not separated from its end; on the contrary, his end is invisibly present in him and moves him. From this comes that high *worth* and that high *responsibility* which is inevitably coupled with the military calling.

An army is impossible outside of the idea of *worth* and *the feeling of honor*.[10] Worth and its living perception in oneself form the very essence of the soldier: the citizen, affirming the warrior in himself, affirms the spiritual rightness of his State and the sacred significance of his native land; and conversely: only by accepting the native land through love, and the idea of the State through will, can he apprehend his true worth and assert it in life. A warrior, separated from the political end, becomes an adventurer; a soldier deprived of patriotism is like an instrument of execution or a professional killer. The worth of the army is determined by the worth of spirit and spiritual culture; the military calling is *a spiritual calling* and the business of war is a feat of spirit and done in the name of spirit. Precisely for this reason military victory remains either an ephemeral accident or a *spiritual ascent*; and only a genuinely spiritual ascent can communicate to the soul the force necessary for a practical solution of the fundamental moral contradiction of war* and for the defense of the native land.

Thus, *spiritual self-affirmation* is essential for the warrior. He must believe in the spiritual rightness of his native land, of his State and of his vital concern. He must cultivate in himself an objective possession of the political end and precisely through this *objectivity* of his will and his life is determined his *honor*. The sword of the warrior possesses a single purpose: political. To preserve faithfulness to this purpose means for the warrior to preserve his honor and his calling. The army, moved by the sense of honor, is the real support of the native land and the guarantee of its political being; the army, having lost its feeling of honor, is a rabble of rapists, marauders, and killers.

[10] This should be read in the light of the article by Paul F. Robinson, "'Always with Honour': The Code of the White Russian Officers", *Canadian Slavonic Papers/Revue canadienne des slavistes*, XLI, no. 2 (1999).

* **See my essay "The Fundamental Moral Contradictions of War".**

Training himself for death, the warrior must remember *in the name of what* he is doing this; imparting to himself the capacity to kill others, he must derive his motive and his resoluteness *from the political end and the will to it.* Military training, separated from the sense of spiritual worth, is training for systematic and unprincipled killing; but that is no longer cultivation of the soul, but its ethical extermination and spiritual perversion.[11] Precisely for this reason military preparation is absurd and fatal outside of the *spiritual cultivation* of the person. The technical ability of the warrior must have an inviolable facet of *objective-spiritual* motives and impulsions: the internal and the external ability to kill while dying, and to die while killing requires not only formal-volitional discipline, but also the capacity to motivate one's own behavior by an authentic, objective relation to spiritual contents and ends. A warrior without spiritual self-affirmation is a real danger for his native land and his state. An army without worth and honor is ephemeral as a military force, but genuine as a source of destruction and death of the State. The first axiom of legal consciousness formulates the living basis of its legal consciousness, its force, its being.

And thus spiritual worth is the root of *any true* life, and respect for oneself is the source of *the force of the State and political health.*

Such is the first and the fundamental axiom of legal consciousness.

[11] See also Paul F. Robinson, "On Resistance to Evil by Force: Ivan Il'in and the Necessity of War", *Journal of Military Ethics*, II, no. 2 (2003), pp. 145-159.

Chapter Sixteen
Diseases of Self-Affirmation

A person unaware of his own spiritual worth, that is, not experiencing it, leads a deformed, degraded, sick life; and its diseases are deeply instructive: they can be described as the diseases of spiritual self-affirmation.

At the foundation of spiritual respect for oneself must lie *a true perception* of oneself, and not an illusion and not an unhealthy self-conceit; an authentic *spiritual worth*, and not a spent external sign of obsolete privileges; a *personal* act of self-affirmation, and not someone else's perhaps mistaken or mendacious pronouncement. Perceiving oneself as a force for the good [благой силы] must be not accidental and not ephemeral, but an *authentic and objective self-perception*. It cannot and must not be replaced by any kind of surrogate whatever: neither by a dreamy imagining of one's supposed virtues and of one's "historical destiny", nor by an empty pride or a cultivation of formal "honor", nor by the accidental and changeable verdict of "social opinion", nor by the self-seeking and capricious "ripples of public opinion". The perception of one's own spiritual worth has at its base experience which is *independent, personal,* and at the same time *objectively valuable*. A legal subject must be a living, self-sufficient depository of spiritual worth; and any deficiency in this experience – a defect in *self-sufficiency* or a defect in *objectivity* – makes this legal consciousness unsteady, rickety, weak in vitality, and unstable.

A person respecting himself only because and to the extent that others respect him strictly speaking *does not respect himself*: his spiritual health depends upon others' secondary impressions, that is, on the ignorance and incompetence of others; in actual fact a feeling of his own inferiority, vanity, and a lust for external success gnaws at him; and if this success and popularity betray him, then he ceases to feel his own spiritual worth, and his personality loses its form. Similarly, a person who respects himself only for his supposed, or purely external, or empirically accidental, qualities, that is, for what does *not* constitute his *spiritual essence* (for strength, for beauty, for wealth), practically speaking *respects not himself*: his spiritual health depends on that which may belong to him, *but is not him himself*, that is, on the accidental and non-essential, on what does not have its own value, on transitory accidents of his personality; in actual fact he amasses a supposed wealth and multiplies his power [силу] or his property, but does not affirm the inner worth of his spirit.

Still more deplorable is the state of that person who is completely unable to respect himself, and is so accustomed to it that he does not experience his own spiritual worth at all. Once, perhaps in childhood, the soul of such a person could not endure some trial, placing a heavy burden on his sense of selfhood; it could not stand the pressure of external circumstances or of its own instinctive inclinations, could not cope with some vital task and responsibility. It gave into it, yielded, and in that very subjection found the poison of a certain enjoyment. The act of spiritual self-affirmation did not succeed; the soul did not stand its ground in the struggle and consented, dispirited and humbled, to its humiliation. It did not succeed in asserting itself as a *force*; rather, having consented to humiliation, it shook its *belief in itself* and in its *beneficent* nature. Once having submitted to its passions or to another will, and having discovered the sick sweetness in subordination and humiliation, the soul turns out no longer to have the strength to forge for itself a personal form of spirit. It does not see its own worth and does not respect itself; and since to conceal such a perception of oneself is impossible, others imperceptibly become accustomed not to respect it and in this way strengthen its disrespect for itself. The person gradually acquires the psychic make-up of a *slave*, accustomed not to respect himself. And the tragedy of his situation is revealed with particular force precisely when he attempts to free himself through an external rebellion or an uprising: this rebellion does not free him, for his shackles have an *internal* nature; this rebellion reveals only what a person deprived of the feeling of his own worth is capable of, while the burden of disrespect for oneself drags the rebel back to a state of abjection. Such, for example, is precisely the consequence of corporal punishment, particularly when endured in early childhood, and only spiritual blindness could have created the folk saying concerning the superiority of one who has been beaten over the one who has not.

It is obvious that the legal consciousness of such people who do not respect themselves, or respect their "not-selves", suffer from profound diseases. Their personality is, as it were, deprived of root and trunk; it leads a ghostly, dependent existence; strictly speaking it possesses only a figuratively-human semblance of existence. It is only a medium for its passions and the influences of others, individual and social; these influences at each given moment enter into a compromise among themselves, which determines its behavior. For that reason it is not in a condition to be determining its life through independent decisions, to be building its future, and to be struggling for the goals it has set for itself. Having lost its spiritual center, it weakened or even destroyed the center of its own volition in that way, and replaces the will by stubbornness, respect for oneself with pride, the feeling of one's own worth with vainglory. The soul experiences spiritual degeneration or even corruption.

The sense of one's own worth unasserted and unstrengthened, or once wounded and not healed, undermines a person's *faith in himself* and in his powers [силам]. In the depth of his personal spirit is formed a certain emptiness and hollowness, robbing his life activity of strength, and rendering him incapable of firm and courageous resistance to the forces of things and people. Any trial arouses in him dismay, doubt in himself, and fear; trepidation and cowardice take hold of his soul and lead him down the path of unworthy pliancy and passivity. Such a person turns out to be capable neither of spiritual *self-assertion*, because he converts it into an outburst of passions; nor of psychic *self-denial*, because he does not possess a living relation to the highest value, to the sacred object. True self-denial is not a denial of spirit, but of the soul, in the name of spirit; and for that reason it presupposes a true respect for spirit and for oneself, and leads not to humiliation, but to the assertion of personal worth.

Not to respect oneself means to experience one's own *weakness in the good.* And one who accepts this weakness and becomes reconciled to it nurtures in himself a diminished well-being and stands perpetually on the threshold of new humiliations; once having "washed one's hands" of oneself, one dwells constantly on the verge of a new spiritual collapse, always more easily overstepping the bounds of the moral and the legal. And one who does not become reconciled with his weakness, but also cannot assert himself for the good, tries to assert his power apart from the good or counter to it, and converts his life into a mixture of cynicism and hypocrisy.

And if, to crown it all, in the soul of a person there stirs a *consciousness* of his own unworthiness or badness, while *pride* is elevated and exacerbated, there arises a so-called *underground* character,[1] in all its misery and deformity. A person begins to experience his own lack of respect for himself as the disrespect of others toward him; the feeling of his own original misfortune gives him no peace; every advantage of another is for him, as it were, an insult, and his life is gradually converted into a continuous, galling and unforgivable injury. His soul is tormented by *meagre self-regard,* which it sometimes is not even aware of; this self-regard cannot be satisfied by any external success whatever, cannot be sated by any flattery, for its redemption cannot in general come from without. Reassurance can come only from a turning inward of the soul, only from a healing act of spiritual *self-affirmation*; and this act cannot be realized by a conscious, arbitrary decision, for the soul flees from the unbearable sight of its own emptiness, unworthiness and deformity, and conceals its disease and its suffering in the deep underground of the unconscious; and forcing out its own disease,[2] it loses access to it and power over it, becoming entangled in a tragic hopelessness.

And amid all these outcomes the person does not find an objective basis for life and wanders through sufferings and humiliations, depraved and miserable, rejected by himself, unjustified and unreconciled.

To lose the objective basis of life means to lose the *spiritual dimension* of things and deeds, to lose any criterion of objektive value. The life of such a person becomes a true realm of *vulgarity*, for vulgarity

[1] Presumably a reference to the character of the narrator in Dostoevsky's *Notes from Underground.*

[2] That is, into the unconscious. Il'in was thoroughly familiar with the works of Freud and had daily sessions of psychoanalysis with Freud himself in Vienna for a period of six weeks during the spring and early summer of 1914. These were interrupted by the outbreak of the First World War, at which point Il'in was declared an enemy alien and forced to leave Austria.

is *a blindness of the soul toward the objektive significance of objects.* A spiritually blind soul lives by wretched contents and scant measures of a personal way of life; it perceives everything on the plane of its *needs and passions* and measures life in terms of *interest and power*. And precisely for that reason its life is converted into a bog of confusion, weakness and vice. But its principal confusion is in the non-recognition of spirit, its objektivity and unconditional value. The person dwells in a naive, immediate certainty that "the main thing in life is himself"; and in himself the most important thing of all is the purely personal, the "intimate", the empirically-singular, the subjective; and from this it is already not far to preferring one's own needs, flaring up on the instant, to everything else. Precisely in this lies the spiritual root of all *corruption* whatsoever.

At the base of all corruption—bribes, public corruption, every sort of demagogy,* and mercenary international treason—lies a *spiritual blindness and an absence of one's own spiritual worth.* Blindness gives rise to an incapacity for a gradation of ends according to value, and a defect of spiritual worth creates a seriously impaired will, an unprincipled readiness to give up the spiritual, the objektive, the universal, for personal interest and acquisition. That is why a political regime not nurturing in the people a feeling of its own worth is doomed to disintegrate eventually from the triumph of *private self-seeking* over the common interest and *vulgarity* over spirit.

From this it is already clear that a person deprived of the feeling of his own worth can maintain the guise of humanity only under the pressure of an *alien power*—landowners, State power—and *personal advantage*; with the collapse of both factors he easily loses the form of humanity, and passions draw him into downfall and chaos. Spiritual disability can always plunge him into a condition of irresponsible weakness of will and mental deficiency. And in the political sense he is not a legally competent being. Neither a sound legal consciousness, nor true loyalty, nor a political form of thought, nor patriotism are accessible to him: for all of this possesses a spiritual nature toward which he is blind and indifferent. Therefore he cannot intelligently carry public authority or build a social organization. Not respecting himself, he also does not respect the *citizen* in himself; not understanding his *own* spiritual worth, he fails to see spiritual worth either in *other* citizens, or in the *State*, or in State *power*. He perceives others' *worth* as an alien *power*, and sees in it either an *instrument* for himself or a *danger* for himself. Standing face to face with State power, or at least with its representatives, he draws from the soul not respect, not trust and not a feeling of vital unity, but a *covert submissiveness* which manifests itself, depending on circumstances, either in cunning *flattery* or in a daring *threat*. Such a person does not maintain his own worth either before superiors or before inferiors. With superiors he is ingratiating, obsequious, and servile; in the best case he serves them as a true lackey; in the worst case he conceals behind servility a spiteful

* **See Chapter Fourteen.**

readiness to humiliate his master just as he was humiliated before the master. With inferiors he is contemptuous, crude, and despotic; in the best case he uses them as his own instruments; in the worst case he vents on them all the insults of his own meagre self-respect and transfers to their shoulders the entire burden of his own slavery. The range of his psychic alternations is defined by the groveling of a Caliban and the daring of a Ham, the disrespectfulness of a Thersites and the ferocity of a Pugachev. And if such a psychic structure turns out to be typical of people in a certain epoch, or even dominant, then the life of the people is a picture of true degeneration: a benighted trepidation is replaced by a benighted rebellion, "senseless and merciless"; and there where ruled the "yoke and the lash", arises a profanation of sacred things, and a snatching of the inviolable.

A people unable to respect its own spiritual worth creates a diseased *ruling power*, brings forth a sick *sense of self* and a sick *ideology*.

In creating its ruling power, such a people are unable to convey to it either a feeling of personal worth or respect for oneself. It establishes a ruling power which does not believe in the spiritual mission of the State, does not see its own spiritual tasks, and does not observe the forms of life necessary for spiritual culture; a ruling power which does not understand in what consists the essence of the State idea and for which a self-active legal consciousness is necessary; which does not respect its own people and does not nurture them; which pampers itself by its own despotic absolutism and perverts the idea of the State into an empty form of submissiveness and order. It does not understand that domination over a slave diminishes and corrupts the master himself, and does not notice how the disease of enslaved legal consciousness corrupts its own will and its political creativity. Such a ruling power recognizes the appearance of political submission and political flattery as a true and sufficient manifestation of its worth and harbors behind that appearance a public venality, the corruption of morals, and a politics directed against the State; it takes flattery and groveling for respect, formal discipline for obedience to law, a frightened submissiveness for legal consciousness, absence of will for loyalty, the absence of a political sense in the people for a guarantee of legal order. But, clearest of all, it will discover its insolvency when the people's dissatisfaction begins to threaten its existence. Then it, deprived of respect for itself, will place its *self-preservation* higher than its *worth* and will prefer utterly to destroy the legal consciousness of the people, to degrade its purpose and its status, to unravel the foundations of the State, its powers and its international position, in order simply to preserve its structure, its form and its direction of will. Following the rule, fatal in politics, of "*divide et impera*", it begins to arouse and intensify discord among citizens, kindling artificial differentiation and hurling nation against nation, class against class, children against fathers. The lie and oppression, political investigations and provocations, graft and terror it spreads open-handedly throughout the country, undermining what is most important in the population—*the will to political unity*. And all this is unsurprising and clear: such a ruling power respects neither itself nor its mission; and in the struggle for its existence it betrays what it is unable to value: the deepest link of its State, squandering this most precious spiritual achievement in outbursts of personal and group despotism or in party interests.

It is natural that such a people, in composing their national sense of self and their political fate, proceed along false paths and prepare for themselves a heavy historical ordeal. In particular, it is precisely out of this that arise all *tyrannies* and especially the worst of them: the tyranny of the *totalitarian State*.[3]

The totalitarian State, even in its less severe version (Italian fascism), is not inclined to attribute any particular significance to the feeling of personal spiritual worth. There where the individual respects this feeling, as its fundamental condition of life, a totalitarian regime does not arise. It is necessary for this feeling to have wavered, for a people to have damaged or lost it, for a totalitarian regime to arise. This is precisely how it was with the Italians at the end of the First World War (the battle of Caporetto), with the Germans (after the defeat and demoralization of 1918), in Russia after the defeat of 1915 and during the revolution, and finally, in China after a protracted revolution and endless external and civil wars. A sharp sense of one's own helplessness and the public shame brought about by it, distrust in one's own good forces, a wrenching feeling of impending doom, humiliation, and most important, the absence of a lively and deep religious feeling—all of this prepares in the people that *particular feeling of dishonor* on which all demagogues and tyrants build their success. This dishonor leads to the degeneration of legal consciousness: there arises disillusionment with discipline and loyalty and responsibility in people's souls—a readiness for any sort of disloyalty, for a scorning of prohibitions, for treachery and violence; people seek an authority which would give them permission for dishonorable conduct, and convey power to them. It is noteworthy that Mussolini succeeded in the beginning in creating a new, authoritarian power which not only did not grant permission for dishonorable conduct, but advanced an ideal of a new fascist honor.

From its side, the totalitarian power builds the whole of its regime on the suppression and perversion of the feeling of personal spiritual worth. It demands blind and humiliating obedience, including voluntary and compulsory political espionage on one another by the citizens. It demands boundless adulation and humiliating public sham-confessions from the insufficiently loyal; it strives to involve in its political crimes the largest possible number of citizens, to force everyone to their knees and break their spiritual backbones. Born itself of dishonesty and dishonor, it creates a new, previously unprecedented regime of dishonesty and

[3] It is interesting to compare Il'in's analysis of the pre-conditions of a totalitarian State, which follows, with that of the much-discussed (but controversial) analysis supplied in T. W. Adorno, et al., *The Authoritarian Personality* (1950). Both were written in approximately the same time-frame: the late 1940s versus the early 1950s, in the aftermath of the Second World War and the holocaust.

dishonor, and unfolds shocking pictures of ethical degeneration. After the political experience given to us by the history of the first half of the twentieth century, scarcely anyone could bring themselves to dispute the significance of the first axiom of legal consciousness.

It is impossible to grant that a people's feeling of mutual belonging to a national and political order could remain in a confused, immature, helpless condition; that a people did not experience its unity, did not seek it, did not desire it, and was unable to create it; its instinct for self-preservation must not only maintain a *personal* form, but also rise to a *national* form. Then it will learn to struggle for its own political existence, to see dangers threatening it, and will never abandon the cause of public salvation for private desire and profit. Experiencing itself as spiritually unified, it will see its spiritual worth, will respect itself, and turn out to be capable of an active, enterprising self-affirmation; then it will be able to maintain its political unity not only in the form of *institutions*, and not become scattered in the transition to a corporative order. A great war will not present itself as a trial beyond its strength, and great historical humiliations will not be needed by it for the stimulation and strengthening in it of the capability for spiritual and political self-affirmation.

It is clear that these and similar diseases inevitably find expression in the *spiritual creativity*, and in particular, in the *ideology* of a people.

To be separated from one's spiritual worth means to lose either the self-sufficient form of spirit, or its unconditional content, or, both one and the other together. A people not yet having realized its spiritual self-affirmation does not respect spirit either in itself or in the object, or in the idea of the State; therefore it develops morbid forms of spiritual life and produces morbid phenomena of spiritual culture. These forms and phenomena may be apparently lacking mutual connections, but in substance they reveal a single organic spiritual disease.

Not being able to find a fitting mean between self-abasement and self-exaltation, such a people forever oscillates between these two extremes, and often *combines* them in the most bizarre fashion. Its religiosity proceeds either from a feeling of personal insignificance, and then feeds on fears and superstition; or from a feeling of seductive all-permissiveness, and then preaches the *sanctity of sin* and takes the form of a collective perversion (Khlysty);[4] or from a feeling of the feebleness of spirit, and then preaches the *sinfulness of the flesh* and transforms human beings into monsters (Skoptsy).[5] Its art either repudiates the independent service of

4 Khlysty (Flagellants) were an underground sect committed to the practice of asceticism, thought to have originated in the late seventeenth century as an off-shoot of Russian Orthodoxy, enduring until the early twentieth century. Il'in seems to be referring to their alleged belief that God most loves the human being who has committed great sins and then truly repents. One of their most distinctive religious rites was rumored to culminate sometimes in sexual orgies.

5 Skoptsy (castrati) were another underground sect, which first appeared in the 1770s, and viewed sexual lust as the greatest stigma of fallen humanity. They attempted to overcome

the beautiful and becomes an instrument of socio-political struggle and advocacy; or suddenly falls into a spiritual blindness, lyrically celebrating the insignificant trivialities of life, or idealizing spiritual collapse and vulgarity; or turns into a cult of sick passions, assuming that aesthetic form can be comfortable with any content whatever; and then it destroys the very form of the beautiful and the worth of art, converting it into a delight for blind or sick souls ("modernism").

These diseases also pervert the national *ideology* of such a people. On one hand, the failed or not yet successful spiritual self-affirmation undermines its faith in its own capabilities and violates the integrity of its self-respect. This hinders it from approaching its shortcomings and vices with a feeling of its own worth: it views them in an exaggerated, caricatured, at times nightmarish form, perceives them as something exceptional and incurable, as a kind of national curse. And then its ideology is filled with a feeling of national insignificance and impending doom; it gives itself over to an excessive and therefore fruitless self-flagellation, implanting in souls a dejection and depression of spirit. From this sense that "we are rotten" flows an exaggerated evaluation of other nations, historically more advanced; there arises a faith in the foreign teacher, in "Varangians",[6] and this faith feeds and strengthens lack of faith in one's own powers, passivity, lack of will, a readiness to submit to other peoples and to serve them. However, the presence of such a sense and such an ideology does not hinder it from indulging in its own condemned vices, indulging with provocative frivolity and self-satisfied posturing.

On the other hand, meagre self-esteem and self-respect instill in the national consciousness, which is creating the ideology of the country, an extraordinary self-certainty and self-satisfaction. A healthy need for self-respect, not finding proper satisfaction for itself, arouses an irresistible inclination to self-idealization, to isolating in the national character solely the bright qualities, and beyond that to an exaltation of national shortcomings. Consciousness discovers a sentimental tenderness toward its offended sense of self and affectionately rewards itself with the incense of reverence. There is formed a doctrine of the "greatest among nations", of a nation-messiah, the chosen leader; there is advanced an

this through male castration and the removal of female breasts. It persisted into the Soviet period, but is believed to have been extinguished before the middle of the twentieth century.

[6] A reference to the well-known theory, deriving from the Kievan Primary Chronicle of the early twelfth century, according to which the first Russian (Kievian) State was founded by a group of Scandinavian people known as the "Varangians" who were *invited* to come and rule over the Slavic tribes: "Our whole land is great and rich, but there is no order in it. Come to rule and reign over us!" The theory has been thoroughly criticized, and the preponderance of evidence seems to contradict it. However, it has been continuously debated since it was first elaborated in the eighteenth century as a serious account of the origin of the Kievan State. It is commonly known as the "Norman theory" ("Norman" being a shortened form of "Norsemen"). Il'in's wife Natalia. a historian by profession, published a critique of the Norman theory: *Изгнание Норманов: очередная задача русской исторической науки* [The Banishment of the Normans: the Immediate Task of Russian Historical Science] (Paris, 1955). 186 p.

ideology of self-glorification, intoxicating the mind and enfeebling the will; there emerges an ideology of national infirmities, demonstrating the moral advantage of spiritual backwardness and ignorance (Tolstoianism); ideologists who perceive in immaturity and the deformity of public legal consciousness the key to the resolution of the social problem (anarchists). There arises a blind and ruinous nationalism advocating contempt for foreigners, deadening the national conscience, and corrupting the roots of true patriotism. Objective self-consciousness falls silent, and ideologists turn out to be the blind leaders of the blind.[7]

Such are the spiritual diseases arising from the violation of the first axiomatic basis of spirit and legal consciousness. To lose one's spiritual worth means to lose in oneself that vital center from which spiritual life is created, which needs natural law, formulates it and establishes a legal order; that means to be deprived of that vital root from which *legal consciousness* grows, *that is the will to law, the will to the end of law and the capacity to motivate one's deeds autonomously through the recognition of that end.*

Such is the first of our axioms.

[7] This severe critique of Russian national chauvinism as rooted in a kind of spiritual collapse is among the more extreme since Chadaaev's first "Philosophical Letter" of 1829, though Il'in's critique embraces not Russia alone, but all those nations that succumbed to totalitarian politics in the twentieth century.

Chapter Seventeen
The Second Axiom of Legal Consciousness

It is impossible for a human, as a spiritual being, to live on earth outside the law, for the law *determines and maintains the social boundaries of the individual spirit.* Precisely for this reason, law is necessary for a living spirit; it is peculiar to it and only to it. As a material thing, a human has no need at all of law: a pile of stones or corpses is indifferent to any legal determination whatsoever; it is simply not subject to the legal dimension. But as a living organism, even though ensouled and conscious, a human can get along without law in its true and profound significance; he will replace it with surrogates: with arbitrary commands; with developed psychic mechanisms; with habits, reinforced by fear, deception and persistence; and at critical moments—by outright violence: single combat, "treachery", a raid, murder, war. Precisely the spiritual and only the spiritual make-up of a human can resolve the collision of human claims on the basis of the *idea of law*, proceeding from an authentic will to the *objektive good.*

But in such a case law is a *sign of spirit*, its creation, its instrument, its mode of life.* It must express, and in reality more or less completely expresses the nature of spirit. Thus, the absolute *value* of spiritual *contents* imparts to law its *significance*, its unconditional basis, its worth; and the *form* or *mode of its life* necessary to spirit imparts to law its fundamental law$_z$: *autonomy.*

The second axiom of legal consciousness is determined precisely by this.

Autonomy or self-lawgiving is the authentic, fundamental form of spirit: it is inherent in it, essential for its *mode of being and activity.*

To be spirit—an individual or a social organization—means *to determine oneself and govern oneself*; it means to possess a *power* directing life to *beneficient ends*. To govern oneself means the will *to decide* on one's actions and *to choose* one's vital contents; *to affirm* one's own worth and powers, and, at the same time, to establish and to observe one's limits; *to assert* one's legal powers and *to fulfill* one's obligations. It befits a spiritual being to perceive and to know *for himself* what is good and evil, where right ends and where duty begins; to seek and find *for himself*, to find and decide, to decide and act in accordance with his own decision; and, having performed the deed, to openly confess that he performed it consciously and intentionally, following his own *conviction* and accepting for himself in advance all *responsibility* for what was done. And if the deed turns out to be mistaken and guilty, then to courageously accept and bear his guilt, not searching for sham justifications and not

*** See Chapters Nine and Fifteen.**

lowering himself to a pusillanimous lie; if the deed turns out to be correct and right, then he calmly acknowledges his accomplishment, not lapsing into disparagement, not indulging in pride, and praying for humility before the face of God.

Spiritual life is *self-activity* in the realization of the *highest objective values.*[*]

It is above all activity. To be spirit means to define oneself *through love* for a certain objektively-valuable object.[**] But spiritual love is not an enfeebling state; rather it creatively exerts spiritual powers. To love means to possess an *active* longing, it means to nourish a certain objective hunger, to seek what is unrealized, or, in Plato's words, to experience an ascent and a wealth of power from the feeling of deprivation. Love is the most powerful motivator; a passive love is not love, but a dream of love or a sick craving. For that reason the spiritual state is an *active* state; it naturally issues in a system of organized activity, in realized struggle. And there where passivity reigns, where activism is halted by calculation, by fears, laziness or simply by an instinct for self-preservation, there love is not; there is no spiritual life; there is neither patriotism nor religion. To be a spiritual being means to find within *oneself a lively source* of activity in the name of the object loved. That is why spiritual life is *self-activity.*

However, it is self-activity directed precisely to the realization of *higher, unconditional values.* It is self-determination in thought, *actively* ascending to *true* knowledge; in volition, *freely* finding its own *conscientious* root; in imagination, *distinctively* realizing the laws of genuine *beauty*; in feeling, *sincerely* loving all that is alive, and *fully* rejoicing in the perfection of the *Divinity*;[***] in work, increasing the property and wealth of the family and the native land. Such is the mode of being and the vital contents intrinsic to spirit. Outside of these values and outside of autonomy there is no spiritual life; drawing near to them is drawing near to it. And everything that disrupts this mode of life and this self-activity, everything that does not serve the *autonomy and objectivity*[****] of human life—all of that is hostile to the sole, common interest of the people, the State, and humanity.

Accordingly, the citizen is not an abstract unit, not an object of ruling power, and not simply a psycho-physiological individual, but a *spiritual* being, one for whom *autonomy* is as necessary as air. To be a citizen in the true meaning of the word means to lead an *autonomous* spiritual life, to possess an *autonomous* legal consciousness and to construct through it *one's own* life and the life of one's *State.*

[*] **See Chapters Nine and Fifteen.**

[**] **See Chapter Ten.**

[***] **See Chapters Five, Six, Nine, Ten and Fifteen.**

[****] **Under "objectivity" one should understand the faithfulness of the soul to the intuited and realized object. See Chapter Fifteen.**

To be a citizen means above all to possess an *independent conviction* concerning what is good and what is evil, what constitutes the essence of the human and his purpose, what is law and the State and what is their highest end. It is essential for the citizen to possess independent convictions on questions of *politics*: he must understand the essence of the State and of ruling authority; he must understand the spiritual nature and purpose of politics, and above all he must possess a conscious and mature *will* to the objektive end of law and the State. Without this the citizen is incapable either of personal or of political self-governance and, if all the same he is called a citizen, he shows himself to be something not corresponding to this title. The title of one able to function as a citizen presupposes in a human intellectual and volitional, that is, *spiritual maturity*. A suppressed, oppressed personality "participating in reason only to the extent of being able to comprehend an alien will, but not sufficiently to possess his own convictions and decisions" (Aristotle)—is incapable of arranging a life—neither his own, nor a family's, nor a community's, nor a State's. For recognizing the good, choosing an end, and organizing its realization is beyond reach for a being suffering from *spiritual mental deficiency*.

On the contrary, the citizen leading an autonomous spiritual life is a true builder of life, both inner, spiritual, and outer. And for that construction it is absolutely necessary for him that his *inner autonomy* find for itself an *unfettered outward manifestation*. He must possess the possibility *of determining* himself outwardly just as he determines himself inwardly: legal recognition and a legal guarantee of *personal freedom* is essential for him. In vain did the Stoics and ascetics strive to construct life outside of the rights of personal freedom: a renunciation of the outward manifestation of spiritual autonomy cuts short the flourishing of spiritual life and diminishes the productivity of its passion. This renunciation introduces a profound split within the wholeness of the human being, depriving the individual spirit of its true sign and plunging the outward make-up of the human into a state of dispiritedness; not to mention that the refusal to realize these rights itself and the renunciation of the struggle for them is already the realization of an outward freedom of spirit--although a negative one. In vain also do partisans of despotism strive even to the present to consolidate a legal order and the idea of the State in the absence of the autonomous legal subject: law and the State are meaningless and ephemeral outside of legal consciousness,* whereas legal consciousness is powerless and fruitless outside the sphere of free—private and public—volition. The connection between citizenship and personal freedom is one of mutual conditionality: a human completely deprived of the right of external self-determination will never become a citizen, for it is impossible to learn to breathe without air; and at the same time it is absurd to grant the right of freedom to one who is completely deprived of a civic legal consciousness, for what will a being who is

*** See Chapters Two, Four, Nine and Eleven.**

completely unable to breathe do with air? Freedom of self-determination, the highest spiritual good, can turn out to be the most dangerous poison, fatal for the individual and for the nation. However, this discovery of a harmful aspect of freedom will witness not to its lack of necessity or to its being doomed, but to the necessity of a *systematic inner preparedness* for it. Freedom of conscience is holy; but it is dead and indifferent for one who lives without faith or convictions. Freedom of speech is a precious means for the formation of spirit; but how does one present it to a person capable of pronouncing only abuse and insults?

Freedom of the press is not a right for the dissemination of lies and slander; freedom of association is not a right of pogrom; freedom of property is not a right of chicanery, that is, of the abuse of one's own property. For always and everywhere *external autonomy makes sense only as a manifestation of inner autonomy*. In other words, a legal order is not possible without legal consciousness; and legal consciousness requires spiritual autonomy. And conversely, none other than spiritual autonomy brings about a healthy legal consciousness and only such a legal consciousness is capable of *supporting the burden of external freedom.*

That is to say: at the basis of self-determination for a human must lie *spiritual maturity*. For that reason a *slave* can in truth be freed not externally, but internally, and only internally. And if he receives external freedom prematurely, then he will not be able to use it until he has freed himself *spiritually*. To lead a person out of the condition of slavery does not mean to take from the slave the external chains and prohibitions; but it means to *help him cease to need them*. To liberate does not mean to unbridle, rather it means to teach *free recognition of rights and duties*. Liberation is a way out not into lawlessness, but into autonomous conformity with law. This signifies that, essentially speaking, it is impossible to liberate someone else; one can only acquire freedom *for oneself*, in an independent, intense struggle for *spiritual autonomy*. Freedom is obtained only through self-liberation, and moreover, through objective self-liberation. A human unable to free himself internally cannot be a creator of external, social freedom, but in the best case, only a passive participant in it; for external freedom, in its true meaning, is the simple and natural manifestation of inner freedom. That is why the wise statesman, introducing political freedom, takes account of the cultural and spiritual level of the masses: he is firmly convinced that the spiritual maturity of the population will inevitably take the form of political freedom; just as the premature seizure or the untimely bestowal of freedom can turn out to be a vain and fatal gift.

Thus, self-governance is a unitary principle. For spirit, everywhere it breathes, introduces the very same forms, intrinsic to it, and remains true to itself, both in the moral self-obligation of the individual and in the self-determination of the private corporation, and in national-political autonomy. The life of a human is impossible outside of a legal form; but it befits him to apprehend this legal form independently: to apprehend the limits of his own freedom and uphold that limit as a necessary and holy facet of his behavior. This *self-obligation* remains for spirit the fundamental mode of life, regardless of whether it is realized in the form of an *imperative norm* or in the form of a *self-imposed agreement*: for although the social differentiation of will in the two cases differs—in the first case the law-establishing will is socialized and marked out; in the second case it remains dual (or multiple) and individual—but its autonomous character can and must be observed on all paths.

The nation and the individual must treasure the *autonomy* of their legal condition. However, a human treasures freedom only when he feels a vital need for it; but a vital need for freedom arises only from the authentic *objective depths of spirit.* Only he is able to defend and preserve his freedom who, moved by objective need, was able to secure and consolidate it in an independent struggle that disciplined his will; whose need for freedom was so great that he invested in that struggle his *chief, vital interest*, risking his property, well-being, and perhaps his life. But to risk one's life makes sense only when there is in the world an object deserving of a *self-sacrificing* love, precisely for the reason that it is *dearer than life*; and such an object is comprehended and acquired only on the paths of *spirit.* For that reason true autonomy is obtainable only for one who has accomplished a *spiritual self-affirmation* and has affirmed in himself *spiritual worth.* Such is the connection between the first two axioms of legal consciousness.

Autonomy, or what is the same thing, freedom, is a property of spirit; and for that reason the fate of *political freedom* is determined by whether the nation *leads or does not lead a spiritual life*, that is, whether it is growing intellectually, ethically, aesthetically, and religiously. *The spiritual growth of the nation is the sole path to political freedom*; and any other path creates only an empty and dangerous semblance. *Politics is the social form of spiritual life*—and for that reason it is always determined by the extensiveness and intensity of that life, its level and its dimensions. From this follows the deepest connection of politics with the religion, ethics, art, science, and philosophy of the nation. This connection is the truest guarantee that an atheistic, amoral, non-objective politics is always doomed to collapse, regardless how "refined" and "clever", "self-sacrificing", and motivated by "love for the people" it may at times seem to be.

Thus, *legal freedom*, in its fundamental essence, is a *spiritual, inner freedom.* It consists in that, in the life of the individual and of the nation, the antithesis between "ruler" and "ruled" is inwardly removed, but not because all governance whatever ceases, but because it acquires the meaning of *self-governance.** Self-governance cannot at all be reduced to the fact that the process of political stratification, according prominence to particular organs of the ruling authority, ceases to operate or is reduced to a minimum; the identification of political self-governance with *unmediated*

* **See Chapter Six.**

means of realizing it is a mistake, characteristic of naive or immature legal consciousness. Self-governance does not at all exclude the fact that some make decisions *instead of* others, *for* others, and *for the sake of* others: for self-governance is by its very nature not a system of external order and external actions, but an *inner spiritual structure of individual legal consciousness and a particular connection between them.** To wit, social self-governance presupposes an objective *solidarization* of wills, a unification of individual desires for a *common object, that is, for law as an end.*** Such a solidarity in the question of the end permits each to find like-minded persons in the understanding and formulation of this end and in this way guarantee himself the possibility of *participating by means of will in the decision* of matters, *not* participating in terms of personal powers in the *development* and *implementation* of this decision. The political solidarization of wills provides the possibility of accepting *another's direction of will* as *one's own*, and another's *decision* as one's own, not renouncing autonomy and freedom: absent and apparently without voice, the citizen expresses and is present with his autonomous will in the words and decisions of his like-minded associate and of his government; in these circumstances he preserves his spiritual *loyalty to himself in the content* of the will's direction, and at the same time, preserves his *formal* autonomy, first by the fact that he *freely* selects for himself his like-minded associates, and second, by the fact that he *voluntarily* consents to the non-autonomous appearance of governance. As a result, his "independence" apparently turns out to be pared-down, but in essence this truncation conceals behind itself his *autonomous self-obligation*, that is, a free volition, choice, and decision. The economy of spiritual forces rewards him richly, more than enough for this seeming diminution of freedom: for it opens up to him the possibility of a vital creativity and self-assertion in more valuable and, possibly, absolutely valuable objective contents; *personal autonomy* is observed, protected, and deepened through the creation of a national government, of a certain self-lawful "we" taking shape through a solidary unification of a multitude of self-lawgiving "I's".[1]

One could say that freedom not only does not exclude obedience but grounds and organizes it: it assumes at its basis an *objective autonomy of individual spirit*, freely having recognized necessary law and freely bowing before it because of its rightness. The human spirit liberates itself not by overthrowing the law, but through the *assertion of it from oneself and of oneself in it*; and this is true of any and all law—ethical and aesthetic and legal. In the normal construction of life, the law is accepted by legal consciousness by way of self-persuasion, and legal consciousness is recognized, revered and empowered by the law; and at the same time the individual soul finds for itself in the law a limit and an instructive

[1] Yet another allusion to Hegel's definition of spirit. See Chapter Ten, footnote 2.

*** See Chapter Nineteen.**
**** See Chapters Five, Six, Twelve and Fourteen.**

discipline, whereas the law finds in the person of individual spirit one who implements and perfects it. There arises a certain organic, concrete unity between the legal norm and the individual spirit. And this unity has always been the source of a spiritually-worthy social order of law. For a legal order consists in just that fact that legal consciousness, voluntarily filling itself with the content of law, carries out the law in life, or what is the same thing, fills the requirement of the law with inner and outer life—through will and deeds. Then the law becomes not a *formula* abstracted from life, but a *form* drawn into life: life becomes an order, while the law becomes a creative force.

From this it is clear that the task of any individual, any ruling power and any regime consists in inculcating *legal consciousness* in the soul, and honoring its *autonomous* nature. That legal consciousness is autonomous, the will of which not only remains *true* to the law, but remains *true to itself* in the law: fulfilling the requirements of law, it does not coerce itself, because it itself seeks the same end that the law serves. Obedience does not deprive it of freedom; the preservation of the legal order does not violate its autonomy; loyalty does not shake its respect for itself. Such a legal consciousness remains true to itself not only in will, but also in action; for its deeds are the mature fruit of its convictions and decisions. A human, possessing mature legal consciousness performs not those legal acts which he wishes; but he wishes to perform only those which conform to the end of law and to law. His actions are as true to the end of law to the same degree as they are to his own will. Will and act, act and norm stand in unity, coinciding in terms of their content, and equally serving the end of law. This constitutes the spiritual and vital *force of law* and at the same time, *the objective power of legal consciousness*.

Inculcating such a legal consciousness in the nation is the sole path to freedom and autonomy. A nation, having grown into it, will possess an autonomous *citizen*, an autonomous *ruling power*, and a powerful *army*.

A *citizen* with an autonomous legal consciousness does not need coercion; for him it is sufficient to sense the voice of the law in order to carry out the *obligatory*, as *the only possibility for him*, without compulsion or coercion, without dispute or a lawsuit. The sense of one's own spiritual worth and the will to the end of law guides his actions and motivates him to assert his legal powers, not exceeding them, and to fulfill his duties, not diminishing them. The struggle for his own interests remains for him always a struggle for the law, whereas the struggle for law never places him in the position of a rebellious slave.* Obeying the law, he remains its creator; serving the State, he is also capable of constructing it through his volition. The centrifugal inclination of his life rests always on the centripetal; his act in accordance with law preserves always the character of self-determination; and as a consequence his life acquires the imprint of a *psychic equilibrium, tranquillity and empowerment*: for he knows

* **See Chapters Seven and Eight.**

and feels himself to be a participant in the ruling authority even when by outward appearances and, perhaps, according to judicial forms, he is *not* a participant in it. For that reason the autonomous citizen feels a much greater responsibility than is usually thought: he considers the entire business of his State to be *his* business, and in each act of his government he is present through consciousness and will, as though he himself were a part of it. He experiences the autonomy of his nation in the structure of power, and the autonomy of his State in the structure of life, as his own autonomy; and from this his soul's readiness to fight to the end of his days for political and patriotic self-determination, for the inculcation of legal consciousness in the nation, and for the liberation of his native land from a foreign yoke.

A State authority must work on instilling in its citizens such an autonomous legal consciousness; for it forms the vital basis of any state in general, the source of its power [силы], the pledge of its indestructibility. A nation with an autonomous legal consciousness will always stand higher than a nation with a heteronomous legal consciousness: all of its spiritual culture will be more mature, deeper, more distinctive, productive, perfected; the existence of the State will be more secure, vital, organically unified. Autonomous legal consciousness forms that *spiritual essence of democracy* which alone imparts to it a certain spiritual meaning. A democratic order, in itself, is only an external form, harboring within itself many senseless traits and dangers. But in any event this form is meaningless and fatal in the absence of a certain mature and true structure of the soul; and this structure of the soul is indeed *autonomous legal consciousness*. However, an autonomous mode of life and activity is in itself essential for a human as a spiritual being, regardless of this or that political regime; and autonomous *legal consciousness* is only a consequence or a manifestation of a deep and substantive *spiritual* autonomy. For that reason it is necessary to recognize that the spiritual growth of the nation nurtures autonomous legal consciousness and in that way prepares in souls the capacity for corporate self-governance. In a democratic structure what is important is not the system of external activities, but the *inner structure of the soul, the inner mode of governing one's own conduct*, motivating one's acts, forming one's direction of will and conduct. And if this mode of inner life degenerates and disappears, then democracy can turn out to be the worst of political regimes. Such a mode of inner life, called autonomous legal consciousness, can gradually settle in and grow stronger in souls also under insufficiently developed external democratic institutions; democracy, as an external political regime, possesses not a self-sufficient, but only a secondary significance, for self-sufficient value is present only in an inward *autonomy of spirit*. Cultivating autonomous legal consciousness in a nation, the State authority fulfills its mission; but by the same means nurtures and strengthens the spiritual basis of the native land and national existence.

In order to cultivate autonomy in one's nation, the tate authority itself must be possessed of autonomous legal consciousness; it must form its direction of will, first of all, *objectively*, and second, *self-sufficiently*.

A ruling authority which is truly autonomous determines its actions by an objective insight into the political end; it is aware of the *responsible nature* of its business and seeks for itself a *spiritual correctness and an objective inspiration.* This awareness and this search become apparent in turning to religious sanctions, in the idea of "anointing"[2] and in the claim of "Divine grace" for itself. The State power is called to serve a single, objektive good; it is bound by the law of God and conscience; its mission is true and grounded in the ultimate, unconditional dimension, and precisely in this sense "there is no power, except from God".[3]

But relating further to the very essence of State authority as such is *self-determination* by objective content, that is, the *autonomous* affirmation of itself in the political end. Insofar as the ruling authority is not autonomous, insofar as it does not rule, but subordinates itself; to that extent not it, but some higher-standing authority rules, for which it is only a transmitting agency, an intermediary. A ruling authority is a force fully empowered to determine *itself* to the determination of *others, to autonomously create for others an external heteronomy.* Thus if an *autonomous legal consciousness* is necessary for an ordinary citizen, then it constitutes *the very essence of State authority.*

And thus the task of any State authority lies in *autonomously*, that is, on paths of its own conviction and volition, understanding the essence of legal consciousness and *determining itself to the cultivation of autonomous legal consciousness in the nation.* The self-determination of the ruling authority must lead it to the nurturing of the self-determination of the population; through the autonomy of its own legal consciousness it must grasp the fact that autonomy is as necessary for spirit as air, and that *to establish a State means to establish in the people the capacity for spiritual autonomy.*

The "autonomy" of the ruling authority by no means implies its formal unboundedness or still less, its non-subordination to law; it implies that its legal consciousness is *spiritually competent* to establish law and to establish an order externally binding others through a heteronomous form. But precisely this places before it its fundamental task: to bind itself with the legal consciousness of the people, to receive their recognition and to *sink the heteronomous form of its rule in the autonomy of popular recognition*;[4] and only then can it employ this recognition in order

2 That is, of a monarch at coronation.

3 "Несть власти, аще не от Бога."

4 This is perhaps the closest approach Il'in made to an explicit acknowledgement of the modern principle that legitimate political power can only be derived from the consent of the governed. Although he hinted at this conclusion in other passages also, his view of the matter seems to have been clouded by the unambiguous aristocraticism and the deeply ambivalent attitude toward democracy evident throughout much of his argument. In this he can be appropriately compared with Plato and Aristotle. Like these ancient Greeks, Il'in was obviously convinced that a just political order depended upon the proper structuring of the individual soul, and only those with well-ordered souls could be entrusted with rule.

to educate the people to autonomous legal consciousness and self-governance: for autonomy of spirit is cultivated only through its orderly, systematic *realization.*

A ruling authority with autonomous legal consciousness determines its will in accordance with the end of law. For that reason it sees itself as the guardian of national spirit and its dignity; in its autonomy it sees the autonomy of the national spirit of its people; and therefore it derives its legal authority from the national spirit, even when the current make-up of its people is not empowered to change its structure or its personnel. It is concerned most of all to impart spiritual truth to the form and content of national life; and therefore its guardianship always remains *enlightening and educational*, and it maintains the heteronomous form of the state structure only to the extent that it is required by the unity of political will, by the political economy of forces, and by the immaturity of popular legal consciousness.* And adopting this form, it remains true to its own guardian and educational activities—the end of law and the law. And in this lies the basis of its self-respect, the pledge of its spiritual productivity and its historical solidity.

Finally, the *army* no less than the rulers needs *autonomous legal consciousness.*

In actual fact, without autonomous legal consciousness the army cannot even *emerge* and begin its existence at the level of the State. However strong the fear of punishment, fear alone is insufficient for mobilization to produce the necessary results. An awareness of obligation and a sense of duty, ithat is, a spiritual *recognition* of military duty and military honor always remain the basic stimulus leading the summoned citizen into the ranks of the army; if the *military draft* does not meet with a lively *response* and readiness, then the army being formed remains an ephemeral organization – fragile, not battle-ready, concealing within itself the beginnings of disintegration and demoralization. Coercion and fear may temporarily and conditionally make up for a defective sense of military duty; but they cannot serve as a basis for the army: coercion always remains here a *reciprocal* coercion and the mechanism of this reciprocity can easily break down under the influence of the dangers of war and exhaustion, and, having broken down, ruin the entire matter, if behind it there is no recognition of the individual soldier's military obligation and honor. A correct mobilization is a result of autonomous legal consciousness.[5]

[5] Although Il'in himself never served in the military, it should be remembered that he was a close confident of General Wrangel' in emigration, was surrounded by remnants of the defeated White army in Western Europe, had had ample opportunity to observe the collapse of the Russian army during the First World War, and during the 1920s was generally believed to favor resumption of the military struggle against the Bolsheviks. During these same years, he came to be viewed as the "theorist of the White idea", owing to the extensive writing he did on legal, political, and military matters of concern to the White

* **See Chapters Six and Thirteen.**

However, the autonomy of motive necessary for war is not only for reporting in response to conscription, but also for the execution of military work with its dangers. The business of war requires a strict, steadfast organization, which is impossible without discipline. But it would be a cruel mistake to confuse discipline with submissive blindness and mechanical sluggishness. A blind, mechanical discipline is a deadening principle and for that reason spiritually destructive. And perhaps no one understood that better than Suvorov, and no one knew how to struggle against the "blindness" of a soldier's subordination than he. True discipline is a form of *living spirit*; it is a *spiritual* state and moreover *volitional*, that is, accepted willingly, and integrally grown into the will, assimilated by it, as its own law. A disciplined human is not a dumb machine but an *autonomously* acting being; true, the mode of his activity is determined by others' commands, but this command is autonomously accepted by his will and realized through his activity. In other words, military discipline is a *volitional organization of the individual soul*, preserving for a human *the character of autonomously acting spirit* with its conscientiousness, heartfelt loyalty, and resolute initiative.

A military calling cannot and must not kill the spiritual principle in a person; on the contrary. A discipline which destroys the spirit in a person destroys the soul of the army. The military calling requires not blindness, but a sharp-eyed awareness; not submission, but obedience; not abjection, but a heightened sense of honor and a feeling of responsibility; not passivity, but a resolute self-control and creative initiative. For war is a *vital struggle*, and, moreover, guided by *spirit and for the sake of spirit.* The organization of such a struggle is unrealizable in an environment of deadened spirit.

Thus, *at the base of all legal and political life lies the capacity of a human for inner self-governance, for resolute spiritual self-discipline.*

This is the second axiom of legal consciousness.

emigration, with the express encouragement of General Wrangel' himself.

Chapter Eighteen
Diseases of Autonomy

A legal consciousness which has not forged for itself the form of autonomy is an immature or *ailing legal consciousness*; and for that reason life can always lead it to suffering and humiliation.[1]

A citizen deprived of an autonomous legal consciousness is incapable of *self-control* or of *self-activity* or of *self-governance*. He can observe order and faithfulness to law only under the pressure of another's will. He is *in need* of threats not to become a law-breaker; punishment is necessary for him because he is continually inclined to become a guilty criminal.* In violating the law and committing crimes, he does not feel the burden of his lawless State, however, because law is not recognized and not accepted by his will. If the law directly contradicts his vital interest, he will quickly elevate an unpunished violation of law into valor, and imperceptibly be converted into a professional criminal.

Such a disease becomes a disaster if the heteronomous form of life for some reason falls away: if, for example, the State authority turns out to be helpless or adopts the principle of "non-resistance". Then there ensues a political *licentiousness* which arouses the *beast* in the soul, and turning into a system, creates a war of all against all. Political non-resistance demoralizes and corrupts the soul deprived of autonomous legal consciousness; it teaches the soul that everything is permitted and grants freedom and debauchery to the soul's instinct, not imparting to it the form of *a noble will*. And then the human soul loses all guidance and lapses into complete lawlessness. Social life becomes deprived of any legal form whatever and turns into a formless chaos.

But if the ruling power, defending the legal order and organizing a rebuff of defective legal consciousness, permits inertia to entice it, and creates a stable and systematic regime of political oppression, then it will

[1] In this chapter Il'in paints a rogue's gallery of defective political actors, all of whom fail in one way or another to be capable of autonomous action on behalf of the objectively necessary ends of law and State. Each portrait is in some measure abstractly executed, but anyone familiar with nineteenth and twentieth century Russian history will have no difficulty picking out the models: "People's Will" terrorists, the alienated radical intelligentsia, the revolutionary underground, Bolsheviks in power, the Stalinist regime, and so forth. There are also hints of some of Dostoevsky's failed human beings for whom "everything is permitted"; indeed, Il'in may in one or two places have been influenced as much by Dostoevsky's own character sketches as by the models from Russian history. After all, Dostoevsky and Il'in were engaged in somewhat similar undertakings; both achieved acute insight into the inner lives of the destructive characters who drove so much of nineteenth century Russian history. Il'in had the advantage of also being able to trace the twentieth century consequences of much of that history.

* **See Chapter Eight.**

reinforce the incapacity for legal self-determination and prepare new disasters and collapses.

Coercion does not educate the soul to autonomy, but intimidates it and saturates it with malice and hatred. One who is intimidated "does not dare" until he has become bolder;* and once having become bold, he pours out his malice and acts on his hatred without restraint. Coercion "forces" a person without imparting to him objective convictions, and therefore its victory is a sham victory and represents an abasement of the soul. The abasement, turned into a system, cripples the soul, injures its spiritual roots** and distorts its life. An autonomous legal consciousness lives by personal, free conviction; but free conviction cannot be found in the soul of a suppressed and frightened person. Having become accustomed to living by another's mind and another's decisions, he imperceptibly loses the center of gravity of his spirit and morphs into some sort of tragi-comic appendage of another creature or of some totalitarian party; he becomes accustomed to external guidance, but does not learn internal guidance; he can only adopt commands from the side and no longer hears the voice of his own spirit and reason. The activity of his mind is gradually extinguished, his volitional initiatives are weakened, the sphere of his self-activity diminishes. He can no longer live without supervision and tutelage; he is no longer in a condition to bear full responsibility for his own acts; his spirit withers, his life becomes degrading.

Thus a regime suppressing autonomy of spirit cultivates *silence and passivity* in the citizenry. Suppressed by the yoke of the ruling power and its prohibitions, a human becomes accustomed to see something forbidden in any spiritual self-activity: in self-sufficient volition, thought and action. In order to act, he requires an order, or at the very least, permission of the governing powers; and his life passes as he forever awaits an order, and forever fears a prohibition; and, when he receives a permission, he is no longer able and does not want to use it; and when he receives a prohibition, he sighs with relief and calms down. People become accustomed to regarding themselves as passive instruments of another's commands, and this frightened sense of self definitively kills in them respect for their own spirit. *Creative initiative* is not characteristic of a frightened soul; its *noble* activity is suppressed, and therefore its enterprise is nourished exclusively by greed and malice. But precisely for that reason, a person having grown up in such a regime turns out to be incapable of social self-activity—due to weakness of will; or of political creativity—due to malevolence and depravity. No totalitarian regime whatsoever inculcates in people a self-sufficient character or a capability for self-governance. Precisely for this reason revolution often culminates first in a leftist, and then in a rightist despotism.

*** See Chapter Four.**
**** See Chapter Fifteen.**

A *passive individual* comes to feel himself free of political burdens and responsibilities; he places his hopes on the ruling power, counts on it, and only in the best case is able to coherently express his claims. But, on the other hand, carping without action produces genuine satisfaction for him; essentially speaking he is perpetually dissatisfied with everything and is secretly convinced that he would be able to do everything incomparably better himself; therefore he rejects and reviles with pleasure, exalting in an empty imagination, and not seeing his own spiritual powerlessness. He becomes accustomed to living on the support of his native land and wishes to receive everything in an already-prepared form; he knows how to take, but does not know how to serve; and, receiving from the native land all the benefits of a legal order and culture, he does not consider State business *his own*, does not value his participation in the State, flees from duty, and does not know how to love his native land. What he takes, he takes as a natural tribute, and, not noticing that this tribute has become a sop, saucily rebukes the donating power for giving him "too little". Such a person is not a citizen, but a subject, carrying in his soul the mentality of a lazy lackey. And it sometimes happens that an entire generation lives and is acculturated to this mentality, able to utter in politics only an assertive "no" and a meaningless "down with!", but incapable of pronouncing a responsible "yes" or a creative "yes, it will be".

When political oppression begets a protest in the souls of people and gives them no way to express it, then its persecutions bring to life a new, profound disease, already prepared for an objectless propensity for opposition: the sick legal consciousness of the *revolutionary underground.*

In idea the underground revolutionary is an "heroic type" rebelling against political oppression and leading a selfless struggle for freedom and justice. However, political protest, turned into a profession, and a revolutionary disposition, substituting itself for legal consciousness—gradually deform his spirit to such an extent that his heroism turns into a diseased opposition, and his selflessness does not respect the worth of that very spirit whose freedom he is apparently fighting for.

Systematic protest accustoms his mind and will to pure and unbending negation; a negation directed against the political order and economic structure of his own State places him in open and intense conflict with the existing laws$_z$, tears his legal consciousness away from the positive law, puts him in opposition to the condemned political and economic mode of life and imperceptibly turns him into an enemy not only of the regime supporting the legal order, but also of the *legal order* itself. Having set himself the task of forcibly overthrowing the existing regime, he revolts equally against the personnel of the ruling power, against its direction of will, its policies, finally, against its very existence. His negation extends already not to the specific distinguishing features of *this* regime and *this* ruling power, but also takes in, unnoticed by him, the essence of law and State. Condemning the loyal citizenry, he endeavors to destabilize their legal consciousness by means of propaganda and agitation, and in this way undermines the very *basis* of the legal order, the very foundations of the idea of the State. The revolutionary refuses consciously and willfully to acknowledge the State center of his country; he extirpates in himself the will to political unity and strives to eliminate this will from others as well. He answers to prosecution with hatred; to repression, with bitterness and revenge; he abandons his legal status, and his entire life is converted into organized deceit, into dissimulation, into concealment and the deliberate, planned violation of law.

Prompted by hatred and bitterness, he begins to conceive his immediate revolutionary task as an end in itself, breaks away from the sole and objektive political end,[2] and concludes that his mission justifies any and all means; and therefore any violation of law whatever strikes him as admissible, any lie whatever as permissible, any success whatever as desirable; the sense of elementary decency falls silent in his soul; morality is declared to be a prejudice; legal consciousness disintegrates at its very root. Persecutions fan his malice to unnatural dimensions; for the failure and disgrace of his enemy—the ruling power—he is prepared to pay any price, though it be the humiliation of his native land (defeatism) or the destruction of his own State (the inclination toward internationalism). Gradually he breaks away completely from the spiritual-national ground, makes himself a political outcast and is definitively transformed into an "internationalist". He loses any tie with the spiritual culture of his nation, no longer lives through it, does not treasure it, and from the entirety of his national connection there remains only an antipathy to the State, fed by a hatred from the underground. His revolutionary zeal loses its former content, which was originally determined by *the law's end*; it becomes a complete and utter negation, a sick inclination of the will, and correspondingly, is filled with sick, spiritually unnatural, fatal chimeras. His heroism is converted into an empty form, into an unwarranted personal vestige: because the former "hero" lives and acts as a rootless, embittered seeker of world revolutionary adventures, as a stateless adventurer, an enemy of his own State, a destroyer of his own native land.

It is clear that, given such conditions, it is impossible to maintain a sense of one's own spiritual worth. To repudiate the law and State of one's own nation means to repudiate the living *form* of its national spirit; and this break from the living form inevitably deforms both the holistic perception of spiritual *contents*, and creative work on their development and deepening. In the soul of the revolutionary all spiritual standards are imperceptibly but definitively shifted and all criteria of value are degraded. Abandoning himself to abstractly rational and doctrinaire, though formally

[2] Literally, "breaks away from the sole and objektive *State* end" (or end of the State). However, Il'in insists that the well-ordered, legitimate State has but a single end, which is simultaneously the sole end of any legitimate political activity. Thus, "political" activity and "State" activity are effectively one and the same, and he appears to use the adjectival forms "political" and "State" more or less interchangeably. Similarly, in the ideal case, the "political union" appears to be a synonym for "State" in his vocabulary. Accordingly, the adjective 'государственный' [State] is sometimes translated herein as "political" if it produces a smoother English text.

correct, critique, he ceases to trust the depth of his own immediate feeling, and renders his intuition powerless; intuitive degeneracy of soul makes his inductive thinking dead and near-sighted, and *revolutionary "deduction"* becomes the main and even the sole source of his *ideology*. At the same time, "revolutionary zeal" is converted into the main and even the sole *criterion of value*, by which he measures all objects and all vital attitudes. Correspondence to revolutionary goals leads to a positive evaluation; non-correspondence, to a negative one. Finally, the class interest defended by him, at whatever cost, fills in all the rationalistic and revolutionary futilities of his worldview, and degeneracy of spirit becomes inevitable. Religion is rejected entirely as not corresponding to reason, revolutionary relativism and class interest. Philosophy deteriorates into revolutionary publicistics and a blind, embittered struggle with all impartial investigation whatever. Science loses any independent value and is converted into a tendentious service to party slogans. Art is either rejected in its entirety or becomes an instrument of political and social struggle ("direction"). The ethical is either ridiculed or identified with revolutionary submission or revolutionary "self-sacrifice". Legal consciousness is directly destined for destruction; the will of the people, to demoralization; the instinct of the masses, to unleashing. In this way the soul of the revolutionary gradually breaks with all spiritual content whatever; "politics" becomes the highest and a self-sufficing value; his entire life is a spiritless and an anti-spiritual striving, and the capacity for *spiritual self-affirmation* is gradually lost completely.

But precisely because of this, his self-sacrifice loses its spiritually-true characteristics and becomes *a rejection of spirit*. The revolutionary intelligentsia ceases to value spiritual culture; it no longer feels itself to be a qualified organ of the *unified* nation and regards spiritual life an inadmissible privilege; it renounces its own spiritual mission, condemns culture as a product of class interest and begins *to serve the spiritual impoverishment* of its native land: the salt of the earth loses its power. Thus is formed nihilistic "populism", with all its delusions and diseases: with its foolish tendentiousness; with its advocacy of "the simple life"; with its idealization of physical labor and intellectual ignorance; with its ideology fed by popular prejudices and historical vestiges. The spiritually senior bow before the spiritually junior and the juvenile; the senior renounces his own seniority, renounces the title of *leader* and adopts the features of a demagogue; he faint-heartedly disavows his own *spiritual worth* and his "self-sacrifice" betrays the *self-value and autonomy of spirit*.

All this reveals that "revolutionary zeal" constitutes not dignity and valor, but a profound and dangerous disease of spirit. This disease consists in the successive separation of *legal consciousness* from *law*, *the State from power*, and after that, in a separation of *the will* from *the end of law*; a person, while seemingly remaining a citizen of his State, exits the legal community, breaks with the form of national spirit, destroys his spiritual self-affirmation, injures his spiritual worth and corrupts his personality and his life. Revolutionary legal consciousness is a *sick and degenerate* legal consciousness, for it loses its autonomous structure; the loss of autonomy is the loss of essential spiritual form; it disfigures the very deepest roots of human existence and inevitably leads to a substantive degeneration of spirit.

Thus the non-recognition by a person of his citizenship deprives him of autonomous legal consciousness and places him in a distressing and ambiguous position in relation to that State which counts him among its members. A citizen, included in a certain State, knowing of this, but not recognizing his political membership, stands before only two honest outcomes: either to accomplish, with the permission of the authorities, a legal expatriation, that is, a formal exit from membership in the state; or to make a unilateral declaration of his extra-political, "non-obedient" status, so as to accept all the consequences of his act (repression). Both of these outcomes put and decide the entire question consciously, openly, and in a principled fashion, leaving no room for ambiguity and lies. However there is a third, unhealthy outcome, leading to the path of *political simulation.*

A citizen not recognizing his political membership may not reveal this openly. While not leaving the given political union and not exiting from its membership, remaining formally and to external appearances its citizen, he prepares the collapse of the State from his very existence alone. Counted as a member of the State mechanically or involuntarily, he remains alien or hostile to it *on the basis of autonomy*. He does not merge with it in terms of will, does not accept it in feeling, does not serve it with consciousness.* *Formally*, it is impossible to recognize him either as a traitor or a revolutionary; however, while apparently observing the laws of the State, fulfilling his public duties and obligations, he harbors even within his loyal manifestations a whole deposit of attitudes antagonistic to the State. In his soul an anti-political poison secretly ferments, taking the form of perpetual opposition or apathy toward patriotism, a superficial cosmopolitanism, a malicious joy or an inclination toward unprincipled political intrigue. Consciously or unconsciously, he develops his life into a system of political parasitism and quasi-treason, converting it into a simulation of citizenship and preserving in the soul an easy receptiveness to any and all revolutionary propaganda. And if there are many such people in a country, deprived of *autonomous, patriotic legal consciousness* and not bonded to their State by a profound personal acceptance, then the political unity of the nation deteriorates into an empty, formal appearance, into some sort of collective self-deception, as degrading spiritually as it is ruinous in its consequences. Then the life of the State is reduced to everyone giving the impression of being genuine citizens. Deluding themselves in this way, they also delude others, and naively consider both themselves and the others actual members of the State; and all together build political life on a common mutual parasitism and quasi-treason, lead the State to ruin and, not noticing their own naiveté, forgetting their hypocrisy, are non-hypocritically amazed by such painful consequences.

* **See Chapters Ten, Eleven and Fourteen.**

This disease of non-recognized citizenship acquires a deepened, tragic significance in cases of the involuntary annexation of *conquered nations*. Then the citizen counted as a member of one State, continues *to live in terms of feeling and will in the structure of another State*; he remains a patriot of the native land now left behind, and his legal consciousness experiences a tormenting crisis: he loses the autonomous form, and his spirit turns out to be in a state of profound division. Entering into the membership of a political organization alien to him, he loses his spiritual wholeness, for the spiritual content in himself is torn away from its legal form. He cannot break away from his own native land, because it is not within his power to re-make his spiritual structure and undertake anew a spiritual self-affirmation; the entire make-up of his spiritual and psychic life binds him to that country the citizenship in which he lost. Therefore he continues to cultivate what formally he must reject. But what he acquired in exchange does not compensate for the spiritual injury. He cannot arbitrarily establish a spiritual homogeneity with a national womb alien to him, and therefore cannot bind himself to his new, supposed "fatherland". Formally, he takes upon himself public-law duties and obligations which his spirit does not accept and which his soul does not value. He is burdened by his new citizenship and recoils from it; and every legal act of his life is tinged with traces of repugnance and falsehood. As a citizen he is dead in his soul and deceitful in his spirit; as a patriot he is torn away from his native land and obligated to take up arms against it in the measure of alien need. He is forced to serve matters that he does not love; and he loves those matters which he has no right to serve. And the more true he remains to his spiritual roots, the more he loves his true native land, the more inevitable for him becomes the path to international treason in a period of inter-State struggle. He experiences a genuine political tragedy: the very deepest and most sacred patriotic motives lead him on a path of political betrayal, repulsive both for legal consciousness and for conscience; and conversely: the very most fundamental and essential acts of public legal consciousness are experienced by him as spiritually false and patriotically dead. And his disease can be healed only through a restoration of autonomous legal consciousness and a reunification of spirit with legal form: he must restore the citizenship he lost and become once again formally a son of his native land; for the path of spiritual assimilation is a matter for entire generations.

Such is the condition of the citizen with an immature, damaged, or degraded autonomy of legal consciousness. He cannot create a legal order or a State; he himself can only fill in their empty appearance while he is passive, and destroy or degrade them as soon as he shifts into action. For that reason the self-activity of a people possessed of immature, *non*-autonomous legal consciousness conceals within itself an inner, vital contradiction fraught with a fateful outcome. And since a certain degree of popular self-activity—conscious or unconscious, organized or scattered, constant or periodically intensifying—takes place in *any* regime, then *every* regime must not repress it, but cultivate and strengthen it for fear of its own destruction.

However, in order for such a social and political education to be possible, autonomous legal consciousness must be present in the *State power* itself. A ruling power deprived of autonomous legal consciousness cannot educate its people; it either fastens the life of the people to a given, more or less low level, or directly corrupts its legal consciousness. The spiritual growth of the nation, as the growth of its self-activity, strikes it as undesirable and dangerous. Not sensing in itself the capacity for *autonomy* and at the same time for *objective* self-determination, the ruling power completely fails to take account of this outcome and task in regard to its people and does not value at all the spiritual self-activity of the nation. It does not value autonomy in general, as a form of spirit and spiritual culture, and therefore views the idea of political or even religious freedom as an idle and harmful prejudice. Precisely from these mistakes arises the anti-natural and fatal idea of the party-totalitarian State, in which State power turns out to be seized, enslaving, and obsessed with a false mission, and deprives the subjects not only of any self-governance whatever, but also of any and all legal consciousness. It is clear that the proper direction of will of such a ruling power is fulfilled in an accidental fashion, heteronomously and, most often, non-objectively. Not perceiving the objektive end of the State, not seeing the spiritual nature of political intercourse, it *formalizes* the regime created by it and reduces the political structure to external order and submission. The bombast of a formalized system of rule separates its actions from the living legal consciousness of the people and imparts to it the character of a groundless and pernicious abstractness. And since a living form of activity cannot fail to possess *substantive* ends, the ruling power's formal bombast inevitably fills its emptiness with *substantively-false, arbitrary and non-objective* missions. This leads in the best case to an international aggressiveness, to a cult of militarism and war, and in the worst case to socialism and communism. A ruling power deprived of autonomous legal consciousness does not itself know what its *calling* is and what it serves in actuality. It remains under the power of *traditions* or deduction and cannot distinguish the political and the valuable from the anti-political and the harmful. It does not know where lies prejudice, where lies an absurd doctrine, and where lies objective wisdom, what the interest of the State requires and how to distinguish the common good from openly advocated class greed. It does not lead its own State, but is dragged along by anti-natural doctrines or by partisan lusts and passions; it does not create culture, but destroys it, mobilizing and encouraging anti-cultural forces. Its willing loses the character of political wisdom and rectitude; its policy turns into a devastation of the country and a danger for all neighbors.

A heteronomous will is a spiritually *weak* will; heteronomous legal consciousness is a *diseased* legal consciousness. If the spiritual weakness of the ruling will is expressed in its objective falsity and the ruler converts autonomy into arbitrariness, then he enters on the path of *tyranny*; if spiritual weakness of the will is expressed in its lack of independence and the ruler subordinates his will to another's, then the State turns out to be in the hands of a *minion*.

The essence of tyranny is determined not by the order of its coming to be, and not by the defectiveness of its public law empowerment, but by the *anti-political nature of its volitional content*, a distinctive combination of power and weakness. The tyrant is a powerful ruler, but not in the good; by appearance "autonomous" in terms of will, but defining himself by arbitrary caprice; his will is strong not in what it ought to be, and weak in what it is called on to be. Arbitrariness is a *disease* of autonomy; it converts the will to willfulness, undermines the authority of the ruling power and trust in it, and prepares destruction for the State. A tyrannical ruling power is a ruling power diseased in *its content*; and in this lies its fate and its sentence. This is revealed with particular clarity if this tyranny is realized in totalitarian forms.

The danger of the second path is revealed from that moment when the ruling power turns out to be in the hands of a person of weak will or intellect. Such a ruler, incapable of spiritual or volitional self-affirmation, becomes exhausted under the burden of power and its volitional nature: for State power is the socially demarcated and concentrated *will* of the political union, which can arrive at a lively movement only from the personal, individual volitions of the legally empowered. Therefore, the ruler, through a weak will, harbors in himself an inner contradiction requiring continuous elimination and overcoming; State power cannot be inactive, but it cannot initiate activity through the volition of a being without will. From this follows the natural inevitability of *personal heteronomy* for the weak-willed ruler: he becomes the passive medium of non-legally-empowered persons, periodically subordinating him to their influence and indicating to him this or that direction of will. A minion—whether one person or a collective—is an irresponsible person, concealing his private interest behind organic imperfections in the structure of the State. He rules without legal empowerment; decides without responsibility; realizes his own interest under the guise of State interest. His very existence is a trampling under of political form; his very position creates for him the possibility and the temptation to pervert the content of the State. The spiritual emptinesses of the ruler are filled by the anti-political will of a whispering double, and the personal level of the latter may become the scourge and the doom of the country. Power deprived of autonomous legal consciousness is a guarantee of political disaster and collapse.

Such are the diseases of legal consciousness deprived of autonomy.

Chapter Nineteen
The Third Axiom of Legal Consciousness

Humanity lives on earth in the form of a multitude of self-enclosed distinct beings, as individual spiritual centers separated by body and soul, and, at the same time, connected by a single, common sphere of existence.* In this common spatio-material sphere a human inevitably manifests his inclinations, satisfies his needs, takes possession of things, transforms them, and lays claim to dominion over them. Given this, the individual claims of people turn out to be in a competitive existence, in a state of rivalry, mutual negation, and exclusion. The conflict of interests gives rise to a contest among the interested parties, and this contest must find an end and a resolution. However, it can be decided along paths worthy of spirit, and along paths unworthy of it; and thus law converts this contest into *an objective argument over a worthy mode of life*.

The right of each individual to a spiritually worthy life can be regarded as a self-sufficient attribute of individual spirit; but in actual life it is manifested as a *connection* between people: that facet which connects them through its boundary, or what is the same thing, that tie which demarcates their commonality. In actuality law is possible only where there is a living relation between people: law arises first as a disposition of will and is realized initially as *a relation of spirit to spirit*. This relation takes shape as *a mutual spiritual recognition*.

From this follows the third axiom of legal consciousness.

It is impossible for a human to live on earth not entering into *relations* with other people: this is determined by his very origin and his upbringing, and is consolidated economically by the development of needs and the growth of the population. But, at the same time, it is impossible for a human to build his relations to other people without paying attention to their psychic makeup. His task is not to escape from such relations, but to ensure that such relations are at *a spiritually and objectively worthy level*. For this it necessary to address precisely this *spiritual* makeup of other people, appeal to it, influence it, and in this way organize a life in common.

People can relate to each other in different ways, and the modes of this relation are absolutely not of equal worth—neither in terms of motives, nor in terms of inner structure, nor according to manifestation. This difference of value has not only the personal, subjective character of "pleasantness",** but also the unconditional, objektive character of *ethical truth and spiritual worth*. And thus relative to himself and for

*** See Chapter Five.**
**** See my essay "On Courtesy", Русская мысль [Russian Thought], no. 5 (1912).**

himself, each person desires the best and moreover the objektively-best relations: each desires that he be loved and respected, that others trust him and wish him well; it is distressing for anyone to be an object of malice and suspicion, scorn and hate. But this "best" relation is created precisely by *spirit* and is a mature manifestation of spiritual life and a spiritual condition. Everywhere that the spiritual level of people is low and unstable, their mutual relations are base and unworthy: they are formed by motives of blind self-interest; they convert a human being into a mere means; their structure turns out to be primitive and overly simple; their manifestation, vulgar and violent. The structure of social relations is determined in the final analysis by the *spiritual* level of the people, and any social organization whatever rests precisely upon spiritually mature and spiritually strong souls.

One could say that a *legal relation* is a *spiritual relation*: for law indicates to people the objektively-best behavior,* and all that is objektively best is perceived, understood, and realized precisely by spirit. In other words, since law is the necessary form of spirit,** a legal bond connects not only soul with soul, but precisely *spirit with spirit*. One who speaks of *his legal empowerment* and of his obligation, affirms of *himself* that *he* is spirit, that is, that he possesses unconditional worth*** and the capacity for self-governance;**** moreover, he declares thereby that he professes certain objektive and unconditional values; that he recognizes the very *idea of law*, that is, orients his life on the ideas of good and justice; that he, in the words of the Bible "goes before the face of God". To enter into a legal relation means precisely *to ascend through thought and will to the idea of law and to the end of law*,***** that is, to spirit as to the source of living rectitude. A legal relation as such introduces a person to the sphere of spirit, for it presupposes a living relation of the soul to the idea of *objektive good*, as the measure of life and action. "Juridical form" in relations possesses *not* only the lesser significance of "usefulness", "solidity", "determinateness", and "compulsion"; but it is above all filled with a higher meaning: it presupposes in a human being *spiritual worth, a will to the end of law* and the capacity for *autonomous self-determination*; it places personal legal consciousness before the face of the objektive good and forces the individual to determine his behavior, to bind himself on the bases of *self-affirmation and self-limitation*. A legal order, as a living system of legal relations, rests on people keeping in their souls *the spiritual dimension* of things and actions, and constructing their lives in this way: affirming the spiritual principle *in themselves*, they establish their *own* legal status; and in just the same way they affirm the spiritual principle *in others* and establish *their* legal status.

*** See Chapters Four and Seven.**
**** See Chapters Five and Fifteen.**
***** See Chapter Fifteen.**
****** See Chapter Sixteen.**
******* See Chapters Five, Six, Eight and Nine.**

This means that a legal relation rests upon *the mutual spiritual recognition of persons*. He who speaks of his empowerment implies a corresponding obligation to him by another; but to recognize a legal obligation on someone else's part means to affirm his legal capacity, that is, to recognize his *spiritual nature*. And in just the same way, he who speaks of his own obligation recognizes the legal empowerment of another corresponding to it; and this means to affirm his legal capacity, i.e., *spiritual essence*. A legal relation with a thing or with an animal is unrealizable precisely because there is no *living spirit* in them; they are not capable of *autonomous manifestation of will*, of *autonomous self-obligation before the face of the objektive good*. A legal relation in its genuine and complete makeup is possible only between beings possessing *legal consciousness*; only *they* can bind themselves as a manifestation of their decision and answer for the obligations taken upon themselves. But these beings need, besides a personal capacity for law, *mutual spiritual recognition* as well.

At the foundation of any legal relation lies a three-fold recognition, twice realized. First, each of the subjects entering into a legal relation recognizes *the law* as the basis of the relation, as a form of life, as an objektively significant idea.* Second, each of the subjects recognizes *his own spirituality, that is, his own* worth and *his own* autonomy, as a law-creating power [силу].** Third, each of the subjects recognizes *the spirituality of the other subject, that is, his* worth and *his* autonomy, as a power [силу] capable of the creation of law. None of these acts of recognition is required *formally*; and *in actuality* they may be absent; they are, as it were, silently presupposed; but precisely this silent presupposition contributes to the forgetting of them, their loss, their vital lack of power [бессилию], and their degeneration. However, in the construction of legal consciousness all these acts are not only necessary, but constitute the most profound essence of a legal relation. To enter into a legal relation means to agree to *a joint subordination to law*; it means to recognize both oneself and the other as *capable* of the cognition of positive law,*** of the perception of its objektive significance,**** of the recognition of law in general***** and, moreover, precisely of its *end and its worth*.****** But an understanding of legal norms and a consent to subordinate oneself to them presupposes in a living being not only the presence of spiritual powers [силы] in general, but also a significant intellectual and spiritual maturity.******* In the absence of these conditions a legal relation is either impossible or absurd. For that reason they must

*** See Chapter Four.**
**** See Chapters Fifteen and Sixteen.**
***** See Chapter Two.**
****** See Chapter Three.**
******* See Chapter Four.**
******** See Chapters Five and Nine.**
********* See Chapters Six, Seven, Nine, Ten, Eleven, Fifteen and Sixteen.**

be present in each of the participants; and each must know, of himself and of the other, that he will comply with these requirements. In other words, *at the basis of any normal legal relation whatever lies mutual spiritual recognition*; and therefore actual, everyday legal relations stand on the height and correspond to their function only to the extent that they are filled with such recognition, created by it and consecrated by it.

Therefore, *a legal order* must be regarded as *a system of mutual spiritual recognition.*[1] Such recognition is realized not only by law; it lies at the foundation of all the spiritual association of people: of any argument, presupposing the capacity for thought and a will to the truth; of any aesthetic compatibility, presupposing a judgment of taste and the will to beauty; of any ethical bond, resting on an act of conscience and on the will to the good; finally, of any religious association, possible only among people capable of prayer and of searching for an authentic perception of God. Spiritual association requires, objektively speaking, *a two-sided spirituality*, while subjectively speaking, *a reciprocal spiritual recognition.* But legal association is precisely a spiritual association; and therefore it is *a variety* of such recognition. In this lies the very deepest meaning of any legal and political union. Such an understanding of law and the State once again reveals the spiritual brotherhood of all people;* it affirms also the absence of any difference in principle between a legal order and the evangelical doctrine of love:** for a relation "in law" and a relation "in love" are equally types of *spiritual recognition.*[2]

To accomplish the spiritual recognition of a human means, first, to recognize in him an unconditional *worth*, intrinsic to spirit, and to establish an appropriate relation to it. As a result of this there arises a *respect* for the person. This means, second, to recognize in him a *will* to the objektive good, in the given case, a *will to law* and to the end of law. As a result of this, there arises *trust* in the person. *Mutual respect and mutual trust* lie at the base of *any* legal relation, both private and public; by these means are connected both citizens with one another, and citizens

[1] This fundamentally important doctrine of mutual recognition was introduced and developed by Fichte and Hegel. In his commentary on Hegel, Il'in explained that the implicit psychic "monadism" of Descartes, Leibniz, and Kant was replaced by Hegel with a conception of the spiritual as "*primordially continuous and grown-together everywhere*", which "only later, already in its internal development . . . breaks into a multiplicity of singular and apparently self-sufficient individual "souls". The science of spirit intuits its object adequately precisely when it has before it a *concrete unity, having internally differentiated itself into a discrete multitude*". I. A. Il'in, *The Philosophy of Hegel*, vol. 2, p. 116. For a fuller account of the doctrine of recognition see ibid., Chapter Eighteen, esp. pp. 115ff., 119ff. For a thorough analysis of the doctrine of recognition in Fichte and Hegel, see Robert R. Williams, *Recognition: Fichte and Hegel on the Other* (1992) and *Hegel's Ethics of Recognition* (1997).

[2] For Il'in's account of the role of the Gospel doctrine of love in Hegel's philosophy, see Il'in, *The Philosophy of Hegel*, transl. Grier, vol. 2, pp. 227ff.

* **See Chapters Five, Nine and Ten.**
** **See Chapter Twelve.**

with the ruling power, and the ruling power with the citizenry. Outside of these forms of mutual recognition a legal order cannot exist, for with their disappearance any *unity* and any *solidarity* inevitably disappear.

If at the base of *respect for oneself* lies a feeling of one's own worth, then *respect for the other* presupposes a living perception of *his* spirituality and *his* worth. But in order to perceive in another these fundamental signs of humanity, it is essential to possess in one's own self an organ and a measure of them; one must know from one's own experience what is spirit, what is its worth and what are its modes of life. And this is achievable only through spiritual self-affirmation. Only in immediate respect for *one's own* spiritual worth does a person learn to respect *another's* worth, and, if the school of this immediate experience betrays him, then there is nowhere he can learn respect for others. That is why a person not respecting himself is unable also to respect others; and conversely, the art of respecting others is the best sign of successful spiritual self-affirmation.*

He who recognizes the spirituality of another person and his worth, affirms in him the principle of absolute good as *the living essence of his personality*; the one respecting perceives the one respected as a *beneficent power*,** a capacity for realizing unconditional values; he affirms his affinity with the nature of the objektively highest and the objektively perfect, or, what is the same, he affirms the genuine presence in him of the *divine principle, that is, of spiritual power*. One person cannot respect another if he does not perceive him as a manifestation of absolute worth. One can and one must always *presuppose* in another the presence of such worth; what is to be ascertained in each separate case is not the spiritual capacity of a person, but its absence, to a greater or lesser degree. By reason of principle, he who prefers to respect a few selected ones, for something exclusive, is not right; rather, he is right who is ready to respect every person, making an exception only for those *not worthy of respect*.

However, in order for this readiness to be converted into a living, authentic disposition, it must receive an objective foundation in the soul of the one who lays claim to respect. Spiritual self-affirmation must be present not only in the one respecting, but also in the one being respected. He who demands spiritual recognition from others must recognize his own spirituality himself and affirm it in feeling, will and vital deeds. He must actually, objectively *deserve* spiritual recognition, feel himself worthy of it, and hold himself as worthy. Respect arises and is formed autonomously; it most often grows in the soul unnoticed and usually enters into consciousness when it solidifies and matures. It is impossible to respect on command or under compulsion; but each one can cultivate respect for himself in others. And for that, one must not seem to be spirit, but *be* spirit; not simulate the feeling of one's own worth, but *possess* it.

* **See Chapter Fifteen.**
** **See Chapter Fifteen.**

The nature of spirit is such that its living presence imparts to a person a particular power and an objektive respectability; a person acquires a certain authenticity of being, a particular intensity of life; his personality becomes significant in its own right, for himself as well as for others; and this power of his becomes still greater from a calm self-recognition. Therefore, in order for a person to be recognized spiritually, he must himself bring about a spiritual self-affirmation; in order for people to respect a person, he must respect himself, and possess an actual foundation for it. He who is unable to respect himself will neither be able to respect others, nor be able to keep or solidify others' respect for him. The third axiom of legal consciousness is organically connected with the first.

And thus respect for other people enters into the very essence of legal consciousness. A true perception of legal relations is a perception not only of *one's own* legal powers, obligations and prohibitions, but also of *others'*. To objectively experience another's legal status means not only to be truly aware of its content and its boundaries, but also *to recognize* its objektive significance; this recognition is realized through *will*, directed to *the end of law* and to its natural roots.* That is why an active will to the observance of another's status is characteristic of a person with normal legal consciousness; and not only because in the inviolability of another's rights he sees a pledge of *his own* protection, but because he perceives the *spiritual* nature of other people and recognizes their *right to rights*. To be a spirit means to be worthy of law and capable of law; to perceive the spirituality of another person means to recognize him as worthy of law and capable of law; that is, *to respect* in his person the subject with a capacity for law. He who has learned to respect the subject of rights and duties in himself will inevitably respect it also in others. A legal relation is absurd and meaningless outside of legal consciousness: in separation from an understanding of law, a recognition of law, and a will to law, it constitutes an empty, formal appearance: in the profound and authentic meaning of the term 'legal relation,' it *absolutely doesn't exist*. But legal consciousness is already a respect for spiritual other-being and its rights. Therefore at the basis of any normal legal relation lies not only a respect of each for himself, but also a mutual respect of the parties.

This mutual respect lies at the foundation both of private and of public legal relations.

`In a private legal relation where it is not the case that one party rules over the other, but both are equally subordinated to the legal authority rising over them, the idea of free and equal consent reigns: *a contract concerning rights and duties*. But a contract concerning rights makes no sense without mutual respect: to consent to the conclusion of a contract means to recognize that a person is capable of measuring his actions and relations by law; that he is capable of being aware of his legal powers and observing his obligations; that he is capable of binding himself through

* **See Chapters Four and Nine.**

the manifestation of will and carrying responsibility for his decisions, words and deeds; in a single word, this means to recognize the spiritual autonomy and spiritual worth of the person, i.e., *to respect him*. A party not respecting his own contractual partner performs an absurd deed: concluding a contract, he himself does not believe that he is concluding it; he does not attach importance to it, doesn't value it and does not consider himself secured; the inner insolvency of his act speaks for itself.

In a public legal relation, where one of the parties possesses the power of rule, and the other, an obligation of obedience, mutual respect is still more necessary. It is natural for a citizen to respect his ruling authority as the creative source of law; for he who spiritually recognizes the law and reveres its worth cannot fail to respect the will empowered to create the law and apply it. The dignity of the law is transferred to the one who establishes it imperatively; the ruling authority is perceived as a competent judge in the question of "the best" and "the worst"; the legal consciousness of the ruler is the living criterion of juridical "good" and "evil". Moreover, in a normal public legal relation the legal consciousness of the individual recognizes in the commands of the authority his own voice, his own direction of will;* thanks to this the citizen preserves his autonomy in loyalty and respects his ruling authority as he respects himself. It is natural for the citizen not to separate himself from his ruling authority and not to counterpose himself to it. He must feel himself in it and it in himself, conveying that in the word "we", "our". And then he transfers into it his feeling of his own spiritual worth and experiences *its* worth, *its* honor, *its* glory, as his own. He respects himself in it and it in himself, sanctifying it by means of his own legal consciousness, and forming his legal consciousness by means of its authoritative commands.

But it is likewise natural also for the ruling authority to respect the citizen subordinated to it, perceiving in him *an autonomous spiritual center, a subject with the capacity for law*. Addressing the citizen with legal imperatives, the ruling authority cannot make what is obligatory, inevitable, or what is forbidden, unrealizable; therefore it is always *forced to rely on the legal consciousness of the citizenry*, on their own reason and on their own will.** Moreover, a normal ruling authority is connected with the citizenry through identity of the political direction of will, through a common end, through spiritual solidarity. It experiences itself as *their* political will; it not only leads them politically, but it recognizes itself to be spiritually borne by them. It obtains sanction and power from their legal consciousness; and only thanks to this does it turn out to have competence; and only through this is it in a position to create their common, national-spiritual cause. *Its* worth is determined by *their* self-affirmation; *its* authority is measured by *their* spiritual recognition. Respecting itself, it cannot fail to respect them; and conversely, if the

* **See Chapters Six and Sixteen.**
** **See Chapter Sixteen.**

ruling authority does not respect the citizenry then it does not respect itself either; then it is not in a position to sustain its own worth; it loses its authority, ceases to be the political center of the country and is converted into an empty appearance.

Thus, the *mutual respect* of the people and the ruling authority turns out to be the necessary basis for the existence of the State. However, equally necessary as a basis for society, the legal order, and political existence is *mutual trust*.

If respect affirms *spiritual worth* in a human, then trust affirms in his soul a *noble will, as the living basis of behavior*.

The one trusting perceives in the one being trusted above all *a spiritual being*; this means that trust rests upon *respect* and presupposes its presence. Every human, building his behavior on a noble will, i.e., on a *will to the objektive good*, is thereby a spiritual being; for this will is one of the fundamental manifestations of spirit. Such a person objektively deserves respect; not only respect, but also trust: for trust is born when a person begins to take into account the *practical*[3] side of the life of the person respected, that is, his will, his direction of will, the very *creative* sources of his personal spirit. One can respect a person in one relation and not trust him in another; but then in this "other" relation lacking in trust, respect will also be lacking. True fullness of respect is always accompanied by fullness of trust; precisely in this way are people guided in friendship, in the choice of a confessor, and in the appeal to God.

Thus, the one trusting perceives in the one being trusted not simply a spiritual being, but precisely *a will to objektively correct behavior*, and moreover a vitally-effective *will*. This means that trust presupposes the *spiritual responsibility* of a person, that is, the capacity to distinguish the "better" from the "worse," to measure one's states and deeds by these standards, to choose the better, and to determine one's behavior by the choice and the decision made. An irresponsible person[4] remains beyond the bounds of trust and leaves the other's soul indifferent in this sense. But responsibility does not create trust by itself; for this, *a positive result of the imputation*[5] is necessary, and, moreover, not in a single instance but on a general scale, in a fundamental sense ultimate for a given person. The one trusting recognizes that the one being trusted determined himself to the "good" not just once, and then perhaps accidentally, but that he is capable of doing it consistently, that this choice and this decision are essentially characteristic of him and stable, for such is the *fundamental direction of his will*. Trust affirms precisely a *beneficent direction of will* in the soul of

[3] *Practical* here appears to have the Kantian sense of a conclusion of reason grounded in *will*, as opposed to a *theoretical* conclusion grounded in *intellect*.

[4] *Невменяемый человек*: a legally incompetent, or imputable, person, one judged not responsible for his or her own conduct.

[5] That is, the imputation of spiritual responsibility.

a person; it not only ascertains abstractly his capability for the good, but recognizes the *power* of this capability, its creative significance in life; it as it were appeals to this capability and to its power, to beneficent motives and to beneficent ends of the will: and in appealing, *relies* on them, that is, calmly counts on their victory and on their vital determining action. This is *faith in another's good will, as the real basis of the other's behavior.*

The one trusting does not simply note the presence of "good wishes" in the soul of a person; rather he considers specifically their power and their true victory. He nourishes a confidence that the will to the good, in the face of *foolish* desires, will enter into a struggle with them and overcome them; that it will be able to command not only the disposition of the soul, but also its creative *unconscious* powers; that the will to the good will be able to find for itself an adequate *verbal* expression which truly expresses its decision; and, finally, that it will be able to forge for itself a true vital manifestation, an appropriate and worthy deed or *act*. The vital effectiveness of the will consists precisely in the holistic, organic agreement of it, first, with the unconscious powers of the soul, which can encroach upon, weaken a decision, ruin an act, or instill in it another, unworthy content; second, with a verbal expression which can conceal a decision, communicate it falsely and bring another to confusion; and third, with external deeds, which may correspond neither to the decision nor to the words. Every such divergence violates the trust of one person in another and deprives him of wholeness; for it interferes with the confident *objective* perception of the other's soul, its authentic sources and its fundamental direction of will. Genuine trust is a holistic trust: it relates not only to the rational will, but also to the unconscious dispositions of the soul, to the word as well as to deeds. Every time that a person, in taking a decision, splits internally and does violence to his desires and inclinations, he loses his wholeness and in that way shakes trust in himself; conversely, everyone turns to the whole, *instinctively* good person with an easy, quick, joyous trust. In similar fashion, every time that a person is attracted not to what he decided to do; or says something other than what he is thinking; or does not do what he decided; or does not do what he said; or does something other than what he is talking about, he shakes, diminishes, fragments and weakens others' trust in himself. He either does not *allow* others to perceive himself as a will *strong in the good and in life*; or he forces them to perceive him as *weak-willed* in life. Therefore, if trust is something spiritually precious and necessary, then falsity and any lack of spiritual wholeness are fatal and ruinous. He who lies by means of words *or outward actions* destroys the wholeness of mutual trust; he destroys it in a different way, but not less, than one who reveals a steadfast *will to evil*, or one who *splits internally* and lies to himself. For genuine trust requires from the one trusted *a noble, strong and whole will.*

For that reason, he who claims trust on the part of others must above all *trust in himself.* Trust, just as respect emerges and forms autonomously; it arises in the immediate perception of another's direction of will, its content, its power and its wholeness. It is impossible to trust under compulsion; but to shake trust in another is easy. A person vacillating in his direction of will, unable to maintain fidelity to his own spirit, not whole of soul or strong of will, loses the energy in spiritual self-determination and ceases to *have faith in himself.* Trusting neither his own decision nor his own word, he begins to cause the distrust of others in himself, and, judging others as he judges himself, also loses trust in them. And since without mutual trust *an ethical bond* among people is impossible, and a *legal relation* inevitably degenerates, then any lie or crookedness, any breaking of faith or betrayal turns out to be absolutely injurious and even fatal in the life of people. A lie is not so much morally reprehensible as it is spiritually destructive: it destroys the unity of people, their community, their solidarity, their organization.

But this also signifies that trust in other people enters into the very essence of legal consciousness. Trust becomes here faith in the *lawfulness of another's will,* in its good intention and loyalty. The one trusting recognizes in the one trusted *a will to law* and a will to *the end of law*; he believes that the one being trusted *recognizes the law*, its objektive significance, its binding power; that he actually *measures by law* his own decisions, states and deeds; and that he does this for the sake of finding *true motives* for a loyal form of activity. To trust means as it were to address oneself to a person with such a declaration: "you are a living will to spirit, to law and lawful behavior; I know this and confidently expect from you corresponding deeds". And this address is essential, both for the one trusted (for it corresponds to his spiritual self-affirmation and permits him to participate in legal relations), and also for the one trusting (for it permits him to confidently construct the legal limits of his spirit and by this means to serve his spiritual self-affirmation). This address must be mutual; and this mutual legal trust is necessarily reciprocal.

Mutual trust lies at the foundation both of private and of public legal relations.

Private agreement on rights and obligations loses its meaning given mutual distrust. The very agreement to negotiations presupposes a lawful direction of will in the other; for where the will to law is completely absent there awaits indubitable trickery or transgression; there it would be absurd to converse about mutual obligations and come to an agreement about legal powers. The very essence of private-law arrangements consists in resting one's own empowerment on another's duty and in a readiness to support another's empowerment with one's own obligation; but such an agreement is already a trust in the other, and such readiness, first, presupposes trust in oneself and second, lays claim to the other's trust. To conclude a private-law contract means to trust another's will and to focus its trust upon onself. Thus a commercial credit is not only a calculation on another's fortune and on another's resourcefulness; credit-worthiness is not at all measured simply by property, experience and connections. Commercial credit possesses a *legal dimension* and is determined in the final analysis by guarantees of a common legal order and of personal legal consciousness; it is a manifestation of *trust* in the level of legal consciousness in the country and in the maturity, the steadfastness of individual legal will. Precisely by this is explained the connection between forms of credit, loans, payments, between the tempo and productivity of commercial transactions in the country, on one side, and the level of the population's legal consciousness on the other. A contracting party who does not trust his contracting partner engages, essentially speaking, in an absurd business, and only the acuteness of vital need justifies his risk.

In a public-law relation mutual trust is still more necessary. For a citizen it is natural to trust his ruling authority, that is, to recognize its *will* to the end of law and to law; for this conforms to the spiritual nature of the ruling authority, its social function, its mission. The ruling authority is the authoritative source of positive law, the servant of the national spirit, the intermediary between natural law and personal legal consciousness; for that reason trust lies at the very basis of the legal order. Trust in the ruling authority is a recognition of its law-creating competence, its rightful will, and its well-intentioned force [силы]; distrust of the ruling authority is non-recognition of it, a rejection of sanctions, a repudiation of its authority; in other words, it is *the beginning of its overthrow*. Revolution arises in a country not at the moment of street disturbances, but in that moment when trust in the ruling authority begins to waver in souls; for that reason he who shakes this trust enters onto the path of revolution. Trust in the ruling authority is the silent accord that it should take upon itself the matter of law-creation and thereby remove this burden and this responsibility from my soul, from my legal consciousness; it is an accord to divide up the business of the construction of the State, to separate out from it the imperative function and transfer it to precisely such and such an order, to precisely such and such people; it is an accord to recognize these people and their competent commands, to support their undertakings, to follow their direction, to assist them and answer for the consequences of their policy. A citizen trusting his ruling authority establishes his solidarity with it, merges *his* will with *its* will. But precisely for that reason, trust alone preserves for citizens their spiritual autonomy and permits them to convert governance by the state into *self-governance*;* trust alone fills the inevitable void between the ruling authority and those subordinate to it; trust alone grows these juridically isolated parties together and converts the state into a living unity. Trust in the ruling authority is that spiritual power which makes the ruling authority an actual organ of the people, and at the same time produces in the people an actual volitional unity.

But it is equally natural also for the ruling authority to trust the citizenry, that is, to recognize their will to law, to rely upon their loyalty, to count on their legal consciousness and on their good intentions. The most elementary, everyday work of the ruling authority presupposes a certain minimum of trust in the people, that is, a confidence that the citizenry are capable and agreeable to heeding the summoning voice of

* **See Chapter Sixteen.**

the law and the law$_z$, to do what is prescribed, to refrain from what is forbidden and so forth. The ruling authority lacking in this confidence admits that the citizenry in general are not capable of heeding the law, or in particular do not want to heed *its* commands. Such a ruling authority either obtains this capability and readiness, and in this way secures for itself the possibility of trusting the people, or it ceases to exist. A legal command in itself already presupposes in the citizenry the will to law; for the legal order rests upon the *interaction of legal consciousnesses*. If this will does not exist, then the legal order is converted into an order of continuous, systematic coercion; for distrust in the popular legal consciousness and popular recognition forces the ruling power to count exclusively on an apparatus of compulsion, preventing by it, and repressing by it, every manifestation of independence. However, on this path it will never succeed in solving its fundamental task: to cultivate in the people an *autonomous legal consciousness* and the capability for *self-governance*. A normal ruling authority sees in the citizenry its own worthy and desired collaborators in the business of political construction; it trusts in their will and their recognition; it counts on their support and does not fear their free initiatives: by trusting in the citizenry it affirms its trust in itself and from this derives its trust in them.

Thus at the basis of any legal order and State lies the mutual spiritual recognition of people—their respect and trust in one another.

Such is the third axiom of legal consciousness.

Chapter Twenty
Diseases of Mutual Recognition

A normal legal consciousness affirms that the State, according to its concept, is a living system of *universal respect and trust.* Historical States must continuously strive toward this ideal: both the solidity of the legal order and the might of the political union, as well as the entire fate of the nation, depend on the achievement of it. Conversely, defects of mutual respect and trust call forth a whole series of diseases of legal consciousness and life; it is clear that every nation possesses a common task: to work on healing them.

Every individual who is incapable of respect forms an elementary germ of such a social disease and, not cured, is converted into a breeding ground of contagion. A person incapable of spiritual self-affirmation, not respecting *himself,* negates his own worth, and in that way, as it were, invites all others not to feel respect for him. Consciously or unconsciously, he himself announces that he is not deserving of respect, and his competence in this question is apparently guaranteed by that very mode of being intrinsic to a human: for people are psychically isolated and each one can know of himself what always remains inaccessible for others.[1] Such a person imperceptibly infects others with his disrespect for himself; he forms of himself a kind of breach in the natural legal order, a spiritual void, as it were, around which accumulates an atmosphere of disrespect. He does not respect himself and thereby stimulates others not to respect him; not being respected by them, he lowers and distorts the common level of life. The act of spiritual recognition fails from both sides, and as a result of this there arises a whole nest of diseased relations. In general, respect is very easy to shake and to destroy, but very difficult to restore. Having been formed in people's self-affirmation, a break becomes consolidated; psychic mechanisms of disrespect are strengthened and imperceptibly transferred to others. The disease grows and is deepened. The individual incapable of respect perverts all of his legal relations. Not respecting himself, he loses the spiritual dimension for his deeds* and winds up not being in a condition to apprehend the idea of law: his word cannot be honest; he does not revere in himself either legal empowerment or legal obligation; his capacity for law remains an empty juridical fiction and loses its spiritual nature.

Not respecting the other person, he measures his deeds and words not by the standard of honesty and law,[2] but rather by the measure of self-interest: he does not understand the nature of spirit and the power

1 Il'in's argument for this claim is found in chapter five.

2 This could equally well be translated as 'right'.

* **See chapter fifteen.**

of legal consciousness and therefore does not grasp the true meaning of others' expressions of will; he does not honor in the other either his legal empowerment, or his social bond; he does not value the consent of the other to a joint submission to law, and does not prize the other's respect; and as a result of this his legal relations are filled with unworthy content and become degenerate. If this disrespect is mutual, then the legal relation turns entirely into an evil and dangerous pretense: the private-law matter turns into an organized mutual deceit, the public-law connection turns into organized covert violence. The disease may gradually draw in an entire net of legal relations and destroy the spiritual nature of the association. Then people become accustomed to weaving a legal order while recognizing neither law nor their own and the others' spirituality; legal relations lose their spiritual significance, and the juridical form conceals directly behind itself a *universal animosity*. In the struggle for existence people already seek not legal victories, founded upon mutual recognition, but an unprincipled and predatory "victory at any cost". An agreement of wills creates not solidarity, but a conditional, temporary truce between enemies; neither side takes seriously either their own or the other's expression of will; the idea of law is trampled under, and of the legal order there remains only a deceitful, futile shadow.

Then there settles into life an order perpetually on the point of sudden, complete collapse. The disease of mutual non-recognition, as it were, inflamed from within by the demons of faction, grows stronger and ascends to a peak. Those who do not respect, by their very disrespect, impute evil to the other's soul and awaken malice in it: and the non-recognized, disrespected soul, like an echo, unconsciously answers to the malicious treatment with a malicious response. Hostility breeds hostility and the sound of discord calls forth an echo from all souls. Disrespect, reinforced by enmity, becomes contempt; enmity reinforced by contempt is converted into *hatred*; hatred, combining with powerlessness, infects souls with malicious *fear*. If disrespect repudiates the spiritual worth of a person, then contempt and hatred negate his right to life. Contempt in itself is already a negation of the right to life; hatred is already *murder*. The social order, saturated with these passions, cultivates in souls the disposition of Cain. People transgress against one another with constancy and ease, committing murder—either symbolically or in reality: now abuse and cursing, now mutual destruction of dwellings (pogroms); now in calls to revolution, now in marauding attacks; in word and deed, in articles and in duels. People in fact live in a state of *civil war* and, given their blindness, call this state "a legal order", and cannot overcome their disease, because they are not aware of it; and not being aware of it, remain sick with it – acutely, helplessly, degradingly.

To such a relation of citizens to one another corresponds a diseased political regime, founded on the mutual disrespect *of the rulers and the people*. The State, infected by this disease plays out a political tragedy of the disrespected citizenry and the despised ruling power. *A ruling power, not respecting the citizen*, cannot rely on his reason or on his will; it sees in him not a subject capable of law, but a more or less broken psychic mechanism, which is incapable of autonomy* and therefore in need of petty and obtrusive regimentation. Precisely from here arises the idea of the "police State" and, in particular, of a totalitarian State. An autonomous spirit requires freedom and is capable of it, even if to a small degree; *a psychic mechanism* does not need freedom and is not capable of it: it requires an organized and powerful pressure on its passions and desires—a pedantic tutelage, terror, perpetual political espionage of all against all. Such a totalitarian tutelage, grounded in disrespect, strengthens *evil instincts* in the citizenry and strives not to convert them into *beneficent motives*, but to create an intimidating counterweight for such instincts. There arises a regime of fear and oppression; the ruling power in its every action negates spiritual worth and spiritual self-activity in the soul of the citizen; every minute it, as it were, reiterates to him: "You are not spirit, but a thing, a machine, a robot", or "You are no longer spirit", and backs up that negation with systematic terror from above. And, heeding this voice, the citizen imperceptibly degrades his spiritual life, turns into a slave and becomes accustomed to tremble and betray.** And the ruling power accepts this trembling as its achievement, as political success, and reinforces it with mass murders, with this ultimate limit of spiritual negation and disrespect.

As a consequence of such a relation to the subjects, the ruling power turns out to be separated from them: it is not sustained by their legal consciousness and loses the true source of its own spiritual worth. The art of respecting itself abandons it; and if its oppression succeeds, then it, not encountering resistance, ascends into the void and indulges in *megalomania*; if the oppression encounters resistance from below, then it falls into confusion and indulges in a *mania of persecution.*

Thus, the non-respected citizen is converted either into *a slave*, or into a *revolutionary*, or perhaps, combines the qualities of both; while a non-respected ruling power lives in fear, sowing trepidation and itself trembling, fearing revenge and avenging its fear, warring with the citizenry and cultivating an "internal enemy" in them; and it destroys the authority of the ruling power, the law, and the State in the country. Similarly, the citizen, not respecting his ruling power, possesses a sick legal consciousness and ruins his State. Not respecting his ruling power, he cannot and does not want to build *together with it* the legal order and culture of the country. Essentially speaking, he does not recognize it as a ruling power and does not guard its authority. He does not assist it, but rather hinders it. He either rejects the ruling power altogether, and consciously or unconsciously prefers anarchy (the anarchists); or he does not recognize *this particular* ruling power and wants to create a new one. However, dwelling in this state of disrespect, he little by little *completely* forgets how to value and construct an order of legal rule: he slackens in

*** See Chapter Sixteen.**
**** See Chapter Sixteen.**

himself *the culture of obedience*, but does not develop in his soul *the capability to rule*. On the contrary, he becomes accustomed to seeing coercion in any ruling power, and considers *any* coercion reprehensible and inadmissible. Therefore, he finds himself to be unable either to support the old ruling power, or to create a new one. If a new ruling power is formed without him, he transfers to it his mechanism of disrespect, and if he enters into the structure of the new ruling power, then he is unable either to affirm its authority, or to apply it to affairs: he only teaches others disrespect for the ruling power, and discredits its authority from the top, just as he up to now discredited it from below.

Such a citizen could probably only respect a powerless ruling power, which is useless for anything; however he would be unable to respect even it. A powerful ruling power would only be hindered by his incapacity to act. State power is the *will* of a political union. A political union can be strong only when its will is not only wise and vital, but also strong, and for that above all a general respect is necessary. The ruling power is the creative source of positive law. A citizen, not respecting the source of his own law, ceases to respect the law itself; it loses the will to a legal order and is drawn toward the violation of law. If he *continues to obey* a ruling power he does not respect, he does this for spiritually-false and degrading motives: either from fear, or from personal and class self-interest, or from stupid, unconscious habit. Then he damages the sense of his own worth, ceases to respect himself, and becomes incapable of a public-law relation in general; either he trembles and grovels before the ruling power, conditioning it to be despotic and corrupting it by his slavish submission; or he requires from it constant handouts, conditioning it to political bribery, and ruins both himself and it along paths of open corruption; or, in the best case, he non-objectively and senselessly worships it, not suspecting himself that behind that reverence is concealed a readiness for an equally non-objective and senseless outrage on it. If he *ceases to obey* a ruling power not respected by him, then he turns either into a brigand, openly undermining the legal order, or into a revolutionary, corroding the basis of the State through covert agitation. Then all the diseases connected with the loss of a loyal will and autonomy strike his soul: he loses the spiritual bond with his people, with his own ruling power and with his State, and, drawn by the spirit of destruction, wrongly imagines himself as a constructive creator. Not respecting his ruling power, he sets about its destruction, and, drawn by hatred and scorn for the enemy, turns to murder: there commence acts of *personal terror*.

A terrorist act destroys not only the personnel of the ruling power, and not only the reactionary disposition of the ruling circles: it destroys the *spiritual basis of the existence of the State—the public law consciousness of the people and its attraction to the ruling authority as a source of law and a center of national unity*. The assassination of a ruler puts into the soul of the people the idea that a citizen not only may not respect his own ruling authority, but that he must *despise* it; naive legal consciousness does not distinguish the person from the agency of the State, the agency from the ruling authority itself, and even the ruling authority from the

State, and spreads its negation, its scorn, on all at once: and as a result of this, souls are infected with a profound anti-State disposition. To reject the ruling authority means to reject at once the *common* power and *one's own* power; this means to disconnect *oneself* from the single, common State center and to untie in one's soul the great knot of political unity. Therefore the assassination of a ruler, even if a "tyrant", is an act destroying the State; this act undermines the will of the people to law and unity; it shakes also the present historical legal consciousness; it demoralizes the State, summons toward destruction, toward the elemental hostility of the multitude, toward civil war.

When the people lose respect for their ruling authority or even begin to harbor scorn for it, then this means that a profound spiritual calamity has overtaken them. Scorn for the State authority is the beginning of a universal spiritual disillusionment and dethronement: behind the rejection of public obligations proceeds the rejection of all ties: scorn for State authority undermines legal consciousness, the destruction of legal consciousness inevitably takes away honor and conscience, kills the sense of measure and justice, extinguishes faith and religion. The people become a victim of *spiritual nihilism*. Therefore he who is invested with power has a sacred obligation to uphold respect for it. The "prestige" of power and the "authority" of power constitute a precious achievement of the nation, its spiritual wealth, a pledge of its might and flourishing: it is the respect of the nation for itself and for its national spirit, accumulated over the centuries. A people scorning its ruling authority scorn *itself* in the person of the State; it lacks a feeling of its own worth. Therefore, it inevitably loses both the respect of other nations and, weakened from inner dissension, becomes a plaything of other's interest and a laughing-stock of other's malicious joy. The whirlwind of history will pulverize it and put an end to its tragicomic existence.

However, no less fatal in the life of a nation are defects of mutual trust. Normal legal consciousness affirms that the State, according to its concept, is a living system of *universal trust*. A historical State must constantly strive toward this ideal; the entire legal life of the nation and its entire political fate depend on achieving it. There is an essential minimum of mutual—social and political—trust: outside of it the State cannot exist. There is an extreme maximum of the absence of trust beyond which the State begins to disintegrate even while alive. The diseases leading to this disintegration arise imperceptibly, hide in the shadows and develop gradually. To live among people not arousing trust in themselves is always a misfortune. A person not trusting another perceives him in the best case as a spiritual void, deprived of indubitable reality and harboring in himself evil possibilities and desires. This assumption of malicious desires and anticipation of evil activities is already a suspicion, always coupled with a certain apprehension, and easily flaring into fear. To suspect means to assume that a person does not reveal what he actually wants, for he wants precisely evil; or that he is doing not what he speaks about, and moreover seeks to occasion harm or evil to another. For that reason suspicion is a disunifying principle: it whispers to people of *the absence of solidarity* among them and sows enmity and hostility. If suspicion *does not* have an objective basis in others' souls, then the sickness finds shelter in the soul of the one suspecting and represents the germ of a mania for persecution, with all its flarings of fear, malice and despair. If suspicion has an objective basis in others' souls, then the one suspecting is actually surrounded by evil-intentioned people: in the best case it is his personal enemies; in the worst case it is enemies of the law, State, and spirit, that is, villains. In all these cases a legal relation cedes its place to a relation of force, enmity, and fear; for with enemies and villains there can be no unity in law.

Mutual distrust is a force destroying the legal order and the State. In the soul of the one suspected, suspicion allows for and recognizes an evil intention. In this way it sometimes for the first time awakens or develops it, strengthens and shapes its existence. The one suspected feels at once estranged, disrespected and to a certain degree expelled from the association. He ceases to waver and is strengthened in malice; but precisely in this way he undermines his own respect for and trust in himself. In response to suspicion he begins to suspect others, and an atmosphere of mutual hostility acquires an open sanction. Any act increasing mutual distrust ruinously affects social life, for it corrupts and breaks the precious living, subtle threads of the spiritual bond; it distorts the very nature of legal relations, for the essence of legal relations is not in enmity, but in unity. Therefore *any deceit is harmful to the State; any malevolence or malfeasance* invisibly destroys its innermost tissue. If social life is filled with mutual hostility and suspicion, if the lie and deceit encounter neither condemnation nor counteraction; if intellect and intrigue become synonyms, if speech ceases to be honest, and honesty turns into a prejudice, if business transactions are based upon mutual fraud, upon shorted measures, shorted weights and the malicious use of bankruptcy; if legal association is formed in an atmosphere of juridical relativism, self-interested double-talk, malicious barratry, and unprincipled legal advocacy; if judges, witnesses, bureaucrats and parliamentary deputies can be bought, while political activity is founded on intrigue; if the parties lie to one another, to the people and to the government, while the parties' programs become an interlacing of ambiguities, omissions and silences, then the ethical basis of the legal order – mutual spiritual trust – inevitably degenerates and perishes. Then the contract loses its sacred character and its unshakable significance; a universal uncertainty settles in, nourished by a universal suspicion and hostility. Perfidy, in former times the most ruinous "divine" merit of Woden,[3] becomes an habitual form of life and gnaws away at the spiritual existence of the nation, its strength, its unity, its being. Social communion perishes, turning into a system of mutual distrust and suspicion. That is why any propagating class struggle, as a principle of behavior and a deepening class contradiction, *destroys*

[3] The reference to perfidy here is not entirely clear; it might point to the mysterious figure of Loki, known for his lies and trickery, who has been associated with Woden/Odin in some scholarly accounts, even depicted as a hypostasis of Woden/Odin.

society and the State. The differentiation of labor already imparts to people different and even opposing interests; if these interests acquire dominance, then the centrifugal forces break down the State and destroy it to the end. Mutual distrust strengthens and ignites the centrifugal inclinations of the various classes, and if a solidarity beyond classes has not formed in souls, has not become firmly established and recognized to a sufficient degree, then legal unity comes to an end in civil war, and the State collapses.

The State in general cannot exist if it turns into a system of mutual distrust and suspicion. If the ruling power is not trusted by the citizenry, then that means that it expects from them evil and contradictory deeds; it does not count upon their legal consciousness and therefore considers them to be "unreliable"; it perceives their direction of will as being opposed to the State or opposed to the government, looks upon their activities as "sedition" or "sabotage" and at the first opportunity pronounces them "internal or class enemies". But enemies dwell not in a legal unity but in a state of war; and thus *the ruling power declares civil war on its people.* All the devices of international war, in all their repulsiveness, are transferred to the internal life of the State and applied to the subjects, and moreover with such contrivances and perversions as were first introduced in the history of humanity by the totalitarian regime: these are slave concentration camps, this torture by starvation, by cold, the breaking up of families, degradations, fear, interrogations prolonged for nights and days, beatings, hypodermic injections, poisoning, gassing (Auschwitz), and so on. The ruling power develops a strenuous and all-embracing vigilance and foresight: internal enemies are covered by an entire network for surveillance, guarding, and apprehending; political investigation and espionage are developed; entire organizations are created which must search out citizens' "plots", report on them, prevent their "plots" and even more, take charge of them by means of pretended participation in them, and in case of need, directly organize supposed conspiracies. Proceeding along this path, the ruling power takes upon itself a monstrous task—the mobilization and formation of an intractable will in the country, with the aims of weakening and extirpating it: political provocation produces the most evil techniques of international villainy, and the state administration experiences the greatest spiritual degradation. The ruling power comes forth in relation to the citizenry in the role of *traitor, provocateur,* and executioner: it does not hide its contempt and its enmity for the people, and openly strives to raise dissension and treason in the camp of its internal enemies. The policy of the ruling power becomes *cynical* and infinitely cruel; it takes on the character of unconcealed viciousness and this forces the government to fill its ranks with *openly vicious people*. The paths of guile and coercion become for the ruling power the habitual paths, and its fate turns out to be the fate of evil itself: it becomes an object of loathing and infects souls with the dream of its destruction. To suspicion, espionage, and provocation the legal consciousness of the citizenry responds with fear and scorn; it gradually becomes accustomed to merging the idea of State power with a conception of evil intent and viciousness; the administrative agencies become living centers of popular hatred; and the collapse of the State turns out to be near.

Distrust of the people toward the ruling power is equally ruinous for the State. The people, accustomed to suspecting their own ruling power, suspect in its person *their own will*; they believe neither in their own power, nor in their own nobility, and therefore remain in the condition of a *rabble*.

Accordingly, State power can rest on a sham or on a true basis; and the former always guarantees for it weakness and degeneracy. The sham bases were always fear and violence, intrigue and deceit, flattery and demagogy, graft and usurpation; in a word, everything that is particularly characteristic of the totalitarian State; a vicious ruling power, seeking roots in the viciousness of the people, is thus a doomed ruling power. The true basis of ruling power will always be *the spiritual respect and trust* of the people for the government and of the government for the people: each side must recognize the legal consciousness of the other party as its own legal consciousness, and thereby merge with it in a certain *unity of will*. The State is precisely a unity in multiplicity: *a multiplicity of subjective wills, bound together by a unity of end and an identical direction of wills.*

Such is the third axiom of legal consciousness. Together with the other axioms it indicates the two main sources of any falsehood [кривды][4] in legal relations: they are either *an insufficient recognition of the law* or *an insufficient recognition of the human spirit*. A legal relation will be sick every time that its participants do not recognize *the end* of law, or *law in general*, or *positive law*, or *a specific* positive law, or a specific *subjective status*; it turns out to be diseased every time that its participants *do not respect* spiritual worth *in themselves* or *in the other*, or *in their ruling power*, or *don't trust* their ruling power, or the other, or themselves. Law is something *of the spirit and for the soul*; in this consists its function; in this is the source of its being; in this way are determined both its might and its fate.

[4] Or, injustice.

Chapter Twenty-One
Legal Consciousness and Religiosity

Humanity will have to experience a profound renewal in the understanding of the law and the State. It must definitively reject the fatal prejudice of the "external" nature of the law and the State; their "inner" *psychic-spiritual essence* must be seen and assimilated. Law merely "manifests itself" in the external, spatio-corporeal world; the sphere of its real life and activity remains the human *soul*, in which it appears with the force of *objektive value*. The State in its realization "presupposes" the presence of a multitude of corporeally-disunited people, territories and external things; but the human *soul* remains precisely that sphere within which there arises, matures, and proceeds both the political life of the individual and the life of the State, as a unified whole.

Outside of the spiritual condition of the multitude of individual souls there is no State, nor can there be one: the political condition of people is above all, and most importantly of all, their *spiritual condition*. If the law possesses fullness of being, it is only through *legal consciousness*, that is, through legal feeling, legal volition, legal thinking, and finally, legal action. If the State possesses fullness of being, it is only through psychic-spiritual experience and the realization by people of its end and its means, its content and its form. In the true and full meaning of the word, the law and the State do not exist outside of the *multitude of individual legal consciousnesses*, connected through continuous association.

Precisely in this way is the connection of the idea of the State with the entire spiritual culture of the nation, and particularly with its *religious culture*, determined.

The element of the *State* is the element of the *human spirit*. But precisely in this element are conceived and developed both fine art and true knowledge as well as ethical perfection; here also descends divine revelation. The sole and indivisible (in-dividu-al) structure of the more or less inspirited soul brings about, or in any event, is destined to bring about, all unconditional values; and that is why all the lines of spiritual ascent arising from here dwell in a certain—unconscious or conscious—interaction.[1] This does not mean, however, that all of these lines remain equal in rights, or that any one of them can, *while preserving its compass and its competence*, subordinate to itself all the remaining lines. Thus, the interaction of cognitive thought and legal consciousness, legal consciousness and conscience, aesthetic choice and legal consciousness—may be considered predetermined *a priori*. But aesthetic taste, in itself, cannot lay claim to superiority in questions of legal consciousness; scientific thinking, in itself, is not in a position to direct the statesman;

[1] The "lines of spiritual ascent" are presumably the just-mentioned fine art, true knowledge, ethical perfection, etc.

and even conscience may leave in a certain state of helplessness one who leads the struggle for law. *Religion alone turns out here to be in an exclusive position.*

Religion, by its very essence, lays claim to the guidance *of all* matters and relations. It seeks and finds the *highest* word and the *ultimate* word; it indicates to a human that through which his very life becomes *truly* a life, and through which each activity obtains its essential *meaning*, its ultimate *consecration*. Art, or knowledge, or virtue, in themselves, do not encompass the entire human spirit and do not indicate to it its highest and ultimate end; if they obtain such all-embracing and guiding significance, then they exceed their bounds and acquire the significance of *religion*. Then a person makes a *religion of conscience*, or a *religion of thought*, a *religion of the beautiful*; the testimony of artistic feeling, or self-manifesting cognitive truth, or conscience, becomes for him the voice of divine revelation and obtains in his eyes a corresponding compass and competence.

This *supreme, guiding significance of religion* could be expressed thus: that which guides a human in life as the highest and subjectively most valued content—that constitutes his "religion". Every human being, however small or bad he may be, possesses a need to attach himself through faith and love to something which is to him an unconditionally "primary", precious content; and that to which he so attaches himself becomes the content and object of his "religion". The self-sufficiency and power of this devotion varies among different people; but only a certain *fullness* of it makes it possible to speak of *authentic* religiosity. The content calling forth this devotion is also subject to changeability and diversity; and only a certain *qualitative level* of it provides a basis for speaking of *genuine* religion. Religious experience is manifold in its empirical appearances; but in its deep essence it possesses certain stable, homogeneous [однородные] qualities and this *uniformity [однообразие] of the religious act* is determined in the final analysis *by the unity of the religious object*—God. The very object of religion and its essential nature inevitably impart to it that central guiding significance which remains with it under all circumstances. Just as there is nothing higher, more significant, or more perfect than the Divinity, there is for a human being nothing higher, more significant or beneficial *than authentic and genuine religion*, that is, one which is based on an objective perception of God. Such a religion possesses the capability and the mission of determining the personality and the fate of a person, transforming the whole of his character, all of his worldview and all of his vital activity. It is natural that it should acquire a decisive influence both on his legal consciousness and on his political form of activity.

The legal consciousness of everyday life may not possess a religious root; it may even be indifferent to what is usually called "religion". *But authentic religiosity cannot pass by law and the State*: it is forced to define its relation to them and to legal consciousness. And, in exactly the same way, *normal* legal consciousness in its mature realization inevitably acquires *a religious character*, although a person may be *aware* of this character to a greater or lesser degree.

Taking possession of the individual soul and determining its character and its fate, religiosity *cannot pass by law and the State*, not least because law and the State lead not an external-mechanical life, but an inner, psychic-spiritual one. If religion affirms in the soul of a person a particular, blessed State, termed in Christianity "the kingdom of God", it sets into motion in this way *all* the powers of the individual spirit: feeling, lying at the basis of patriotism; and will, supporting the right of the individual to spiritual autonomy; and thought, composing the form of the law and the State; and imagination, objectively constructing a system of legal relations. *Legal consciousness and the kingdom of God* live by one and the same psychic tissue, realize themselves in one and the same spiritual sphere. A mechanical separation of the "Divine" from "Caesar" will always remain a lifeless fiction, deprived of being and practical significance. The word of the Gospel of course intends no such mechanical separation; it establishes only the *compatibility* of "God" and "Caesar," *not* their irreconcilability, the possibility of giving "To Caesar what is Caesar's" without sinning against Divine law and, accordingly, the possibility of serving God while not committing a violation of law. This indication of *reconcilability* is wrongly interpreted as a doctrine of *indifference* or opposition; and the medieval comparisons ("two swords", "the sun and the moon", etc.) not only did not resolve the issue of the relation between religion and the State, but imparted to it from the very beginning a false positing.

However, the matter is not reducible to the fact that legal consciousness lives by means of those same creative powers that religion governs, that is, to the *inevitability of their "meeting" in the individual soul*. Religion itself, as the realization of "the kingdom of God", *is impossible outside of law and its recognition*, that is, *outside of legal consciousness*. Religiosity is a *spiritual* state and therefore it possesses meaning and value only given *an autonomous acceptance of revelation by the individual soul*. *Un*free, *non*-autonomous belief dictated or constricted by prohibitions, not accepted in voluntary conversion, not having matured in self-active seeking, loses its meaning and is diminished in its "religious" value and power precisely to that degree. A human being possesses a *natural* and inalienable *right* to autonomous perception of the Divinity, to a free profession of Him and to a self-active vital realization of His will as his own; and he who satisfies his need for a vision of, and living service to, God, who puts into practice his capacity for religion, realizes by the same means his most precious *right*, for the sake of which the best people of all ages and nations were able to renounce all other rights, were able to suffer, and went to their deaths. *To possess religion is a human right and this right—the right to be spirit—lies at the basis of all his other rights*. A person rejecting that right loses his spiritual worth and falls into all the diseases connected with this loss; a person not exercising this right leads a vain life and unworthily burdens the earth. The need for religion gives rise to the need for *spiritual freedom*, and therefore also for *a legal order*; that is why religiosity more than once appeared in history as the most profound source of legal consciousness, while *the right of religion became the unconditional and sacred foundation of the struggle for political freedom.* None other than the struggle for freedom of conscience is capable of imparting to national legal consciousness that spiritual basis which subsequently places the imprint of genuine nobility on all its political history.

Genuine religiosity requires spiritual freedom and is nourished by it; it brings about *human natural law*, treasures this law and therefore develops *natural legal consciousness* in the soul. An authentic craving for cognition of God stimulates in the human soul a *will to spiritual autonomy*, and this will is already a will to natural law. That is why authentic religiosity can reject a certain legal content or a certain mode of legal organization, *but cannot reject law itself in its principle without falling into misunderstanding.* Law is the necessary form of the spiritual being of the human; and religious being is spiritual being; therefore *outside of law there cannot be religion.* It is possible to be a religious person and doubt the necessity of this or that *positive* law and this or that form of the State; for *their* necessity is established not by the very fact of the spiritual being of the human, but by the entire ensemble of concrete historical conditions. But law in itself and particularly *natural law* must be recognized *by each believer*.

Such a recognition of natural law however forces each religious person subsequently to turn to the question of those paths on which natural law can be and must be *confined in actual life*. And here before them inevitably stands a dilemma: either to *reject* positive law and the State, or to *sanctify* them in their noble essence and mission. A religion tends toward rejecting them, first, if it *in principle rejects the very task of accommodating to life on earth*, or, rejects the reality of the sensible world, or insists on a systematic extinguishing of earthly existence, or recognizes earthly life as a religiously indifferent State; such a rejection of earthly existence witnesses, on one hand, to a substantive *poverty* of religious *revelation*, not uncovering the most fundamental secret of being—the secret of *the presence of God's power in the sensible* earthly element; and on the other hand, to a creative lifelessness of the religious act, letting slip the fundamental *mission* of any religion: the mission of transforming earthly life by the power of divine revelation.

Religion is inclined to the rejection of positive law and the State, *second*, if it recognizes the task of a renewal of life, but *rejects as inadmissible the principle of compulsion by the ruling power*, or sees in compulsion a compromise unacceptable for a morally upright bearer of revelation, or values the unlimited freedom of the human in the choice of good or evil, or combines both these bases; such a rejection of the idea of the State witnesses, on one hand, to the *naivete of the religious worldview*, overlooking the *tragic* nature of the creation, due to which the very *mode* of earthly life of the human *already* conceals within itself a "compromise", whereas the moral innocence of a person contains within itself a secret inner contradiction; on the other hand, it witnesses to the naivete of legal consciousness, mistakenly reducing the idea of the State to coercion and heteronomy, and mistaking the *unfreedom* of the human, mired in evil, for his "freedom" in choosing evil.

Finally, third, religion is inclined to the rejection of positive law and the State if it rejects as *unnecessary* the principle of *heteronomous rule*, or overvalues the power of a *good* will and individual autonomy, or undervalues the power and stubbornness of *evil* human passions, or, commits both mistakes together; such a rejection of the idea of the State witnesses on one hand to the naiveté of that understanding of psychic life which supposes that spiritual autonomy is already inherent in each person, that it does not need heteronomous assistance and that an objective insight into the good is always accessible to everyone; on the other hand, it witnesses to a vital blindness and to a lack of objectivity of *historical* insight.

In this way, religion, rejecting positive law and the state, either *consciously turns away from the empirical life of humanity* or *unconsciously loses from view the objektive properties of this life, of humanity itself and the State*. In all these cases it becomes necessary for it one way or another to enter into a vitally important struggle with positive law and the idea of the State. In this struggle religion will be trying to separate natural legal consciousness from positive legal consciousness, removing from the former the historically discovered paths of realization, and from the latter, its noble source and criterion; it will inevitably be drawn into the destruction of the entire *political will and capacity* of humanity, accumulated over thousands of years, and will *merge its cause with the cause of anarchism*. And, working on the destruction of the whole of political culture, it will on its side either insist on the rejection of *earthly life*, which will continue all the same, or *construct an "autonomous" order of external life for people incapable of inner autonomy*. It is clear that the first outcome will lead to absurdity, and the second, will realize all the diseases of a defective will and return humanity to a heteronomous order. Under all these outcomes religion *will not fulfill its fundamental mission: to transfigure the earthly life of humanity on the basis of divine revelation*. And in the face of this failure, it will be forced to re-examine anew its negative relation to the principle of the State.

But if religious consciousness turns to the *acceptance* and recognition of the State principle, then *that does not at all mean that it sanctifies the entire historical structure of the idea of the State or that it falls into some sort of "idealization" of the political lowland*. In the historical idea of the State there rules a certain mixture of the worthy and the unworthy, the healthy and the diseased, good and evil; only that which corresponds to the *idea* of the State in that history is subject to recognition and sanctification. Idealization results from an unseeing or nonobjective perception, taking evil for good, collapse for flourishing; such a perception leads, however, to mistakes and delusions not less than an inclination to the opposite side: to assert, absurdly, *that the historical State had no creative relation to the idea of the State*, or that in the struggle with evil positive law created only evil, and, moreover, due to its own unconditionally evil nature. It would be useless to mix up the State with *one* of its possible means: the idea of *heteronomous regulation*, by itself alone, by no means coincides either with the principle of "coercion," or, still more, with the principle of evil. Indisputably, the evil with which the historical State struggled not only [did not][2] give way to the power of legal regulation, but to some extent subordinated such regulation to itself; there arose "evil" law and the evil State, in which good and evil were intermixed, both in terms of nature, and in terms of action, and in terms of results. But in this complicated and tragic intermixing, evil was never able to force out either the good *end* of law, nor its good *form*, nor its good *influence*. And thus normal legal consciousness affirms that the essence of the idea of the State appeared precisely in this *good influence of a good end* through the means of *a good form*. This means that the idea of the State is *a force for the good in the history of humanity*; and for this reason it deserves a religious understanding and is in need of it.

A religious understanding of positive law and the State rests upon seeing in it a certain vital *value*, and moreover one such that it *possesses justification before the face of God* and therefore summons in the soul of humanity a certain *religious attitude*. Such a value is the fundamental motivating end of law and the State—*the spiritual culture of the nation and humanity*, that is, its constructive power, its creations, its creators, and its necessary conditions. The *flourishing of the human spirit and spiritual life is truly a Divine cause and religion cannot fail to recognize it as its own cause*. Therefore the State, called to serve it, must receive and does receive from religion, *recognition and a consecration*. Moreover, precisely religious intuition indicates to the state its conceptual purpose: *to establish in the earthly life of people by means of heteronomous regulation, the most favorable order for the spiritual flourishing of the nation and humanity, and educating the citizen to the gradual ennobling of the positive law through the powers of brotherhood and autonomous legal consciousness*. This higher, guiding end of all politics is revealed precisely through *religious* intuition, measuring every phenomenon by the ultimate, absolute scale of divine perfection. Through such a religious intuition political creativity obtains that most profound idea and that vital guidance which connects *the idea of the state with natural legal consciousness*, and by the same means protects it from spiritual degeneration.

This means that the ultimate root of healthy legal consciousness possesses *a religious nature*, for the spirit of instinct, just as the *will to spirit*, is in its essence a *search for divine perfection*. Accepting positive law and the State, a healthy legal consciousness includes in them that same will and that same search; it discovers in them a religious worth

[2] This phrase does not occur in the original 1956 edition, but was added in the Собрание сочинений [Collected Works] edition, ed. Yu. T. Lisitsa, IV, p. 393.

and indicates to them their religious task; it saturates their lives with *religious energy* and in this way imparts to them the qualities of authentic spiritual *reality*. The authentic idea of the State is constructed by *healthy legal consciousness, that is, by religiously intuiting will.* The greater this will in the rulers and in the citizenry, the higher the spiritual level of political life, the more solid and spiritually productive the political union [государственный союз]. Similarly to *any* human life, *political* life needs a *religious source and religious intuition*; for only hence can it receive that true scale of vital values and ends outside of which there is no salvation from political relativism and lack of principle, from political banality and cynicism, from self-interested compromises and treason, from petty political intrigue, from "wobbliness in intellects" and sedition. Without a *higher and ultimate*, unconditional guiding meaning, the idea of the State is doomed to degeneration; but it is *precisely religion* which discloses such a meaning. For that reason to begin living through the idea of the State in truth means to *begin living through it religiously*, that is, to introduce it as an essential member in the creative order of religious intuition and volition, or, what is the same thing, *to connect legal consciousness with the absolute root of life*.

This purposeful (teleological) connection between religion and the State is expressed in the fact that the State will serve religion in its highest ends, recognizing them as *its own*. The State will not guide religion where it needs to go; but *religion will indicate to the State where and how it must proceed.* Faith will not become a device for the ruling power and the church will not become an instrument of political intrigue and political ambition, but the ruling power will become an instrument of that end which is the same for religion and the State: *the inspirational transformation of life*. This does not mean that this or that historical church or confession will prevail within the state and make it its own instrument: not the church and not a confession of faith, *but a religiously renewed legal consciousness*. The State needs not obedience to ecclesiastical guidance, and not confessional quarrels, but *an authentic, free religiosity of the people*. The ruling power does not have the ability to summon this religiosity to life; but it is a direct obligation of the State to protect its *rise and flourishing*; moreover, it is an *existential problem* for it. *Freedom of conscience* is a pledge of political flourishing; and only it can create what no artificial planting of confessions of faith can create.

All of this can be expressed thus: At the basis of a worthy and mighty legal order, of a worthy and mighty State idea, lies *a religious disposition—religiosity* in the profound and authentic meaning of that word. None other than religiosity reveals the ultimate depth of the human soul and imparts to it *an unconditional devotion and an unconditional steadfastness*. None other than religiosity makes a human capable of viewing himself and his people before the face of God, accepting the life of his people as a service to God, and becoming a *patriot*. Patriotism, if it is not a zoological passion, if it is a spiritual state, is a certain *religiously rooted, unconditional devotion and an unconditional steadfastness of the soul in relation to his own God-serving nation.* Thus, at the basis of the State lies patriotism, and at the basis of patriotism lies a religious breathing of the soul.

One must not identify a *religious* state of the soul with its "ecclesiastical" or "creedal" state. This is clear already from the fact that a religious person may belong neither to any sort of creed nor to any church. A free intuition of God may not lead a person either to dogmatic formulas of a confessional character, nor to a social unification with other people on the basis of a creed, a cult, or law (a church). Revelation may live in a soul unrecognized, unarticulated, unformulated, while remaining an actual revelation, guiding personal life and inspiring personal creativity. A religious fire of spirit may not fit into any kind of historically-formed dogma: and nevertheless it may be authentic and mighty. Thus, the Christianity of the first century did not yet have a mature ecclesiastical organization; Christianity before the Council of Nicaea lacked the creed of faith, and nevertheless it led and renewed souls by the power of genuine religiosity.

Conversely, *any* ecclesiastical or creedal state of the soul, it would seem, must be necessarily a *religious* state, similarly to the way in which a species concept always possesses all the signs of a generic one. However, historical phenomena do not submit to the laws of logic. A religious fire may get extinguished in the bowels of an ecclesiastical organization, while a *creedal* union may lose *faith* and not be realizing the *creed*. Then the dogma is separated from authentic, personal religious experience and becomes a moribund, abstractly rational formula; a praying cult degenerates into an aggregate of outward actions and habits; the sacrament no longer sanctifies life; the beneficent power of religion vanishes from the ecclesiastical union and converts it into a routine scheme of everyday life. *The routine* swallows up religion and religion loses *being*; while "the church" and "the creed" remain as signs of a previous, but lost, religiosity.

In such situations it turns out that for the idea of the State and legal consciousness, the precious connection is not with "ecclesiasticism" and not with "creedalism," but with *religiosity*, in its fundamental and authentic, so to say, "generic essence." In the same way that a *musician* must first be an *artist*, and above all, a *spiritual person*; in the same way that a *ruler* must first of all be a *citizen*, and above all, a mature *individual spirit*; so an *orthodox believer* or a *catholic* must be first of all a *Christian*, and above all, a person with *self-sufficient and authentic* religious experience. What is important here is not the routine and not the outward appearance, not the tradition and not the habit, but the fire of genuine spiritual life, of a religiously-deepened and concentrated fire providing light to the will, and energy to feeling and action. For that reason the apparently "secularized" idea of the State is not thereby an "*extra-religious*" mode of life; it is historically possible for there to be a situation in which *a religious renewal* of the idea of the State will be realizable only given an open break with traditional, but degenerate ecclesiasticism.

A healthy and powerful legal consciousness, in terms of its basis and of its structure, possesses a *religious character*. This is determined by the very essence of such consciousness and *of religion*.

Religiosity in its fundamental essence is a *spiritual, holistic, vital and unconditional* acceptance of the Divinity, as the *perfect and real focal point of life*.

Religiosity always consists in something being experienced as *perfect*. It begins where the soul gets beyond a state of *indifference* and distinguishes between "better" and "worse"; where the soul is drawn precisely toward what is "better" and, following that, ascends to what is *perfect*. Religion is *a passion for perfection*; precisely for that reason it is impossible where *indifferentism* reigns.

Ascending toward perfection, religiosity perceives it not as conditionally "better", or relatively "better", or "subjectively" the most acceptable, but as *unconditionally,* non-relatively, *objektively* perfect; as perfect *in actual fact*, in itself, and then also for all. The religious soul lives not by simple pleasantness of subjective contents of consciousness, but *by objektive perfection*. Precisely for this reason there is no religion where *subjectivism and relativism* hold sway. Religiosity is a *joy* of the soul, accepting the *objektive* quality of the object and *captivated* by its perfection. This captivity is inevitably transformed into *love* and *gratitude*; this joy gives to the soul a feeling of *flight* and *liberation*. Precisely for this reason there is no religion where *love has died* and where *bitterness* reigns.

Having risen toward perfection, religiosity affirms it as something *real*, as actual being or as a creative *power*. Religiously perceived perfection is not an abstract idea, not a dream, and not merely a remote ideal; within it not only the quality or value is objektive; it is *itself* objektive, it *authentically is*, even when it is drawn into a process and is still realizing the fullness of its being.[3] Religiosity makes of a human *a living participant* in this being; it *really introduces him* into the system of this reality and gives him a living feeling of *unity* with it; it introduces the soul to this highest *power* and thereby imparts to the human a certain *creatively intense calm*. Religion is not only a passion for perfection, but also a *passion of real power*. It is obvious that *nihilism and illusionism* exclude any religiosity whatever.

[3] This extremely compressed statement on the nature of Divinity can be loosely compared to Hegel's conception, which was discussed (and criticized) at length in Il'in's two-volume commentary on Hegel. See I. A. Il'in, *The Philosophy of Hegel as a Doctrine of the Concreteness of God and Humanity*, transl. and ed. Philip T. Grier (Evanston, Ill : Northwestern University Press, 2010 and 2011). See especially vol. 1, Part 2 "The Doctrine of the Divine Path," as well as the final chapter of vol. II, "Conclusion: The Crisis of Theodicy". See also footnote 2 in Chapter 12 of the present volume.

Further, religiosity is a *spiritual* condition.* Its spirituality is determined not only by its turning toward the *objektively* valuable, but also by its *autonomy*. It rests on the self-sufficient and unforced perception of perfection, on personal and authentic *experience*, opening up, deepening and renewing the soul. The religious condition cannot arise from others' words or on a foundation of *others'* experience; the content of others' experience must be actually *assimilated* by the soul. Religion requires from a person self-sufficient *experience and sincerity*; it requires authentic, free *presence* of the soul in the professed content; precisely for that reason it is impossible where the soul is afflicted by *falsehood, pretense and hypocrisy*.

But religiosity is not only a sincere state, but also a *holistic* one.** The unforced, authentic perception of perfection inevitably seizes the *entire* soul and attracts it into a new life *as a whole*. Not one of the fundamental psychic-spiritual powers of a human being stands apart in this state and counteracts the others. Thus, for a truly believing human, *thought* does not break apart the soul and does not weaken it with doubt. One can believe only in that which is *in actual fact* so, in what is "true";[4] it is absurd to believe in something *knowing* that it is in actual fact not true; but it is impossible also to know something, believing that in actual fact it is otherwise. Genuine faith does not fear thought, but is strengthened and purified by it; genuine thought is not alien to faith, thought is borne by faith, made strong through its strength. In general, feeling without thought turns out to be a source of blind passion, leading the soul to licentiousness and degradation; while thought without feeling steps forth as cold reflection, lifeless, idle argument. Religion requires an organic combination of feeling and reason, believing love and knowing thought; for thought *alone* begets dead philosophizing and *skepticism*; while feeling *alone* begets careless intoxication and *superstition*. Skepticism and superstition signify the absence of religiosity.

In similar fashion, religion requires an organic combination of feeling and thought *with will*; for the absence of this living unity splinters the soul and enfeebles religiosity. Will without feeling is like a dead machine; it is a cold force, monstrous in its biased schematism. But at the same time feeling without will degenerates into a sentimental passivity, into a sterile, falsely lyrical volition, into a mystical sensibility. Will without thought remains an indeterminate, blind craving, a formless longing or a foolish caprice and an objectless arbitrariness. But at the same time, thought without will degenerates into a lifeless doctrinarism, obligating one to nothing, into an unprincipled, needless rearranging of possibilities.

[4] In English one cannot duplicate the parallel in Russian here between "to believe" (*веровать*) and "to be true" (*верно*).

*** See Chapter Two, "On the Spirituality of Religious Experience", in my book *The Axioms of Religious Experience*, vol. 1.**
**** See Chapter Eighteen in *Axioms of Religious Experience*, vol. II.**

Religion is not formed on this path, rather falls apart and perishes. If religiosity without reason leads to superstition or depravity; and without feeling, to skepticism or empty dogma; then in separation from will it turns into a *sentimental sanctimoniousness* or an *apathy of theorizing.*

For that reason religiosity is a *holistic* state of the spirit: here is what is accepted by faith, loved by *feeling*, and comprehended by *reason*; it objectively occupies the *imagination* and calls forth an effort of *will.* What is professed, loved, believed, and desired simply coincide.

But precisely this spiritual *wholeness* imparts to the religious soul that *vital intensity* which naturally finds expression in *practice*, in *a system of creative deeds*. True religiosity is a *devotion to perfection*; and this devotion summons forth an *energetic service* to it, a *creative realization* of it on earth. Faith is not only dead without deeds; it simply does not exist. For a religious perception of the object engages the *entire* soul in a new life and inevitably becomes a *life-determining* force. It is not possible that religious faith should stand by itself, while everyday activity stands by itself; for that would signify that religiosity lost its wholeness and ceased to be itself. A truly religious person loves that perfection in which he believes; professes what he loves; and realizes with his life what he professes. The calling of religion becomes *his* own creative calling; and he voluntarily accepts it for fulfillment. Precisely for that reason a *lackadaisical* life is not a religious life.

Finally, this vital devotion to perfection is an *unconditional* devotion. A religious relation to the object binds the individual spirit *without* conditions, limitations, or reservations; it impels the soul to subordinate to the beloved perfection its powers, and its interests, and any other interest. Religious self-determination consists in a person *loving* a certain object (for its perfection) more than himself, more that his life and his interest; it instills in a person a certain ultimate certainty that in the absence of this object there is no life for him; and from this arises the motive to struggle for the realization of this object and for its victory: through good will, devoting to this all his strength and life itself; and not due to "duty," and not as a "sacrifice", but with a light wholeness of spirit and with an awareness that this is truly worth dying for. Precisely this *unconditional* devotion to perfection teaches humans that scale of valued ends which protects the soul from *banality*, this worst foe of true religion;* precisely this holistic good will makes a person a *hero* and teaches him that self-denial which affirms the highest spiritual worth of the one renouncing. This signifies that religiosity is not reconciled not only with contemplative, but also with active, *relativism.*

Such is the fundamental nature of any truly religious act, notwithstanding to which creed or to which metaphysical doctrine it leads the individual soul later on. Religiosity reveals to a person his spiritual

* **See Chapter Thirteen in *Axioms of Religious Experience*, vol. I.**

essence and connects him with the perfected focal point of life; this instills a *feeling of one's own spiritual* worth, an absolute measure of any value and real energy of life and will; and this imparts to the soul the capacity for *spiritual autonomy, for inner self-discipline*, and teaches the soul the spiritual acceptance of other people. Religiosity awakens in the soul the capacity for a life-determining *love* and indicates to it a vital calling; it develops in a person a *spiritual sightedness*, a spiritual wholeness and an everyday heroism. The religious conversion of a person regenerates the very sources of his life and rebuilds the whole of his personal character: he is renewed in reason, in feeling, in will, and in imagination; he passes through *a spiritual cleansing and obtains power over the evil element of life*.

Precisely these fundamental qualities of religiosity reveal its connection with normal legal consciousness. Genuine religiosity affirms in the soul of a person *the axiomatic roots* of legal consciousness: *the sense of one's own spiritual worth, the capacity for autonomous life and the art of recognizing the spiritual principle in other people.* Arousing *spiritual sightedness* in the soul and bringing to life in it *the power of love*, religiosity leads a person to *patriotism*, to a cult of *solidarity*, to mutual spiritual *respect and trust*; for all these States are born precisely through the union of *spiritual understanding* with the feeling of *love*. Religiosity brings to legal consciousness all its gifts: the highest calling and an absolute measure of value, and a wholeness of character, and the power of inspiration, and everyday heroism.

This means that *in the soul of a religious person there are aroused precisely those most noble powers which are essential for the flourishing of a noble idea of the State*. The idea of *a religious citizen* not only *does not* hide within itself any inner contradiction, but *is one of the greatest ideas with which humanity is concerned.* The religious citizen unites in his soul the power of *authentic religiosity with the power of* healthy and true *legal consciousness*; and, moreover, in such a way that *his legal consciousness is a mature manifestation of his religiosity*. Uniting with legal consciousness, religion finds a new, mighty path for the transformation of life; uniting with religiosity, legal consciousness gains for itself an unconditional basis, affirming "a will to spirit", as *a will to God. From this atmosphere there arise both religious leaders of the nations and unknown hero-patriots, silently devoting their lives to the native land. With the deepening and solidifying of this atmosphere is connected the future of all States and the whole of humanity.*

Thus true religion is not hostile to the true idea of the State; it does not lead away from it, but leads to its flourishing. The encounter of the two "kingdoms" in the soul of a human is *organically necessary and spiritually fruitful*. Humanity must recommence its thousand-year work on the organic reconciliation of "the kingdom of God" with political construction. But it is impossible to gain this reconciliation either by means of a new syncretic "ideology," or by means of an external unification of "the State" with "the church", or by merging several "creeds" among themselves. What is necessary here is not a new mode of "organization", but *a new mode of life*.

This new mode of spiritual life may be acquired and realized only as a result of a great humanity-wide ascent and protracted exertion of will which takes on the features of *a religious renewal and a political renewal* at once. Its essence will consist in a restoration of *an authentic and immediate* association *with the unconditional object*, and therefore in a liberation and renewal of the spiritual mode of life. The personal-psychic root of our religion—Christianity—and the root of the historical idea of the State—legal consciousness—must be renewed through living and authentic, suffering and inspired experience. This will be an epoch of great disillusioning from false paths, and a great casting-out of moribund arrangements and prejudices. But from the fire of this epoch will be born a new religiosity, a new legal consciousness, and a new humanity.

I believe that we have already entered into this epoch. And in the light of this idea I assess and make sense of everything that is taking place around us.

Chapter Twenty-Two
Conclusion

The entire history of cultured humanity witnesses to the fact that law and the State periodically enter into a state of profound crisis. The reason for these crises is that humanity, in constructing a legal order, loses from sight *the sole, unconditional end* of political union and turns it into an instrument for conditional, lesser tasks and private desires; from this follows the degeneration of legal and political life: the absence of principles in the ruling power and the diminution of its authority, the absence of solidarity among citizens and classes, civil war within the state, and open warfare constantly breaking out among the nations. According to its objektive purpose, law is an instrument of order, peace, and brotherhood; in actuality it too often covers up falsehood and violence, litigiousness and discord, insurrection and war. People join together on the basis of law, as it were, only in order to bring about an extra-legal separation;[1] two establish solidarity in order to attack a third; brotherhood serves animosity; under the guise of order there smolders and develops a new strife; peace turns out to be a truce, while the truce prepares the way for war, and having prepared it, cedes its place to war. A crisis sets in when history begins to sum up the results of an entire period filled with such self-interested encroachments, unprincipled incursions and impotent outbursts. Then, as it were, it is suddenly revealed that the law and the State have acquired a false content and an unworthy form; that they have lost their sole purpose, and perhaps any end at all; that they have been made into an instrument of evil, and not of the good; that they need a profound renewal and rebirth. And, having sensed disaster, but having not understood its significance and its roots, humanity begins to extricate itself from it with that same instinctive blindness and spiritual impotence with which it permitted the disaster to overtake and overwhelm it. And blindness and impotence lead it again to palliatives, to an external ordering of life, to new dangers, diseases, and disintegrations.

In order for law and the State to actually enter on the path to renewal and rebirth it is essential to become truly aware of their nature, their end, their basis, and then to make that awareness an object of will and vital activity. At the foundation of a cure must lie a true understanding of the *healthy organism and its diseases*. To establish such a true understanding of legal and political association is the task of philosophy of law: to resolve this task means to create a doctrine of sound and true *normal legal consciousness*.

A doctrine of normal legal consciousness is as necessary for humanity as is a doctrine of the self-manifesting theoretical truth,[2] of conscience,

[1] "Separation" here is presumably intended as the opposite of "solidarity".

[2] Il'in's term is *очевидность*. See footnote 7 in Chapter One above.

of aesthetic taste and of the axioms of religious experience. The object of such a doctrine is a certain *objektively true and unconditionally valuable state of the human soul*, which in its structure possesses not only a cognitive but also a sensuous and a volitional character. That is not only a truly knowing, but also a truly feeling, and a truly desiring psychic state; and precisely its objective truth and spiritual wholeness impart to it a living might and that unconditional value which permits one to call it a sound and true legal consciousness. Knowledge, feeling, and volition are mutually conditioned here: only *love* can give rise to true knowledge and a powerful will; only *will* can assist knowledge in its impulse toward the object and toward mature form, assist love in its living creation; only *knowledge* can impart *objectivity* to love and will. Patriotism must nourish the thought of the learned jurist and the will of the citizen; the science of law must illuminate the citizen and the patriot; volitional self-assertion must lead the patriot and the scholar. Then *the scholar* will have access to authentic legal and political *experience*; then the *patriot* will make his feeling objectively *conscious and fruitful*; then the *citizen* will construct his volitional act on a clear *understanding* and passionate *feeling*. That is why normal legal consciousness is an object of cognition, accessible only for objective philosophy: here, to cognize means to experience the object; to experience the object means to come to love it; to come to love it means to affirm in oneself the will to it; and all this together means to enter on the path of immediate realization of what became known, loved and desired. Such is the path (the method) of *any* philosophizing; such is the path also in the philosophy of law, and in the investigation of normal legal consciousness.

From this it is already clear that the doctrine of normal legal consciousness rests neither upon historical induction, mechanically registering *any* "legal consciousness" and identifying the qualities common *to any and all* modes of experiencing law and the State (such an induction would create in the best case a barren generalization, abstracted from pathological material); nor upon deduction, setting out from a preconceived idea and drawn toward a non-objective completeness in an arbitrary construction. No, the philosophy of law moves, as does all philosophy, by the path of *systematic intuition*, directed at the objektively subsisting object. In order to describe the structure of normal legal consciousness and truly fix its content, it is essential to realize it in oneself. This means that the investigator must organize in himself a thinking, feeling, and desiring association with the single unconditional end of law and the State. This end is determined by two coordinates: the ultimate *purpose* of human life in general and *the mode of being* inherent in the human as such. Ascending toward this unconditional end, the investigator places before himself the problem of *the objektively-best* order of human life, that is, of the best law in terms of content, and of the best State in terms of form. Experiencing through thought, feeling and will this end and this best order of life, the investigator assimilates the objective *content* of normal legal consciousness and works out in his soul its spiritually-true "act". Thus: the experience of the unconditional end *of law* leads to an investigation of the nature of the human *spirit*, while the nature of the human spirit determines through itself the deepest nature of the law and the State; and as a result the essence of natural law, the basis of normal legal consciousness, the axioms of legal consciousness, the essence of the idea of the State and the axioms of ruling power are revealed.

All of this investigation is realizable only through the concentration of attention, feeling and will on the question of the objektively best, and moreover, *of the very best*. This means that sound legal consciousness is here not only *the object under study*, but in a certain sense also *the organ of investigation*, i.e., the means of cognition. Similar to the way in which the essence of conscience can be studied only *in realizing* acts of it and experiencing its call, that is, *living with conscience*; one can investigate spiritually sound legal consciousness only by *tracking it down in oneself, developing, strengthening and deepening* it in *living experience and realization. The basis* of normal legal consciousness is given to each person in the form of a *will to spirit*, giving birth in the soul to a feeling of law, a feeling of its necessity, its worth and its end. This obscure feeling can be and must be strengthened and cultivated in souls and brought to a state of *legal conscience*, i.e. an objectively true and life-determining *volitional love for right law.*[3] And thus the process of *cognition* coincides here to a certain degree with the process of *cultivation*; what is cognized is created for cognition and in cognition in such a way that each success in creation opens to cognition something new and each success in cognition solidifies the cause of self-cultivation: *normal legal consciousness must live and grow in him who investigates it: and only he who develops it in himself can investigate it*. This is not induction and not deduction, but *a systematic intuition of the object, created in the process of self-perfection*, or, what is the same thing, this is "self-knowledge" in the sense of Socrates.[4]

It is clear that the doctrine of spiritually sound legal consciousness does not investigate and does not depict the life of humanity in its actual fullness; but neither does it draw an abstract "ideal", an unreal idea or an "infinite" task. It investigates one of the best *potentialities* of the human soul, as *already* real, but still *not* standing on the peak of the ideal and of might [могущества] and far from determining through itself the entire life of the human. Spiritually, true legal consciousness is given in embryo to *each* human being, if we leave out of account the psychically ill and deformed; it lives and acts in souls even when it proves to be weak, obscure, depressed, or muffled; similar to the self-manifesting truth

[3] Правому право. Alternatively, "just law".

[4] Il'in's discussion of philosophical method in this and the two preceding paragraphs parallels his account of philosophical method in general, and of Hegel's philosophical method in particular, in his commentary on Hegel. It is also explicated in other essays he published during the same period in which he was writing his Hegel commentary. For a discussion of these matters, see *The Philosophy of Hegel as a Doctrine of the Concreteness of God and Humanity*, vol. one, *The Doctrine of God*, transl. and ed. Philip T. Grier, pp. xxxi-xxxviii and pp. 6-9.

or conscience, it preserves its nature and its importance even when its essential power is reduced to a minimum. For that reason it is appropriate to consider it as *one of the factors of the historical process*, as *a really present force*, having not yet unfolded its activity, however, in the whole of its compass and with all of its possible intensity. A sound and mighty legal consciousness is, however, a certain "ideal" state of the soul, but not in the sense that it *does not exist* in actuality; it is *really* in souls, even though its vital power can and must become immeasurably greater. It is an historical force which is subject to strengthening; the future belongs to it more than the past belonged to it. The real power of this factor is expressed in the fact that everywhere that it operates with greater intensity and in greater compass, the order of social life turns out to be not only more perfect, but also more *solid and stable*. The vitality and solidity of the State is determined, *ceteris paribus*, by *the level of national legal consciousness: the spiritual soundness and force of legal consciousness* is the main basis for political organization and the national spiritual culture protected by it. Philosophy here, as everywhere, teaches perception of the fact that *the good is a real power*, *already given* to humanity as a fact, as a possibility of what is greater, and as an object of desire, and, at the same time, yet *assigned* to humanity for cognition and full realization.[5]

Precisely such an understanding of legal consciousness creates the possibility of overcoming in practice the abstract, methodological opposition of *law and power*. For normal legal consciousness is that vital power which concentrates in itself the *worthiness* of law and at the same time, the possibility of real, vital *activity*. It is that spiritual force which is a depository and "source" of law, in such a way that precisely by *its* "competent" desire is conditioned a valuable "igniting" and "extinguishing" of legal norms. A legal norm acquires its significance precisely through legal consciousness, and therefore also its vital effectiveness; precisely through it legal force acquires its sanction, its consecration, and loses its odious character. Legal consciousness is that noble source in which are reborn both lawless force and impotent law: law becomes a noble force, and force becomes a rightful force.

To perceive the presence, the worth, and the competence of normal legal consciousness means to find a path for the solution of all the vital, fundamental difficulties stemming from the nature of law and creating not a few theoretical controversies and even "antinomies" in juridical science.

Thus, first, law, according to its essence, prescribes and forbids *only the external* behavior of people and presupposes in a human the presence of corresponding psychic states, so long as the opposite is not proven. Law cannot and does not try to regulate by its prescriptions the psychic-spiritual life of a human, and concentrates its attention on what is externally-perceptible and outwardly manifested: it would be absurd to prescribe to a person in a heteronomous order such deeds *the value*

[5] There are obviously some distinct echoes of Hegel in these claims regarding legal consciousness and the good as actually operative in human history.

of which is determined by their *autonomy* and the realization of which does not lend itself to counting or verification. Law is an *external* order of life. But if this external order gets disconnected from the *inward* states of spirit, and is not created by them, is not received, or does not emerge, from their maturity, from their autonomy, from their substantive truth and wholeness, then it degenerates, becomes paralyzed, degrades the person and, collapsing, destroys the life of spirit. *At first glance*, law does not need legal consciousness and often does not even have access to it. However, *in actual fact* it *lives* though legal consciousness and fulfills its purpose the better, the more mature and perfect is legal consciousness. Thus, a parliamentary order does not exclude corruption; free elections do not exclude class-based programs; dueling or murder is not preventable by external measures; the mobilization of the army is not realizable through universal compulsion; and *only a mature legal consciousness* can extirpate bribery, class politics, murder and desertion in life. Law can create an *external order* of life only through the *internal orderliness of the soul*, that is, through legal consciousness.

Further, second, law can establish only *general, abstract* rules and therefore it speaks in its norms only of people *in general*, of features *in general*, of deeds, relations, empowerments and obligations *in general*, treating as essential some aspects and properties, and ignoring others. If the legislator were to try to replace general norms with singular imperatives tailor-made for individual behavior, then he would have placed before himself the absurd task of fruitlessly chasing after an infinite variety of individual material; the number of imperatives would turn out to be infinite and the order of life would turn out to be unregulated. A legal norm is an *abstract* rule; this rule regards humanity as an *abstract* content. However, in actuality there exist not "people in general", but "human beings in particular", possessing not *abstract features, but concrete characteristics.* An individual human being is a living, concrete whole, with a numberless multitude of distinctive traits and characteristics, the only one in his genus, and an unrepeatable complex of bodily, psychic and spiritual powers. This complex can never be reduced to common features, or exhausted by abstract categories. An abstract qualification of it would not only be forever conditional, forced, inadequate, but in its consistent and extreme realization, it would lead to the highest injustice (*summum jus, summa injuria*). For that reason *the problem of the application of legal norms* to living people, their statuses, deeds, and relations, is a problem absolutely not resolvable by way of formal induction and deduction: a *mechanical* matching of "features", stipulated in a norm, and in "characteristics" given in life, is an operation destroying law, disfiguring life, and undermining in souls the will to legal order. A perception of concrete givenness must be an act of *artistic justice*; the understanding of an abstract rule must rest on *an intuition of the unconditional end of law* (not simply the goals of the "legislator", which may remain unknown, or not have had a definite content, or were developed *per compromissum* from opposing desires, or were simply false and pernicious).[6] But an act of artistic justice and an intuition of the unconditional end of the law can be accessible only to *normal legal consciousness*. The application of legal norms requires an objective understanding of that for the sake of which law in general is created, applied, and maintained. The one applying the law must *have in mind* not only the formal "legality$_z$," of the norm and not only its objektive content, but also its objektive *purpose*, its spiritual mission, and its living function; and this means that it must proceed on *the basis* of normal legal consciousness and be guided by its *axioms*. The law can regulate concrete living material by means of abstract rules only through the means of a living, intuiting and true legal consciousness.

Further, third, law is a phenomenon of *spiritual rightfulness*; it possesses objektive significance and this significance rests, in turn, on the unconditional value of spirit, its contents and its states. For that reason law *always* harbors within itself a certain *unconditional worth* and with good reason lays claim to recognition and obedience; law is something objektively "true", "right", and "valuable". However, in actuality, each historically developed codex probably has norms which are *incorrect, unjust*, and perhaps divergent from the fundamental nature of spirit. Positive law is not a system of perfect and mistake-free rules of behavior, and a positive legal order frequently contains in its make-up spiritually anti-natural stipulations. And thus, only normal legal consciousness is capable of getting out of this living and philosophical contradiction, not breaking away from the spiritual value of law and not corrupting the soul through legal unscrupulousness, nihilism or rebellion. The problem is resolved along the path of *a creative recognition* of law: such a recognition, which actually perceives its spiritual worth, maintains the freedom of the recognizing spirit, and, at the same time, *pours the energy of individual will into the transformation of positive law*; this recognition achieves the significance of law-creation: the renewal of law is born from that same depth which perceives and knows its unconditional worth, so that recognition obtains the form of a struggle for law, while the struggle for new law doesn't shake spiritual recognition. Clearly, such a relation to law reveals in the soul of a human the presence of a spiritually healthy, creative legal consciousness.

Fourth, law in its true and profound significance expresses and protects the nature of the human spirit and, for that reason, it rests upon *the spiritual self-sufficiency* of the subject and his self-activity; on the other hand it protects the autonomy of the person and, in turn, is nourished by this autonomy as by air. However, in actuality law is realized in a *heteronomous* order: it is established, supported, and protected by an *organized and fully empowered* ruling authority which authoritatively prescribes and forbids people to do certain external acts;

6 One might compare this statement to Savigny's observation that laws (*Gesetzen*) passed by emperors, senates and legislators may constitute "a baleful corruption of the *Recht*" for reasons quite similar to the ones cited here by Il'in (though Il'in's standard of *Recht* is not the "common legal consciousness of the culture" but the natural law).

it creates a complex apparatus of coercion, courts and punishment; it requires obedience and, in case of need, forces people to submit. To resolve this apparent contradiction means to open to humans a means of *asserting their autonomy while preserving the heteronomous order of rule.* To reject the autonomy of individual spirit means to violate the end of law and undermine its vital force; to reject the ruling authority means to destroy the means necessary for this end, and the paths by which this force proceeds to realization. And that is why *autonomy must become the creative source of heteronomy*, accepting it as one's own essential handiwork, consecrating it and then *making it an instrument of one's own expansion and flourishing.* The individual spirit must pour its autonomy into the structure and activity of the ruling authority; while the ruling authority must see in spiritual autonomy the form of its being, the principle of its life, and *the end of its practice.* Clearly, this outcome can be revealed and realized only through a spiritually sound and true legal consciousness.

Fifth, law in accordance with its true and profound nature is a manifestation of *spiritual solidarity*, connecting person with person; this connection is essential for people precisely as a consequence of their psychic and bodily separateness. Law can exist and operate in the life of people only when they feel and understand their solidarity, that is, not only the similarity of their egoistic inclinations, but their identical interest in the maintenance of a single order common to all. Arising out of solidarity, law in its turn cultivates solidarity in souls; needing a certain minimum of mutual respect and trust, law is destined to strengthen respect, to organize it and approach the maximum. However, in actuality a legal order seemingly grows by way of *struggle and compromise.* Precisely the *struggle for existence* governs the historical life of humanity and gives rise to private and public competition of citizens, classes, parties and states. The boundaries set for the natural rights of persons and nations develops as a result of the struggle for law: and precisely in this way are explained the attempts to examine private transactions and peace treaties, courts and ruling authority, the law$_z$ and the structure of the State, as compromises of interests that have *not* achieved solidarity. And thus normal legal consciousness affirms that the struggle for law leads and must lead to the establishment of solidarity, and that solidarity lies in the very foundation of the social struggle, if only it really is a *struggle for law*. A sound and mature legal consciousness is able to treasure the law and struggle for it; but it knows that in the struggle for *just law* all people are solidary and that the task of each person defending his law [его право][7] consists in leading others to the *awareness* of this solidarity. The social struggle excludes solidarity, both at its root and in its achievement, only if it is conducted *not* for the sake of law, but for the sake of violence and subjugation. But this also means that he has defended his law who has achieved a universal, solidary recognition of it on the part of others. Not just any struggle for existence is a struggle for law; and not just

[7] Presumably "his law" in the sense of "his (national) *system* of law".

any compromise possesses, in terms of content and of form, a legal nature. The task of people is not to find a "compromise", but *to convert any compromise into a manifestation of legal solidarity.* Historically, humanity is doomed to suffer in the struggle for existence, to become aware of, obtain and affirm their spiritual and legal solidarity. However, both the basis of these sufferings and the crowning of this struggle are clear from the very beginning to a sound legal consciousness.

Sixth, law in its true and profound significance establishes a world-wide natural brotherhood of people, connecting all in a living order of subjective-legal mutuality and correlativity. In accordance with natural law, *all* people are united by legal association and by mutual legal recognition; *universal spiritual culture* forms the immutable foundation for this unity, while international positive law works on the creation and strengthening of this supra-national supra-state legal unity. However, hand in hand with this, positive law and the historical idea of the State *break apart* the world-wide legal brotherhood, close the disconnected legal organization in on itself, counterpose State to State, and periodically throw people into a life and death battle; the struggle for national spiritual culture and for its empirical basis leads to international wars and always imparts to them a spiritual significance, and occasionally even a spiritual justification. It is given only to normal legal consciousness to resolve this predicament and furthermore, through a true understanding of the nature of spirit and the nature of the State: this resolution confirms patriotism as the *true* state of spirit, as the *necessary* basis for *spiritual* internationalism and as a living, actual path to the *positive-law organization* of international brotherhood. Sound legal consciousness not only does not reject the political form of thought and patriotic feeling, but cultivates these States as unconditionally valuable and necessary—not only for the individual, but also for the State, and not only for the individual State, but for all of humanity as a whole.

Finally, a whole series of other complicated and subtle problems of life and jurisprudence find a resolution for themselves only through the doctrine of legal consciousness, through its systematic deepening and strengthening. Such are the problems of natural law and its grounding, of positive law and its overcoming, the violability of law and the non-violability of its significance, the problem of criminal guilt and punishment, the problem of aristocracy and democracy, of State power and the political party. All these and other problems require for their solution *an objektive criterion,* which would possess not only strict contents and credibility, but also a living creative power. And precisely a spiritually sound and true *legal consciousness* provides this criterion, connecting its volitional nature with the sole, objektive end of human life and contemplating law and the state as products and instruments of the human spirit in its unconditional and sacred significance.

The entire history of humanity must be examined in the light of such a legal consciousness, as *its* history, as the long line of *its* victories and *its* defeats.[8] The entire history of political *institutions* appears as a pantheon of *its* embodiments in life. The entire history of political *doctrines* is comprehended as a great, universally-human search for *its* adequate formula. In the light of normal legal consciousness again and in a new way is revealed the objective unity of the human family, the continuity of its *volitional* culture, the maturing of its *spiritual self-consciousness.* The history of the human family is revealed immediately as a process of great suffering and as a process of gradual healing, and, moreover, in such a way that precisely the suffering produces the healing, for they teach objective feeling and volition, true knowledge and action.

The life of humanity has always been formed in such a way that the ascent to unconditional objects was accomplished only in spiritual elevation, and spiritual elevation was achievable only as a result of authentic and great suffering. This ancient path is reproduced also in modern history. And from this follows the task for new generations: *to accept the ordeals granted; to comprehend anew the essence of law and the state and realize what is comprehended—through the power of renewed legal consciousness,* which has accepted not only the experience of past genuine suffering, but also the great, thousand-year tradition of spiritual seeking. The modern world will return to the political tradition of Socrates and Aristotle. But it will seek and find its root in Christianity; precisely there will its political achievement be confirmed. The modern world must create and will create a new legal consciousness resting upon *love for spirit* and on the *will to the unconditional good.* This legal consciousness is already being born and has been born and the task of humanity as a whole is to not extinguish the flaring up of the fire, but to maintain its precious flame and ignite hearts by means of it.[9]

8 That is, the history, victories, and defeats of *legal consciousness*.

9 Presumably another reference to the sacred central fire in the ancient Greek Prytaneum. See Chapter Ten, footnote 2.

APPENDIX

I. A. Il'in

The Concepts of Law and Power

The Concepts of Law and Power: an Essay in Methodological Analysis[1]

Chapter I

The question of the interrelation of law and power deserves particular attention from the jurist for a whole series of reasons. On one hand, this problem plays a prominent role in the *history of political doctrines*. The most varied philosophical, political, and juridical doctrines approach this problem in order to give it this or that interpretation and resolution, and if we take only those doctrines which in one way or another *approximate* law to power, then before us unfolds a long series of views, often completely heterogeneous as a whole and in essence. In one or another modification we find this approximation in the sophists, and in the flaming republican Machiavelli, and in the monarchomachs (Hubert Languet), and in the naturalist Hobbes, and in Spinoza, and in the extreme individualist Stirner, and in the reactionary Haller, and in the sociologist-legal scholar Gumplowicz, and in many others. Doctrinal material from the centuries has been accumulating around this problem, and the essence of it has acquired an ever more subtle and intricate character. The presence of similar resolutions in the most varied doctrines should alone arrest the attention of one investigating this problem.

To this is further joined the *practical relevance* of this question. The most varied social groups are interested in this or that practical resolution of the conflict between law and power, in the establishment of a so-called "correct" interrelation between these aspects of *social life*. And although the practical interest forcing one to struggle for the triumph of "impotent law" or to sympathize with "lawless power" is capable of arousing theoretical interest in the problem, the importance and the necessity of a preliminary systematic analysis of the problem is still far from being recognized to a sufficient degree.

[1] In this first footnote to the German translation of his essay ("*Die Begriffe von Recht und Macht: Versuch einer methodologischen Analyse*" [hereinafter: *Die Begriffe*] in the *Archiv für systematische Philosophie* [Berlin]. Sonderabdruck, Band 18 (1912), pp. 63-88, 125-144), Il'in added the following clarification of what he meant by "power": **"It should be emphasized explicitly from the outset that in the present investigation, from among the multiple meanings of the concept 'power' (*Macht*), we have in view only that aspect which draws near to the concept of force (*Kraft*): 'power' is to be understood here as a species of the generic term 'force' (*entelecheia*). This is sufficient for our investigation, since according to the universal rule, the species retains all the defining features of the genus. So too here: because power is always force, it is merely sharpened and refined as a concept for other special sciences, and applied accordingly in them".**

The *theoretical complexity* of the problem is the third aspect of it capable of arresting the attention of the researcher. Among jurist-theoreticians the problem of the interrelation of law and power can and must arouse interest in the representatives of all separate disciplines: issues of the definition of law, of its formation, application and content are near to every jurist-theoretician as such, and this problem is tightly connected with these issues. The very concepts of law and power are numbered among the most difficult and complicated in the history of scientific thought in general. To say anything exhaustive concerning these concepts is to this day an unattainably difficult matter, and it *may* in general *seem* that the question of their interrelation should be allocated to the number of so-called "cursed" questions.[2]

Therefore, if we take upon ourselves the task of saying something concerning it, that is not because it seems to us by its very nature uncomplicated, and a resolution of it easily achieved, but rather that certain general viewpoints recently taking shape in philosophy[3] and the philosophy of law mark out in our opinion that *path* movement along which might permit introducing into this problem the necessary analytical light.

In order to enter upon this path it is necessary above all to recognize that the historico-philosophical and practical illumination of it must without fail be preceded by theoretical analysis. The essence of an opinion on law and power cannot be understood in a single historically familiar doctrine if we do not accomplish a preliminary attempt to define these concepts in terms of contemporary science: for the process of explicating obsolete doctrines consists essentially in translating them into the language of contemporary concepts. In just the same way the critical evaluation of these doctrines presupposes that the problem has been solved in one way or another, that the "correct" interrelation of the *concepts* has been found. Finally, the practicing politician speaking of the "power of law" and of the "law of power" must clearly and precisely represent for himself all the inner logical significance of these verbal phrases, and it is a theoretical analysis of the concepts that can place his reasoning and actions on the necessary height of meaningfulness. And so for the jurist, whoever he may be, it is necessary to begin with a theoretical examination of the problem.

We will attempt here to pose the problem of the interrelation of law and power from a universal-juridical point of view. This means that we will abstract from all those formulations which it receives in separate

2 Stemming especially from the reign of Tsar Nicholas I, the so-called "cursed questions" concerned in the first instance the meaning of Russian history, and expanded to include the meaning of life, the existence of God, and the destiny of humanity. They were initially debated by aristocratic intellectuals, then eventually by the radical intelligentsia as well. –[PTG].

3 Among these Il'in is likely to have had in mind the early phenomenology of Edmund Husserl, some influence of which may be detected in this text. – [PTG].

juridical disciplines and from these special problems and complications which arise for it in the separate sciences, and we will approach it from the point of view of a *general jurisprudence*. Accordingly, *the analysis of the concepts* of power and law moves to the foreground for us – however, in a single definite respect.

Let us isolate our formulation still more fully and precisely. We abstract from the question of which, in the *ethical* or *socio-philosophical* respect is *more valuable*—law or power; or what must serve what in the *political* respect, i.e., is law the *end*, and power the *means*, or the reverse. We leave aside likewise the question of what triumphed over what in the process of *historical* development, as well as what turned out to be the *cause* and what the *consequence*. We are not interested in what *ought to be* in social life, and not in what *was* in historical actuality. All these are questions of great importance and interest. But, for the moment, the center of gravity is not in them. We are attempting to carry out here an analysis of the concepts of power and law from the point of view of the *general methodology of juridical disciplines*.

Contemporary jurisprudence is more and more arriving, with great determinateness and a principled awareness, at a recognition that law is in itself a certain complex and many-faceted formation, possessing a whole series of separate aspects and forms of "being". Each of these aspects enters into the substance of what is named by the one common term "law", but each of them is in its very essence something distinctive to such a degree that it presupposes and requires a special definition and examination alongside the others. If a general study omits even one of these aspects, then it is not complete; if the study of one of these unconsciously merges with another, then there arises the danger of a methodological confusion, sometimes capable of invalidating the entire study. This viewpoint recognizes in this way that there is no single universal and exclusive method for the study of law which would supplant and replace all others, rendering them superfluous, unnecessary. Methods of the study of law are many; each of them in separation is valuable, necessary and irreplaceable. Belief in a salvific methodological monism perishes and cedes its place to a principled recognition of *methodological pluralism*.[4]

[4] To the number of adherents of this point of view in Western science belong: Laband, P., *Das Staatsrecht des deutschen Reiches*, vol. I, pp. *vii-x*. Jellinek, G., *Allgemeine Staatslehre*, pp. 23-48. Lask, E., "Rechtsphilosophie," article in the Festschrift für K. Fischer. Weber, M. R., "Stammlers Ueberwindung der materialistischen Geschichtsauffassung," article in *Archiv für Socialwissenschft*, vol. XXIV, and others.

In Russian science:

P. Novgorodtsev, "Государство и право," [State and Law] in Вопросы философии [Questions of Philosophy], no. 74-75.

A. Alekseev, *К учению о юридической природе государства* [On the Doctrine of the Juridical Nature of the State].

Th. Kistiakowsky, "Gesellschaft und Einzelwesen".

G. Shershenevich, *Курс гражданского права* [Course of Civil Law], vol. I, 1901, pp. 79-118, and others.

From this point of view the whole of legal theory starts to become complicated, stratified, differentiated. The juridical disciplines begin to be divided not only according to the character of the relations regulated, but by *the method of examination* of law as such. Approaching the law in all its complexity from its particular viewpoint, each methodologically particularized discipline separates out precisely that aspect of the law which is important for it, and declares just that aspect of law to be vital, forming the supposed essence of law. This results in not one definition of law, but several, perhaps many, and none of these definitions can or should pretend to exclusivity. Only all of them together, conjointly, may lay claim to an exhaustive comprehension of law.

Among these separate methods of examination, among these *methodological orders of legal inquiry*, may be greater and lesser proximity and remoteness. The mutual remoteness of separate orders may extend to complete and full, cardinal isolation. And precisely in this last case, the concepts belonging to one order stand in relation to the concepts of another order in the plane as in essence divergent, other, alien. There are orders of legal inquiry which not only do not supply answers to questions arising and standing in another order, but cannot even tolerate the transfer and posing of them *in its own sphere*. Such orders must be characterized as *mutually indifferent in the methodological respect*, and the recognition of this indifference is one of the most immediate and important tasks of legal theory as a whole. Thus, for example, an *historical* examination and a *sociological* examination of legal *phenomena* are related to one another; sometimes they flow together and modulate one another. In just the same way a *philosophical* evaluation of *legal phenomena* and a *politico-teleological* examination of them possess certain points of contact. But, for example, a *dogmatic* working-out of *the norms of law*, having the goal of constructing a system of juridical *concepts*, and a *sociological* explanation of *legal phenomena,* move on two completely different planes; in a certain relation they may come to be in the position of mutually indifferent orders, and on certain questions may reveal even a direct opposition.

Let us further notice that *the principle of methodological indifference* by no means has, and must not have, the meaning that certain *phenomena of social life* do not stand in any sort of *real* connection with each other, don't condition or determine one another. The essence of this principle consists in a certain provisionally admissible cognitive device of *logical* abstraction from some aspects of law during the examination of other aspects of it. More concretely and definitely speaking: studying law in a logical order, we abstract from those aspects of it that characterize it as a real phenomenon. Here are counterposed not two phenomena, but rather, on one hand, law as a phenomenon, and on the other, law as something examined outside the plane of the real. But we will get to the point of this later.

To carry out that analysis of the concepts of law and power which we are here undertaking means to attempt to discover whether there is a possibility that a certain methodological order of jurisprudence, or perhaps several methodological orders, will turn out to be related to that scientific plane in which the concept of power stands. And if it turns out that such a relation or intersection of these methodological orders is possible *in general*, then it remains for us to follow the trail and indicate for precisely which orders this is possible and to what extent. This is how a correlative question will be decided: is there an aspect of law such that it *in no way whatever* tolerates a methodological approximation to power, or still less, an identification with it? And if there is, what is this aspect? This will also give us the opportunity to say: is it possible in general to regard law as power; is this admissible in general from a methodological point of view, and if it is admissible, with respect to which subtleties of both concepts is it possible? Only then would we have in hand a criterion both for understanding and for a critical evaluation of the entire series of historically known doctrines approximating to each other, or especially merging, the concepts of law and power. Only then would the practicing politician acquire the possibility of understanding with complete clarity and precision the senses in which law becomes power, and what measures can facilitate or hinder law in the realization of its functions.

Chapter II

Let us establish above all that the concept of power, however it be defined, lies always in the order of *the real*, possesses always an *ontological* significance, whereas the concept of law may not be located in the order of the real, may not have numbered among its predicates the sign of being (however construed).

Thus, the concept of power always possesses an ontological meaning.

If it is examined from a *naively-realistic* or, in particular, from the usual naturalistic point of view, then by power is ordinarily understood a certain property, more precisely, a capacity of objects and things, possessing concrete reality. In such a case, power is a *real* (no matter whether active or inactive) *capacity* of empirically *real things*.

If we approach the concept of power from a *metaphysical* viewpoint, then power will receive a threefold meaning: power either forms the essence of substance itself (so it was for Leibniz),[5] or it is manifested as an attribute of substance (so it was for Spinoza),[6] or it receives the meaning of an attribute self-supporting in its essence, free of belonging

[5] [from *Die Begriffe*]: **See Leibniz, *Die philosophischen Schriften* (Philosophical Writings). Gerhardt Edition. Vol. 4, p. 472. *Leibnitii Opera Philosophica.* Ed. Erdmann. Pars Prisz. pp. 146, 158, 191. *Monadologia.* 18.**

[6] **One can accept this designation conditionally from the conjunction of Spinoza's *Ethics*, Part I, Def. IV and Part I, prop. xxxiv, not entering into the examination of his doctrine of attributes. Kuno Fischer defends the understanding of Spinoza's "attribute" as a primordial power. *Geschichte der neueren Philosophie*, Vol. II, pp. 235, 383-395, u.a.**

to a substantial substrate (so it was for Fichte[7]). In all these three cases power has metaphysical reality (regardless whether it is self-supporting or not).

Finally, if the concept of power is taken from the point of view of a *critical theory of cognition*, it acquires the meaning of a concept applied by the understanding to the givenness of sensory intuition (i.e., to phenomena and only to phenomena), creating experience as a conjunction of scientifically-valid assertions; this is a concept serving for the explanation of *sensorily-real phenomena*. In this case power itself is *not* something real, but is a concept, applicable only to that which is itself sensorily real.

So it was, for example, in Kant.[8]

These three different viewpoints on "power," while converging and intertwining, can also form new, more complex doctrines, joining, for example, empirical nuances with metaphysical ones (so it was with Nietzsche), or critical ones with metaphysical ones (Schopenhauer), and so forth.

One thing is common to all doctrines of power: that is, *locating it in the order of the real*. Power is either real on its own—empirically or metaphysically, temporally or extra-temporally, independently or dependently—or it is a principle for cognizing the real. That is why we said that the concept of power always possesses ontological meaning. If, given this, the reality in the order of which the representation of power lives and moves is constructed beyond the given, from a concept, then we will speak of the metaphysical reality of power; if this reality is constructed from the given, from intuition and perception, then it will inevitably be thought in the temporal order and acquire empirical meaning. Therefore, we can agree that everything that is conceived within time – for example as arising, developing, as having its cause in the past, as "conditioned" by what is past or co-existing – is conceived as empirically real. For that reason we can say that everything located within that cognitive order in which our conception of power dwells, is located from the methodological point of view in the *real* order, and itself acquires the meaning of *the real*, the metaphysically-real or the empirically-temporally-real. This is explained still more from the following considerations.

Namely, we can also establish something else, as common to all understandings of power, and as revealing in essence the cognitive role of this concept. By "power" is always understood *the capacity of the real for action*.

7 [from *Die Begriffe*]:**This we can conditionally accept in the sense that Windelband advanced in his *Geschichte der neueren Philosophie*, vol. II, p. 211, however without losing sight of places on pp. 41, 45, 393, 439 and a series of others of his [Fichte's] *Wissenschaftslehre* of 1794**.

8 [from *Die Begriffe*]: **See, e.g., Kant, *Kritik der reinen Vernunft*. Erdmann Edition, p. 108.**

Power is always a *capacity*, whether it forms the very essence of the thing, or only its property, or plays the role of a category of the understanding: with the concept of power is always connected a conception of a certain *capacity*, either remaining in a purely potential state, or already realizing itself. This capacity can further bear a *physical* or a *psychic* character (interpreted from a metaphysical or an empirical viewpoint), or become manifest in the most remote subspecies of this species, but it is always conceived as a capacity.

Given this, it is ordinarily connected with a conception of some sort of a bearer which is itself a member of the *real* order: an element of the external world or an element of psychic life.

Finally, it is a capacity for *action* in the most indefinite and general sense of this word, whether this action should be manifest in self-maintenance, as in Spinoza, or in self-development, as in Fichte, or in the causal determination of other elements of the real order, as in Kant and the empiricists. And to the extent that we have in mind precisely the empirical order, to that extent we will speak precisely of the *causal* significance of power, of power as a *capacity to be a causally-determining moment in the physical or psychological sphere*.

In order to have done with this necessarily schematic analysis of the concept of power, let us add the following. The possibility of interpreting power as a perfectly "ideal" principle, not unlike the idea of "Spirit" in Hegel, or not unlike a purely transcendental Kantian category freed from psychological or anthropological aspects, in no way refutes our thesis of the "real" meaning of this concept. That conception of the "ideal", which in this case absorbs the conception of power, is either itself, perhaps, a new, refined species of the real, or is defined in its essence and meaning as a logical instrument for the establishment or the grounding of judgments concerning the real. And in this case power, even though interpreted as an "ideal", is either something existing and a property of the existing, or a predicate applicable only to the existing. Thus Hegel's "Spirit" is real with the highest reality; a transcendental category is applicable only to the "temporal", and therefore to the real. Thus from the cognitive viewpoint power always belongs to the real order because either the predicate "being" is applicable to it, or it is itself a predicate of the "existing", or finally, both together.

From this it is clear that in order for the concept of law to be approximated to the concept of power, or still more, to be absorbed by it, it is necessary for it itself to be transferred to the *ontological order*, so that law one way or another should itself become a member of the *real* order, acquire the significance of something *real*. Outside of this the concepts of power and law cannot be brought together, and if we see that these concepts in some doctrine or other fall together in such an interrelation, whereby *the concept of law is defined through the concept of power* (i.e., power is the generic concept, and law is the specific), then either the characteristics of the concept of law and the characteristics of the concept of power have been united *in a third concept*, somehow as their logical offspring, or we can be certain that *law* in one way or another has become a member of the real order, *has acquired the significance of the real*. In such a case we can with certainty say: this doctrine conceives law as something real. Given this (still not entering into the methodological analysis of *law*), if power is conceived as a metaphysical essence, then law acquires the significance of a metaphysical reality; if power is conceived in an empirical spirit, then law acquires the significance of an empirical reality, i.e., law is conceived as real, existing in time.

Chapter III

Now we can cross over to the question of which methodological orders are accessible for law, i.e., with which methodological points of view it is possible to approach this concept. If among these orders there turn out to be those with the character of the real, then we will have to decide how to define the concept of law in them, and in which forms it can be approximated to the concept of power. If there turn out to be orders alien to the real, free of any ontology whatever, what significance does the concept of law acquire *in them*, and what does the intrusion of the concept of power into these orders bring about?

First of all, speaking of law, the jurist usually has in mind two general and fundamental meanings of it: law in the objective sense and law in the subjective sense, i.e., legal norms and empowerments[9] derived from these norms. With this, the question of the interrelation of law and power breaks up into two fundamental channels, since the concept of law may be approximated to the concept of power in an *objective* sense or in a *subjective* sense. Accordingly, it is necessary to clarify whether a legal norm can acquire the significance of power, and whether a legal authority can acquire the significance of power. We will begin with an analysis of the first question.

If there is some sort of thesis which might count on wide recognition among jurist-theoreticians, then it is the thesis asserting that *law is a norm* or *an aggregate of norms*. The jurist who would refuse to recognize this would probably throw everyone into astonishment. But if the concept of law, defined in a strict logical order, *per genus proximum*, comes up against the concept of a norm, then it is necessary to ask what is a norm. By a norm I mean *a judgment establishing a certain order*[10] *as obligatory.*[11]

[9] *Полномочия*: authority, power, plenary powers. A grant of legal *authority* is in effect a conferring of a legal *power*, hence, an ***empowerment***. Although it is often translated simply as "power", it will normally be translated as "empowerment" here to distinguish it from two other terms also translatable as "power". – [PTG].

[10] Note: not an "order" in the sense of a command, but, as Il'in explains in the next paragraph: "a certain standing relation among elements of a multiplicity". – [PTG].

[11] **Let us note here that *a norm* is *always* from our point of view a certain sort of *judgment*, but *law is not always a norm*, as we defined it. That state of law in which it acquires a settled logical meaning, fixed in a strict verbal form, is a product of**

Given this, the terms "order", "obligatory", and "judgment" are composed in the following way.

An order is a certain *standing relation among elements of a multiplicity*. Thus an order absolutely presupposes the presence not of a single element, but of two or *many*. The minimum is two; the maximum is a positive infinity of elements. An "order" conceivable within the internal relations of a single element to itself, presupposes this element being conditionally divided into several elements of a lower rank. Under this circumstance it makes no difference to the concept of an order what the elements are, be they people, experiences, planets, and so forth.[12] Further the concept of an order presupposes that among these elements is established a certain *relation*, for the elements, conceived outside of any relation to each other, as taken from various mutually indifferent planes, can form neither an order nor a disorder: one has only to attempt to understand "*the absence of relations*" as an order, and we are instantly convinced that "the absence of relations" itself acquired the significance of a certain type of relation. Given this, for the *generic* concept of an order, and we now have in mind precisely that, it makes no difference what the type of this "relation" is: be it the interaction of human souls, or an associative connection, or gravitation. Finally, this relation is conceived as permanent, and "permanence" constitutes that special mark which distinguishes the specific concept of an "order" from the generic concept of a "relation". This permanence may be conceived as in succession, or in coexistence, or in both together; it can be conceived as "stability" or as "repeatability", but it must always be present and always have at its basis a certain *schema*, permitting one to ascertain this stability or

comparatively late and high development; law can dwell for a long time in a state of logical formlessness and a lack of verbal fixity (for example, customary law in general, or certain spheres of English public law, or the legal basis of parliamentary rule), and in this shape it turns out to be not a *norm* (or, correspondingly, not an aggregate of norms), but an *experience* (or a series of experiences) *of a normative character*. The entire "juridical" mode of examination established below is either in general inapplicable to these shapes of law or applicable to them only to the extent of the possibility of clarifying their logical and verbal form. From this point of view law becomes a norm and a judgment only at the highest stage of its development, and the later apprehension of the "juridical" method in its purity and independence (*the process of this apprehension is not complete even now)*, is fully understandable also to a high degree as a significant consequence of this. Speaking of the *tasks* of further legislation and of *the paths* of the further development of law, it would be possible, if you will, to establish as a *goal* and as an *actual tendency*, the gradual brightening and strengthening of the logical element in "effective" legal norms.

12 I *do not* refer here to *concepts*, not because in relations among them it would not have been possible to have a certain type of order, but because in relations among them only an order is possible, moreover one such that its *permanency* is guaranteed by their very essence; it lies in a plane of the sort that knows no temporality, and accordingly, knows no change, inconstancy or norm. For the *thinking of concepts* is involved in temporality and is subject to a norm; concepts themselves are not involved in temporality and are not subject to a norm.

repeatability. Thus an order is a certain standing relation among elements of a multiplicity.

This order is established in a norm as *obligatory*. If a judgment establishes a certain standing order among elements of a multiplicity as a generalization, achieved by analysis of the temporal or spatio-temporal given (i.e., actuality), then it formulates a law which can be characterized as positive. In such a case we have before us the result of an inductive investigation, stating something about what is, and moreover not concerning the question of *whether* it is, but concerning the question of *how* it is, i.e., concerning the typical relations among elements of the existing.[13] In its concrete application this relation is itself conceived as existing, real, independently of whether it *must* be such, or not. If the judgment establishes a certain standing relation among elements of a multiplicity, not basing itself on an analysis of actuality, and not intending to give an abstract formula for what is taking place in actuality, but asserting the significance of that standing relation as *valuable*, and moreover also valuable outside of reality, but able to achieve the completion of its "significance" in the general sense of this word, indefinable here, precisely through being realized,[14] then it formulates a *norm* in the general meaning of that word. In such a case we have before us a judgment stating that something must be, and moreover, independently of whether it *is* in actuality or not. A norm establishes a certain standing relation among elements of a multiplicity, precisely as something obligatory.[15]

Finally, speaking of a judgment, we have in mind the following. A judgment can be examined *either* as a psychic act, and then it is a moment of a real process in all its given empirical complexity; or as a connection between two concepts (in the simplest case), i.e., conceivable contents, subject and predicate; this connection is denoted by the conditional term "is" (having no ontological significance), and is expressed in a "partial" logical coincidence of the two concepts. We say "partial", having in mind that complete coincidence of them would result in a single concept, and

[13] [from *Die Begriffe*]: **At the same time we conditionally accept that the singular is identical with the concrete-empirical, and the concrete-empirical, with the existing. This is in order to simplify the exposition.**

[14] **We limit ourselves with this observation to the definition of the category of obligation, having in mind that to develop it is possible only in a special investigation in connection with the concepts of value and end.**

[15] [from *Die Begriffe*]: **The norm, according to its general, formal sense, always constitutes an "ought", because in its content it deals with "can", "may", "must," "want", "have", and the like. At the same time, we must expressly emphasize that according to its genesis, even though the *consciousness of the ought* in some special cases shows a connection with the "will", as for example in legal practice, in connection with "another's will", still, the ought in the logical respect and in the normative view of this real connection, as also of every other, can and must be thought as distinct. The determinateness as real here turns out to be not at all a constitutive feature of the logical essence of the concept.**

would convert the judgment into an identity. This connection always remains, and cannot fail to be expressed in words. In using the term "judgment" we take it precisely in the second of its meanings[16] and consider it necessary to stipulate this especially because the Russian language still does not have a particular term for the logical concept of a "judgment" and a particular term for the psychological concept of "judgment".

Thus the thesis that "law is a norm" more fully developed reads: *law is a judgment* (i.e., a connection expressed in words between two conceivable contents, expressing their partial logical coincidence), *which establishes a certain order* (i.e., a certain stable relation among elements of a multiplicity), as *obligatory*. Or: law is a norm, a norm is a judgment. And from this must necessarily flow the possibility of examining law as a norm and as a judgment. For if the concept of a judgment is the genus, and the concept of a norm is the species, and all the marks of a generic concept according to the general rule are inherent in the specific concept, then in law there must be present all the marks of a norm; and if we consider that such a relation of species to genus lies between the concept of a norm and the concept of law, then it becomes clear that in law must be inherent also all the marks of a judgment. Thus, law can be examined as a norm and as a judgment.

Establishing this thesis, we must stipulate that a legal norm may consist not only of a single, but of several judgments, that it may be (and often happens to be) formulated in the form of an deduction, and that each judgment included in a legal norm may in its turn establish a connection not between two concepts merely, but among several. These concepts may be folded into one by means of subordination (e.g., the concept of the administrative office of the chancellery of the State Duma", Article 29. Establishment of the State Duma) or may stand in separation and form a complex subject of judgment (e.g., "guilty of ...; guilty of ...; guilty of ... is punished by ...". Article 73, Russian Criminal Code, 1903). Let us add further that we completely consciously omitted a demonstration or grounding of the second premise necessary for the conclusion just formulated, the premise asserting the actual presence in positive legal material of "norms-judgments" in our sense of this word. It is sufficient to refer to *all "written" law* in order to free oneself from a demonstration of this premise. All so-called dogmatic working-out of the law, consciously or half-consciously, takes law precisely as a norm and as a judgment, although in the vast majority of cases it also interweaves the examination of them with elements taken from other methodological orders. The latter circumstance forced us to dwell on these concepts with great attention, for only a strict methodological purity and restraint in the determination and

[16] i.e., as "a connection between two concepts (in the simplest case), i.e., conceivable contents, subject and predicate". – [PTG].

examination of the legal object can provide the possibility of a resolution of our fundamental question.[17]

The essence of the matter is that both indicated examinations (treating law as a norm and as a judgment) may be completely abstracted from any temporality and actuality whatever, i.e., move in an order alien to being and reality. This is possible *first* thanks to the fact that it is possible and interesting to subject a norm, as a rule concerning what is obligatory, to scientific analysis *in the formal regard* and *according to the "content" of the prescription*, independently of whether the norm is efficacious or not, i.e., whether it is applied or not applied, and if it is applied, then how, and to what does this lead. Such an analysis of a legal norm is being conducted and will be conducted, and its scientific value consists precisely in the fact that it is the *sole* path to the cognition of *norms as such*. We will see shortly that other methods of examination cannot be substituted for *this* method, for they pose for themselves other tasks, and moreover, these other tasks presuppose that *this* task has been resolved. *Second*, the abstraction of norms from time and actuality is possible also because a "*norm*" and "*consciousness of a norm*" are not one and the same. A norm can be examined according to content in such a way that it will be viewed not as the thought of someone, i.e., not as the thought of that or another definite person or definite group of people, but as a conceivable content of a normative character in general and in itself. Something is established as required; I can be interested in what is established and what is obligatory without asking in whose consciousness the conception of this obligation dwells, how it was formed there, how it influences his thought, feeling and actions, and so forth. This does not mean, of course, that this last group of questions is not important, not necessary, or presents no scientific interest. Not in the least; on the contrary. But this entire group of questions revolves in a completely different plane, in a plane foreign, heterogeneous to the formal order.

The same is also repeated in the examination of law as a judgment. If a *normative* investigation is interested in law as a *juridical norm*, i.e., its juridical character and the content of its prescriptions, then a *logical* investigation is interested in law as a *juridical judgment* and sets itself the task of a scientific clarification and systematic working-out of these juridical concepts (we called them above the conceivable contents of

[17] **We don't provide here a developed determination of the concept of a "*legal* norm" in its specific distinction from other types of norms because the center of gravity lies for us not in the question of *what kind* the legal norm is (the resolution of that question requires independent investigation, and we conditionally set it aside), but in whether law is a norm and merely a norm, or something else. [Continuation from *Die Begriffe*]: The investigation undertaken by us does not have the aim of providing for the concept of law [*Reichts*(?)] a complete, thus also objective, so to say "material" definition, but only the aim of preparing the way for such a definition through a methodological analysis of what defining the law can and must involve; as proposition, as norm, as individual experience, as social experience, and so forth. We cannot here indicate even the pattern of a proper definition of law; the solution of this problem requires a special investigation.**

a judgment, the subject and the predicate), which are connected in the judgment. But again, this analysis can be conducted in complete abstraction from the temporal sphere and temporal conditions. A judgment in its *logical make-up* and a judgment as *someone's thought*, i.e., as the content of the consciousness of a definite individual or definite group, or even an indefinite aggregation of people, are completely different things. I can be interested in the logical contents of a judgment and its concepts, while not being interested in the fact that it is *in actuality* being thought or, perhaps, that someone is not thinking, not inquiring *in which* consciousness it arose and lives, how it influences his thought and feelings, in which associative connections it stands in him, and so forth. These questions are important and valuable, but they revolve in the psychological plane, not in the logical.[18]

The possibility and the value of a *normative* examination of law in separation from the political, sociological, historical and psychological, and the possibility of a *logical* examination of judgment, in contrast to a psychological one, must receive, and in recent years have been gradually receiving recognition in various fields of scientific thought, in logic and in jurisprudence. This is undoubtedly the important fruit of a methodological deepening of knowledge which, so it seems to me, is interesting and valuable in many respects. An example is our problem of law and power.

Chapter IV

We can agree to combine the *normative* and the *logical* examination of law in the general term of *juridical* examination, by no means however counterposing this juridical examination to the moral, the aesthetic, etc. The term "juridical" in our *conditional* usage of it by no means presupposes a ready definition of the concept of law, as is evident from the entire course of our discussion; on the contrary, the method we designated by the term for the first time opens up the possibility of acquiring a narrow, but strictly logical and methodologically pure definition of the concept of law. To examine it as a *norm* and as a *judgment* is possible not only for law, but also for morality, and the logical, as such, and the aesthetic—in a word, all those spheres of cognition which have a normative character according to their object; and there this methodological order may be (also, of course, conditionally) characterized as specifically moral, logical, aesthetic, etc. In a word, when we characterize the normative and

18 [from *Die Begriffe*]: **We would wish to be understood here as saying that the methodological-systematic relation between the logical order and the normative order of a legal judgement is such that the former is logically a priori. In respect of methodology, the logical analysis of law as a proposition precedes the normative analysis. What is normative in the law cannot be understood and must not be investigated before the meaning, the intended objective content of the corresponding propositions is clarified. On the further methodological-systematic articulation of the legal judgment there is more below.**

logical examination of law as "juridical", this term has for us a "formal-methodological" significance, and not a "material-objective" one.

And thus if we recognize that the methodological isolation of this "juridical" order from the temporal orders is possible and valuable, treating *legal actuality* in one way or another, then we will see that within the concept of law (as a norm and a judgment) is revealed thereby the familiar aspect which does not tolerate approximation to the concept of power. For to conceive law as power means to conceive law as something real, while the juridical order is characterized in its methodological essence precisely by a complete and consistent abstraction from everything real, from any "ontology," as such. To abstract from the order of the real, in order imperceptibly or unconsciously to reintroduce concepts of the real, is obviously a bankrupt operation. Either a juridical study of the law is admissible, and then it must consistently maintain to the end its methodological determinateness, which we strove to establish above, or it must be rejected as such—in principle and generally; but then an unfillable conceptual cavity in the study of the law is formed.

Establishing this separation of "juridical" analysis from the psychological, the historical, and the political, since they move in the order of the real, we see ourselves as completely immune from rebuke for infusing into law any sort of new extra-temporal reality, and immune from rebuke for anti-historicism,[19] from granting to logic some sort of exclusive supremacy in political institutions (the objection of Deslandres to Laband[20]), from belief in real definition (the objection of Gierke to Laband[21]), and so forth. The normative and logical examination of law does not see in it anything real whatsoever; what is more, the very putting of the question whether law is real in these methodological orders makes no sense: here it neither *is* nor *is not*; to it cannot be ascribed either *being* or *non-being*, for the predicate "real" is dead for this order. Given this, the separation of law from the historical and the psychological and any other actuality is, like any other methodological device, a *conditional* operation, pursuing the greatest possible logical comprehension of the object studied, and the methodological purification of modes of investigation for the sake of the productivity of scientific cognition. The conclusions achieved through "juridical" analysis relative to legal norms, it goes without saying, will subsequently be referred back to the framework of the historical epoch and the temporal conditions, for the jurist will never forget the "artificial" and conditional isolation carried out

[19] [from *Die Begriffe*]: **Thus, for example, can Stoerks' objection to the method applied by Laband be understood: *Zur Methodik des öffentlichen Rechts.* See pp. 70-90.**

[20] [from *Die Begriffe*]: **Deslandres, M., *La crise de la science politique et le problème de la méthode.***

[21] [from *Die Begriffe*]: **Gierke, O. *Labands Staatsrecht und die deutsche Rechtswissenschaft.* In *Jahrbuch für Gesetzgebung, Verwaltung und Volkswirtschaft.* 1883.**

by him in the beginning. But precisely this *preliminary* and *subsequent* turning of cognitive thought to an awareness of the *unity of the object* and to an awareness of the necessary mutual belonging of separate aspects of it—at first to an "irrational" synthesis of the *untheorized* object, as to the given, and then to a "rationalistic" synthesis of the *theorized* object, as adjusted—secures the possibility of observing a strict methodological consistency and purity in the isolation and investigation of separate aspects of the object being *cognized.* A necessary correlate of methodological *pluralism* is a methodological *purity* in cognition, and an "adjusted" synthesis of the object cognized (in our case of "law" in the most general and broad sense of that word) will be naturally the more exhaustive and profound, and the more completely reflective of the endless complexity of the "irrationalistically" presented, "given" object, the more finely was the latter differentiated in the process of cognition, and the more consistently and strictly was that methodological differentiation carried out. It is as important *before* entering into a certain methodological order, and *upon exiting* from it, to remember that in essence the thing cognized is one and whole, as it is perhaps to forget about that unity and that wholeness while *within the boundaries* of that separate cognitive order, and this concerns especially those orders which are constructed according to the principle of "methodological indifferentism."

Thus, precisely in our case, all the disciplines moving within the "juridical" order, treat and must treat law in such an understanding as would exclude from its make-up the marks of the category of the real order and, in particular, the category of power. The concept of law and other juridical concepts must not be determined here through the mark of power; for the jurist in the narrow sense of that word, law is a norm and a judgment and is *not*, in any respect at all, power. Law as a norm and a judgment, and law as power, are concepts lying in methodologically-indifferent orders. For that reason all these constructions of legal concepts which immediately, or in a masked and subtle form, introduce into juridical determinations the moment of power, merge two methodologically-indifferent orders and either must be recognized as not juridical (in the narrow sense), or must be critically re-examined.

And this concerns above all the fundamental *juridical* definition of the very concept of law. The general theory of law can and must, in that part where it examines this definition, take account of and subject to analysis all separate aspects of law. But its first and primary obligation is to give a purely "juridical" definition of law as a norm and a judgment with certain specific marks. This is absolutely necessary because in the *logical* order juridical (in the narrow sense) definitions precede other examinations and determinations. For all remaining modes of examination, and consequently, for all remaining methodological orders, juridical definitions are the necessary presuppositions without which they cannot take the first step. This is clear already for the two fundamental real orders of legal theory—the psychological and the sociological.

Thus, above all in the psychological conception of law there is nothing other than legal experience, or the experience of law. This is law introduced into a temporal stream of individual consciousnesses, or a series of individual consciousnesses as one of their contents; precisely in such a real meaning does the psychologist analyze law. But the concept of "the experience of a legal norm" or a "legal empowerment" (correspondingly, "obligation") presupposes that a legal norm and a legal empowerment have already been defined somewhere; otherwise, the psychologist would have no definite schema for the delimitation of his object. The "jurist" must provide this definition to the psychologist, if the psychologist does not wish to wander in the darkness and dissolve his object in a broad and indefinite atmosphere of accidental insights. Thus the psychological examination of law presupposes a ready juridical definition, and rests upon it.[22]

The situation of sociological legal theory is exactly the same. If the sociologist examines, describes, and explains the process of the interaction of human psyches,[23] then the sociologist-legal theorist will be concerned with law in two respects: 1. Law turns out for him to be a *phenomenon* in the sense that it, being an individual experience, determines the relations of the experiencing individual to other members of the community; in this case the sociologist has the same understanding of law as the psychologist, but in a different aspect—he is interested in the experience of law and its influence not on the inner world of the experiencing individual, but in the relation of the individual to those around him, and the relation of those to him. In this case the methodological correlation of the sociological and the juridical orders is determined by analogy with a psychological examination: the concept of the individual experience of law; and in this respect it presupposes a ready juridical definition of law. 2. Law in the sociological order turns out further to be a *legal phenomenon* in a narrower and definite meaning. Law in this understanding is a legal norm, introduced *through its application* into the factual makeup of social relations, as the *schema* of these relations. Law at the moment of its application acquires a new significance, a factual one: if in the juridical order law was a norm, then in the sociological order, after application, it acquires the significance of one of the elements in the real makeup of social relations.[24] It is again here an experience, but is experienced by

22 From this viewpoint the circumstance turns out to be extremely interesting that the most subtle, original and consistent of the psychologist-legal theorists, Prof. Petrazhitskii, in establishing his definition of law, analyzes law not only as an experience, but also as a norm, revealing the imperative-attributive character in the very logical essence of the legal norm. See *Теория права и государства* [Theory of Law and State], vol. 1, pp. 56-59. In the methodological respect this is hardly consistent, but it witnesses to the importance and inevitability of the "juridical" path.

23 Here I abstract from the problem of the delimitation of sociology from collective psychology; this question is by no means decided, and perhaps not even clearly posed in the literature, and requires specific independent investigation.

24 The "application" of the law is sometimes called a *logical deduction* from a certain

an indefinite aggregation of psyches, experienced not only as a norm, but also as a schema actually being realized, and as deduced from a norm in application to the concrete case of a structure of empowerments and obligations, ordinarily with an awareness of a definite sanction (in the form of prospective real consequences for deviation) and so forth. In one word, *a legal phenomenon* for a sociologist is the relation of people *after* the application to them of a *norm of law* and *throughout the period of its real* "efficacy." It is obvious that the concept of a legal norm or (in the particular case) *the content of a given* legal norm, and consequently its *formal significance* as such, as well as the *concepts* used in it – all this is presupposed here as being known, ready, necessary (for the *delimitation of the object* of a sociological theory of law)[25] and established somewhere else, in another place. Thus, sociological jurisprudence also presupposes a ready juridical definition and rests upon it.[26]

Finally the political examination of law, moving according to its essence in the real order, also presupposes the prior accomplishment of a juridical analysis. The political point of view places law in a teleological chain, i.e., in an order of ends and means.[27] In this order every link except the highest and the lowest (the "ultimate" end and the "initial" point) has a double significance: for each higher link it is a means, for each lower link, it is an end. The supreme link—the ultimate end—is grounded in its content transcendentally (a deduction from the system of values); all remaining links are grounded through an empirical causal connection (inductively verified or hypothetically constructed), asserted in the order of temporal succession among all lower links and the next

legal norm applicable to a certain case concretely given or abstractly indicated (a case-book). Understood as a psychological process in the mind of the judge, this operation enters as a constituent aspect into that understanding of application which we have in mind here; by itself it cannot and must not be called "the application of the law", but at the very most "an analysis of the applicability of a legal norm".

25 [from *Die Begriffe*]: **The thought that a norm can serve for the delimitation of an object to be comprehended—to be specific, the actuality governed by it--we find (though in a somewhat different meaning and application) in the brilliant essay by Max Weber, "R. Stammlers Überwindung der materialistischen Geschichtsauffassung." *Archiv für Sozialwissenschaft und Sozialpolitik*. Vol. XXIV, pp. 134-136.**

26 **This relates also to *historical* jurisprudence, insofar as it has to do with an object near to the sociological; it puts in the foreground a schema of temporality in real processes of legal "functioning", not immersing itself usually (because of the objective impossibility) in the psychic bases of "legal relations", limiting itself to description and to a comparatively superficial explanation of the *external* results of an internal psychic process, does not raise itself to broad generalizations, withdrawing more into the concrete empirically-singular, etc. In a word, to the extent it deals with legal phenomena (I abstract in the present moment from the "historical" comparison of the results of "juridical" examination, obtained from the working out of various aggregates of legal norms, taken from various epochs—this order remains essentially juridical and non-real); to that extent it presupposes ready "juridical" definitions.**

27 **From the entire doctrine of telos, I give here only those definitions which are necessary for the confirmation of the fundamental thesis of the work; the examination of the rest I conditionally postpone.**

higher one (correspondingly, with the still higher ones). In this way the *entire* teleological (political) order is conceived in the schema of the temporal, is conceived as real. Whether "law" here is *merely* a end or simultaneously both end and means—it is conceived as something subject to realization, realized or being realized: it will be *law as a phenomenon* or a *legal phenomenon*. Both one and the other concept presuppose that the principle of the selection of the "lawful" over the "unlawful" has been established, presuppose that law has been defined as a norm and as a concept. Thus the political examination of law also presupposes the prior accomplishment of a juridical analysis.

But if a juridical definition and examination of law is the logical prius of the psychological, the sociological, the historical and the political definition and examination, then the translation from the first order to the remaining orders can also be characterized, from our point of view, as the *ascription to law of the meaning of power*. Precisely in the remaining methods of examination indicated, law is made a member of the real order. It acquires the significance of a psychic- or socio-real moment, standing in *real interaction* with other moments of that same order. Thus *consciousness of a legal norm* may determine and does determine in the mind of the individual other contents of his consciousness; it may arouse in him certain new feelings, desires, thoughts, or support and modify the older ones. Law as the consciousness (or more broadly—experience) of a legal norm is here capable of being a causally-determined moment in the sphere of the psychic: it is "*power*".

In precisely the same way the application of law, as the introduction of it into the real processes of the social, makes it a factor determining the *reality* of the social. Law, as they say, is here a "*social power*".

Chapter V

In this way there is obtained an answer to the question posed by us of the coincidence and non-coincidence of law and power. We were always interested not so much in what is common and similar in these conceptions as we were in the methodological possibility and necessity of distinguishing them in the theory of law. It is possible to examine from a certain point of view *both* law *and* power as *reality*; from another point of view it is possible to examine *both* law *and* power as *value* (law as a value of the moral-practical order, power as a category of constitutive knowing, i.e., as a "value" of the theoretical order); from the third point of view *both* law *and* power can be examined as *abstract concepts*. But it is not what is "*common*" to law and power that interested and interests us. We are striving to explain not so much cases of the co-subordinated positioning of these concepts, when both of them alike are subordinated to some third concept standing *over* them; but cases of their immediate, so to say, logical contact, when all the marks of one of them are intrinsic to the other (the relation of genus to species), and when the marks of both one and the other concept are merged in a certain new conception, which doesn't have for them the significance of a generic concept, but uniting within itself in an inadmissible way categories taken from various planes, representing a conceptual formation subject to analytical decomposition.

And in this direction we succeeded in clarifying the following.

Law can be regarded as power, but it can also be conceived in such a way as does not admit of being approximated to power. All the marks of power are inherent in law in a "*real*" theory of law, i.e., in the psychological, sociological, historical and political orders of examination; not a single one of the marks of power is inherent in law in a "*juridical*" theory of law, i.e., in a normative and logical order. In other words, insofar as law is regarded as having been introduced into the order of the real, to that extent its being approximated to the concept of power is admissible; here power is the generic concept, while law is a specific one. To the extent that law is separated methodologically from reality in its various forms and understandings, to that extent such an approximation is inadmissible, since law and power lie in mutually indifferent methodological orders.

From this it is clear that those definitions of law and other concepts of jurisprudence which include in themselves openly or tacitly an aspect of power in one or another of its conceptions, must be recognized as *not* juridical in the narrow and strict sense of the meaning of this word, or must be corrected--so to say, methodologically cleansed and freed from this aspect. Given this, from our point of view one must never reject the possibility and necessity of such non-juridical definitions; but it is appropriate to argue tirelessly that in general, and for those definitions themselves, it is necessary first to establish a juridical definition.

Thus so long as, e.g., Gumplowicz[28] approximates law to power historically and genetically, one can object to it only within the boundaries of history and sociology, i.e., setting out from an analysis of the factual material of legal phenomena, but not from the methodological point of view. But, at the same time, from the methodological point of view one must never fail to recognize that the juridical essence of the concept of law remains completely untouched by Gumplowicz's sociological and historical investigations into the genesis of law from power. A juridically understood science of State law is occupied not with the investigation of factual social relations, similarly to Gumplowicz,[29] but with an analysis of the norms of State law.

Or Ihering's thesis, declaring that law is "a concept of power" (*Kraftbegriff, Machtbegriff*), and not a "logical concept"[30] from our point of view must be divided into two parts for evaluation: into a first

[28] **Gumplowicz, L. *Allgemeines Staatsrecht*, p. 388 among others. *Die sociologische Staatsidee*, pp. 108-111.**

[29] **Gumplowicz, L., *Allgemeines Staatsrecht*, pp. 377, 438-439. *Die sociologische Staatsidee*, p. 40.**

[30] **R. v. Ihering, *Der Kampf um's Recht*, pp. 9, 11.**

asserting that law is "a concept of power", and into a second asserting that law is *not* "a logical concept". Leaving aside the formulation of the thesis, which is unsuccessful from a logical point of view (logic knows no counterposition of "concepts of power" to "logical concepts"), we must recognize that the first part of it contains nothing inadmissible, for law can in certain orders be regarded as power; the second part of the thesis turns out to be unacceptable, because the meaning of law as real is fully compatible methodologically with its logical examination. The latter must not and cannot be rejected just because in the sociological order law turns out to be power, and Ihering himself in one of his best early works came out as an advocate of this consideration (although in a methodologically inconsistent way[31]). And when in his very latest work that same Ihering speaks of two paths by which a legal norm becomes power, while power becomes a legal norm,[32] then he is moving at all times in the real sociological order, and in his treatment of a "norm, which became power," is opposed not by a "norm, methodologically indifferent to the concept of power". but by a "powerless norm", i.e., the *consciousness* of a norm *incapable* of becoming a "compulsorily" determining factor of the social.

Or when Merkel speaks of the fact that law in an objective sense is a social factor,[33] we see in this a methodological confusion: a prescription of law is, as we just said, a social factor, as is the consciousness of a norm, or still more, due to its application; in just such an understanding does it become "power" but precisely in this understanding it is *no longer* law in an objective sense, for law in an objective sense is an aggregate of *norms* as such, and not the normative contents of consciousness, and not an actual schema of real relations.

From all this it is also clear that in a "*juridical*" definition of law a whole series of features containing aspects of power in a *hidden* form do not fit.

Thus the definition of law as an "expression of will"[34] ("expression" taken in the real sense)[35] will be related, from our viewpoint, not to the juridical, but to the psychological order. For it introduces law into the real order, as a result of examining its psychological genesis and establishing between it and the will a real connection of origin. This provides the possibility of regarding law itself as a causally-determining power.

31 **R. v. Ihering, *Geist der römischen Recht*, Part I, pp. 25-32.**

32 **R. v. Ihering, *Der Zweck im Recht*, vol. I, pp. 248-249.**

33 **A. Merkel, *Gesammelte Abhandlungen*, II, I, *Recht und Macht*, pp. 403-404. *Juristische Encyklopädie*, p. 7, § 42.**

34 **A. Merkel, *Juristische Encyklopädie*, p. 22, § 42. [from *Die Begriffe*]: Also Thon: *Rechtsnorm und subjektives Recht*. pp. 1-4, and Bierling, E.: *Juristische Prinzipienlehre*, vol. I, pp. 19 and 29. See note 13 above in Section 3 of this essay.**

35 The parenthetical material was added at this point in *Die Begriffe*. – [PTG].

Thus, the definition of law as "the expression of an interest" will also not be included in the juridical order from this point of view, for it also introduces a causal consideration into logical analysis and in this way ascribes to law itself the real meaning of power, for law born from psychic "power", naturally, is itself power.

It is just as incorrect from the methodological point of view to introduce into a juridical definition of law the mark of "compulsion", unless what is meant is simply the unchanging presence of a sanctioning norm (then there arises an objection of an inductive character). The question of whether any "legal norm" as such brings about the manifestation and action of a socially-compulsory apparatus, or *not*, is a question which can be decided only by a description and typing of the real process—of the individual or social experience of law. Compulsion in this sense is a moment of the real embodiment, the real action of law; it presupposes that law itself crossed over into the condition of reality, that it acts in reality, that it is power.

A more subtle aspect of the approximating of orders is the introduction of the mark of a threat or of a social sanction. In this case there is established that typical fact supposedly needed for the consciousness of any legal norm, that this consciousness is always accompanied by a conception of the possibility or even the inevitability of psychic or physical pressure on the individual on the part of more or less definite social strata. Even if we recognize that law actually is always *experienced psychically* as an aspect of power, the jurist takes law precisely *not* as an experience, but as a norm, and does not draw in to the analysis of a norm all the complexes of associations that accompany law.

In precisely the same way the understanding of the *obligatoriness* of the legal norm as *power* does not have a juridical character. If the obligatoriness of a norm is defined as its action upon the human will, then this definition introduces the legal norm into the psychological order, for what acts on the will is *not a norm*, but the *representation of a norm*, the experience of a norm. Of course, from the *psychological* point of view the degree of obligatoriness of a norm is measured by that intensity with which the representation of it acts upon the will. But *juridically* a norm also preserves its obligatoriness where, perhaps, for an expanse of a hundred versts,[36] there is not one human being who would have a representation of it.

It is also troubling to speak in the juridical order of the "ethical" power of law. This question is important to a high degree from the viewpoint of a psychologist, a sociologist, a politician, and a moralist, but a juridical examination would strive for the clearest possible faceted delimitation of the concept of a legal *norm* from the concept of a moral *norm*, recognizing

[36] A measure of distance in the older Russian system, equal to very slightly more than a kilometer. – [PTG].

that insofar as a juridical examination touches morality, the latter is treated by it not as a psychic power, but as a moral norm.

From this it follows further that the concept of "efficacious law" will have for the jurist not that same meaning as for the jurist-psychologist, sociologist and in part the politician. The latter recognize law as efficacious only if it has entered the consciousness of people or passed through a process of application. For them is important not the juridical obligatoriness of the law, i.e., not the formal moment of authoritative sanctioning and publication, as for the jurist, but the passage of the law from a "moribund" state, as they say, to a "living" state: in the eyes of the psychologist and the sociologist that law is "efficacious" which has become a "power". The jurist does not require this moment of realization.

The methodologically incorrect approximating of orders [*рядов*, *von Reihen*] that we have in mind here is also facilitated by the introduction between law and power of certain neutral and in appearance completely innocent terms as, e.g., "order" [*порядок, Ordnung*].[37] We indicated above that the concept of an order [*порядка*] is a methodologically two-faced concept. An order may signify, on one hand, that structure of relations which is established by norms as obligatory; or on the other hand, that structure of relations which is observed as empirically-actual. In the first case order is a juridical term; in the second case it is a term of the real order. In employing the term "legal order" [*правопорядок*] researchers usually do not indicate in which sense they are using it; a bridge is formed across which one may always easily pass from one order [*ряд*] to the other. Therefore, those definitions of law that characterize it as an order [*порядок*], must be reexamined from the juridical point of view. Thus, Regelsberger[38] and Kohler[39] define law as a legal order; Gareis defines law as an order of the world; Roussel as an order of equilibrium, and so forth.

To such terms are also related the concepts of a "legal attribute" and a "legal relation". In the broadest and most indefinite sense one can call

[37] Up to this point in the Russian version of the essay, the term being translated as "order" has consistently been "*ряд*" (although in his German translation, Il'in early on dropped the equivalent term *Reihe* in favor of *Ordnung*). Current dictionaries in both languages provide only "linear" synonyms for *ряд* and *Reihe*: row, line, rank, file, series, etc. However, nineteenth century dictionaries contained another meaning in both languages: the Russian dictionary Dal' added 'строй' (structure), and the *Deutsches Wörterbuch* of the Brothers Grimm contained the (Latin) term "ordo" (order), as additional meanings. Only a non-linear concept such as "order" or "ordering" would work as a translation, because Il'in defines an "order" (*ряд*, *Ordnung*) as "a certain standing relation among elements of a multiplicity". In this paragraph Il'in introduces a second Russian term for "order", *порядок*, paralleling "*Ordnung*" in the German. From this paragraph on, *ряд* and *порядок* are used fairly interchangeably for "order" (as in the German translation, *Reihe* and *Ordnung* were used interchangeably from much earlier in the essay). – [PTG].

[38] [from *Die* Begriffe]: **Regelsberger, F., *Pandekten*, vol. I, p. 58.**

[39] [from *Die* Begriffe]: **Kohler, J., *Einführung in die Rechtswissenschaft*, pp. 1-3. *Lehrbuch des Bürgerlichen Rechts*, pp. 8-28.**

everything that in one or another sense and understanding is ascribed to something else an "attribute"; and precisely this broad meaning of the term, justifying its use in logical examination, turns out to be one of the paths leading to an approximation and confusion of methodological orders. For in the narrowest, most strict and definite meaning of "property", one can call only that which is ascribed to (or correspondingly, is inherent in, or belongs to) something else *in the order of the real*; in particular this must be a real potential or *power* of a thing. For this reason, in examining law in the juridical order, we must speak of the *marks* of law; in examining it in one of the real orders, we will speak of its *properties*. Thus "compulsion" in the sense indicated above may be a *mark* of law and a *property* of law, depending on whether the jurist or the sociologist is speaking. We will see how the concept of a property is decomposed methodologically into another combination.

In just the same way the concept of a "legal relation" has various methodological tendencies. One can speak of "relation" in natural science, and in jurisprudence, and in logic in the broadest and most common meaning of the term. But from the point of view of juridical methodology it is in the highest degree important, in speaking of a "relation", to clarify whether is intended a concrete, singular relation, which is conceived as "real" (we abstract here conditionally from the critical point of view, according to which a relation is always a category) or the common generic *concept of a relation*. It is essential, further, to clarify to which order this "relation" belongs, to the order of actuality, inductively ascertained, or to the normative order, the obligatory, the prescribed. Then in a logical examination a relation will always be a concept, methodologically indifferent for a real examination; in a normative examination it will acquire the significance of a formula of the obligatory; in real orders it will be conceived as a real, concrete, singular relation, or as a concept providing a pattern, an abstract schema of what is brought about *in reality*. And only in the real orders is a "relation" not indifferent for the category of power. We can refer to all of this only in passing; a systematic working-out of these distinctions would inevitably require their application to the material of jurisprudence.

From among other conclusions we dwell for now only on the concept of "explanation" in jurisprudence and on the idea of a "dogma of law".

Often the establishment of this or that *juridical construction* is designated by the term "explanation"; the same term is also used to denote the establishment of these or those *connections among the phenomena of life under law*. This lack of *terminological* distinction is an indicator of much more substantive *logical* confusions. Namely, it is always necessary to have in mind that a "juridical" construction, in the strict and definite meaning of this word, sets out from an analysis of legal norms as judgments, and not from the analysis of legal phenomena; therefore, moving in an order alien to reality, it *does not provide* and *cannot* provide anything whatever for the cognition of what is real; a juridical construction, if we only wish to be methodologically clear and consistent, does not strive and must not strive for an "explanation" of legal phenomena: its task is "interpretation" (i.e., the logical analysis and systematic reworking of legal norms as norms and as judgements), and a juridical concept, constructed in such a fashion, *explains nothing* in real social life, for it is taken as an abstraction from judgments formulating *not the existing*, but *the obligatory*. And the content of norms may diverge quite sharply from the characteristics of social phenomena "embodying" these norms. Thus, it would be appropriate to relate the term "explanation" exclusively to the real orders; there "to explain" means to place the concrete thing being studied under the abstract thing that has already been cognized, the unknown real under the known abstracted from the real; or to establish a genetic connection between two concrete moments of the real order. The task of juridical examination should be formulated not as "explanation", but as "logical interpretation". Given such a delimitation, it is revealed with particular clarity that for the categories of power there is a place only in the "explanatory" orders, but not at all in the "interpretive" ones.

Finally, from all that has been said, it follows self-evidently that the idea and the task of a "dogma of law" acquires a new formulation from the standpoint occupied by us. Historically, a dogma, as a particular means for the examination of law, grew up under the influence of practical needs; it was an aggregate of methods facilitating the jurist-practitioner in applying the law, a matter of an orientation within the material of the legal norms being applied. The spirit of roman dogma, composed in the formula, do not "study in order to know", but "study in order to apply", shifted the center of gravity from the theoretical aspect of the working out of legal norms to the practical, and in this form its influence has been preserved to the present day, and still hinders jurisprudence from becoming an independent science, i.e., a *theory* in all the significance of that word. From our point of view, such a thesis of the dogma must be replaced by another, purely theoretical. Similar to the way in which the history of natural science knows a gradual emancipation of theory from the guiding and determining influence of practice, so also in jurisprudence it is long since time to recognize that the practical needs of the court and of political life can serve at the most as a stimulus, a reason, for awakening an independent theoretical interest in legal norms and their content. In the idea of "jurisprudence", theory must be differentiated from practice, and in essence this will be expressed in a recognition of the permissibility of the inclusion into "juridical" concepts and constructions, of marks obtained from the analysis of legal norms independently of whether these marks have found practical application and actual realization or not, or, perhaps, this realization is no longer found as a result of historical development. From this viewpoint the dogmatic development of the norms of the French constitution of 1793, which failed to find application, is just as interesting and essential in regard to science, as the juridical analysis of the norms of "obsolete" Roman law or the development of a new Russian criminal code in the period between its confirmation and its "being put into effect".

But this "practical" spirit of ancient and contemporary dogmatics has other, far deeper and more dangerous consequences, since it leads to the approximating of essentially different methodological orders. Namely, in the process of application, a legal norm usually passes through an interpretation, i.e., through a series of operations called for by the lack of correspondence, or less than full correspondence between the marks of the relation *in abstracto*, providentially indicated in the legal norm, and the essential properties of the "concrete" relation having received its legal form from the interpreted norm. These operations must elucidate the inner meaning of the norm so as to link the abstract pattern given in it with the concrete relation, and through this accommodation create the possibility of an infusion into the concrete relation of that aspect and those consequences which are indicated in the norm. As a result of the interpretation, the legal norm, as they say, "approximates to actual life" and, as it were, absorbs into itself certain properties of actuality; the interpreted norm forms that middle order between the "norm" and "actuality", which leads many jurists into temptation, giving them a ground to see in it a generalization of everyday facts, as though it were a positive sociological law_z. Abstracting from a whole series of weighty objections, which the sociologist with his point of view must bring against such an understanding, we point out that for the jurist the inclination of dogmatics not to distinguish the analysis of a norm from the analysis of an interpreted norm is unacceptable, and especially to forget about the normative significance of any legal norm, as such. Here it is essential to carry out consistently those methodological lines of which we spoke above, if only we wish to avoid such complex and continuous mental formations which in contemporary jurisprudence constitute the concept of a "legal institution". Thus, for example, under the "institution of property" one may intend: 1. an aggregate of generic and specific *concepts* of property *abstracted from the norms* of a certain code; 2. an aggregate of the same *concepts* abstracted from *interpreted norms* of that same code;[40] 3. an aggregate of *norms* regulating relations of property;[41] 4. an aggregate of those *same norms*, of the same code,

[40] **We do not provide with this a developed systematic analysis of the concept of "interpretation" and an explication of those technical difficulties which are connected with the attraction to the dogma of the interpreted make-up of the legal norm.**

[41] [from *Die Begriffe*]: **Thus *Windsheid*: The institution of the law is "the aggregate of *legal prescriptions* relating to a *legal relation*." *Lehrbuch des Pandektenrechts*, p. 140. Also *Puchta*: "The *legal propositions* which form the Law of a people are collected in certain masses according to the *relations* which define them; such masses of legal propositions are called legal institutions. Law consists of legal institutions, and these, once again, consist of legal propositions." *Kursus der Institutionen*, vol. I, *Geschichte*, p. 8. Similarly, *Gierke*: "An embodiment of *legal propositions*, which corresponds to a determinate *living relation*, is a legal institution." *Deutsches Privatrecht*, vol. I, p. 124. And *Erxleben*: A legal institution is an "embodiment of *legal propositions* related to a determinate *living relation*." *Einleitung in das römische Privatrecht*. p. 1. From this we can provisionally foresee that Windsheid speaks of "legal prescriptions" and "legal relations," while the others speak of "legal propositions" and "living relations." As opposed to these determinations, *Dernburg* (*Pandekten*, p. 91) distinguishes between norm and legal institution, and *Brinz* (*Lehrbuch der Pandekten*, p. 4), between legal statute and legal institution.**

but having passed through the process of interpretation; 5. an aggregate of *concepts*, abstracted *from real social processes* and states, referred to as "relations of property";[42] 6. an aggregate of these *concrete* social *relations*, referred to as "relations of property."[43] It would be interesting in the highest degree to discover how in various writers all or some of these meanings of a "legal institution" are spliced together.[44] And indeed for our basic problem of the interrelation of law and power there is given here a series of the most substantial indications. The first four meanings of a "legal institution" lie in an order alien to reality and, consequently, to the categories of power; the last two lie in the real order. The dogmatist, forgetting about this distinction, joins together separate orders of jurisprudence and insensibly introduces the categories of power there where there is no place for them. As opposite to that, the dogmatist who maintains these delimitations, obtains the possibility of creating an independent "jurisprudential" theory, of approaching the law from that logical side of it which Ihering,[45] Laband,[46] and Muromtsev[47] felt with such power and formulated in various directions and understandings.

Thus does the resolution of our basic problem take shape within the limits of objective law.

[42] [from *Die Begriffe*]: **Thus *Savigny*: "in fact...every legal relation...stands under a corresponding legal institution as its type." At the same time Savigny speaks of the "living connection of the constituent parts of the legal institution" and of its "progressing development." *The System of Contemporary Roman Law*, p. 9. Unfortunately the logical presuppositions of these statements were not laid out here. Similarly also *Regelsberger*: "Legal institutions are the legally ordered basic forms within which communal life moves." They were abstracted from "legal relations as phenomena" and form, as it were, "typical abstract legal relations." *Pandekten*, p. 73.**

[43] [from *Die Begriffe*]: **Thus, from *Dernburg*: "Legal institutions are legally regulated arrangements of civil society." *Pandekten*, p. 91. It is interesting to note in this connection that, for example, *Theodor Kipp*, the publisher of Windsheid's *Lehrbuch* [*des Pandektenrechts*, observing that] The definitions of a legal institution which belong to *Windsheid, Dernburg, Regelsberger* and *Gierke* hang together, adds: "Also, the differences here are probably not great." See Windsheid, *Lehrbuch*, § 37, note 2, p. 140. So also is very much from Jhering fused together: "Individual *legal relations*...group together...toward greater systematic unities—to legal institutions." *Geist des römischen Rechts*, Part I, p. 36. "Legal propositions come together to a certain extent in a higher state of aggregation and form elements and qualities of legal institutions." *Ibid.*, p. 37. At the same time one must keep in mind that for Ihering "legal propositions" and "legal norms" do not coincide. And therefore it is completely incomprehensible when he speaks in another work of the "historical development of the individual institute" and immediately again speaks of "institutes lying systematically far from one another." *Entwicklungsgeschichte des römischen Rechts*, pp. 10, 11.**

[44] **See, e.g., in Ihering, *Geist des römischen Rechts*, Part I, pp. 25-27, 30-31, 34-35.**

[45] **Ihering, *ibid.*, pp.25-32.**

[46] **Laband, P., *Das Staatsrecht des deutschen Reiches*, vol. I, pp. *vii-x*.**

[47] **S. Muromtsev, *Что такое догма права?*** [What is a Dogma of Law?]. **German translation: *Was heist Rechts-Dogmatik?* Prague, 1885.**

Chapter VI

It remains for us to touch on the question of the possibility and admissibility of approximating the concept of power to the concept of law *in the subjective sense*. However we define the concept of law in the subjective sense, whatever we see as its essence, we will always have to recognize that law in the subjective sense presupposes law in the objective sense, and moreover, in a twofold relation. First in the order of juridical grounding, second, in the order of logical determination. Whether we dwell on the aspect of empowerment [*полномочия*][48] or on the aspect of duty, we always recognize that both empowerment [*полномочие*] and duty acquire and only can acquire a *legal* character exclusively by virtue of a certain connection with legal norms. Thus, empowerment [*полномочие*] is *legal* empowerment [*полномочие*], or law, only because it is established, recognized, etc., in the *content* of legal norms. Law in the subjective sense obtains its significance, as such, through law in the objective sense; that is why in the logical order as well, the mark of being established, of being deducible from the content of legal norms, is a necessary part of the concept of law in the subjective sense. But if this concept is one of those which are defined and constructed through the analysis of the content of legal norms, then everything that we established in a methodological respect for all juridical concepts belongs to it; we could directly refer to this and consider the matter closed. However, certain particularities of this concept have aroused historically, and frequently arouse also in the present, a series of specific difficulties which must be examined.

Under law in the subjective sense from the juridical point of view we mean *an empowerment* [полномочие], *established in the content of a legal norm*. In a broader sense also any duty, established in the content of legal norms, may be brought in here as a correlate, although *terminologically* the idea of duty is not covered by the conception of law in the subjective sense. Given this, an empowerment [*полномочием*] from our point of view will be called any *permission* or *conferral* contained in a norm, whereas duty is obligation established through norms *and defined according to the subject*, whether it is positive or negative in meaning. Both a permission and an obligation, defined according to the subject, must be expressed in a judgment and fixed in words, while this judgment may be contained in the text of the legal norm itself, or deduced from such a text within the logical order. This opens up the possibility of constructing for law in the subjective sense essentially that same schema of methodological orders

[48] *Полномочие* (authority, power, plenary powers) is being translated here as "empowerment", as indicated above, in order to distinguish it from two other terms used here which *also* mean power: *сила* and *власть*. *Сила* is the most general term for "power" employed by Il'in (see also note 1 above). *Власть* is an inherently ambiguous term in the Russian language, meaning here both "ruling power" and "ruling authority". (Il'in uses it in both senses). Thus, Il'in is dealing throughout this section with three terms potentially translatable as "power", two of which can also mean "authority". To minimize the inevitable confusion, we have frequently inserted the appropriate Russian terms in the text. [PTG].

that we constructed above for law in the objective sense. Thus, in the logical order law in the subjective sense will be regarded as a concept and a judgment; in the normative order, as empowerment and obligation; in the psychological order, as the individual experience of empowerment and obligation; in the sociological, as the experience of empowerment and obligation introduced into the order of psychic interactions, etc. And conclusions applicable to the question of power [*силе*] will be analogous: law in the subjective sense may be regarded as power [*сила*], i.e., as the capacity (as an aspect of the rèal order) to causally determine other aspects of that same order; and conversely, it may be examined in abstraction from the real order and the categories of power [*силы*]. A consistent delimitation of the orders of the real and the non-real is also here a necessary condition for avoiding misunderstanding.

Therefore, those definitions of law in the subjective sense which include the category of power [*силы*] in one form or another, explicitly or implicitly, cannot be recognized as juridical in the narrow sense of the word. In exactly the same way those definitions of other concepts in jurisprudence, which merge the properties of law in the subjective sense, taken from the real orders, with marks of it taken from the non-real orders, require reconsideration, and cannot be recognized as consistent in a methodological respect.

Here we need first of all to mention those cases where law in the subjective sense is defined through the concept of *ruling power* [*власти*],[49] and is recognized as a species concept, subordinate to the latter.[50] In the concept of ruling power [*власти*] is concealed an undoubted methodological duality. Under ruling power [*властью*] in jurisprudence is conceived something concerned with, on the one hand, legal empowerment [*полномочию*], and on the other, power [*силе*]. Of course, ruling power [*власть*] may also not have a legal sanction, but precisely to that extent it will not be a category of jurisprudence. Ruling authority [*власть*] is power [*сила*] sanctioned by law; it is as it were objectified and hardened legal power [*сила*] *par excellence*. And it is precisely the boundary position of the concept of ruling authority/power [*власти*] that makes it a member of two different methodological orders: the juridical and the real. Therefore from the point of view that we are attempting to advance, the concept of ruling power [*власти*] must be broken down into two component parts and each part must be ascribed to a corresponding order: then the jurist will speak of ruling power [*власти*] in the normative order as of *the authority to rule*, and from the logical viewpoint will study this authority to rule as a judgment, and as a concept derived from a judgment or judgments; while the psychologist, the sociologist, and the political scientist will understand by ruling power

49 *Власть*, power or authority, especially in the sense of ruling power or authority. – [PTG].

50 I.e., where 'law' is a species-concept subordinate to 'power' as a genus-concept. – [PTG].

[*властью*] *a power* [*силу*] *sanctioned by legal norms*. That is why, for example, those definitions of the *State* which ascribe to it not the authority to rule, but *ruling power* [*власть*], and also those definitions of the concept of *sovereignty* which construe it as a real property, or as something divisible, or as a certain form of *ruling power* [*власти*], must be critically reexamined in a methodological respect, for they introduce into the non-real order the real category of power [*силы*].

From this it is clear, further, with what care it is necessary to employ the term "*property*" in application to law in the subjective sense. Similar to the way in which ruling power [*власть*] in the juridical order is not a "property" of the State, but an empowerment [*полномочие*], similarly, in the same order, "law" is not a "property" of the subject; the legal status of a person consists from the juridical point of view in an aggregate of permissions, conferrals (of obligations and prohibitions), derived from legal norms "as applied to"[51] a specially given combination of generic properties, causally encountered by the jurist. *Properties* of the person must be (concretely or abstractly) given to the jurist for this deduction, in order for the jurist to deduce the person's *legal empowerment*; these legal empowerments in the juridical order must not be regarded as properties. *Consciousness of an empowerment* may, of course, be regarded as a property, though not of a *person* in the juridical sense, but rather of a *human being*.

In just the same way, the definition of law in the subjective sense as a "*defended interest*" or as a "*supremacy of the will*" conferred by means of legal norms is unacceptable for the jurist. Both the one and the other definition introduce law into the psychological order, for a "defended" interest does not cease to be an interest, i.e., the *experience* of a human being, and "supremacy of the will", although also granted through legal norms, remains a *phenomenon* of the inner world of a human being (of course, accompanied by external manifestations). In the one and in the other definition the object studied is taken in a methodologically non-partitioned form. From our point of view aspects of "the defended" and "the conferred" will interest the *jurist*, whereas aspects of interest and will, in the measure of their recognition through law, will interest the psychologist-legal theorist.

It is further clear that the use of the categories of "*possibility*" and of "*freedom*" in defining the concept of subjective law must be accompanied by a certain prescribed methodological caution, with clarifications and reservations. Indeed if empowerment is regarded as a particular form of "possibility", then it is important in a high degree to know whether "possibility" of a juridical nature, or of a factual, a real nature, is intended. What is *juridically* possible is what is permitted by norms of law, and this possibility does not depend upon the *actual* realizability or non-realizability of what is permitted. Factually speaking, possibility lies in its turn, beyond the limits of normative determinations and is expressed in

[51] **See footnote 24 above.**

a certain favorable realization of something, a combination of elements of the psychic or the physical order. Accordingly, when the jurist speaks of possibility, then he must have in mind legal *permission, conferral*; when the legal theorist-psychologist, sociologist, or political scientist speaks of possibility, then he must have in mind *empirical realizability*. The history of philosophy of law knows an entire series of classic examples of law in the subjective sense having merged with the concept of power [*силы*], and, consequently, having been translated into the real order, precisely as a consequence of missing this distinction. Thus, in Hobbes[52] the idea of legal authority and the conception of power [*силе*] are merged in the neutral term "*potentia*", bearing a real empirical character. Thus, in Spinoza the idea of legal empowerment is completely dissolved in the concept of power [*силе*], present in every natural thing; this "*potentia rei naturalis*", is nothing other than "*ipsissima Dei potentia*" and bears a definitely expressed metaphysical character. Thus, finally, law in the subjective sense is approximated to power [*силой*] in Haller, and in the doctrine of Stirner[53] it is absorbed in a refined conception of power [*силы*], a conception of personal capabilities, of the potential of an individual in all of its distinctiveness. In the history of jurisprudence the essence of law was long regarded precisely in its subjective aspect, and this makes it possible to significantly enlarge the number of examples indicated; thus it turns out to be all the more essential to maintain the established distinction.

The concept of "*freedom*" in its application to law in the subjective sense can be subjected to an analogous analysis. It is extremely important for the jurist to clearly understand that in the order of his examination, this concept must be alien to a realistic comprehension, whether in a metaphysical or an empirical sense. The jurist understands "freedom" not as an absolute exemption from *all* determinateness, or from the effects of *empirical* laws_z *in general*, or from the effects of *only certain* empirical laws_z, but as a permission, established in legal norms, and the "*sphere of freedom*" signifies on his lips *an element of empowerment* [*полномочий*] *in the legal status of the subject*. In just the same way "*being bound*" on the lips of the jurist must not have a factual coloring: a subject may have many juridical "bounds" in his status and be factually not "bound" "by circumstances". The methodological significance of this distinction is revealed with particular clarity in the sphere of criminal law; the latter rests entirely on the recognition of a permanent divergence between "being bound" juridically and "being bound" factually, giving rise precisely to the necessity of a "criminal" response. "Freedom" and "being bound" in the eyes of the jurist lie beyond the limits of the real order, beyond the limits of the reach of the category of power [*силы*].

52 **See, e.g., *De Cive*, Chap. XIII, § 2 and others.**

53 [from *Die Begriffe*]: **Stirner: *Der Einzige und sein Eigentum*, pp. 121, 133, 196, 220-223, 227, 239-240, 244, 249, 294, 299, 348, among others.**

Chapter VII

On this we can conclude the essay we undertook on the methodological analysis of the concepts of law and power [*силы*]. We came to the conclusion that for a resolution the usual question: "*Is* law power or *not*?" must be changed in its very *formulation.* One must never claim that "Law *is* power" or that "Law *is not* power" because both answers can be understood in the sense of a *real* coincidence or non-coincidence of the two aspects. Precisely a *methodological* approach to the problem exposes it in all its significance and indicates a path to its resolution. And this approach poses the question differently: "*is it possible for law to be regarded* as power and *can it be regarded* as *not* permitting an approximation to power"? To answer the question posed in this way means, in our belief, to deploy a doctrine of method in jurisprudence applicable to it, and moreover, it means in a methodological analysis to touch on *all* spheres of *jurisprudence* as such, and to attempt to uncover in it the possible and the actual linkings of these concepts from the viewpoint of their methodological admissibility or inadmissibility.

Our attempt at such an analysis is, unfortunately, due to certain external conditions, compressed and schematic; it accepts certain definitions provisionally and without a developed scientific justification; it passes by many paths and branchings leading off to the side, only alluding to many others, and not fully discussing many. It presupposes, of course, further, that the general rule according to which any abstract methodological investigation can be counted as fully justified only after a series of attempts at the applied working-out of its fundamental conclusions, also applies to it. But it rests at the same time on the assumption that the first link in a scientific study may be an *abstract* investigation of the presuppositions and paths of study, all the more if this investigation has the possibility of pointing out the past and present experience of science as having nurtured and nurturing related methodological tendencies.

From the viewpoint of methodological pluralism professed by us there can be no doubt that all the suspect categories deconstructed by us revolve around the essence of law, taken as a whole, in all its complexity. The categories of "will", "interest", "compulsion", "social sanction", "obligation", "efficacy", "order", "property", "relation", "power", "possibility", "freedom", "being bound", and so on, must enter into and do enter into a general, comprehensive theoretical analysis of law. But each of them must track down for itself a methodological order corresponding to its essence and not encroach on orders methodologically alien to it; those concepts which can be involved in various orders must pass as a preliminary through a process of analytic breakdown and, where possible, receive a differentiated *designation*. Scientific knowledge is always knowledge of a *determinate* object or, if you will, a determinate, conditionally abstracted, aspect of an object, and the issue of the greater care and purity of such an isolation of aspects, varied in terms of their logical essence, is undoubtedly a question of greater productivity and comprehensiveness of scientific inquiry.

Glossary

A number of terms in this list have been marked as "obsolete" either because they are not currently in use, or because Il'in may have used them in a sense which is now obsolete. Terms involving "pravo" [law] have been listed separately to facilitate comparisons among the numerous compound forms and phrases in which they are used in the text.

веление	command (obs.)
властьruling	power, ruling authority
влачитсяto	drag oneself along (obs.)
влечение	inclination
государственной	State, political (adj.)
государственность	the idea of the state
государство	State
действие	activity
действовать	to function
делание	doing(s), practice
деяние	deed, act
должное	what is owed, what ought to be
изволение	will, willing, volition (obs.)
наверно	certainly, for sure (obs.)
непредметным	non-objective (obs.)
обязанность	duty
обоснование	grounding
обстояние	situation, circumstance(s), subsistence (obs.)
обстоящее	standing (situation), (circumstances) obtaining
оригинальничанье	a fetish for originality
основание	foundation
побуждение	motive
поведение	conduct, behavior
повинность	obligation

покориться	submit (to)
полагать	to lay, to place (obs.)
полномочие	empowerment, plenary power
полномочный	plenipotentiary
попирание	trampling (on)
порыв	impulse
поступки	acts, deeds
почиющий	quiet, restful (obs.)
правительство	government
предусмотреть	to stipulate in advance, to anticipate, to foresee
прилепленность	clinging (obs.)
приятие	acceptance, taking up (obs.)
самостояние	independence, self-standing
состояние	status (obs.)
установление	statute (obs.)
чувствилище	sensorium

TERMS AND PHRASES INVOLVING "ПРАВО"

бесправие	lawlessness
внеправовая расправа	extra-legal reprisal
неправовой	nonlegal
неправое право	unrightful law, unjust law
неправомерность	unlawfulness
неправомерный	unlawful, unrightful
неправость	wrong, wrongfulness
неправота	injustice, wrong
неправый	unrightful, unjust
право	law, right
правоведение	jurisprudence
правовой	legal , under law

праводательство	legislation
правосозидание	law-making
правочувствие	sense of right
правое право	right(ful) law, just law
правомерность	lawfulness, rightfulness
правомерный	lawful, rightful
правопознание	theory of law, legal theory
правота	rightness, right, innocence
правотворчество	law-creation, law-creating activity
правый	rightful, just
правый правопорядок	just legal order, rightful legal order
справедливость	justice
противоправность	wrongfulness
противоправный	anti-legal, anti-lawful

Bibliography

Primary Readings by I. A. Il'in:

Il'in, Dmitrii Aleksandrovich (ed.). Русский колокол: журнал волевой идеи [Russian Bell: Journal of a Volitional Idea], ed. Iu. T. Lisitsa. Moscow, [Fund Khristianin], 2012-. 999 ptd.

Continuation of journal founded by I. A. Il'in and published in nine issues from 1927 to 1930; numbering of the journal continues from 1930, thus no. 1(10) (November-December 2012). Early issues entirely devoted to reprinting pieces by I. A. Il'in.

Il'in, Ivan Aleksandrovich. "Die Begriffe von Recht und Macht: Versuch einer methodologischen Analyse", *Archiv für systematische Philosophie* [Berlin], XVIII (1912), pp. 63-88, 125-44.

Also known as separate offprint with continuous pagination.

___. *Foundations of Christian Culture*, transl. Nicholas Kotar. N.p., Waystone, 2019.

___. О русском национализме: сборник статей [On Russian Nationalism: Collection of Articles], Preface Nikita Mikhalkov. Moscow, Rossiiskii Fund Kul'tury, 2006. 160 p. 2000 ptd.

___. О сущности правосознания [On the Essence of Legal Consciousness]. Munich: Тип. Обители преп. Иова Почаевскаго, 1956.

___. О теме и просветлении. Книга художествноой критики. Бунин, Ремизов, Шмелев [On Darkness and Lucidity. Book of Belles-Lettres Critique. Bunin, Remizov, Shmelev]. Munich, Тип. Обители преп. Иова Почаевскаго, 1959. [v], 196 p.

___. Общее учение о праве и государстве: Основы Законоведения [General Doctrine on Law and State: Fundamental Principles of Jurisprudence]. Moscow: 1915.

___. Огни жизни [Flames of Life], ed. and comp. Iu. T. Lisitsa. Moscow, Russkaia kniga – XXI vek. 2006. 544 p.

Contains: I Glance into Life; Singing Heart; and A Glance into the Future.

___. *On Resistance to Evil by Force*, transl. K. Benois. Zvolen and London, Taxiarch Press, 2018.

___. Основы борьбы за национальную Россию [The Bases of the Struggle for a National Russia] (Narva, Издание Национально-трудового союза нового поколения, 1938.

___. Основы государственного устройства. Проект основного закона России [Fundamental Principles of State Structure. Draft Basic Law of Russia]. Moscow, тоо Rarog, 1996. 160 p. 5000 ptd.

___. "Понятия права и силы: опыт методологического анализа" [The Concepts of Law and Power: Essay in Methodological Analysis], Вопросы философии и психологии, XXI, kn. 1 (1910), pp. 1-38.

___. Проблема современного правосознания [Problem of Contemporary Legal Consciousness]. Berlin: Товарищество "Presse", 1923.

___. Пророческое призвание Пушкина [Prophetic Calling of Pushkin]. Riga, Russkii akademicheskoe obshchestvo v Rige, 1937. 43 p.

Solemn addresses delivered at Riga from 27 January to 9 February 1937 celebrating the anniversary of Alexander Pushkin.

___. Путь духовного обновления [Path of Spiritual Renewal]. 2d ed.; Munich, Тип. Обители преп. Иова Почаевскаго, 1962. 269, [ii] p.

Based on the 1935 version, with three additional chapters.

___. Путь духовного обновления [Path of Spiritual Renewal], ed. and comp. Iu. T. Lisitsa. Moscow, Russkaia kniga – XXI vek, 2006. 336 p. 2000 ptd.

Contains three works: Path of Spiritual Renewal; Foundations of Christian Culture; and Crisis of Godlessness.

___. *The Philosophy of Hegel as a Doctrine of the Concreteness of God and Humanity*, transl. and ed. Philip T. Grier. Evanston, Illinois, Northwestern University Press, 2010-2011. 2 vols.; paperback edition, 2019. 2 vols.

Vol. 1, *The Doctrine of God*; Vol. 2, *The Doctrine of Humanity*.

___. *The Singing Heart: A Book of Quiet Reflections*, transl. Alexandra Weber. Memphis, Orthodox Christian Translation Society, 2016.

Collected Works of Il'in

___. И. А. Ильин: Собрание сочинений [I. A. Il'in: Collected Works], ed. Iu. T. Lisitsa Moscow, Russkaia kniga, 1993-. The collected works commenced in ten numbered volumes (in twelve): volume 2 is in two parts, and volume 6 is in three parts; volume 9-10 is a single book. These twelve volumes were followed by another twenty-five unnumbered volumes, making a total of thirty-seven, of which volumes 34 to 37 consist of correspondence between Il'in and Nikolai Medtner and are in press as the present volume is being published. Commencing in 2006 these supplementary volumes have been published by the Orthodox St. Tikhonov Humanities University Press [Изд. ПСТГУ]. From 2019 (volume 31) publication was undertaken by the Heritage Institute, the publishing arm of the D.

S. Likhachev Russian Scientific Research Institute of Cultural and Natural Heritage.

[1] Vol. 1: 1993. 400 p.

[2] Vol. 2(1): 1993. 496 p.

[3] Vol. 2(2): 1994. 480 p.

[4] Vol. 3: 1994. 592 p.

[5] Vol. 4: 1994. 634 p.

[6] Vol. 5: 1996. 608 p.

[7] Vol. 6(1): 1996. 560 p.

[8] Vol. 6(2): 1996. 672 p.

[9] Vol. 6(3): 1997. 560 p.

[10] Vol. 7: 1998. 608 p.

[11] Vol. 8: 1998. 608 p.

[12] Vol. 9-10. 1999. 513 p.

[13] 1999. 608 p.

[14] 1999. 513 p.

[15] 2000. 560 p.

[16] 2000. 576 p.

[17] 2000. 528 p.

[18] 2001. 560 p.

[19] 2001. 576 p.

[20] 2001. 528 p.

[21] 2001. 582 p.

[22] 2002. 448 p.

[23] 2002. 608 p.

[24] 2002. 608 p.

[25] 2003. 608 p.

[26] 2004. 624 p.

[27] 2006. 576 p.

[28] 2008. 856 p.

[29] 2013. 716 p.

[30] 2015. 656 p.

[31] 2019. 920 p.

[32] 2021. 736 p.

[33] 2021. 704 p.

[34-37] 2022/23.

___. И. А. Ильин. Сочинения в двух томах [I. A. Il'in. Works in Two Volumes]. Moscow, Moskovskii filosofskii fond. Izd-vo "Medium", 1993. 2 vols. 7000 ptd,

Vol. 1 contains seven works devoted to the philosophy of law and moral philosophy, including "Concepts of Law and Power" and "On the Essence of Legal Consciousness".

Vol. 2 contains four works devoted to religious philosophy and an extensive bibliography of Il'in's publications and works about Il'in (pp. 513-559) compiled by Iu. T. Lisitsa.

Other Primary Sources

Hegel, G. W. F. *Grundlinien der Philosophie des Rechts,* Berlin: Nicolai,1821. English translation: *Elements of the Philosophy of Right*, transl. H. B. Nisbet, ed. Allen W. Wood. Cambridge, Cambridge University Press, 1991.

___. *Lectures on the Philosophy of Religion*, ed. Peter C. Hodgson, transl. R. F. Brown, P. C. Hodgson, and J. M. Stewart with the assistance of H. S. Harris. Berkeley and Los Angeles, University of California Press, 1984-1987. 3 vols.

___. *The Phenomenology of Spirit*. transl. A. V. Miller. Oxford: Oxford University Press, 1977.

Petrazhitskii, L. I. *Л. И. Петражитский, Теория и политика права: избранные труды* [L. I. Petrazhitskii, Theory and Policy of Law: Selected Works], ed. E. V. Timoshina. St. Petersburg, University Publishing Consortium "Law Press", 2010).

Savigny, Friedrich Carl von. *Vom Beruf unserer Zeit für Gesetzgebung und Rechtswissenschaft*. Heidelberg: Mohr und Zimmer, 1814. (2d ed.; Heidelberg: Mohr, 1828; 3d ed.; Heidelberg: J. C. B. Mohr, 1840). Translated as *The Vocation of our Age for Legislation and Jurisprudence*, transl. Abraham Hayward. London, Littlewood & Co., 1831; reprint edition: New York, Arno Press, 1975 (a translation of the 2d German edition).

___. *System des heutigen Römischen Rechts.* Berlin, Veit und comp., 1840-1849. 8 vols.

___. *The History of the Roman Law during the Middle Ages*, transl. E. Cathcart (1829; reprinted 1979).

___. *The System of the Modern Roman Law*, transl. William Holloway. Madras, J. Higginbotham, Pubs., 1867.

Stammler, Rudolf. *Die Lehre vom den richtigen Rechte.* Berlin, J. Guttentag, 1902.

___. *The Theory of Justice*, transl. Isaac Husak. New York, Macmillan, 1925; Reprint ed.: New York: Augustus M. Kelley, 1969; South Hackensack, N. J., Rothman Reprints, 1969.

Velikodina, I. L. (ed.), Каталог библиотеки Ивана Александровича Ильина. Из собрания Отдела редких книг и рукописей Научной библиотеки МГУ [Catalogue of the Library of Ivan Aleksandrovich Il'in: From the Collection of the Section of Rare Books and Manuscripts of the Scientific Library of Moscow State University], comp. I. V. Ovchinkina. Moscow, izd-vo Moskovskogo universiteta, 2011. 200 p. + ill. 550 ptd.

Secondary Sources on Il'in and His Times

Adorno, Theodor W., et al. *The Authoritarian Personality*. New York, Harper, 1950.

Aleksandrov. A. I., Ivliev, G. P., Rozinskii, M. G. (eds.). Учение И. А. Ильина о праве, власти и социальной культуре России: Материалы научно-практической конференции, посвященной 125-летию выдающегося правоведа и философа И. А. Ильина. 19 июня 2008 года [Doctrine of I. A. Il'in on Law, Power, and Social Culture of Russia: Materials of a Scientific-Practical Conference Devoted to the 125th Anniversary of the Leading Jurist and Philosopher, I. A. Il'in. 19 June 2008]. Moscow, izd. Soveta Federatsii, 2008. 242 p. 250 ptd.

Babb, Hugh W. "Petrazhitskii: Science of Legal Policy and Theory of Law", *Boston University Law Review*, XVII (1937), 793; XVIII (1938), 511.

Butler, W. E. *Russian Law and Legal Institutions*. 3d ed.; Clark, New Jersey, Talbot Publishing, 2021. viii, 516 p.

Butler, W. E. and P. T. Grier, "'Legal Consciousness': Some Comparative Legal Aspects", *The Journal of Comparative Law* VII (2012), pp. 40-62.

Cohen, Morris R. *Law and the Social Order: Essays in Legal Philosophy*. New York, Harcourt, Brace and Co., 1933.

Cotterrell, Roger. *The Sociology of Law: an Introduction.* 2d ed.; London, Butterworths, 1984, 1992.

Drozdova, Oksana, Robinson, Paul, "In Others' Words: Quotations and Recontextualization in Putin's Speeches", *Russian Politics,* II, no. 2 (2017), pp. 227-253.

Ehrlich, Eugen. *Grundlegung der Soziologie des Rechts* (1913).

___. *Fundamental Principles of the Sociology of Law*, transl. Walter L. Moll. Boston, Massachusetts, Harvard University Press, 1936; reprint ed.: New York: Russell & Russell, Inc., 1962.

Evlampiev, Igor Ivanovich. Иван Ильин [Ivan Il'in]. St Petersburg, Narva, 2016. 249 p.

Field, Daniel. "Kavelin and Russian Liberalism", *Slavic Review*, XXXII, no. 1 (1973).

Filonova, L. G. (comp.). Религозно-философская мысль русского зарубежья первой половины XX века: библиографический указатель [Religious-Philosophical Thought of the Russia Abroad of the First Half of the Twentieth Century: Bibliographical Index]. Moscow, Pashkov Dom, 2011. 240 p. 200 ptd.

Gessen, V. M. *Возрождение естественного права* [The Revival of Natural Law]. St. Petersburg, 1902.

Grier, Philip T. "The Complex Legacy of Ivan Il'in", in James P. Scanlan (ed.). *Russian Thought after Communism: The Recovery of a Philosophical Heritage*. Armonk, M. E. Sharpe, 1994.

___. "Ivan A. Ilyin: Russia's 'Non-Hegelian' Hegelian", in Marina F. Bykova, Michael N. Forster, and Lina Steiner (eds.), *The Palgrave Handbook of Russian Thought.* Switzerland: Palgrave Macmillan International, 2021, pp. 317-337.

Gritskov, V. V. (ed.). Быково [Bykovo]. Zhukovskii-Moscow, izd-vo Kuchkovo Pole, 2005. 272 p. 2000 ptd. Contains an account of the Il'in country estate in Bykovo where Ivan Aleksandrovich spent his summers.

Gurvitch, Georges. *Sociology of Law* (International Library of Sociology and Social Reconstruction founded by Karl Mannheim), London, K. Paul, Trench, Trubner, 1947 (a translation of *Éléments de sociologie jurdique* Paris: Aubier, 1940. Reprint: London and Boston, Routledge and Kegan Paul, 1973).

[Haka, Clifford H., Berg, Peter I.], *The Ivan Aleksandrovich Il'in Papers and the Michigan State University Libraries*. East Lansing, Michigan, Michigan State University Libraries, 2013. [viii], 51 p. Text in English and Russian throughout.

Hertogh, M., ed., *Living Law: Reconsidering Eugen Ehrlich.* Onati International Series in Law and Society. Oxford, Hart Publishing, 2009.

Heuman, Susan. *Kistiakovsky: The Struggle for National and Constitutional Rights in the Last Years of Tsarism*. Cambridge, Massachusetts, Harvard University Press, 1998.

Hodgson, Peter C. *Hegel and Christian Theology*, Oxford, Oxford University Press, 2005.

Il'ina, Nataliia Nikolaevna (*née* Vokach). *Изгнание Норманов: очередная задача русской исторической науки* [The Banishment of the Normans: the immediate task of Russian historical science]. Paris, 1955.

___ . *Одиночество и общение* [Solitude and Communion], 1916 manuscript. Published in *И. А. Ильин*, *Собрание сочинений*, ed. Iu. T. Lisitsa. Unnumbered supplementary volume *Философия как духовное делание* [Philosophy as a Spiritual Doing]. Moscow, Изд. ПСТГУ, 2013.

Kholmogorov, Egor. «Правый гегелянец в окопах Сталинграда» [Right Hegelian in the Trenches of Stalingrad], Самопознание [Self-Knowledge], no. 2 (2015), p. 24.

Kiselev, A. F. Иван Ильин и его поющее сердце [Ivan Il'in and His Singing Heart]. Moscow, Logos, 2006. 272 p. + ill. 1000 ptd.

Kistiakovskii, B. A. *Социальныя науки и право: очерки по методологии социальных наук и общей теории права* [Social Sciences and Law: Essays in the Methodology of Social Sciences and General Theory of Law]. Moscow, Издание М. и С. Сабашниковых, 1916.

Klimoff, A. E. (comp.). [E. E. Klimov: Selected Works]. Riga, University of Latvia Journal "Latvijas Vēsture" Foundation, 2006. 64 p.

Kornilov, S. V. (ed.). Идейное наследие И. А. Ильина и современность: Сборник научных трудов [Ideological Legacy of I. A. Il'in and Modern Times]. Kaliningrad, izd-vo RGU im. I. Kant, 2008. 172 p. 400 ptd. Fourteen articles by leading authorities on Il'in.

Kudinov, O. A. Конституционные проекты Белого движения и конституционно-правовые теории российской белоэмиграции (1918-1940-е гг.), или За что их расстреливали (для тех, кто хочет понять смысл права) [Constitutional Drafts of the White Movement and Constitutional Legal Theories of the Russian White Emigration (1918-1940), or for What They Were Shot and Deported (For Those Who Want to Understand the Meaning of Law)]. Moscow, Os-89, 2006. 224 p. 1000 ptd.

Lahusen, Benjamin. *Alles Recht geht vom Volksgeist aus* [All Law Comes from the Spirit of the People]. Berlin, Nicolai, 2012.

Laruelle, Marlene, Karnysheva, Margarita. *Memory Politics and the Russian Civil War: Reds Versus Whites*. London, Bloomsbury Academic, 2021. [viii], 155 p.

Lisitsa, I. T. (comp.). Иван Ильин и Россия: Неопубликованные фотографии и архивные материалы [Ivan Il'in and Russia: Unpublished Photographs and Archival Materials]. Moscow, Russkaia kniga, 1999. 192 p. 2500 ptd.

___, «Ильин искал сущность свободы как подобия божия в человеке: Интервью с Юрием Лисицей» [Il'in Searched for the Essence of

Freedom as the Likeness of God in Man], Самопознание [Self-Knowledge], no. 2 (2015), p. 12.

___. "Ivan Il'in on the Foundations of Christian Culture", in Artur Mrowczynski-Van Allen, Teresa Obolevitch, and Pawel Rojek (eds.). *Apology of Culture: Religion and Culture in Russian Thought*. Eugene, Oregon, Pickwick Publications, [2015]. x, 241 p.

Lisitsa, I. T., Lisitsa, O. V. Иван Ильин: провозвестник грядущей России [Ivan Il'in: Prophet of the Coming Russia]. Moscow, Izdanie Nikita Mikhalkov, 2005. 64 p. 3000 ptd.

Manigk, Alfred. *Savigny und der Modernismus im Recht*. Berlin, 1914; reprint, Aalen, Germany: Scientia, 1974.

Merryman, John Henry. *The Civil Law Tradition*. 2d ed.; Stanford, California: Stanford University Press, 1985.

Novgorodtsev, Pavel Ivanovich. "Ethical Idealism in the Philosophy of Law (On the Question of the Revival of Natural Law)", in Randall Poole (ed.). *Problems of Idealism: Essays in Russian Social Philosophy*. New Haven, Yale University Press, 2005.

___. *Кризис современного правосознания* [Crisis of Contemporary Legal Consciousness]. Moscow, 1909. Reprint edition ed. V. N. Kudriavtsev. Moscow, Nauka, 1996.

Oakshott, Michael. *On Human Conduct*. Oxford, Clarendon Press, 1975.

Pipes, Richard. *Struve: Liberal on the Right.* Cambridge, Massachusetts, Harvard University Press, 1980.

Pogrebnaia, Iu. K. Кризис современного российского правосознания [Crisis of Contemporary Russian Legal Consciousness]. Moscow, Al'fa-M, 2013. 192 p. 500 ptd.

Poltoratskii, Nikolai. Иван Александрович Ильин: жизнь, труды, мировоззрение. Сборник статей [Ivan Aleksandrovich Il'in: Life, Works, World Outlook. Collection of Articles]. Tenafly, New Jersey, Hermitage, 1989. 320 p.

Pound, Roscoe. "Mechanical Jurisprudence", in George C. Christie and Patrick H. Martin (eds.), *Jurisprudence: Texts and Readings on the Philosophy of Law.* St. Paul, Minnesota, West Group, 1973, pp. 828-832.

Pribytkova, E. A. Несвоевременный современник. Философия права В. С. Соловьева [Untimely Contemporary. The Philosophy of Law of V. S. Solov'ev]. Moscow, Modest Kolerov, 2011. 480 p. 500 ptd.

Rampton, Vanessa. *Liberal Ideas in Tsarist Russia: From Catherine the Great to the Russian Revolution.* Cambridge, Cambridge University Press, 2020.

Rehbinder, Manfred. *Die Begrundung der Rechtssoziologie durch Eugen Ehrlich*. 2d ed.; Berlin, Duncker & Humblot, 1986.

Reimann, Mathias. "Nineteenth Century German Legal Science", *Boston College Law Review*, XXXI (1990), p. 837.

___. *Historische Schule und Common Law: Die deutsche Rechtswissenschaft des 19. Jahrhunderts im amerikanischen Rechtsdenken.* Berlin, Duncker & Humblot, 1993.

Rinaldi, Giacomo. "Neo-Kantianism versus Hegelianism". *Jahrbuch für Hegelforschung*, XXI (2020), pp. 11-100.

Robinson, Paul F. "'Always with Honour': The Code of the White Russian Officers", *Canadian Slavonic Papers/Revue canadiénne des slavistes*, XLI, no. 2 (June 1999).

___. "On Resistance to Evil by Force: Ivan Il'in and the Necessity of War", *Journal of Military Ethics*, II, no. 2 (2003), pp. 145-159.

___. *Russian Conservatism*. Ithaca, Cornell University Press, 2019. viii, 288 p.

___ . *The White Russian Army in Exile, 1920-1941*. Oxford: Clarendon Press, 2002.

___. Русский мыслитель. Иван Александрович Ильий. Творческая биография [Russian Thinker: Ivan Aleksandrovich Il'in. Creative Biography]. Moscow, izd-vo Glavarkhiva Moskvy izd-vo "Delovoi ritm". 2008. 304 p. 500 ptd.

Rosenberg, William G. *Liberals in the Russian Revolution: The Constitutional Democratic Party, 1917-1921.* Princeton: Princeton University Press, 1974.

Snyder, Timothy. *The Road to Unfreedom: Russia, Europe, America*. New York, Tim Duggan, 2018.

Tomsinov, V. A. Мыслитель с поющимь сердцем. Иван Александрович Ильин: русский идеолог эпохи революций [Thinker with a Singing Heart: Ivan Aleksandrovich Il'in: Russian Ideologue of the Era of Revolutions]. Moscow, Zertsalo-M, 2012. 192 p. 500 ptd.

Ulianova, Liubov'. «Скрытое славянофильство в творчестве Ильна» [Concealed Slavophilism in the Creative Work of Il'in], Самопознание [Self-Knowledge], no. 2 (2015), p. 38.

Valliere, Paul. "Ivan Ilyin: Philosopher of Law, Force, and Faith", in Randall Poole and Paul Valliere, *Law and the Christian Tradition in Russian Thought* (2021).

Walicki, Andrzej. *The Flow of Ideas: Russian Thought from the Enlightenment to the Religious-Philosophical Renaissance.* Frankfurt, Peter Lang, 2015.

___. *Legal Philosophies of Russian Liberalism.* Oxford, Oxford University Press, 1987.

Williams, Robert R. *Recognition: Fichte and Hegel on the Other*. Albany, New York, SUNY Press, 1992.

___. *Hegel's Ethics of Recognition.* Berkeley, University of California Press, 1997.

___. *Tragedy, Recognition and the Death of God: Studies in Hegel and Nietzsche*. Oxford, Oxford University Press, 2012.

The Authors

Butler, William E.: J.D.; LL.M., Ph.D., LL.D., доктор юридических наук (*honoris causa*). John Edward Fowler Distinguished Professor of Law, Pennsylvania State University; Emeritus Professor of Comparative Law, University of London (University College London); Foreign Member, National Academy of Sciences of Ukraine and National Academy of Legal Sciences of Ukraine; Associate Member, International Academy of Comparative Law.

Grier, Philip T.: Ph.D.; Thomas Bowman Professor of Philosopy and Religion Emeritus, Dickinson College, Carlisle, Pennsylvania.

Robinson, Paul: Professor, Graduate School of Public and International Affairs, University of Ottawa and author of numerous works on Soviet and Russian history, including *Russian Conservatism* (2019) and the forthcoming *Russian Liberalism*.

Index of Names

www.ingramcontent.com/pod-product-compliance
Lightning Source LLC
LaVergne TN
LVHW091341101126
852199LV00002B/31